MUSIC
AND
TRANCE

MUSIC
AND
TRANCE

A Theory of the Relations
between Music and Possession

GILBERT ROUGET

Translation from the French
Revised by Brunhilde Biebuyck
in Collaboration with the Author

THE UNIVERSITY OF CHICAGO PRESS □ CHICAGO AND LONDON

GILBERT ROUGET is the director of research at the Centre
Nationale de la Recherche Scientifique, chairman of the
Department of Ethnomusicology at the Museé de l'Homme in
Paris, and lecturer at the University of Paris X—Nanterre.

The original edition of this book was published as *La musique
et la transe: Esquisse d'une théorie générale des relations de la
musique et de la possession,* © Editions Gallimard, 1980.

THE UNIVERSITY OF CHICAGO PRESS, CHICAGO 60637
THE UNIVERSITY OF CHICAGO PRESS, LTD., LONDON

© 1985 by The University of Chicago
All rights reserved. Published 1985
Printed in the United States of America
94 93 92 91 90 89 88 87 86 85   5 4 3 2 1

LIBRARY OF CONGRESS CATALOGING IN PUBLICATION DATA

Rouget, Gilbert.
    [Musique et la transe. English]
    Music and trance.

    Translation of: La musique et la transe.
    Bibliography: p.
    Discography: p.
    Filmography: p.
    Includes indexes.
    1. Music, Influence of. 2. Music—Physiological
effects. 3. Trance. I. Title.
ML3920.R813 1985   154.4   85–1107
ISBN 0-226-73005-0
ISBN 0-226-73006-9 (pbk.)

For Aurélie

Contents

Contents

The figures occur on pages 251–54

Preface to the American Edition

What cultured Westerners, anthropologists included, most commonly think about the effects of music on trance sometimes reminds me of an old story.

Some fifty years ago, the son of a great Kakemba rain maker, first of his tribe to visit England, was taken to a football match which made a great impression on him. Back in his village, he told his father about it: "There was an enormous crowd. You would have thought it was a king's funeral or something. People were seated in tight rows, around a huge empty plot of grass. After a while, a troop of twenty men or more came running in. They scattered and stood there for a moment. One of them put a round ball down on the earth, right in the center of the green. Suddenly someone blew a whistle. A chap rushed forward and kicked the ball away with his foot. Immediately the rain started to pour down." His father replied: "These big white rain makers! Their medicine must be very strong!"

Now what about those black drummers who can make people fall down and faint on the spot? Their music must be very strong too! Both are cases of what could be called an ethnology of the cause-and-effect relationship.

If by virtue of its topic this book leads us into the very heart of ethnology, it does so for another reason as well. It happened to be written in French by a native of Paris. But most of the data gathered in the following pages concern other ethnic groups belonging to other parts of the world, speaking other languages that express other systems of thought. Now that this work is presented in English and meant to be read by natives (not only those of the British Isles) whom the author did not originally have in mind, one may ask whether the reader will get the right idea of both the ethnological facts cited and the theory proposed to interpret them. A question of translation? Of course! But translation is *par excellence* a matter of ethnology.

I will not linger on the ethnographic data that constitute the raw material of this book. They raise the ordinary problem of compilation. Suffice it to say that the ethnographers' texts have always been strictly respected and quoted as fully as it seemed necessary. Of course, whether the authors correctly reported the native thoughts or not still remains to be seen. This is the usual—and central—problem of ethnology (others would say of cognitive anthropology, but this does not matter). What I will linger on is my interpretation of those data, such as it is now presented to the reader, in English and translated from the French.

However cosmopolitan one may be, one is always to some degree a native (if not on occasion, even nowadays, an aboriginal). I do not escape the rule. The only difference between me, the author of this book, and all the anonymous people whose notions and behavior are its very substance, is that, contrary to the latter, who were not asked their opinion about the way their words and gestures were reported by foreign observers, I was given the chance of checking what had become of my writing once it was translated into a foreign language and of defending my own train of thought.

Since each language is a particular organization of meaning, translating a text implies a change of organization. The relative flexibility of the latter allows the change to be more or less important depending on the type of translation required. In the present case, I wanted it to be as slight as possible—which of course was not always obtainable. Revising the translation first made of this book, Brunhilde Biebuyck and I tried to keep the English as close as possible to my personal way of thinking, a way which is, *nolens volens,* a French one. To achieve an acceptable result, we had to work in close cooperation since it was necessary to adjust not only the expression to the thought but sometimes also the thought to the expression. Naturally, this procedure may have resulted at times in a rather marked literalness. I hope the reader will be ready to accept it. I would like to add that if in a number of places a French phrasing was preferred to an English, in return the final formulation chosen for the American version quite often proved to be better than the original one and induced me to revise it. If some day there is a new French edition of this book, I do hope it will take advantage of these improvements. My lifelong faithfulness to the practice of ethnology would find in this its best reward.

No one could have carried out the exercise of gobetween required by this revision with more competence, more talent and more gentleness than Brunhilde Biebuyck. I am glad to express all my gratitude to her.

Because of editorial constraints, the preface Michel Leiris kindly wrote for the original edition of this book has not been reproduced here. I regret it deeply, not only because the presence of a text by Leiris at the beginning of this work did me great honor, but also because his views on trance and on music would have interested the reader all the most since they are those of an author well known both for his studies on possession—among the very first ever made—and his literary writings.

For this American edition, I have brought certains corrections to the original French version. A few additions have been made as well. But the only change of some importance concerns the chapter on Greek antiquity, which has been somewhat augmented and reshaped. Photographs have also been added.

G. R.
Paris, December 1984

Acknowledgments

In 1968, Roger Bastide and Jean Rouch, at whose instigation the Centre National de la Recherche Scientifique organized in Paris an international conference on possession, asked me to present a paper on music. It was inconceivable, in their view, that such a conference could take place without at least one session on music; this would have meant that an essential aspect of the facts would be ignored. Since no one better qualified than I offered to shoulder the task, I agreed to participate. However, it took all the friendly persuasion they could muster to make me do so, since at that time my knowledge of the subject was confined to the very limited field observations I just mentioned above. The sheer scope of the problem appeared formidable to me. Imprudently, but because it seemed to be the fundamental question, I entitled my paper "Music in Its Psychophysiological Relations to Possession." In June 1972, when Roger Bastide sent me the typescript of my talk, with a request to revise it (otherwise it would have been published as it stood), its inadequacies seemed so glaring that I committed the second imprudence of deciding to rework it entirely. This was how I gradually embarked on the writing of this book. My great regret will always be that I was unable to show Roger Bastide the first draft before he died. We owe him the most perceptive observations yet penned on the relations between music and possession. His criticisms would undoubtedly have been invaluable to me. I nevertheless dare believe he would have approved of the general direction of the pages that follow since they tend to show how music contributes to the socialization of the trance state, a process whose great importance he himself had pointed out. May this book be a modest tribute to his work.

The encouragement I received from my friends while I was working on this book has been of the greatest value to me. My thanks go first of all to Michel Leiris, Eric de Dampierre, and Pierre Smith, all of whom were kind enough to read a first draft and greet it favorably. Leiris subsequently maintained an unfailing interest in my enterprise and comforted me constantly with his advice and friendship for which I am deeply grateful. It was at Dampierre's suggestion that I greatly enlarged the chapter on the Greeks, a task I could not have accomplished without his help and that of Jacques Lacarrière, as well as the valuable advice of Samuel Baud-Bovy.

Jean-Pierre Vernant was later kind enough to read this section and offer a number of observations that I hope to have taken sufficiently into account. Stella Georgoudi was kind enough to check my transliterations of the Greek. My heartfelt thanks to all of them. As for the chapter dealing with the Arabs, since I am even less of an Arabist than a Hellenist, it would have been quite impossible for me to write it without the friendly help of Bruno Halff and Schéhérezade Qassim Hassan. I thank them both from my heart, as I do to the late R. P. Nywia for the comments he sent me after having kindly consented to look over my text.

Among all those to whom I owe helpful comments, information, criticism, or support—a group too large to name—I would like to express particular gratitude to Maguy Andral, Elena Cassin, Gisèle Binon, Laurence Delaby, Jean Gouillard, Roberte Hamayon, Georges Lapassade, François Lesure, Ariane Macdonald, Jean-Bertrand Pontalis, Jean Pouillon, Jean Rouch, Pierre Verger, and Andras Zempléni. Various colleagues and friends in the Department of Ethnomusicology at the Musée de l'Homme have also earned my gratitude for the help they have often given me during my research, as has the Library of the Musée de l'Homme for the reading facilities always so kindly and freely put at my disposal. My thanks also go to Lucile Garma for her attentive and critical perusal of this work at each of its many stages. Lastly, I would like to say how much I owe to Jeanne Goussé for the friendly and tireless kindness with which she assisted me in a task that, without her, could never have come to term.

Pierre Nora also played a decisive role in the publication of this book in France. To him I feel a most particular debt of gratitude.

Introduction

The trance state, a phenomenon observed throughout the world, is associated most of the time with music. Why? That is the question this book will attempt to answer.

Why? people will no doubt ask. Quite simply because it is music that throws people into a trance. There is no need to look any further. Now what if things were not in fact quite so simple? Looking at them a bit more closely is enough to show that the relations between music and trance could not be more changeable or more contradictory. In one place music triggers it; in another on the contrary, it calms it. Sometimes thunderous drums send the subject into trance; at others, it is the very faint susurration of a rattle. Among certain people a musical instrument is said to produce this effect, whereas among others it is the human voice. Some subjects go into trance while dancing, others while lying prone on a bed. Under these conditions, one asks oneself, How does music act? Plato attributed the trances of the Corybantes to the effects of the aulos, Aristotle to those of the Phrygian mode. From the very beginning the facts have given rise to the most opposed theories. To use Jean-Jacques Rousseau's words, is it a physical effect or a moral one that is at work? In the twelfth century, among the Arabs, Ghazzali upheld both possibilities, and as proof of music's physical effects he advanced the case of camels driven into a frenzy by the cameleer's singing. During the Renaissance, the poets and musicians of the Pléiade thought that music was capable of its greatest effects only through its union with poetry. Rousseau, who constantly took a great interest in the problem, hesitated a long time before categorically siding against the theory of "the physical power of sounds."

A few years ago, Andrew Neher, an American neurophysiologist, proved—or rather thought he had proved—that, on the contrary, the "mystery" of the effects of drums on trance was due simply to the purely neurophysiological action of the sounds of that instrument. A fair number of ethnologists and ethnomusicologists at present accept this theory as a given. Twenty years earlier, Melville J. Herskovits advanced another very different thesis explaining the effects of music on trance as the result of conditioned reflex. Some years later, Roger Bastide took up this last theory again, but added to it the notion of an overall situation, without which the reflex in question would not come into play. If we now leave possession, which was Herskovits's and Bastide's concern, to turn to shamanic trance and Shirokogoroff's reknowned description of it, we find what could be called, ultimately, a theory of the emotional power of music. In yet another and totally different view on the effects of music on trance, Alain Danielou, an "ethnomusicologist of worldwide reputation," wrote quite seriously in a recent number of *The Unesco Courier* that "in all regions of the world the rhythms employed [to produce trance states] are always odd, in 5, 7, and 11 time." And he added, unabashed by the contrary evidence of a thousand examples, "square rhythms in four or eight time have no hypnotic effect."

As we have just seen, we do not lack explanations. Apart from Daniélou's, which is pure fantasy, and Neher's, which is false, each has some truth to it; yet none is completely satisfactory. The truth is that the facts are so varied and so complex they evade any single explanation. In a general way, all—or almost all—those who have dealt with trance believe, more or less unconsciously, that music has the secret power to trigger it, and that it does so all by itself, by the interplay of its own properties. They then go on to call upon either the power of the rhythm, which is the most frequent argument, or the magical effect produced by chants, as in the case of that otherwise admirable scholar, Jeanmaire, who, when speaking of the "possessed person thrown into a trance by the demonic call of incantatory melody," attributes to music qualities which it by no means has. These are received ideas that do not stand up to examination.

Demystifying the conception, too often adopted, of the role played by music in inducing trance states will be one of this book's aims. The importance of music will not be diminished for as much; quite the contrary. Music will ultimately appear as the principal means of manipulating the trance state, but by "socializing" much more than by triggering it. This process of socialization inevitably varies from one society to another, and takes place in very different ways according to the systems of representations—or, if one prefers, the ideological systems—within which trance occurs. In each case a different logic determines the relationship between trance and music. It is this logic that I shall try to elucidate.

Although trance is a quasi-universal phenomenon, it is nonetheless a practice much more widespread among those peoples constituting the very object of ethnological research than among others. This book is therefore a book of ethnology, or, more precisely, of ethnomusicology. Consequently there will be almost no mention of trance states observed in the modern Western world, whether among European or American Christian sects, devotees of pop music, or bioenergy adepts. Not that I regard such phenomena as less interesting, but a line had to be drawn somewhere. In addition, especially in the last two cases, information is rather scarce.

This book had its origins in my long-term interest in the music of possession cults practiced in the People's Republic of Benin (formerly Dahomey), a stronghold of trance, the country that gave birth not only to Haitian voodoo but to a great many other Afro-Cuban and Afro-Brazilian cults. Ten or so periods of varying length spent in that country allowed me to attend—usually in order to record music—a fair number of ceremonies directly connected with possession among the Gun, the Fon, and the Yoruba. But my first encounter with the trance state dates to a day in 1946, during a visit to the Congo, when right before my eyes a Babinga Pygmy was suddenly entranced in the very midst of a hunting dance, whose music my companions and I were recording. Two years later, in Bahia, Pierre Verger introduced me to the *candomblé* of Nuestra Senhora on the occasion of a beautiful nighttime ceremony for the water of Obatala, which was followed on the next day by a feast during which a number of possessions occurred. On various occasions I have been fortunate enough to attend other such rituals elsewhere: in Dakar, in particular, where in 1952 I was a wide-eyed spectator at a *ndöp* ceremony which I shall never forget, and several days later a witness—and one who was somewhat too roughly handled for my taste—to a "devils" ceremony among the Sarakole. Twenty years later, in Niamey, having providentially missed my plane, I was able to attend, in the company of Jean Rouch this time, the ritual enthronement of a *holey* daughter among the Songhay. However superficial they may have been, these contacts with other aspects of possession have been extremely instructive for me.

In recent years, and with this book in view, I have organized my readings around these direct observations of the relations between music and trance; they have progressively extended themselves to other regions of Africa, then the Mediterranean world, Asia, Indonesia, and from there, through shamanism, to Indian America. Quite arbitrarily, and in order to limit the already broad scope of my research, I have excluded not only China and Japan but also Polynesia and Melanesia. I must also add that even within the boundaries just indicated, I do not in any way pretend to have exhausted the available literature, which I have only gleaned. Immense lacunae remain. Nevertheless, I do feel that the sample cases I present here are representative enough and that the different types of relations that emerge from them are to be seen as a valid basis for further research. If this proves to be the case, this book will then have amply fulfilled its aim.

I hope I may be permitted one last observation. This work covers too many different domains not to be vulnerable—abundantly, I fear—to criticism from the specialists concerned. It is the overall picture that is important, however. If it finds favor in their eyes, then I trust they will consider that the weaknesses of detail are the inevitable price to be paid for such an enterprise, and that they should be weighed accordingly.

PART ONE

As long as we choose to consider sounds only through the commotion they stir in our nerves, we will never have the true principles of music and of its power over our hearts.

J.-J. Rousseau, *Essay on the Origin of Languages*

1 Trance and Possession

Axiomatically, trance will be considered in this book as a state of consciousness composed of two components, one psychophysiological, the other cultural. The universality of trance[1] indicates that it corresponds to a psychophysiological disposition innate in human nature, although, of course, developed to varying degrees in different individuals. The variability of its manifestations is the result of the variety of cultures by which it is conditioned.

A state of consciousness, trance consists, for the subject, in a particular experience composed of a series of events that can only be described by those who have lived through them. Although it constitutes the very essence of the phenomenon, for all sorts of reasons I shall not make use of such subjective experience in order to delimit the concept of trance. Instead, I shall define it by referring to its external manifestations, the context in which they can be observed, and the representations of which they are the object. However, those who have dealt thus far with trance have not always used the same vocabulary to identify the same manifestations, associated with similar contexts and representations among different populations. Sometimes, in fact, the very same author uses two or three different terms to refer to one and the same phenomenon. It is important at this stage to unify our terminology, since otherwise we will not know what we are talking about. The first point to be clarified relates to the use of the words "ecstasy" (*extase*) and "trance" (*transe*). I shall deal with the word "crisis" or "fit" (*crise*) later.

Trance or Ecstasy?

In French, the word *transe* is often used in ethnological literature as a synonym for *extase*. In everyday usage, however, the two words signify very different things. The same holds true in English, with the one exception that whereas "ecstasy" and "trance" stand in more or less the same opposition in medical and colloquial usage, their usage is the reverse of the French. Two quotations, both from medical dictionaries, make this clear. The English work[2] defines trance as "a sleeplike state, as in deep hypnosis, appearing also in hysteria and in some spiritualist mediums, with limited sensory and motor contact, with subsequent amnesia of what has occurred during the state." The French work[3] defines *extase* as "a mental state characterized by profound contemplation accompanied by a loss of sensitivity and motricity." Thus one calls *transe* what the other calls *extase*. Let us now shift from medicine to social anthropology, beginning with English. The word "ecstasy" does not appear at all in the index of Jane Belo's work, *Trance in Bali* (1960). Both "ecstasy" and "trance," on the other hand, occur in I. M. Lewis's *Ecstatic Religions* (1971), which begins with a chapter entitled "Towards a Sociology of Ecstasy." One would expect the author to define ecstasy, but he only proposes a definition of "trance" (taken from the *Penguin Dictionary of Psychology*, and very close indeed to that from Taber quoted here above), a term that, as he says, he uses in "its general medical sense" (1971, 38). In the course of his book he certainly uses "trance" most frequently, but this does not prevent him from using "trance" and "ecstasy" as if they were absolutely synonymous.[4] In the volume of collected papers edited by Beattie and Middleton under the title of *Spirit Mediumship and Society in Africa* (1969), one might search in vain for the word "ecstasy," which does not appear in the index either: "trance" is used throughout. On the other hand, the Arabic word *wajd*, which among the Sufi denotes a state that both British and French ethnologists would indisputably render today by the word "trance" or *transe*, was invariably translated as "ecstasy" by Macdonald in his 1901 translation of Ghazzali's well-known book.[5] In his work on Sufi sects, Trimingham (1971) remains faithful to this tradition throughout, with one very significant exception. When he needs to describe precisely what the *wajd* consists of in practice (1971, 200), he introduces the word "trance," and uses the terms "ecstatic trance" or "ecstasy or trance-like state." Lastly, Erika Bourguignon (1965, 1968, 1973, 1976), to whose works on possession I shall often refer, constantly uses the word "trance." On rare occasions she also uses "ecstasy" in order to denote the paroxysm of trance.[6]

We can thus see that the meaning assigned to the words "trance" and "ecstasy" poses a very real problem. Finally, I should point out that neither "trance" nor "ecstasy" figures in the general article on possession published in the *Encyclopaedia of Religions and Ethics* of 1918 (the first of its kind?). There are several references to "nervous crisis." "Ecstasy," on the other hand, does appear in the articles dealing with possession among Greeks, Muslims, and Christians.

In French the situation is just as complicated. When dealing with possession among the Ethiopians of Gondar (1958), Michel Leiris more often than not uses the word *crise* (crisis), but he sometimes also uses *transe*, particularly with reference to dancing, a "classic means of inducing trance" (1958, 18), and occasionally speaks of "ecstatic techniques" (ibid., 93). The same terminology prevails in the work of Andras Zempléni (1966). When describing possession ceremonies among the Wolof in Dakar, he generally uses *crise*, like Leiris, but in the context of dancing, he also makes use of *transe* (1966, 408) and refers elsewhere to *la transe extatique* (ibid., 434). In her contribution to research on the Hausa *bori* cult in Niger, Jacqueline Monfouga-Nicolas (1972, 177 ff.), on the contrary, constantly uses the word *transe*, never uses *extase* at all, and scarcely ever uses *crise* except to designate a very specific case of profane possession induced by drugs (ibid., 198–99). To provide a final example, not itself African but at least of African origin, when describing the Brazilian *candomblé* in Bahia, Roger Bastide (1958) uses *transe* and *extase* as practically synonymous. Moreover, although his chapter devoted to this aspect of the cult is entitled "La structure de l'extase" (ibid., 173 ff.), the same phenomena are examined under the title "La transe" in a later collection of articles (1972) entitled *Le rêve, la transe et la folie*. It is true that the four cults I have just mentioned, the *candomblé* in Brazil, the *bori* cult in Niger, as well as the *rab* cult in Senegal and the *zār* cult in Ethiopia, do display a certain number of differences. But all four are cults of possession and, except for the degree of violence involved, they are comparable not only in their manifestations but also in the conditions under which they occur and in the ideas associated with them. As we have seen, what one writer calls a "crisis" the other terms "trance" and the third "ecstasy."

Let us now move on to two equally renown works, both very different from those already mentioned: Jeanmaire's *Dionysos* and Mircea Eliade's *Le Chamanisme*, both of which appeared in 1951. Although the second of the two is subtitled "Les techniques archaiques de l'extase" (Archaic techniques of ecstasy), the word *transe* is nevertheless employed almost as often as *extase*.[7] We read, for example, that among the Samoyeds "great shamans undertake the ecstatic journey in a trance." Jeanmaire, for his part, uses *transe* much more frequently than *extase*, but when referring to the dithyramb, for example, he speaks of "collective ecstasy" (1951, 248), and often resorts to the adjective *extatique*, particularly in the phrase *transe extatique* (ibid., 252). The same use of *extatique* can be found in Luc de Heusch (1971), in which we find "ecstatic religions," "ecstatic crisis," and "ecstatic theater" side by side with the word *transe* on its own, which he uses far more frequently than *extase*. (It should be noted that the frequent use of *extatique* by so many authors can clearly be attributed to the fact that this word is an adjective. If there were an adjectival form of *transe*, the authors I have quoted would in many cases undoubtedly have preferred it.) One final word on the interchangeability of *extase* and *transe*: in the collection *Les danses sacrées*, published in 1963 by a group of orientalists, numerous passages are specifically devoted to trance; under the term *transe* in the index, however, one is referred to *extase*.[8]

This brief summary of the use of the words *transe*/trance and *extase*/ecstasy in modern ethnology clearly demonstrates that their usage is very inconsistent.[9] The two words are never used to establish an opposition between two different states. Yet, as we shall see, this opposition does exist, and it is essential to convey it. Within the perspective of this book, it is even more indispensible to make this distinction since trance and ecstasy each stand in very different relationships to music. We will, therefore, have to establish the distinction between them clearly, so that we can put an end to the confusion and agree upon exactly what we will mean from now on by the words trance and ecstasy.

Everyone will admit that in French it is the word *extase* that springs to mind when we think of the mystical experience described by Saint Teresa of Avila, and it is this very word (Spanish *extasis*) that she herself uses in her writings. But she is careful to make a distinction between its two aspects: "union" (*union*), which constitutes the weaker form of ecstasy, as it were, and "ravishment" (*arrobamiento*), which "goes far beyond union," "produces much greater effects,"[10] and thus corresponds to ecstatic plenitude. "Union," a frequent state with Teresa of Avila, can be achieved under almost any circumstances. "Ravishment," on the other hand is linked, as we shall see, with silence, solitude, and immobility. Before describing her famous vision of the angel, which recurred on several occasions, Teresa of Avila analyzes her state as it comes to her: "The whole body is broken and can move neither feet nor arms; if it is standing it collapses as though drawn downward by some great force and can scarcely breathe."[11] So much for immobility. As for solitude and silence, we all know they are the rules that she herself wanted for all Carmelites. Speaking of a cloister dear to her heart, she writes: "Those who seek *solitude*[12] in order to enjoy Christ, their Husband, have every possibility of living constantly in his company."[13]

Silence, solitude, immobility, three conditions that represent the exact opposite of those required by the shaman when he officiates or by the possessed person when he dances. In these two cases an altered state is achieved in public, accompanied by music, and manifested, often very violently, either by dancing, chanting, or both—in short, by the very opposite of immobility. I could cite such other examples as Dionysiac dances in ancient Greece, the Haitian voodoo cults, the brotherhoods of the Maghreb, such as the 'Aïssāoūa, Gnawa, or others, the tarantula victims in southern Italy, and, lastly, the shamanic curing ceremonies, be they Siberian, American Indian, or Eskimo. All these examples involve noisy, more or less frenzied behavior, and call for a greater or lesser degree of physical agitation. There could thus be no greater dissimilarity between these two types of behavior, that of Teresa of Avila on the one hand and of the shaman or possessed person on the other. In current French usage, the term *extase* rather than *transe* is applied to the first, and *transe* is more frequently used than *extase* for the second.

Considering the primary meaning of these words, this is hard to justify. The Greek *ekstasis* signified first and foremost "the action of moving through space, displacement, deviation." Hence "disturbance, agitation, wandering as applied to the mind."[14] (One might have expected Plato to use it in the context of *mania,* but he never does. In fact the word did not figure in his vocabulary at all.[15] It was only fairly late that *ekstasis* acquired the meaning it still has today in the vocabulary of mysticism.) On the other hand, *transe* also designates a change of state, but of a different kind, originally related to the act of *transir,* that is to say of passing away, and thus of entering into a state of definitive immobility. (It should be noted additionally that death—as a transition—is very often accompanied by agitations of greater or lesser degree, by convulsions. For this reason, "trance" is doubly suited to a description of states of possession, since such states often entail a convulsive stage, and in numerous cases are linked to symbolic death.) It was apparently spiritism that first gave the word "trance" the meaning it currently has today in the anthropology of religion. It was used in the late nineteenth century to denote "the state of the medium when depersonalized, as though the visiting spirit had taken him or her over."[16] But the life of words is not governed solely by the logic of their etymologies. If "trance" has gradually replaced "ecstasy" in descriptions of possession states, it is perhaps because, in both English and French, the word trance in some way evokes both trembling and dancing, and so summarizes, or better yet (like Lewis Carroll), telescopes the two aspects that are particularly characteristic of such states.

Whatever the case may be, it is evident that despite certain hesitations and some inconsistencies associated with using the adjective "ecstatic," the tendency today in both languages is to use "trance" to designate, in a general way, the agitated states I just mentioned, and to use "ecstacy" less and less. Personally, I would be in favor of specializing the use of the two terms, of using "ecstasy" solely to describe one particular type of state—altered states, let us say, attained in silence, immobility, and solitude—and of restricting "trance" solely to those that are obtained by means of noise, agitation, and in the presence of others.

In order to demonstrate the distinction between ecstasy and trance I have thus far referred to only one example of ecstasy—not because it is particularly representative, but because it is well known—that of Saint Teresa of Avila. Before going further, I would like to broaden our comparative base by adding further examples to the "ecstatic" category: the state that the early Church Fathers[17] hoped to attain in the deserts of Egypt; the one sought by certain Tibetan monks in their walled-up solitude;[18] and that still pursued in our own day in Senegal by the Wolof "marabouts" who withdraw into grottoes in order to practice *khalwa,* and in this way obtain divine visions or *jenneer.*[19] Let us also include the state of annihilation in God (*fanāᶜ*) sought by the Sufis when they practice a certain kind of prayer (the *dhikr,* said to be "of the intimate," to which we shall return later),[20] the state of *samādhi,* that is to say, annihilation attained by Indian yogi, and lastly the one achieved by Japanese mystics through *nembutsu.*[21] In his comparative study of mystical practices centered on *dhikr,* which is to say the recolleciton of Allah by ceaseless repetition of the divine name, Louis Gardet, subsequent to Louis Massignon, stresses the shared aspects of Sufi and yoga experiences in their quest, the former for the state of *fanāᶜ* ("annihilation" in God), the latter for *samādhi* (the "abolition of all action"). These two experiences, however, occur within general conceptions of the world that are by no means the same. To quote Jean Filiozat's comment on *samādhi,*[22] the "true nature of this state" consists not in "being ravished out of oneself" but in stabilizing "one's thoughts and latent psychic tendencies" and to succeed thereby in discarding "all representation." The Teresian state of ravishment, *fanāᶜ,* and *samādhi* can certainly all be seen as ecstasies. But they are three very different forms of ecstasy. Mircea Eliade (1948, 93) suggested use of the word "enstasis"[23] to designate the State of *samādhi,* precisely in order to distinguish it from ecstasy. This word has often been used since, notably by L. Gardet (1953; 205ff.) Other distinctions must still be made if we are to seriate the various aspects of "ecstasy" in any definitive order, since the word encompasses such a vast variety of phenomena. This is not our purpose here. From the viewpoint of this book, what we need to remember is that enstasis and ecstasy must be seen as forming together a category that is distinct from that of trance.

Whether experienced by Christians, Muslims, or Buddhists, whether observed in Spain, Senegal, Tibet, India, or Japan, the states with which we are dealing here all are achieved in solitude. "Loss of everything by means of radical withdrawal and aloneness," is how Gardet (1952, 676) defines *fanāᶜ,* the "annihilation in God" of the Sufis. Elsewhere (1953, 208) he writes that *samādhi* is achieved "when the accent is placed on aloneness, solitude filled with self in self." And what do the marabouts of Senegal seek in the depths of their dark grottoes, or the Tibetan monks in their walled-up retreats, if not a similar radical solitude? Such a solitude therefore seems to be a necessary condition for the blossoming of or preparation for ecstasy. The contrary is true for trance. And there are still other features that distinguish the two states. As we shall see, trance usually comprises a convulsive stage, accompanied by cries, trembling, loss of consciousness, and falling. Nothing of this order occurs in *fanāᶜ,* *samādhi,* or in the weak form of Teresian ecstasy. There is also another, even more important difference: ecstasy is a keenly memorable experience which one can recall and ponder over at leisure and which does not give rise to the dissociation so characteristic of trance. The great Christian mystics, Saint Teresa of Avila, Saint John of the Cross, Saint Ignatius Loyola, and many others, have abundantly commented on their ecstasies. The same is true of the Church Fathers and of Indian ascetics. Trance, on the contrary, be it of a possessed person or of a shaman, is characterized by total amnesia. The relationship of the self to the trance state is, in this respect, diametrically opposed to that of the self to ecstasy.

Oesterreich (1927, 23–24) perceived this essential difference between possession trance and states of ecstasy. "On the latter," he wrote, "we possess a host of autobiographical sources. . . .Descriptions of possession by those who have experienced it are, on the contrary, extremely rare." And he added: "This scarcity of accounts by those who have undergone the experience has a profound psychological explanation that stems from the very nature of the state of possession. We are dealing in part with states that entail more or less total post facto amnesia, so that, generally speaking, the majority of those who are possessed are in no position to describe their condition."[24] He does nevertheless cite a few exceptions—including some very noted ones: Sister Jeanne des Anges, the most famous of the Loudun nuns, and Father Surin, one of her exorcists who in turn became possessed[25]—in whom the state of possession remained, to use his expression, "lucid," meaning that the subject was conscious of being inhabited by the "demon" (since he usually is concerned) and subsequently recalled that state. In these cases we are dealing exclusively with a type of possession I shall subsequently term "reprobate"[26] in order to distinguish it from "cultivated" possession, the kind that will primarily concern us in this book. This being so, the exception represented by this "lucid form of possession" as opposed to what Oesterreich calls the "sleepwalking form," which is always followed by amnesia, does not invalidate the rule. The latter, which has been described numerous times, states that the possessed person never, in principle,[27] remembers anything about his trance following his return to consciousness. One may question the sincerity of this forgetfulness or wonder about the mechanism at work, but this would change nothing. The same holds true of the shaman, as is evident from many examples including what G. Morechand says in his study of shamanism among the Hmong of Laos (1968, 202): "No Hmong shaman will ever admit to remembering the trance he has just experienced, or ever agree to calmly, 'intellectually' repeat any previously experienced trance. . . . This is an absolute rule among the Hmong. No one will ever be able to persuade a shaman to perform his chant outside of the trance itself. Shamans unanimously agree that once they have returned to their

normal state, following the trance, they remember nothing. . . .: they
have 'trembled,' then 'woken up again,' and none of them will accept deni-
al of this rupture."

Among the Shakers of Saint Vincent in the Antilles—a Christian sect
whose trances belong to the type I shall subsequently term "communial,"
since there is no possession in the strict sense—the trance state is similarly
followed by amnesia (Henney 1973, 239), even though it is only partial
and—significantly enough—relates solely to the context. Still other types
of trance are accompanied always or usually, totally or partially, by amnesia. Even though it is not possible to say as much, with no exceptions, for
all the forms figuring in the general table of trance drawn up at the end of
the book (see p. 289), amnesia characterizes the principal types of trance
strongly enough to justify using it as a distinctive trait differentiating
trance from what I propose to term ecstasy.

Two further traits can be added to the list of oppositions already cited
with a view to distinguishing between ecstasy and trance. The former is
frequently accompanied by visual or auditory hallucinations. In the first
of his series of three volumes entitled *Ecstasy or Religious Trance* (a perfect example of what has been said previously about the usage of these two
words!), Arbman reserves an important place for visions and hallucinations. These are indeed characteristic of Christian ecstasies, with which he
mainly deals in the first part of his work. "The ecstasies of Saint Anthony
(. . . and many others. . .) have explicitly the character of a vision," we
read in the chapter on ecstasy among the Church Fathers in the *Dictionnaire de spiritualité* (1961, col. 2104). Trance is usually free from such
hallucinations. I should also observe in passing that as far as possession
trance is concerned—the type that interests us the most here—the absence
of hallucination conforms to the very logic of the relations between the
possessed person and the divinity possessing him or her. Since the divinity
takes the place of the possessed person's everyday personality, it does not
constitute an apparition for the subject, contrary to what often occurs
during ecstasy.

Finally, ecstasy and trance differ in that while trance is always associated with a greater or lesser degree of sensory overstimulation—noises,
music, smells, agitation—ecstasy, on the contrary, is most often tied to
sensorial deprivation—silence, fasting, darkness. Nothing could be more
striking in this respect than the contrast one can observe among the Wolof
of Senegal between the behavior of marabouts who seek out ecstasy in the
silence, solitude, and darkness of their grottos and that of the practitioners of the *ndöp,* who enter into trance in the midst of a dense crowd, stimulated by drink, agitated by wild dancing and the din of drums.

Ecstasy and trance may therefore be characterized in relation to one another by two series of terms forming the following oppositions:

Ecstasy	Trance
immobility	movement
silence	noise
solitude	in company
no crisis	crisis
sensory deprivation	sensory overstimulation
recollection	amnesia
hallucinations	no hallucinations

When all the characteristics in one of these two series are present, we then are dealing with what one might term the full form of either ecstasy or trance. Clearly, however, such completeness is not always realized, or the configuration of features provided by a given state may in fact be composite. In the first case, when we are dealing with full forms, the difference between the two states is quite clearcut, in the second much less so. Ecstasy and trance must therefore be regarded as constituting the opposite poles of a continuum,[28] which are linked by an uninterrupted series of possible intermediary states, so that it is sometimes difficult to determine which of the two is involved. To cite only one example, that of Teresa of Avila (which, as we have seen, can be justifiably said to provide the very model of ecstasy), in at least one case (albeit a very exceptional one, it seems) we are confronted with what I shall henceforth identify as trance. I refer to the "ecstasy of suffering" that overtook her one evening when "in the company of the sisters. . . , we sang a number of verses about the torments we suffer from living without God." "Since I was already experiencing this torment," Saint Teresa writes (1949, 500), "I was so gripped by it that my hands stiffened despite all my efforts. . . ," and she adds that the suffering, "now so intolerable. . . forced me to utter loud cries that I was powerless to repress." One cannot help but compare this account with other examples mentioned in the chapter on the Arabs, involving the particular form of trance I will suggest we term "emotional."

Finally, I would like to observe that trance and ecstasy may both be practiced, albeit within the context of different rituals, by the same individual within the same religious faith. Thus the Shakers of Saint Vincent in the Antilles, who still practice trance as I have just defined it, also attain ecstasy when they withdraw into the "secret room" (Henney 1973, 242–43) in order to weep away their sins. In isolation, immobility, and through corporeal chastisement, they then undertake a "spiritual journey" that is apparently strongly characterized by "hallucinatory activities."[29]

Now that the difference between trance and ecstasy—and also, I hope, the gradations existing between them—have been adequately established, let us move on to that which for us is the essential point: the differences between trance and ecstasy in their respective relations to music. Whereas trance, as we shall see throughout this book, is very frequently and very closely associated with music, ecstasy, as it has just been defined, never makes use of it at all. There is an inherent incompatibility between the practice of ecstasy and music. This is, after all, only logical. Excluding certain deliberately contrived experiences, immobility, silence, and sensorial deprivation are incompatible with music. Indeed, in order to escape from her ecstasies—which were so strong that she succumbed to them against her will (F. Jette 1961, 2147)—Marie de l'Incarnation, more or less a contemporary of Teresa of Avila, would begin playing the spinet. In a quite different form of ecstasy, that of the yogi, it may happen that music does play a role under the form of what Mircea Eliade (1948, 254) calls "mystic sounds," which are heard during yoga meditation. The voice of the divinities heard in such states is said to be "similar to the sound of a golden bell." In other words, the sounds that are heard are auditory hallucinations, and thus a further confirmation of our definition of ecstasy. In her laboratory study of yoga techniques, Therese Brosse (1963, 116) tells us that in *bhakti yoga* a song is transmitted mentally and silently from guru to disciple as a means of enabling the latter to attain *dhyāna,* the higher stage of *samyama,* which represents the fullest stage of ecstasy. Here again we may view the music in question as hallucinatory in nature. As we can see, this case does not constitute a counterexample any more than the preceding one; quite the contrary, in fact.

To put an end to the debate on the possible relation between music and ecstasy, suppose someone says that a Mozart quartet plunged him into ecstasy at a concert. This is, of course, pure verbal inflation, or, if one prefers, hyperbolic use of language. Besides, how does this ecstasy manifest itself? Not by noise or frenzy, certainly, but rather by a great desire to prolong it in silence. In practice, applause usually brings it to an end. It is, then, trance—or enthusiasm, to which we shall return later—that drives ecstasy away. Ultimately, we could also invoke Scriabin and his *Poem of Ecstasy.* This would lead us far astray.

All this having been said, I shall not return to the subject of ecstasy in this book. The task facing us now is to isolate and describe all the other signs by which trance may be recognized.

Manifestations of Trance: Hysteria and Madness

Trance is a temporary state of consciousness, or, as the word itself indicates, it is transitory. One leaves one's usual state when one enters into trance, and at the end of a certain period of time, the duration of which varies considerably from case to case, one returns to one's previous state. Trance is thus an unusual state. One might conceivably say of someone that he or she lives in perpetual trance, but the fact remains that such a state is regarded as unusual, or in this particular case as unusually usual.

But what are the telltale signs of trance? Let us divide them into two categories: symptoms and behavior. I shall term symptoms those signs that constitute merely the simple, unelaborated expression of a certain perturbation experienced by the subject at, let us say, the animal level (being seized by trembling is a sign of great fear in both men and animals). "You tremble, carcass!" Turenne said to himself. On the other hand, the runaway horse perhaps represents the most striking example of what we would call "animal trance." I shall term behavioral those signs that no longer constitute a simple reaction, as do symptoms, but a positive action endowed with symbolic value. (It must be acknowledged in passing that the boundary between these two categories is impossible to draw with any precision. This difficulty, however, is inherent in any, or almost any, attempt at categorization. Such categorization still remains indispensible, however, since without it the multiplicity and diversity of such signs would remain sheer chaos. The choice lies between inevitably arbitrary and reductive categories—which remain open to reconsideration, be it said—and confusion.)

Without attempting an inventory, let me list the principal symptoms of the trance state: trembling,[30] shuddering, horripilation, swooning, falling to the ground, yawning, lethargy, convulsions, foaming at the mouth, protruding eyes, large extrusions of the tongue, paralysis of a limb, thermal disturbances (icy hands despite tropical heat; being hot despite extreme circumambient cold), insensitivity to pain, tics, noisy breathing, fixed stare, and so on. In addition, there are two signs that are difficult to categorize as either purely symptomatic or behavioral. First, the subject gives the impression that he is totally engaged in his trance, that the field of his consciousness has been completely taken over by this state, that he has lost all reflexive consciousness, that he is incapable of coming back to himself (unless enjoined to it by some external intervention); in short, that he is plunged into a sort of bewilderment. It is impossible to attract his attention; if he turns his eyes in your direction he does not see you. Second (somewhat complementary to the first), once the subject has emerged from his trance, he has no recollection of it.

As for the behavioral signs, which are even more diverse—not surprisingly so, since in their case the predominant factor is no longer nature but culture—ultimately they all seem to be merely the various "signifiers" of one and the same "signified."[31] One could say that in practice they always symbolize the intensification of some particular faculty by means of an action endowed with certain extraordinary or astonishing aspects. Thus trance may be recognized, among other signs, by the fact that one can walk on burning coals without being burned, pierce one's own flesh without bleeding, bend swords one would normally be unable to curve, confront danger without flinching, handle poisonous snakes without being bitten, cure diseases, see into the future, embody a divinity, speak a language one has never learned, swoon or die of emotion, be illuminated by the Eternal, enter into contact with the dead, travel in the land of the gods, confront those gods, emit totally unhuman cries, give acrobatic displays beyond one's normal ability, bend backwards to make a perfect arc, compose poems in one's sleep, sing for days and nights on end without a break, dance without difficulty despite being crippled. Thus trance always manifests itself in one way or another as a transcendence of one's normal self, as a liberation resulting from the intensification of a mental or physical disposition, in short, as an exaltation—sometimes a self-mutilating one—of the self. In the early days of Christianity, people in trances were called *energoumenoi*[32] since they were thought to be prompted by a supernatural *energeia* attributed, according to circumstances, to God, the Holy Ghost, or the Devil. The word *energumène* was still in current use in seventeenth-century France to designate people who were possessed, notably the nuns of Loudun.[33]

These behavioral signs can vary, needless to say, from the very spectacular to the extremely discreet, just as the symptoms listed earlier can vary from the extremely visible to the almost imperceptible.

The individual in a trance state is thus recognizable by the fact that (1) he is not in his usual state; (2) his relationship to the world around him is disturbed; (3) he can fall prey to certain neurophysiological disturbances; (4) his abilities are increased (either in reality or otherwise[34]); (5) this increased ability is manifested by actions or behavior observable by others. The picture can obviously be either more or less complete or incomplete depending on the individual case. In case of doubt, the context will indicate whether or not one is justified in saying that trance is involved.

The word "liberation" has just been used. It is in connection with the quest for a liberation of this kind that, in an article intended to situate his work in relation (and in opposition) to the "human potential movement" in California, Max Pagès speaks of trance: "When I conduct a seminar I have no fear of admitting that I am in a sort of secondary state akin to *trance,*" he writes (1973, 171). This "liberation of the body" constitutes the goal of the "new trance groups," especially those stemming from the bioenergy movement, also mentioned by Georges Lapassade (1976, 215). What is there in common between trances of this kind and those I shall examine in this book? We know too little about them to decide on this point. Accordingly, I shall not take them into account, especially since their relation to music seems very uncertain. With reference to the seminars he describes, Pagès (ibid., 170) notes that in the "expressive equipment at the disposal of the participants," there are "rudimentary musical instruments, particularly those requiring no previous training that serve to produce simple rhythms: tom-toms, drums, kettle drums, cymbals, xylophones, flutes. . . ." Rudimentary instruments, simple rhythms . . . A strange conception of music, indeed!

Whether one likes it or not, the signs I have listed as characteristic of trance are far too clearly reminiscent of hysteria[35] to avoid a discussion of this matter here. Nor is it merely hysteria that should be considered. Trance states have also commonly been associated with madness. In his work on the relationship between trance and disease, Luc de Heusch entitles the sequel to his chapter "Possession and Shamanism" "Divine Madness and Human Reason." "Trance can be seen as the cultural aspect of mental illness or as the 'madness of the gods,' as the Thonga put it," he writes (1971, 256). The title of Roger Bastide's last work, *Le rêve, la transe et la folie* (1972), is also significant, and although the author actually begins his book by claiming he will not "confuse dream, trance, and madness," one of the sections devoted to trance is nevertheless entitled "Mystic Trance, Psychopathology and Psychiatry." Jean Rouch's most famous film on trance is called *Les Maîtres fous.* Jean Gaborieau entitled the second part of his study, "Ritual Trance in the Central Himalayas," "Madness, Avatar, Meditation." And this is by no means the end of the list.

Ever since Plato (and doubtless before him), the question of the psychiatric aspects of trance has caused a great deal of ink to flow, if we may say so. The debate seems to have made little headway, however, and I shall not, of course, enter into it. First, because it is absolutely outside my competence; second, because the only valid way of doing so would require an interdisciplinary approach. All the same, it is of twofold interest to us. First for its own sake, and because it is fundamental; second, because the psychiatric problem posed by trance is closely linked to that of the relationship between its psychology and its physiology. And it is at the juncture of these two components of trance that the problem of the "effects" of music lies, at least in part. It must be acknowledged that, for an undertaking such as mine, the absence of any general theory of trance as a reference point does not simplify the task.

Seen from my perspective, the problem of trance is clearly a "cross-cultural" one, as the Americans say. But to the extent to which they deal with hysteria, the very writings on trance also raise in and of themselves a cross-cultural problem. In the United States, for instance, the words "hysteria"[36] and, more recently, "neurosis,"[37] have been erased from the psychiatric lexicon. Yet in France this is far from being the case; there hysteria as a concept continues to have a healthy livelihood, both in psychoanalysis and in psychiatry.[38] All the same, opinions on the psychiatric nature of trance could not be more opposed. Subsequent to many other writers, Georges Devereux[39] peremptorily declares that there is every reason to "see the shaman as suffering from serious neurosis, or even as a psychotic in a state of temporary remission." Roger Bastide, on the other hand (1972, 67), supports Herskovits's thesis "which considers mystic trances as 'normal' cultural phenomena in certain societies."[40] I. M. Lewis, for his part, in his chapter entitled "Possession and Psychiatry" (1971, 186, 196) proposes that shamans and possessed persons be classified among "the mass of ordinary 'normally' neurotic people." Is trance a normal phenomenon or a pathological one? Although he has not offered a solution to this question, Claude Lévi-Strauss has at least provided a clear formulation of the problem. Scarcely abridged, the essential part of what he writes follows.

Having observed that "it is convenient to compare the shaman in his trance state, or the protagonist in a scene of possession, to a neurotic," and that "in societies where scenes of possession are prevalent, possession is a form of behavior open to all . . . ," he poses the question: "On what grounds may we assert that individuals corresponding to the average of their group. . . and occasionally manifesting a significant and approved form of behavior, should be treated as abnormal?" To which he gives this answer (1960, xviii–xix):

> The contradiction I have just spelled out can be resolved in two different ways. Either the forms of behavior described by the terms "trance" and "possession" have nothing to do with those that we, in our society, call psychopathological; or one may regard them as being of the same type, in which case it is the connection with pathological states that must be regarded as contingent, and as resulting from a condition particular to the society in which we live. In the latter case we would be faced by a further choice of alternatives: either so-called mental illnesses, in reality outside the realm of medicine, must be regarded as sociological events affecting the behavior of individuals who have been dissociated from the group in a particular way by their personal histories and constitutions, or we must recognize in these sick people the presence of a state that is truly pathological but of physiological origin, a state that tends to create a terrain favorable, or, if you wish, 'sensitizing,' to certain symbolic forms of behavior that still fall solely within the realm of sociological interpretation.

A relativist theory, then, and one that moreover leaves open the possibility of "one day seeing physiologists discover a biochemical substratum for neuroses," without it being invalidated thereby.[41]

In the United States there are those who have attempted to resolve the problem by resorting to a psychiatrically neutral concept, that of "altered states of consciousness."[42] According to this line of thought, trance, whether it is shamanic, possessional, mediumistic, or of any other kind, would be just one "altered state of consciousness" among many others, and this term would cover not only that which ethnographical literature identifies as "states of dissociation or fugue, hysteria, hallucinations, catalepsy, epilepsy, hypnosis, somnambulism, and so on," but also such states as those induced by highway hypnosis or brainwashing on the one hand and possession by the Holy Ghost on the other (Bourguignon 1973, 4, 8).

To consider dreaming as well as just another state of altered consciousness, as Erika Bourguignon herself does, can only inspire doubt as to the validity of this concept. My feeling is that it actually is not a concept at all, but that it only serves as a convenient means of sidestepping the problem. If the purpose of using it is to avoid "committing" oneself to "any particular explanatory theory" to account for the trance state (ibid., 5) and falling into "amateur diagnosis" based on the more or less appropriate use of the language of psychopathology (and this is indeed the danger), then why not simply content oneself with calling a trance a trance and leave it at that? This is the solution I shall adopt here, although I nevertheless reserve the right to return briefly to the question of hysteria in a later chapter.

In ethnology, one may say, evaluating the right or wrong of relegating trance to one or another category of contemporary Western nosography is not of crucial importance. The real interest lies in finding out the category to which the "native" assigns it within his own system of thought. Certainly! But it so happens, first of all, that in the great majority of the cases to be examined here, information on this point is either nil or unreliable. Consequently, any attempt to generalize in this domain would be vain. Second, we shall see right away that even if information is available, and even if it is actually reliable, this does not necessarily help matters.

Gaborieau (1975, 165), in his study of trance in the Himalayas from which I quoted earlier, tells us that the possessed person is referred to as the god's "beast of burden," and that to describe the "psychological transformation" he undergoes when he enters into trance "they say that he becomes mad (*baulino*) or that he is mad (*baulo*)."[43] "A person is referred to as mad," Gaborieau observes, "when he can no longer carry out his familial and social obligations." He then adds: "The same term is applied to the ethnologist who, arriving from who knows where, with no familial or social insertion, occupies the same marginal position as the madmen belonging to the society he is studying." Such information invites us to reconsider the whole situation so radically that we had better forget about it on the spot!

The Representations of Trance: Shamanism and Possession

Although trance can manifest itself in a profane context—and we shall treat such an example among the Arabs in the second part of this book—throughout the world it is usually associated with religion. Religious trance will therefore be our main concern from now on. This said, it occurs in such a variety of forms and is the object of such a multiplicity of representations[44] that it would be impossible to establish its relations with music—or indeed with anything at all—if one did not begin by making a few broad distinctions within such a vast domain.

Everyone will agree that trance is associated, in an overwhelming number of cases, with two aspects of religion: shamanism and possession. But as we shall see later, the relations between music and shamanic trance on the one hand, and possession trance on the other, are by no means the same. It is therefore essential to establish clearly, from the outset, what differentiates the two—and needless to say, to do so without resorting to music since this would make our argument circular.

Shamanism and possession have so many points in common—trance, in particular—that the distinction between them is not always self-evident, to say the least. Certain authors—Mircea Eliade (1951), Luc de Heusch (1971)—think it is very important to distinguish between them. Others on the contrary, and most notably I. M. Lewis (1971), think there is no basis for such a distinction and that there is therefore no reason to draw one. Others still—Erika Bourguignon (1968), for example—recognize the distinction but blur it with so many nuances that it almost disappears. In my opinion shamanic trance and possession trance constitute two very different—and indeed opposite—types of relationship with the invisible, and this is why they give rise to manifestations as different from one another as, for example, a shamanic séance in central Asia and a tarantism séance in southern Italy.

Borrowed in the seventeenth century from the Tungus, "a people, small in numbers (25,000) but scattered across the whole of Siberia from the Jenissei to the Amur and from Lake Baikal to the Tamir peninsula,"[45] the word "shaman" has gradually achieved widespread dissemination in ethnological writings, and its use, once restricted solely to Siberia, now extends not only all the way to Southeast Asia and Melanesia but also, via the Arctic, through the two Americas as far as Tierra del Fuego. As a result, the word "shamanism" has come to include religious practices of the greatest diversity, yet all presenting—at least in principle—common features. Seen from the perspective of this book, what are these features? For my answer to this question, I shall turn to Mircea Eliade and his work on shamanism.[46] However disputed certain parts of it may be,[47] this work nevertheless is the only available, general synthesis of this vast domain. All the same, the examples I shall borrow from it are entirely dissociable from Eliade's overall interpretation of shamanism.

In the chapter describing shamanism in central and northern Asia, which deals successively with the Tartars and the Kirghiz, the Samoyeds, the Ostiak and the Lapps, the Buryats and the Yakuts, the Chukchi, the Yukaghir and the Tungus, with all their various subgroups, besides "shaman"—naturally—and along with "ecstasy" (or "trance"),[48] "chant," and "drum," the two words that recur most frequently are "journey" and "spirit." The shaman's trance is thus conceived as a journey undertaken in the company of the spirits he embodies. The shaman's soul leaves his body and voyages through the invisible regions in order to meet the dead or the spirits, and his journey usually takes the form either of an "ascent to heaven" or of a "descent into hell," to use Eliade's words, or better yet, of an incursion into the "upper" or "lower" worlds. "Among the Xingan Tungus, the shaman vigorously strikes his drum three times and raises it in order to indicate he is ascending into the upper world. He strikes it three times and lowers it when he is descending into the lower world."[49]

Among the Eskimos, it is in the "depths of the ocean" that the shaman undertakes his journey "to seek out his patient's soul and bring it back to his or her body." In addition, he is a "specialist in magical flight. Some shamans have visited the moon, others have circled the earth," Eliade writes (1968, 223). Among the American Indians, shamanism also takes the form of a journey. Besides the examples mentioned by Eliade, an account of such a shamanic journey, collected among the Cuna Indians of Panama, made famous by Lévi-Strauss's interpretation (1949) should be cited here. The same situation exists in Southeast Asia and the Indian archipelago.[50]

Nothing of this kind occurs in what is by general agreement termed possession. In possession the communication between visible and invisible worlds operates in quite the opposite direction: it is no longer the man who visits the inhabitants of the invisible world but, on the contrary, the latter who visit him. One could perhaps say, by oversimplifying the opposition, that since religious trances are essentially private and dramatic communications with the dead, the spirits, or the gods—depending on the particular religious system concerned—men dispose of two major means for achieving such communications: either they have to go to the spirits, or the spirits have to come to them. Whether we examine menadism in ancient Greece or demoniac possession during the Renaissance, the *zār* cult of Ethiopia or the *rab* cult of Senegal, the *orisha* and *vodun* cults in the Gulf of Guinea and Brazil, *basangu* in Zambia or *hàu bóng* in Vietnam, or any of the various forms of trance to be found in Bali, nowhere do we find any evidence of trance being viewed as a journey made by man into the spirit world. In every case it is interpreted as involving the arrival of a spirit or a god in the world of men. This difference is a radical one: in the first case we have shamanism; in the second, possession. Since in both cases the event is experienced from the viewpoint of the human involved, in the first case a journey is taken and in the second a visit is received—considerable distinction indeed.[51]

Starting from these two basic schemes, however, many combinations can be constructed. There is nothing to prevent someone, for example, from setting out on his or her journey only after having "incorporated" auxiliary spirits to assist him or her in the other world.[52] This is in fact what happens in shamanism, so that the shaman has sometimes been described as "possessed." In this case journey and "possession" are combined. Arguing from the fact that shamanism and possession by a spirit regularly occur together, Lewis (1971, 51) is of the opinion that, contrary to the views of Eliade,[53] and de Heusch,[54] the distinction between shamanism and possession is "in fact untenable." But this ignores the fact that the "journey" component is regularly present in trance manifestations observed among the Asian populations listed earlier and regularly absent from those in my second list. This presence, or absence, is an essential feature, since it is the factor that not only underlies all representations related to trance but also governs most of its ritual and external manifestations. Flanked by his auxiliary spirits, the shaman—or rather his soul—leaves his body in order to travel to the invisible world and meet its inhabitants. During his trance, he recounts the events occurring during his journey, which is often undertaken with the aim of recuperating a sick person's soul. "The main function of the shaman in central and northern Asia is magical healing," Eliade observes (1968, 179). His "journey" is for him the supreme method of exercizing that function. His "possession" by his guardian or auxiliary spirits is ultimately no more than a secondary aspect of it.

One may object that there are cases, notably among the Tungus, in which the shaman "incorporates his familiar spirits and undergoes a shamanic trance without going on a journey" (Eliade 1968, 199). In reply, it must be noted that in the functioning of any institution, the logic of things accentuates sometimes this, sometimes that feature.[55] The fact still remains that among such peoples the "descent into hell"—which in their "pusillanimity" present-day shamans "do not dare to undertake" (Eliade 1968, 195)—is the great model of the shamanic adventure.[56] Laurence Delaby, for her part, also stresses "the importance attributed by the Tungus to the perilous journey into the lower world that only the great shamans were able to make" (1976, 130).

Let us now move on to the role played by the incorporation of spirits in shamanic trance, and consider whether this incorporation occurs in the same way in shamanism and in possession.[57] We shall find that it emphatically does not, and that once again the relations involved in the two phenomena are diametrically opposed. How is such incorporation seen in shamanism? A brief summary of what happens among the Gold[58] will provide very significant insights. As among other Siberian tribes, the Gold shaman is a "psychopomp"; in other words, he is the one who guides the souls of the dead into the lower world. Each person who dies has two funeral ceremonies. The second, which is the more important, "takes place some time after the first" and "terminates with the soul being led to the underworld." Based on Eliade's description (1968, 174–76), I shall now provide a summary of this ceremony.

The funeral ceremony lasts several days. The first day, after donning his costume, the shaman takes up his drum and sets out in search of the soul in the area around the yurt [the tent of central Asian nomads]. While searching, he dances and recounts the difficulties that lie ahead on the path to the Underworld. Finally he captures the soul and brings it back into the dwelling. . . .The feast continues late into the night. . . .The next day, he dons his costume again and awakens the dead person with his drum. . . ;[there is then] another feast. . . .Finally, one morning the shaman begins his chanting and, addressing the dead person, advises him to eat well but to drink very little, since the journey to the underworld is extremely hazardous for someone who is drunk. At sunset, preparations are made for the departure. The shaman chants, dances, and smears his face with soot. He invokes his auxiliary spirits and asks them to guide the deceased and himself into the beyond. He leaves the yurt for a few moments and climbs up a notched tree. . . ; from there he can see the path down to the Underworld. . . .Returning to the yurt, he summons the aid of two powerful guardian spirits: *buchu,* a kind of one-footed monster with a human but feathered face, and *koori,* a longnecked bird. . . .Without the help of these two spirits the shaman could never make his way back up from the Underworld, because the most difficult part of the return journey can only be made sitting on the *koori's* back. After dancing and chanting himself into a state of exhaustion. . . .the shaman calls upon the spirits to harness the dogs to the sledge, then asks for a "manservant" to keep him company during the journey. Several seconds later he "leaves" for the country of the dead. The chants he intones, the words he exchanges with the "manservant" enable those present to follow his itinerary. . . .They arrive in the Underworld. The dead at once cluster around and demand to know the name of the shaman and of the newcomer. The shaman is careful not to utter his real name. He seeks among the crowd for the spirits of the kinsmen who were closest during their lives to the soul he has brought with him and consigns it to their care. He then returns to the land of the living as quickly as possible and, once back, recounts at length all that he has seen in the land of the dead.

I ought to add, since Eliade takes it so much for granted he does not mention it, that throughout this time the shaman is in a trance.[59]

Nothing could be more different from this account than trance as it is observed in Africa. Among the Gold the shaman acts as the master of the spirits he embodies: he uses them as "guides," he sits on the back of one of them, he makes them harness his dogs, he converses with his "manservant." In order to return from the underworld, as we saw, he rides one of his auxiliary spirits as though it were a horse. Among the Ethiopians of Gondar, on the contrary, as well as among the Songhay of Niamey, the possessed person—or "possessee"—is the one who is ridden by the genius! As Eliade says (1968, 89), when shamans among the Chukchi, the Eskimos, the Lapps, and the Semang transform into a wolf, bear, reindeer, fish, or tiger and imitate these animals' actions and voices, they are not being "possessed by these creatures; rather, *the shaman takes possession of his auxiliary spirits:* he is the one who *transforms himself*[60] into an animal, in the same way that he achieves a similar result by putting on an animal mask. . . ." In Africa, the possessee does not imitate the god he embodies, he *is* that god. In Asia, the shaman coexists with the guardian or auxiliary spirits he has embodied by means of his magic chant, and this is why it is possible for him to converse with them. Unless I am mistaken, in Africa (at least in all of the cults I have mentioned) such coexistence, within one and the same individual, of the subject in trance and the spirit possessing him, never occurs. The persona of the divinity is substituted for that of the subject but does not coexist with it. Any dialogue between the two would be unthinkable.

Possession, or more precisely the possession fit as observed so frequently in Africa (a subject we shall subsequently discuss at length) can nevertheless be found among Siberian peoples who practice shamanism, and particularly among the Tungus. In these cases we are dealing with disturbances brought about in certain individuals by spirits who torment them. These possessed individuals, who are "for the most part frustrated or disappointed women" on whom the "visitation of spirits" confers "a certain social importance" (Delaby 1976, 28), are not called shamans but something quite different. However, as with the possessed person in Africa, it is frequently through disturbances of this order that the shamanistic vocation first manifests itself, or, more correctly, as Delaby puts it (1976, 37), that the future shaman is elected. Shamans, "when they begin," thus also fall into the category of the possessee, but "they transcend that category by mastering the spirits that torment them" (ibid., 28). Once embodied within them, the spirit of the shamanic ancestor who has chosen them (ibid., 38) becomes their principal auxiliary spirit. From then on, the shaman is the one who "summons" that spirit, together with all those fellow spirits that ordinarily accompany him, and who embodies him "at will" and expels him "when he has no further need of his services" (ibid., 28).[61]

Master over the spirits he embodies, the shaman is also in control of his trance, another factor that helps us to distinguish him from the possessee who, as we shall see later, merely undergoes this state. Thus it has recently been proposed that we define the shaman as someone "who can enter at will into a non-ordinary psychic state (in which either his soul undertakes a journey into the spirit world or he himself becomes possessed by a spirit) for the purpose of making contact with the spirit world on behalf of members of his community."[62]

There are cases, however (and the Kahm-Magar in the Himalayas, filmed and described by Michael Oppitz [1981] are an example), in which in the course of the same ritual the entranced person appears sometimes as a shaman who voyages and controls his trance, sometimes as a possessed person who totally submits to the will of the possessing spirit, identifying with him but not mastering him at all, quite the contrary. Shamanic trance and possession trance—this time in the full sense of the word—can thus alternate in one and the same person. Or, if one prefers, one and the same person can undergo in succession these two forms of trance. It seems that no one can experience them simultaneously. The distinction to be made between shamanism and possession, consequently, remains valid. The difference between the shamanic and possession trance thus seems to rest on three factors: the former is a journey made by a man to visit the spirits, the latter is a visit by a spirit (or divinity) to the world of men; in the former the trance subject gains control over the spirit embodied within him, in the latter the reverse is true; and lastly, the former is a voluntary trance whereas the latter is an involuntary one.[63]

However, here, as in so many other fields, displacements can occur from one model to the other, hybrid forms arise, contacts are made or lost, giving birth to mixtures that are continually done and undone. This is why the configurations of religious trance are so extremely varied, and also why, in many cases, it is difficult to be sure whether one is dealing with shamanism or with possession. In this respect, based on an analysis slightly different from mine, and one to which I do not wholly subscribe, Luc de Heusch[64] described the complexity of this situation very clearly. It is unnecessary to belabor his points here. But even though there are all sorts of possible intermediary forms between shamanism and possession, we must not forget the difference that separates the two. It is fundamental.

In my view, I. M. Lewis commits a great error in refusing to recognize this difference. Let me give a concrete example. In his book[65] he reproduces a photograph of a priest of Ogun, the Yoruba's iron god, taken in Dahomey (now the People's Republic of Benin) around 1950–60. I know the priest in question, having seen him perform his functions on several occasions in 1952 when I was in the company of Pierre Verger, who also published several photographs of the same individual to illustrate his description of the weekly ceremony in which this particular priest was the principal officiant at the time.[66] The caption to Lewis's photograph reads: "The god Ogun speaks through the mouth of the shaman who incarnates him, in Dahomey." Why baptize (if one may so express it) this priest a "shaman"? Among the Yoruba, the trance state associated with the worship of Ogun, the god of iron, has never been regarded as a journey. As depicted, the priest in his trance state is absolutely not recounting what is happening to him in the otherworld. Nor is he imitating one of the guardian or auxiliary spirits whom he has embodied as the result of his summons. Ogun is within him and he identifies himself to Ogun, whose symbols—iron cutlass and bell—he wears, but he is so little master of the god that he is accompanied by a priestess whose function is "to calm Ogun

when he becomes too violent (Verger 1957, 151). *"Ogun kpęlę o"*—
"Ogun gently!" the choir of women sing when the divinity takes possession of his follower too abruptly (ibid., 195). When the shaman in his
trance returns from his journey to the underworld, bringing news of the
dead he has just encountered there, he, the shaman, is the one who speaks.
When the priest of Ogun, as seen in this particular photograph, addresses
himself to the people around him, it is not he, the priest, who speaks; it is
Ogun. To say in this instance that Ogun "is speaking through the mouth"
of the individual embodying him, as Lewis does, is to suggest that Ogun
and the priest are coexisting inside one and the same person, as does in
fact happen with the shaman. But this is absolutely not the case. The personality of the priest as priest has been totally replaced by that of Ogun.
The chorus, which continues its chanting throughout the priest's dance,
sings about Ogun and Ogun alone. To view this priest as a shaman is completely to misunderstand the representations that underlie his trance and
to create a wholly unnecessary confusion in a situation that is already
quite complicated.

The responsibility for this confusion does not fall entirely on I. M. Lewis, who is only perpetuating that made long before by S. F. Nadel in his
well-known article, "A Study of Shamanism in the Nuba Mountains"
(1946). Nadel presents the cult he observed among the Nuba of Kordofan
as corresponding "in all essentials to the classical shamanism of Central
Asia and North West Africa" because, like the latter, "it rests on the belief
that spirits may possess human beings and on the practice of establishing
communication with the supernatural through human beings so possessed" (1946, 25). In fact, it constitutes a case of possession at the service
of mediumship, and conforms in every respect with the case described a
few pages further on in this book.

This is not to say that trance in black Africa only has one possible cause,
which is spirit possession. In Africa there are in fact trances not attributed
to a spirit. Such is the case, for instance, among the Zande, in Central Africa. The witch doctor, "who is both diviner and magician" (Evans-
Pritchard 1937, 149) and whose task "in both roles is to counteract witchcraft," performs these activities in "séances" during which he is entranced
("How Witch-doctors Conduct a Seance," ibid., 147–82). Evans-
Pritchard's description leaves no doubt on this point, even though he himself only dares say, prudently, that the witch doctor "speaks as though in a
trance" (ibid., 165) or "is now entering in a trance-like condition" (ibid.,
167). To what do the Zande attribute this state? Evans-Pritchard does not
provide the answer. Had we not known it was in Africa, however, we
would have believed that the séance was taking place in Siberia and that
the witch doctor was indeed a shaman. But of course to be valid such an
interpretation would require much more information.

Other forms of trance in Africa raise as well problems of typology. I am thinking here of those associated with various cults in equatorial Africa (the Mbwiti in Gabon, notably), in which taking hallucinatory drugs plays an important role. But I shall limit myself to mentioning the fact, for fear of being led too far away.

Let us now return to the essential point. What we need to remember above all is that shamanism and possession are the products of two quite different ideologies of trance. As we shall see later on, these two ideologies correspond—most logically—to two quite different uses of music.

Possession, Inspiration, Communion: Identificatory Trance

To speak of personality substitution, as I have just done in the case of the priest of Ogun, to see it as a relationship "between a spirit thought of as acting and an individual thought of as acted upon," as Michel Leiris (1958, 78) puts it with reference to the zār cult, and to consider that this constitutes a relationship of "possession," certainly is, as Leiris says, a "reductive qualification." Nothing could be more hazy, less sharply focused than the concept of possession, so that despite its great convenience it is also the source of a great many confusions. Here again, several broad distinctions need to be made.

Jeanne des Anges, the most notorious of the possessed nuns of Loudun, was described by everyone, including herself, as "possessed." Jean Cavalier, the famous Camisard, was described by himself and everyone else as "inspired"—with the exception of the papists, who described him as possessed in order to make people believe that the devil was in fact possessing him. We can apply neither of these terms to the Sufi in trance: "possessed" would mean that he was so by either God or the devil, which would be erroneous; "inspired" would imply that his state was due to the presence of the Holy Ghost, which is a religious concept foreign to Islam. He is in the state of having found (*wajd*)[67] God. Leiris (1958, 78) refers to adepts of the zār cult in Ethiopia as being possessed because the Amharic vocabulary used there does in fact convey "the very general idea of seizure of the spirit by force—the exact equivalent of our 'possession.'" When an adept of the *vodun* cult in Benin enters into a trance, the *vodun* is said to have "come into his head."[68] In Brazil, the *candomblé* adept is said to be "in a state of *santo*" (Binon 1970, 163). In the case of the Hausa *bori,* in Niger, the woman in trance is said to be the "mare" of the god, or to "have the gods on her head," or again, to be "in *bori,*" which is to say in a state of ebullition (Monfouga-Nicholas 1972, 193). The list could be much longer still, but let us stop there. The question is to understand how the relationship between the subject in trance and the divinity responsible for that state is conceived.

In the case of a relationship of this kind, however, we must not expect to find very clearcut notions capable of providing us with precise and clearly defined categories. By definition, we are confronted here with the domain of the unspeakable, the vague, the subjective, and the emotional. Nevertheless, by taking as our base the vocabulary used to designate this relationship, the behavior by which it is expressed, and the internal logic of the religion of which it forms one aspect, we are able to distinguish three broad types of mystic trance.

The first is characterized by the fact that, during trance, the subject is thought to have acquired a different personality: that of a god, spirit, genius, or ancestor—for which we may use the general term "deity"—who has taken possession of the subject, substituted itself for him, and is now acting in that subject's place. In a later chapter we shall return to the manner in which this representation of things is often founded on the idea that an individual possesses several souls, so that, using the *bori* of the Niger Hausa as an example, there is one soul that "the gods send away during possession in order to take its place" (Monfouga-Nicolas 1972, 194). For a longer or shorter period the subject then becomes the god. He *is* the god. We can call this possession in the strict sense of the word.

In the second category, rather than having switched personalities, the subject is thought to have been invested by the deity, or by a force emanating from it, which then coexists in some way with the subject but nevertheless controls him and causes him to act and speak in its name. The most frequent example of this relationship is that found in trances attributed to the Holy Ghost. I shall refer to this category of trance not as possession, but as inspiration.

In the third category the relationship between divinity and subject is seen as an encounter which, depending upon the individual, is experienced as a communion, a revelation, or an illumination. Unlike the previous two relationships, this one does not involve embodiment of any kind. I shall therefore refer to the trance state brought about by *wajd,* and achieved by the practice of *dhikr,* which will be described in the second part of this book, as communion or "communial" trance. For a Sufi, or for any Muslim, there can obviously be no question of embodying Allah, or of identifying oneself with him.

Having defined these three categories—not as abstract models but on the basis of concrete examples—let me hasten to add that, in reality, things are not always as simple as this division might suggest, and that it is often difficult to know with which of the three categories one is dealing. To return to the case of the Sufi, it can happen, contrary to all the principles of the Muslim faith, that it does take the form of an indisputable embodiment. Among other examples, there is this description of a *dhikr* séance by a Fez derqⁿwa votary[69] in which, speaking of God (Allah), the trance sub-

ject cries out: "He is in me! He is in me! *Huwa! Huwa!* [meaning He! He!]"
Many people would say that this, whether one wishes to accept it or not, is
purely and simply a case of possession. For my part, I shall say that it is inspiration, but that in any event more than mere communion is clearly involved, contrary to what the logic of Sufism might lead us to expect. In
other cases the distinction I have suggested between "possession" and "inspiration"—which implies a differentiation between two different modalities of embodiment—will not seem either self-evident or necessary to everyone. The Shakers of Saint Vincent in the Antilles regard their trances as
resulting from the presence of the Holy Ghost. They say they are "shaken"
by him (Henney 1973, 238), but they do not identify themselves with him
in any way. Jeannette Henney nevertheless explains these trances as resulting from possession by the Holy Ghost. Further justification of my point
of view is therefore necessary, and this brings us back to the identificatory
aspect of possession.

Let us take the case of the *candomblé,* practiced in Bahia, Brazil. The
divinities (*orixá*) venerated there form part of an extremely populated
pantheon; Roger Bastide (1958, 141) names ten without claiming his list
is complete, and each of those on the list is plural. Each of these deities (all
of African origin), Ogun (god of iron), Yemanja (goddess of fresh and salt
water), Shango (god of lightning), and so on, is capable of incarnating
him or herself into an adept, and thereby bringing on the trance state. The
adept then identifies himself with the divinity and manifests this identification by carrying the deity's symbols (a double-headed ax for Xango, a
sword for Ogun, an articulated fish for Yemanja, and so on), by assuming
his or her humor, by imitating his or her behavior, and by executing dance
steps expressing the deity's individual characteristics.[70] One must admit
that in a cult in which possession can be attributed to a variety of deities, it
is essential to know which one is involved, hence the necessity to identify
him or her. The same can be said of many other cults. To name but a few,
there is the Vietnamese *hầu bóng,* the Ethiopian *zār* cult, and that of *rab*
in Senegal. Identifying the spirit or divinity responsible for the possession
occupies a very important place in the initiation rites of these cults: unless
one knows to which deity any particular possession should be attributed,
how is one to address him, make the correct sacrifices, and generally behave toward him in the appropriate manner? In the case of tarantism—
which is not, properly speaking, a cult—identifying the particular spider
whose bite is responsible for the trance state constitutes a crucial moment
of the ritual, since here again there are several different spiders that may
have bitten the sick person. The first thing to do, therefore, is to ascertain
which one is involved (a process carried out with the aid of music). Moreover, one of the dance figures through which the trance is expressed consists in imitating the spider by walking, if that is the right word, on all

fours with one's back to the ground. So there are trances whose ritual is identificatory in nature, and in a double sense, moreover: on the one hand it is essential, before anything else, to identify the deity responsible for the perturbation, and on the other, once this has been done, it is then necessary to become identified with him or her. I shall say, therefore, that there is possession when the ritual is identificatory, and only in this case.

Nothing of this kind occurs in what I have proposed we call inspiration or communion trances, even though in one of them there may be embodiment (as in possession) and not in the other. When the dervish, as a result of *dhikr* or *samāꞋ*,[71] falls into a trance and dances, he is not identifying himself in any way with Allah, even when—an extreme case inadmissible to the purists—he cries out "He is in me!" Neither (on the orthodox side) the followers of the Shlustes (a Russian flagellant sect),[72] who dance in a trance induced by the presence of the Holy Ghost, nor (on the Protestant side) the Camisards of the Cevennes (France), who are moved to prophesy by inspiration, identify themselves with God or the Holy Ghost. The latter causes them to shake and dance, or talks through their mouths; but those he inspires do not in any way imitate him. Would imitating Allah, Jehovah, or the Holy Ghost be conceivable? The same may be said of Elisha's trance in the Bible, when he feels the hand of Jehovah upon him before he begins to prophesy (2 Kings 3:10–15): he senses the presence of God upon or within him, but there is no question of identifying with Him or imitating Him.

Thus nonidentificatory trance inspiration or communion trance appears to be characteristic of Islam, Christianity, and Judaism. In other words, it seems to be linked with the logic of religions of transcendence. It nonetheless signals the presence of a divinity. It is an epiphany, and in this respect it should be ranked alongside possession, even though the latter is identificatory, rather than alongside shamanism, even though shamanism is also nonidentificatory. We shall see later that identificatory and nonidentificatory trances each make very different use of music. This is why I have insisted on the importance of making this distinction.

Divinatory Trance and Mediumship

Shamanism, possession, and inspiration have in common the fact that they all—each in its own way—usually lead to divination. Divinatory trance is not their prime goal, but it does constitute a natural extension of such states. Shamans are not specialists in divination, any more than those who are possessed or inspired, but while they are in a trance they are asked questions, their advice is solicited, and they are requested to predict the future. Besides this kind of trance in which divination occasionally figures, there is also another type in which divination is the sole purpose. I shall label this type mediumistic trance or mediumship.

Mediumistic trance also manifests itself in numerous ways. In Greek antiquity, the most famous example was the Pythia of Delphi. As we know, she was inspired by Apollo, but her trance did not in any way involve identification with or imitation of the god. People came to consult her and she simply delivered her oracles. In Tibet the so-called government oracle has a comparable function, but in this case the trance is triggered, and manifests itself, in a very different way; I shall have occasion to refer to it several times later. There also are numerous examples of mediumistic trance in both Africa and Asia. Since by its very function it is triggered on command (frequently at close intervals), it is only logical that it would often manifest itself in fairly nonviolent ways, and that on occasion, it would occur so discreetly as to be imperceptible. This is the case among the Mofu of Cameroon, for example, where one finds both male and female soothsayers. J.-Fr. Vincent (1971, 108) writes that the women "identify with their genius to the point of saying 'I' or 'we' instead of using the third person." Their trance manifests itself in an extremely reserved manner. The men, who practice divination in what one might call a more professional way, are described as being "inspired" (ibid., 76, 77, 104), and their possession by the "genii of devination" is thought to be a "permanent state." When they converse with these genii, and question them, their trance, if it is a trance, does not manifest any external signs, and there is nothing to indicate they have entered an "altered state" (ibid., 104). On the surface, then, there is no trance state at all in these cases, even though the soothsayer's vocation was originally determined by trances or possessions displaying all the usual characteristics of those states (ibid.).

For all sorts of reasons, mediumistic trance—which one can observe without going to the other end of the earth—can take an almost infinite variety of forms. Its relations with music do not therefore have the same regularities that can be found in the case of shamanism or possession. I shall devote a section of a later chapter to this subject.

To conclude this attempt at classifying religious trance, I should note that we shall be dealing, a little later on, with yet another type of trance, one closely connected with possession but quite distinct from possession trance, and which I feel is best labeled, for reasons I shall provide later on, as "initiatory trance." Lastly, it hardly need be said that I do not claim to have exhausted all the possible aspects of trance in this typology, and that there are many more than those I have described. I have limited myself here to those with which we will be concerned in this book.

THE DYNAMICS OF POSSESSION
Possession Cults and Reprobate Possession

Of the various types of trance we have just investigated, possession trance is the one that will concern us most. It is therefore important for us to investigate in greater detail the characteristics of possession as a religious phenomenon. In his "Prolegomena to the Study of Possession Cults," Roger Bastide (1972, 84) defines such cults as sets of "functional variables" in which manifest and latent functions are articulated in different ways and give rise to a very complex series of combinations. Without entering into the details of these variables, let us simply say here that (1) possession cults are forms of religion characterized by a certain type of relation between a given deity and certain categories of his or her zealots whom I shall call adepts, this relation causing the adept to become possessed by the divinity; (2) possession itself is the socialized behavior of an individual consisting, given certain circumstances, in a change taking place within him, with the effect that his usual personality (which governs his everyday behavior) is replaced by the persona of the deity, who dictates different forms of behavior to him; this substitution being accompanied by an alteration in psychic activity generally termed trance; (3) the identification brought about in this way constitutes an alliance (sometimes reduced, one might say, to a pact of peaceful coexistence), the major function of which is to lead the divinity either to exert his power in favor of the possessed person and / or his group (by increasing their strength, say, or protecting them from adversity, or curing them of an illness, or revealing the future to them) or, alternatively, to cease exerting his power against them.

There are also cases in which, far from being cultivated by society, possession is reprobated either by the whole of society including the possessed individuals themselves, or by one section of the population, sometimes a majority, sometimes a minority, according to circumstances. The notorious possessions of Loudun, which were the talk of France in the seventeenth century, were unanimously disapproved of, since they were demoniac in nature, and regarded as such not only by public opinion but also by those subject to them. They were nevertheless "possession" in the sense of the word we are using here, since they were identificatory: "Three types of references—to the social body, to the angelic Orders (whence the demons formerly fell) and to the physical body—constitute the coordinates by means of which an *identity* is conferred upon these women," observes M. de Certeau (1970, 135). "The evil spirits were commanded in Latin to speak their names . . ." he writes elsewhere (ibid., 28). We cannot help but compare this identification of the spirit by its name, in Loudun, with what Andras Zempléni describes as happening among the Wolof of Dakar, in his chapter on "the naming of the *rab*" (the *rab* being the spirit responsible for the possession), naming without which there could clearly be no possible "identificatory behavior" on the part of the adepts (Zempléni 1966, 356 ff., 402 ff.).

In the opinion of one of the most important protagonists of this much-publicized affair, Father Surin (the principal exorcist of these extraordi-

cults
France ?

nary victims of possession, before succumbing to possession himself), the Loudun possessions took a truly "theatrical" form.[73] This does not mean that they became the object of a cult. Quite the contrary in fact. Far from cultivating possession, the point was to exorcize or put an end to it. This explains why this "theater" was totally devoid of music, and why we shall consequently not deal any further with this type of possession in this book except, very briefly, in a later chapter devoted to exorcism.

Music and Possession: An Approach to the Problem

Widely distributed throughout the world, possession in its cultivated forms is associated everywhere with music and dance. Associated, moreover, not merely in a general way, as is the case to varying degrees with so many forms of religion, but in a very particular one, since trance, which is the central phenomenon here, is often regarded as the direct result of music and dancing. We are therefore faced with the problem of understanding the origin of this power, so frequently accorded to music, of triggering possession trance. Of what order is it? Psychic? Somatic? Symbolic? Effective? Imaginary? Real? On the other hand, we shall see later that music, even within one and the same cult, may sometimes appear to be indispensible to triggering the trance and then, at others, quite unnecessary. Why? How are we to explain the fact that its effects are, as we shall discover, so variable? Or that they take such different, sometimes even contradictory forms from one cult to another? Or that they have been so variously interpreted by those who have described them? There is something paradoxical in the relations between music and possession. Seen from afar, in their totality, they appear most of the time to be absolutely necessary. Yet when one looks closer, the nature of that necessity appears incoherent and escapes all attempts at formulating it. This is because possession cults, of which there are so many various types, must be regarded as so many discrete systems whose internal logic will govern the articulation of their elements differently in each case. Music occurs as one of the component parts of those systems, and the role it plays varies with the models upon which those systems are structured. But, since music is itself a system, its relations with each model are equally determined by its own organization, thus accounting for their protean character. How can we try to grasp such a constantly shifting reality?

Since the essential feature of possession cults is the change of state that occurs within the adept's psyche, these cults must be considered first of all in terms of their dynamics. But this dynamic must itself be viewed from several angles.

Trance being by definition transitory, possession must be first approached from the viewpoint of the dynamics of trance. The modification of the state of consciousness characteristic of trance follows a process comprising a sequence of distinct phases whose sequential order obeys a particular internal logic. These successive phases—preparation, onset, climax, resolution—each present particularities that vary significantly from one cult to another. As for the modalities of this modification—more or less imperceptible or brutal, mild or convulsive, calm or dramatic— their variations are equally significant. The relations that trance may have with music can vary not only from one phase to another but also according to the type of modification involved. This being said, however fleeting or brief the state of possession may be, it is always more or less durable. It is therefore important to consider it also from this aspect, the one it takes on during its culminating phase. This phase, which varies in duration and can, I repeat, be very fleeting, consists in a state of consciousness characterized by a form and a content that are both set and stable. It is a slice of time experienced under an identity other than the one of everyday life, and which we can justifiably isolate from the let us say normal state of consciousness that precedes and follows it. During this phase the adept is no longer a Niger peasant or a Bahia street vendor but Dongo, god of lightning, or Yemanja, goddess of water. What is significant, then, is the behavior of the spirit incarnated within the possessed person.

In addition, trance, both as an experience and as a corporeal technique, represents different types of events from the adept's standpoint depending on whether he is integrating this experience and learning this technique— during initiation—or whether he exercises previously acquired knowledge and skill. Initiation, which is the discovery of a new state of consciousness and an apprenticeship in the various ways of reaching and then leaving it, is a unique experience that will not be repeated, and one that results in an irreversible modification of the person's relations with himself, with the divinity, and with society. Once this initiation has been undergone, the modification is permanent. On the other hand, the inner change that the votary undergoes when he passes from his everyday state to his possessed state, and then reverts to his former one, naturally recurs every time he goes into a trance throughout the remainder of his life. But, and all the descriptions concur on this point, the behavioral patterns characterizing trance differ according to whether it involves a novice, a recent initiate, a confirmed adept, or an officiant experienced in the trance state. The behavior of the possessed person thus varies during his career, and his trance takes different forms depending on the stage he has reached. It is therefore essential to set trance within this dynamic process when one investigates its relations with music.

Lastly, trance, as an event, is linked with the successive stages of a ceremony, and does not generally occur at just any time. A possession ritual is an architecture of time also composed of various phases connected with different kinds of music. It is thus within the dynamics of the ceremony that we need to consider the relations between music and trance.

Investigating the relations between music and possession, ultimately means asking ourselves what role music plays in the preparation for trance, in the onset of trance, in the maintenance of trance, then in the emergence from trance, all this being seen in terms of the stage the adept has attained in his career and of the particular moment in the ceremony that has been reached. It is within this threefold dynamic—of trance itself, of the adept's life, and of the ritual's development—that we will therefore examine these relations.

So what means do we have at our disposal to conduct an investigation into these relations between music and possession? To begin, let me observe that although the various manifestations of possession have often been likened—whether rightly or wrongly—to those of hysteria, we do not know a great deal about the actual state experienced by those who have become possessed. The descriptions at our disposal have all been made from the outside, apart from the one by G. Cossard (1970), which despite its qualities, is nevertheless extremely brief. On the other hand, although we know that music does have dynamogenic effects, although experiments have shown that certain sounds or certain kinds of music encourage the growth of plants, the lactation of cows, or the resignation of saleswomen in department stores, although, in short, we can be sure that music does have the capacity to act upon the psychological or physiological behavior of living beings, these effects tell us nothing about the way music may act in the case that concerns us here, which is totally distinct from all those listed above. The only research carried out in this field, that of Neher (1962), is unfortunately devoid of all scientific value, as we shall see later. We therefore have no experimental data available for advancing any hypothesis on the psychophysiological role of music in trance states. Given the present state of things, the only means of understanding this role is to turn to the existing evidence we have on possession cults, which is to say, essentially, the writings of ethnographers. These ethnographers (or anthropologists) provide us with three kinds of information, depending on whether they offer accounts of the correlations natives make between music and trance—unhappily the rarest kind—whether they themselves make such correlations—unconsciously more often than not—or whether they simply describe the facts in such a way as to enable us to discern concomitances between music and trance ourselves, which is the most frequent kind, though in this last case precise observations are much less numerous than one would wish.

In examining the relations between music and possession as they emerge from such texts, or rather from those I have selected as being particularly significant, I shall conform to the principle stated earlier, that of considering possession cults as dynamic wholes. I shall therefore proceed by following the various stages the adept goes through in the course of his career as a possessed person, beginning with the stage I shall label as prepossession. But first it is important to provide a broad outline of this career and of its principal stages.

Possession and Vocation

Whether explicit or not, the autochthonous theory is that possession is produced by the will of a divinity who, for one reason or another, wishes to incarnate him- or herself within a particular individual. The god is the one who selects the person in whom he wishes to incarnate and not the reverse: a person does not select a god for whom he then becomes the vessel. On the surface, at any rate, the relation as experienced by the possessed person is passive rather than actively willed.

In Vietnam, in the *hàù bóng,* "it is accepted that Genii themselves are the ones who select their mediums, 'catch' them, and oblige them, willy nilly, to serve their masters" (Simon and Simon-Barouh 1973, 33). In the Niger, among the Hausa, "societal viewpoint requires that adepts be chosen by and solely by the gods. Any initiative on the part of the woman concerned would only be merely presumptuous and sacrilegious" (Monfouga-Nicolas 1972, 95). In Dahomey, among the Gun, "the *vodun* himself selects *vodunsi* from members of the families who make up his followers (Akindélé and Aguessy 1953, 113). In Brazil, among adepts of the *candomblé,* "a deity's supreme requirement is that one of the faithful become his 'horse' by means of trance, so that he can come down among mankind and dance" (Cossard 1970, 95).

Perhaps we ought to detail the nature of this relationship. The fact that initiation is sought (as it is in many but not all cases, as we shall see) does not, in practice, mean that it has been deliberately willed. To be initiated into the worship of a divinity when you know, thanks to the intervention of a soothsayer, that the divinity has chosen you, constitutes a submission to that choice, not an act of choice on your part. Whether in Bali (Belo 1960, esp. 2, 47 ff.), Tanzania (Gray 1969, 175), or in Dahomey (Akindélé and Aguessy 1953, 114), the witchdoctor or soothsayer is the one who, in answer to the questions of a person who has come to express his or her troubles, unveils behind the client's difficulties either the anger of an offended divinity or that divinity's quest for a receptacle, a visible envelope. If the soothsayer's interpretation meshes with the client's unconscious aspirations, so much the better; as with good matrimonial agencies, good soothsayers are those who can arrange alliances satisfactory to both parties. "Officially," to use the term employed by Jacqueline Monfouga-Nicolas (1972, 93), he has simply translated the wishes of the invisible element that governs the world.

Thus, if one becomes an adept of a possession cult, it is not because one has willed it oneself—or at any rate not because one has willed it consciously—but because a god wishes it. I should add that it is not always a soothsayer who discloses this fact, and who identifies the god requesting the initiation, as is the practice in Chad, for example, among the Mundang (Adler and Zempléni 1972, esp. 87, 118). In a neighboring country, Niger, among the Hausa (Monfouga-Nicolas 1972, 97), on the contrary, "the healer of the *bori* [the woman in charge of the college of possessed women] is the one who decides whether or not a woman had definitely been chosen by any particular god." But this does not affect the problem in any way. The significant point is that in each case divination is involved; that is to say, a method of acquiring information about the will of the gods so that their wishes may be obeyed.

In all cases, that is, except for tarantism, in which recourse to any kind of divination is never described. This exception, however, is neither complete nor significant. Obviously, tarantism is an institution in an advanced state of decadence. Although it still attracts "new recruits" (cf. De Martino 1966, 41), we know nothing about the way in which they are recruited. But in any event it offers a case of the "selection by illness" mentioned by J. Monfouga-Nicolas (1972, 97), a selection process that does in fact constitute a system of divination, either in itself or as an element of a broader divinatory system, as in the case of the Mundang (Adler and Zempléni, ibid.). Moreover identifying the tarantula responsible for the bite, in other words the possession, is carried out by means of a "musical diagnosis" that also functions as a divinatory system. We shall return to this subject later.

Alongside possession by personal vocation, if one may so express it, which is a response to a particular state or unhappy event in the life of an individual (as is the case, among other examples, with the *sadeg* "trance medium" in Bali, and with other categories of possession: *zār* in Ethiopia; tarantism in Europe; the *candomblé* in Brazil; and usually with *bori* adepts), there also exists a kind of possession that affects the person undergoing it not as an individual but as a member of a group. Two ways are possible here. In the less frequent of the two, possession is handed down as an inheritance, which can occur in the case of *bori*: "*Bori* can be transmitted as an inheritance, in extremely rare cases, without the intervention of any pathological elements" (Monfouga-Nicolas 1972, 93). The same thing has been observed in Bali, but here again, as an exception (Belo 1960, 19–20). Among the Fon of Dahomey, Herskovits tells us (1938, 2:195, 197), albeit without clarifying whether or not the practice is common, the adept of a *vodun* can designate his successor before dying. In the other way the family, group, or village consecrates an individual to the gods, usually at a very early age. This was the case in Bali—Jane Belo (1960, 4) speaks of it in the past tense—with girl dancers, under the age of

puberty, whose trances owed nothing to illness. These girls were in practice chosen by the village when it decided to form a "club" around two female dancers in the hope of driving out epidemics. Little girls, Belo tells
us, "were chosen apparently for their ability to go into the disassociated
state and to perform in this state dances which it was said they could not
possibly have executed if they were not entered by a god, since they had
received no previous training in the dance." This is also most frequently
the case in *vodun* cults among the Gun of Dahomey, at least when a lineage *vodun* is concerned. Since filiation among the Gun is patrilineal, the
child is consecrated as a general rule to the *vodun* of the father's lineage,
on the advice of—or at any rate after consultation with—the soothsayer.
The recruitment of *vodunsi,* the "wives of the *vodun,*"[74] thus follows a
path opposite to that of the *bori* or *zār.* In the case of the *vodun* it is a family matter, and the individual concerned (usually a girl) is not even consulted (a situation comparable to the marriage process prevalent among
the Gun, in its traditional form at least); in the case of *zār* or *bori,* on the
contrary, it is above all an individual matter,[75] and although it may involve
familial components, these are not decisive. This does not mean that in
the case of *vodun* personal predisposition does not play a certain role. In
order to choose future *vodunsi,* and thus prepare for the next "class" of
adepts, "several months before the ceremony of their entry into the convent," the kinfolk, with the agreement of the priest of the *vodun* concerned, consult Fa, the god of divination. The list of "pupils selected by
the vodun" is established in this way (Akindélé and Aguessy 1953, 114).
Among other things, this consultation obviously bears upon a particular
child's predispositions with regard to the status of a *vodun*'s wife, and the
final choice certainly takes this into account. The fact remains, nevertheless, that the decision ultimately rests with the family. *Vodun* and lineage
live in a reciprocal relationship, since the more powerful the *vodun* the
greater the protection for the lineage, and the more the lineage honors its
vodun (notably through lavish ceremonies, and therefore by large numbers of faithful followers) the more the deity's power is consolidated. This
being so, it follows that the lineage must ensure its bonds with the *vodun*
do not become attenuated in any way. It must therefore, regularly supply
its *vodun,* if one may so express it, with new wives as the generations age
and renew themselves. It can happen, however, that the family's zeal
slackens, or, as is becoming more and more frequent, that new recruits,
influenced by marabouts and missionaries of various denominations, are
recalcitrant, refuse to enter the convent when the moment arrives, or even
run away from it. Any misfortune befalling the family or the country is
then interpreted as a warning to restore order. We know that the 1973
drought was regarded by a number of Africans as a sign of the gods' anger
at being deserted by mankind. Attempts were consequently made to revive

old forms of worship that had either become extinct or were on the verge of becoming so (de Sardan 1973; see filmography). Possession is thus sometimes a given group's response to adversity, a situation analogous to the one we already mentioned, in which it constitutes an individual response to illness.

Vocation of the impersonal type, by which I mean that in which the god's choice (since, let us recall, it is always the god who does the choosing ultimately) affects the person involved (usually a child) not as an individual but as the representative of a lineage, can take other forms as well. It often happens that if a woman remains sterile, or regularly loses her children very young, for example, her parents decide to consecrate any future child in advance to the *vodun* from whom, always on the advice of the soothsayer, assistance will be sought.[76] The *vodun* in question will then be one of those that Akindélé and Aguessy term "private *voduns*," particularly Dan, the snake god, or Sakpata, the earth god, who controls the incidence of smallpox. It should also be observed that although he may be a "private *vodun*" for certain families, Sakpata (one of the most popular of all *vodun* in the Gun region) may equally be a lineage *vodun* for other families.

The *orisha* cult among the Yoruba, neighbors of the Gun, has two types of recruitment process, one personal and one impersonal. In the Nago territory[77] of Benin, Shango, who is the dominant *orisha*, recruits his votaries young, sometimes as very young children, I am told by Pierre Verger, who once saw a novice of about two years old still being carried on his mother's back. It is clear that such recruitment, classified by age, and intended to renew the alliance between family and divinity as well as to ensure the succession between generations, takes place at the family level, without consulting with the individual selected. In short, it falls into the category of what I have termed impersonal vocation, because it is unconnected with the individual's personal history. Pierre Verger observes (1969, 51) that the most frequent form of recruitment occurs at the moment of birth, when the oracle indicates that "such is the child's destiny." But it can also happen, and apparently this is not exceptional, that the *orisha* acquires recruits the other way. Verger (1957, 159) recounts the case of a woman whose children had all been stillborn, victims of an evil spirit. Ogun, god of iron, the village's predominant *orisha*, then took this woman under his protection (after she had lost consciousness at the door of his temple); she underwent initiation, and then became an Ogun votary. Here, the recruitment is of the same type as the one that predominates in the *bori, zār,* and *ndöp* cults.[78]

The *vodun* and *orisha* cults share one feature that distinguishes them from a whole group of other interrelated cults: they are both, not at the collective but at the individual level, strictly monotheistic. The votary is, indeed, consecrated to one and only one *vodun* or *orisha*,[79] who in the great majority of cases is the adept's lineage deity. To use the term employed by Luc de Heusch (1971, 254), possession in this case is the deed of an endogenic spirit. In *bori*, as in *zār* or *hầù bóng*, the votary is possessed by several spirits in succession. In *bori* it would seem that these spirits are mostly unconnected with the votary's lineage, in other words they are allogenic. In *zār* the spirits are most often seen as coming from another district, and therefore are once again allogenic; but this rule is not absolute.[80] Let us remember in passing that Jeanne des Anges of Loudun was possessed by seven demons (Certeau 1970, 136). In tarantism, on the contrary, the person affected is associated with one particular species of tarantula and no other, a fact that results in his selective sensitivity to a particular form of the tarantella. On the other hand, the *vodun* and *orisha* cults are distinguished by the fact that in the first, initiation entails apprenticeship in a series of secret languages,[81] whereas in the second, Pierre Verger tells me, there is no such component.

Trance, Crisis, Fit, "Wild" Possession

Three words constantly recur in texts describing possession cults: possession (of course), trance, and crisis (*crise*).[82] But all authors do not use the last two terms in the same way. Some talk mainly of crisis: Michel Leiris (1958) and Andras Zempléni (1966) in particular, in their descriptions of possession in Ethiopia and Senegal respectively. Other writers mostly use the word trance and employ *crise* solely with reference to one of its particular aspects. This is true for Jacqueline Mofounga-Nicolas (1972), among others, and limiting ourselves to texts in French. Other writers use both words almost interchangeably. The word *crise* is used to denote sometimes a convulsive form of trance, sometimes the paroxysmic aspect of trance when it displays periods of variable intensity, sometimes the onset of trance if it is characterized by a moment of more or less distressing agitation, and finally sometimes—and this last is a very different usage— to refer to the troubled period a given individual may undergo, and which will lead him to seek an outlet in possession. It is in this last sense that H. A. Junod (1913, 2:438), among others, uses the word: "Thus the first signs of a possession seem to be a nervous crisis, but also the occurrence of certain suspicious symptoms. . . .However these symptoms are not sufficient ground for a diagnosis, and the bones are always consulted to come to a conclusion," he writes in his famous monograph on the South African Thonga. But several pages later Junod uses the word in another sense, to denote the onset of possession: "Conquered at length by this noisy concert, the patient enters a condition of nervous exaltation. The crisis occurs, the result of evident hypnotic suggestion. He rises and dances wildly . . ." (ibid., 443).

E. De Martino, in his work on tarantism, also uses *crise* in two different senses: "The real therapeutic ritual begins with music. At first there was solely the crisis, that is to say, the culturally conditioned imitation done by the poisoned victim. . . .Within the framework of this symbolic imitation, the tarantulees refer to themselves as feeling 'broken,' 'torn,' 'bruised,' 'shattered,' or else—as I have so often heard said during our fieldwork—'wounded,' or 'upset,' in other words filled with a profound distaste for oneself and for everything. The extreme form of this imitation is an abrupt collapse, which means that the tarantulee is enacting the role of a person in danger of dying . . ." (1966, 142). On the preceding page, the word crisis is used to denote a quite different stage, the one in which the tarantulees, after having already danced a long time, meet together in the chapel of Saint Paul and communally attain the paroxysm of their trance, a paroxysm Martino describes elsewhere in these words: "in the interweaving of the individual crises. . .the general and desperate agitation was dominated by the stylized cry of the tarantulees, the 'crisis cry,' an *ahiii* uttered with various modulations, that sounds more like the yelping of a dog than a human cry" (ibid., 121).

A. Métraux, in his study of Haitian voodoo, reserves the word *crise* for the initial stage of possession, in which "the trance manifests itself by symptoms of a clearly psychopathological character" (1958, 106). Roger Bastide, on the contrary, sometimes uses *crise* and *transe* interchangeably, so that in his series of studies on trance states we can read, only a few pages apart, "the *crise* brought on by the *bossal* god" and "trance brought on by the *loa bossal*" (1972, 88, 92). Elsewhere (on p. 74), he writes of possession by the *bossal* god.[83] Luc de Heusch (1971, 228) uses the terms *transe* and *crise,* or even *crise de possession* and *crise extatique* without differentiation. For our purposes, however, it is indispensible to assign a clear meaning to each of these words, or, rather, to make it quite clear to which precise phase of possession they refer. Further, it is essential to realize that the various possession cults throughout the world differ greatly in the type of temporal development they exhibit. Some go through numerous, very ritualized stages, the milestones of a long initiation; others, on the contrary—and tarantism in particular—display a very telescoped type of development. Certain distinctions that are thus indispensible when describing certain cults have no relevance for others.

First, let it be said that if crisis and trance are so often used interchangeably it is because they both designate an abnormal and transitory state. But although trance is, in this sense, always a crisis or a fit, crisis, on the other hand, is not always a trance. Moreover, viewed as a temporal development, trance contains a particular stage—entry into the trance—which itself often takes the form of a crisis and, consequently of a crisis within a crisis. Finally, as we have seen, the word crisis is also used to designate the state of crisis, either chronic or acute, that leads the individual who experiences it to enter the path of possession. It is therefore important to clarify the ambiguity inherent in this term.

The chronic crisis to which I have just referred—illness, misfortune, troubles of all kinds affecting the individual's person, human relationships, or possessions—leads in general to an acute nervous fit interpreted as the sign that a divinity desires embodiment. Who this divinity is remains to be discovered. If it has already been identified, an alliance with it remains to be made. This nervous fit often consists in falling unconscious to the ground. Frequently, this event occurs without any kind of ceremony, as in tarantism, where, as we have just seen, this sudden collapse represents the paroxysm of the fit. Describing an initiation in the Yoruba region of Dahomey, P. Verger (1957, 159) relates how the woman in question had previously "fallen to the ground in a rigid state" outside the temple of Ogun, god of iron. In Chad, among the Gula Iro, all possessed women "start their career" as the result of a fit of this sort that floors them quite unexpectedly (Pairault 1969, 258). In Tanzania, among the Segeju (Gray 1969, 175), the victim is brutally thrown to the ground "as if by some invincible force." The day and precise time of the fall are used by the diviner to identify the *shetani* genius responsible for it. But the fall may equally occur during a ceremony. In Benin this is usually the case in the rituals involving Sakpata, god of the earth and master of smallpox. This also holds true for the *candomblé* (Cossard 1970, 158–59), but Cossard specifies (ibid., 162) that the future adept "may also fall at any other given moment outside the ceremonies."

I would like to propose we label this first sort of crisis, which resembles a nervous fit or attack much more than a possession crisis, a "prepossession" crisis or fit. Whether or not it takes the form of a fall, such a crisis constitutes in many cults a unique and decisive type of event in the life of the future adept. In many cases, the crisis (and fall) does not merely signify that the divinity has taken possession of the individual, it also indicates, above all, that the individual has been "killed" by the divinity. The fall occupies a particularly important place in the *ndöp* cult among the Lebu and the Wolof of Senegal. Whether a "nonritualized possession crisis" (in other words a "prepossession" crisis) or a "ritual crisis" is involved, the "fall" constitutes the "terminal event," the "natural conclusion" of the crisis (Zempléni 1966, 314, 400, 410, 414). As the resolution of a ritual crisis, it of course occurs during the ceremony. As the resolution of a nonritualized crisis, on the other hand, it may also occur—like the crisis itself—outside any ceremony, usually "at home."[84] In the *ndöp* the fall does not therefore constitute a unique event but rather a recurrent one. Nevertheless we should note that those adepts who preside over the cult, the "officiants" or *boroom rab bu mag* (ibid., 306) fall only very rarely.

In the case of tarantism, as with *ndöp,* the fall exhibits two distinct characteristics. As we have seen, it occurs on the one hand as a sign of prepossession, and on the other as the end product of the dance itself (De Martino 1966, 69 and photo 7). In the case of the Balinese *barong,* the possessed dancers, having attained the paroxysm of excitation during their *kriss* dance, then fall to the ground (Belo 1960, 98). In Tibet, mediums fall unconscious after they have delivered their oracles.

Zempléni (1966, 419) interprets this fall in the case of the *ndöp* as "the fatal outcome of the meeting with the double," which is, moreover, what the "symbolic burial" episode illustrates.

Among the Gun, the enclosure where the novices live during their reclusion—an enclosure situated within the boundaries of the *vodun*'s temple—is sometimes referred to as *kuxwe* or "house of death" (Tardits 1958, 53). Several days after the entry of a graduating class of recruits into the convent, their parents thank the *vodun*'s priest for "having restored their children to life" (Akindélé and Aguessy 1953, 114), a fact clearly demonstrating that the children, upon entering their new state, have undergone a symbolic death. It would seem that their "death" and subsequent resurrection occur out of sight, within the secrecy of the convent. In fact, the ritual always differs to a certain degree depending on the *vodun* concerned. In the case of Sakpata, the recruits' death and resurrection are public and take on a particularly dramatic and spectacular character.[85] But this is the exception, not the rule, contrary to what is usually assumed.

The amalgam of possession crisis (or rather prepossession crisis) and ritual death is also found among the Yoruba, as is implied by the following phrases extracted from an *oriki* (sequence of praise mottoes) of Shango, god of lightning (Rouget 1965, 102–3):

> The earth does not eat for ever
> Leopard-Death, Death that sends the child to sleep!
> Death that bruises many times before taking a wife!

Behind these esoteric phrases one should read that the ritual death is merely temporary ("not . . . for ever") and that Shango, who is Death insofar as he kills ("sends the child to sleep") and also Leopard insofar as he is king, subjects the novice to a long ordeal ("bruises many times") during the reclusion before finally making him or her his adept ("his wife"). This text poses the problem of the relations between ritual death (however realistically acted out in the case of Sakpata) and the first possession crisis. How are we to accept that the recruit can be at the same time dead, since the god has just killed him or her, and also possessed by him—since our authors indicate, in the case of both *vodun* and *orisha,* that this first crisis is a possession? This contradiction might perhaps be resolved if we viewed the matter from the standpoint of native thought, which believes that human beings possess several souls. In Métraux, for instance (1958, 106), we read that "the explanation given by members of the voodoo sect for mystic trance is among the simplest: a *loa* takes up residence in the head of an individual after having first driven out the "big good angel," one of the two souls that everyone carries within him. The abrupt departure of the soul causes the twitching and violent movements that characterize the onset of trance. Once the "good angel" has left the possessed person experiences a feeling of total emptiness, as if he were losing consciousness."[86] We know that initiation into the cult of a *vodun* or an *orisha* is a long process intended to produce profound modifications in the individual's personality structure, so that he or she will become a receptacle fit for the divinity. It is characterized by a sequence of phases during which the novice's head is subjected to a variety of treatments: in *candomblé,* the *bori* ritual[87] intended to "strengthen the novice's head" (Cossard 1970, 176); in Haitian voodoo, the "headwash" (*laver-tète;* Métraux 1958, 107); in the *orisha* cult the imposition of *oṣu,* a mystic preparation placed on the novice's shaved head at a certain stage in the initiation in order to aid reception of the *orisha* (Verger 1957, 71).

The structure of possession thus appears to be related to that of the person, in as much as the latter is formed by the conjunction of several souls. Perhaps it is in these terms that it can best be described. Maybe its different phases could be satisfactorily defined in every case if we could always refer them to an indigenous theory of the conjunction and disjunction of souls. This is what we are led to believe, for example, by what Adler and Zempléni (1972, 130–31) tell us about the Mundang, among whom possession gives rise to a spectacular "coming and going of the souls of the *sinri*"[88] between the sick person and the therapist. During this coming and going, they note the patient is not guided by his or her own "small soul" but by the souls of the *sinri* who possess him or her, and one hears dialogues such as the following between the patient and his or her initiated sister who asks: "Has your little soul come back?—Yes, it has come back." Among the Songhay, J. Rouch writes (1973, 531), "the most widespread *zima*[89] theory is that during possession the "double" (*bia*)[90] of the god has taken the place of the horse's "double." Elsewhere, the Dogon themselves describe the mechanism of the crisis undergone by a candidate for the function of totemic priest as the direct result of the contradictory movements of his different souls (*kikunu*). "The struggle between antagonistic *kikunu* in this crisis symbolizes the struggle between reason and affectivity, which is the source of disequilibrium,"[91] Geneviève Calame-Griaule tells us (1965, 46).

Let us now return to symbolic death and to the *vodun.* During their period of reclusion, the *vodun*'s new recruits are in a state of partial death, since, although they remain quite alive all the while, as each one can see, they nevertheless display behavior associated with death, such as eating with their left hands, for example, or going through doorways backwards. In *bori,* the initiation is described by J. Monfouga-Nicolas as composed of two successive stages, the first an exorcism,[92] the second an imposition. The former is accompanied by symbolic death: the future adept lies flat on the ground, and this is referred to as "lying with the worms,"[93] an expression evoking an interred body eaten by worms (Monfouga-Nicolas 1972, 117). But this death occupies no more than a very secondary place in the ritual. The "struggle with the dark gods," on the contrary, which terminates this first phase, plays an essential role and takes a very spectacular form. We might be justified in seeing this as a form of what R. Bastide (1972, 92) has termed "wild trance," which leads us to distinguish it from the prepossession crisis.

Unlike prepossession crisis, "wild" possession crisis as described in Dahomey, Brazil, and Haiti occurs when initiation has already begun. Among the Fon, Herskovits (1938, 186–87) describes it as a "war" with the *vodun*, who suddenly attacks the new recruits.[94] In Haiti, wild possession is caused by a *loa bossal* according to Métraux, who in this context observes that "the nature of the nervous attack depends. . . on the ritual condition of the possessed person; the less experienced he is the more he struggles. Until his head has been 'washed,' that is to say, as long as his *loa* has not been fixed in his head by a special ceremony, he behaves wildly" (1958, 107–8). In the *candomblé* it seems that the possession crisis by a *santo bruto* or "wild saint" may correspond either to what I label a prepossession crisis—as Bastide's (1958, 22) description suggests—or to what Bastide himself refers to elsewhere (1972, 92) as wild possession, in other words possession that has not yet been "socialized." This possession by a *santo bruto* does not necessarily take a brutal form, however. G. Cossard, in effect, simply likens the *santo bruto* to an *orisha* who has not been "educated, does not know how to behave. . .and still has everything to learn." On the other hand, she also describes (ibid., 204) a phase of the initiation ritual, which has now fallen into disuse, that very closely resembles the one described by Herskovits to which I just alluded. This would imply there is yet another aspect of "wild" possession in the *candomblé*. In any case, the important thing to remember is that wild possession, whatever form it takes, corresponds to a period during which the adept is not yet completely initiated.

Important as it may be to distinguish between prepossession crisis and wild possession crisis, it is just as important to differentiate between wild possession and the wildness of possession.[95] We have already seen that possession by a *santo bruto* in the *candomblé* is not necessarily brutal. Extremely violent and brutal possession trances, such as those filmed in J. Rouch's *Les Maîtres fous*—possessions involving such truly savage forms of self-mutilation as can be observed in the Ivory Coast or Togo—are not in any way examples of possessions of adepts undergoing initiation. By their very nature, such trances demand frenzy. The same is true of Balinese possessions during which men in trance states turn their *krisses* against themselves. But we must not forget there also are nonviolent—even calm—trances, and others—as is often the case in the Dahomey *orisha* and *vodun* cults—in which possession is so interiorized as to go almost unperceived by an inexperienced spectator. To take two cults studied by Andras Zempléni as examples: possession among the Wolof of Senegal is as brutal and convulsive as that among the Mundang of Chad is gentle and relaxed. As two films demonstrate[96] the behavior of the possessed is totally different in each of the two cases. The music involved is just as different, a significant point to which I shall return.

Finally, as far as making a general distinction between trance and crisis or fit is concerned, perhaps it might be best to reserve the word "trance" for the more or less durable period during which the adept fully identifies himself with the god possessing him, and the word "crisis" or "fit" for the very temporary, often painful and more or less convulsive state marking the transition from a normal to a trance state, or, on the contrary, as in *ndöp,* the end product of that state.

We would, in this way, be led ultimately to distinguish between trances with and without crises or fits; crises with and without falls; and, reciprocally, between crises or fits and falls with and without trance.

Possession and Obsession

Before broaching the subject of initiation, whose goal is to help the adept enter into ritualized possession, or possession in the full sense of this term, let us return for a moment to the state that is an antechamber, as it were, of true possession and which I proposed we call prepossession. We have seen that this latter state is frequently characterized by what Zempléni calls "non-ritualized possession crisis." Clearly, to speak of prepossession is to imply that this state precedes another, possession itself, and by the same token, to speak of "nonritualized possession" would be meaningless except with reference to "ritualized possession," which it will become sooner or later. Frequently, however, states corresponding to the picture just given of this prepossession—or, if one prefers, this nonritualized possession—are not subsequently transformed, through initiation, into a state of full possession. What term should we consequently use to designate such states?

During the Renaissance—and without doubt long before that—a distinction was made between two states, "obsession" and "possession," the first being regarded as the effect "of the Demon as an external agent," the second as that of the Demon "as an internal principle."[97] In the case of obsession the Demon was thought to act upon obsessed individuals "by appearing to them often and visibly so, regardless of their will in the matter, by striking them, by troubling them, and by exciting in them strange passions and movements far exceeding the scope of their capacities," whereas in the case of possession the Demon "disposes of the faculties and organs of the person possessed in order to produce, not only in her but also through her, actions that the person could not produce by herself." In Loudun—for these quotations refer to the Loudun possessions—it does indeed seem that only those nuns whose demons had been identified were seen as possessed; the others, whose "symptoms" were "not so clear" were viewed as merely obsessed. In ecclesiastical language, obsession is "the state of a person thought to be disturbed, besieged by the devil, which is different from possession, which signifies actual habitation by the devil within a body."[98]

Leaving aside its Christian context and its reference to the Demon, this obsession/possession distinction corresponds exactly to the one I am trying to make. Nothing is more common throughout the world than the belief that certain troubles occurring in peoples' lives, certain bizarre forms of behavior, certain illnesses, particularly those of a mental or emotional kind, are to be attributed to the spite of malevolent spirits, baneful forces, or wrathful divinities, who torment such victims with their presence and afflict them body and soul. Everything that happens to such a person is then interpreted by him as being brought about in such a way. From our present perspective, we could say that obsession refers precisely to such a state. There are two possible ways to put an end to this condition, which is always experienced as a disorder: either by transforming and organizing the relationship with the spirit or divinity seen as responsible for the disturbance—which entails recourse to possession rituals—or else, by bringing it to an end—which entails recourse to exorcism. Naturally, however, these alternatives leave room for a number of intermediary solutions.

In Benin, when one says in Fon *vodún wá ta éton mę,* "the vodun has come into his head," one is speaking of true possession in the sense we have agreed to assign this word. When, on the contrary, one says *vodún wa nú xę,* "the vodun has tormented him,"[99] one is speaking of the state of prepossession just described. As Fon clearly expresses it, this latter state is conceived and experienced in a completely different way from the first. To designate it in English or in French, it would therefore also be preferable to use a completely different word. Why not "obsession," since this is precisely the meaning the word once had? This would certainly make for greater clarity.

Moreover, if we further agreed to apply the term "obsession" not only to prepossession states but also to those generally labeled possession but that call for exorcism and not initiation as a response, we would be spared the opposition between "happy" and "unhappy" possession—or "authentic" and "inauthentic"—proposed by Luc de Heusch (1971, 232) as a means of distinguishing between accepted and welcomed possession and possession that is rejected and treated by exorcism, an opposition that has the disadvantage of introducing into the problem a value judgment that can lead to all kinds of confusion.

It may be objected that in this case the Loudun possessions, since they called for exorcism as a response, should not be regarded as possessions, even though I have already accepted them as such. Does this mean I am contradicting myself? A few words will show I am not. Loudun in fact illustrates a situation in which both identificatory possession and exorcism were involved; but here the exorcism was of a very particular nature, in that the victims were not the ones who asked for it; society (or the Church, which comes to the same thing) imposed it. Contrary to what happens in a society that proposes possession as a remedy for people's ills, at Loudun society entirely rejected possession, and it was the individuals concerned who resorted to it, thereby conforming to an illicit model. Hence exorcism, which was repressive instead of curative, and which did not try to remove a tension between the visible and the invisible, but to resolve a conflict between the individual and society. Above, I proposed we term the Loudun possession reprobate. With the exception of reprobate possession, then—in which case this qualification must be specified—we will consider that the difference between obsession and possession lies in the fact that obsession calls for either initiation—thereby becoming possession—or exorcism, whereas possession, which can only occur after initiation (the latter being eventually reduced to mere identification of the one responsible for the trance, as in tarantism), never in any case leads to exorcism.

INITIATORY TRANCE AND MUSIC

Initiation, whose duration and complexity vary a great deal from one cult to another, is in most cases the moment at which the adept undergoes his or her apprenticeship in possession, and at which music and trance establish within him their tightest relationship. Consequently, it is of the greatest interest for us here. But the very word initiation almost inevitably implies secrecy. This is why we are, as a rule, badly informed about it. The most notable exception undoubtedly is the Brazilian *candomblé*. Initiation into this cult has in fact been remarkably well described by Gisèle Binon-Cossard (1970, 157–217) in a study[100] rendered all the more fascinating because it was conducted from the inside, as it were, since the author was herself an adept. I shall therefore begin this chapter with initiation to the *candomblé*. I will then deal with the *orisha* cult in Africa, the *candomblé*'s continent of origin, followed by the *vodun* cult, which is geographically and religiously very close to that of the *orisha* and has similarly spread abroad, to Brazil, Cuba, Haiti, and various islands in the Antilles.

Initiation, Possession, and Dispossession in the Brazilian *Candomblé* and the African *Orisha* Cult.

In the *candomblé,* as described by Gisèle Binon-Cossard, initiation lasts in theory for a period of three months, but the most important stage consists of a three-week period of confinement or reclusion. During this entire period novices live in a state of consciousness completely different from the one usually considered normal; this state is characterized by two quite distinct aspects, one termed the *santo* state, the other the *ere* state.

The state of *santo* (saint) is experienced when the *orisha* is embodied, in other words when the novice is effectively possessed by the divinity. However, Cossard writes: "this state never lasts more than a few hours; it is extremely tiring physically and, in addition, since swallowing scarcely occurs in the course of it, it is impossible for the novice to take nourishment; consequently it cannot be continued for long with impunity. It is therefore necessary to put the novice into a different state called the state of *ere*" (1970, 167). This latter, we are told, is a "less violent state of trance" (ibid., 164). Even though the alterations of consciousness are much less marked than during the *santo* state, the *ere* state is still accompanied by phychophysiological disturbances: extremely reduced faculties of taste and smell, a diminished sense of touch, almost no need for sleep, and dissociation from affectivity relating to normal life. In order to provoke this the *ere* has to be summoned, for the *ere*[101] is in fact a child whom "the *orisha* leaves behind" when it leaves. As a result, the novice in a state of *ere* behaves in a wholly infantile manner. "Her intellectual activity never exceeds that of a very young child," Cossard tells us. "The initiates who look after them provide them with small pieces of wood, rags, and ribbons, that then become dolls, boats, or kites" (ibid., 165). At the same time the novice experiences a sort of "splitting of the self" such that the "*ere* is aware of all the novice's preoccupations when in a normal state but envisages them with total detachment, as though he were dealing with a complete stranger. He refers to her in speech as "my daughter" (ibid., 164). We can therefore say that the novice exists in a state of double consciousness. But this state is also a trance, since, apart from the disturbances already mentioned, it also gives rise in certain cases to "phenomena that fall into the province of parapsychology: projection into space, projection into past and future time, hence, prophecy, prediction, divination." During the various initiation ceremonies, Cossard writes, "the little mother summons the *orisha* by calling out the ritual words of greeting specific to that particular spirit, and by shaking the *adza*.[102] The state of *ere* then gives way once again to the *santo* state. After the ceremony, the *ere* state is induced again as described earlier" (by summoning the *ere* three times in a loud voice).

In his study of the *candomblé* in Bahia (which differs slightly from the one in Rio de Janeiro described by Cossard), Bastide (1958) investigates the *ere* state[103] at great length in his chapter entitled "The Structure of Ecstasy." "The crisis brought on by the *ere*," he sums up elsewhere (1972, 88) "is of two kinds: imitation of childlike behavior (after initiation) or else a semitrance (after total trance)." Herskovits (1943, 505),[104] writing about yet another region of Brazil, tells us that "when the possessed person returns to her normal state she must pass through the *ere* condition, a 'type of semi-possession' described as a childlike state that accompanies the personal divinity." Thus the *ere* state is described by Cossard as a "less violent trance," by Bastide as "semi-trance," and by Herskovits as "semi-possession," all three terms being slightly vague and, it must be said, somewhat unsatisfactory. Although closely linked with possession trance, since it alternates with it throughout the initiation period, the *ere* trance is clearly distinct from that of possession proper, and even in opposition to it. What ultimately characterizes the *ere* trance from the subject's viewpoint is that he or she is no longer possessed but at the same time has not yet returned to his or her normal identity. Strictly speaking, this involves a double dispossession, since the subject is dispossessed both of the god and of himself. It may be objected that he is said to be possessed by a child. This objection cannot be sustained, however, since apart from the fact that this possession may well be purely metaphorical (the texts are not absolutely clear on this point), identification with a child in these circumstances does indeed constitute a dispossession, since the child in question is anonymous. Possession proper is the diametric opposite of anonymity. Indeed, one is possessed by a precise deity who has a well-known name. In the *ere* state, on the contrary, it is not the personality of any particular child but the childlike state as such that is involved. Everything shows, therefore, that the *ere* state is one of depersonalization, whose role in the initiation process is easily understood. For this process consists, in practice, as much in losing one's former personality as in acquiring a new one, and this loss is indeed a necessary condition for this acquisition process.

I would suggest, therefore, that we label this *ere* state a "trance (or state) of dispossession." And since the state is so closely associated with initiation, we could further qualify it, among other things, as "a trance (or state) of initiatory dispossession." One observation made by Bastide confirms that this qualification is justified: with the impression made on him by the novices in the *ere* state in their "initiatory chamber" still fresh in his mind, he writes (1958, 200) that "this childlike behavior during religious initiation" could well be "a survival in deepest Brazil of the childlike behavior observed in tribal initiation." Later on we shall have the opportunity to compare the behavior of novices in the Dahomey *vodun* cult with the one observed in another region of Africa among a group of boys undergoing a tribal initiation entirely unconnected with possession.

So what are the relations of this initiatory *candomblé* trance to music? The extremely detailed descriptions given by Gisèle Binon-Cossard, who never fails to record carefully the part played by music in the ritual, answers the question quite clearly: when the novices are in a state of initiatory trance (*ere* state), it so happens that they occasionally sing, and when they do, they sing alone, unaccompanied by any instrument. When, on the contrary, they are in a possession trance (*santo* state) they are always totally silent,[105] and if there is music (whether vocal or instrumental), it is always made on their behalf by others, either by the men or women who conduct the initiation, or by a group of drummers. The opposition of the two states with regard to their relation to music is, therefore, absolutely clearcut. I shall return on several occasions in later chapters to the music specifically associated with possession trance in this initiation process, and shall therefore limit myself here to the music involved in initiatory trance.

Twice a day, morning and evening, the novices sing "the *ingolosi* prayer, which is very long and must be known absolutely perfectly by the end of the period of reclusion" (Cossard 1970, 168, 169). The author says no more about this prayer in her book, but I know from her first-hand account that it consists in a very slow chant presenting specific musical characteristics totally different from those in the remaining repertoire of the *candomblé*. Everything suggests that this sung prayer is equivalent to the long thanksgiving song sung morning and evening by novices in the *vodun* cult in Benin, which we shall discuss a little later in this chapter. Other ritual songs, all much briefer, are sung by the novices during the course of the day: first upon awakening, then while going single-file to and returning from the place of their morning ablutions,[106] before their meal, and lastly at nightfall, when they ask for lights to be lit (ibid., 167–70). Since I do not know the wording of these songs, I cannot say whether or not they have any direct relationship with the initiation process, but it seems probable since they are in fact sung while in a state of initiatory trance. We can be fairly certain, however, that they have no connection whatsoever with possession, since they are never sung when the novice is in this state, or for the purpose of entering it, or inducing it in his or her companions. This is what we need to remember for the moment.

We have a great deal less information on what happens during the initiation process into the *orisha* cult as practiced among the Yoruba in Nigeria and, above all, in Benin. In his article entitled "The Role of Hebetude [*hébétude*] during Initiation to the *Orisha* and *Vodun* Cults," Pierre

Verger does tell us, however, that "during the period between the day of resurrection and the one on which the novice receives a new name [in other words during the initiation period], the latter appears to have lost his reason and is plunged into a state of hebetude and mental torpor. . . . While in this state, the novice is referred to as ọmọtun or newborn child.[107] It is in this state, when his mind has been washed clean of all previous memory, that the *orisha's* particular rhythms, his songs, dances, and all the god's forms of behavior, will be inculcated in him" (1954, 337).

This "state of hebetude and mental torpor," with which we shall deal at greater length later on, is clearly nothing other than the *ere* state, as everyone will agree.[108] Here again, therefore, I shall say that the state involved is one of dispossession. Verger does not elucidate whether during initiation the novice alternates, as in Brazil, between the possession state and the dispossession or initiatory trance, but there is every reason to suppose that this is the case. Elsewhere, describing the annual ceremony for Shango[109] as celebrated in Benin, Verger (1959, 52–53) records that the man charged with embodying Shango throughout the entire ritual, which lasts seventeen days, is possessed by the divinity only episodically. During the remainder of the time he is possessed, Verger tells us, by "a secondary spirit who accompanies the *orisha*" and causes the man to behave "like a child or as if he were simple-minded, so that he smiles idiotically all the time." When in this state he is treated with a familiarity very different from the respect accorded him when he is possessed. In this childlike state he is able to eat, drink, sleep, and fulfil his natural functions, but "when possessed by the *orisha* himself, his body must be totally exempt from such prosaic obligations," Verger adds. If this alternation of possession and dispossession trance is observed during this comparatively brief ritual, there is even greater reason to suppose it must also occur during the initiation period which, to my knowledge is much longer. As far as this particular aspect of the *orisha* cult is concerned, therefore, the process is by and large the same in Africa as in Brazil.

Is the same true of music and of its relations to the two forms of trance, possessional and initiatory or else possessional and dispossessional? It is extremely probable, but we lack sufficient information to be able to say so categorically. We can, however, say so with certainty in the case of the very similar *vodun* cult. Therefore, we shall now turn to it.

Hebetude, Initiatory Dispossession, and Music in the *Vodun* Cult in Benin

In the *vodun* cult of Benin[110] the length of the initiation period varies from one *vodun* to another, but it is in general remarkably long. Herskovits (1938, 2:181) mentions a tradition according to which reclusion in olden times lasted eight years. In Porto-Novo, I was told about one *vodun,* called Bodo, for whom the initiation lasted seven years. The length and strictness of the requisite reclusion period discouraged the followers of this *vodun,* however, so that to this day he has not made any new recruits for the last forty years. Only ten years ago in the Porto-Novo region, it sometimes happened that the initiation period lasted for two years, and it frequently lasted six months or more.[111] The size of the new graduating class—if one may use that term to denote a group of novices undergoing initiation together—also varies a great deal. It can happen that only one individual is initiated at a time. Most frequently, however, the new class comprises between three or four and a dozen novices. In 1969 I personally attended the coming-out ceremonies of a graduating class consisting of sixty or so young initiates whose age varied from about two to about fourteen years old. It was the largest I ever saw myself, and it is worth describing one episode of the ritual in detail for several reasons.

The *vodun* involved was Ohwe, whose "convent"[112] is about two miles outside Porto-Novo. When the first "coming-out" ceremony had been performed, the "new ones"[113] were convened, on an appointed day, to go to pay homage to the king. Led by their monitress and escorted by women carrying their baggage, they formed a long procession stretching for over a hundred yards. Dressed in their finest clothes, heads newly shaved, wearing pearl headdresses, shoulders oiled, shiny looking as if sculpted by freshly incised scarifications, torsos barred by two broad belts of shells, ankles encircled with metal rings, they[114] moved rapidly, single-file along the path, looking neither to the right nor the left. From time to time they sang in perfect unison their walking song, a beautiful tune, ample, supple, alert, and at the same time impregnated with a certain melancholy. Having reached the palace, where the king, seated on his cushioned throne, awaited them in the court of justice, they prostrated themselves before him and began to sing, presumably[115] for the last time in their lives, a long song of thanksgiving diligently learned during their reclusion. These novices made a superb sight, lying prostrate in a vast, spectator-packed inner court, pressed so tightly against one another that one could scarcely make them out save for their pearl crowns and strings of purple-dyed cowrie shells undulating to the slow rhythm of the melody. They sang the song twice, which took about twenty minutes, after which the king addressed a few words of congratulation to the "new ones." The monitress then translated his speech into their "secret language," since the novices, who had not yet returned to everyday life, could neither understand nor speak any other. In answer, and still in perfect unison, they sang a second song of thanksgiving, much shorter than the first but in the same style. After that, still at the order of their monitress, they withdrew into another court of the palace, where they were served a large meal of beans.

Several days later the very same ceremony was repeated in the palace by the novices of another *vodun,* Siligbo,[116] who had likewise come to salute the king. This time there were only four of them, but events unfolded in exactly the same manner. Indeed, this is how they had unfolded, or at least had had to unfold not many years ago, for all *vodun* in Porto-Novo.

This seemingly anecdotal aspect of initiation perfectly illustrates the problem at hand: In what state exactly are these novices who sing on their way to salute their king, and, once there, sing a very particular song, then another, and then return to their convent still singing? They certainly are not in their normal state. Their robotic behavior, their totally "absent" gaze, the fact that they can neither understand nor speak everyday language, makes this quite clear. They certainly are not possessed, either, since this state manifests itself by quite a different form of behavior. We are thus forced to assume they are in the same state as the one experienced, as we have seen, by novices initiated into the *orisha* cult, both in Brazil and in Africa; in other words, here again we are dealing with initiatory trance. However, in the *vodun* cult this state displays particular forms that we need to examine a little more closely.

We have just seen how novices behave at the end of their initiation. Now let us observe them at the very beginning of that process, as described early in the twentieth century by Le Hérissé in his historic work on the former kindgom of Dahomey (1911, 135):

> "The 'féticheur' who was showing us around his establishment
> summoned his pupils. Approaching us we beheld three groaning
> creatures dripping with palm oil, crouching very low, one arm thrown
> across their backs, the other pressed to their chests, fists clenched and
> bent down at the wrists. Two of them were bedecked with flashy objects
> and clothed in a simple, short, brightly colored skirt; the third, more
> recently admitted, had no covering other than a piece of greasy cloth
> around his loins. They all kneeled down and, in shrill voices, recited a
> monotonous chant that we were told was a greeting and a prayer for our
> benefit. When they had finished they left us, still groaning and
> crouching, to sit in their hut, where they immediately took on the most
> bestially absorbed air we have ever seen.

Despite the quite colonial contempt inspiring this passage (which causes the author totally to misinterpret what he is seeing), this description could very well apply to novices undergoing initiation as it can still be seen today (if one is permitted to do so), or at any rate as it could still be seen only a few years ago. The photograph in Verger's article (1954, fig. 2) on hebetude in the *orisha* and *vodun* cults provides a perfect illustration of this,[117] and the word hebetude is indeed the one that seems best to characterize this particular state.

In the early stage of initiation—weeks or months depending on the cases—this dazed state is apparently very pronounced, actually verging on total hebetude. The new recruits live completely apart from the rest of the world in a "convent." In theory, they are seen by no one other than the priests and priestesses looking after them. Dressed in an unwashed, raffia loincloth, hair neither shaved nor dressed, they are "dirty things," as I have been told twice when I was permitted to see them in two different convents in the Alada region. Heads stubbornly bowed, gaze obstinately absent, they display absolute docility to their monitress. According to Verger (ibid., 338), this dazed state is due, at least partially, to the effect of herbs and medicinal leaves whose use "is the most secret part of the ritual." Let us say that they, like the *candomblé* novices, are drugged during the entire initiation.[118] But as time passes, this giddy state becomes modified. From all appearances, the "new ones" I was able to see in certain convents, who stood up straight and were no longer doubled over, had shaven heads and were wearing extremely clean loincloths, were in a less deep state of hebetude, representing, in all likelihood, a more advanced stage of initiation.

In the *vodun* cult, initiatory reclusion is characterized by an important ceremony during which the novices receive the scarifications that constitute the mark of the *vodun* or the *vodun* group to which they are being consecrated. These scarifications, which are certainly symbolic but also highly decorative, are incised on the shoulders, the neck, and a section of the torso. Blisters are produced by rubbing in certain powders, and the resulting scars remain raised. By remodeling the body in this way, treating the skin as sculptural material, profoundly altering the individual's physical appearance, "statufying" it as it were, these scarifications are part of an even broader cosmetic undertaking which will acquire its full meaning during the ceremonies that accompany the novices' coming out from the convent, when they file out and dance in public, glistening with oil and bedecked with their finest ornaments. As distinctive signs of the *vodun,* however—and therefore in most cases of a lineage—these scarifications can also be likened to body painting, scars, or tattoos that are done elsewhere in Africa during initiation rituals and that are destined to display membership to a particular tribe or clan, and have nothing to do with possession. A bloody and even dangerous procedure, these scarifications are done in the secrecy of the convent, far from profane eyes. The novices are drugged, I am told, in order to withstand the ordeal, which takes place in an atmosphere of great excitement maintained by continuous loud drumming. Anyone who has seen "fetishists" in Dahomey cannot have failed to notice a particular kind of reserve, of dignity that radiates from them, an inner bearing, as it were, that is different from that of ordinary people, a quiet energy that emanates from them and distinguishes them from everyone else. The long initiation they had to undergo must certainly have produced a very special ripening of their personality. In this slow restructuring of consciousness and character achieved by *vodun* initiation, what is the real importance of the scarification stage? We lack the data to answer that question. But there is every reason to suppose that the novices emerge from this ordeal at least partly transformed. At all events, it is certain that as initiation proceeds, the profound hebetude which they displayed at first gradually gives way to a different state.

Once the initiation is concluded, the coming out of the "new ones" is the occasion for a number of ceremonies, the details of which naturally vary from *vodun* to *vodun*.[119] At this point let me simply say that they are sumptuous feasts all of which, in their different ways, are ostensibly intended as a triumphal proclamation of the social group's vitality. Everything unfolds as if the intention were to show that the coming out of the initiates is a kind of victory for the group. Decked in finery and jewels, the new initiates look like precious beings whose molding—one is tempted to say gestation—accomplished ever so slowly and secretly in the heart of the convent and now brought to term, is a dazzling triumph for which everyone congratulates himself. Unquestionably, they no longer are "dirty things." On the contrary, the new initiates are now displayed as objects for general admiration. Their youth, their beauty, their wealth, their skill as dancers, their capacity to accomplish extraordinary feats—a subject to which we shall return—are there on show to excite pride in all the onlookers. True, their gaze is still abstracted and their docility still absolute; they move like automata and behave like beings who have become totally reified in the hands of those who have molded them. But their state is no longer one of hebetude. The state of hypnosis in which they seem to exist appears, on the contrary, to be a mark of their invulnerability, their indifference to the external world, a sign that they no longer have anything to fear from it. (The childlike and totally stereotyped poses they adopt in certain circumstances, and described by Verger, do not alter this in any way: unawareness and innocence are manifestly their lot.)

After their coming out, the "new ones" then spend several weeks leading a life intermediate between reclusion and normal life. Every five or seven days, depending on the calendar of their particular *vodun*, they must return to sleep in the convent and remain there throughout the following day, which is the "*vodun*'s prayer day." The rest of the time they wander about the countryside, visiting houses and markets, performing their dances, begging for food, and singing brief thanksgiving songs in return.[120] This is the stage when it is easiest to observe them. They only go somewhere under the guidance of their monitress, who is on the regular staff of the convent and is also the one who looked after them during their initiation. They speak to no one else, see no one else, and obey her orders, given in the cult's "secret language," like robots. They give the impression of being somewhere else, of moving in another world, but in no way of being in a state of diminished or dimmed consciousness. On the contrary, as one watches them passing by single-file, peregrinating from one village to another, what emanates from them is a sense of determination, comparable to some extent to that of marching soldiers whose eyes are fixed straight ahead with never a glance to either left or right. When they perform their begging and thanksgiving dances and songs, which they always execute to perfection, they give the impression they are somehow floating, in a state of somnambulistic ravishment. In fact they give the appearance of being in a trance, but a restrained, internalized, reticent kind of trance, one might say, a state very different from the unbridled and paroxysmal trances one usually sees during possession ceremonies. They are clearly not in a state of possession, but one is tempted to say that they are in a state of grace. Seeing them, one thinks of those little Balinese dancing girls described by Jane Belo (1960, 4), who perform in a state that she too describes as somnambulistic. In this state, identified by a doctor as "hypnotic trance" (ibid.), these little dancing girls execute acrobatic dances they would be incapable of doing, the Balinese think, "if they were not possessed by a god." Some of them, Jane Belo adds, sometimes "would dance through hot coals without being burned." Yes, one may say, but these little Balinese girls are in a state of possession, whereas the "new ones" I have been describing are not. The moment has come, in fact, to consider their behavior during the "coming-out" ceremonies, when, having received their new names, they are possessed.

Although, in this possession state, they do perform actions different from those executed when they are in initiatory trance, the fact is that their general behavior nevertheless remains the same. In the case of certain *vodun* these ceremonies include a spectacular rite that is a kind of ordeal by fire.[121] Outside, large jars—one for each initiate—containing food floating in palm oil mixed with some other liquid are prepared for cooking over as many separate hearths. At a given point the vapors produced by the cooking process spontaneously ignite above the jar, an event that is seen as a "miracle" (Herskovits 1928, 2:165). Each new adept then goes to his or her jar, thrusts his or her hand inside it, and removes the cooking food without burning him- or herself, a sign that "the god is present." During this entire ordeal the behavior of the new initiates does not differ in any apparent way from that they display the next day, or the following days, when they wander from village to village singing their thanksgiving songs. During these coming-out ceremonies they also perform dances—usually in pairs, accompanied by drums, and sometimes song—which although not acrobatic are of sufficient virtuosity to be one of the highlights of the festivities. These dances form part of the repertory of possession dances they will perform henceforth on various occasions, in particular at their *vodun*'s annual feast. While executing these dances, during which they are possessed, their behavior is identical to that displayed during the

begging dances already described, performed when they are not possessed: they manifest the same abstracted air, the same robotic gait, the
same hypnotized appearance. It is only some years later, when they are
fully adult both as individuals and as initiates, that they give themselves
up to the violent and extrovert dances in which possession manifests itself
so plainly, since it is expressed without restraint and can be recognized as
what it is without a moment's hesitation.

If we thus consider initiation to the *vodun* cults by obeying the rule we
imposed upon ourselves in order to study possession in general—that is,
looking at it as a dynamic process—we notice that its accompanying state
of initiatory dispossession is modified considerably as initiation unfolds.
Between the state of deep hebetude into which the new recruits are
plunged during the first weeks of their reclusion and the state of somnambulistic grace they attain at the time of their coming-out ceremonies, a
great change takes place. And indeed, what could be more natural? An upheaval of the self as total as the one they experience during initiation could
hardly take place without a similarly total modification of the altered state
in 'which they live. This altered state nevertheless remains, from start to
finish, one of depersonalization or, as I have termed it, dispossession. Further proof is that these "new ones" are given a name only after they come
out from their reclusion and are solemnly presented to the outside world.
This being so, are we then really justified in saying that this dispossession
is simultaneously a trance?

If trance is to be defined as an altered, transitory state of consciousness
conforming to a cultural model, everything proves, as we have seen, that
we are justified. True, it has the peculiarity of being extremely durable,
since it can last for several months, even years. And the fact that it can last
so long is explained in part at least by the use of drugs. The fact remains,
nevertheless, that it is transitory. There is therefore no incompatibility
with the definition just proposed. Even though some trances are very
brief, even verging on the momentary, this does not mean that others cannot be very long and follow, moreover, certain specific stages of development. What is important ultimately is to make a clear distinction between
dispossession and possession trance. "A less violent trance" is how Cossard describes the *ere* state. True, but it is neither "semitrance" nor "semi-
possession trance," contrary to what Bastide and Herskovits have written.
What we are dealing with is initiatory trance, and this should be underscored. In the *candomblé,* as in *vodun* cults, initiation has two ultimate
objectives, which are complementary but nevertheless distinct. The first is
to train the initiates, which means transforming them not only in terms of
their internal structure (by conferring a certain knowledge and a certain
power upon them) but also in terms of their social relations (by making
them members of a brotherhood which, in this case, can be likened to a se-

cret society, since initiation is closely linked with secrecy). The second objective is to create receptacles for the gods, by which I mean individuals capable of becoming possessed. Once initiation is accomplished, the initiate will never be the person he or she used to be, and will never again bear the same name, at least in Benin. But this does not mean that he or she will permanently become the divinity to be embodied. The initiate will only be possessed by that divinity from time to time. And even if he or she is never to be possessed again, he or she would still remain an initiate. Even though the goal of initiation is possession, training an initiate is, nevertheless, an operation in its own right, and the initiate in his normal state is very different from the person he becomes when possessed. Initiatory trance affects initiates, not those who are possessed. The fact that it is easier, so it seems, to trigger possession trance in a subject already in a state of initiatory trance (which is to say, in a state of dispossession) than in a subject in a normal state does not in any way suggest that initiatory trance is an intermediary state between the normal and the possession state. It is another form of trance, which should be considered in and of itself and quite independently from possession.

Bastide, as we noted earlier, had already seen that a connection could be made between the *ere* state and "tribal initiation." Describing the graduation of a group of initiates among the Kissi, in Guinea, A. Schaeffner (1951, 31) writes: "heads slightly lowered, these automata seem to see *nothing* around them." Everything in his description reminds one of the coming-out ceremony for the "new ones" of a *vodun* in Benin, with the single exception that among the Kissi there is never for a moment any question of possession. Would these young Kissi boys also be in a state of initiatory trance? And could we not ask the same question in other cases? The evidence leads us to believe we could. If this hypothesis could be verified, then initiatory trance might possibly appear as having no connection with possession, and as constituting a particular and autonomous form of trance, which is usually linked with religion, of course, but which, a priori, could as well not be.

However different initiatory trance and possession trance may be from one another, they nonetheless constitute, at least in *vodun* cults, a continuum between whose two extremities all the intermediate states observed occur. I must stress, however, that this does not mean that the distinction I have tried to establish between them is either nonexistent or even purely convenient. It is just as real as the one that differentiates a "u" sound and an "i" sound, a distinction that in no way prevents us from moving from the first to the second, and vice versa, without being able to say exactly where one begins and the other ends. The phenomena we are studying here never display oppositions of the type that Troubetzkoy, in the field of phonology, termed "privative," which is to say that they are based on the presence or absence of some distinctive feature or, if one prefers, on an "all-or-nothing" basis. The oppositions we are dealing with here are "gradual" ones, in other words they operate on the basis of a "more-or-less" type of distinction and this is what frequently makes analysis so difficult and uncertain. This means that any valid interpretation of the facts can only be made from a structural viewpoint, that is, by taking into account the whole situation in which the phenomenon occurs and the system within which it is at work. During initiation, the novice will probably have moved very gradually from the profoundly giddy state into which he or she sinks at the beginning to the state of inspired somnambulism displayed at the end. The same holds true of the following phases. The transition from initiatory dispossession trance to possession trance experienced during the ordeal by fire described earlier, for example, also seems to be very gradual; in any event, it is imperceptible to the spectator. During a period as changeable as the end of initiation, it is also very difficult to say which particular state is involved at any point. Moreover, it often happens in Benin that the most evidently genuine possession trances manifest such discreet external signs that they go totally unnoticed by the uninitiated. It is not surprising, therefore, that, in the case with which we are dealing here, external behavior is insufficient to identify the type of trance involved.

Having stated these points, we can now ask ourselves in which way initiatory (or dispossession) trance and possession trance differ in their relation to music.

The Musical Repertoire of Initiation

During the entire initiation period a large part of the novice's time is devoted to daily musical activities. These can be divided into two quite distinct repertoires. On the one hand, there are *a cappella* songs that the novices sing themselves, and that no one else ever sings; on the other, there is drum music, sometimes accompanied by singing and sometimes not, which is executed by specially appointed musicians so that the novices will dance. The first repertoire is made up, for the most part, of chants closely connected with the initiation itself, and which the novices will never sing again once their initiation is over and they have graduated from their novice status. This will be labeled the initiatory repertoire. The second repertoire, on the contrary, comprises the rhythms and tunes that will be played and sung at all the cult's public ceremonies, particularly during the *vodun*'s annual feast, in order to trigger and accompany the possession dance. This will be labeled the possession repertoire.

The same kind of distribution of the music can also be observed in the *candomblé*. On the possession side we find, first, the invocations sung by the "saint's father" while he rings the sacred bell in order to trigger the *santo* state, and second, the drums and songs used to incite the novices to dance while they are in the *santo* state. On the initiatory side, we find various songs executed by the novices in their *ere* state, and in particular the long prayer, *ingolosi,* that we mentioned previously. This chanted prayer is characterized, as I said earlier and without being able to go into greater detail, by a particular musical style completely different from that of the singing heard in the public ceremonies. This same distinction, between initiatory and possession repertoire, can also be found, as we know, in the *vodun* cults; but in the latter case, I will be able to describe their contents in rather more detail.

The long thanksgiving song, sung when the "new ones" are prostrate in front of the king, is[122] performed during the entire reclusion period by all the novices twice a day, at dawn and just before sunset, except on the "day of the *vodun*" or, in the case of Khevioso (god of lightning), unless he has thundered that day. Each *vodun,* or *vodun* family at any rate, has his or its own particular song or chant, but all these songs display the same stylistic features, which are extremely marked.[123] Without going into the musicological details, let me say first of all that the long thanksgiving chant (since there is a short one too, which I shall come to later) is performed using a type of vocal emission totally different from the ordinary singing voice used in this region of Benin. Thus when singing for the *vodun* Sakpata[124] (god of the earth), one sings in a fluted voice and in a high-pitched register. The song is purely vocalized—meaning that no actual words are involved—with very long note values (whole notes, half notes) that are connected by melismas using successions of short or very short notes (quarter to sixteenth notes). All notes may be dotted or not, but the melismas are always sung—one would like to say drawn—with the greatest precision. The voice completely lacks vibrato, which gives this very slow melody, punctuated by carefully measured silences the aspect of a zen painting, whose spirals would vanish slowly into the air even as they were formed. The song, which lasts for about ten minutes, is made up of a sequence of seven stanzas, each repeated two or three times with variations. The word "hieratic," had it not been so misused, would perhaps best characterize this music, which is so impregnated with spirituality, so otherworldly, that it conveys an overwhelming sense of strangeness. Nothing could be less like "black" music than this. The voices, so light, so purged of materiality, so disembodied, move through space without any rhythmic support and create a totally abstract architecture. The same melodic motifs are employed throughout, but linked into sequences that are constantly varying, so that one never quite knows where one is. It is an immaterial, seraphic music, suspended between heaven and earth, as far removed as it can be from the music one usually hears in this region, a sound that creates a feeling of complete remoteness and of projection into another world. Yet it conveys at the same time a sense of great perfection, both in form and in execution. The perfection of art. If the phrase were not pejorative, one would be tempted to say the perfection of artificiality, since nothing could be further removed from nature than this singing. It begins with a long, held note sung in the very highest register of the voice,[125] and almost cried out, it then slides very slowly down to the semitone below. The chromatic effect is striking. It ends on the same note, sung to conclude the repetition of the first stanza in a mirror form *da capo,* which completes the extraordinary impression of atemporality this music produces. Everything is done to conjure up a sense of the unusual, to create by musical means a world apart, a world far removed from this one, as far apart as the life the novices lead during their reclusion.

The strangeness of this singing, its formal perfection, its impassibility, the disembodied timbre of the voices, the atemporality of the melodic development, the total absence of meaningful words—all this gives the music an abstract, almost geometric character. What does this mean? Obviously, nothing could be less gratuitous than this sort of Greek temple, as it were, of African religious song. For me—and here we inevitably enter the realm of total subjectivity—this music is the very expression of the zero state of the self, of depersonalization, in short of dispossession. This is the music of a being somehow floating between essence and existence, and it succeeds admirably in its purpose, which is to express the experience of dispossession.

Apart from this long thanksgiving song (which is always sung twice in succession, so that the performance lasts more than twenty minutes and constitutes an amazing vocal feat, since the voices are under extreme pressure from beginning to end), there is also a much shorter one which is sung at other times and in other circumstances. In this case the song has words. Its melodic structure—in accordance with the brevity of the piece, which lasts anywhere between twenty and forty seconds depending on the case— is totally different from that of the long one; but it too makes use both of a certain chromatism and a, let us say, bizarre method of voice production, two features that conjointly produce the same feeling of strangeness.[126] Different as they might be from one another, these two thanksgiving songs, the long and the short, therefore unquestionably belong to the same repertoire. And the same is true of the third category of song, already mentioned, which is sung like the short thanksgiving songs during the period when the young novices have emerged from their reclusion and proceed from place to place begging for food. Unlike the thanksgiving songs, however, which are sung in a prostrate position, the begging songs are executed while dancing, although, like the former, they also make use of chromatism, which, I must repeat, is extremely unusual in the music of this region.

Both the thanksgiving and the begging songs, which constitute the essential core of the initiatory musical repertoire in *vodun* cult, are thus characterized by musical features that differentiate them from the music of the Fon and the Gun as a whole. The beating of the drums and the songs that make up what I have labeled the possession repertoire belong, on the contrary, to the region's habitual musical language. In a later chapter we shall see that this is a general rule, and I shall go into the reasons for this. If these two repertoires differ so greatly, both in their musical structure and in their function (the initiatory repertoire is sung *by* the initiates whereas the possession one is played *for* them), this is because they are concerned with two distinct aspects of the cult, initiation on the one hand, possession on the other. The latter, possession, is directed toward the outside since it has no meaning unless it is public. Initiation, on the contrary, is directed inwards. It is the secret side of the cult. Music of secrecy, this initiatory repertoire is kindred to that music of masks and of secret societies which occupies a very distinct place in African music as a whole. The bizarre voice production and the chromatism by which they are characterized seem to be somewhat similar to a vocal mask and a disguise of the person. In the case of possession, on the contrary, it is essential to know by whom the subject is possessed.

The role played by initiatory music in the *vodun* cult posed a problem made even more interesting by the fact that this cult occupies an important place in the general picture of possession cults. We therefore could ask ourselves if the unusual musical devices it brings into play—its strangeness, in short—could be directly connected to that equally strange event we call possession; if the disorienting or distancing effect it produces could be cultivated in order to trigger that separation from the self, that loss of the self in the beyond experienced by the possessed person. We find, in fact, that this is not the case at all. In practice, this music has no connection with possession, or at any rate only indirectly. It is never associated with the triggering of possession trance, which it never precedes and with which it is never simultaneous. This being so, one might say it would have been enough to state it, certainly. But we also needed to understand the why and the wherefore of the matter. Why this music then? Because the *vodun* cult is not solely a possession cult. It is just as much an initiatory religion and a social institution that lays great stress on the integration of age groups. This music is not associated with apprenticeship to possession; it is associated with the training of the initiate. But the two are linked. Hence the importance of the dispossession trance which, in the context of these very long initiations, constitutes a sort of backdrop that makes the alternation of initiatory and possessional practices possible.[127] The function of this initiatory music is both to express this dispossession and to assist in bringing it about, since in and of itself it manifestly constitutes an ascesis. Hence its strangeness. As for its beauty, I shall not venture to attempt an explanation. It is a kind of beauty that the art of music can achieve whenever it is at the service of religious fervor, and when that fervor represents for the whole of a society the most essential form of vital force.

2 Music and Possession

THE WORD "MUSIC"

"Everything is music," John Cage once said. If this were true, this book would have been pointless from the start, since the relations it seeks to bring out between trance and music would necessarily be relations to everything, or to anything. But this is in fact untrue, or rather it is neither true nor false. There are some statements that should not be taken more seriously than their authors expected. Everything, silence and emptiness included, can in effect be heard, or seen, or felt, as a piece of music might be: it is ultimately a matter of good will. A squeaking door, a faulty loudspeaker, the sound of a flushing toilet can all be appraised with a musical ear. Some find it pleasurable and if they say so we must believe them. Equally, nothing prevents one from saying that a landscape can be viewed as music for the eyes. If "everything is music," then we are dealing with metaphor, which is a perfectly legitimate way of using words and doubtlessly as old as the world; but I shall attempt to avoid it since it is of minimal profit for our enterprise.

What will the word "music" mean in this book? Given its context, that of trance, the word music will be used to signify any sonic event that is linked with this state, that cannot be reduced to language—since we would then have to speak of words, not music—and that displays a certain degree of rhythmic or melodic organization. Music will therefore be taken in its most empirical and broadest sense. In other words, it will not be treated here as an art but as a practice displaying the greatest possible variety of aspects, extending from the most discreet rustling sounds produced by the shaking of a basketry rattle to the deafening unleashing of a large group of drums, from the solitary tinkling of a tiny iron bell to the orchestral splendors of a Balinese gamelan, from the most elementary monody, chanted *recto tono,* to the most complex vocal polyphonies (such as those of the Bushmen), from the linearity of a simple motif produced by clapping hands to the extremely complex interplay of a large percussion ensemble, from the refinement of a violin tune skillfully varied by a professional virtuoso to the rustic sound of a summons bellowed through an animal horn or tapped out with a nail on the side of an empty beer bottle.

Now that I have empirically delimited the field covered by the word "music," we should ask ourselves whether the concept at work is or is not adequate to the kind of investigation I am undertaking. In practice, such a definition emerges from the delimitation of a concrete world of sound that is totally foreign to the one practiced by the majority of the societies in which the facts we will consider can be observed.[1] By working with a concept of this kind we are thus turning our backs on the system of thought proper to these societies. But let me not hedge on this point; this book is not aimed at these systems. Not that I ignore nor wish to minimize their importance or their interest; quite the contrary. If, in the case of certain societies at least, we possessed a truly indigenous taxonomy of notions relating to what we term music,[2] and a matching theory of how those notions relate to the trance state, I would certainly use it as the primary basis for my research. To my knowledge, however, no such documentation exists. Since we are unable to conduct our analysis with indigenous concepts, we must therefore use our own. It must be noted, however, that this would ultimately have been the case anyway. A demonstration, had it been possible, of the relations a particular system of thought—be it African, Asian, or European—establishes between trance and particular sound events falling within our definition of music, could never have constituted more than the first stage of our work. My aim can only be to bring out these relations by going beyond interpretations necessarily belonging to cognitive processes different both from each other and from our own. Whatever materials are used, whatever degree of elaboration is reached, whatever language is used to convey the findings, we will always have to reinterpret them in our own terms. When I am told by a Songhay musician in Niger, via the work of Jean Rouch, that he transmits his music to the ears of the spirits by means of a rattling device extending from the neck of his single-stringed fiddle,[3] I take note of this information, which is indeed of the greatest interest; but I must then go on to reinterpret it within the framework of a more general system of symbolics. When I read, in the work of Henry Skoff Torgue, that for pop musicians the double bass "lends security" with its low notes, that the percussion is "never frenzied," and that it is the voice, or those instruments deriving from it (in other words, those of medium or high pitch), that furnish the "hysterical cries," I am then led to consider these observations, which are scattered throughout his book, as significant of an underlying system. Whether it is clearly expressed, implied, or ignored altogether—which is usually the case—is of little import. Just as I am within my rights to include within a single category—the one of "music" as I have just defined it—facts that others would assign to different categories, so am I at liberty to organize into a system facts that others would not link together at all, or would organize on the basis of different viewpoints. The question is to know if the result of such a rearrangement is logically conclusive or not. The reader will be the judge.

Any music can be considered from three different viewpoints: first, in and of itself, as an object (independent of its maker and of anyone listening to it); second, as something produced either by composition or by execution (as a subjective creation); third, as something listened to (from the viewpoint of perception). To use the terms proposed by R. Jakobson (1963, 214) for the analysis of language, music may be considered from the viewpoint of the "message" it constitutes, from that of the "addresser" who transmits it, and from that of the "addressee" who receives it—or, if one prefers, from that of the "transmitter" and the "receiver."[4] In the normal conditions of musical communication, the transmitter and receiver share a common code, so that the message sent by the former refers to a context understandable by the latter, and communication is established between them by the action of a certain contact. "Each of these six factors (transmitter, message, receiver, code, context, contact) gives rise to a different linguistic function," Jakobson tells us. Although we must guard ourselves from systematically applying what has been said about language to music, since the one can by no means be reduced to the other, the same proposition can nevertheless be made for music, and with equal chances of leading to interesting observations. Throughout this book we will see that, depending on whether the music is made *by* the person in trance or, on the contrary, *for* that person, music and trance have quite different relations to one another.

WHEN DOES MUSIC ACT?

We have just seen that possession should be viewed as a dynamic process. Therefore, we will begin by asking the question, *When* does music act?

The individual in the process of experiencing those physiological, psychological, or emotional disruptions that will orient him toward possession will, generally speaking, gravitate toward the milieu of possessed persons, and will consequently be present at their ceremonies. Since these ceremonies are accompanied by music, he becomes impregnated with the musical atmosphere of such possession sessions. But the chronic crisis he is experiencing and the acute crisis that will follow it most of the time do not necessarily have any direct relation to that music. Indeed, they often have no relation to it at all. As Louis Mars very rightly points out (1953, 225)—with specific reference to Haitian voodoo (but his observation could as well be applied to other cults)—"We have to distinguish the ritual possession crisis from the possession sickness that arises (generally speaking) independently of any ceremonial atmosphere." Music can undoubtedly sensitize a subject to the call of possession, and can thus contribute to awakening his vocation; this, however, does not mean that music is responsible for the psychological disturbances he encountered and which led him to follow this path.

In Bali, Jane Belo (1960, 48) describing the initiation of a medium, tells us that it was as the result of a series of trances—in my terminology crises or fits—undergone in various places and circumstances (but always outside of any ceremony and thus in the absence of music) that the person concerned, after having consulted a priest on the meaning of these attacks, became convinced that "the gods were calling him." In this case we are clearly in the presence of what we have labeled the prepossession crisis. Similarly, J. H. Nketia (1957, 5), writing about possession in Ghana (which he interprets as being essentially a renewal of man's alliance with the gods or with his ancestors), observes that "individuals are known to get possessed in private life outside the context of music and dancing." We may suppose that here again we are dealing with prepossession crises. In any case, let us remember that such crises can take place without music and without dancing. Among the Dogon, future priests of the *binu* (mythical ancestors) undergo crises or fits that occur unexpectedly, not only during ceremonies that include music—and are not necessarily related to *binu* worship[5]—but also outside of any ceremony and consequently with no music at all.[6] This is no longer the case after their ordination, however, and I shall return to this point later (p. 98). In the *candomblé*, on the other hand (Cossard 1970, 158–59), it is usually while the future initiate—of either sex—is attending a ceremony that he or she is suddenly struck by the divinity and collapses to the ground. This is a sign that a god has chosen him or her as his "horse." But at this entirely preliminary stage of possession, neither the victim nor anyone else yet knows which god is involved. Contrary to what happens to those who are already initiated, and who go into trance only when summoned to do so by the song or rhythm specific to the god who is to inhabit them, here the person cannot have answered such a summons since he or she does not yet know the code. Gisèle Cossard further points out, as we saw earlier, that the "candidate" can also be struck and fall in this way at any time outside of any ceremonial context. Thus, despite appearances, prepossession crisis must be regarded in the *candomblé* as well as being independent of music.

In Chad, among the Mussey,[7] it often is while she is out in the bush that the person about to be possessed is seized by an unknown god and struck to the ground. She will then lie where she has fallen, unconscious, until women belonging to the college of the possessed come near her and blow into a gourd trumpet until the right notes awaken her. In this case then music does not trigger the crisis, but on the contrary, terminates it, by establishing communication with the god who is responsible for it.

Among the Hausa, noninitiated girls experience possession crises by ingesting a drug, betel datura (J. Monfouga-Nicolas 1972, 200). This "profane possession" displays all the symptoms of normal possession crisis except for the fact that "the gods clearly do not manifest themselves." These false possessions occur when girls, who want to imitate *bori* adepts, swallow datura seeds in order to do so (ibid., 199). But formerly they also used to occur in a more institutionalized way. On particular evenings when the girls congregated to spin cotton together, they amused themselves by introducing the youngest among them to the intoxicating effects of the betel datura. "When the girls began to shake, dribble, and spin endlessly around and around, mouths filled with froth, the young people's griot[8] came to play the plant's motto on his drum, then immediately afterwards that of the god *Kure*.[9] The girls were then told to sit down, given cool milk to drink, and the griot tapped them on their heads with his drum. The crisis subsided and order was restored." In this example music is used not to trigger the crisis but, on the contrary, to make it subside, which corresponds to what was just mentioned for the Mussey. The crisis subsides owing to the symbolic alliance effected with the god and obtained, first, by beating out his motto, second, by bringing the drum, the sacred instrument, into contact with the head of the falsely possessed person. When it is simply a case of false possession in little girls imitating the grownups' *bori*, also induced by datura, the young people's griot is likewise summoned. He "plays his drum and touches the girl's head with it. She then calms down and dances to the sound of the music. Everyone knows that if the griot were not summoned, the child's belly would swell up and she would die. . . ." A Hausa woman explains the situation as follows: "When they go into trance you have to call for the griot and he plays his drum; the girls dance like fools. It is because they dance that the *babba jiji* (the datura) leaves them." Here again, we find that music is used to end the crisis and not to provoke it, but this time it does not act symbolically; it spurs the girls on to dance.

Exactly the same thing happens in tarantism, as we know from the following text dating from 1621 and quoted by E. De Martino:

> True, the action of music is miraculous, and if one had not seen it with
> one's own eyes, one would never believe it possible that the person who
> had been bitten by the tarantula, almost moribund because of the
> venom, moaning, anguished, agonizing, almost bereft of his senses,
> external and internal . . . , [could] come back to his senses as soon as he
> has heard the sound of musical instruments, open his eyes, prick up his
> ears, rise, first begin to make slight movements with his fingers and toes,
> and then, keeping the rhythm of the melody, which he finds pleasant and
> helpful to him, start dancing with the greatest liveliness, gesticulating
> with his hands, his feet, his head, with all the parts of his body shaken in
> all of its limbs by the most varied agitations. [1966, 385]

In the Hausa *bori*, dance is used as a means of counteracting the effects of the betel datura; in tarantism it cures the bite (real or imaginary) of the spider. We should remember that in both cases the function of the music involved is not to trigger the crisis or fit but, in fact, to cure it, to provoke its resolution in dance. All the same, there is one notable difference between these two cases. In the *bori* we are in fact dealing with a false possession dance, which prefigures the real one by skipping the initiation phase. In tarantism, in which the crisis leads directly to possession without skipping this phase (since it functions without initiation by nature), we are dealing, on the contrary, with real possession dance.

It should be observed in passing that this absence of initiation, which is perhaps tarantism's principal characteristic, is undoubtedly due to the fact that it is not a completely socially integrated religious practice. Since there is no initiation, the prepossession crisis is never entirely resolved, which is why it recurs periodically. This would explain the fact that in tarantism, contrary to the general rule, the prepossession crisis is not a unique event in the possessed person's life but an annual recurrence.

In the *ndöp*, prepossession crisis, or, to use Andras Zempléni's term (1966, 314), "non-ritualized possession crisis," often occurs during a ceremony, but can equally well occur without any ceremony and thus in the absence of music,[10] which conforms to everything we have said up to now. On the other hand, as we have seen, the normal climax of ritualized possession trance in the *ndöp* is a crisis resolved by a fall to the ground, and in this respect it has the same exterior signs as prepossession crisis. This time both crisis and collapse are directly related to music, as we know from Zempléni's (ibid., 358–60) description and what he tells us about the behavior of a new *ndöpkat*[11] at her first public séance. She must, "if possible, achieve a crisis leading to collapse. If necessary, she will be dragged in front of the drums in order to force this outcome" (ibid., 375). So whereas the "unorganized crisis" (ibid., 415) and the ensuing collapse do not seem to be necessarily related to music, the ritualized crisis and collapse, on the contrary, appear to be directly provoked by it.

Let us now pass on to initiation. The role of music seems to differ according to whether one is dealing with the *bori,* for example, or the *candomblé.*[12]

In the *bori,* possession is always accompanied by music throughout the entire initiation, both during the exorcism phase (dark gods) or the ensuing imposition phase (white gods).[13] In the *candomblé,* on the contrary, the majority of possessions that occur during initiation do so without music, or almost so. As we saw earlier,[14] the novices live in the *ere* state throughout their reclusion period, and this state is interrupted by short periods when they go into the *santo* state, which is to say into a possession trance. The day begins with a morning purification bath. Wakened before dawn, they walk to their bathing place in silence with their "little mother"[15] walking ahead of them ringing the *adza*[16] or sacred bell. Each in turn is bathed with cold water by the "little mother." The shock they experience,

Cossard writes (1970, 168), is usually enough to ensure a return to the *santo* state. There is every reason to believe that the bell is not rung during the bath ceremony itself, so that here we are faced with possession occurring in the absence of music. There is another possession trance that occurs without music: the one caused by drinking *abo*—an infusion of leaves collected from plants that have the "property of provoking and reinforcing the trance state" (ibid., 181). As with *bori*, the *candomblé* thus provides examples of trances induced solely by the action of drugs and in which music plays no role whatsoever.

Continuing with the *candomblé*, at least seven days after the beginning of the reclusion period, a first ceremony takes place, at the end of which the novice becomes a *jawo*, or the *orisha's* wife. "The saint's father summons the *orisha* with the appropriate salutations while ringing the *adza*. This is the dramatic moment of the ceremony, for it can happen that the *orisha* is slow in coming" (ibid., 176). This possession, which marks an important phase of the initiation process, is thus accompanied musically by nothing more than the tinkling of a sacred bell.

Several days later another ceremony takes place in which the *jawo*, while in the *santo* state, is bathed in blood in order to establish the mystical bond that will henceforth bind her to her *orisha*. The ritual, Cossard tells us (ibid., 184), is identical to the *assamento* ceremony she describes elsewhere, which means that it too takes place in the complete absence of music. On the evening of the same day the naming feast takes place in the presence of a large audience. When the *jawo* make their appearance they are already possessed. Upon the invitation of a woman who accompanies them and to whom the "saint's father" has entrusted the *adza*, the new *jawo* then cries out her name. At this point the drums are beaten "to greet the birth of a new *orisha*" (ibid., 185). This is another example of a possession trance associated with the sacred bell but owing absolutely nothing to the sound of drums.

Among the Wolof, as among the Thonga, it is at the end of a ritual in which music plays a central role that the possessed person is induced to utter publicly the name of the divinity possessing him. This is, of course, a crucial episode in his initiation, since by uttering this name, the possessed person not only identifies the divinity but, in so doing, enables himself to become identified with it. There are broad analogies between the kind of music used in the two cases. Zempléni (1966, 356–60) in his work on the Wolof and H. A. Junod (1913, 438–43) in his study on the Thonga, both place equal emphasis on the violence of this music, the purpose of which is to reduce the sick man to a state of nervous exhaustion: "almost intolerable noise of the drums," Zempléni writes; "hideous din," notes Junod. We shall later examine what exactly this music consists of. For the moment we need only recall that in both cases music attempts to induce the crisis through the same method. "Conquered at length by this noisy concert the patient enters a condition of nervous exaltation. The crisis occurs, the result of evident hypnotic suggestion. He rises and dances wildly in the hut. The hubbub is redoubled. They implore the spirit to declare his name. A name is shouted . . . " (ibid., 443). This is very close to what Zempléni describes as occurring among the Wolof. In his account of a long and theatrical *ndöp* ceremony he describes the musicians once more beginning their drumming, the chants resuming, the bells ringing "louder than ever." Finally, the sick man's trembling "gives way to organized movements." This is the ritualized crisis, followed by a long cry and then the declaration of the name "that they were waiting for."

We have another example from Tanzania. Among the Segeju (Gray 1969, 178) the sick man's public declaration of the name of the *shetani* possessing him occurs at the climax of a seven-day ceremony characterized by "noise, dancing, blood, and frenzy." This declaration takes place on the sixth day. On the seventh the spirit leaves the patient.

In the case of a quite different form of crisis, the wild possession crisis mentioned earlier, what happens differs considerably since, in this case, music is used not to provoke the crisis or fit but, on the contrary, to make it subside. At least, this is what Herskovits (1938 2:186–87) found among the Fon.

"On a given night the *voduno* informs each candidate that one of the *vodun* of the pantheon will 'declare war' on him." The candidates are awakened before dawn by a gun shot and loud cries. They leap up "from their sleeping mats, run about wildly, throwing stones at anyone within reach, and beating those who approach them." A drummer will then succeed, with some difficulties, to calm them down, by beating out rhythms that "will bring them their gods." And it is at this point, after the name of the divinity has been proclaimed, that the candidates, calmed by the drum, go into trance. As among the Thonga and the Wolof, this episode is thus linked to the declaration of the god's name. In the *candomblé,* or at least in the old *candomblé* ritual described by Cossard (1970, 204), which, as we have seen, constitutes one aspect of wild possession in this cult, events unfold in ways comparable to the example just described among the Fon. The *ere* in the process of initiation were "released into the countryside where they lived a solitary existence, hiding from the eyes of the lay people and living on wild plants, or even on whatever they could steal from people's homes." Summoned back after a period of several days, the *ere* would return "in a state of extreme savagery, beating anyone they encountered on their path" (ibid.). Possession of the *ere* by their respective *orisha* was then induced by a specific drum rhythm, the *adarum* (to which we shall return) thereby causing them to pass from a state of wild possession to what we may call, antithetically, "cultivated" possession. Here again music clearly plays the role of calming the wild possession, not of provoking it.[17]

Now let us examine possession when the people concerned are no longer candidates or adepts in the course of initiation, but initiates. Here again the relations between music and possession appear to be quite variable. Possession ceremonies are organized in various ways depending on the ritual to which they correspond: the coming out of new initiates, for example, enthronement of a new dignitary, the annual feast of the divinity, seasonal rituals, conjuration of calamities, therapeutic sessions, and so on; the calendar and frequency of such ceremonies naturally vary a great deal from cult to cult. In a general way, however, crises or fits and possession trances do tend to occur at certain specific points in the ritual and not at others. In the majority of cases they occur while music is being played, and are closely related to it. It is essential, all the same, to stress not only that the rule is far from being absolute but also that the same music, or rather the same type of music, does not have the same effect on all adepts, regardless of circumstances. Thus adepts in a state of impurity must never under any circumstances be possessed. This means that the effect of music is not as constrictive or as automatic as some people have sometimes wished to believe. P. Simon and I. Simon-Barouh (1973, 42 n.) provide a well-substantiated example in their description of the *hầu bóng*. But although this restriction on account of impurity, which concerns women above all, seems to be universal, there are others, on the contrary, that are specific to certain cults.

Among the Yoruba the annual feasts for Shango, god of lightning, are attended by a great number of adepts. All of these, and there may be several dozen of them, are capable of being possessed by Shango. But in practice the god must never be embodied by more than one of them throughout the entire feast, which lasts for seventeen days.[18] On the first day the man chosen goes into his trance under the following circumstances: at a given moment in the ceremony, soon after a kid has been sacrificed to the god, the drums fall silent; an officiant then chants an invocation[19] during which his female counterpart holds out the animal's freshly severed head toward those who are present. Suddenly one of the adepts goes into a trance, dashes forward, and seizes the kid's head between his teeth, which is a sign that the deity has accepted the sacrifice. From that point on the man is possessed by Shango. He will remain in this state during the following seventeen days, although he will alternate between the possession state and the *ere* state described earlier. In the course of one season the feast moves from village to village, and in each one a different adept will in turn embody Shango. The same invocation, chanted in the same context, thus triggers the trance in this or that person, leaving all others unaffected. The effectiveness of the music thus appears to be largely governed by convention.[20] And it should be remarked in passing that the convention is different among the neighboring Fon and Gun. Among them, Khevioso, a homologue of Shango, can be embodied by several dancers simultaneously. The same is true in the case of Sakpata, who admittedly has a great many hypostases, which is not the case with Shango.

As a general rule, it seems that whatever the cult concerned, the reaction to music varies according to the seniority and importance of the adept. Writing about the relations between trance and music, Cossard observes that "the more recent the initiation, and the stronger the sensitization to the rhythm, the greater the likelihood for the occurrence of trance" (1967, 175). In the *ndöp*, to which we will return later, trance, under the effect of music, must normally result in the crisis and then the fall. Although new adepts are "grounded by griots in a few seconds" (Zempléni 1966, 416), the veterans, on the contrary, do not succumb for quite a long time, the actual period varying according to the individual. When, for their part, women officiants (those who oversee the cult) go into trance, they are in theory not supposed to go "as far as crisis and fall," unlike the adepts already mentioned. (ibid., 400, 417). If it so happens that one of them does—and the honor in such a case goes to the first drum, who uses every ounce of his talent to produce this end result—"the session then attains its highest peak of intensity."

The efficacy of music thus varies according to the status of the adept, who can be more or less vulnerable according to age, experience, and position in the hierarchy of the cult. We shall return later to the role played by the musician, as opposed to music itself, in inducing the trance state. For the moment we can say that, regardless of the particular cult, the officiants, who by definition have had a long experience of possession, can control their behavior to a much greater extent than new initiates. This means that they are less slavishly controlled by the music, so that they can either resist it, as our *ndöp* example has just shown, or in fact do without it altogether, as we learn from Michel Leiris's descriptions (1958, 61–71) of the possessions of Malkām Ayyahu, a practitioner of the *zār* cult, who could show off the possession state at the drop of a hat, as it were, outside any ritually defined occasion and also, needless to say, without any musical stimulus. Generally speaking, moreover, since the role of officiants is to control the possession of others, it is natural enough they should first know how to control their own.

These few examples will have made it clear enough, I trust, that the relations between music and possession vary to a very great extent depending on the particular cult, the stage reached by the adept, the state of that adept at a particular moment, and the ritual in which he or she is taking part. In certain cases, music triggers the fit, in others, on the contrary, it brings it to an end. Sometimes it seems to play a decisive role in inducing trance; sometimes it seems to have none whatsoever.

As for coming out of trance, as opposed to entering into it or being in it, music can again play a role. In Bali, the trance of the little girl dancers is ended through specific songs (Belo 1960, 198). In Chad, among the Mundang, in order to return the possessed persons to their normal state, the musicians play a particular theme while the chief officiant taps them on the back.[21] In the *candomblé* it is a rhythmic theme played by the drums that tells the dancers embodying the *orisha*s to leave the room at the end of the ceremony (Cossard 1970, 117).

WHAT MUSIC?

There are certain cases, as we have just seen, in which the triggering of crisis or the entry into trance can in no way be attributed to the effects of music, for the very good reason that at that particular moment there is none. This is exceptional, however. As a general rule, possession fit or trance is accompanied by music, and music is almost always regarded as being more or less responsible for its onset. In what does this music consist? A swift glance at the evidence shows that from the viewpoint of its formal characteristics it varies considerably, if not totally, from one country to another. Ultimately, we have to accept that there are as many different kinds of possession music as there are different possession cults. Yet all these different kinds of music are regarded as being responsible for inducing trance. How can it be that, despite their respective differences, they all have the same effect? That is the question. The answer is that in order to have the same effect—and a very specific effect, let us note—they must share, despite their differences, the same characteristics. We shall now attempt to identify these characteristics by examining one by one the principal aspects of these various kinds of music.

Vocal or Instrumental?

Let us begin with the acoustic characteristics of trance music. Of what is it made up? Is possession music generally vocal or instrumental, or both at the same time? When it is instrumental, is one instrument more frequently used than any other? In what case is a certain instrument used? Let me say at once that possession music is, as a general rule, both vocal and instrumental, but that the relative importance of the vocal and instrumental elements varies a great deal from one cult to another and that it also varies in any given cult according to how the ritual unfolds and how the trance develops. There are, nevertheless, several exceptions, some of which I shall now cite.

There are examples of possession accompanied by singing alone. In Java, a possession ceremony centered around a doll, and whose principal goal is to induce rainfall, is accompanied by purely vocal music (Kartomi

1973, 179–82). In Bali, the trances that Jane Belo labels as folk trances, which are due to possession by *sanghyang* spirits, not by gods, seem also to be accompanied by purely vocal music; at least Belo's descriptions (1960, 201–25) do not mention anything but songs.[22] These trances are very violent and usually end with a crisis and fall. We shall see in a later chapter[23] that in Tunisia, *dhikr* chants[24]—here purely *a cappella*—whose primary function is to accompany communion trance, can in a particular context trigger *possession* trance, but in this case those who are affected are not the ones who sing the chants but those (women, in the present case) who listen to them. Black Africa, too, provides us with specific examples of purely vocal possession music. I have already mentioned one of these a little earlier with reference to the *orisha* Shango. In the *bori* cult, at the end of the novice's purification ritual, the *bori* women who participate in the ceremonies enter into trance when they hear the two women officiants singing the mottos of their gods (Monfouga-Nicolas 1972, 109). These women can also become possessed under quite different circumstances, when they hear these same mottos sung by their handmaiden-wives (their *el-biya*), who, in truth, accompany their singing with the rustling of cowries they hold in their hands (ibid., 160ff.). In other words, all these songs, contrary to the usual practice in the *bori,* take place without the presence of an instrumentalist. Among the Wolof, during the *samp* ritual, which is a variant of the *ndöp* reduced to its "essential symbolic moments" (Zempléni 1966, 426), the music consists solely of sung *bak,* which are the mottos of the genii (*rab*). As for the neophyte's possession, it is reduced to a simple trance accompanied neither by dancing, nor fit, nor fall. The drummers, who play such a crucial role in the *ndöp* ceremonies, do not take any part in the *samp*—a ritual that is "very strongly associated with the Moslem *rab.*" This absence of drums is explained in various ways, all connected with the fact that the *samp* appears to be "the principal means of effecting a compromise between Islam and the *rab* cult" (ibid., 428). This absence must therefore be seen as connected with the disapproval of musical instruments so characteristic of Islam. Be that as it may, it is nevertheless true that whether we are dealing with the *bori,* the *rab* or the *orisha* cults, such purely vocal music must be seen as the exception in black Africa, since the music accompanying possession is generally provided, there as elsewhere, by a combination of instruments and voices.

Inversely, we can also cite rare examples of purely instrumental possession music. In Bali, in the *barong,* the music that accompanies the trance during the final episode of the *kriss* dance is provided solely by gamelan instruments, and is not accompanied by any songs (Berthe 1970, discography). In Brazil, in the *candomblé,* there is a particular kind of drumming, *adarum,* that may not have any vocal accompaniment (Bastide 1958, 20), and which is specifically intended to provoke possession not in one par-

ticular adept but in all the adepts at once. In ancient Greece, the dances of
the Corybantes were performed to the sound of purely instrumental music; this is at least what the writings of Plato and Aristotle indicate, as we
shall see later.[25] In southern Italy, tarantism would at first sight seem to
constitute a ready-made example of purely instrumental possession music,
the tarantella being this cult's central musical expression. This dance is
performed to music provided by an instrumental ensemble unaccompanied by any sort of singing. But if we look more closely we notice that there
also exist "singing" tarantulas who require a vocal form of "iatromusic"
(Carpitella 1966, 362), and *pizziche tarentate*,[26] which are sung. In tarantism, song, compared to the tarentella, has little importance. It can, nevertheless, take the most diverse forms, from stanzas ladden with erotic allusions to funeral laments—the use of a particular type of music being
dictated by the circumstances and being dependent upon the ritual and the
type of possession concerned. It is in fact quite difficult, as must be clear by
now, to find possession rituals in which the music is always and exclusively instrumental.

In the majority of cases, as I have said, possession music makes use,
either simultaneously or alternately, of both song and instruments. The
combinations of the two are quite variable, however, and it would seem
that songs tend to be interrupted more frequently than the instruments.

But what are these instruments? Although the distinction may not always be valid, they may be assigned to one of two categories according to
whether their function is melodic or rhythmic, with those in the second
category most frequently serving to accompany the first category of instruments or the voice. Certain instruments, such as rattles or bells,[27] have
a rhythmic function by their very nature, as it were, while others have a
naturally melodic function, like the fiddle.[28] Others, such as the drum,
can perform one or the other function depending on the way they are
used. In regions where tonal languages are spoken, the drum can be made
to "speak" in such a way as to perform the function of a melodic instrument and acts as a substitute for song. Apart from this particular case, it
may be played in such an expressive manner that the drumming can become, as in the *ndöp,* a melodic combination of timbre, stress, and intensity. In short, if the drum is the instrument most often used for possession
music, this is because it can be melodic as well as rhythmic, and because,
when fulfilling the second of these functions, it can be incorporated into a
great many different instrumental ensembles.[29]

This being so, if we look at the various kinds of possession music as a
whole, there does not seem to be one single type of melodic instrument
that noticeably prevails over the others. The violin, nowadays, is the preferred instrument in tarantism, but in earlier times its role could be filled
by a great variety of instruments, among them musettes, shawms, trum-

pets, bombardons, and other wind instruments, which are sometimes replaced today by the accordion (Carpitella 1966, 361).

Piano has never been mentioned in this context, as far as I know, but it
has been in another, not so far away. In Paris, around 1780, Mesmer, the
well-known inventor of magnetic trance (which has thousands of adepts
nowadays in Latin America) and also the sponsor of Mozart's *Bastien and
Bastienne,* used to play "moving tunes" on this instrument to trigger the
trance of his patients when they could not attain the "perfect crisis"
(Rausky 1977, 104).

Leaving Europe now for Africa, we see that among the Songhay of Niger (Rouch 1960), the fiddle is the instrument used to play the spirits' music. This is also true among the Hausa, though in certain cases the fiddle
may be replaced by the flute (Monfouga-Nicolas 1972, 105). Let us also
observe only in passing—since the trance concerned is one of communion,
and not of possession—that the flute plays an essential role in the orchestra used to accompany the Mevlevi whirling dervishes in their dancing and
trances. We should add, though, that there are many dervish sects and
that the Mevlevi one is among the few that uses the flute (*nay*)—an oblique one, incidentally—for the *dhikr*. In Iraq, to cite only one example,
the dervishes who practice "body beating"—in other words corporeal mu-
tilation—during the *dhikr* do so to the sound of an orchestra made up
solely of drums, with no accompanying melodic instruments (Hassan
1975, 223–26). But in the domain with which we are dealing here, truly
every rule is immediately contradicted by a counterexample.

In ancient Greece the double clarinet (aulos) was the chosen instrument
for the Dionysiac rituals during which the maenads and Corybantes sur-
rendered themselves to the manifestation of their enthusiasm or mania.[30]
As soon as they heard it, they fell "into the trance of divine possession"
(Jeanmaire 1951, 175). But although there are conclusive texts (notably
Plato's *Symposium*) that connect the triggering of trance with the sound of
the aulos, and although both the maenads and satyrs are often represented
as blowing into twin clarinet-like instruments, the Pan flute (syrinx) is also
the instrument of the sileni (*Symposium* 215b) and thus of the musicians
of Dionysiac "enthusiasm." The maenads are sometimes depicted as striking tambourines in order to induce other entranced maenads to dance.
One vase shows Dionysus himself playing the seven-stringed lyre[31] in a
scene of bacchic dance (Emmanuel 1914, 397). Another vase shows a sa-
tyr also playing a lyre, but a five-stringed one this time (ibid., 395, 396),
while a dancing maenad executes "swaying movements of the torso, arms
outstretched," in a pose that Jean Rouch's films on possession among the
Songhay have made familiar to us. True, it is clear from the texts that the
aulos was the most typical instrument of corybantism and maenadism,
but it is also true, as we have seen, that the Greeks associated other instru-

ments with trance, up to and including the lyre itself, which since it was Apollo's instrument, one might have expected to be excluded from Dionysiac rites, and which, in Crete, was associated with the aulos in the ecstatic dances of the *kouroi* (Jeanmaire 1939, 432).

In Tibet, just as the already entranced diviner[32] is about to be totally possessed, "two priests approach the oracle and taking up positions at his left and right sides, each of them blows a thighbone trumpet into his ears" (Nebsky-Wojkowitz 1956, 430). When he hears this sound "the intensity of his convulsions increases." Among the Sumerians it was the harp that was "used during the oracles of the high priest" (Farmer 1957, 235). Among the Hebrews (and we will return to them later), stringed instruments, the harp and the lyre, were associated with prophetic trances. But in certain cases the stringed instruments were complemented by clarinets and drums.[33] In Iraq (Hassan 1975, 181), the lyre is the typical instrument of possession cults practiced by the blacks originating from Africa. In Chad, among the Kotoko (Brandily 1967, 53ff.), the characteristic instrument of possession rites is the harp, accompanied by the water drum; among the Gula Iro it is again the harp, but even more prevalent is a series of spherical whistles (Pairault 1966, 259 and fig. 179); among the Mundang (Adler and Zempleni 1972) it is the gourd trumpet, and among the Mussey (Garine, filmography) it is the gourd trumpet with vibrator. In the Central African Republic, among the Ngbaka-Mandja (Arom and Taurelle 1968), it is the xylophone. In Zimbabwe, among the Shona, it is the *mbira*, a set of plucked lamellae (McEwen 1970 and Tracey 1970, 37–38). In Madagascar, among the Vezo (Koechlin 1975) it is the accordion, which has replaced the zither for this purpose. In Bali, unlike the "folk" possessions mentioned a short while ago, which are accompanied by purely vocal music, possessions attributed to the gods are accompanied by gamelan music (or rather, to use the Balinese word, by "gongs"), sometimes in association with song and sometimes not. In Laos (J. Brunet, discography), mouth organs accompanied by small cymbals are used "to make the shamans go into trance." In Vietnam, possession songs are normally accompanied by a moon-shaped lute and a little drum.[34]

What can we deduce from this series of examples—which could easily be extended although multiplying them would only serve to increase the variety of cases—except for the fact that no constants emerge from it, or, more correctly, that the one thing that does emerge is the lack of constants? The conclusion, in consequence, is that among all the instruments used for possession music not one stands out as the rule. Practically speaking, they can all do the job; at least, this is what the facts indicate. One may wonder if some particular instrument, by virtue of its specific sound—violent, strident, piercing, screeching, enveloping, haunting, percussive, who knows?—might perhaps have turned out to be more capable than any other of contributing physically, in one way or another, to the preparation for and the triggering of trance. Clearly this is not the case at all. If there were such an instrument, then one would come across it, if not invariably, at least more frequently than any other. The facts indicate the contrary. One may also wonder that, despite their great variety, the musical instruments used for possession do not manifest some commonly shared acoustic property that might perhaps explain why they all act upon the listener in the same way. But no family of instruments is missing from our list above; the hypothesis is thus untenable. Drums of all sorts—and heaven only knows that their variety of forms, dimension, materials, and sonorities could hardly be greater—bells, rattles, harps, lyres, fiddles, xylophones, gongs, trumpets, clarinets, mouth organs, whistles . . . Every one of these instruments, which somewhere or other is closely associated with trance, delivers acoustic signals too radically different from one another to be able to produce, at the level of auditory physiology, the same effects on the listener. So that if one of them could by chance produce such effects—that is, were capable of triggering trance by virtue of its sonority alone—another would certainly lack this ability. Although all these instruments are associated with trance, and more particularly with entry into trance, this association is not related to the physical impact created by the sounds they produce. At the beginning of this chapter we asked ourselves what particular characteristics instruments used for possession could share? We now see they have none.

Rhythmic, Dynamic, Melodic?

Music, we have seen, can be vocal or instrumental, but whether it is one or the other still does not explain the sort of action it might have on trance. Its effects cannot be attributed to some special virtue of the voice, since in trance sessions there might quite often be no singing at all, nor can it be attributed to any *sui generis* power of a particular instrument since, in fact, all instruments can be used, contrary to the commonly accepted idea that the drum is the major cause of the great hurly-burly of possession. We must now investigate if the effects of music could be due not to its acoustic characteristics, but to the manner in which they are shaped; by this I mean by the rhythmic, dynamic, or melodic—or more correctly modal—features of the music.

Are there such rhythms that in and of themselves, because of their intrinsic musical structure, are more suitable than others for inducing trance? Concretely (and presenting the facts in a rather simplistic way), would 4/4 time be more likely to produce such an effect than 3/4 time? A syncopated rhythm more than one that is not? A staccato more than a legato rhythm? A rhythm with strong stresses more than one almost without stress? A monotonous rhythm more than a continually changing one?

Carpitella (1966, 361), who considers "rhythm to be the determining factor in tarantism's iatromusic," asks if the original rhythm of the tarantella was in "'perfect' or 'imperfect' time." Danielou, for his part (1975, 14), asserts that "the processes and the characteristics of these [ecstatic] dances are the same in all regions of the globe, in India, in the Middle East, in Africa," and that "the rhythms used are always of 5, 7 or 11 beats." Such an assertion can not be taken seriously: no study has yet been undertaken that would allow us to state this universal a rule, and a great many observed facts contradict it. The question posed with respect to the tarantella is, however, legitimate, and we are justified in asking the same sort of questions about any music used to accompany trance dances.

As far as I know, no work, either monographic or comparative, has been published on this subject. However, it seems valid to ask, for example, what exactly were those rhythms among the Greeks "that had the property of provoking trances, by possession of the Corybantes and also, no doubt, of the Sileni-Satyrs" (Jeanmaire 1951, 497). Plato himself scarcely had any opinion on this point. In *The Republic* (400 a–b), when discussing what I shall label for simplicity's sake the "ethos of rhythms," he admits he does not know either "which rhythm represents such and such a character," or "which rhythms are suitable (for producing) *mania*," in other words trance. We know from other sources that the dithyramb was originally closely associated with Dionysiac rituals. And as a poetic genre, we are told that it was essentially iambic, so its rhythm must have consisted of a foot made up of one short syllable followed by a long one. In a text attributed to Plutarch and presented by Jeanmaire (1951, 289) as "a development that is basically no more than a paraphrase of the Platonic theory concerning the divine origin and character of *mania*," we read, concerning the relations of possession to rhythm and melody, that "in the case of Bacchic and Corybantic leaps, it suffices to change the rhythm by abandoning the trochee, and the air by abandoning the Phrygian mode, for them to become less violent and cease" (Amatorius 16. 31). Here, then, the trochee (a long syllable followed by a short), and not the iamb, is associated with possession dance. Elsewhere, apropos the word *iambos,* Jeanmaire (1951, 234) wonders whether it refers "in one case to a dance step in duple time and in the other to a rhythm that may be in triple time." Uncertainty on this point is evidently considerable. What we do know, on the other hand (ibid., 242), is that "the celebration of the dithyramb manifested itself by noisy exclamations, outcries underscored by music in which the flute [read: aulos], which incites *mania*, played a role that has always remained preponderant, but which nevertheless included other instruments, small drums, kettle drums, castanets. The rhythm must have been dominated by repeated ritual acclamations." Interesting though it is, this text does not tell us much about exactly what this rhythm was (a point to which we shall return later, but from a different angle).

Just as the lyre, Apollo's instrument, is sometimes associated with Greek Dionysiac cults, so in Egypt the paean, an essentially Apollonian literary form as well, seems to have been incorporated, with its own specific meter no doubt, into the Greek Dionysiac tradition.[35] Such is the information we have concerning the rhythm accompanying trance and to which Dionysiac dances were performed. As we can see, it is rather scant, but there is enough to let us suspect that no one rhythm was especially associated among the Greeks with possession dance, or, to say the same thing differently, that there must have been several rhythms, and that none was specific to trance. As a matter of fact, this is the same conclusion we shall reach again later on, albeit by way of dance, in the chapter devoted to possession music among the Greeks.

From ancient Greece let us now pass on to modern-day Brazil and the music in *candomblé,* about which we do possess a fair amount of information, owing in particular to the work of Gisele Cossard. The repertoire of twenty-five rhythmic themes published in her study (1967, 180–207) of *candomblé* music contains, with only one exception, duple meter rhythms, in many cases employing triple subdivisions. As for the tempo indicated, they show that the smallest pulse unit varies according to the theme from MM 288 to MM 576.[36] Thus we are faced with a group of rhythmic themes that are extremely uniform as regards meter, but extremely varied as regards tempo. Apart from one or two, including the one for the entry of the *orisha,* these themes are all intended to trigger trances. Each of them is specific to a particular *orisha,* with the exception of the *adarum* rhythm,[37] which we already mentioned, and is valid for all the *orisha,* without any distinctions. "This swift and insistent rhythm is a veritable imperative," says Cossard (1967, 176). "Rare are the initiates who can resist it, even those among the most senior." On the day of the center's annual closure, it is this theme that the saint's father orders to be played "so that all the initiates present will go into trance" (1970, 145). It is also played during any other ceremony when the *orisha* "delay from incorporating themselves" (ibid., 108).

In fact, the *adarum* does not have a particularly quick tempo, since Cossard records it as being MM 69 to the quarter note. It contains no note shorter than a sixteenth note and frequently makes use of both eighth and quarter notes. Its rhythm is nevertheless very particular. The first three bars contain accented and unaccented eighth notes, an eighth note against the beat, and a triplet of eighth and sixteenth notes; the next three bars are made up, on the contrary, of a regular sequence of quarter notes. Rhythmically, then, this theme has an extremely uneven profile. As for its "insistent" character, it evidently stems to a large extent from the four accented quavers with which it begins. Is the efficacy of the *adarum* due to rhythmic factors comparable in some way to those Métraux (1958, 161, 169) de-

scribes in Haiti when he writes about the drummer's "feints," defined as
"breaks" against the beat ("brisures et cassees") that "interrupt the flow of
the dance and produce a state of paroxysm propitious for *loa* crises?" Does
this device belong to a musical system specific to trance? Are not the same
devices equally used in music having no connection to possession? An in-
depth study would be needed to ascertain it.

However, let us note that evidence of the same kind has been collected
by Alain Daniélou (1967, 92) in Asia, "in the *kîrtâna-s*, which in Bengal
are the mystic chants danced to in groups, and in the prophetic dances of
primitive peoples in Southern India." Here is what he writes: "The dancers
are first of all drawn into an easy rhythm with which they identify completely and thus sink into a sort of hypnotic half-sleep. The musicians then
create a shock by means of several violent drum strokes and embark on a
new, much more complex rhythm. After hesitating an instant, the dancers
are taken over by this new rhythm without even consciously willing it. In
some of them, this provokes a trance state and a complete loss of self control, as though the rhythm were a kind of spirit that had possessed them.
This trance state is characterized by insensitivity to pain, complete loss of
modesty, and visionary perceptions."

Let us also remember, even though it lies somewhat outside our domain
since it involves shamanism and not possession, that according to F. Densmore (1948, 36–37) the healing songs of the North American Indians she
studied are characterized by changes of stress and rhythmical irregulari-
ties that distinguish them quite clearly from the tribes' other songs.

Although there are not enough data at our disposal to enable us to state
that such rhythmic breaks constitute one of the universal features of possession music, it is nevertheless true that they recur very frequently, and
this is something we need to remember. On the contrary, it does seem that
we can consider another rhythmic feature, the acceleration of tempo, to
be universally used as a means of triggering trance. Discussing the dithyramb as a ritual, which is to say as a "chorus arranged in a circle that sings
and dances," Jeanmaire (1951, 240) writes: "The movement was imparted
only gradually to the cyclical chorus, which for a while at least gave the
impression of crawling on the ground like a heavy cable, the goal being a
progressive approach to the ecstatic state, which is achieved precisely by
the monotony of the acclamations, repeated at first to a deliberately slow
rhythm, and *by the progressive acceleration of their cadence.*"[38]

Writing about the *candomblé*, more specifically in reference to the *toque
adarum* and after having stressed that "it is not accompanied by chants,
since this time not just one divinity but all of them at once are summoned,"
Roger Bastide (1958, 20) notes that "the ever more rapid rhythm,[39] the
ever more imploring tone finally opens up their muscles, their viscera,
their heads, to the penetration of the god they have awaited so long." Simi-

larly in Tunisia, in the case of the possession dances performed by women as they listen to the *dhikr* chanted in the neighboring room by the men, it is when the rhythm of this chanting accelerates that they begin to dance and fall into trance (Ferchiou 1972, 56). The same is true of other marabout-type sessions in which the music, which is quite different, is in fact true possession music, since it is played specifically for the purpose of inducing possession. Here again, the session has two phases: "during the first, the atmosphere is relaxed, the rhythms are slow, and the words distinct; this is the phase in which all those who are present participate. The second becomes progressively more intense, and the rhythms, which steadily accelerate, are those of the possession dance" (ibid., 57).

In Tibet, the invocations chanted in order to trigger the oracle's trance and addressed to the divinity who is to descend into him, are first chanted slowly, but soon "the tempo [is] increased" (Nebesky-Wojkowitz 1956, 433). In Bali, Jane Belo (1960, 35) describes how the orchestra accelerates suddenly in order to trigger the trance of the *barong* carrier. One could go on and on listing such examples. But even this rule, needless to say, is not without exceptions. To mention only one, again in Bali, the orchestral music accompanying the trance of the *kriss* dancers at the end of the *barong* ceremony maintains an even tempo from start to finish.[40]

As is frequently the case with all sorts of music, acceleration of tempo very often goes hand in hand with an intensification of sound. The record entitled *Fête pour l'offrande des premières ignames à Shango* (Feast for the offering of the first yams to Shango; G. Rouget 1965) provides us with a typical example of simultaneous *accelerando* and *crescendo;* in this case the *accelerando* is achieved not so much by an acceleration of the tempo as by an increase in the number and insistence of the drumbeats within it; as for the *crescendo,* it results both from the intensification and dramatization of the singing and of the horn call. In Bali, describing the ceremony during which "the official entrance of the god" into the medium who is to embody him will take place, Jane Belo (1960, 50) observes that in order to encourage trances in the mediums present, people were singing loudly while the orchestra played "as loud as it could." Elsewhere (ibid., 20) she notes that, again in order to trigger the trance state, "the singing and the music of the orchestra redouble their intensity." Among the Thonga of Mozambique, H. A. Junod (1913, 438–43), describing a session held for the purpose of inducing the sick man to declare the name of the spirit possessing him, emphasizes the violence of the percussion, which is composed of single-skinned drums, drums made of large tin cases, and calabash rattles shaken so as to almost "slightly touch the head or the ears of the unfortunate sufferer," the total result being "a hideous din." In addition to these instruments there also are "incantations" remarkable for the singularly incisive and penetrating nature of their melody, whose disturbing effect is intensified by a "very pronounced *sforzando* when the chorus took up the dominant phrase" (ibid., 442).

In the *candomblé,* "when possession is long in coming," Roger Bastide writes (1958, 18), "the priest or the priestesses ring the *agogo*[41] close to the girls' ears as they dance, and then it is by no means rare for the divinity, spurred on by this deafening noise, this barbaric sound, to make up his mind at last to mount his horse." Here the crescendo is achieved not only by louder playing but also by playing closer to the one for whom the music is destined. The same is true, as we have just seen, with the Thonga and their rattles. In Tibet, as we saw, horns are blown into the ears of the oracle on the verge of possession. In Bali, Jane Belo (1960, 50) describes how the singers leave their places and move to a spot just behind the medium who is about to be possessed, so that they can sing very close to him and thus make him go into a trance. These facts are not without importance, and we shall return to them later.

In Madagascar, among the Vezo, B. Koechlin (see discography) notes that when the god takes a long time to come down, the tempo increases, while at the same time "interjections ring out: 'your hands!,' 'louder,' 'clap all of you'"; and among these exclamations, he selects "it's getting hot now, sister!" Zempléni, for his part, has demonstrated the great importance of the "warming-up" process in *ndöp* ceremonies (1966, 395, 399), which follow a carefully staged dramatic scenario. All the participants— officiants, musicians, and spectators—contribute in varying degrees to the general warm-up. Although the chanting plays an important part in this process, the decisive role seems to be played by the drummers, the "griots"—who themselves are well aware of this fact: "We summon and excite the *rab* with our drums," they say (ibid., 395). The lead drummer seems to be the "master in these rhythmic dialogues between the public dancing and the crisis." With the first "crisis labor," the beat of the drums speeds up, then a little later, as they announce and at the same time cause the possessee's collapse, "the movements and the drum become very fast." The possession séance for the "naming of the *rab*" (that is, for identifying the spirit possessing the patient) as described by Zempléni (ibid., 356–60, 369–70) becomes one immense and increasingly dramatic *crescendo,* in which the drama (the fit and final collapse) is carried to its climax by a constant and progressive amplification of the sound. His account is littered with observations relating to music. After a certain number of rituals have unfolded, first without any musical accompaniment and then to the sound of a rattle (a small horn filled with cowrie shells), an officiant begins to ring "a little bell close to the patient's ears." A short while later, with the bell still tinkling, "the drums thunder out. The atmosphere in the room changes totally." The ritual continues as the officiant "shakes his little bell tirelessly in the patient's ears. The din grows louder still." The treatment of the sick person takes ever more violent forms, and "the dry clicking of gourd rattles is now added to the almost intolerable noise of the drums and the insistent tinkling of bells." The sick woman howls. She is about to speak the name of the *rab*. Silence then dramatizes the situation: "the drums abruptly fall silent." If no answer comes, "the drums, bells, and chanting resume." The acceleration of the tempo is described elsewhere (p. 416) in these terms: "The drum beats and the gestures then become so rapid that the ear perceives a qualitative change in the music (even though the rhythmic pattern stays the same)." The collapse, "the terminal point of the crisis," is "marked by a resounding blow on the first drum." The *ndöp*, as described by Zempléni, is probably the most spectacular example of increasing dramatic tension by an acceleration of momentum and an intensification of sound. But degree of intensity aside, other examples of *accelerando* and *crescendo* abound, as we have seen, and the list could be extended without difficulty—so much so that these two features may well be regarded as constituting veritable universals of possession music. Yet here again several reservations must be made.

In the first place, it would seem that this dramatization of the music is to be found solely in the possession cults in which trance is accompanied by crisis, whether the latter precedes the trance (as with the Shango ceremony cited earlier) or, on the contrary, forms its climax (as in the case of the *ndöp*). When the trance is totally nonconvulsive in character, and when there is no fit, then the music maintains the same intensity and tempo. At least this is the case among the Mundang, as the films and recordings of Zempléni, Pineau, and Adler demonstrate.[42] In this case, the dances performed by the possessees are always characterized by a great gentleness (even the panther dance, so very different from what one observes during the ceremonies for Agè, god of the hunt, in Abomey). The music used to accompany them—double-skinned drum, gourd horn alternately blown and sung into, and rattle—is likewise devoid of all violence. It flows gently, always yielding the same delivery and it renews itself in a manner that owes nothing to changes of tempo or intensity, but results from expressive modulations always occurring on the same registers. The character of the music, the character of the dances, and the character of the trance thus appear to be completely interdependent. And nothing, indeed, could be more natural.

Although the violence of music and of trance may well be closely allied, this does not change the fact that an outburst of music may perfectly well not lead to a fit, or, inversely, that a fit can occur without musical violence. Although the relation between musical violence and the onset of a crisis seems to be extremely close in the *ndöp*, in other cults it appears to be much less so. True, in Haitian voodoo, as in the *candomble*, to cite only two examples, trances most often occur at the moment when emotions are at their strongest and the music is at its most dramatic, but it is not exceptional for things to happen quite differently. Michel Leiris told me recently he had noticed this several times, as did Alfred Métraux, during the voodoo ceremonies they attended together. It is by no means rare, they both observed, for trances to occur precisely at a moment when the music slackens. No one would think of relating such slackening to the entry into trance. Yet the opposite seems quite normal, and if trance occurs at the moment when music reaches its climax, no one fails to connect the two. This is what has usually happened, and it explains why music has so often been perceived, quite improperly, as the very springboard for entry into trance. Michel Leiris, for example, remembers a voodoo ceremony in Haiti toward the end of which, at a moment when the music had ceased completely, a lemonade seller, who was of course at a slight distance from the dancing area and thus from the musicians, was suddenly seized by a violent crisis and began rolling frenziedly in the dust and howling. And Pierre Verger, too, has told me how often it happens in the *candomblé* that whereas the drummers have unsuccessfully attempted to send someone into trance by unleashing the full force of their instruments, the trance is brought on by the mere tinkling of a little bell gently shaken close to the subject's ear!

In fact, we see that in the domain of the relations between music and trance, the connection between causes and effects offers a very wide margin of freedom. To illustrate this point, I will cite as examples two ceremonies for Ogun, god of iron, that I attended with Pierre Verger in the Yoruba region of Dahomey. In both cases the ceremony was held on a weekly basis in honor of this *orisha,* and during it the officiants went into trance almost as a rule. The music and drumming were quite spectacular (Verger 1957, 150–70). And as the recordings make plain,[43] the music attains the same paroxysmal climax on both occasions. Yet on the first occasion the expected trances ensued and on the second they did not. There must undoubtedly have been a reason for this; but the fact remains that the same music did not produce the same effects on both occasions. I can cite yet another example of entry into trance, which I witnessed personally, again in Dahomey, that was not linked to any kind of paroxysm. In this case (during a ceremony for Dan, the snake *vodun*) it occurred while the officiant was chanting rather quietly and shaking a rattle smoothly and evenly. The woman, who was quite close to the officiant, it is true, went into a trance within a matter of minutes. As for East Africa, K. P. Wachsmann (1957, 8) underscores the many different aspects possession music can assume there. Although certain possessions are triggered by the sound of an extremely noisy gourd rattle, others, on the contrary, are induced by the sound of very gentle chanting accompanied by an almost inaudible zither. Then there is the extreme case of the "deaf" tarantulas (Carpitella 1966,

362) who inspire in their devotees a behavior consisting in "a nonchalant dance, as though the tarantulee were deaf to the music."

Investigation of a number of different possession cults therefore shows that, although the dramatization of the music by *accelerando* and *crescendo* often plays a role of primary importance in triggering trance and/or fit, this rule is nevertheless far from absolute. Even in cults that make systematic use of these techniques, trance and fit can occur in the absence of any musical paroxysm. Frequent though its use may be, this dramatization cannot therefore be seen, contrary to what people often tend to think, as the quasi-inevitable means of inducing possession. Moreover, such techniques are in no way specific to possession. As far as I know, Ravel's *Bolero,* which is one enormous *crescendo,* does not habitually induce possession in our concert halls. In Africa, an outburst of music, particularly drum music, can reach the intensity described for the *ndöp* in the course of feasts or ceremonies that have nothing to do with possession.

Yes, one may say, but what about the *ndöp,* all the same? Is not the violence of the music in this case, if we are to believe Zempléni, the *sine qua non* of the fit and fall? Let us leave aside the fact, significant though it may be, that agitation and collapse also form part of "nonritualized" crisis (Zempléni 1966, 314) which can occur, as we saw earlier, outside any ritual framework and therefore in the total absence of music. In "ritualized crisis," in other words during a *ndöp* ceremony, it is the crisis and fall, that is to say, the frenzied and convulsive dance and the fall that follows it, that seem to be directly associated with the explosions of the drummers, and not the entry into trance. Moreover, the crisis and the fall are the normal (or even required) end products of trance only for the neophytes. Experienced possessees go into trance and dance, but do not go as far as a crisis or, needless to say, a fall. But in what does this crisis or, to use the author's own terms, this "labor of crisis" consist? Zempléni describes it as a "motor sequence" containing two consecutive phases, during which the possessee, who is now "at the drummers' mercy," executes an increasingly violent and convulsive dance. The second phase consists in "a rapid extension and bending of the arms, in an oblique line to the axis of the body, and a violent swinging of the head up and down." The drummers accompany these movements, "causing them to become still more rapid and violent all the while." Then comes a phase of disordered movements, contortions, raucous cries, and then the fall. "The physiological cause of the fall," Zempléni writes (ibid., 417), seems to be autostimulation of the inner ear: owing to the increase in volume and pace of the music, the possessee is led to—or, more exactly, drives himself toward—muscular exhaustion and extreme spatial disorientation. This seems to correlate with the remarks of Dr. H. Aubin quoted by Leiris (1958, 18–19) on the "frenzied movements of the head . . . subjected to repeated shaking in every direction," on "the violent excitation of the labyrinth" engendering a "special state of drunkeness," and on the shaking "to which the thoraco-abdomino-pelvic viscera involved in some of the previously mentioned movements" are subjected "to a lesser degree." It is true that this frenzy is governed by and relies upon the drumming (even though for their part the drummers, as we shall see, pay the closest attention to the behavior of the possessee), but the possessee's loss of balance and fall are due to the frenetic movements of his dance and his own frenzied agitation in general, and not to the music. Or, rather, the music is only indirectly responsible for them; it spurs his dancing on, but it is not a source of vertigo or auditory dizziness, as it were.

Without ever explicitly formulating the hypothesis, numerous authors, in remarks scattered throughout their work, more or less insidiously lead the reader to believe that the violence of the sound involved—particularly that of drums, rattles, and bells—is capable of producing a phenomenon of this nature. "A din growing ever louder," "almost intolerable noise of the drums" (Zempléni), "frightful hubbub" (Junod 1913, 441), "deafening noise" (Bastide). We have already encountered "voodooish drums of the *rada* ritual, unbelievably percussive. . . . Orchestral convulsions. Thunder" (Leiris 1955, 18). One could add other quotations that highlight the unbearable, intolerable intensity of sound to which the individual who is either possessed or on the way to becoming so is subjected. Going from these observations to thinking, or causing others to think—even if involuntarily—that any convulsions, crisis, or collapse are in fact signs that the intensity of sound can no longer be tolerated, involves only one step. This step, moreover, is all the more easy to take because it is sometimes taken (and for good reasons, at the level of appearances at least). Describing the first possession crisis of the saint's daughter-to-be, an event usually taking place during a feast, "when the *orisha* are embodied and the drums play the rhythmic compositions intended to summon them," Gisèle Cossard (1970, 158–59) writes: "The person seems at first unable to go on tolerating the sounds she is hearing. She puts her hands over her ears as though to protect herself from them, she sways, she loses her balance. . . ." And this person, it should be noted, is only a mere onlooker; she is not part of the group of "embodied *orisha*"; she is not dancing. So in this case the giddiness and the collapse are to be ascribed directly to the music, which "she seems unable to go on tolerating." Thus we are faced here with a very different process from the one observed in the *ndöp*.

But collapse following a convulsive possession crisis can also be found without accompanying music. In Tibet, the medium goes into trance, as we have seen, as a result of "special prayers" chanted "in a peculiar, quick rhythm" (Nebesky-Wojkowitz 1956, 547), accompanied, depending on the case, by drums, bells, cymbals, and sometimes thighbone trumpets.

He is seated (ibid., 433–34), but as he enters his trance he begins "to swing the upper part of his body rhythmically with a rotating movement from left to right . . . rolling at times limply as if it were only loosely attached to the trunk." After having delivered the oracles demanded of him—and after the music has stopped, of course—the medium is once more seized by convulsions, again rotates his trunk as at the beginning of his trance, and suddenly falls backward into the arms of his helpers, stationed behind him to break his fall. The text does not specify it, but one assumes that the rotation of the torso is also accompanied on this second occasion by the headrolling mentioned earlier. So here we find the same bodily movements as those associated with the final collapse in the *ndöp*. The physical context and the relations to the music, however, are very different. There is no deafening music or, in fact, as in the second episode, no music at all. There is no dancing properly speaking, or any frenzied agitation, except for a very brief period at the beginning of the trance. But the medium does display an extreme state of inner concentration, achieved through meditation that sometimes lasts for several days (ibid., 440) and through a wholly corporeal technique that is not described but that includes the swaying and rotation of torso and head already mentioned, breath control, and an exercise that prepares the medium to bear the weight of an extremely heavy metal helmet, which is placed on his head as soon as the first signs of trance manifest themselves and which he wears throughout the séance. At certain moments the trance nevertheless evidences very marked convulsive aspects. Like the priests of Ogun in Dahomey,[44] the seated oracle suddenly leaps "several feet" into the air at the beginning of his trance (ibid., 434). Moreover, as in Bali and Madagascar, his entry into trance is encouraged by the burning of a great deal of incense. What role does this incense play exactly? Is it simply part of what one might call an overall program of overstimulation? Or does it in fact act as a true drug? The authentic oracles all abstain from any stimulant (ibid., 440) as a means of entering the trance state. But there are "impostors" who make use of a mixture of Indian hemp and Guinea pepper that "is supposed to make one feel the blood running hot through the veins and become rather excitable by the music made at the beginning of the ceremony" (ibid.). Clearly an intensification of musical perception is consciously sought here, which means that it must play some role in the system. It is worth noting that in Niger too, in the *bori,* during the ceremony for the "raising of the dark gods," the neophyte is likewise subjected to fumigation, and J. Monfouga-Nicolas tells us (1972, 116) that "just like the music . . . the smoke from certain plants is a summons to the gods, a sign they recognize just as well as their motto." In Niger, however, the plants utilized produce an "acrid and evil-smelling" smoke that chokes the initiate. In other words the stimulation sought is not at all the same as that in Tibet, but its physical effect is accompanied by a symbolic action that figures in a system of signs which here again is related to music.

Let us return to the final collapse of the Tibetan oracle and to the collapse of the possessee in *ndöp*. They each occur in contexts as different from one another as could be imagined. In *ndöp,* the collapse is very closely connected to the frenzy of the dance and the music; in the case of the oracle, it is not. In the first case it is taken to represent "the lethal outcome of the encounter with the double," writes Zempléni (1966, 419), who then adds: "in order to let oneself be invested by, then fused with, one's double [the *rab*], one must erase the foundations of one's own identity, one must die." In the second case, on the contrary, the collapse represents "the moment in which the *dharmapala* [deity] is supposed to have left the body" (Nebesky-Wojkowitz 1956, 429). However, it is true that in both cases the collapse occurs after a period of intense emotion, extreme tension, and great convulsive muscular exertions. It is probable, therefore, that in both cases the fall is simply, in part at least, the effect of a brusque decompensation. However, on the level both of physical technique and symbolic representation, the conditioning involved is so different in each case that one is tempted to think there must be something else at work, and that the something else is a behavioral convention, a stereotype. This does not mean to say, of course (imagination being the powerful force it is), that the behavior is insincere. Let us go back to the *ndöp* example, for instance. If what I am tempted to think happens does in fact happen, then neither the numbing effect of the music, nor that of the dance, supposing they exist, is sufficient to explain the collapse—any more than either suffices on its own to explain entry into trance.

In tarantism, in which collapse occurs before as well as after the trance, albeit in a form very different from that of *ndöp,* the role of the rhythm is to provide a regular (and rapid) pulsation for dance music. As we know, this dance music is regarded as a remedy for the crisis (and for the collapse that was its manifest symptom). But during the entire time that the tarantulee is entranced, the dance, in its turn, is intended to lead to collapse (De Martino 1966, 68) except at the end, when he is granted "grace" (ibid., 73) and returns to his normal state. De Martino shows how important are the intensity and proximity of the sound: "During the upright phase, whenever the tarantulee—still dancing to the beat of the music—lingered in front of the musicians, or amongst them, the drummer would hammer out loud rhythmic strokes close to his ears, but still keeping time . . ." (ibid., 70). But in his general interpretation of the part played by music in tarantism (ibid., 145–46), he lays the most stress on the *moto perpetuo* aspect of the tarantella. After giving an account of an episode that "provides an excellent demonstration of the relation between the crisis and its musical resolution" he concludes: "Everything that occurs seems to suggest that a certain rhythmical ordering of sounds unleashes that most elementary sign of life which is movement, while, at the same time, the discipline of that rhythm prevents the movement from sliding into pure psychomotoric convulsions. . . . Tarantism begins, runs its course, and ends—as ritual and action—in the very elementary perspective of a fresh breakthrough into historical existence by placing itself, *pro tempore,* under the protection of rhythmic repetition, as certain and as predictable as the orbit of a planet. . . ." In this case, we are far away from the "feints" and "breaks" that Metraux tells us are so propitious to *loa* crises.

Now let us pass on to another aspect of the relations between rhythm and trance. So far we have examined them only with respect to a certain number of specific cases. It is equally possible to consider them from a much more general point of view, and that is what I propose to do now, very briefly. To make things as general as possible, let us take three musical regions: black Africa, Southeast Asia, and Indian America. And I should make it clear, because some may have doubts in this respect, that however impressionistic or disputable it may seem, this particular division—in my opinion at least—does correspond to a certain reality. It will be agreed that the musical styles of these three regions all possess rhythmical aspects, specific to themselves, that can be decisive factors in identifying them. There are certain unmistakable characteristics that enable us, without the possibility of error, to attribute a particular way of drumming to one specific region rather than to another. There is a rhythmics particular to Amerindians[45] that could not under any circumstances be black African. I would be tempted to go further and say there is an incompatibility between certain fundamental aspects of American Indian rhythmics, on the one hand, and black African rhythmics on the other. The fact that in the present state of musicology it is difficult to say exactly what it is, does not affect the matter. In the same way there is a radical difference between the rhythmics of Vietnam, let us say, and those of Amerindia and Africa. This being so, in all three regions we find the same relations between music and trance (possession trance, as is usually the case in black Africa, or shamanic trance, as is the case for Amerindia; the difference is not important). If one particular rhythmic is thought to trigger trance in one region, and in another quite a different rhythmic performs the same function, the reason must be that any rhythmic, or any rhythmic system—for any rhythmic is a system—can do the job as well as any other. Or else, which comes to the same thing, no rhythmic system is specifically related to trance. This totally contradicts the assertion by Daniélou, quoted at the beginning of this chapter, that certain rhythms possess the particular virtue of being able to trigger trance in all regions of the world. If this were the case, it would mean that the action of rhythm—and therefore of music—in triggering trance is of a physiological order. Everything points to the contrary: the relations between rhythm and trance operate at the level not of nature but of culture.

As a conclusion to these remarks on rhythm in possession music, two observations should be made. First, contrary to what we found out about instrumentation, which, as we saw, revealed no particularities, the rhythmics of such music have two frequently recurring characteristics: on the one hand breaks or abrupt changes of rhythm, on the other an *accelerando crescendo,* which recurs so frequently one might view it as a universal of possession music. Second, again contrary to what we found to be the case for instrumentation, which we examined only in and of itself, or, if one prefers, from the point of view of acoustics, rhythmics must be considered from a double viewpoint: in and of itself, that is, as a message received by the person in the trance, or preparing to enter it; as a dance performed by the entranced person; that is, as a modality of his or her perception. For dancing to music (or rather "dancing the music," if one may say so) is in fact perceiving it in a particular way. For the dancer, it means reenacting it on his own account. It means retransmitting the message in the form of movement and not merely receiving it. One is tempted to say that it means "acting" the music rather than simply undergoing it. At any rate it certainly means substituting a totally or partially passive relationship to music with an overtly active one. In a later chapter, we shall once again observe that as far as the relations between music and the subject in trance are concerned, it is important to distinguish between those that are active and those that are passive. We shall see, in fact, that depending on whether one is dealing with shamanism or with possession, either the active or the passive relations are involved. This is therefore an important distinction to make. As for dance, it too will have a short chapter devoted to it later on.

Let us now pass to facts about the melodic order, or, more precisely, to facts about the organization of the relations between pitches, in other words, to facts about mode, using the word "mode" here in its most general sense. Are there musical modes specifically propitious to trance, or more frequently linked with trance than others? The ancient Greeks and Chinese, the civilizations of India and of Islam, all the "high cultures" in fact, have associated musical scales with emotions, passions, the cosmic order, and ultimately, with man's moral and physical health. These relations were established for the most part, it is true, at the level of learned music, and consequently do not necessarily or directly involve popular melodic systems. In a civilization in which there are grounds for distinguishing between learned and popular music, possession usually occurs at the popular level. The question thus remains: Are there any connections between musical scales and possession?

In Greek antiquity, Aristotle observes (*Politics* 8. 7. 1341b), the philosophers classified melodies according to three categories: "ethical" melodies, linked with various ethoses or, let us say for simplicity's sake, various states of soul; "practical" melodies, linked to certain occupations; and "enthusiastic" melodies, associated, as their name indicates, with possession. Elsewhere in Aristotle's *Politics* (1342b) we read:

> "All Dionysiac transport and all analogous agitations find their expression in the flute [read: *aulos*] rather than in any other instrument, and these emotions receive a melodic accompaniment in the Phrygian mode, which among all others is best suited to them. The dithyramb, for example, is in everyone's opinion a Phrygian meter, and to prove it, experts in the matter adduce a mass of examples, among others, the fact that when Philoxenes attempted to compose a dithyramb, the *Mysians*, in the Dorian mode he was unable to do so, and fell back, following the natural course of things, into the only suitable mode, the Phrygian mode.

We know that the entire Greek system of modes may be regarded as resting, originally at least, upon a fundamental opposition between the Dorian and the Phrygian modes. Since it used the Phrygian mode exclusively, "enthusiastic" music must have displayed very specific characteristics. But what were they? In other words, in what way did the Phrygian differ from the Dorian? This is a complicated question, and one to which we shall return at greater length in a later chapter; suffice it to say that Samuel Baud-Bovy's recent findings (1977) lead us to believe that in its "primitive" form the Dorian was a pentatonic mode without semitones and that the Phrygian was, on the contrary, a diatonic mode with semitones. The difference, from the viewpoint of expressive resources, is considerable. Should Baud-Bovy's views be confirmed, we could be certain that the two modes were clearly distinct from one another. The fact remains, however, that Plato, who of all the Greek writers tells us the most about the relations between music and possession, does not even refer to the Phrygian mode when dealing with the subject. Just as he so frequently cites the *aulos* as the instrument specific to mania, so he remains as utterly mute on the matter of modes. This fact is extremely important, and, combined with a number of others (to be treated at length later), suggests that Aristotle's views on the effects of the Phrygian mode are but a much later interpretation and rationalization of the relations between music and enthusiasm. Plato, for his part, sticks to the *aulos*. Aristotle also acknowledges that this instrument plays a great role in triggering trance (*Politics* 8). But the *aulos* is also the instrument of Marsyas, as Plato tells us in his *Symposium* (215c), and Marsyas is a Micrasian. In a roundabout way, we are back in Phrygia.

So we find that in Hellenic Greece, not only the musical mode of possession but also its favored instrument were seen as coming from elsewhere. Maurice Emmanuel (1914, 440), taking his lead from Aristotle, underscores that Greek music is divided into two antithetical worlds, that of the Dorian, "harmony of European Hellas" and that of the Phrygian, "music of the Asians, imported by the *aulos* players of Phrygia." One easily recognizes that broad antitheses of this kind—and the one first made by Nietzsche between Apollo and Dionysus naturally springs to mind—are rather reductive; so let us not give this one any more importance than it actually merits. However, we do not lend it too much credit if we simply note that—as many other texts confirm—the music of enthusiasm or Dionysiac *mania* was strongly felt to be Phrygian. It was indeed from Phrygia (or Thrace, but in any case from Asia Minor) that the Dionysus cult spread (Jeanmaire 1951, 22) or, as the Greeks themselves believed, that it originated. We are therefore justified in saying that although Dionysiac music was Phrygian in instrumentation and mode, it was not because the musical characteristics of this instrumentation and mode in and of themselves (that is to say, their particular timbre or set of intervals) were thought to have any remarkable effect on triggering trance, but rather because they were the clearest sign of Dionysus' identity. This would in any case concur with the general logic of possession. For what in fact is possession other than an invasion of the field of consciousness by the *other,* that is, by someone who has come from elsewhere? Insofar as he is the other, Dionysus is at the same time an elsewhere; whether he is or not really is of little importance. This is how he was thought to be, and how his music was experienced. In Dahomey, people of Gun or Fon origin speak Nago[46] when they are possessed by a *vodun* of Nago origin. Elsewhere, people who ordinarily speak a given African language talk in Arabic if the spirit possessing them is thought to be of Arab origin. When she was possessed by Beelzebub, Jeanne des Agnes spoke, it is said, in Hebrew (Certeau 1970, 66–67). What is true of speech could also be true of that other language, music.

Whatever our interpretation of the facts may be, it seems clear that among the Greeks the music of Dionysiac possession was characterized by its use of one particular mode and no other. A comparable situation may be found among the Thonga of southern Africa. Among them, possessions are said to be caused by foreign spirits, either Zulu or Ndau. Songs relating to possession by Zulu spirits are pentatonic, we are told by T. F. Johnston (1972, 13), whereas those relating to possessions by Ndau spirits are heptatonic. The fact that one rather than the other scale is chosen is directly related to the fact that Zulu music is pentatonic and Ndau music is heptatonic. In other words, the scale is not chosen for its particular me lodic potential or expressive resources, but as a sign of the identity of the spirit with which the melody is connected. This considerably strengthens the above interpretation of similar facts among the ancient Greeks.

With respect to tarantism, Diego Carpitella (1966, 361) observes that if the musicians are to be believed, "the tarantulees are incited to dance" by certain tonalities only, "and remain insensitive to others." This is because each tarantula "likes its own tune." Consequently the repertoire contains "a traditionalized series of tunes and songs from which one must choose the one (or ones) best suited to each particular case" (De Martino 1966, 153). At least, this was the situation some time ago, when tarantism still flourished in southern Italy. Nowadays, because the cult is in a state of decadence, this "aspect of tarantism is on the decline and has disappeared from general awareness," Carpitella observes (1966, 351), and adds that during his fieldwork, in 1959, his own observations did not confirm what the musicians had told him. Whatever the present state of things may be, let us keep in mind that, traditionally, the different tunes played for the tarantulee were in principle related to the different species of tarantula that may have bitten him or her, and they thus served to identify the particular one responsible for the bite. Moreover, the tunes varied in their key signatures. Here, then, we are confronted with evidence showing that music is identified not with the region or people whence the spirit regarded as responsible for the possession originated, but with the species of the creature whose bite triggered the crisis. The choice of key or mode is thus dependent in all three cases (the Greeks, the Thonga, and tarantism) upon considerations external to the music itself, and not upon the use of any expressive possibilities the music may possess.

Everyday Language

To conclude, let me turn to another aspect of the matter, even though it really concerns timbre rather than melody. Writing about the "low notes" of the single-stringed fiddle, Rouch (1961, 141) tells us: "According to the Songhay, it is these raucous, wavering, and tragic notes that speak to the gods, that summon them and calm them." A comparative study of both profane and sacred tunes that make up the repertoire of the fiddle (*godye*)— which can itself be used as either a sacred or a profane instrument—would let us formulate some judgment about the use of these notes in the "spirits' tunes" and would thus help isolate the melodic system used in the Songhays' possession music, if such a system exists. Similarly, among the Wolof, one could make an inventory of the mottoes sung during the *ndöp* and then attempt to isolate the stylistic characteristics of this repertoire. Among the Yoruba, similar research could be applied to the mottoes that, in this case, are played on drums, rather than sung, or played on the fiddle. For my own part, however, I doubt whether such research—which must still be done—would succeed in isolating styles that could be clearly distinguished from the style of the profane popular tunes belonging to the same literary genre. At the risk of jumping ahead too fast, I will say that, on the basis of the possession music I have heard so far (some of it from all over the world, but in particular that of the Songhay, the Wolof, the Gun, and the Yoruba) it does not seem at all probable that any such music uses a musical system specific to it; that is to say, one that constitutes a separate and distinct system within the general musical system to which it belongs. Indeed, paradoxical though it may seem, it is quite logical that possession should speak, on the musical level, the language of the everyday. The reasons for this will be investigated later.

The same is not true, however, of initiation and initiatory trance, which are expressed, on the contrary, by a specific musical language characterized by its deliberately unusual nature. At least, this is what we find both in the Benin *vodun* cult and in the Brazilian *candomblé,* as we saw earlier. In Benin, the songs relating to initiatory trance are distinguished from all the other music of the region by their very unusual use of chromaticism. Are there other such examples? One may well wonder whether a certain liturgical chant sung in the Buddhist repertoire, described as constituting an "essentially ecstatic"[47] music and performed in a state that could be one of trance, should not also be placed in the category of initiatory music. This chant has, of course, no connection with those already described for Benin, but it too makes systematic use of chromaticism. Compared to the usual Buddhist music one hears, it does strike one as being very unusual indeed. On the contrary, the hymns for the genii sung during possession séances in the Vietnamese *hàu bóng* cult, as described by Simon and Simon-Barouh (1973), belong to the most banal popular style.[48] Whereas in both Africa and Asia trance that is not linked with possession expresses itself in a musical language constituting a separate and distinct system within the population concerned (I have given two examples, but the list could certainly be extended, particularly in the area of shamanism and of communion trance), contrariwise, possession trance seems to require, everywhere and at all times, a form of music belonging to the most everyday and popular system. Despite appearances, what I said a moment ago about the use of Phrygian music by the Greeks and Zulu or of Ndau music by the Thonga does not violate this rule. Among the Greeks, the Phrygian mode, despite its foreign origin, was perfectly integrated into the general musical system and was as much part of the popular tradition as the Dorian mode. And in all likelihood the situation is the same among the Thonga.[49]

What Does This Music Mean?

The brief (and very incomplete) survey I have just provided of some of the formal characteristics of possession music thus tends to indicate that, although such music does play a part in triggering and maintaining the trance state, it does not owe its effect to the properties of its musical structure, or if it does, it does so only to a very small degree. Let us therefore abandon this aspect of music, by which I mean the signifying side of the musical sign, and turn instead toward the signified one.

What does possession music signify? What is its meaning? What are the words of the songs saying? What do the dance rhythms express? Or, rather, to what dances do those rhythms correspond and what do those dances signify? We can say in a general sense that the vast majority of such songs concern divinities that have come to be embodied, or that are expected to do so. They can concern these divinities in several different ways. Sometimes they are addressed directly to them, summoning them or, on the contrary, asking them to go away; sometimes they describe them, usually in a flattering way, and often by referring to their genealogies or their mottoes, which comes to the same thing.

Jane Belo, in her book on Bali, does not provide very much information about the texts sung during trances caused by the gods. But the songs for the popular trances brought about by *sanghyang* spirits (the *sanghyang* who inhabit the dolls and the little girl dancers on the one hand, and the *sanghyang* of animals on the other [Belo 1960, 180–225]) fit in well with what I have just said. Judging from Simon and Simon-Barouh's chapter on the subject, the same is true of the "hymns of invocation to the genii" sung in Vietnam during *hâu bông* ceremonies. In Tibet, the chant used to trigger the oracle's trance is formed of two parts (Nebesky-Wojkowitz 1956, 429). The first is an "invocation to the *dharmapâla* who is asked to take possession of the medium. The invocation usually starts with a detailed description of the *dharmapâla* and also of the abode in which he is supposed to reside." Then follows "a litany . . . praising the *dharmapâla*— who by now should have occupied the body of the oracle—enumerating and eulogizing his various capabilities" (ibid.).

In Madagascar, the songs (*àntsa*) sung to summon the divinities (*tsumba,* a dialectical variation of *trômba*) are "fairly slow." The words "aim to describe and flatter the god" (Koechlin, discography). "These solemn chants" alternate with other songs accompanied by a board-zither, an instrument "also used on a schooner, to summon the winds when the boat is becalmed." Once the trance is well established and the dances take on a purely playful character, it is dynamism of movement that is mainly required. The importance of the words decreases, and they are often reduced to simple exclamations. But for slower dances, the words may acquire importance again, and the singing consists of "success songs," occasionally humorous in content but no longer connected with possession as such. Among the Thonga of Mozambique, the importance of the rhythm and sound level provided by the drums in possession séances have been strongly emphasized by H. A. Junod, as we have seen, but "that which is the most essentially necessary," he also writes "is the *singing*" (1913, 441). This is provided by experienced possessed persons: "They address the spirit in laudatory terms, trying to cajole it by flattery, to get the right side of it, and thus to induce it to grant the signal favour of a surrender" (ibid.). Such phrases as "Rhinoceros, thou attackest man!" show that these songs obviously fall into the category of mottoes.

In Ethiopia, "apart from the songs used to evoke the *zār,* which are called *wadāgā* like the gatherings during which they are performed," and apart from "songs with prophetic intentions . . . often contributed by professional possessees" and consisting most often of "a very general lament about vicissitudes of the times," Leiris (1958, 43) also describes a great many songs "performed for the purpose of entertainment." Elsewhere, however, (ibid., 80, nn. 2, 93) he makes reference to a "song intended to make the *zār* descend onto a novice" and also mentions—though without expressly linking it to the singing—the use of mottoes (*fukkarā*) which he defines as a "fairly free accumulation of stereotypes recalling Homeric epithets."

In Niger, in the *bori,* the songs used to trigger trance (and on occasion to calm it too, when the possession is a false one) are essentially mottoes. At least this is what emerges from the work of Jacqueline Monfouga-Nicolas (1972, 109–59, 160, 201, etc.). Still in Niger, among the Songhay the "musical mottoes" (that is to say, the ritual texts) which are sung "usually with instrumental accompaniment" (Rouch 1960, 135), but which are also frequently played on the fiddle without being sung, provide the very substance of their possession music. "Each divinity has one or several musical themes specific to him," writes Rouch, who then assigns these themes and texts, the dance steps associated with them, and even such objects as altars, ritual furniture, and costumes, to one and the same general category of "more or less materialized signs of the divinities."

In Senegal, the *bak,* a "theme-song or motto-song is one of the *rab*'s attributes. . . . It is with the aid of the *bak,* a short and more or less explicit phrase, that the spirits are summoned one by one during the *ndöp* and the *samp*" (Zempleni 1966, 304). In the warming-up phase, chanting of the *bak* plays a decisive role. At the start of the session, after the drummers have played the summons, the *ndöpkat*[50] form a procession, enter, stop in front of the drums, and "consult over the choice of the first *bak.*" Then, when everything is ready, the women officiants, in order to achieve "a suitable degree of excitation," "summon those possessees who are particularly easy to excite, by manipulating the appropriate *baks* (ibid., 399–400). In the course of the extremely important session known as the "naming of the *rab*," whose description I quoted earlier several times, various *bak* are intoned in succession. At the end, "it is when a new *bak* is called out by the assistants that A. G. . . . suddenly utters a long cry, then announces: '*Wali Ndiaye Sene!*' This is the name they had been waiting for." We shall return later to the role of chanted mottoes in the process of identifying a deity.

Among the Dogon,[51] in the course of the ceremonial enthronement of one of the priests of the *binu* (mythical ancestors), when the priests hear the drum theme of their own *binu*, "they move into the center of the circle and dance more quickly, or give themselves up to a ritual crisis that a colleague then calms with an application of sacred bastard-mahogany bark" (de Ganay 1942, 41). What is happening here is that "when the *binu*'s rhythm is played that *binu*'s *nyama* [life force] possesses the priest, who then performs the movements specific to the theme being drummed out." "For each *binu* there is a specific drum rhythm (*binu boy*),"[52] G. Dieterlen writes. When he hears the rhythm specific to his *binu*, the priest goes into trance, because "at the mere beating of the drum, the *binu*'s soul is thought to rise onto [his] head . . . and provoke the crisis."[53] Here again, then, among the Dogon, we are dealing with musical mottoes (which must not be confused with verbal mottoes, *tige*) that trigger possession. But possession can equally well be induced, not by rhythms played on a drum, but by songs. At least this is implied in a remark made by S. de Ganay (1942, 43), who relates the trance of a *binu* priest "crawling on his belly to imitate the *Nommo* [water spirits] who move in the deep holes in the earth" to a song about the god *Nommo*.[54] But at the level of myth, the onset of the trance is attributed neither to the singing, nor to the musical instruments, nor to the dance, but to the sound of speech. It was when he heard *Nommo* utter the first word intended for the first men that Binu Seru, the first totemic priest, "underwent the first fit, analogous to those that still make all priests seized by inspiration 'tremble' today" (Calame-Griaule 1965, 97). Here again, then, in every case a sound bearing a meaning is seen as being at the origin of trance.

In Nigeria and Dahomey, among the Yoruba and also among the Fon or the Gun, the *oriki* of the *orisha* and the *mimlan* of the *vodun* respectively occupy an important place in the invocations chanted to summon the divinities to manifest themselves, or to make them dance once they have been embodied (Verger 1957; Rouget 1965). These *oriki* and *mimlan* are nothing other than mottoes, which may be spoken, sung, or drummed depending on the circumstances. In Brazil, in the *candomblé*, each deity has his or her specific "canticles," which "constitute, together with the sonorous drum rhythms that accompany them, so many leitmotifs, to borrow a Wagnerian term, intended to attract the orixá" (Bastide 1958, 19). "As these canticles unfold," Gisèle Cossard writes, "so the initiates go into trance" (1970, 107). The texts she quotes elsewhere (1967, 172–75) demonstrate that we are once again dealing primarily with mottoes.

The sung invocations requesting the divinity to come and take possession of the adept combine mottoes, exhortations, prayers, and, on occasion, insults—a sign of the familiarity that reigns between men and gods. Thus among the Vandau: "They are not afraid to insult the possessing spirit, like the chief's daughter who is mocked for being a prostitute, or like the almost untranslatable song of the *Mandiki*" (Junod 1934, 281). In nearby Zimbabwe, among the Tonga, A. Tracey (1970, 38) reports that when people grow tired of waiting for the medium to become possessed, a certain *mbira* player specializes in singing a song so insulting to the *mhondoro* (spirit), who is usually addressed in flattering terms, that shame forces him to "come out" immediately. Whether they are prayers, praises, or insults, these songs are addressed to the deity, and this is the important thing to remember. They constitute communication with him.

When they are specific to a particular deity, melodies played on an instrument have the same function as sung mottoes:[55] they are call-signs. Indeed, these melodies often are mere instrumental versions of the sung mottoes which are deprived of their text; but, when they hear them, "men and gods also hear the words that relate to them" (Rouch 1960, 135–36). Whether linked to a text or not, these tunes are used for dancing, and the resulting dance constitutes the motto's choreographic aspect; it expresses the deity's personality just the same, but in movement rather than words. Whether it is a rhythmic theme played on a drum or a melodic theme played on, say, a fiddle, this theme, when linked to a particular deity, has a "signified" referring to that deity, either because it is related to him or her by some expressive correspondence (it depicts the deity) or because it simply has been arbitrarily attached to him or her. Thus the rhythmic themes specific to the various *orisha* in the *candomblé* are described by Gisèle Cossard (1967, 177) as "dramatic," "full of vivacity," "aggressive," "tempestuous"—each of these adjectives corresponding to the nature of the divinity in question. On the other hand, I am unable to say whether or not the "tunes of the genii," which constitute the repertoire of the *holey* (genii) cult among the Songhay, also have an expressive content. In tarantism, each variety of tarantula has its own particular tune. But is the correspondence in this case expressive or is it purely arbitrary? We do not know. We do know, however, that in order to cure tarantulees "the piper or zither player plays for them various motifs related to the quality of the venom, so that they are ravished by the harmony and fascinated by what they are hearing, and the venom either dissolves away within the body, or is slowly eliminated through the veins" (early sixteenth-century text quoted by De Martino 1966, 144). Since each tarantula "likes its own tune" (ibid.,

153), there is "a traditionalized series of tunes and songs from which one must choose the one (or ones) best suited to each particular case." It is the "right" music, in other words the one that best fits the case, that "will make the tarantula *scazzicare* (leap about)" (ibid., 65), just like the appropriate canticle in the *candomblé* or *bak* in the *ndöp* will attract the corresponding *orisha* or *rab*. But although there are different varieties of tarantella, each differing from the other in tune, key, and rhythm, it seems that the dance—or rather the sequence of the dance's various movements—always remains the same, no matter which tarantula is involved. One of these movements consists in imitating the spider. It is thus a figurative dance, as are so many other possession dances in Bali, in Vietnam, and in Africa. Depending on whether it involves a warrior (sword dance), a loving woman, a wild animal symbolizing power (tiger or panther) or fertility (snake), the dance will naturally differ in character, and with it the music that sustains it. And in this case one is also dealing with more or less directly figurative music.

The situation offered by tarantism, in which the same dance is performed to different tunes, corresponds among the Mundang to an inverted situation where, on the contrary, different dances are performed to the same music. The film and recordings made by Adler, Pineau, and Zempléni, already mentioned earlier, show that different possessed women all dance at the same time, one the panther dance, one the sun dance, one the rain dance, and still another the milling dance. In a small group, they all dance to the same music. This music varies only in its details and, as we have seen, nothing shows it is linked to one or the other choreographic figure. We are thus dealing here with music that, in contrast with the figurative music in tarantism, one might describe as abstract. Another example of nonfigurative music is the *adarum* rhythm already mentioned several times. The saint's daughters, who ordinarily respond only to the summons of the rhythm specific to their own particular *orisha,* all go into trance when the *adarum* is played. In the *ndöp,* while the *rab*'s *bak* (the genius's tune) is what most distinguishes one genius from another (Zempléni 1966, 405), and while each class of *rab* has its own mimicry (its "identificatory behavior"), contrariwise certain dance movements, particularly those of the "labor of crisis," together with the drum music directing them, of course, are the same for all *rab*. This is true among the Songhay as well: "Although each *Holey* has one or several specific mottoes, one or two special musical themes, the dances that lead to his incarnation are not particular to him" (Rouch 1960, 146–47). These dances comprise several distinct phases, characterized by different figures and following one another at a steadily increasing pace until they finally lead to the crisis, but here again, as with the "labor of crisis" in the *ndöp,* the drumbeats, and not the played or sung melodies, control the dancing. And since the same drum music works for all the *holey* or for all the *rab* and is thus impersonal in a way, it does not function as a musical motto,[56] which is also the case with the *adarum* rhythm. The list of such examples could be extended considerably. It is consequently necessary, with respect to music accompanying possession dances, to distinguish between sung or played themes on the one hand, which are usually musical mottoes, and on the other drum music which may or may not function as a motto. This does not, however, alter the fact that in practice the music may be an intimate mixture of melodic music and of rhythmic music, the two being associated in combinations that vary from cult to cult, and in which one or the other sometimes predominates.

Let us now return to the musical motto, which, as we have seen, plays a central role in possession. It can be defined as a sign whose "signified" is the god to which it refers and whose "signifier" has three facets: linguistic, • musical, and choreographic. The signifying power of this sign is peculiarly extensive, since it involves spirit and body, intelligence and sensibility, and the faculties of ideation and movement, all at the same time. This is evidently what makes it, for the adept, the most powerful means available for identifying himself with the divinity possessing him. In certain cases when the deity's unknown identity must still be established, it will also be the principal means of identifying him or her.

Tarantism provides a particularly striking example of this use of music or, more precisely, of the musical motto, as a means of identifying the divinity (here, the spider) responsible for the possession. In the late nineteenth century, one could still find "in Naples twelve different tarantella themes used to diagnose tarantulees in order to establish which one corresponded with which particular case, and consequently triggered the dance," writes E. De Martino (1966, 160), who elsewhere quotes a passage from G. Baglivi, the celebrated iatromechanist of the late seventeenth century, describing "musical exploration" (or diagnosis) as follows: "The musicians who were summoned asked the patient the color and size of her tarantula so they could adapt their music accordingly; but the patient replied she did not know if she had been bitten by a tarantula or by a scorpion. They began trying out their themes: at the fourth, the tarantulee immediately began to sigh, and at last, no longer able to resist the call of the dance, she leapt half naked from her bed, without a thought for conventions, and for three days kept up a sprightly dance, after which she was cured." We find the very same process at work in the case of the Sardinian *argia,* a variant of tarantism that departs considerably from the Apulian model. Like the tarantula in Italy or Spain, or the scorpion, in Sardinia a mythical creature, the *argia,* is responsible for the patient's poisoning. This creature "is categorized under three distinct species, the nubile, the wife, and the widow, and the treatment of the poisoned person differs according to the type of *argia* that bit him or her. In particular, the widow *argia,* symbolically associated with the color black, always requires dirges . . . the musical exploration [is] intended to determine the type involved in the given case [and] it unfolds through the successive use of musico-choreographic themes and songs traditionally associated with each type" (ibid., 214–15).[57] The success of this musical "exploration" depended on the skill of the musicians, as did the efficacy of the cure, once the "right music" had been found, De Martino also tells us (ibid., 161).

This "right music" is, in fact, to give another example, what Plato speaks of when he describes the Corybantes "falling into a trance when they hear the melody specific to the divinity by whom they are possessed" (Jeanmaire 1951, 134). And again, it is the "right song," played for the medium among the Tonga that proves irresistible: as soon as the deity hears it "he is unable to refuse to incorporate him" (Tracey 1970, 38).

Among the Thonga,[58] as among the Wolof, it does not suffice for the possessed woman to declare the name of the divinity possessing her—a crucial episode in her initiation, as we saw earlier: she must also sing the deity's theme. In the *ndöp,* after they have extracted the name of her *rab* from her, the officiants continue to press the sick woman: "They begin shaking her again in order to get the *rab's* song-motto out of her. It was some time before the young woman began to sing in a staccato voice, the *bak* required of her, and which all those present then repeated in chorus" (Zempléni 1966, 370). Among the Thonga (or Tsonga), things unfold slightly differently. The patient sings his song, but he has to invent it himself: "Every possessed person invents a song which will be henceforth *his,* and by means of which crises, or trances will be provoked or cured" (Junod 1913, 445). If the spirit responsible for the trance is a Zulu one, as is most frequently the case among the Thonga, the words will be in Zulu, even if the man involved does not know this language (ibid.). This is an extreme case of personalization of the sung theme, which, among the Tonga, corresponds to the inverted case of "songs, which while identified with *mhondoro* spirits in general, are not tied to any one" (Tracey 1970, 38). This recalls what I said above about the *adarum* rhythm in the *candomblé,* at the sound of which all the *orisha,* without distinction, go into trance.

WHO MAKES THE MUSIC AND IN WHAT STATE IS HE?

Who makes this music played at various points in the ritual, which triggers adepts' trances and which makes them dance when they are possessed? Who plays these instruments, who beats these drums, who sings these songs? Whatever the cult in question, in most cases it is important to make a distinction between two categories of individuals: those whose activity is expressly and exclusively to make music, in other words, those appointed to make it and whom I shall call the "musicians," and those whose activity is to make music only episodically, or accessorily, or secondarily, and whom I shall call "musicants" (*musiquants*).

A short parenthesis about this last word will perhaps be useful. In using the French word *musiquant,* I was returning to the verb *musiquer,* which is hardly used nowadays, but which was used not so very long ago and figures in the well-known French *Littré* dictionary, with reference to excellent sources such as Rousseau and Diderot. Present usage in the French language does not make it possible to express in a single word the act of making music (*faire de la musique*). The same holds true for English. This situation is often, and particularly here, a constraint. Using in French the verb *musiquer* or in English the coined expression *to musicate*—which I would propose as its equivalent—opens up a number of possibilities, such as making a distinction between "make music" and "musicate," which is not necessarily the same thing, or between "musician" and "musicant," as I have just done, or again, as I will do later, between a "musicant" and a "musicated" person. Let us add that the series "to musicate, musicant, musicated" could as well take the form of "to musicize, musicizer, musicized." The reader will choose which one of the two seems preferable . . . or less horrible to him.

Every, or almost every possession cult has two aspects, that of its private rituals, reserved for the initiates or those being initiated, and that of its public rites, in which both adepts and followers of the cult take part and which more or less always take the form of a performance in which possession dances constitute the central element. For simplicity's sake, we will only examine this second aspect. One part of the music for these performances—dance music, to be sure, but also the music of overtures, preludes, interludes, postludes, divertissements, and others—is furnished by people especially appointed for the task and whom we shall call—whether they are instrumentalists or singers or both—the musicians. They often are professionals, and in this case they are always paid for their services. The rest of the music—invocations to the divinities, sung mottoes,[59] calls, playing of various accompanying or punctuating instruments, handclapping, and so on—is provided by the adepts (we shall later see which ones) and by the spectators, all of whom we shall call musicants when they fulfill this function. The difference between musicians and musicants does not reside solely in that they participate in the general musical performance in different ways, even though this difference is essential and is sufficient in and of itself. They also differ in their relation to the cult and particularly to trance. It is this last point that is of interest to us.

As far as the musicians are concerned things are relatively simple: they do not, in principle, go into trance. Indeed, to do so would be incompatible with their function, which is to provide for hours on end and sometimes on several consecutive days, music whose execution must continuously adapt itself to the circumstances. It is therefore important that they should be constantly available and at the service of the ritual. This is probably the reason why these musicians frequently are not adepts themselves. Since they have never been possessed there is no fear that they will enter into trance. Paradoxically, then, these musicians, who seem to be the very pillars of possession séances and without whom possession dance would be inconceivable, are in a way external to the cult. In any case, they occupy a place apart. Like the officiants, and in collaboration with them, they control the adepts' possessions and play a part in inducing them, particularly in the case of neophytes, but, unlike the officiants, they have never lived through the experience themselves. In certain cults, however, it can happen that they are adepts themselves. In this case they have to be very experienced in order to be able to resist possession in all circumstances. Incidentally, it does happen that they cannot resist it.

But it is equally possible that they may have every outward appearance of being in a trance, when in fact they are not at all. Speaking in general terms about Haitian *tambouriers* (drummers), Métraux writes: "Looking at them, with turned-up eyes and contorted faces, hearing the rattle escaping from their throats, one would think they were in a trance, but this apparent frenzy is not due to any god. It is in fact rare for them to be possessed by a *loa*" (1958, 159). The musicians can certainly reach states of very great overexcitation, but this should not lead us to confuse inspiration with trance. However, as an example of a borderline case in which the musician is not possessed but "inspired," let me quote what Jean Rouch tells us when writing about the Songhay: "It is the fiddler's (*godye*) left hand that is 'inspired' (guided) by the genii who are collectively summoned at the start of the ceremony by the 'hunters' theme' (*gawey-gawey*)" (1973, 532).

In Vietnam, in *hầu bóng* ceremonies, the task of providing the music is assigned to a group of musicians, some instrumentalists, some singers, who in principle are professionals (Simon and Simon-Barouh 1973, 40). But, the authors of the description tell us, in the ceremonies they have observed in France, the musicians were "amateurs," either adepts of the cult or simply "disciples of the Genii." These musicians do not go into trance. The instrumental music dominates the ceremony from beginning to end, with preludes, interludes, and postludes framing the tunes to which the genii dance. Contrariwise, the singing of the hymns breaks off during the periods when possession is at its climax. It is worth noting, in passing, that this seems to be a general rule: in cults in which the music for possession dance is both instrumental and vocal, the instrumental music always prevails and is always more continuous than the vocal.

With respect to tarantism, the instrumental music, which predominates to a great extent, is provided by a small group of professional musicians who specialize in this function. Quoting Kircher, E. De Martino writes about the "musician-therapists . . . who, in seventeenth-century Tarento, were civil servants receiving set wages and who, in 1876 still, were regarded as persons of great social prestige" (1966, 212). Civil servants? This is perhaps an exaggeration on Kircher's part, but they were hired for a price and were the cause of great expense for the patient or the patient's family. Unless I am greatly mistaken, it has never been recorded that one of these musicians was, or could be, a tarantulee himself.

In Bali, when trances are caused by gods, the musicians of the village orchestra are the ones who provide the music. In the case of trances caused by spirits, the music is mostly, if not exclusively, vocal. The people of the village are the ones who provide it, and anyone who wants to is free to join in the singing that regulates the possessee's dance or pantomime (J. Belo 1969, 40, 202).

In the *ndöp,* the musicians are "griots," in other words professionals who belong to a particular caste. They only play drums and do not take part in the chants intoned by the officiants and repeated in chorus by the ordinary adepts. The spectators participate by clapping their hands. In the *holey* cult, among the Songhay, the principal instrumentalist, who plays the single-stringed fiddle, and the gourd-drummer(s) who accompany him, are likewise professional musicians. The fiddler—who is not a griot (Rouch 1960, 141, 144)—is often also a *zima* or a priest of the cult. He plays and sings at the same time. The situation is more or less comparable in the *bori,* except for the fact that the fiddler is not a priest of the cult. In Dahomey, in both *vodun* and *orisha* cults—and in many other cults in black Africa as well—the musicians, who are drummers, are not professionals; at the most they are semiprofessionals. This is also true in the case of the *candomblé.* But whether in Africa or Brazil, whether professional or not, whether they play the fiddle, the xylophone, or the drum, whether they are purely instrumentalists or whether they combine playing with singing, none of these musicians goes into trance.

If we turn now to the musicants, in other words the adepts[60] (officiants or ordinary members) insofar as they are musical actors, and their relation to trance when they are in this role, their case is much more complex than that of the musicians. In a general way we find that the role of the adept as musicant varies according to his seniority in the cult and his place in the hierarchy. The more neophyte he is the less he takes part in the music; the more he grows in seniority and importance the more he takes part in it, or at least the more he is likely and able to take part in it, for the situation changes from one cult to another.

It would seem, moreover, that more often than not (but not always, as we shall see), whether he is a neophyte or not, the ordinary adept does not take part, or takes very little part, in the music when he is possessed. For him, the only expression of his possession state is dance and mimicry. The officiant, on the contrary, a veteran adept who is used to possession, can sing and can play the ritual musical instrument he or she is carrying (if he is carrying one) while possessed. All of them, however, neophyte, ordinary adept, and officiant alike, enter into trances at the sound of music (instrumental, vocal, or both) made *by the others,* and not by themselves. This at least seems to be the rule, whatever the cult involved.

In the *ndöp,* as in the *candomblé,* the officiants sing the themes of the deities while ringing bells, and their vocal and instrumental contributions play an important role in triggering trance in the adepts in their charge. But, and let me stress this, while fulfilling their functions as officiants and musicants, which go together, they are not themselves in trance. The ordinary adepts, for their part, also sing the divinities' tunes, but without playing any instrument. In the *candomblé* (Gisèle Cossard, personal communication) an adept is only permitted to "start a canticle" after seven years of seniority. Before that she is only allowed to sing the refrain in chorus with her companions. During the entire period of their apprenticeship, which lasts seven years and ends with a special feast, new adepts thus participate in the music only passively, which is a very good illustration of what I just stated on the relation of neophytes to music in general.

Although in most cases officiants only "musicate" during ceremonies when they are not in a state of possession, it can nevertheless happen that they are in fact possessed at the time. The *orisha* cult in Dahomey provides us with two examples of this exception, the first involving instrumental music, the second vocal. Among the Nago-Yoruba of the Sakété region, in the course of the weekly ceremony for Ogun, god of iron,[61] the god's priest goes into trance together with other priests who are embodying kindred deities. The music is provided by a number of musicians divided into two groups, drummers and bellringers on one side, a chorus of women on the other. The officiants, four or five in number depending on the circumstances, all hold a pair of large iron bells with internal clappers. During the entire time they are waiting for their trance to begin, that is, while the musicians (instrumentalists and singers) summon the gods to incorporate themselves, the officiants remain seated and silent. At the moment they enter into trance, they utter a great cry and leap into the air, after which they embark all together upon a long ritual deambulation taking the form of a quadrille that is half walked and half danced and during which they continually bang their bells together in time with their steps, so that the resulting din mingles with the rest of the music. Here, then, we are dealing with officiants in a state of possession who are "musicating," but it should be noted they are not "musicating" in order to induce either other adepts or themselves into the trance state. The same observation also applies to a priest of Shango, god of lightning, who sings while he is possessed during a ceremony at which the first yams are offered to this deity.[62] It is only once he is actually in trance, which was induced by sung and drummed calls played *by others* on his behalf, that he begins to sing, limiting himself to intoning the first words of a song known to all and that everyone takes over in chorus.

Among the Ga of Ghana (Kilson, 1971) the adepts of the traditional religion (*kpele*), which is a possession cult, frequently sing *kpele lala* (*kpele* songs) during ceremonies when they are in a state of possession. But, we should note, they may also sing them during the same ceremonies without being in a trance (ibid., 26–27), and these same songs can, moreover, be sung outside of any ceremonies by the laymen. When an adept wishes to dance during the *kpele* dances, which are in fact public possession séances, she stations herself in front of the drummers and sings a *kpele* song; this serves as a sort of prelude to her dance and also gives the musicians the required rhythm. Whether the adept is entranced or not does not affect the way in which this is done. The author tells us no more on the subject; what she does say suffices to make it plain, and again this is what we need to remember, that the action of singing is unrelated at this point to the triggering of possession.[63]

What has just been said concerning the Ga of Ghana could as well fit the Gun of Porto-Novo (Benin), among whom I have often seen a possessed *vodunsi* (adept of the *vodun*) come and plant herself in front of the drummers in order to sing the first words of a given air, thus showing the musicians the tune she wanted for her dance. But here again the singing had nothing to do with inducing trance. Whereas the majority of these tunes can be sung by the *vodunsi* whether or not in trance, some of them can only be sung when the adept is possessed and when the dance takes place inside the convent. The study of this last repertoire, which is, of course, much less accessible than the first one, remains to be done.

On the other side of Africa, in Ethiopia, the evidence provided by Leiris, already mentioned earlier, concerning "songs with prophetic intentions . . . proffered by professional possessed persons," or "songs with a moralizing tendency" sung by Malkâm Ayyahu while she is possessed (1958, 43, 66), again does not invalidate the rule that the possessed person is not the one who sings in order to prepare his or her entry into trance. These songs, which are not possession songs, are not sung by the possessee during the phase preceding his trance, but only after he has already entered it: "Malkâm Ayyahu covered her head with a handkerchief and, *having become Abbâ Yosêf*, sang several moralizing songs and quoted some proverbs," writes Leiris. Describing entry into trance and the preparatory phase preceding it, he notes elsewhere (ibid., 83) that when the patient has had his soul already "partially 'veiled' by listening to the *wadāgā* song,"[64] he remains silent, sometimes for a long while, "without singing or clapping his hands with the rest of the assemby" before gradually slipping into a state of possession. Using his informant's own terms, Leiris adds in a note, to make things even clearer: "Before making them do the *gurri* [the convulsive dance of those who are possessed], their *zār* gives them ants and makes them stay quiet during both the singing and the clapping." One could hardly express more clearly the fact that in the *zār* the possessed person is neither the musician nor the musicant of his own trance.

In Tunisia, Sophie Ferchiou (1972) describes an extremely curious situation: that of women entering possession trances upon hearing chants that are not only not intended for their ears but also are being performed by men who are trying to induce a quite different type of trance in themselves. Here is a brief summary of what happens. Within the context of what in Maghreb is generally called the Saints Cult, men of a certain Sufi brotherhood (that of the Sāduliyya) gather once a week in a sanctuary in order to take part in the well-known practice of *dhikr*.[65] While these adepts, secluded in a "totally dark" room, dance in place and rhythmically chant the name of Allah, until they attain the trance state, in a contiguous room, women, who are "kept at a distance" and who do "not participate in the ritual," devote themselves to their own possession practices:

> They do not chant with the men; they are interested, not in the words but the rhythm to which they are chanted. When the rhythm becomes fast enough they begin to dance, and, keeping time with the rise and fall of the collective, guttural drone (made by the men), they swing their torsos forward and backward, backward and forward. Now and then they make gestures that are thought to be dictated by the spirits possessing them. . . . Once the *dhikr* session is over, when the men fall silent next door, all the possessed women swoon to the floor. Attempts are then made to revive them by murmuring in their ears phrases intended to appease the spirits possessing them. [Ferchiou 1972, 56].

The relation between the trance of these possessees and music thus conforms to the usual scheme in the sense that they are not the ones who make the music.[66] The unusual aspect in this case is that although the music is not made *by* them, it is also not made *for* them. In a way, they appropriate it for themselves, which shows that many combinations are possible even within the boundaries of the restrictions established earlier.

The fact that the musicants, that is, the men practicing *dhikr,* are either in trance or seeking to enter it, does not invalidate our rule, since they are not "musicating" for the women. On the other hand, they are, it is true, acting as musicants for their very own entry into trance. But in their case the trance is not a possession trance, an aspect to which we shall return in a later chapter.

Besides this example, which, with respect to the relations concerned, represents the height of paradox, Sophie Ferchiou provides yet another example that is so reassuring in its classicism it deserves to be quoted. This time she is dealing with possession dances performed in another sanctuary and by another brotherhood, that of the Tidjaniya (ibid., 57ff.). Here, the music is provided by four women singers seated around a drum. These women are "descendents of the saint" (ibid., 59), as are the two young girls who take care of the possessed women and make sure they do not harm themselves. The musicians and the healers "never become possessed themselves; they are immune on account of their birth, since their ancestor has transmitted to them a little of the power he has over the spirits," Ferchiou tells us. These women musicians who never go into trance thus confirm the rule observable in the majority of possession cults, since it conforms to the inherent logic of possession itself.

Finally, let us look at the case of adepts who are still neophytes. Among the Thonga of Mozambique, as among the Wolof of Senegal, we have seen that the first ritualized crisis, a very dramatic event, is intended to make the sick person, who is completely entranced, utter the name of the spirit possessing him or her, or, in other words, to identify that spirit. After having uttered the spirit's name, the possessee must then sing his tune. Among the Wolof this tune is a *bak,* that is to say a motto-song already known to everyone and long associated with that particular divinity. Among the Thonga, on the contrary, the possessee must make up the song.[67] Be that as it may, we should note that in both cases, even though the neophyte in a state of possession does sing during the course of his or her first ritualized crisis, the singing does not serve to trigger this crisis but, on the contrary, to induce and express its resolution.

The same observation applies among the Lovedu of southern Africa, neighbors of the Thonga, where the first ritualized trance also shares many features in common with that of the Wolof. The main purpose of the séance is to make the patient dance to the point of exhaustion in order to force the spirit to manifest itself. Quoting Krige (1943), Luc de Heusch writes the following: "The first exit of the pathogenic spirit is painful. The patient sways when it approaches, his movements become more and more frenzied, he drags his feet with great effort and finally collapses in a trance. He then chants the song for the arrival of the spirit who is saluted by the attendance" (1971, 265–66). Among the Kongo, quite some time after the first ritualized trance, at the end of the initiation period, during the coming-out feast which takes place at the end of three months, the neophyte is invited by the master of ceremonies to sing in order to appease the spirit responsible for her possession (de Heusch 1971, 263, quoting Van Wing 1938). Here again, in both cases, we see that the point is to resolve the crisis, not to induce it.

So far we have seen adepts acting as musicants and not as musicians, in the sense that singing or playing an instrument is only but one aspect of their activity, and not its principal goal. Among the Mussey of Chad (Igor de Garine, see filmography), on the other hand, the adepts do seem, on certain occasions at least, to act as musicians properly speaking in that making music appears to be their essential activity. When taking part in certain rituals, the college of possessees (men and women) constitutes a veritable band of instrumentalists in which everyone plays the gourd-horn, an instrument characteristic of possession. All of them are entranced while they play, and they do nothing else. To my knowledge this is the only case of its kind. The reason for this exception must certainly be sought in the particular logic of the Mussey possession system, and in the position this system occupies within their religious organization as a whole. But whatever the reason for it, by behaving as musicians and not as musicants the Mussey must be regarded as an exception.

What is it that should be remembered from the examination we have just made of possession music in its relations with the people who make it and with the state in which they are at the time? First, that a large part of the music is provided by people—the musicians—who do not go into trance, who often are not themselves adepts, and who consequently are marginal with respect to possession. Second, that possessees never figure as either the musicians or the musicants for their own entry into trance. For the possessee, it is the music made by others that triggers, or helps to trigger, his trance, never the music he makes himself. This fact is significant: in shamanism, as we shall see later, the reverse is the rule. Third, that the adept's activity as a musicant increases only in proportion with the degree to which he becomes more and more capable of controlling his own trance state. It is as though the adept becomes capable of "musicating" only insofar as he has become less vulnerable to the music. The adept thus passes from a stage of zero musical activity to one in which his musical activity is relatively large. This coincides with his passage from the status of neophyte to that of officiant; in other words, from a state of total submission to the deity to one of relative independence. Last, that the officiant "musicates" in order to trigger the trance of those adepts for whom he is responsible only when he is not in trance himself. When he is in trance, his activity as musicant no longer serves his efficacy as an officiant, at least insofar as he is in charge of others.

We thus find there is a kind of incompatibility, total or partial depending on the case, between the state of possession and the act of making music, or, if one prefers, between the state of possession and music as active behavior, or, again, between being possessed and "musicating." When the relation of the adept to music is examined at two particularly significant moments—that is, when the adept is still a neophyte and when, either as neophyte or as officiant, he goes into trance—it turns out to be one of total passivity. At the outset, it will be remembered, we found that the adept's general relation to possession is, in a similar way, also fundamentally passive; it now turns out that possession is a form of behavior involving a double submission: to the will of the gods, on the one hand, and to the effects of music on the other. The inherent logic of the system basically requires that the possessed person be neither a musician nor a musicant, but a "musicated" person.

Uttering Cries

As a general rule, then, the possessee is not a musicant. This does not mean, however, that he or she is necessarily silent. "*Crier comme un possédé*" (shouting like a possessee), for instance, is a current French expression. Uttering a cry often is a part of trance behavior. In tarantism, for example, the "crisis cry" has been described as being sometimes "more like a yelp than a human cry" (De Martino 1966, 121), sometimes, on the contrary, as approaching a sort of music. According to D. Carpitella, to whom we owe the ethnomusicological observations appearing as an appendix in De Martino's work, "the characteristic cry of the tarantulees [is] based on two syllables 'A-hi' in accordance with a time-ratio that may be codified as: A = hi! A − hi! A + hi! This time-ratio develops within a tessitura going from approximately the interval of a diminished second to a ninth" (ibid., 365). Others have referred to this cry as a "baying" sound. In tarantism then one has several ways of uttering cries when one is entranced.

The same can be said of the *vodun* and *orisha* cults in Benin. Frequently the priest of Ogun emits, at more or less regular intervals, little yelping sounds. Adepts who are possessed by Sakpata, on the other hand, will at certain moments utter modulated cries of extraordinary violence that very closely resemble those just described for tarantism. This cry sometimes, but not invariably, accompanies mimicry quite clearly meant to represent the efforts of parturition. In Niger, as Rouch's films show, it often happens that those possessed by *holey,* and even more so those embodying *hauka,* do literally bark when they are in the most violent phase of their trance. Other, similar examples could be cited. Moreover, we all know the great importance that bioenergy adepts attach to the cry in their quest for liberation through trance.

There is no doubt, therefore, that uttering cries is a very significant manifestation of trance, and that it needs to be decoded on several levels. For the moment, let us simply state that in and of itself, the trance cry merits a book-length study.

MUSICIANS AND THE POSSESSED

What is the relation of the possessee, not to the music this time, but to the musicians? It is essentially characterized by the submission of the former to the latter, and this follows logically from what we have just seen.

In Haiti, Métraux tells us that "the *tambourier* [drummer] may not be a professional musician, often is not even an initiate, but he nevertheless is the mainspring of the entire voodoo ceremony . . . a talented drummer can induce possessions or halt them just as he wishes." (1958, 159). This shows how great his power over the adepts may be!

During *ndöp* séances, where, as we have seen, the crisis and subsequent collapse are crucial, the honor of "bringing down" mainly falls on the first drummer (Zempléni 1966, 416). When the possessee has already been dancing for a while, and the crisis is drawing near, "her whole body begins to quiver. At this sign the first griot moves nearer and quickens the tempo." The "labor of crisis" then ensues: "the possessed woman is at the mercy of the drummers, who accompany her movements and force them to become ever more rapid and violent" (ibid., 415). In fact, a close interpersonal relationship develops at this point between drummer and possessee.[68] The drummer takes charge of her, so to speak. Keeping very close to her, never leaving her side, concentrating on her slightest movements, incessantly observing her behavior in order to: speed up the tempo, or, on the contrary, relax it; select the necessary types of beat; and adjust the intensity of the stroke. Communicating the rhythm of the dance to her, he holds the possessed woman in his sway and leads her into the ever more violent whirlwind of his music. But if he is able to lead her in this way, and finally guide her where he wishes, it is because he has been able to establish a close understanding with her. It is because he can follow her that he is able to dominate her and impose his will upon her. He is the master of the game, but within a dialogue. He speaks music and she replies dance.

Among the Songhay, the principal instrumentalist, the fiddler, is also sometimes a *zima,* a priest of the *holey* cult. Jean Rouch (1960, 148) similarly emphasizes the personal relation established between the possessed person and the musician-priest during the preparation for and triggering of trance: "At an imperceptible sign, the priests and musicians sense that one of the summoned genii is beginning to manifest itself . . . the orchestra now plays only one tune . . . the dancers as a group continue to move as before, but one of them has now become the sole object of the solicitude demonstrated by the priests, who surround him and recite mottoes of ever-increasing efficacy. . ." Here again we find that in order to induce trance in a particular person the priests and musicians establish a special relationship with him, "surround" him, make him the object of their "solicitude," address themselves to him in an exclusive way, and become at the same time very attentive to what he himself is feeling.

In his description of a memorable tarantism séance, at which he was present with his team in Salento in 1959, E. De Martino (1966, 69) demonstrates the very close bonds woven between possessee and musicians. The latter, "in a passionate musical offering . . . brought their instruments to her ear. . . . At one point during the phase on the ground, we saw the tarantulee crawl over to the feet of the violinist and linger there as though hypnotized; the violinist then knelt beside her, enveloping her with his music to such a point that his bow seemed to be using the woman's quivering body as its violin." In Bali, as we saw earlier, Jane Belo describes how the singers move very close to the individual concerned in order to make him enter into trance.

Instrumentalists or singers, professionals or not, when they attempt to trigger the trance state, the musicians, as we have seen, enter into very close contact with the possessees. Communication is established between them, not only at the level of the code involved (words of the songs, dance movements), but also at the personal level, the emotional level of direct person-to-person relationships.

Here again, however, there are distinctions to be made depending on the type of cult involved. In ceremonies like the first coming-out of the new initiates in a *vodun* cult, or the *vodun*'s annual feast, or the "Customs" in Abomey (during which, as we shall see later, princesses embody the royal family's departed ancestors), the musicians and the *vodunsi* form two separate groups, each of which remains compact, and from which no one separates him- or herself at any point.[69] The possessions in these cases are, it must be remembered, of the kind we have termed "impersonal." Similarly, the relations between musicians and possessees operate not at the individual level, as in *ndöp, bori,* or tarantism, in which possession is a personal matter, but at the group level, a fact corresponding to the logic of the system.

The power musicians have over the possessees is not entirely due to their talents; it also stems from the instruments they play, or rather, from what those instruments represent. In the *orisha* cult, "the drums are very much respected, for they are not just musical instruments. They are seen as being the voice of the gods themselves; through them one summons the gods and, at the same time, replies to them" (Verger 1969, 59). They are consecrated, moreover, just as the *adza* bell of the *candomblé* and the fiddle of the *holey* cult are consecrated, to name but two examples. As a result of this consecration, Rouch tells us, the use of this particular fiddle becomes restricted "since even a single note played upon it is a summons that cannot go unnoticed in the invisible world" (1960, 144). This is because the instrument is in fact equipped with a rattling device whose discreet clicking "guides the music" to the genii's delicate ears.[70] In the *bori,* Jacqueline Monfouga-Nicolas writes, the single-stringed fiddle, which is "capable of forcing the gods to embody themselves" (1972, 139), is "the most sacred of all" the instruments (ibid., 159). According to information given to Michel Leiris in 1931 (personal communication), but which needs to be verified,[71] among the Bambara the water spirit (*dyiro dyina*) responsible for possession is supposed to come and position himself on an iron rod placed in the water drum[72] (the instrument used for possession) after the drummer has begun to play. The musical instrument is thus seen sometimes as the voice, sometimes as the more or less temporary seat of the divinity. Evidence of this sort is so plentiful and well known it is unnecessary to cite any more. But the symbolics of musical instruments does not interest us here solely as an element of the very complex system of signs constituted by a possession cult. This symbolic efficacy is twofold. On the one hand it reinforces the effective power of communication these instruments establish between not only gods and men, but also musicians and dancers. On the other, it helps strengthen the power of the musicians who play them and thus increases their ascendancy over the possessees for whom they play.

MUSIC AND DANCE

Whereas, as we have just seen, the task of playing music during possession ceremonies does not fall on the possessee but on the others, the possessees are the ones who do the dancing. Dance should thus be seen as doubly more important than music; first because it is the possessee's own business, and second because music, or at least a large part of the music, is played for the purposes of dance. A theory of the relations between dance and possession is thus even more necessary than the one for which I am attempting to gather together the basic elements in this book, and which will only concern music. It is hardly worth saying that for all kinds of reasons (chiefly because dance is a vast subject that lies outside my domain), I will not even attempt to propose such a theory here.[73] At the same time, I cannot altogether avoid mentioning dance. But I shall do so only insofar as it is indispensible to situating it in the perspective adopted here.

In a number of cults it is possible to distinguish between two types of dance. There are what I shall term abstract dances, whose function is to trigger trance, and figurative dances (or simply mimes), whose function is to manifest the possession state. Among the Songhay, the dance proper, which is made up of three "principal movements" (Rouch 1960, 147–48), does not represent anything—it is abstract—and remains the same regardless of which genius is expected to become embodied. This dance helps to summon him: "the music, the words of the mottoes, the dance steps, trigger the strange mechanism"; and, when a certain stage is reached, the dance indicates that the genius is on the verge of becoming present. After having been grounded by the fit marking the deity's descent, then "calmed by the attentions of the 'quiet women,'" the possessee adopts the behavior befitting the god he is embodying, and which consists in stereotyped mimicry. In the *ndöp*, besides the dance and the "labor of crisis" resulting in collapse and which are the same for all genii, there is also a mimicry repertoire—or "identificatory behavior patterns" (Zempléni 1966, 402ff.)—having the same function as that among the Songhay. In theory, adepts of long standing perform only the mimed dances, since convulsive dance, crisis, and collapse are restricted to neophytes.

In *hàù bóng* ceremonies, the dancing also includes two phases (Simon and Simon-Barouh 1973, 44): "The first is the descent of the Genii. . . . It is reproduced identically in all cases; only the sign of the raised finger is changed." While the drum "beats out the rhythm of possession," the women singers "summon the Genii" (ibid., 42). The dance consists of the adept's head "turning, slowly at first, then more quickly, drawing the whole torso into its rotation. By means of a coded sign made with the hand—the number of fingers raised indicating the order number . . . the Genius . . . discloses his identity." When the embodiments have been completed, the various genii execute figurative dances: the sword dance, flame dance, oar dance, unicorn and lion dance, and the "wands with pellet-bells" dance (ibid., 45). In the middle of this last dance, that of the Princes and Little Princes, "the Tenth Prince inserts an episode in which he mimes a bowed musical instrument while the notes of the scale are sung as an accompaniment." Although in the *hàù bóng,* contrary to what we have seen in the *ndöp* or among the Songhay, the dances contain no elements of violence (the only dance which does is that of a much-feared genius whose descent is "heralded by violent somersaults [ibid., 57]); there are clearly great similarities between these Vietnamese ceremonies and the African ones just described. The same could be said for tarantism, with its "regular choreographic cycle" (Carpitella 1966, 359): the sword dance, spider dance, convulsive figures (that of the arched back in particular), and the step "more properly agonistic" consisting in rhythmic stamping. These are just a few examples, but they will situate the problem within the perspective of this book.

It would no doubt be difficult—and possibly futile—to draw precise boundaries between abstract dance, figurative dance, and mimicry. A particular dance may seem to be nonfigurative only because we do not know (or it is no longer known) what it represents or symbolizes. These three categories do nevertheless exist, and they furnish the elements of a system of combinations that varies from cult to cult, and which undoubtedly tells us a great deal about the underlying logic of these cults.

For the adept, dance is the best possible means of exhibiting, if one may so put it, his state of possession, since his movements, steps, mimicry, and costume are in reality those of the god inhabiting him. But in certain cults dance is also a means of compelling the gods to become embodied. "If the music and the dance are pleasing to the spirits, to the point of ensnaring their will, this is because they are themselves dancers who become carried away by the supernatural power of the rhythm," Métraux writes (1958, 168). "They danced, these powerful genii," Rouch tells us, "because the music forced them to do so" (1960, 145). "A deity's supreme requirement is that one among the faithful become his 'horse' by means of trance, so that he can come down among mankind and dance," Gisèle Cossard writes (1970, 95). Music incites the gods to dance, but in order for them to dance, they must have a visible support, and this forces them to become embodied. Whether we are dealing with voodoo, the *holey* cult, or *candomblé,* the symbolic system is the same. Of course, this does not mean it is the only one.

Whereas Rouch and Zempléni see dance as one of the principal means (if not *the* principal means) of inducing crisis and fall (which we must remember do not have the same function among the Songhay as among the Wolof), Leiris, on the contrary (1958, 18), says that the *gurri* (the dance of the *zār* cult) which is also characterized by violent movements, is the "symbol of trance" rather than the "means of provoking it."[74] While referring to it as "a classic procedure for inducing trance," Leiris observes that the *gurri* has the particularity of marking "both the departure and the arrival of the spirit," so that it is thereby associated with both the beginning and the end of trance. We must therefore rule out the idea that its role is to trigger trance in a mechanical way, as it were. Further on, Leiris notes that "certain great *zār* . . . do not make those they possess dance the *gurri*" (ibid., 92), which is proof that entry into trance can perfectly well take place without dance. As with music, the problem is to find out whether or not dancing plays a role in inducing trance. If we say it does, then we also have to ask: Is this role real or symbolic? And in either case we still have to ask whether this role should be attributed to the ethnographer's discourse or to that of the adepts themselves.

The relations between the two aspects of dance—figurative and non-figurative—and the two forms of music—instrumental and vocal—emerge so clearly in a note on the *dyide* (water spirits) cult among the Malinké of Mali provided by Chéron (1931) that a long passage of his text merits quotation in its entirety. This passage also reveals that, as in the *ndöp,* the female officiants (the "high-ranking members") want to avoid the fall, which is to say, ultimately, the full trance state, since this is the business of the "ordinary members," who are, broadly speaking, new adepts: a significant rule since it reflects an entire section of the cult's internal logic.

> The dances are always accompanied by one or two *dyidunu* (water drums) played by a woman, the *dyidunufola* (she who makes the water

drum speak); this music is supported by songs, whose tune and words are given (*donkili la*) by a woman musician, then repeated in chorus by the audience. Each dancer executes steps and gestures, which mainly consist of rapid movements of the legs, arms, and head.

The ordinary members dance more often than the others; they enter the circle when the woman singer intones the tune specific to their particular genius, which immediately sends them into convulsions. They then perform their *jinn*'s dance, a special dance that simply mimics the *jinn*'s habitual actions; both song and dance are taught to the adept by the chief, the only person, given his infallible power of identification, who knows the genius of the ordinary members.

As for the high-ranking members, they dance as little as possible, as a precaution, for should they happen to fall to the ground during their revels, this would be a sign of the imminent death of an adept. They cannot, however, abstain from dancing altogether for fear that their genii, thinking they are rebellious, would oblige them to do so. When it is their turn to dance, they require the assistance of ordinary members whose duty it is to watch over them and hold them up should they fall.

If, in possession, dance oscillates between two poles, the figurative and nonfigurative, the one being dance as identificatory behavior, the other dance as trance behavior, this is because it provides the adept with the means of assuming his new personality and living intensely at the motor level. Depending on the type of cult, one or the other of these aspects will predominate, but both usually seem to be present; either simultaneously, if the trance takes on both aspects at once (as in the case of the spider dance in tarantism), or else alternately.

In possession, then, dance is a representation of the gods, in other words theater—sacred theater, but also theater that one enacts not only for oneself, as Leiris has shown, but also for others. But dance also is physical exercise, as it is by definition, in any circumstance. Viewed from either of these aspects it is esthetic activity and play. But in all of its aspects it is, above all, communication—with oneself and with others.

For the possessed person it is a system of signs both in relation to himself, in that it "signifies" his borrowed personality for him, and in relation to the group, in that it expresses this personality and marks out his role (in the ordinary and the theatrical sense of this term) in the "representation" of the world constituted by the possession ceremony.[75] During the course of the dynamic process presented by possession in its succession of changing states, dance also "signifies" the stage that the possessee has reached in his metamorphoses. Moreover, whereas it is by no means certain that possession music has purely physiological effects on the possessee (or the person about to be possessed), dancing—be it in conjunction with possession or not—undoubtedly brings about modifications in the dancer's state, both at the physiological and psychological level. These physical effects are the ones sought after, and this explains why dancing can be seen as a form of ascetic exercise and why it is often used as a trance technique. But no matter how important its nature as a sign may be, or its symbolic function, esthetic power, or ascetic possibilities, dance is still a motor activity that finds an end in itself. Dance is always, at least in part and sometimes despite appearances, the pleasure of dancing, of using one's body in play. If it is nonfigurative, dance is pure physical expenditure. In this sense it is already liberation, catharsis. If it is figurative, particularly when erotic or warlike, dance is manifestly a means of release; when it imitates animals, it is also a means of release, albeit through a symbolic route. Here again it is cathartic, this time in the classical sense of the term. At once "mimesis and catharsis" (to borrow one of the subtitles of Jeanmaire's book), dance can ultimately be seen as the true realization of the state of *enthusiasm*. The identification experienced by the individual with the god he embodies takes place through dance and because of it. It is also through dance that this identification is made manifest in the eyes of others. This second function is as important as the first, since apparently the very existence of possession cults requires that possession be public behavior.

I spoke earlier, with reference to music, of the importance of the "right" tune, which makes it possible both to identify the divinity and to make him or her dance. If this tune is said to be "right," is it not so because the dance with which it is associated reveals, over and above the apparent behavior of the divinity, the deeper nature (or the hidden aspirations) of the possessed person? Or at least one aspect of his or her nature. It seems, according to Gisèle Cossard, who made reference to her personal experience of the *candomblé* (personal communication), that multiple possessions would provide a means of adding light and shade to the inner portrait of an individual by organizing, around the principal divinity he is embodying, a constellation of secondary divinities (also identified by divination, of course) who might unveil other traits of his character. But the relations of individual to divinity can be of another kind, notably that of filiation, as is generally the case with impersonal possessions.

It can happen that possession trance is achieved without music, and consequently without dance, since the latter does not occur without the former. In an earlier chapter we already noted one example of this for the *candomblé* during initiation; but this happens much more frequently in inspiration or mediumistic trance than in possession in the strict sense of the word. This is confirmed, among other examples, by the situation found in southern India, where the possessee's main function is to deliver oracles. The possessed man, L. Dumont tells us, "is described as he who 'dances the god' . . ." (1957, 350). But he adds that although "dance is a means of inducing or revealing possession, it is not indispensible to this process. Certain *kodangis* [possessees] are thought to be able to provoke possession all by themselves. This is why they were sometimes consulted without either music or dance, either during preliminary meetings, or on a day after a cult ceremony for familial oracles."

Before putting an end to this rather brief summary of the relations between dance and trance, shamanism must at least be mentioned. A musician (as will be shown in the next chapter), the shaman is as much a dancer, and the role of dance in shamanistic trance deserves in-depth treatment. Suffice it to say here that shamanic dance is as much of a show as is possession dance, although in quite a different manner.

However paradoxical it may be, the only example I shall give will not come from Siberia but from Africa, and will concern a case whose shamanic character remains to be proved. I refer here to the Zande witch doctor who, when entranced, acts both as a diviner and a healer (see p. 24). We owe to Evans-Pritchard (1937, 149–82) the most extraordinary description of a "seance" in which dance appears as a means of divination. Indeed, for a Zande witch doctor, divining is a highly corporeal technique (as Mauss would have said) achieved through dancing. "A witch doctor does not only divine with his lips, but with his whole body. He dances the questions which are put to him," Evans-Pritchard writes (ibid., 176). To sum up very quickly, he describes the witch doctor's dance ("violent, ecstatic . . . the most spirited performance of the art that I have ever witnessed") as being the principal way of stirring and enhancing divinatory intuition within himself. This is, to be sure, an unexpected aspect of dance, although it deserved to be cited.

Music, Gods, Illness

I hope the reader will forgive me for now entering the realm of commonplaces and basic truths. At this particular stage in my argument I feel it necessary to recall a few of them. They will bear first upon the manner in which music is experienced, then upon the manner in which the presence of the gods and the weight of illness are experienced, since in matters of possession the latter two frequently go together.

How is music experienced?[76] We respond to it in several ways; to simplify matters, let us say physiologically, psychologically, affectively, and esthetically.

Physiologically speaking (at the sensorial level), although music is mainly perceived by the ear, this is not the only path it can take. Musical vibrations are wave movements whose amplitude is relatively large when compared to the scale of the human body. The movement of the objects that give rise to these vibrations—or the movement that they excite in objects, since the transfer of energy can take place in either direction—is always palpable and often even visible. It is thus directly perceptible as material and concrete. A musical vibration can be something palpable. If one touches the soundboard of a violin while it is being played, one can feel the sounds quivering against one's finger tip. If one nears one of the extremely large drums the Yoruba beat at their secret *oro* ceremonies, one will hear the sounds through one's abdomen—which vibrates in sympathy—as much as through one's ears. Similarly, if in the same ceremonies, one comes close to one of the small drums (whose tightly stretched skin is whipped rather than beaten, *prestissimo,* with extremely slender sticks), one's entire head vibrates. In an organ loft, when the organ plays loudly, one absorbs the music with one's whole body. The whole world trembles, the very air resounds. "To bathe in music" is not just a metaphor. It happens that we truly perceive it through the skin. The candle flames flickering in churches at the sound of the organ provided Louis Roger (1748)[77] with one of the observations on which he began constructing his theory of the effects of music on the human body. The curious use that Tibetans make of the vibrations of a drum skin[78] is also based on the same type of observation. To blow into a clarinet is to feel the reed quiver between one's lips. To ring a bell held in one's hand is to be in direct contact with the vibrations of the metal one is striking. To shake a rattle is to feel the skin of the gourd vibrate as it is struck by the seeds inside. To play a Jew's harp is to feel the metal tongue moving in one's open mouth.

But this external sensitivity is not the only thing involved. One's internal sensitivity is also aroused by music and likewise functions as a path of reception. It is well known that when we speak, and even more when we sing, we hear ourselves from inside. But in fact we are doing more than hearing ourselves sing. We are *feeling* ourselves sing. We are feeling our larynx (let us say, more simply, our neck or throat) vibrate, quiver. And this is true of many other areas of the body too: the entire head, the thorax and abdomen, the pelvic region.[79] Music is thus simultaneously an animation of things and a palpitation of the being. Both are felt more intensely when one is making music than when one is simply listening to it. We should be able to say "to act" music, as opposed to "undergoing" it, for these are indeed two very different ways of experiencing it. Be that as it may, what we need to remember is that music has a physical impact upon the listener and that it produces a sensorial modification in his awareness of being. This physical impact, of course, is what pop music is consciously striving for. Through the din of vast amplifiers, such music obtains effects of violence and acoustic turbulences never before achieved. Having told us that the amplification of pop music can "reach 10,000 watts" (!), and that it "was possible to hear the pop festival on the Isle of Wight from three kilometers away," Alain Roux observes that "this amount of power acts directly upon the body and creates a feeling of participation that many people never attain even during the sexual act. There is no resisting it except by flight. Amplified to this extent, the human voice affects the larynx. . . . The sounds of the electric bass (infra-sounds) produce vibrations localized in internal erogenous zones of the abdomen. . . . The ‹ repetitive melodies and perpetual thrumming instantly produce a light hypnosis" (1973, 130). Clearly, this is the kind of effect that certain forms of possession music are aiming for; that of the *ndöp,* for example.[80]

Music is in essence movement. Its origins lie in bodily movements—to sing is to move one's larynx, to drum is to move one's arms, to play the fiddle is to move one's fingers along the stem and a bow across a string—and in return music is an incitement to movement. Since by definition sound is actualized in the unfolding of time, its relations with itself are constantly changing (even if it remains the same, for continuing is inevitably also changing, since it implies change of duration) and these changes are integrated, at several levels, into the "thickness" of time. Even in its most immaterial aspect—sound totally isolated from its source—music is perceived as movement being realized in space. This is even more true when it is made simultaneously with dance, or to make people dance. To dance is to inscribe music in space, and this inscription is realized by means of a constant modification of the relations between the various parts of the body. The dancer's awareness of his body is totally transformed by this process. Insofar as it is a spur to dancing, therefore, music does appear capable of profoundly modifying the relation of the self with itself, or, in other words, the structure of consciousness.

Psychologically, music also modifies the experience of *being,* in space and time simultaneously. Like the sound of speech, the sound of music defines the space in which *I* am situated as a space inhabited by men, and at the same time it situates *me* within this space in some particular manner. Silence is the sign of an empty or motionless space—death or sleep. Sound is the sign of a space that is filled and in movement. The sounds of nature bring me information on the movements of nature, the sounds produced by men bring me information about the presence of men, and the types of sound I hear tell me something about their activities: they are cutting down a tree in a wood, they are machine-gunning one another, they are dancing, she is rocking a baby to sleep. People are there, they are doing something. The sounds I hear mark out the space around me and enable me to integrate myself into it.

In the dimension of time, music modifies our consciousness of being to an even greater extent. It is an architecture in time. It gives time a density different from its everyday density. It lends it a materiality it does not ordinarily have and that is of another order. It indicates that something is happening in the here and now; that time is being occupied by an action being performed, or that a certain state rules over the beings present. The drumroll that resounds throughout the circus ring as the trapeze artist makes

his death-defying leap is one example. Another is borrowed from my recollection of a ritual for the enthronement of a new holder of the power of
Ogun Edeyi (god of iron) that took place in a particular village of the
Nago-Yoruba territory. Around the sanctuary a crowd of several hundred
people had gradually collected since nightfall. Noise and bustle. People
coming and going in a darkness broken here and there by the light of kero-
sene lamps. Very gradually, the lamps go out unnoticed, one after the other.
Total darkness. The night dozes. At about midnight a cry rings out, a ball
of fire hurtles from the sanctuary scattering bright sparks, and suddenly
the drums sound. Their thunder takes possession of the world. The universe has changed. Something is happening. The drums will go on beating
for eight or ten hours. Dawn will drive out the night, day will drive out the
dawn, the sun will drive out the coolness of morning, but never for an instant will the drums cease to beat. More correctly, *the* drum: the little
drum mentioned a moment ago that is also beaten for *oro*. It is placed on
the ground and played by two drummers at once, facing each other; while
two more are aligned on the other diagonal, ready to take over. Unlike the
other drums in its drum section, this little drum does not "speak." Nor
does it play the metronomic role so often assigned to small drums. It is
played more or less quickly and more or less loudly, sometimes frenziedly,
sometimes almost in a doze; in fact it possesses no rhythmic function
properly speaking. Everything suggests that its role is to maintain a certain vibration in the air, and thus ensure the continuity of the action. In
short, to establish a different order of duration. Or, if one prefers, to bring
about a sort of crystallization of time. In this case it is a matter of crystal-
lizing time for a relatively long period (half a day), over a relatively large
area (the sanctuary and the space around it), and for the benefit of a relatively large number of people (a good twenty protagonists and several
hundred spectators). Given such conditions, the crystallization of time
cannot be maintained constantly to the same degree. It inevitably goes
through periods of rise and fall. But this is not of great importance. What
is important is that it should never completely cease.

   Music does not organize time only at this elementary level but also at a
higher one, thus giving birth to a real architecture of time. Possession music does not operate solely by means of repetition and accumulation, as is
too often thought. The musical mottoes are melodic or rhythmic statements, and consequently temporal forms. They are capable of being varied and ornamented. In the course of a ceremony they follow one another
and thus form sequences that should be seen as the multiple ways of re-
newing and developing musical time, which preserves its unity all the
while since the pieces following one another belong to the same genre. By
thus transforming our awareness of time and space, in different ways, music modifies our "being-in-the-world."

The state of affective resonance that music—or at any rate certain kinds of music—creates in any individual is another aspect of the upheaval it creates in the structure of consciousness. Nothing is more laden with emotional associations than music, nothing is more capable of recreating situations that engage one's entire sensibility. It induces the individual into a state in which both his inward feelings and his relations with the outer world are dominated by affectivity.

Finally, as art, when it is a success, music creates the feeling of total adhesion of the self to what is happening. In this sense it again brings about a transformation in the structure of consciousness, by effectuating a particular and exceptional type of relation of the self to the world.

These very brief remarks were intended solely as a reminder that music • modifies—profoundly, and in several dimensions—the consciousness we have of ourselves in relation not only to ourselves but also to the world. These modifications bear essentially upon the perceptible dimensions of those relations. We shall now see that relations with the gods also fall within this selfsame category of data.

It is clear that possession cannot be understood unless it is set in the system of representations of the society concerned. These representations, in their turn, must then be brought into relation with the way in which they are experienced in daily life, and in particular with the way the presence of the gods is experienced in day-to-day life, outside any form of ceremony. The least one can say is that we are very ill-informed about this last kind of experience. What we do know, however, is that in societies having preserved an archaic way of life, which are precisely those in which possession cults are frequently found, the individual lives in constant sensorial contact with nature. He lives in perpetual intimacy with the elements, plants, animals. For him, the frontier between the animate and inanimate worlds is extremely vague. Men, beasts, plants, and things—all have souls or are the receptacles of souls. Every phenomenon is interpreted as resulting from the action or presence of a soul. The visible is constantly animated by the invisible. For him, the presence of the gods is materialized in all sorts of objects, localized in all sorts of familiar places, associated with all sorts of day-to-day activities and concrete phenomena. Given all this, we are justified in thinking that he sees the gods as beings who are very close to him physically. Their existence does of course become the object of abstract representations on his part, but everything suggests that he strongly responds to it on the level of sensory experience. I should add that, in many societies, the majority of the souls peopling the invisible world are those of the dead, of dead persons with whom the individual sometimes lives in very close physical proximity (in Fon and Gun territory, which is to say in *vodun* country, the dead are buried in the family dwelling) and to whom he refers at every occasion.

We know, moreover, that he often attributes illness either to the presence of a spirit within him who wishes him ill or wants something from him, or to the theft of his soul, or of one of his souls, by some such spirit. In such a context it seems to me that nothing could be more sensible, or more logical, than to interpret sickness as the dispossession of one's self by some other who robs you of your forces, divides you, alienates your physical or mental capacities. Physical illness is an invasion of the consciousness by sensations coming from a part of the body—a more or less important, more or less narrowly localized part depending on the particular complaint—that is at odds with the rest. For an individual who does not picture his body in terms of the biological categories of our modern world, and who does not interpret its dysfunctions as caused by bacteria or chemical imbalances, nothing is more natural than to believe that illness results from a foreign presence: since one does not recognize oneself when one is ill, the ailing limb becomes a foreign body, the afflicted organs take on an independent existence as though they had a life of their own. On the mental or nervous level, sickness—or simply fatigue, irritation, anxiety, frustration—also take the form of inner sensations one is receiving from one's body. To be "overcome by anger" similarly expresses that the state in question is experienced as a physical modification of the self. To "feel drained" very clearly conveys the idea of feeling dispossessed of one's vital energies. "*Etre dévoré par la fievre*" (literally, to be "devoured by fever") or "*rongé par la maladie*" ("eaten away by an illness") both express that illness is experienced as though there were some other living being residing in one's body. And such expressions exist in all languages, so that we can be certain they are representative of a universal experience. In the societies that concern us here, these internal states are perceived all the more intensely at the sensorial level for the simple reason that daily life is dominated by manual labor, which keeps one constantly aware of one's body. Given these conditions, it makes good sense to draw a connection between such internal states and the physical presence of one of the souls, spirits, or genii, in short, one of the divinities that people the external world and regulate all of its phenomena—good sense that indeed fits in perfectly well with the commonly held theory on the general functioning of the world.

We are thus led to think that, in the societies concerning us here, the ways of being affected by music, of experiencing the presence of the gods, and of undergoing illness all derive, in the sphere of the structure of consciousness, from one and the same type of relation to the world and to oneself. This doubtlessly explains why gods, sickness, and music can be so closely interwoven in possession cults.

3 Music, Shamanism, Mediumship, Exorcism

The question of who makes the music in possession rituals and what part the possessee plays in such music (if he takes a part at all) led me earlier to refer to shamanism. The active or passive character of the possessee's relation to possession music is not in fact fully significant unless one compares it with the shaman's relation to music. This is why we are now going to examine this other aspect of the relations between music and trance.[1]

An in-depth study of shamanic music still needs to be written. Since possession is our principal interest here, I shall do no more than skim the surface of this subject, pausing only when it is important to clarify just how different things are in the two cases. After a digression on mediumship, which often is simply one aspect of either possession or shamanism, I shall move on to a quite different question, also common to both; that of music and trance viewed from the standpoint of exorcism.

MUSIC AND SHAMANISM

By now, I hope it is sufficiently clear that in possession the relation of the possessee to music is most often passive.[2] On the contrary, the shaman's relation to music is active, since he sings and drums while he exercises his functions.[3] We must, nevertheless, ask ourselves if this inversion is verified when in the case of shamanism we take into account as we did for possession the stage the individual involved has reached in his career.

In possession we saw that the relation of the possessee to music is totally passive during initiation, and that it becomes progressively more active as he passes from the status of neophyte to officiant. In shamanism, on the contrary, the shaman's activity as musicant begins from the moment of initiation. Describing the consecration ceremony of a young female shaman among the Araucan of southern Chile, Métraux (1967, 191ff.) tells us how the new initiate, in a state of trance, climbs the *rewe*—the tree made into a ladder—which is the "symbol par excellence of her condition." She climbs it "dancing and drumming."[4] Having reached the top, she utters a long prayer during which she begs for clairvoyance, effective chants, and the art of drumming. Her behavior is thus the opposite of that of a *candomblé* neophyte, for example, who cannot take the lead in beginning a

song until he or she has been an adept for seven years. The Araucan shamans perform as both singers and instrumentalists from the very outset.
Among Asian shamans, on the other hand, full mastery of the drum (shamanism's musical instrument par excellence) is not achieved until after a
certain length of time has elapsed. In Siberia, among the Tungus (or
Evenki), after having made a stick for his future drum, the apprentice shaman "remained seated outside for several days chanting shamanic chants.
One or two years later, he saw in a dream the reindeer whose skin would
cover his drum" (Vasilevič 1969, 251),[5] and it was only after the making
and "animation" of the drum[6] that "the apprentice shaman was granted
the right to shamanize." As a beginner, the Buryat shaman has no right to
use a drum; he can only play a Jew's harp.[7] Among the Ammasalik Eskimos, while the shaman is still a postulant he does not use a drum: "If he
wants to provide the rhythm for the chants he learns far away from men,"
he uses "two wooden sticks struck one against the other" (Gessain 1973,
153). Although the Tungus or Eskimo shaman becomes an instrumentalist only gradually, since to play the drum (the geometric locus of all the
symbols of shamanism) is to have mastered all the powers, he is nonetheless a singer from the very start, just like his Amerindian homologue, a
fact that distinguishes him radically from the possessee.

The most important difference, however, is that in every case the shaman is the musicant of his own entry into trance. In other words he goes
into trance not by listening to others who sing or drum for him, but, on
the contrary, by singing and drumming himself. All the accounts agree on
this point. And herein lies the great difference between shamanism and
possession. The possessed person is never the musicant of his own trance;
the shaman always is. For the shaman, shamanizing and musicating are
two aspects of one and the same activity. So much so that among the Yaruro, in Venezuela, he is called *tõewame*, which means "musician" or,
more precisely, "he who sings and dances."[8] As for the word shaman itself,
which as we saw originates with the Tungus, it has now been established
that it derives from the root *sam-*, "common to all the Altaic languages,"
which "contains the idea of dance and leap on the one hand, trouble and
agitation on the other" (Lot-Falck 1977, 9). In Tungus there also exist
"three other series of terms expressing the idea of shamanizing" (ibid.,
11).[9] The root of the first is *jajar-*, which is the "only one that furnishes a
term, *jajan*, designating the shaman, a term of ancient and frequent usage" which originally meant "to sing, to pray to the fire for good fortune";
in Chukchi it gave way to *jajar*, "drum." The second has two meanings:
"narrate, sing, hand down the tradition" and "shamanize" (ibid., 12).[10]
Among the Tungus, then, language itself identifies the shaman as he who
dances and sings; in short, to express the matter in general terms,[11] as a
musicant. But we should note that he is seen as a singer only with refer-

ence to words, to what is said,[12] and not with reference to the tune or rhythm to which those words are sung. I shall return to this point shortly. We briefly saw in a previous chapter that this is not true for possession, since the term used to identify the possessee has no connection with dance, words (whether they are sung or not), or musical instruments.

As we did with respect to the possessed person, we must now ask what role music plays (only this time it is the music of the shaman himself) in triggering the shaman's trance. And let me say right away that this is a vast problem indeed, and one I shall only touch on.

Let us first talk about the shaman's musical instruments. Naturally one's thoughts immediately turn to the drum,[13] an instrument closely associated with the image everyone has of the Siberian or Eskimo shaman. Eliade believes that if it contributes to inducing trance, it does so for magical reasons. "It is *musical magic*[14] that has determined the shamanic function of the drum," he writes (1968, 149). According to him, this magic can be explained by one of two hypotheses, depending upon whether it derives from the charm of the drum's sounds, considered to be the "voice of the spirits,"[15] or whether "an ecstatic experience had been achieved as a result of the extreme concentration induced by prolonged drumming." Why "prolonged drumming" should create "extreme concentration" is not explained. Like so many others, Eliade is, I fear, falling into the trap of stereotypical ideas about the power inherent in the physical sound of the drum.[16] In the case of possession, we were led to conclude that although the drum is frequently used to induce trance, any instrument at all can perform the same function. And the facts plainly demonstrate that the same holds true of shamanism, even though the actual variety of choice is less great.

Among the Tungus, "many groups of Transbaikali have replaced the drum with a pair of canes that fulfill the same functions" (Delaby 1976, 112–13). In fact, these canes serve as "supports for spirits," musical instruments (they are furnished with small bells and various kinds of jangles—all highly symbolic), and a "means of locomotion" (like the drum, but by virtue of a partly different symbolism, they enable the shaman to undertake his journeys into the upper and lower worlds). We have seen that at the outset of his career at least, the Buryat shaman does not use a drum but a Jew's harp. Among the Mirghiz it is replaced by a lute, the *kobuz* (Eliade 1968, 150). We know that the Araucan shamans in Chile use a frame drum that displays curious similarities to the one belonging to their Siberian homologues.[17] But among the Amerindians the shaman often uses a rattle as his musical instrument, at least when he has one, for he can do without one just as well, as is the case among the Selk'nam (or Ona) of Tierra del Fuego, who shamanize without any instrumental accompaniment.[18] To end, let us also mention the rather paradoxical case of the Eskimos who, unless I am mistaken, all know the drum but do not all use it in order to shamanize. Alongside an active form of shamanism on the Arctic coast as far as Greenland, in which the shaman makes great use of the drum to induce his trance, there is also among certain "Central Eskimo" a more passive and contemplative way of shamanizing (Holtved 1967, 26). The shaman has his visions when he is seated or lying down. And the drum is not used in these circumstances. Triggering trance in shamanism thus appears to be no more linked to musical instruments in general, and to the drum in particular, than it is in possession.

On the other hand, in order to trigger trance, shamanic music, in some cases at least, does make use of the simultaneous *crescendo* and *accelerando* that, as we have already seen, are at work in possession. Shirokogoroff, who in his monumental study on Tungusian shamanism stresses the "exceptional psychological power of the musical part of shamanic performances" (1935, 327), refers on several occasions, and in different chapters, to the increased tempo and volume of both drumming and chanting, which he says strongly contribute to inducing trance[19] owing to the resulting intensification of emotions. This applies both to the shaman's incorporation of his auxiliary spirits[20] and to his journey into the lower world.[21] According to him, the shaman's aim "is to put himself into a state of ecstasy, which is achieved by various means—rhythmic drumming with an increase of tempo, singing, 'dancing' and even drinking wine" (ibid., 339).[22] Similarly, the audience's entry into trance—for it can happen that the spectators go into trance as well—is achieved by the repetition of refrains, "with gradually increasing emotion chiefly produced by an increase in tempo, intensity, and expression" (ibid.). But let us first stress that *accelerando* and *crescendo* do not always have the effect of triggering trance. Shirokogoroff himself tells us that "the increase in the tempo of drumming and the singing and dancing become a ritual when the shaman does it for influencing the patient, but does not himself feel to be in ecstasy (ibid.). Second, sometimes different, if not diametrically opposed, musical methods are used. Describing the shaman's preparations for achieving his state of "doubling," Shirokogoroff says that "at the beginning the shaman drums, continually increasing and decreasing the tempo and the intensity, with a definite rhythm empirically discovered, in order to produce a physiological and psychic state in which a suggestion—the coming of a spirit—made by the shaman himself, may have an immediate effect of 'doubling.' " (ibid., 363). Sometimes, then, trance is triggered by the constant acceleration of tempo, at other times, on the contrary, by an alternation of acceleration and deceleration. It seems, too, that whatever its rhythmic form may be, the sound of the drum is thought to possess within itself the power to call upon spirits.[23] And finally, the "content of the text of the shaman's songs" also plays a part (ibid., 330).

As with possession, then, in shamanism the musical means used to trigger trance are varied. Moreover, they operate only within the framework of an overall situation. For in fact, although the Tungus shaman may certainly be regarded, according to Shirokogoroff's account, as the principal musicant of the shamanic séance, he is nonetheless supported in that role both by his assistant, who frequently takes over the drumming, and by all those who are not only present but also participate in the séance. They all help him by chanting and maintaining the rhythm, which has the effect of intensifying his trance. Several shamans told Shirokogoroff (ibid., 363) that they were unable to perform without an audience. "All people present," one of them told him, "helped me go to the lower world." In other words, the shaman, just as much as the possessed person, but in a different way, must have an audience.

Among the Selk'nam of Tierra del Fuego, the shaman (male or female) went into trance by singing (again without instrumental accompaniment) and giving in to frenzied physical activity, dancing, leaping into the air, striking the earth violently with his feet and fists,[24] repeating, all the while, the same incantations again and again. Was this repetition also accompanied by an acceleration of the rhythm and an increasing intensity of the singing? We just don't know. We can be quite sure, however, that the techniques used to induce trance vary—or varied—a great deal from one country (or continent) to another. Among the Selk'nam, who did not use drugs at all, trance was achieved by entirely natural means of autoexcitation, but recourse to artificial means is common in both Asia and America. Among the Yaruro of Venezuela, S. Dreyfus tells us, "trance is, if not induced, at least facilitated by the absorption of a very large quantity of stimulants (fermented beverages, alcohol, tobacco)" (1954, 3).[25] In Siberia, among the methods used by the Yakut shaman to "reach the altered state," E. Lot-Falck (1968, 2: 264) cites mycophagy as "the surest method, provoking hallucinations automatically."

But let us get back to music. The exteriorization of the shaman's soul during his journey "manifests itself in two diametrically opposed ways," E. Lot-Falck tells us, "through cataleptic trance and through dramatic trance" (1973, 9). The music is clearly not at all the same in the two cases. During cataleptic trance, the shaman's body is "rigid, no more than an empty envelope, abandoned by the soul, which has left to accomplish some mission," and it is the shaman's assistant who is the musicant. During dramatic trance, on the contrary, the shaman describes what he is seeing during his journey into the upper or lower world and recounts his adventures by chanting and beating his drum, thus providing a truly theatrical performance, or, more accurately perhaps, a one-man show, which includes episodes drawing upon the most varied musical styles: songs, recitatives, invocations, spoken passages, dialogues, imitations of

animal cries or sounds of nature and other onomatopoeias, and voice dis-
guises.[26] Dramatic or epic moments alternate with comic passages. The
drum provides a constant support for the sung action, underscoring the
vocal effects and providing links between one episode and the next. Its
function is sometimes rhythmic, and to be sure, it always accords with the
character of the particular song or narrative—hurried, panting, solemn,
peaceful, and so on. At other times, its function is one of pure punctua-
tion, and the meaning of the drummed phrases is sometimes symbolic,
sometimes descriptive, sometimes simply a kind of signal. At least, this is
what one gathers from one of the rare available recordings of shamanic
music originating in Siberia.[27]

At the antipodes, among the Wayana Indians of Guyana,[28] another recording suggests that, all things being equal, we are also dealing with a
theatralization of the shamanic séance that is rather comparable to the Siberian example. Since there is no musical accompaniment proper, the
sung action is supported by "skillful sound effects" (Hurault 1968, 4) produced by very rudimentary means. Among the Yaruro of Venezuela, the
shamanic séance held for the purpose of curing a sick person also begins
with a narration of the journey made by the shaman's soul "into the realm
of Kuma, the mother goddess" (Dreyfus 1954, 1). The shaman sings, accompanying himself with a gourd-rattle "engraved with figures and signs
representing inhabitants of the supernatural world" and depicting, "arranged around Pwana, the great water serpent, husband of the anthropo-
morphic goddess Kuma, the tribe's male and female ancestors dancing in
the dwelling place of the dead." As he sings, the audience replies in chorus.
The "auxiliary spirits" are incorporated in the course of this journey.
When the shaman leans over the patient and "tries to extirpate the sickness . . . by aspiration and suction of the painful parts," he stops singing,
and his assistant then takes over this function for him. Having successfully
"extracted the pathogenic element, he utters a cry, throws himself backward, falls to the ground, and remains unconscious for some moments"
(ibid., 3). This crisis, which is directly related to a particularly dramatic
moment of the healing process, does not seem to be linked to any simultaneous dramatization of the music.

Although the pantings, cries, whistles, sighs, hoarse breathing, yelps
("which are the sign of the spirits' presence"), and the occasionally quivering voice of the shaman do create a certain theatralization of the séance
and introduce some variety into the development of the sung action, for
the listener who cannot understand the language and is consequently unable to follow what is being sung, this action would tend to seem very
monotonous, despite the introduction of new themes that form a kind
of suite. If I had to characterize the style of this sequence of songs in a
single word, I would say they are incantations (though this is an entirely
subjective evaluation, and based mainly on the monotony I mentioned, on

the one hand, and on a certain quality in the intonation of the singing on the other). This is precisely the term Claude Lévi-Strauss uses (1958, 205) in the case of the famous shamanic "song" whose purpose is to "aid a diffi- cult birth" and that comes to us from the Cuna Indians of Panama. This long narrative, which undoubtedly relates the most extraordinary sha- manic journey imaginable, inspired Lévi-Strauss to draw comparisons between shamanism and psychoanalysis that are too well known to be repeated here. In his interpretation of the "symbolic efficacy" of this "great magico-religious text," he makes no mention of the connections that might exist between the shaman's song and his trance. And he does not do so for two reasons; first, because this was not his subject, and second, because the shaman is not, or at any rate does not seem to be, in a trance. Whereas "transition to an altered state" is not necessary for the shaman to undertake his journey, which is required for his curative action, we are told that clairvoyance, which the Cuna consider as the shaman's "innate talent," is absolutely indispensible (ibid., 206–7). Among the Buryat, R. Hamayon tells us (1978a, 63), when the shaman goes into the state we have termed "trance," they say he "enters into a visionary state." When he describes his journey he is, after all, describing what he is seeing. Clair- voyance or journey, what he chants has a meaning, and it is the meaning of this sung text that is important. The reasons why the words have been set to music probably have much more to do with the difficulty of memorizing a very long text, or with the need to render it expressive or en- dow it with a certain magical effect, than with any attempt to engender trance.

One of the great differences between possession and shamanic music lies in the fact that the latter is often endowed with magical power, where- as the former is not. It speaks, it identifies, it induces movement. Its efficacy is of a mechanical order. Its effects are of a practical order: it summons the gods, makes the dancers whirl, creates contact between men and gods, arouses emotion. It has no other powers. The shaman's music, on the con- trary, claims, in certain cases at least, to transform the world. To use Lévi- Strauss's words (1962, 292), it seeks to intervene in natural determinism in order to modify its course. It is in this respect that it is magical: through the power of incantation when it is vocal and when the words and their musical shaping are what count, or through the power of sound when it is instrumental, the symbolic nature of the instrument being then as much at work as the spell of the sound. Of the thirty-four shamanic songs Anne Chapman (discography, 1972) collected among the Selk'nam of Tierra del Fuego, sixteen[29] relate to notions of journey and magical power that con- cern not only healing but also such actions as conjuring a lunar eclipse, aiding whale hunters, or preventing rain through rituals.[30]

Incantatory: such is the main characteristic of shamanic music. But what is an incantation? This is a vast problem I can only touch on here.

In his description of the six basic functions of verbal communication, R. Jakobson defines "the magic, incantatory function" as "chiefly some kind of conversion of an absent or inanimate 'third person' into an addressee of a conative message" (1981, 24). The third of the three examples he uses to illustrate this definition is taken from the Old Testament (Joshua 10:12): "Sun, stand thou still upon Gibeon; and thou, Moon, in the valley of Ajalon. And the sun stood still, and the moon stayed." This type of text, which juxtaposes conative messages employing, first, the conversion of a "third person," and, second, referential messages also concerning the second or third person, but in which "the stress is at the same time laid on the message itself . . . which is characteristic of the poetical function of language" [(ibid.)], corresponds fairly well with what we know of shamanic incantations. As for the musical character of the words, that is, the singing itself, it seems that its particularities are, first, to be very repetitive; second, to use a type of vocal delivery nearer to the spoken than the sung; and third, to make use of unusual vocal effects—cries, onomatopoeias, imitations of all kinds of noises—all of which combine to give shamanic singing a distinct position within the musical system characteristic of the population concerned.

In a previous chapter,[31] I tried to isolate the difference between shamanism and possession and came to the conclusion that it could be expressed by a series of three oppositions: journey to the spirits/visit by the spirits; control over the spirits/submission to the spirits; voluntary trance/involuntary trance. This triple opposition could be further condensed into only one: acting/undergoing. Shamanism appeared to be, if one may say so, essentially *acted*, possession as *undergone*.

To use Pouillon's terms (1972, 94), "the orientation of the relation" between subject and trance appeared to be diametrically opposed in the two cases. We just found a similar opposition in the relations between subject and music. In possession, as we saw, music is made *for* the possessee. In shamanism it is made *by* the shaman. The latter is a *musicant*, the former is *musicated*. This opposition musicant/musicated should be considered, therefore, together with the three previous ones, as a factor contributing to the distinction to be made between shamanism and possession.

Shamanism or possession: in both cases the imaginary content of trance is of course totally socialized. By this I mean that the representations underlying this content are shared by the group as a whole. The musicant/musicated opposition means that the shaman is a musicant since he imposes his imaginary world upon the group, whereas the possessed person is musicated since the group imposes the imaginary content upon him. Moreover, in possession the subject goes into trance because he changes identity; in shamanism he goes into trance because he changes worlds.

The role of music in shamanism is thus doubly different from the one it plays in possession: first, because music is experienced differently depending on whether one makes it oneself or whether others make it; second, because it serves two different imaginary constructs (or, if one prefers, two different ideologies) of trance. In possession, uttering musical mottoes associated with the identificatory aspect of trance plays an important role in triggering that trance. In shamanism, it seems this function is performed by the incantatory character of the music. But in shamanism as in possession the facts are quite variable. The available accounts lay emphasis sometimes on the shaman's physical agitation,[32] sometimes on the chanted summons, and sometimes on his use of the drum. In maintaining the trance state, as opposed to triggering it, music constitutes in every case an essential factor guaranteeing continuity during the shamanic journey. Among the Tungus, after the shaman has entered his trance by chanting and drumming, his assistant takes the "drum and continues the drumming, both for maintaining the shaman's state of extasy and for controlling the behaviour of the audience," Shirokogoroff tells us (1935, 329). In fact, the journey is pursued from episode to episode through a musical dimension, and it is both the words and their musical shaping that endow the singing, when necessary, with its incantatory and magical value.

MUSIC AND MEDIUMSHIP

Shamanic and possession trance have in common the fact that they both frequently lead to divinatory practices, as we saw earlier.[33] Insofar as shamans and possessed persons behave like mediums who prophesy or are consulted, I have nothing to add here about the relation between their trance and music. But it can happen that the exercise of mediumship, or, if one prefers, of divinatory trance, acquires a certain autonomy, so that it must then be distinguished from shamanism or possession in the strict sense of the term. From the standpoint of its relations with music, the situation is thus a somewhat hybrid one. I shall now examine this aspect of the matter.

With a view to distinguishing between possession in the usual sense of the term (spirit possession) and mediumistic possession (spirit mediumship), R. Firth (1969, xi) points out that, in the first case, the possessed person's behavior does not necessarily "transmit a particular message to others," whereas in the second "communication is emphasized." The spirit responsible for mediumistic possession has something to say to an audience. And obviously when the divinity is speaking through the medium's mouth, he should be heard clearly. This means that there cannot be any music at the same time. I will only cite three examples. In Porto-Novo (Benin), when the priest of Hwonse, a vodun who utters the oracles, prophesies in public or answers questions put to him (something I have witnessed on several occasions), one could have heard a pin drop. In his description of a mediumistic trance séance among the Shona in Zimbabwe, Paul Berliner (1975/76, 137) tells us that as soon as the climax marking the possession of the medium by the spirit is over, the music stops and the participants all sit down to listen to what he is going to say. Later, when the spirit has left, the music resumes. And we have already seen in an earlier chapter that when the Tibetan oracle begins to prophesy the music stops.

The medium's entry into trance, on the other hand, often requires music. When it does, two possibilities exist. Either the music is provided not by the medium but by musicians or musicants grouped around him, which seems to be the case most frequently, or else the medium himself is the musicant of his own entry into trance. In other words, in the first case events follow the pattern of possession and in the second that of shamanism. Let us look at a few examples of both kinds, beginning not with identificatory possession trance—the trance state central to this book—but rather with the type of trance I proposed to term inspirational or communial. When the Hebrew prophets were in their state of prophetic frenzy, they were accompanied by a variable number of musicians.[34] Elisha went into trance and prophesied while he was listening to music.[35] These prophets are never described as their own musicants. During the religious wars in the Cévennes (France), it was quite usual for people to go into trance and prophesy during the assemblies in which there was singing; but often they were also "seized by Inspiration"[36] and prophesied without any music whatsoever. Everything depended on the circumstances, but I shall not delve any more deeply into this aspect of divinatory trance. Prophetism is a vast subject that extends far beyond my present aims. Let us thus move on directly to possession.[37]

In Tibet the music is provided exclusively by the medium's assistants and consists, as we have seen, in sung invocations accompanied by drums, bells, or cymbals, and sometimes by a horn. At least this is what happened in the case of the "State" oracle; I shall cite a different case later. Black Africa, where possession and mediumship frequently coexist within the framework of the same religious system, provides a perfect terrain for comparing the relations of these two aspects of religion with music under particularly favorable conditions. And the comparison is very instructive, as we shall see. In Zambia, among the Tonga (Colson 1969, 76), before entering his hut to answer questions put by those consulting him, the *basangu* medium may sometimes go into trance publicly while others clap their hands and sing to summon the spirits. As a general rule, however, he does not enter into trance until he is inside the hut, and does so without any stimulus other than fumigations. On the contrary, possession in the

usual sense of the term—a state due to the *masabe* (a quite different category of spirits) and one that has given rise to a cult mainly concerned with
therapeutic activities—is always accompanied by drums and singing. The
difference is thus very marked. Contrary to what we find to be the case in
possession, the medium's trance is not necessarily accompanied by music,
and if it is, the music is of no great importance. Among the Nuba of Kordofan, during mediumistic "séances" organized for "clients" (Nadel 1946,
36), the medium[38] goes into trance without music of any kind.

Among the Kalabari of Nigeria (Horton 1969) different forms of possession are found, some due to the spirits of the group's founding heroes,
others to those of water genii. They all, however, give rise to two categories of manifestation: possession dances integrated into a variety of rituals
on the one hand, and mediumistic séances on the other. In the case of the
possession dance (*oru seki* or dance of the spirit) associated with the cult
of the founding hero, the priest's trance is triggered by a deafening din produced by drums, praise songs, and the sound of machete blades struck
violently together to a very insistent rhythm (ibid., 19). In the case of the
mediumistic séance *oru bibi n'ekwen* (speaking through the spirit's
mouth; ibid., 25), the medium, who is a different person from the priest
who dances the *oru seki*, goes into trance after the clients (who have come
to consult him) have summoned the spirit by means of an invocation and a
libation of gin. Perhaps this invocation is sung; the account is not clear on
this point, but there is nevertheless no mention of music. There is thus a
total contrast between these two entries into trance. Moreover, the same
contrast can be observed in the possession attributed to water genii: when
it takes the form of possession dance there is music (ibid., 30–33), and
there is consequently every reason to believe—although the text does not
say so—that entry into trance has musical accompaniment; when it takes
the form of consultation with a medium there is none, but I shall return to
this point a little later.

Now let us go on to the second case, in which the medium triggers his
trance himself by acting as his own musicant. The most striking example is
provided by the Sukuma of Tanzania (Tanner 1955). Among them, the
medium is possessed by the spirit of an ancestor. He goes into trance in order to reply to questions put by people who come to consult him, diagnose
the causes of their misfortunes or illnesses, and prescribe a remedy for
them. Seated on his stool, he begins turning his rattles in front of him,
close to his head, and then starts to mutter increasingly loudly. This is how
he triggers his own trance. When the moment comes, he suddenly stops
shaking the rattles and begins to talk. "The stopping of the rattling is said
to be done by the ancestor spirit, and not under the direct volition of the
magician" (ibid., 276). This is because the spirit has been disturbed by the
noise of the rattle and therefore hurries to "assist in the séances in order

that the noise may stop." This medium can also, if the need arises, trigger possession in the patient consulting him, still, of course, in the hopes of finding a remedy for his ills. In this case he does not enter into trance himself. Having whistled to summon the spirits, he begins to shake his rattles close to the client's ears, slowly at first but then more and more quickly. "The slow crescendo of the rattling allows for the gradual arrival of the spirit concerned, since if it arrived too quickly it would have a harmful effect on the patient" (ibid., 277). This, then, is a doubly interesting case: it demonstrates that the very same person is capable of triggering trance both in himself and in others; it shows that the musical means are the same in both cases, but that the interpretation of the effects they produce differs in each.

In Nigeria, among the Kalabari mentioned earlier, when a woman possessed by a water genius acts as a medium, she triggers her own trance once her clients are there by placing offerings on the altar of the spirit possessing her and "by calling upon it to mount her" (Horton 1969, 29). The reverse is the case, as we have just seen, when the medium is possessed by the spirit of a founding hero: the trance is triggered not by the medium himself but by the clients who are consulting him. In both cases, however, the means are the same: summoning the spirit and giving offerings; there is no music, unless perhaps the summons is sung, something we do not know. Let me sum up the situation among the Kalabari: possession in the usual sense of the term is most often triggered by music, and by music that is never made by the possessed themselves; mediumistic possession, on the contrary, is triggered without the aid of music, or at most by chanted invocations, and entry into trance can be induced either by the medium's clients or by the medium himself.

Benin (formerly Dahomey) supplies a slightly different example. The Gun of Port-Novo have a *vodun*, called Hwonsè, whose principal function is to deliver oracles. He is also consulted in order to establish the truth and settle legal wrangles; occasionally he is thus summoned to assist the king in making judicial decisions. Like all *vodun* he has his annual feast, and on one of these occasions (in December 1964) I was able to observe him exercising his functions. For this feast the ceremonies begin with a solemn reopening of the sanctuary, which had been closed for several weeks, followed by an exhibition of the *vodun* and an offering of the first yams. All this takes place, naturally enough, in an atmosphere of great rejoicing. In the open space between the sanctuary entrance and the houses facing it, a small band of drums, rattles, and bells plays music so that the faithful and the local people can dance. The final day is reserved for a great processional during which the *vodun* emerges from his temple and is carried around the sanctuary precincts on the head of the high priest. This is followed by a public séance during which Hwonsè speaks through the mouth of his bearer.

How is the medium's trance achieved? First he washes his head with lustral water. Then he places the *vodun*, which is rather heavy, on top of his head. A drummer then plays on the *agbla*, an instrument used exclusively for such cult purposes. A note in passing: this type of drum, which is not specific to Hwonsè but is found in the worship of other *vodun*, is not meant to produce very loud sounds. The drum itself is shallow and entirely open beneath, while the skin is relatively loosely stretched. It is played with the hands, by gently tapping the membrane, just hard enough for one to hear the calls, greetings, and mottoes the player addresses, in drum language, to be sure, to the divinity. There is no singing. While the drum is being played to summon the *vodun*, the priest also utters mottoes (*mimlan*) and speaks to Hwonsè with the help of words "that he alone knows and that force Hwonsè to come and incorporate him." At least, this is what I was told when I made inquiries following the event, since circumstances prevented me from being in the sanctuary precisely when the medium went into trance.

For our present purposes there are two facts to be noted here. First, that words, spoken or drummed, play an important role in this entry into trance, but that music plays almost none, since it would be improper to view the *agbla* as a musical instrument, at least as it is played in this situation. This drum is talking. If need be, one might say it "musicates" a bit, but one cannot really say it "makes music." Second, that Hwonsè's medium does play a role in his own entry into trance, but he is not alone in bringing it about. Although he himself pronounces the words that force the *vodun* to incorporate himself, it is equally necessary for the drummer to address words of praise to the divinity through the *agbla*. With respect to how the trance is triggered, then, and to the role played by the medium himself in this process, the example of Hwonsè illustrates extremely well what I said earlier about the hybrid situation that mediumship, in its relations to music, occupies between possession and shamanism.

Lastly, from Tibet we have an example of a medium triggering his own trance by acting as his own musicant; but this time the process is presented as being far from usual. As we saw in the case of the State oracle, trance is, generally speaking, triggered by music played by the medium's assistants. But Nebesky-Wojkowitz (1956, 437–38) tells us that another diviner, whom he knew very well personally, confided that he sometimes proceeded in a different way: "If he is asked to deliver a prophecy for one of his customers and there is no priest present who would be able to chant the necessary invocation, he will sing the prayers himself. He assured me that this method, too, proves most effective, and that before concluding the chant, he looses consciousness and falls into the trance. Should, however, the first prayer have no effect, then he will chant once or twice again." Insofar as it is self-induced (like those encountered by Tanner among the Sukuma), this trance is an exception among Tibetan mediums. In all other respects, however, it conforms with the general model of Tibetan mediumistic trance, which exhibits a very different aspect from the one seen in black Africa.

As we have seen,[39] the medium in Tibet prepares himself by meditation and purification, by fast and abstinence. R. A. Stein (1962, 155) describes his behavior while in trance as follows: "Not only is his face transformed—it swells and becomes red, the eyes become bloodshot, the tongue thickens and hangs out, etc.—but he also shows proof of superhuman strength, supporting an extremely heavy helmet, bending swords, etc." This trance, we must remember, owes absolutely nothing to the drugs. Nebesky-Wojkowitz observes that "medical authorities who examined my material expressed the opinion that the trances of the oracle priest may be partly induced by tetany, the attack being initiated by controlled respiration" (ibid., 440). This would imply that trance is produced by voluntary behavior using a form of self-control, an ascetic practice that is much more reminiscent of shamanic practices than of those used in possession. Nebesky-Wojkowitz himself devotes a chapter to what he calls Tibetan shamanism, and in it he compares Tibetan religious practices (particularly those concerning the oracle) and Siberian shamanism. Perhaps we could say that whereas the possession of the Tibetan oracle, seen as a religious practice, falls within the domain of possession, the corporeal technique he uses in trance falls within the domain of shamanism. The Tibetan oracle would thus provide a particularly striking example of a situation intermediate between these two major forms of trance religion.

Moreover, whereas the Tibetan medium can only occasionally trigger his own trance, the "true bards" of Tibet, who go into trance before singing, do so as a rule. In order to enter into trance and "summon a hero into himself" (Stein 1952, 156) the bard "begins by purifying himself with a prayer and by singing a description of the hero." This is thus a self-induced trance, one that involves possession rather than shamanism, since as Stein writes, "the god of the epic comes down [and] falls" onto the bard. On the other hand, the act of singing while in trance, which is characteristic of shamanism, thus seems to be characteristic of a certain form of possession in Tibet. In this respect, it would be interesting to know how things stand throughout those areas in which shamanism and possession coexist, particularly in Asia among the proto-Indochinese (Pottier 1973 and Condominas 1973, 141).

All the cases of mediumship we have reviewed thus far involve at least a minimum of music, for one must assume, even when the authors do not say so explicitly, that the invocations or summons addressed to the spirit must be chanted to some degree. To what extent was this also true of the Pythia of Delphi, that most famous of all mediumistic possessions? "How was the 'enthusiasm' evoked by ancient writers induced?" asks J. Defradas (1968, 192). On this point, authors are quite divided (cf. Dodds 1957,

70–74). J. P. Vernant (1974, 11) has recently commented on our state of ignorance as to the workings of "the oracle par excellence, the oracle whose fame and prestige eclipsed all others, and whose authority, from the eighth century onward gradually extended over the whole Hellenic world: the Delphic oracle." In order to answer the questions put to her, the Pythia either went into a "true state of trance," and spoke in so unintelligible a manner that her answers required "prophets" to interpret them, or else she "answered the questioner directly" in which case we must suppose she spoke "in cold blood." In either case there is no question of music being involved. And even supposing that music was used in order to trigger the trance, it must certainly have been limited to a few chanted invocations, at the very most. In any case, we can be sure that unlike the "telestic" trance of the Corybantes,[40] which always required music, and a great deal of music, the "mantic" trance of the Pythia, on the contrary, required very little or, more probably still, none at all.

The relations between divinatory trance and music are thus quite variable. The fact remains, however, that if the medium is a shaman then in every case in which music is involved he is the musicant of his own entry into trance, but if he is a possessed person, then he is in general musicated. It can happen, however, albeit less often, that the possessed medium too can be a musicant, and in this respect his situation then becomes more like that of the shaman. Not because his trance changes in content—the visitation of the spirit never becomes, as in the shaman's case, a journey to the spirits—but because the relation of the possessee to the spirit possessing him is no longer characterized by submission, nor even, quite often, by identification, which is the defining factor of identificatory possession.

The Sukuma medium in Tanganyika, whose trance Tanner describes as self-induced, ultimately is a professionally possessed person, and his constant relations with the spirits who come and inhabit him in order to speak through his mouth have given him a greater or lesser degree of mastery over them. Like the shaman, or almost so, he becomes master of the spirits, and thereby master of his own trance. Any gradation between the two extremes is of course possible, however, and this explains why the relations of mediumism to music are so variable.

This variability also results from mediumship's vast variety of forms and techniques. The latter are doubtless attributable, at least in part, to the fact that mediumship is often practiced in a completely private way, in conditions favorable to individual initiative and consequently very likely to encourage change.

THE CASE OF THE BUSHMEN

Among the Bushmen,[41] music plays a determining role both in trance, which is itself linked to dance, and in the treatment of illnesses. Trance, dance, and the treatment of the sick among these people all fall into the category, not of possession, but, as we shall see, of shamanism. This topic is of such interest from the standpoint of this book that it merits fairly detailed examination here.

The Bushmen attribute illnesses to the will of the creator god, who distributes good and ill fortune among humans through a secondary god and his messengers, the spirits of the dead (Marshall 1969, 350). Treatment consists in attempting to drive the sickness out, together with its agents, by using the "supernatural potency" (*n/um*, which Marshall terms "medicine") wielded by their "medicine men," a potency or a power that also resides in their "medicine songs" and in their "medicine plants."[42] This power is usually possessed by men,[43] and medicine men make up more than half of the group's male population; but women can also possess it. In order to be effective, this power must first be activated. It is awakened by singing medicine songs, then heated by manipulating glowing coals and by dancing. "Eventually the *n/um* becomes so hot that it boils," and "it is at its strongest when medicine men are in trance and the songs being sung with utmost vigour." At this point the healing power reaches its peak of efficacy (ibid., 352–53). The medicine men exercise this power either in the course of medicine dances in which the whole group takes part—and occurring frequently though not necessarily in connection with any particular illness[44] (ibid., 354)—or during healing séances that are more private in nature and aimed specifically at the treatment of a particular illness. To simplify, one might say that the first involves preventive medical practices whereas the second involves curative practices.

Broadly speaking, roles in the medicine dance are distributed as follows: the women sit in a circle around a fire, forming a compact group, and sing the medicine songs while accompanying themselves with loud handclapping; the men dance around them in single file, gradually go into trance one after another, then exercise their healing power, both for the afflicted and for the group as a whole.

In the medicine dance, treatment of the illness involves two stages. The first consists in capturing and driving out the illness: the medicine man, in a trance, massages the sick person's body, anoints it with his own perspiration, lays hands upon him, thus drawing the illness out into his own body; he then rids himself of it by ejecting it violently in the direction of the secondary god and his messengers, the spirits of the dead (ibid., 370). The second stage consists in driving away the spirits themselves by hurling sticks and insults at them, and sometimes, too, though more rarely, by trying to conciliate them by calling for their help. When he is entranced, the medicine man is in fact seeing the secondary god and the spirits of the dead, and is therefore able to address them directly. When he is at the deepest stage of his trance, "in half death," his soul (or rather one of his two souls, it seems) leaves him to go meet the secondary god (ibid., 378).

In olden times, the Bushmen say, there were medicine men who actually met the great god himself, when he let down a rope from heaven so they could climb up to him. Clearly then, we are dealing on all counts with shamanism, not with possession.

R. B. Lee (1968, 37), in his article on the sociology of trance among the Bushmen, emphasizes the different roles played by the two sexes in the medicine dance (which he labels "curing dance"). "Only the men dance and enter trances," he tells us; but "the participation of the women is fundamental, for it is they who provide the musical framework which makes the trance experience possible. The men are quick to acknowledge this, and say that the success of the dance is dependent on the perseverance and sustained enthusiasm of the women." If R. B. Lee's account is indeed absolutely accurate, then the medicine dance could be seen as a shamanistic séance in which the music is made not *by* but *for* the shaman, a situation that is in fact characteristic of possession, and that, therefore, contradicts the thesis advanced earlier on the relation of music to shamanic trance. In other words, the opposition I thought I had unveiled between shamanism and possession with respect to "who makes the music" would be unfounded. This point, therefore, warrants discussion.

At first glance, the two descriptions we have of the medicine dance, by Lorna Marshall and R. B. Lee, seem to agree broadly. Examined more closely, and from the viewpoint of their musical details, they contradict one another. Lee (1968, 37) makes a very categorical distinction between the women's and men's role. "There is a fundamental asymmetry in the roles they play in the curing dance," he writes. The women sing, the men dance. The women dance only occasionally, he notes in passing. "Only the men dance and go into trance," he says without mentioning that the men may sing. Lorna Marshall provides a much more detailed account. Indeed, she writes that during the medicine dance, women play the principal role in the singing and the men have an almost total monopoly over the dancing, all of which corresponds to what Lee tells us. But she also indicates several times that the men (the "medicine men") also sing during the dance: "The men dance and sing for some time (usually an hour or two, at least) before trances begin to come on," she writes (1969, 375). The rhythmic stamping of their feet on the ground and the tinkling of small jangles wrapped around their legs is added to their singing (ibid., 359). This acoustic dimension of their dance is so important from the musical point of view that, when she discusses the role of various dance steps (ibid., 364), Marshall concludes that the "primary function" of these steps is not to form choreographic figures but to "produce sound." In other respects, she describes healing practices in the following terms: "The medicine man, singing one of the medicine songs, touches the person, usually placing one hand on the person's back and one on his chest. In a moment or two his singing changes to the formalized sounds called *n//hara*" (ibid.,

370). These sounds emitted by the healer consist of groans, moans, high-pitched cries, and sighs of all sorts; they display a certain formal structure because they are constantly repeated, have a rhythmic organization, and are sometimes slightly sung. Thus the healers take an active part in music making, both before their trance begins, in order to help induce it, and also during this trance, in order to practice healing.

This means that, with respect to the relations between trance and "the one who makes the music," the situation among the Bushmen represents an intermediate state between possession, as we have observed it up to this point, and shamanism as it is generally defined. Contrary to what happens in the case of the possessee, the Bushman healer takes part in the songs that induce his trance, but contrary to what happens in the case of the shaman, the main responsibility for the singing falls not upon him, but upon the chorus of women; that is to say, upon a group that never under any circumstances goes into trance. There are at least two underlying reasons for this situation. First, the Bushman healer, unlike the Siberian shaman, is not a solitary figure: as we have seen, at least fifty percent of all male Bushmen are healers; shamanism among them is thus more a collective affair than an individual one. Second, it is through dance that the Bushman healer attains the trance state. This dance is collective and requires such a continuous flow of music that it can only be provided by a group of people specifically assigned to this task. Once the healer has gone into trance and exercises his shamanic healing power, however, it seems that his own singing, and not that of the chorus, takes precedence from the patient's point of view. This demonstrates that for both shamanism and possession it is important to make a distinction between the different stages of trance.

Now that this point has been cleared up, examining the case of the Bushmen also poses, and in a particularly interesting way, the problem of the therapeutic role of music and that of the relations of music and dance to trance.

We have seen that among the Bushmen, we could to some extent distinguish between, on the one hand, preventive medicine involving the whole group and consisting in the curing dance, and on the other, curative medicine practiced by the healer during private sessions and without the use of dance (ibid., 369). We are thus faced with two different practices. But both use music, or rather curing songs—the songs mentioned earlier that are charged with a magical power. The great difference between the two practices is that the first is indissolubly linked to dance and trance, whereas the second does not make use of dance and is not even necessarily associated with trance. Moreover, whereas the power of healing seems to be exclusively in the hands of men, both men and women can sing the curing songs, either in the group dance or in the private session. Lorna Marshall, describing the healing of a sick baby under dramatic circumstances (ibid.,

374) notes the following: "Instantly the women began to sing a medicine song in full voice (no tentative beginning). Men from both groups began to cure the baby. In minutes, two of the men from the parents' group and one from the other group went abruptly into frenzied trance and soon fell unconscious." She points out that in other serious cases, the medicine men she observed at work also went into trance, but only "into light trances" (ibid., 373). With respect to two healing sessions involving more benign illnesses, on the contrary, she describes the medicine man as working alone, beginning to sing without any preparation, making the *n//hara* sounds, rubbing the patient with his forehead, fluttering his hands over his body. She adds that the medicine man did not show the slightest sign of being entranced in either of these cases.

From all this only one thing, among all those with which we have dealt, appears indispensible to the healing process in every case, and this is the singing, under its double aspect of medicine songs, sung by men or women, and of *n//hara* sounds produced by the healer alone. What are these songs like?[45] For the sake of simplicity, let us say that aside from the *n//hara* sounds, they display the same musical characteristics as those that define the Bushmen's vocal music in general: yodeling, contrapuntal polyphony, and vocalization (that is, a total, or almost total, absence of words). Lorna Marshall makes two extremely important observations about these songs. On the one hand she writes: "Despite their believed supernatural origin and the fact that they are charged with *n/um*, the songs are not set apart exclusively for the curing ritual. They are sung everywhere by everybody, more than any other music, to enliven tasks and miles of walking, to beguile hours of leisure, and to delight and soothe babies" (ibid., 368). Interpreting information she has collected, she adds that it seems to her that "the *n/um* in medicine songs is thought to be inactive until it reacts with the *n/um* in the medicine man" (ibid., 368–69). This interaction of the two powers would obviously not occur under just any circumstances, but only on the condition that the medicine man "actually be intending to cure and thus be seeking to evoke the power of the *n/um*" (ibid., 369). Moreover, it should be added that according to Marshall the dance steps also have nothing specific about them: "In the medicine dance, the dancing is always the same whatever song is being sung, . . . using the same basic step . . . it is this step that a !Kung will use, when spontaneously, on occasions quite unconnected with medicine dance, sudden exuberance leads him to dance along for a moment or two" (ibid., 363). This demonstrates that, as Roger Bastide observes (1955, 501) for possession music, among the Bushmen, it is the "total situation" that confers power to medicine songs.

Unlike the medicine songs, which can be sung (and received in dreams) by either men or women, the *n//hara* sounds are emitted only by the healers, that is to say, by men. These sounds are not necessarily linked to trance or to dance, but they are indissociable from the practice of healing itself, and are thus in a sense its acoustic expression. I may also say in passing, though without drawing the slightest conclusion, that one cannot help but compare these sounds, as described by Lorna Marshall (1969, 370), and as we can hear them on the recordings made by the Marshall expeditions,[46] with those emitted by Amerindian shamans, which have been recorded, in particular, by H. Le Besnerais,[47] J. Hurault,[48] and Audrey Butt.[49]

Viewed within the perspective of the relations between trance, dance, and music, the preventive and curative aspects of Bushmen shamanic healing practices differ from one another because each has a distinct configuration of its components. This is made clear by table 3.1, in which those components present in healing are indicated by the sign +, those absent by the sign −, and those that can be either absent or present by both signs together (±). The letters m and f indicate their distribution by sex. One can see that the healing power of curing songs is not necessarily associated with trance, any more than with dancing or with the participation of women. Earlier, we saw that a medicine song is not effective unless it is sung by a healer and with the specific intention of healing. The songs themselves can possess either a greater or a lesser degree of magical power. Thus whereas one song may be able to "cure any sickness" (ibid., 367), another may have become worn out and lost all of its power (ibid., 368). In every case, however, the minimal conditions that must be present for a song to have healing power are those we just mentioned: the inherent power of the medicine song becomes effective only if it is in synergy with that of the healer. In other words, for the Bushmen a medicine song is not therapeutic in and of itself but it is only one element of a therapy. Let us file this information in the dossier of research about musicotherapy.

Now let us turn to music from the viewpoint of its relations, not with healing, but with trance. Among the Bushmen, trance can occur to very varying degrees, from "light" trance to extremely violent trance resulting in fainting and collapse. From Lorna Marshall's description, we would probably be justified in deducing that two conditions must always be ful-

Table 3.1 The Relations of Song, Dance, and Trance to Healing Practices and Sexual Differentiation

	Practices							
	song		n//hara		dance		trance	
	m	f	m	f	m	f	m	f
Healing								
preventive	+	+	+	−	+	−	+	−
curative	+	±	+	−	−	−	±	−

filled in order for violent trance to occur. On the one hand there must be music (which is to say, essentially, singing), and on the other there must be either dancing ("medicine dance") or serious illness that involves ipso facto the medicine man in a dramatic situation. One might perhaps take the view that the long preparation provided by the dance, which "warms up" the healer's power and brings it to a boil, creates an emotional state within him that is equivalent, as far as disturbance of his consciousness is concerned, to that resulting from the critical situation with which he is suddenly faced when he must heal a seriously ill patient. Whatever the case, although music appears to be indispensible to triggering trance, for all that, it must still be combined with a certain emotional situation.

The situation that interests us here is the one that materializes when the "medicine dance" takes place. This dance lasts for several hours, sometimes for a whole night if not longer. The warming-up period preceding the first trances may take an hour or two. During this time, as we have seen, the women sing and clap their hands while the men sing and dance, loudly stamping—pounding, we could say—the ground, so that the little rattles attached to their legs jingle to the rhythms of the steps. For Lorna Marshall (ibid., 373), "the powers of autosuggestion that induce trance" are greatly fortified by "the loud singing that assails the ears for hours, the exertion of dancing, the repetitiousness of the rhythms, the physical nearness to others and the synchronization of movements with others." This singing is wordless (which is a rule among the Bushmen, whether one is dealing with healing songs or not), contrary to what happens in possession. Its action cannot therefore be attributed to the emotional impact of words, and is therefore purely musical. Marshall and Lee both stress the passion with which the women sing, and also the loudness of both their singing and their handclapping. The trance itself is associated, as we have heard, with heat, fire, and boiling.[50] One is reminded of Zempléni's observations about the warming-up music provided by griots to start off the *ndöp*. Among the Bushmen, as among the Wolof, the role of music is to arouse the dancers' ardor and raise their excitement. At the auditory level, the louder it is, the greater its effect as a stimulus; at the motor level, the more passionate it is, the more pressing its invitation to dance. As we saw in the case of possession dance, music in the Bushmen shamanic dance appears to play an important role in a general program of overstimulation. Above all, however, it appears to be the condition sine qua non for dancing, and it is ultimately the dancing that produces the decisive effects; the fact that only the dancers go into trance, while the seated women do not, makes this quite evident.

In what does this dance consist? Lorna Marshall describes it as tense. The body is "held erect or leaning forward bent at the hips," and the movements of the torso are so controlled that the dancers look "like statues being carried by the dancing legs" (ibid., 363). As we saw, the men violently stamp the ground in an attempt to make as loud a noise as possible. In the long run, does dancing in this manner entail a particularly great expense of physical energy on the part of the dancers, or does it incur particularly significant metabolic disturbances? This is something we do not know.

Let me sum up what we have learned from this visit to the Bushmen. Music fulfills several functions in the "medicine dance": (1) it incites the men to dance; (2) it contributes to the entry into trance of those among them who are healers; and (3) it leads to the practice of magical healing. The greater part of the music is provided by the chorus of women, but the men also sing. The chorus of women is the one that plays the essential role in inciting dance. On the other hand, it seems that the healer's own singing is of prime importance in the actual healing practices. Be that as it may, the healers play an active role in the music, whose purpose is to make them dance and go into trance, which is contrary to what happens in possession, yet at the same time the main burden of the music making rests on a group that does not go into trance (the women), which is contrary to what happens in shamanism. Viewed from the standpoint of the relations between trance and "who makes the music," the case of the Bushmen thus occupies an intermediate position between possession and shamanism, a fact that weakens, but does not invalidate, the oppositions drawn in the previous chapter.

We should also remember that (1) music does not trigger trance unaided and that it can work only in conjunction either with dancing or with an emotional situation; and (2) in the opinion of the Bushmen themselves the efficacy of their "medicine songs" certainly resides in their magic power, but it equally resides in the power of the healer himself and his conscious use of the song for healing purposes.

Last, let us remember that, for Lorna Marshall, the Bushmen's "medicine dance" should be seen above all as a means of reasserting the unity of the group and reinforcing awareness of that unity among all of its members. The words "united" and "unity" recur three times only several lines apart in her conclusion (ibid., 380): "In their singing, clapping their hands, and dancing, the people are united, . . . people unite and dance together whatever the state of their feelings." Even if they hurl accusations at one another in the course of the dance, "the next moment, the people become a unit, singing, clapping, moving together." I shall return later to the importance of this aspect of things.

As a sequel to what we have just learned about the Bushmen, I would like to add a few observations on trance among the Pygmies, their distant neighbors. Both the Bushmen of the Kalahari desert and the Pygmies of the great equatorial forest are, as we know, nomads who live by hunting and gathering. Although they are not of the same "race," both are peoples of very small stature. Although they live thousands of miles apart, without any contact between them and in totally different environments, their music, or more precisely their singing (since they have no instrumental music, or very little) is extraordinarily similar in some ways (Rouget 1957; Lomax 1968; Frisbie 1971). In certain respects their dances are also very similar. Among the Bushmen, as we have just seen, songs and dances are to a great extent used to induce trance, and trance plays a role of great importance in their lives. What about the Pygmies? In contrast to the Bushmen, they are thought not to practice trance at all (Bourguignon 1968, 20). Colin Turnbull (1961) makes no mention of it, so we can be sure that trance is unknown among the Ituri Pygmies he studied. The same is not true, however, of the Sangha Pygmies, or at least of those I was able to observe in 1946, that is to say the Babinga (Bangombé and Babenzélé) of the Ouesso region. One day during a dance, the Bangombé hunter who was leading a file of dancers suddenly became entranced before our very eyes (exhibiting shaking, loss of balance, abundant perspiration, bewilderment and then collapse). A little girl then brought cool water, which was applied to his face as he lay unconscious on the ground, a situation comparable to what Lorna Marshall (1969, 378) describes for the Bushmen. The cold water brought the hunter gradually back to his senses, but he remained sitting there for a long while, obviously exhausted, while the others went on dancing without him. I can report nothing more about this trance, except that the group obviously perceived it as perfectly normal. My stay among the Pygmies was too short for me to discover anything more on the subject.

Let us simply note that, contrary to what has been said, trance, in relationship with dance and song, does occur among certain Pygmy groups, a fact that is of some interest for mapping the distribution of trance and for comparative studies with the Bushmen.

EXORCISM?

The words possession and exorcism are so frequently linked together in ethnographic literature and in Western religious thought—and the association is clearly not fortuitous—that one might almost say the one inevitably trails the other like a shadow. Both are often seen as covering two normally complementary aspects of one and the same phenomenon, or, rather, the one is seen as the question and the second as the answer that the first raises. Given this basic approach—which is evidently not ours—one could define the various types of possession in terms of the greater or lesser importance given to exorcism in the response made to them. If possession were represented as a circle, the position of exorcism could be depicted as going from zero, expressed as a totally empty circle and conveying the total absence of exorcism, to a full 360-degree turn, covering the entire surface.

In this latter case, in which exorcism is the only possible response to possession, we would be dealing with possessions of the Loudun type, which ultimately are rejected by society or, as we labeled them, reprobate. They do not interest us here since they do not give rise to any form of cult.[51] All the same, we ought to note that the Loudun possessions, which occurred outside of the official religion, cannot be reduced—any more than those concerning us here, which are completely integrated into religious life—to cases or a series of cases of individual hysteria. They have so many stereotypiced features—use of a secret language, number and hierarchy of demons corresponding to the personality of the possessed, to mention but a few—that they certainly should be connected with older possession cults, of which the evidence suggests they are (partially at least) a survival or resurgence. However this may be, possession of the Loudun type is not accompanied by music of any kind. As we have seen, the principal function of possession music is to establish communication with the gods. There is therefore no reason to use music when the possession, far from being desired, is rejected. The events at Loudun therefore confirm the logic of our theory. We will linger on them no longer.

In the first case, on the contrary, in which possession is unreservedly welcomed by society, we are dealing with such cults as the *vodun* in Dahomey,[52] which give rise to possession séances totally devoid of exorcism.[53] This does not mean that exorcism practices are completely unknown in *vodun* worship. When someone has been struck by lightning, the high priest of Khevioso, god of lightning, comes to exorcise the victim's house.[54] But such exorcism rituals are one thing and ceremonies in which possessions occur quite another. Each has rather different orientations and, needless to say, only the second kind interests us. In Vietnam, *hàu-bóng* ceremonies are devoted exclusively to the "guardian Spirits, Genii, and, in an accessory way, the Souls of the Dead"; the "evil Spirits . . . do not intervene in any way" (Simon and Simon-Barouh 1973, 76–77). Between possession of the Loudun kind and the one found in *vodun* worship or the *hàu-bóng* ceremonies, between possessions that are rejected on the one hand and possessions that are entirely welcome on the other, there is room for a whole series of intermediate cases.

Possession and Pact-Making: African Examples

Among the VaNdau of Mozambique the possessed are characterized by two types of possession that coexist and are complementary (Junod 1934).

Those of the first type are bound to be exorcised. The function of those of the second type is to exorcise those of the first.[55] Whether they belong to one or the other of these two categories, the possessed are all occupied by spirits of the Ndau ancestors, but the vast majority are possessed by malevolent spirits, whereas the remaining few are possessed by guardian spirits. The first undergo their possession passively since they depend entirely upon the second category to rid them of it. Contrary to the first, the latter, called *nyamusoro*, undergo initiation, at the end of which they are able to fulfill their function—that is, to rid the others of their possession. Junod calls them exorcists. Unlike the passive majority of possessed persons, whose state is caused by spirits "who enter into living beings and torment them until they do all that is demanded of them" (ibid., 273), the "exorcist" derives his "spiritual power" from "the spirit of a dead person who has possessed him, not to harm but to protect him" (ibid., 283).

As described by Junod (ibid., 286), the exorcism séance (during which, at the request of the passively possessed person, the *nyamusoro* rids him of the tormenting spirit) appears almost more like a shamanic séance—albeit without any journey—than a possession séance. I shall not enter into further detail on this aspect of things here. We will, however, take note of the method the "exorcist" uses to liberate his patient (ibid., 287). Junod describes this method as it relates to diverse "categories of ancestral spirits," the majority of whom are Ndau. It varies according to the category and Junod's information is more or less detailed from case to case. In order to be appeased, each of the twelve sorts of spirits mentioned requires offerings and sacrifices, but some are more "difficult to satisfy" than others. There are those who "deign to appear only when everyone is drunk" (ibid., 277). One can make some spirits "rejoice" by playing the flute for them (ibid., 275), others by "handclapping and dancing" (ibid., 280). The spirits of hunters are "propitiated" by imitating the act of hunting. To "please" certain female spirits, one dons animal skins with fringes and pearls (ibid., 280). Clearly, these are very friendly ways of exorcizing. And indeed, although the séance described by Junod does involve "liberating" a possessed person of the spirit "tormenting" him, it is far from being true exorcism. The spirit in question is not driven out; it is appeased, made to rejoice, provided with some kind of satisfaction, and then politely escorted back into the bush: "There is your place, your village" (ibid., 287). There is a certain contradiction in terms involved, in fact, when one speaks, as does Junod, of "the Ndau exorcists' propitiation ceremonies" (ibid., 273): either one propitiates or one exorcises; one cannot do both.

Also in southern Africa, the Thonga, neighbors of the VaNdau were described by H. A. Junod (father of H. P. Junod) as responding to possession with exorcism; possession among them is attributed to foreign (Zulu or Njao) and consequently malevolent spirits from whom one must be relieved. Using H. A. Junod's own description, Bastide has shown (1972, 103–4) that the evil spirit in reality reconciles himself with his victim and becomes his guardian spirit. I should add that the real purpose of the "strange and terrible exorcism" (Junod 1913, 440), which involves an "infernal" or "hideous" din of drums sometimes for days on end, is not to drive the spirit out at all, but to force it "to reveal itself, to declare its name" (ibid., 441, 443). On this particular occasion "the patient will sing his song, . . . a song which will be henceforth *his*"[56] (ibid., 445), and which will serve in the future, at the appropriate moment, to induce further trances in him. In this case, we are clearly at the opposite pole of exorcism and reprobate possession.

In the Central African Republic among the Ngbaka-Mandja (Arom and Taurelle 1968), possession works in the same way as among the VaNdau in the sense that there are two categories of possessed: the healers, who go into possession trances in order to heal, and the so-to-speak occasional possessed person, who comes to the healers to be cured. As among the VaNdau, the healer is similar in many respects to the shaman—he is the one who induces trance in the sick person, sings the appropriate songs while shaking his rattles, and directs the musicians. His songs clearly show the ambivalence of the relations with the deities responsible for the possession and the illness. On the one hand he calls to them, "Come and help me cure the sickness!" and on the other he threatens them: "If you try to come back into her and poison her again, you shall all die!" At the end of the ceremony, after the offerings have been made, the healer addresses the divinities again: "This is for you . . . eat your share . . . do not trouble her any more" (ibid., 102, 103, 104). Here, as among the VaNdau, occasional possession results in a relation with the divinity that could be termed peaceful coexistence: let both sides stay in their own place.

In the Hausa *bori*, which exhibits aspects of possession that are very different from the foregoing, initiation may be broken down into two successive phases, which Jacqueline Monfouga-Nicolas (1972, 110ff.) describes as the "exorcism" phase and the "imposition" phase. During the first, that of exorcism, the *jakeso*—the officiant conducting the initiation—plays a similar role, all things being equal, to that of the *nyamusoro*, the Ndau "exorcist." This first phase lasts for three nights (ibid., illus. p. 112). Its purpose is, as it were, to wipe the slate clean so that the beneficent divinity can then come and take possession of its "mare." This beneficent divinity can belong to the category of either white or dark gods; the latter (*kankama*) can cross over into the category of white gods if it becomes beneficent for the neophyte. There are, however, certain *kankama* who will always remain unyieldingly dark. During the first two nights, the *kankama* manifest themselves when they are summoned by musical instruments. For each one, the initiating *jakeso* goes into a light trance (ibid., 116), and the neophyte being initiated "seems absent." On the third night, however, the "struggle with the dark gods" takes place (ibid., 120). They arrive in a cohort, as on the previous two nights, but this time "each of the gods invoked will swoop down upon" the neophyte. "After each invocation the god refuses to leave the initiate's body," and she must then "fight with him" to make him leave her. At the end of this struggle, which lasts for several hours, one of the white gods, who is assigned "the task of driving out the *kankama* for good" (ibid., 121), comes and incorporates the *jakeso*. The latter then struggles with the neophyte she is initiating, who is still possessed by the dark gods, and finally emerges "victorious from this struggle." As with the VaNdau, then, exorcism involves an exorcist who is possessed by a benevolent god and uses this power to drive out a malevolent god from the body, not of a patient this time, but of a neophyte undergoing initiation. The methods used, however, do not appear to be at all the same. There is no question of "satisfying" the *kankama*; they are driven out. This is, therefore, a true form of exorcism, even though, during the two nights preceding the struggle with the dark gods, the *jakeso* went "into a light trance at the sound of the motto" upon the arrival of each dark god (ibid., 116), which in a way implies paying homage to or at least acknowledging the *kankama*. Be that as it may, the important thing about this type of exorcism is that it constitutes no more than the second part of a process in two stages, since before the dark gods are expelled they are first summoned. Another important point to remember is that the summons to the dark gods does not differ in any way from the one to the white gods. Both are issued by musical instruments on which divinities' mottoes are played.

Let us now move to Chad. In her article entitled "Musical Exorcism among the Kotoko," Monique Brandily describes a ceremony organized for the purpose of exorcizing a sick woman "because she had fallen prey to a genius" (1967, 38). After a considerable length of time spent in organizing various participants—musicians, women singers, members (women) of the college of the possessed, spectators—the séance begins with the possession of the sick woman. The musicians play music addressed to the genius inhabiting her. The sick woman dances and then a number of other women also become possessed and dance. The séance ends when the last woman has been "freed": "All the women have now been freed," the author notes (ibid., 49). The woman singer, who played the central role in the séance, then embodies the "marabout" genius and in this capacity begs the "chief" of the genii to order to all his subjects "to leave the women in peace" (ibid., 50). These data lead Monique Brandily to comment on the ambiguity of the ceremony, which, she observes, "consists at the same time in driving out the genius in order to obtain a cure," and in provoking "several cases of possession among the women present" (ibid., 51). What is its real aim? Is it to drive out the genii—or as she prefers to call them, the demons (ibid., 38 n.1)? Or is it to make them come? To use Luc de Heusch's terminology (1971, 229ff.), is it exorcism or adorcism?

This question, which is posed by so many possession cults, is by no means new. In his work, *La possession et ses aspects théâtraux chez les Ethiopiens de Gondar*, Michel Leiris (1958, 34 n.2) makes the following observation: "It is improper to apply the term 'exorcism' to the practices of the *zār* brotherhoods; their goal is in fact to make a pact with the spirit rather than to expel it." This observation can in fact be applied to all cults in which the rites are directed toward expelling the spirit responsible for possession. All available descriptions demonstrate that this expulsion is only obtained if a pact with the spirit has been made *beforehand*. Before the genii "leave the women in peace," as Monique Brandily puts it, the women must first publicly identify themselves with them, for by reproducing the genii's outward behavior in dances that imitate them, the women, in fact, become identified with them. But this identification, this possession, cannot take place unless one has already summoned these genii, and this precisely is the role of the musicians and women singers. The ceremony's primary aim, therefore, is to summon the genii, not to drive them away.

To return to the healing séance described by Monique Brandily, from the sick woman's point of view, events unfold—whether consciously or unconsciously is of little importance—something like this: I am sick because a genius is tormenting me, I become that genius; satisfied because he has possessed me, he ceases to torment me, I am set free. Is this exorcism? Broadly speaking, it could be, since ultimately the sick woman has exorcised or chased out her illness. Strictly speaking, it certainly is not. We speak of exorcism when the divinity who comes to be embodied is seen as a demon. But there is every reason to believe this is the case only because among the Kotoko, who live in a region converted to Islam, there is a more or less overt conflict between Islam and the old, traditional religion. Although they once were deities—and still are, incontestably, in many parts of Africa—these genii have become demons. Thus people succumb to them because belief in their power is not yet extinct, but they then expel them—at least this is what they say—because this is what the official or dominant religion requires. The trances of the female Tunisian possessees described by S. Ferchiou (1972, 60) take place within a similar religious framework.

In other places, as the example of the Thonga demonstrated, the conflict manifests itself differently: there, the spirits that possess the patient are foreigners and therefore enemies. Again the patient must get rid of them, they must be driven out. But is this exorcism? Here again the same process is used: in order to expel them, one must first enter into communication with them and appease them; in short, one must have established bonds with them, if not through possession, at least by making a pact.

What we need to remember from all this is that in a great many cults, in black Africa at least, possession séances are devoid of any element of exorcism. Whenever there is genuine exorcism the expulsion of the genius, however dramatic it may be, is merely the culmination of a process in which integration of the deity is a prerequisite and a sine qua non. Finally, the term exorcism is frequently used pejoratively, mainly because contact with another religion has led certain people to refer to spirits as demons when, in fact, for the adepts there is nothing demoniacal about them.

We must be careful not to oversimplify, however. Among the Mundang of Chad (Adler and Zempléni 1972, 32–35) the entire system of possession consists, from the sick man's standpoint, in being possessed by a genius who is in fact seen as an "agent of sickness." In this case, should we compare the possession to a kind of homeopathic cure that treats disorder with disorder, illness with illness, or, as Firth puts it (1969, xiv), "fights fire with fire"? However that may be, here again there is identification with the divinity, initiation into his cult, consecration of altars, and performance of sacrifices. This is the important point for us.

Let us sum up. Possession has often been said to require exorcism as a response for reasons that vary from case to case. Sometimes it is because the descriptions are no more than a projection of the writer's own ideas onto the facts observed. More often still, it is because the cult in question, which in the region where it is found represents either the autochthonous religion or an earlier stage of a religion, is in conflict with a monotheistic religion brought into the region more recently and occupying a politically or morally predominant position. The spirits, the genii responsible for possession are then seen by followers of the official religion as demons to be exorcised, an attitude that is frequently disturbing for the adepts. These latter then accept the fiction of exorcism all the more readily because the genii are indeed tormenting them, because by expelling them or by pretending to do so, one keeps everyone happy, and because, in addition, the essential aspect of their cult, which is to practice possession, is safeguarded. There also are cases in which possession is due to foreign spirits, a situation which generally results from recent historical vicissitudes and consequently reflects a conflict situation, but of another type. In this case expulsion can take precedence, apparently, at least, and in certain parts of the ritual, over the making of pacts. Nonetheless, in order to expel these spirits, one must first embody them, which usually entails a preliminary initiation stage.[57]

I hope the reader will excuse me for having spent so much time on the question of exorcism but it is in fact crucial. If, as I believe, the relations of music to possession are of the same order, give or take a few variants, whatever the possession cult, it is because all these cults, notwithstanding their diversity, exhibit one and the same type of religious behavior. If they did not, my hypothesis would then be unthinkable. It was therefore important to establish that side by side with possession cults in which the intrusion of the divinity is not only welcomed but even ardently desired, there also exist others in which possession only calls for exorcism. If this were so, the inner behavior of the possessed person would necessarily be different in the two cases. Indeed, logically it should be diametrically opposite. We have seen that one of the main functions of music is to establish communication with the gods and thus to create a situation of identification and alliance that favors the kindling of possession. If relations with the gods were conflictual, then the music would either have to play a different role or be of a radically different kind. Apparently, this is not the case. This is why I was led to examine exorcism so closely, and to determine whether it does indeed play the preponderant role, which has often been attributed to it, in possession. It does not. Or if it does, the possession concerned belongs to the reprobate (as at Loudun) and not to the cultivated kind—in other words, it is not a possession cult—or else it is obsession (in the medieval sense of the word as it was described earlier) and not possession in the sense we have agreed upon in this book.

One could almost say that the difference between possession and exorcism lies in the fact that possession necessarily calls upon music at some moment or other while exorcism, on the contrary, does not make use of it. This is fully illustrated by the situation Schéhérazade Qassim Hassan describes in Iraq. In her chapter devoted to "the possession ceremonies of black population" (1975, 172ff.) she distinguishes between "non-musical ceremonies" devoted to "exorcizing the spirits of Evil," and "musical ceremonies" whose function is "the invocation of beneficent spirits."

Saul and David

The well-known story of David playing the lyre[58] to calm Saul's delirium is often considered to be the most well-known example of musical exorcism. It therefore merits investigation.

Let us begin by looking at the various interpretations that have been made of it. When he writes, with reference to the role of music in Israel, that "music drove the demons out of Saul's soul when David played for him," Curt Sachs (1940, 105) clearly interprets it in terms of exorcism. The same is true of E. Dhorme (1956, 868), for whom David and his music constitute the "remedy for the possession of which Saul is victim." The same is also true of Combarieu (1909, 86), for whom Saul is a possessed person upon whom David's music exercises a "beneficial" effect. But when he discusses the episode in which Saul, blinded with jealousy, attempts to kill David who is actually playing for him, Combarieu adds that when music "in the spirit of possessed people is associated with painful memories," it is also capable of provoking "terrible crises." For him, Saul is "a well-known example" of this "double role of music," which sometimes consists in "creating a pathological state that is inherent in the musical emotion itself," but which, on the contrary, in different circumstances, "arrests his fury and restores the subject to a normal state." H. G. Farmer (1926, 12), who, like Sachs, pays attention only to the beneficial aspect of David's music, notes that "the evil spirit" who was afflicting Saul is conjured by David's *kinnor*. Here again we are back with exorcism. Unlike the previous two writers, however, he does not speak of possession but emphasizes the magical power attributed to David's music in both Hebraic and Arabic literature. Finally, A. P. Merriam (1964, 111), who like Farmer restricts himself to the calming effect of David's lyre on Saul, sees it as an example of healing music that should be classified under the broad heading of music's physical effects, particularly musicotherapy. What are we to think of all this?

To clarify things somewhat, let us begin by formulating the facts in the terms we have adopted for this book. If the matter is complex, this is because Saul himself has a complicated relation to his trance. He has frequently been described as a possessed person. Barton (1918, 135), for instance, says so in his article on Semitic and Christian possession in the *Encyclopaedia of Religions and Ethics*. In my view, Saul's trance has two aspects which must be clearly distinguished, and neither of the two constitutes possession in the strict sense of the word as I am using it. On the one hand he is tormented by "an evil spirit sent from God." In no case, however, does he identify himself with that spirit. In our terms, therefore, it is not possession that is involved but obsession. On the other hand—and this is something that has not yet been mentioned—he is also a prophet, a *nabi*, and therefore susceptible to being seized by prophetic trances, when the spirit of Jehovah descends upon him. Here again, however, there is no question of identification, since this would be unthinkable. For us then, Saul the prophet is inspired, not possessed. Viewed in terms of its two aspects, what is the relation of his trance to music?

We know the circumstance in which Saul prophesied—and therefore went into trance—for the first time. After anointing Saul as ruler of his people, Samuel tells him, among other things: "and furthermore when you come there to the city, you will meet a band of prophets coming down from the high place with a lyre, a tambourine, a flute, and a harp[59] before them; and they will be prophesying ecstatically. Then the spirit of the Lord shall suddenly seize upon you, and you shall prophesy ecstatically with them and you shall be changed into another man" (1 Samuel 10: 5–6). So it is while listening to music that Saul goes into his first trance. And we should note that among the various instruments listed, those regarded by the Hebrews as specific to trance are the stringed instruments, not the tabrets or the flutes. This is made clear by the story of Elisha. Before he prophesies at the request of the three kings of Israel, Judah, and Edom, and before he performs a miracle to save their threatened army, the prophet demands that a musician be brought to him. And "when the musician played music[60] the hand of the Lord came upon him" (2 Kings 3:15). The Hebrew text does not indicate what instrument the musician played, whether harp or lyre, but the verb translated here as "played" in fact means "playing with one's hands," and refers to a string instrument.[61] In the introduction to his edition of the Bible (1956, xviii), E. Dhorme stresses the importance of this passage and talks about Elisha's "trance." The prophet's entry into trance thus must be attributed to this string music.

This being granted, we can now turn to the text that relates the circumstances under which David was summoned to play before Saul: "Now the spirit of the Lord had departed from Saul and an evil spirit from the Lord terrified him. So the servants of Saul said to him, 'See now, an evil spirit from the Lord is terrorizing you. Let now your servants who are before you speak: let them seek for our Lord a man skillful in playing the lyre. Then whenever the evil spirit comes upon you he will play with his hand, and you will be well' " (1 Samuel 16:14–17). Saul demands that a good musician be found, David is brought to him, and Saul takes him into his service. And verse 23 reads: "So whenever the evil spirit from God came upon Saul, David would take the lyre and play with his hand, and Saul would be relieved and feel restored and the evil spirit would depart from him." Now, if we restricted ourselves to this text alone we would have every reason to think, as Sachs does, that by "playing with his hand" David drives out the evil spirit, or in other words exorcizes it. But in this case we are faced with a contradiction. Earlier, it was by "playing with his hand" that the musician induced Elisha's prophetic trance; now it is also by "playing with his hand" that David succeeds in calming that of Saul. How can this contradiction be resolved?

Let us go back to the beginning of the quotation from Samuel. "But the Spirit of the Lord departed from Saul, and an evil spirit from the Lord troubled him." Elsewhere (1 Samuel 18:12), when Saul, raving under the influence of an evil spirit, tries to kill David, we read once more that God "had departed" from him. This withdrawal of the Spirit of the Lord thus appears to be a precondition for the arrival of the "evil spirit from the Lord." (And one cannot help thinking here of the exchange of souls we mentioned several times in African possession cases.) This being so, why should we not suppose that if the evil spirit departs from Saul when David "plays with his hand" before him, it is less because the music drives him out than because it brings back in Saul the Spirit of God that had left him?

We can then say that by playing his lyre David reconciles Saul with the Spirit of God, a situation that is no longer in contradiction with that of the musician using his stringed instrument to induce Elisha's trance, a trance that is inspired by the spirit of Jehovah. We are now in line with the logic of the relations between music and possession as it has gradually emerged in the previous pages. It is true, as I have said, that neither Saul nor Elisha is possessed in the strict sense of the term as I am using it: they never identify themselves with God. Instead, they are inspired, or prophets (*nabi*). Admittedly, the dividing line between inspiration and possession is often rather thin. In this instance, seen from the standpoint of their relations to music, one might even claim that it has disappeared altogether.

By interpreting David's music as having the effect of inducing God to become present again and thus driving out the evil spirit as an aftereffect, we remain within the general logic of a well-attested system. By interpreting it as exorcism music, not only are we faced with the contradiction already mentioned, but we also run up against yet another difficulty.

What is generally considered to be exorcism music seems to act in only one of two ways, either by virtue of noise or by the magic of incantations. Here there is no question of either being involved. Like the Hebrews, the Babylonians thought that it was necessary for the "good" spirits to have left someone before he or she could be possessed by "demons" (Barton 1918, 133, 135). Surviving Babylonian incantatory texts for use in exorcising evil spirits express this belief very clearly. We thus have good reason to think that if it was a matter of driving an evil spirit out of Saul, whose "good spirit" had left, David would have chanted incantations. No such thing is mentioned in the Bible.

If my hypothesis—that David used his lyre to effect a reconciliation between Saul and God—seems unjustifiable, there is really only one other that could be acceptable; that is, Farmer's. He depicts the lyre as a magical instrument and David as a musician famous for his magical power over beings and things. This places him in the Near-Eastern tradition, which according to Farmer originated in Mesopotamia, that attributes powers to music derived from complex symbolic or numerical relations with the cosmos. We shall encounter this tradition again in the chapter on the Arabs. These powers, which were magical in nature, formed the basis of a theory of healing by means of music. Here we return to Merriam's theory of musicotherapy, which in fact is perfectly compatible with Farmer's ideas.

The contradiction we spoke of earlier could then be resolved in this way: when the musical instrument triggers the prophetic trance in the *nabi* (it does not matter whether it is Elisha or Saul), the mechanism at work is perhaps not exactly that found in possession but it is nevertheless very close to it; when David's lyre calms Saul, on the other hand, another musical tradition is at work; that of magical music.

The case of David playing the lyre to calm Saul's frenzy can thus be interpreted in three different ways. First, it can be seen as a case of musical exorcism. I have already stated the reasons for rejecting this hypothesis. Second, it can be seen as an example of musicotherapy. But this means that we would resort to a notion (musical magic) absent from the text, and that we would ignore an essential situational fact, which is the reference to intrusion by an "evil spirit." Third, one can see—as I do—Saul's obsession by this evil spirit as being in some way the reverse of God's absence. By playing his lyre David reestablishes God's presence, which means that he restores in Saul, in an attenuated form, the state of inspired prophet that he had momentarily lost. Granted, this is a rather complicated interpretation, but it does have the advantage of taking into account all the textual data. It also remains within the general system of relations between music and prophetic inspiration among the Hebrews, a system that is in fact quite close to the even more general one governing the relations between music and possession.

One final point concerning Saul's furor, in his attempt to transfix David with a javelin while David is in the very process of playing his lyre for him. Combarieu interprets the prophet's homicidal delirium as a possession fit brought on by the music. Nothing in the passage from Samuel justifies this interpretation. After it recounts David's military successes and Saul's reasons for taking umbrage with them, the text reads: "On the next day the evil spirit from God seized upon Saul, and he was filled with prophetic frenzy within the house, while David was playing with his hand as he did each day. Now Saul had his spear in his hand; and Saul lifted up his spear, saying, 'I will pin David to the wall.' But David escaped from his presence twice. Saul was afraid of David because the Lord was with him and had departed from Saul" (1 Samuel 18:10–12).

Contrary to what is clearly stated in the two other passages quoted from Samuel that deal, first, with the prophetic trance that seizes Saul for the first time while he is in the company of other prophets, and second, with his state of obsession calmed by David's lyre (passages that both associate music directly with trance, first to induce it; then to end it), this third passage does not in any way imply that the sound of David's lyre is responsible for Saul's furor. An evil spirit from God (read: jealousy) comes upon Saul and provokes his fury. It so happens that at this point David is playing his instrument, as he does every day. The text does not connect the two facts. It is clear that Saul's murderous fury must be attributed to the sight of David as a rival warrior, not to his presence as a musician.

The Case of Tarantism

As we know, tarantism has been long regarded as a particularly characteristic and spectacular form of musicotherapy. Opinions on this subject have had to be considerably revised as a result of the work done by Marius Schneider (1948) and Ernesto De Martino (1961). The interpretations advanced by these two scholars are very different. Both, to be sure, acknowledge that musicotherapy is an important factor. But whereas Schneider sees it as simply one element in a vast system of symbolic representations one might call astrological in nature, De Martino sees it as a form of exorcism functioning within the psychoanalytic logic of a religion based on remorse. Both[62] also associate tarantism as a religious phenomenon with possession cults as a whole, but they do so with what one might term repugnance, so that they present this aspect of things as entirely secondary. Neither the word "possession" nor the word "trance" appears in the index of either book.

Is tarantism possession? Musicotherapy? Exorcism? We return, though in a wholly different context, to the questions we just posed in the case of David and Saul. What is the answer? Here again the exorcism theory has to be discarded, as does that of musicotherapy. Examined closely, tarantism turns out to be nothing more than a particular form of possession. At least, this is the hypothesis underlying everything I have written in preceding chapters on tarantism's relation to music. It is now important to demonstrate this hypothesis, as I hope to do in the next few pages. Indeed, it is particularly important for my present purposes to clarify the relation between tarantism and music, since it represents the best-known example of trance in all of Europe.[63] We have relatively early descriptions of tarantism, and it has been the object of recent investigations. It is, moreover a ritual in which music and dance play an essential role.

Let me begin with broad summaries of the two theories already mentioned. In his *La danza de espadas y la tarentela*, Marius Schneider looks at only one aspect of tarantism—admittedly a particularly interesting one for musicologists—that of "medicinal" rites expressing a cosmological vision of the world characteristic of megalithic civilizations, or at least of those civilizations as they are interpreted by the ethnological theory of *Kulturkreis*. A system of mystical correspondence between nature and man, between the elements, astrological signs, the seasons, and sounds, causes the spider dance, the sword dance, and the music specific to them, to function (by complementing one another) as a form of therapy acting both on the level of accidental reality (that of the illness produced by the spider's bite) and on the level of permanent reality (that of the struggle between life and death, summer and winter, stillness and movement, renewal and decay). Within the overall configuration of these mystic correspondences, musical sounds, musical instruments, and dance steps occupy a well-defined position. It is by virtue of this position, and of the power it confers upon them, that music and dance ensure the triumph of recovery, which should simply be seen as an example of the victory of life. In this vast theoretical edifice the real and the symbolic are closely intertwined, but at no point does Schneider seem to cast doubt upon the very real aspect of the bite and its cure: "cases observed in detail are too frequent, and we cannot ignore them without running the risk of ridicule" (1948, 126). Schneider himself seems entirely prepared to accept completely the general conception of the world within which the cure is effected. Indeed, he seems to see it as superior to any other in providing an account of the ultimate reality of things. Too bad if the "catastrophic theories of Descartes" (ibid., 128) have been responsible for relegating this conception to "the camp of poetry" where "any madness is permitted." It is the only one that contains the truth concerning "the impenetrable mystery of creation" (ibid., 126). Schneider's case thus raises the very problem of a particular mystique and its value as a current system for interpreting the world. I shall of course refrain from entering into the debate. Suffice it to say that in terms of our interest here, the symbolic system he describes seems to be the reconstruction of an edifice whose existence as a coherent whole has never actually been observed. The elements that make it up do indeed all have a reality, but they have been gathered from the four corners of the earth, and nothing proves they have ever constituted a whole.

In his *La terra del rimorso* (1961),[64] which appeared thirteen years after Schneider's work, Ernesto De Martino provides a totally different interpretation of tarantism. His work derives to a very large extent from the team fieldwork he conducted in Salento in 1959 and it is in light of the materials gathered during this investigation that he reinterprets the old texts used by Marius Schneider, to whose theory he refers very little (1966, 301–2). De Martino sees tarantism as a "minor religious form" centered around a kind of "choreographo-chromatico-musical exorcism" (ibid., 71) and as an institution that "is not reducible to a common type" (ibid., 305). Whereas he in fact acknowledges that its origins must be sought in the "orgiastic and initiatory cults of classical antiquity," and whereas he considers there are "African analogues" (ibid., 204) that justify a "common Mediterranean cultural homeland" for the *zār*, the *bori*, and the Iberian and Sardinian forms of tarantism (ibid., 305), he nevertheless thinks it more important to stress its "cultural autonomy." According to him, tarantism should be seen as "an internal episode within an expanding Christian civilization" born in the Middle Ages and related to the Crusades, during which the "real attacks of spider poisoning experienced by the Christian armies in their camps" facilitated "the birth of the tarantula symbol." Having said this, he states that the essential of tarantism, as an institution, is to function on a "mythico-ritual horizon of recapture and reintegration in relation to critical moments of human existence, with a marked preference for the crisis of puberty, the theme of the forbidden eros, and the conflicts of adolescence, within the framework of a peasant lifestyle" (ibid., 304).[65]

De Martino's thesis thus seems to be concerned with establishing the historical perspective of the data and deeply impregnated with psychoanalysis. There would be nothing to criticize in this outlook were it not for the fact that it makes us lose sight of what is, after all, the most obvious aspect of tarantism; that is, identification with the spider. One particular point in his argument, symptomatic of the rest, shows this very clearly. One of the dance figures of the tarantulees—the best known—consists, as we know, in imitating the spider's movements: back to the ground, body arched to a great or lesser degree, the tarantulee moves about like a spider on all fours. One can see this very clearly in D. Carpitella's film, and the sight is a striking one. In certain cases the tarantulee utilizes, or rather used to utilize, since the practice has now died out, another dance figure. When the séance took place in the open air, De Martino tells us, quoting Kircher's seventeenth-century account, "some tarantulees let themselves hang from trees by ropes, showing that this suspension was most pleasant for them . . . ; such a passion affected above all those who had been bitten by tarantulas that had the habit of hanging their webs from trees" (ibid., 138). When the dance took place indoors, they hung from a rope fixed to the ceiling. There is every reason to see in this behavior a pure and simple imitation of the tarantula. Without denying the reality of this imitation, De Martino prefers to see something else in it. According to him, this figure "highlights the particular symbolic value of the swing" (ibid.). Associating this aioresis (ibid., 230ff.)—the act of "letting oneself hang in space"—with the myth of the swing of the hanged virgins and with that of Phaedra's hanging, he interprets the hanging of the tarantulees as a sign of frustrated, unhappy, or thwarted female passions. For him a number of other symbols can be added to this one: "being rocked in a mother's arms"; a game in space that is "always the same, at first granted, then immediately taken away"; and finally, a "prefiguration of the embrace" with a possible husband. The problem with such an amalgam is that it not only proves nothing (in fact, it makes one think that anything can be symbolic of anything), but it also obscures the essential core of the matter, which is that here we have people in trance busy identifying themselves, through dance, with a creature thought to have made them ill; in other words, that we are dealing with a characteristic case of possession. De Martino is certainly correct in seeing behind this behavior impulses strongly tinged with an eroticism whose demons need to be exorcized. But one could say just the same about the Hausa *bori*, for example. For us, the essential thing to remember is not what exactly those involved are trying to rid themselves of, but rather how they do it.

Seen in light of directly observable behavior manifested by the afflicted person rather than from the standpoint of its underlying representations, be they real or conjectural, tarantism displays all the characteristics of possession as it operates in the group of cults recognized as possession cults. In fact it dovetails perfectly well with all the points of the definition proposed earlier:

1. It takes the form of a religious manifestation, since it is placed under the sign of Saint Paul, whose chapel serves as a "theater" for the tarantulees' public meetings. And even though the spider itself is not (is no longer?) a divinity in the ritual, it nevertheless seems to be constantly interchangeable with Saint Paul. The female tarantulees (ibid., 363–64), who still dress as "brides of Saint Paul" (*ibid.*, 240) even today sing:

> Say where the tarantula stung you
> Underneath the hem of my skirt
> . . . Oh my Saint Paul of the tarantulas
> Who stings all the girls
> And makes them saints

2. It is characterized by a change in the behavior of the person concerned, and this change is accompanied by trance. When she is entranced—and her behavior indicates on every count that she is—the tarantulee indulges in all kinds of extravagant behavior, of which the most notorious is that of behaving like a tarantula (that is, of identifying herself with it, as though she were possessed by it), since her dance imitates the spider's movements.

3. Healing is the manifest function of tarantism. But what is it a cure for? This, as we shall see, is where its very particular nature comes in.

Ultimately, then, what is missing from tarantism to make it a possession cult? Simply daring to call it one. Why? Because if it had been, it would have long since ended in the same way as the events at Loudun ended: at the stake. H. E. Sigerist (1948, 114) saw this perfectly well. Whether the origins of tarantism must entirely be sought, as he thought, in the orgiastic cults of Greek antiquity, or whether they became mixed with African contributions, as De Martino seems ready to admit, is of little consequence. The essential point is that the Church of Rome could never for a moment have tolerated its existence as an overt possession cult. The bite of the tarantula, whose effects coincide so extraordinarily closely with the signs that herald the onset of possession, provided a providential alibi. As Sigerist points out, women who gave themselves up to these practices were no longer sinners but unfortunate victims of the tarantula. Fundamentally, then, tarantism is nothing other than a possession cult that dares not speak its name. This does not mean it has no particular traits of its own. Indeed, it has some very marked characteristics that derive, in part at least, from the fact that it had to remain unavowed.

Without wanting to dispute the interest of Schneider's and De Martino's theses, I have tried to identify the reasons that justify integrating tarantism, without reservations, into the category of possession cults. This task, I hope, is now accomplished. We can now move on to exorcism and music.

As we saw, tarantism is regarded by De Martino as "choreographo-chromatico-musical exorcism" that primarily functions, let us say for simplicity's sake, as a psychic release mechanism, so that the spider's bite, which is more often imaginary than real, operates on the symbolic level and provides the opportunity, as it were, for the cure. De Martino cites (1966, 256) a fourteenth-century text, which is "the most ancient document on the musical exorcism of those poisoned by a tarantula bite," that interprets tarantism as a cure operating not on the symbolic level this time, but on the level of reality, since the actual bite is never doubted at any point. Music and dance are seen as a sort of mechanical expulsion, as it were, of the venom. In other words, this text, the *Sertum papale de venenis*, views tarantism as an example of what was to be known three centuries later, in Kircher's time, as "iatromusic" or curing music, or what we would term musicotherapy. The text claims that the "joy" the tarantulees feel at the sound of tunes that please them is apparently responsible for their recovery, but the author adds that, in reality, the joy stems from the fact that "by means of the melodies and songs their humours [body fluids] are drawn from the interior of their body toward the exterior, preventing the venom . . . from penetrating inwards; consequently the most important parts [of their organism] do not suffer from it, but on the contrary are relieved" (ibid., 257). This text is also interesting in that it gives an account of the popular interpretation of tarantism (only to refute it): "the common people and the ignorant affirm that when the tarantula bites, it emits music, and that when the sick man hears melodies or songs conforming to this music, he then derives great relief from them. But in my opinion the situation is quite different" (ibid., 256). Of the two interpretations this text provides, the popular and the learned one proposed in its place, the first is clearly nearer to the truth: it alone takes into account what is, as we have seen, an essential feature of tarantism: identification with the spider. For it is because the melody "conforms"to the music emitted by the spider that it has the virtue of relieving the sick person. We in fact know that there are various kinds of tarantulas, and that the tarantulee is only supposed to react to the sound of the tarantella specific to the tarantula that has bitten her. Indeed, this is how the latter is identified, by means of the "right tune" or, if one prefers, the right musical motto, which as we saw earlier plays such an important role in other possession cults.

This having been said, let us note that the *Sertum* does not actually mention exorcism, either in its own interpretation of tarantism or in the popular interpretation it records. De Martino is the one who is interpreting when he writes that the *Sertum* is a "document relating to musical ex-

orcism": neither the word nor the idea actually appears in the text. In using the word, De Martino is apparently making himself heir to a Christian
tradition whose makeup he himself describes: "The use of canonic exorcism and the elaboration of crisis as a means of doing penance were the ex-
pedients to which the [medieval] Church sought recourse in order to deal
with the situation" (ibid., 265). And it is significant that on the same page
of *La terra del rimorso* we read: "In short, the tarantula appears as a 'possessing spirit' that exorcism controls," and that a few lines later we come
across a quotation from a priest writing in the seventeenth century who
speaks of the Apulian tarantulees as people "possessed by the demon" on
whom "exorcism should be practiced" (ibid., 192). Moreover, De Martino is misusing language: from the standpoint of the *Sertum*, expulsion
certainly is involved, but it is venom and not a spirit that is being expelled,
and moreover not through words but rather through the mechanical action of the music and dance. This would be of little importance were it not
that the use of the word exorcism masks the most important aspect of the
possession: in tarantism as elsewhere, it is not a conflictual relation with
the deity that is involved, but the partaking of an alliance. The fact that,
depending on the case, this relation can vary from alliance proper to a simple pact of peaceful coexistence, as I said earlier, is secondary.

Despite appearances, the divinity responsible for the possession is not
the one that is exorcised. On the contrary, it is the divinity concerned who,
by allowing the possessed person to identify himself with him or her, provides the means of exorcising the illness—real or imagined—from which
the person is suffering. In possession cults in which the "therapeutic dimension"—to use Zempléni's expression—is an important feature, the
hysteriform behaviors displayed by the possessed person are not the disorders for which the cure is intended; on the contrary, they are a remedy for
deeper disorders of a quite different nature afflicting the sick person; that
is to say, for the adversity that strikes him. This means that possession
should be understood as a form of therapy of adversity, bringing into play
an institutionalized hysteria or, if one prefers, a socialization of hysteria.
Music and dance are precisely the principal means of socializing or institu-
tionalizing this hysteria, by providing it with stereotyped forms of trance,
forms that of course depend upon the set of representations constituting
the particular system of a given cult. In tarantism, the tarantella (music
and dance) does not have the function of curing the tarantulee of her hysteria, but on the contrary, provides her with a means of behaving like a
hysteric in public, in accordance with a model recognized by all, thereby
freeing her from inner misfortune. How? By providing her with a means
of "coming out of herself" and of communicating with the world, with society, with herself. But whether possession constitutes itself into a kind of

hysteriotherapy, as in tarantism or in the *ndöp*, or whether it remains un-connected with any therapeutic functions and displays an extremely con-trolled outward aspect, it must in any case be viewed as a response to a need for communication.

If, in tarantism, the spider's bite has been seen as constituting the ill that should be exorcised whereas, in reality, it is the means by which this ill is exorcised, this is because the case is extraordinarily ambiguous. Although the bite is most frequently imaginary, it can, nevertheless, sometimes be real. When real, it produces symptoms that are not imaginary at all: toxic reaction, pains, difficulty in standing, muscular rigidity, sometimes sexual arousal, and, in a later stage, "a characteristic sensation of burning and tingling in the soles of the feet" (ibid., 317).[66] Following a period of "very marked depression accompanied by anxiety and a feeling of impending death," the patient then becomes, on the contrary, "agitated, very anx-ious, and sometimes suffering from hallucinations." Somewhat like the datura used in the *bori* (J. Monfouga-Nicolas), the spider's venom induces the principal symptoms of possession as it manifests itself in the system mentioned earlier. The tingling sensation in the feet and the "intermittent trembling that occurs principally in the lower limbs (sometimes displaying a convulsive aspect)" obviously constitute, in addition, an invitation to dance. In short, tarantism is the very model of the ideal scenario, since within it the symbolic and the real, the signifier and the signified, the manifest and the latent, the anecdote and the hidden meaning, the pretext and the profound motivation or, to refer to De Martino's thesis (ibid., 198–99), *morso* (and *re-morso*) and *rimorso*, (bite, rebite, remorse), co-incide perfectly. We should not forget, however, that although the purpose is sometimes to chase out the venom and always to expel what it symbol-izes, the intention is not to chase out the spider, but, on the contrary, to identify oneself to it, which is done a great deal by imitating it in a variety of different ways.

There would thus be no reason whatsoever for viewing tarantism as "musical exorcism" were it not for the fact that among the texts collected by De Martino (ibid., 154–56), some can in fact be regarded as exor-cisms:

> She has stung you
> She has bitten you
> . . . .
> And we are chasing her away, far away

and

> There where she stung you
> She can be killed

Others accompany dance movements expressing the spider fleeing or being crushed. Still others, however, tend to glorify the tarantula:

> Dance, Maria
> And dance hard
> For the tarantula
> Is living and not dead

or else to minimize its role:

> It was not tarantula, nor tarantella
> But it was wine from the cask

This is done, however, lightheartedly and with acknowledgments to Bacchus, or, in other words, with no intention of exorcising.

As expressed in the first two of these texts, the desire to get rid of the tarantula need not necessarily be interpreted as a wish for exorcism. As Jacqueline Monfouga-Nicolas emphasizes, there is always a certain ambivalence in matters of possession, and possession can very well be felt as a burden by the possessed, even though they may also derive great satisfaction from it, or even have been cured by it. In Dahomey, at the end of an initiation, I remember seeing the *Sakpatasi* (handmaidens of Sakpata, god of the earth and smallpox) delightedly brushing themselves off. This meant the *vodun* was leaving them, I was told. Jean Rouch recently told me that, for a certain Songhay adept of his acquaintance, going to a possession séance with the prospect of being possessed sometimes did not give him the slightest joy. "Playing horse" for a god is not necessarily an agreeable role. Even if they are benevolent, the divinities may not always leave as easily as one might like. In many cases they have to be coaxed before they will agree to go. But this does not mean that they are being driven out.

To be sure, "exorcism" is a word that can easily be used metaphorically. It is significant, however, that it was in an Italian music magazine, *Muzak*,[67] that I read the following statement by a young Moroccan musician, the founder of a group that draws its inspiration from Gnawa music: "I believe in the liberating value of trance through music, as a means of exorcising not the spirits of evil but, symbolically, the spirits of the twentieth century."[68]

4 The Strange Mechanism

In both possession and shamanism it is clear that music usually plays a role in triggering trance. But this "strange mechanism," as Jean Rouch would call it, has been the object of the most diverse, and sometimes utterly conflicting interpretations. Before moving on to the second part of this book, in which we shall look at trance in relation to Greek antiquity, the Renaissance, and Islam, let us examine the theories through which the facts have been viewed thus far. These theories gravitate around two poles: let us call them, using Jean-Jacques Rousseau's words, that of music's moral action and that of music's physical action. Various theories, we shall find, combine both aspects in different ways.

Rousseau and the Physical Power of Sounds

Jean-Jacques Rousseau—whom Claude Lévi-Strauss (1962) has called the founder of the social sciences—could also be seen as the founder of ethnomusicology, since some of the remarks in his *Dictionnaire de musique*,[1] and the *Essai sur l'origine des langues* fundamentally pose for music not only the problem of the "other" but also of the relations between nature and culture. It is therefore particularly interesting to note that he himself wavered between these two poles, that of moral action and that of physical action (another aspect of the culture/nature opposition) precisely with respect to tarantism. In Rousseau's time there was a great deal of discussion about the curative powers of music on the one hand and its physical action as mechanical vibrations on the other. In his *Dictionnaire* (1768, 312) Rousseau writes: "Although *music* has little power over the affections of the soul, it is nevertheless capable of acting physically upon bodies, witness the story of the Tarantula, which is too well known to recount here. . . ." Undaunted at having to contradict himself quite openly, he asserts the following in a passage from the *Essai,* which I feel I must quote in full:[2]

> As proof of the physical power of sounds, some adduce the healing of
> Tarantula stings. This example proves quite the opposite. Neither
> absolute sounds nor the same tunes are required to cure all those stung
> by this insect, for each needs the airs of a melody known to him and

phrases that he understands. The Italian must have Italian tunes, the Turk would need Turkish tunes. Each is only affected by accents familiar to him; one's nerves will respond only to the degree to which one's mind prepares them for it: he must understand the language spoken to him before what he is being told sets him in motion. Bernier's Cantatas are said to have healed a French musician's fever; they would have caused it in a musician of any other nation. [1970, 165]

Even though Rousseau, like everyone in his day, regarded tarantism as a particularly spectacular case of healing through music, whereas I regard it as a case of possession trance, what he relates in this passage is the very mechanism of the musical motto we described in a previous chapter. But for him, this interpretation of things is only one part of a much vaster theory of music as sign. Discussing sensations in the chapter "On Melody" of his *Essai* (ibid., 147), Rousseau writes: "they do not affect us solely as sensations, but as signs or images. . . ." Further on, in the chapter entitled "That Our Most Acute Sensations Mainly Act through Moral Impressions," (ibid., 163), he also writes: "As long as we choose to consider sounds only through the commotion they stir in our nerves, we shall never have the true principles of music and of its power over our hearts. Sounds in the melody do not act solely as sounds, but as *signs*[3] of our affections. . . ."[4]

In his *Dictionnaire de musique,* Rousseau applies this sign theory to a concrete case, that of the famous tune "Ranz des vaches," which among the Swiss can trigger what I, for the purposes of this book, have suggested we term emotional trance. Perhaps it is also worth underscoring that this reference to the "Ranz des vaches" is part of a long passage under the entry "Music," which is devoted to what one might call, anticipating somewhat, ethnomusicology, and that the tune is printed at the end of the volume along with four others, one Chinese, one Persian, and two Amerindian, with the intention, Rousseau says, of "enabling the Reader to judge for himself Peoples' various musical accents." This is what he writes:

> I have added on the same Plate the celebrated Ranz-des-Vaches, that Air so dear to the hearts of the Swiss that playing it in their Troops was forbidden on pain of death, because it made those who heard it weep, desert, or die, so ardent a desire did it arouse in them to see their country again. One would seek in vain in this Air the energetic accents capable of producing such astonishing effects. Those effects, which never take place in foreigners, derive solely from habit, from memories, from a thousand circumstances that, called back by this Air to those who hear it, and recalling their country, their former pleasures, their youth, and their whole manner of living, excite in them a bitter sorrow for having lost all that. The *music* is then not acting precisely as *music,* but as a mnemonic sign. Today, this Air, which is still the same as it ever was, does not have the same effects it once had on the

Swiss; because, having lost the taste for their previous simplicity,
they no longer regret it when reminded of it. So true is it that it is not in
their physical action that we must seek for the greatest effects of
Sounds upon the human heart. [1768, 314]

Elsewhere, replying in advance to those (and they would be numerous)
who would later consider the violence of the music, especially the drums,
as the principal stimulus to trance, he clarifies his thoughts even more by
writing: "musicians who view the power of sounds only in terms of the action of the air and the excitation of fibers are far from knowing in what the
force of this art truly resides. The closer they approach to physical impression the further they take it from its wellspring, and the more also do they
deprive it of its primitive energy."[5] To be sure, Rousseau did not foresee
the explosion of decibels favored in our day by certain types of pop music,
unleashed by multi-thousand-watt amplifiers through loudspeakers that
have become instruments of acoustico-musical aggression.

In adopting this position with respect to the "effects" of music, Rousseau was reacting against the ideas of his time—which he had initially
shared—and forged the way for cultural relativism in the field of music.
("Why is our most affecting music no more than empty noise to the ear of a
Caribbee?" he asked in the *Essai*.[6] "Are his nerves of a different nature
from ours. . . .") His interpretation of the way music acts in tarantism is
clearly the right one, but it was hardly listened to, and the conviction that
in such cases the musical sounds act through the "vibrations they excite in
our nervous systems" would continue to have partisans. In fact, certain recently expressed ideas on the effects of percussion instruments, particularly
those of the drum, belong to this trend of thought. Let us now examine
them.

Percussion and Drums

In an earlier chapter,[7] we considered at some length the possibility that the
triggering of trance may be attributable to a certain *sui generis* power
characteristic of musical instruments. We found, in fact, that this very
widespread hypothesis was unfounded, but certain conceptions are so
deeply engrained that I feel it necessary to return to this point once again,
and to look somewhat closely at the case of percussion instruments, in
particular the drum.

For a variety of reasons the drum is surrounded by such a particular
aura that not only the man in the street but also, very often, the man of science readily lends it very special powers. The often explosive, violent, and
brutal nature of the sounds it produces, and the frequently dramatic or
obsessive use to which it is put, indisputably confer upon the drum a particularly strong emotional impact. Its sound can be a truly aggressive

force, and its vibrations can have an almost palpable impact. Whether we observe it in Europe, where it is an instrument of war, or whether we envision it in those distant and barbaric lands in which literature and the cinema inevitably associate it with the bloody and tempestuous rites of "primitive" religions (particularly those ceremonies often indiscriminately lumped together under the vague term "voodoo"), the drum is regarded as the instrument par excellence of frenzy. If, to use Rousseau's terms, there is one instrument capable of "shaking our nerves," then it must, one would think, be the drum. Moreover, it is also the instrument par excellence of rhythm, and therefore of dance. It is easy to understand how, carried away by their imaginations, some poeple have believed that it is able physically, and as it were mechanically, to project people out of themselves. Hence the literature, often extremely bad, that has developed around the drum—the "piercing call of the tom-tom"!—and subsequently the scientific theories, of equally doubtful merit, that have recently been constructed around it, and which we will have to examine in greater detail later on. Let us begin, however, with percussion and with Rodney Needham's[8] article "Percussion and Transition," which appeared in 1967 in *Man*.

Starting from a number of reflections on the shaman beating his drum in order to establish contact with the spirits, Needham (1967, 607) gradually moves on to the observation that "All over the world . . .percussion . . . permits or accompanies communication with the other world." The problem then, according to him, is to discover what the exact relation is between the concept of spiritual existence and this "non-cultural affective appeal of percussion" (ibid., 610). Why "non-cultural"? Because the means used for this summons change from one society to another, because in some cases the drum is used, in others the gong, and in still others hand-clapping. Needham, therefore, states that the impact derives from percussion itself, and not from rhythm, melody, or the repetition of a particular note or resonance. After observing that "there is no doubt that sound-waves have neural and organic effects on human beings, irrespective of the cultural formation of the latter," he then adds that, of all sounds, those that produce the greatest effect of this kind are those obtained by percussion, since percussion involves the "foundations of aurally generated emotion" (ibid., 611).[9] Next, observing that drums and percussion instruments are not solely linked with communication with the other world, but are also used in many other circumstances, which are very often transition rites, Needham posits "a constant and immediately recognizable association between the type of sound and the type of rite," as a consequence of which, he argues, "there is a significant connection between percussion and transition" (ibid.). I shall not dwell on the validity of this proposition here, or on the argument Needham gives for the use of fireworks in Chi-

nese marriage ceremonies (explosions that represent percussion at its pur-
est, marriage which is the very archetype of the transition rite, fireworks
entirely devoid of any rhythmic character), or on his epistemological reflections suggested by the connection he posits. I would like only to observe that, as John Blacking stressed in his answer to Needham,[10] the notion of percussion constitutes an extremely disputable category in
musicology. This alone is sufficient to cast grave doubt on the validity of
the connection Needham has proposed. We know, moreover, that Claude
Lévi-Strauss devoted a whole section of his work *Du miel aux cendres* to
the "Instruments of Darkness." In a letter published by *Man* in answer to
Blacking, Needham expresses astonishment at not having found any confirmation of his views in the Lévi-Strauss work. The reason is, that although Lévi-Strauss does indeed discuss these instruments in relation to
"transition", he is careful not to regard the notion of "percussion"—which
is precisely what Blacking rejects—as a pertinent one.

Let us now come to the point of interest to us here. Referring to the triggering of trance in Haitian voodoo, Needham claims that it results from
disturbances brought about by the sounds of the drums "in the inner ear,
an organ which modulates postural attitudes, muscular tonus, breathing
rhythms, heartbeat, blood pressure, feelings of nausea, and certain eye reflexes."[11] For Needham, percussion thus should be viewed from a purely
acoustic viewpoint, and its effects from a purely physiological one. For
heuristic reasons (which are not worth repeating here and which I do not
find very convincing, moreover), Needham nevertheless regards the why
of this relation between "percussion and transition" as remaining open.

Two notes that appeared in *Man* the following year, in response to
Needham's article, suggested ways of extricating him from his difficulties
by taking the mechanistic aspect of his theory a stage further. True, both
writers contested the validity of the connection made between "percussion
and transition," judging it too general to be significant, and they were of
the opinion that stripping it of all reference to rhythm, as Needham did,
made it valueless. For it is the rhythm that is important, they both
claimed, not just percussion itself. One of these writers, however, again
resorts to Needham's arguments in order to explain the effect of drums on
the triggering of trance. If these effects are so widespread, W. C. Sturtevant (1968, 134) writes in his letter to the editor headed "Categories, Percussion and Physiology," it is because "some universal psychological or
physiological mechanism is at work." A. Jackson, for his part (1968,
297), in his article "Sound and Ritual" says that "since the brain is a common denominator to all mankind, it follows that what is true at the neurophysiological level must be universally true." Here we are more firmly en-
trenched than ever in the physical-effect-of-sounds camp. And the reason
these two authors feel so secure in their beliefs is that both are basing

themselves upon a neurophysiological theory of the effects of the drum
that they accept as proven, a theory according to which the rhythmic beating of this instrument is capable of producing a particular effect upon the
central nervous system and thereby triggering convulsions.

Sheila S. Walker (1972, 17–24), in her chapter on the neurophysiological aspects of possession, lends central importance to this theory, the validity of which she does not question for one moment. Although in this
same chapter (ibid., 24) she prudently confesses she cannot tell "why some
societies have drum-induced possessions and others do not," in her conclusion she loses all sight of that restriction, and those famous mechanical
effects of drumming are allotted, if not full responsibility, at least the major share of it in the triggering of trance: "The most fundamental element
of possession," she says, "is the presence of neurophysiological changes,
[and these] are most frequently produced by a sensory bombardment, usually in the form of the sonic driving[12] of the drum rhythms." A little later, observing that it is sometimes difficult to separate purely neurological elements from other kinds, she adds: "However, sometimes people seem to
be reacting just to the effects of the drums" (ibid., 148). And with reference to hypnosis and the important role it plays in possession, she notes
that "the hypnotic state is triggered by the altered state of consciousness
and changes in body ego produced by the neurophysiological effects of the
rhythmic drumming." It must be remembered that Walker in fact ascribes
very great importance to the cultural determinants of possession in general.
We see that for her one must nevertheless turn to a neurophysiological theory of the effects of drumming—the same theory invoked by Sturtevant
and Jackson—in order to find an explanation for the triggering of trance.

A Neurophysiological Theory of the Effects of Drumming

Let me begin, without preamble, by saying right away that this theory,
which is advanced by Andrew Neher, does not stand up to examination,
and that it is not necessary to be a specialist in the field to see why. However, the scientific, or rather pseudoscientific, apparatus with which it is
surrounded has earned it a certain credit, as is attested not only by the attention paid to it by the three authors already mentioned, but also by the
pages Raymond Prince (1968, 133–35) devoted to it in his article on en-
cephalography and research into possession states, by the allusions made
to it during the 1968 Paris Colloquium by various ethnologists, and by the
reference T. F. Johnston (1972, 30) makes to it in his article on possession
music among the Tsonga, in which it is clear that he, too, regards it as a
given.[13] I therefore have no choice but to examine this theory in fairly
great detail.

Neher's theory, the subject of an article published in 1962, and the only
one to which the authors just mentioned refer, is based upon the results of

a number of laboratory experiments reported a year earlier in an article dealing solely with neurophysiology and containing no allusion whatsoever to possession. The very title of the main article (that of 1962), "Physiological Explanation of Unusual Behavior in Ceremonies Involving Drums," demonstrates the confusion that reigns from the outset. In whose eyes is the behavior in question "unusual"? Not once is this question even asked. The article deals, Neher tells us, with this behavior, "often described as a trance state, in which the individual experiences unusual perceptions or hallucinations. In the extreme cases contraction of the body and generalized convulsion are reported" (1962, 151). The ethnographical descriptions quoted refer to both possession and shamanism.

The thesis is that intermittent acoustic stimuli having particular characteristics are capable of "driving" the brain's alpha rhythms and thereby triggering convulsions. These particular characteristics are: (1) with respect to intermittency, a bass frequency corresponding more or less to the frequency band of the alpha rhythm, which can vary from eight to thirteen cycles per second, according to the individual; and (2) with respect to the acoustical spectrum, a predominance of bass frequencies (musical frequencies in this case) since they are capable of transmitting more energy to the brain than higher frequencies without doing damage to the ear.

Neher derived the hypothesis from which this theory sprang from research done by various authors on the effects of intermittent light stimuli, which showed that the latter are capable of causing behavioral disturbances and even epileptic fits (Neher 1961, 449; 1962, 153–54).

His arguments are based on: (1) the results of his laboratory experiments using a drum; (2) the results of prior experiments done by various scholars on the effects of light stimuli; (3) musical transcriptions of African drumming and recordings of Haitian music; (4) ethnographical descriptions. This ragbag of arguments, put forward in a very confused way, hardly inspires confidence, but here again, let us move on.

For his laboratory experiment, Neher (1961, 449) used a drum delivering a signal of low frequency (75–150 kh) and high volume (120 db), struck at the relatively low frequency of three, four, six, and eight beats a second, because "it was difficult to beat the drum faster"! The two published encephalograms (ibid., 451), each of a different brain, were obtained by using a beat of four strokes per second, as the trace indicates. They show, Neher says, that the results of the stimulation were, in both cases, (1) a "driving" phenomenon; and (2) blinking of the left eyelid. The blinking was observed in half of the ten subjects taking part in the experiment, the driving phenomenon having been observed in all of them. It seems, however, that the results obtained with the faster speeds of six or eight strokes per second were not good, since the loudness of the signal decreased at these frequencies, "which were not easy to attain" (ibid., 449).

On the strength of these experiments, Neher feels he is justified in concluding that: (1) the responses he obtained in his laboratory with auditory stimulation are "similar" (ibid., 451) to those obtained by others with "photic driving"; and (2) they confirm the proposed; hypothesis, namely, that the "unusual behavior [read: the convulsions] observed in drum ceremonies is mainly the result of rhythmic drumming which affects the central nervous system" (1962, 159).

I should like to point out first that whereas, according to Neher (ibid., 154), light stimulation has indeed brought on behavioral disorders that can reach the stage of "clinical psychopathic states and epileptic seizures," he, Neher, has managed to produce nothing more than "involuntary eyeblinks" (1961, 450). Even invoking, as he does, Fischer's Exact Probability Test, there is some abuse, I would think, in regarding these results as being of equal value, and in claiming, as a consequence, that in other conditions (perhaps by hitting the drum quicker? But this is not easy!) he would have obtained the same responses, or in any case responses that could be diagnosed as "musicogenic epilepsy" (1962, 153). Second, there is no reason to accept without further proof that the behavioral disorders observed in a laboratory under the effect of intermittent stimuli of any kind, visual or auditory, are of the same nature as those observed in possession trances. There are many different kinds of convulsion. Neher makes reference to epilepsy. In Senegal (Andras Zempléni, personal communication), the first duty of those responsible for *ndöp* séances is to ascertain, in the case of nonritualized crisis, whether it is the result of epilepsy or, on the contrary, attributable to possession. Third, *a priori,* the kind of parameters chosen for the stimulation casts doubt upon the experimental value of the procedure. The auditory stimuli used in the laboratory, being totally constant in form and intensity, have in practice very little in common with the constantly varying stimuli provided by drums played in possession séances.

All this should suffice, I believe, to arouse extreme skepticism with respect to Neher's theory. But there are even more decisive reasons for being skeptical. Neher bases his arguments, as I have said, partly on his own laboratory experiments, partly on ethnomusicological data. I shall state later what I think of the latter. Be that as it may, however, Neher considers that (1) *a priori* the frequency most likely to induce the driving of the alpha rhythm lies in "the range of slightly below 8 to 13 cycles a second" (1962, 154); (2) in reality, as described in ethnomusicological documents (musical transcriptions and sound recordings), "agitated behavior occurs with drum frequencies that reach 8 or 9 cycles per second" (ibid.); (3) he has obtained results himself with drumbeats of four cycles per second. This means, ultimately, that the phenomena in question can occur when drums are struck at a speed varying from, let us say, twelve beats per second to four beats per second; in other words, when they are played at anywhere between MM 240 and 720. These cadences cover the whole spectrum of tempi from *moderato* to *prestissimo* and beyond. So, unless it is slow, drumming of any kind must therefore be able to trigger "driving." In other words, every time a drum is played, or almost, we should expect to see people go into convulsions. At least this would be the normal conclusion of Neher's arguments. Needless to say, this makes no sense. If Neher were right, half of Africa would be in a trance from the beginning of the year to the end.

Let me add, just in case it seems necessary, that (1) the musical transcriptions he invokes to support his theory relate to ceremonies that have nothing to do with possession and in which, naturally enough, no trances or convulsions ever occur; (2) although the recordings he cites (made by Courlander, which is no coincidence, as we shall see) are indeed of possession music, I could cite dozens of others, all with the same rhythms, that are not. As for the ethnographical texts, there is no point in even talking about them: not one of them proves anything at all about the subject under discussion, and some are quite simply ludicrous. But the quotation he takes from Courlander (1944, 45) is nevertheless significant. On the subject of drums and possession in Haiti, Courlander indeed says[14] that as a result of preconditioning, "whenever these rhythms are heard possession is induced." Clearly, texts of this kind, and there are a great many, inspired Neher's hypothesis. I have no intention of criticizing Courlander, whose work is justly and unanimously respected. I only wish to emphasize that such information must be used with extreme prudence and that this is precisely what Neher fails to do.

I have dealt with this theory at length, I would like to repeat, only because it has sometimes, quite wrongly, been taken seriously. But because Neher's theory is valueless does not mean that we are not justified in asking ourselves whether the sound of drums, which does incontestably have, at least in certain cases, a genuine physical impact upon the listener, is not capable of inducing certain perturbations of the physiological nervous state and thereby contribute to triggering trance. Others besides Neher have thought so. Dr. Charles Pidoux, for instance (1955, 278), a physician who has been acquainted with possession cults in Mali for a long time and who is also an ethnopsychiatrist, hypothesized that drumbeats might act upon "different levels of the neural axis." The research work on which he bases his ideas has unfortunately not been published, so it is impossible to make any judgment on the matter.

It is my view that given the present state of our knowledge, contrary to what may have been said, there is no valid theory to justify the idea that the triggering of trance can be attributed to the neurophysiological effects of drum sounds. This does not mean that drumming is never responsible for entry into trance, it means only that when it is responsible it is so for reasons of another kind.

From Hypnosis to Conditioned Reflex and from Emotions to Drugs

Let us now leave theories conceived in the abstract and pass on to those resulting from the observation of trance in the field, and even, sometimes, from personal experience of it. How do those who have observed and described trance conceive of the relations that may exist between music and trance on the psychophysiological level? What explanation do they offer, at this level, for that "strange mechanism" which is the triggering of trance?

Some of them regard music as having hypnotic action upon the nervous system. For instance, Nina Rodrigues, a Brazilian doctor of medicine strongly influenced by the work of Charcot and Janet, and whose writings are a milestone in the study of the *candomblé* wrote eighty years ago on the "somnambulism brought on by the hallucination of sacred music" (Rodrigues 1935, 122) and on "the unusual monotony" of the drumming, "capable of rivaling all the various means of inducing hypnosis by fatigue and concentration" (ibid., 111). Moving from Brazil to South Africa, H. A. Junod regarded entry into trance as the result of hypnotic suggestion exerted by a "noisy concert" (1913, 445) to which the patient was subjected hour after hour, a concert in which drums and rattles combined to guarantee the continuity of a terribly intense sound, a "frightful hubbub," or "infernal" or "hideous din." Although, as we saw, he also writes: "That which is the most essentially necessary is the *singing,* the human voice . . ." (ibid., 441), and although he recognizes the importance of the meaning of the words, it is clear that for him the music acts largely by overloading the nervous system, by a physical harrassment, one might say, that reduces the patient to a state of exhaustion and nervous crisis.

Still in the same line of thought, the much more recent description that Katerina Kakouri (1965, 21, 25) gives of the trance of the Anastenarides in Thrace, also presents music as acting directly on the nervous state of those involved, with the "heavy sound" of the drum and its "persistent beat" which gets on the nerves of the initiates or on the "strained nerves of the possessed." It is indeed the physical action of sound on the nervous system that is openly involved here. But behind other, much less explicit formulations, such as that of R. Firth (1969, xiii), who refers to the "monotonous beating of drum," or that of D. Carpitella (1966, 360), who speaks of the "obsessive rhythmic repetition" of the tarantella, one can still perceive the same idea of hypnosis as resulting from the manipulation through music of the nervous system of the person who will be or already is entranced. Many more similar examples could be cited.

To consider the mechanism of entry into trance as a conditioned reflex that is due to a musical stimulus is a quite different idea. We owe this theory to Herskovits, who developed it within the framework of his general interpretation of possession as it can be observed in the *candomblé* of Brazil. Reacting against the views of Nina Rodrigues and her successors, who treated trance as a psychopathological phenomenon, Herskovits thought of reinserting it into the general system of religious representations characteristic of that society. He wanted to show in this way that possession trance should be viewed as a normal state resulting from apprenticeship to a cultural model, itself largely determined by history.

> The psychological process we have in view is that which is very clearly defined by the expression 'conditioned reflex,'[15] which means that every time a specific stimulus is applied, there is a corresponding reaction, the individual having been accustomed to behave in this way in response to an agreed-upon signal. There is nothing abnormal in this process—quite the contrary, since it represents the psychological level at which a large part of our existence is lived. Now let us imagine a person who has been brought up in a cultural environment in which there is a profound belief in divinities, and in which he has been taught since childhood that he will receive, or be capable of receiving, one of these divinities; that these deities are summoned by the intermediary of specific drum rhythms and chants, to which they respond by descending upon the heads of those chosen to serve them. There is a good chance that, in the presence of the stimulus constituted by all the factors of a given situation conforming to the indications I have just given, the response will not be long delayed, and that possession will take place. [Herskovitz 1943a, 25]

The broad lines of this theory were taken up by Roger Bastide (1945) two years later; but Bastide places even more emphasis than Herkovits on the importance of the situation. "The music does not inevitably lead to trance," he writes (1945, 88),[16] for "the selfsame rhythm that on a day of ceremony will produce a possession crisis in an individual, will produce nothing if he hears it outside this context, since the stimulus of the conditioned reflex, as described by Herskovits, is not a physical stimulus, the hearing of a particular rhythm, but a psychic stimulus, the rhythm associated with a certain day and with a certain place. It is also necessary for the initiate to have had his body purified by certain herbal baths. A set of factors, regulated by society, must all be present together, otherwise the music will have no effect at all."[17] This being so, one would expect Bastide to reject the notion of conditioned reflex in this context. This is not the case, however. Despite the restrictive clause that he inserts into its operation and that he opposes to Herskovits's thesis, when he writes (1955, 501) "it is not a stimulus [music] that determines trance . . .it is the total situation that acts . . .[it] is the total situation that causes music to lead to trance, or, on the contrary, prevents it from producing crisis," he still remains faithful to it, for in his last writings on trance (1972, 73) he states that it is because of "conditioned reflexes" that, once initiated, the adept can go into trance again "upon hearing certain musical leitmotifs."

We still must ask, nonetheless, if it is in fact legitimate to speak of conditioned reflex in these circumstances, since either it really is one, in which case it ought to occur in response to its stimulus in any situation, or else the stimulus sometimes does not obtain a response, in which case it is not a reflex of this type that is involved. The question is an important one, since it involves the level of consciousness at which the mechanism of entry into trance operates. I myself am inclined to think that if the triggering of trance by music is subject to so many circumstantial restrictions—and observation undoubtedly confirms that it is—then to talk of conditioned reflex merely adds to the confusion. Hence the rather oblique use that has been made of this term. Thus Pierre Verger (1969, 59) tells us that rhythmic motifs played on drums are the basis of "a sort of conditioned reflex" acquired during initiation. For Jacqueline Monfouga-Nicolas "the musico-gestural whole" (1927, 189) constituted by possession dance should be regarded as the "conditional stimulus" enabling trance to become a "conditioned reflex," but elsewhere she observes that "the music does not induce the trance itself but the form it must take" (ibid., 197). Margaret Field (1969, 7), for her part, uses the word "conditioned" but without associating it with reflex. Having noted that in Ghana "drumming, singing, clapping, and the rhythmic beating of gong-gongs and rattles, alone or all together, are the commonest inducers of trance," she adds: "Most people who are possessed as part of their profession—priests, diviners, priestly auxiliaries, and medicine-men's auxiliaries—are *conditioned*[18] to become possessed when they place themselves suitably, just as most of us are *conditioned* to fall asleep in a comfortable bed in a dark, quiet room. Some priests have only to enter the sanctuary when the drums and gongs are beating and the flute wailing. Some diviners gaze into a black liquid to the sound of gongs. Another may have to hold upon his head, again to the sound of gongs, a weight heavy enough to make his neck ache."[19] But there are occasions when the spirit, like sleep, is wooed in vain.

Other writers have, more or less explicitly, made use of various combinations of the conditioned reflex theory inherited from Herskovits, that of the neurophysiological effect of drumming taken from Neher, and that of the total situation taken from Bastide. Thus Gisele Cossard, whose interpretations are especially interesting because they are based on the personal experience of being initiated into the *candomblé*, on the one hand writes (1967, 175) that "at the time of initiation a correspondence was established between the rhythm and the trance state," and on the other (ibid., 162) that "one is inclined to wonder if there is not some physiological action of certain sounds on the organism."[20] The reference she then makes to "low-frequency vibrations" echoes the Neher theory,[21] although she does not name him. Indeed, she then goes on to say that "when the person goes into trance he makes the characteristic gesture of putting his hands over his ears as if to protect himself from the sounds besieging him." Nevertheless, for Cossard music ultimately is only one element in a whole set of stimuli made up of "auditory sensations: rhythm of drumbeats, song, ringing of the *adza* bell, cries of greeting to the *orisha;* sensations of taste and smell: smell and taste of the *abo;*[22] visual sensations: sight of the consecrated objects representing the *orisha* or used to adorn him" (ibid., 192).

Another category of explanation highlights the disturbances music—and also dance—produce in the inner ear. For Zémpleni, in the *ndöp,* where "the ritual crisis is the normal termination of the dance and collapse is the natural conclusion of the 'crisis'" (1966, 414), the "physiological trigger of collapse" is "vestibular autostimulation," which, "owing to the increasing volume and pace of the music," leads or rather "drives" the possessed person to "extreme muscular exhaustion and spatial disorientation" (ibid., 417).[23] This "spatial disorientation" thus seems to be caused partly by music acting (at the physiological level) on the ear by means of its volume and intensity, which can attain an "almost intolerable" level (ibid., 359), and partly by the set of motor behavior patterns centered around dance and constituting what Zémpleni calls "the labor of crisis" (ibid., 415).

The interpretation proposed by Francis Huxley in relation to Haitian voodoo is very similar. For him, trance is largely due to perturbations in the inner ear produced by drummers who manipulate the music until the "buffets" of the sound have achieved their full effect (1967, 286), while drumming, dancing, and singing combine in order to achieve these perturbations that would set off a process of the dissociation of consciousness (ibid., 287). However, he also says that the drummers succeed in setting off this dissociation only in those who are "ready" for it. In other words, Huxley introduces a restrictive clause similar to the one asserted by Bastide when he writes that if a set of conditions is not completely realized, "music has no effect at all." For the same reason that I doubted earlier the existence of a "conditioned reflex," I am now skeptical about the reality of these "perturbations of the inner ear": either they exist and do in fact induce the trance, in which case they should have the same effect in all circumstances, or else they do not always have this effect, in which case why resort to them as an explanation, since it is in any event no more than hypothetical? We might as well do away with it.

I should point out, however, that this theory of trance as being caused by perturbations of the inner ear was advanced as early as 1948 by Dr. Aubin, a physician, but only in relation to the dance element, which he de-

scribed as including "movements of neck and torso both resulting in frenzied movement of the head, which is subjected to truly vertiginous gyra-
tions and repeated shaking in every direction." "This orgy of movements"
results, he says, in "a violent excitation of the labyrinth." "We know by the
same token that it [the excitation] engenders, from the psychic point of
view, a special state of exaltation,"[24] concludes the author who, as we can
see, confounds reasoning and tautology.

However, I had better make my position clear. Though I am skeptical
about perturbations of the inner ear, I do not necessarily deny that certain
movements (particularly rotating the head or spinning round and round
on the spot) do in fact produce them. What I am disputing is that these
perturbations should be seen as constituting trance, and that they are held
to be automatic. In the *zār* cult, the *gurri* (the dance in relation to which
Leiris quotes the passage from Aubin given above) marks "the departure
of the spirit as well as its arrival" (1958, 18); in other words it is associated
as much with the end of the trance as with its onset. This fact alone is
proof enough that it does not inevitably produce loss of balance in those
who perform it.

It is, moreover, necessary to distinguish between two aspects of these
perturbations of the inner ear. One is linked with the movements just described, and within the limitations I have mentioned there is no reason to
doubt their existence; the other is attributed not to the movements made
by the subject but to the sounds he is made to hear. The intensity of these
sounds is such, the argument goes, that they engender an "oversaturation"
of the ear that causes people to lose their balance. That is the theory. I will
not repeat the objection I made to it in an earlier chapter, and which questions why this oversaturation affects only one particular person and not all
those around him. This objection alone demolishes the thesis. What I
think ought to be stressed here is the very subjective nature of this theory.
Everyday experience tells us that such intensity of sound judged to be intolerable by some people can be considered extremely desirable by others.
Witness our present-day pop concerts, in which the sound level, to the delight of the fans, reaches a threshold that is to me personally (in all my subjectivity) intolerable. It is to be feared that in judging the "violence" of the
drumming that so often accompanies possession dances, those who see it
as a factor in producing sensorial perturbation are only interpreting the
facts in a very subjective manner.

Alongside, or in opposition to, the various theories I have listed so far,
all of which claim the onset of trance results, at least in part, from the
physical action of music on the nervous system, there are others that make
absolutely no use of this kind of explanation. This holds true particularly
of the thesis of Jean Rouch, for whom the onset of trance results from psychological much more than physiological manipulation of the subject by

the *zima;* that is to say, by the priest-musician officiating at the ritual. That Rouch should opt for such an interpretation is made all the more interesting by the fact that possession music among the Songhay is, in fact, characterized by very violent drumming.[25] This drumming is provided, as we know, by large gourds upturned on the sand and fitted with a device that increases their resonance.[26] The drummers play them with sticks arranged in a fan formation, which enables them to obtain percussive effects of unusual intensity. As for the dance, it too is characterized by violence, and often entails rotation of the head at the neck. All these conditions might well prompt an observer to evoke perturbations of the inner ear caused both by sensorial oversaturation and physical overexcitation. Yet Rouch does not once allude to any phenomenon of this kind. Having observed that "a possession dance can last for several hours, even for several days, without success" (which excludes, *ipso facto,* that the dancing and music mechanically produce an effect), he goes on: "But when the *zima* know their job well, these failures are rare: the music, the words of the mottoes, the steps of the dance, trigger the strange mechanism" (1960, 148). There then follows a description of entry into trance that I must quote in full:

> At an imperceptible sign, the priests and musicians sense that one of
> the genii summoned is beginning to manifest itself (they feel "a cool breeze"
> on their faces); at this, they dispense with the usual order of the
> dances, the band now plays only one theme, the *zima* recite only one
> motto. The dancers as a group continue the steps they are performing,
> of course, but one of them, and he alone, has now become the
> object of the priests' solicitude; they surround him and recite
> increasingly efficacious mottoes to him while pointing alternately to his
> left and right: the genius must come neither to the left nor to the
> right, but in the middle, onto the dancer himself. Abruptly, the latter
> quivers, weeps, and halts. Already his movements are no longer those of
> dance but those of convulsion, and when the trembling reaches
> paroxysm the dancer rolls on the ground and howls: the dance is over.
> At this very moment a god incorporates himself in the man's body.
>   When he has been calmed somewhat by the attentions of the 'quiet
> women' and risen to his feet again, the Holey's behavior, voice, and
> gait become completely different from what they were before his
> possession. They are characteristic of the genius present within him, and
> enable this deity to be recognized with unfailing accuracy: for
> example, the paralytic *Hargey* stay on their knees and move about by
> hopping on them; *Kyirey,* who has only one eye, keeps one eye
> closed; *Zatao* covers his head with dust and eats earth; *Nyalya,* who is a
> coquette, on the contrary shakes off the dust that soils her; *Sadvara,*
> who is a snake crawls on the ground; *Dongo,* the spirit of thunder,
> points at the heavens and groans . . .all specific patterns of

behavior: myth materializes in the most singular way, its invisible
characters appear to all the world as they are. And so that this identity
can be even more complete, the genii themselves are the ones who
demand their ritual vestments and props, in that [type of] voice which
also is halting, alien, and distant.

From the viewpoint of our present subject, what is striking in this description is that Rouch lays no stress either on the frenzy of the dance
(even though he does describe it a short while before) or on the violence of
the drumming. What he highlights is the fact that the band concentrates
on a single tune and that the *zima* only recite the one motto. Tune or
motto, it comes to the same thing: a musical message, which is a sign and
which has a psychological, not a physiological impact on the subject
whose entry into trance is being prepared. In fact this description might
have been made to illustrate our Rousseau quotation earlier: "for each
needs the airs of a melody known to him and phrases that he understands." As for trance, it is described as being made up, first, of a crisis,
which is an emotional paroxysm, then of a change of identity, which, of
course, also has much more to do with psychology than physiology.

Another example of an interpretation of the role of music that makes no
reference to any kind of "physical power of sounds" is provided by an African ethnomusicologist, J. H. Kwabena Nketia. Talking of possession in
African society in general, but with particular reference to Ghana, he
writes: "it is believed that the state of ecstasy or of possession can be
quickly induced and sustained by means of special music closely correlat-
ed with specific forms of bodily action. It is believed also that the gods are
sensitive to this music. Opportunities are, therefore, sought to call to
them while the dancing is going on, in the hope that they will 'possess' the
dancers as they are emotionally prepared to receive them" (1957, 5).
Here, then, music and dance act in conjunction to produce an emotional
state favorable to possession.

Curiously enough, the emotional component of trance plays almost no
part at all in interpretations that have been made of the onset of possession, and Nketia is an exception in thinking, as he does, that music paves
the way for it at an emotional level. On the contrary, one of the principal
accounts we have of shamanism, that of Shikogoroff, places a great deal of
emphasis on this component, and presents music as contributing in a decisive way to this "growth of emotion" that leads to trance. But here again,
as we saw,[27] the restrictive clause we have already mentioned twice comes
into play: the shaman still has to will his trance.

In the second part of this book, in the chapter concerning the Arabs, we
shall be dealing at length with musical emotion as a factor in triggering
trance. For the moment I will limit myself to underscoring the fact that
with this emotion we enter the psychological dimensions of trance, and—

to use Rousseau's terminology once again—that in this case it is the "moral action" of the music that is at work, not its physical action.

Ultimately, then, one might search in vain for the reasons why the role of music in triggering the "strange mechanism" has so often been viewed as physiological in nature and, consequently (the final point I wish to make in this chapter), as more or less comparable in its action to the use of a drug. Yet this is implicitly the interpretation that Lewis, for example, arrives at when, in listing the various means used to induce trance, he comes to music (and dance) just after having cited "the inhalation of smokes and vapors" and just before going on to "the ingestion of such drugs as mescaline or lysergic acid" (1971, 39). Nor is it by chance that we read, in a passage devoted by Lenora Greenbaum to possession in sub-Saharan Africa, that possession trance "may be induced by drugs, music, or other methods external to the individual" (1973, 42). To express things in this way is to imply that the action of music is of the same order as that of a drug, which does, incontestably, act in a "physical" way. Although it is perfectly permissible to say, metaphorically, that music is a drug, in the present context, which is not that of metaphor, it simply contributes to general confusion.

I hope I have demonstrated by now that nothing authorizes us to think that music—at least insofar as it is being heard, not made, which is the case in possession—plays any direct role in the onset of trance other than by means of its "moral action."

PART TWO

It is through integration that the quality of things changes.
François Jacob, La logique du vivant

5 Music and Trance among the Greeks

In ancient Greece, trance, although this is too often forgotten today, constituted a very important aspect of religious life. Dionysiac practices, with their wild behavior and violence, do of course form an integral part of the picture we tend to have nowadays of Greek religion. Rohde, and many others after him, have given accounts of these practices. Nietzsche celebrated them at length. Even though Jeanmaire and Dodds (respectively in *Dionysos* and in *The Greeks and the Irrational,* both published in 1951) made it quite plain more than thirty years ago, we still too often ignore the fact that possession trance was the mainspring of the cult of Dionysus-Bacchus. That Bacchus was the god of the vine and wine is obviously no mere chance; to get drunk is ultimately no more than a particular way of no longer being oneself. But Dionysiac frenzy can no more be reduced to drunkenness than Dionysus can be reduced to Bacchus, contrary to what the current usage of his latinized name would lead us to believe. From the standpoint of the history of religions, the feeling of elatedness due to wine is no more than an anecdotal and fairly recent aspect of the much more ancient, and much more universal elatedness due to trance. Moreover, religious frenzy was not limited among the Greeks to the worship of Dionysus. Everyone knows that the actual functioning of the Delphic oracle, another essential aspect of Greek religion—this time linked with Apollo, god of music—relied in part at least upon the practice of mediumistic trance. In addition, like so many other peoples, the Greeks regarded the inspiration of the poet (and of the musician, since the two were for a long while inseparable) as being nothing other than a trance. Finally, Plato, as we shall see, held that there was no true love other than mad love, and that this madness, also stemming from the gods, was a trance.

It is of particular interest for us to examine the relations between music and trance in ancient Greece more closely than it has been hitherto. First, because of the importance Greek civilization has for us. Second, because of its key position, both in space and time: at the juncture of archaic societies (those that have constituted the main areas of our observations up till now) and the Middle East, hence the Arabs, who undoubtedly owe certain aspects (recent ones, actually) of trance as practiced by the Sufis to the

Greeks, but who, above all, have profoundly affected trance as it is observed today in large sections of Africa, both black and white. Finally, because we are indebted to Plato for the most ancient theory of the relations between music and trance. A fascinating theory, moreover, first because of the stature of its author, but also because it has the unique quality of being at one and the same time the theory, first, of an observer who certainly did not practice trance himself and only half-believed in possession, but who belonged to a society in which it was an everyday occurrence; and second, of a philosopher, one of whose major concerns was to integrate the irrational into that essentially rational system of the world that he strove all his life to construct.

I have just written the word *system*. For it is in fact the tireless quest for a vision of things and men at once all-embracing and unified, in short the search for an all-encompassing coherence, that is the very hallmark of Plato's thought. His theory of the relations between music and trance—for it is a true theory, as we shall see—is consequently not separable either from what he thought of music or trance or from his general theory of the world. In order to reach the thick of the matter, that is to say, these very relations, we must begin from the start. I shall do my best, however, to limit myself to the indispensible.

Mania and Its Terminology

That the word *mania* among the ancient Greeks meant what I have been calling "trance" throughout this book is something that will become apparent as this chapter proceeds. For the moment, therefore, let us take this for granted and begin by asking ourselves what Plato's conception of *mania* was. Even so, one point should still be clarified. Although from our perspective, the word *mania* can be considered as the exact equivalent of "trance," depending on the context, I shall translate it sometimes by "madness" and sometimes by "frenzy." The reader should see no inconsistency in this. "Madness" and "frenzy" are in fact more accurate translations of *mania* as the Greeks understood it, and it is their viewpoint that is important to us at the moment. We should note, however, that although "madness" (or the French *folie*) is, along with "frenzy," the most frequently used translation of the Greek *mania,* this has not always been the case. During the Renaissance, to mention only one period, it was rendered in French as *fureur* and in Italian as *furore* (Cicero said "furor"), both of which were just as legitimate as *folie,* albeit signifying another aspect of things. Today, *Orlando furioso* ought to be translated "Mad Orlando" rather than "Furious Orlando." In the seventeenth and eighteenth centuries, Michel Foucault points out in his *Histoire de la folie a l'âge classique,* that *fureur* was a "technical term in jurisprudence and medicine" designating "a very precise form of madness."

This said, what did the word *mania* mean for Plato? The answer is to be found partly in the *Timaeus* and partly in the *Phaedrus*.[1] In the *Timaeus* (86b), having given a general account of the diseases of the body (*sōma nosēmata*), he turns to those of the soul (*psychē*),[2] whose specific disease, he says, is dementia (*anoia*), which is of two kinds: either madness (*mania*) or ignorance (*amathia*). And he adds: "Whatever affection a man suffers from, if it involves either of these conditions, it must be termed 'disease'; and we must maintain that pleasures and pains in excess are the greatest of the soul's diseases." Oddly enough, but significant no doubt, Plato's reflections in the *Timaeus* on the classification of *mania* stop there. It contains no allusion whatsoever to something found in the *Phaedrus*, a much earlier work, in which he makes what is for us a crucial distinction (265a–b) between two different kinds of *mania*, one arising from human diseases (*nosēmatōn anthrōpinōn*) and the other from a divine state (*theias exallagēs*) "which releases us from the customary habits." He then divides this state into four sorts of mania, four different kinds of madness each inspired (*epipnoian*) by a God: "mantic," (by Apollo), "telestic," (by Dionysus), "poetic" (by the Muses), and "erotic" (by Eros and Aphrodite). This is how in a celebrated and often quoted passage, Socrates summarizes and characterizes in one word the four forms of madness he had just described in his discourse to Phaedrus on love.

This manner of characterizing the four forms of madness merits closer attention. Three of the four are defined by means of epithets concerning their function: the one leading to divination is called "mantic," the one stirring the poet to creation is "poetic," and the one inspiring the lover to transports of frenzied love is "erotic." The fourth, however, is defined from a quite different standpoint, a formal rather than a functional one. It is called "telestic," meaning it entails *teletai,* or rites. In other words it is "ritual" madness. As we shall see before long, this telestic frenzy is nothing other than what we have been calling possession trance. For Plato, then, that which characterizes the possession trance first and foremost and distinguishes it from other forms of trance, is the fact that it is ritual. About these rites themselves he provides few details, no doubt considering it pointless to elaborate on facts with which the reader of his day would be familiar, and presuming that the latter would know them well enough. Fortunately, he nevertheless writes enough about them (*Laws* 791a–b) for us to know they essentially consisted of sacrifices, dances, and music. We can also be sure, moreover, whatever the arguments aroused by the interpretation of the word *teletai* (we will return to it), that these rites also comprised an initiatory aspect, of varying importance, and that they must have been secret, to some extent at least.

Now that we have defined each of the four forms of *mania,* and in particular telestic *mania* (possession trance), let us return to what they have in common. Divine madness is the lot assigned to certain humans by the gods; it is their personal and divinely ordained fate (*theia moira*) and at the same time a manifestation of "enthusiasm" (*enthusiasmos*),[3] which is to say the presence of a god in the person who is prey to this frenzy. That person is in fact *entheos* or "engodded," as we ought to be able to say in order to convey that "the god is in him."[4] This is the word that Plato utilizes to designate the Sybil prey to mantic madness in the *Phaedrus* (244b), the lover prey to mantic madness in the *Symposium* (179a), and the poet possessed by the Muse in the *Ion* (534b). It is also the word used by Euripides in Hippolytus to speak of the state of Phaedra,[5] who suffers from a hidden ill (*kryptō pathei*) and who wants to put an end to her life: "O young woman are you not engodded [*entheos*] by Pan or Hecate, led astray [*phoitas*] by the awful Corybantes, or by the Mother who reigns over the hills? Would it be some faults [*amplakiais*] committed against the ardent huntress Dictynna[6] for not having sacrificed victims for her?" asks the Chorus. (We will come back to this fault later on.)

But let us return to Plato and the *Ion*. In this dialogue Socrates pokes fun at a rhapsodist named Ion who is utterly astonished to learn from him that when he recites the *Illiad*, he is possessed by Homer (*Ion*, 536b). Here the words "enthusiasm" and "enthusiastic" alternate with "possession" (*katokōchē*), which stems from the verb *katechō*, meaning "to hold firmly, retain, contain, detain, possess, take hold of, occupy a place," in the military sense of the word, and from there, "to possess," in the sense we use it here. When this passage of the *Ion* deals with poetic madness, enthusiasm and possession are synonymous. When he is inspired, the poet is said to be *entheos* ("enthusiastic"), *katechōmenos* ("possessed"), or *mainomenos* ("enmaddened"), a word not only reserved for humans but also applicable to the gods, as is attested by the appellations of both Dionysus and Heracles Mainomenos.

Other Greek words also serve to signify the state of possession.[7] In the *Ion* (536a–b), speaking of the relation existing between the poets and the divinity inspiring them and describing it under the form of a "mighty chain" hanging down, Socrates says: "One poet is suspended from one Muse, another from another; we call it being possessed, but the fact is much the same since he is held." And he adds that some poets "are filled with inspiration" by Orpheus, others by Musaeus. "But the majority are possessed and held [*katechōntai te kai echōntai*] by Homer." Alongside the verb *echō*, carry, lead, grasp, hold," which also forms part of the verb *katechein*,[8] which we have already mentioned and which is probably most frequently used with reference to possession, the Greeks also used *lambanō* "take in one's hands, grasp, take possession of, occupy," and hence "to take hold of, possess" in the sense we use it in this book. This term is attested in one of the oldest Greek texts we have on possession, that by Herodotus (consequently, one century before Plato), in which we read, in the famous passage recounting how the Scythian Skyles was punished by his own people for having been initiated into Greek possession rites: "You mock us, Scythians, because we give ourselves up to Bacchic transports and the god takes hold [*lambanei*] of us . . ." (Herodotus, 4. 79). To convey the fact that the possession state has become total, that it is at its height, Euripides writes that the god "in his fullness floods" the human body (*sōm' elthē polys*) (*Bacchae* 300) of the one he possesses. And the latter, he notes, is then able to "tell the future," an observation tied to what I said earlier concerning the transition linking possession and mediumship. Among the Greeks, as elsewhere, there is no break in continuity between the two, but only complete possession leads to mantic states, in other words the kind of possession that presupposes a long experience of trances and that is for this reason characteristic of officiants and not neophytes.

The term *theoleptos*, "seized by the god," which expresses the idea that the god is present in the person subject (*entheos*) to frenzy and that the latter has been invested or seized by this god, is more recent and does not occur under this form in Plato. But in the *Phaedrus* (238c) Plato has Socrates say, in a joking mood, that he would nearly feel like a "nympholept," that is to say possessed by a nymph.

Alongside the words *mania* ("madness"), *enthusiasmos* ("enthusiasm"), and *katokōchē* ("possession"), Plato uses, albeit less frequently, another term also important for our purposes: *epipnoia*, "inspiration," which derives from *pneuma*, "breath." He in fact uses this word in the famous passage from the *Phaedrus* already mentioned (265b) in order to describe the four mania: each is an *epipnoia*, an "inspiration." The effect of *epipnoia* is to put the subject "out of his senses" (*ekphrōn*). Thus Plato says of the poet that he is "never able to compose until he has become 'engodded' [*entheos*], and is beside himself [*ekphrōn*] and reason is no longer in him" (*Ion* 534b).

Again, of the Delphic Pythoness and the priestesses of Dodona, he writes that "when they were mad [*maneisai*] they conferred great benefits on Hellas, both in public and private life, but when they were within their senses [*sōphronousai*] few or none" (*Phaedrus* 244b). In the same passage of the *Phaedrus*, the opposition of "out of" and "within" one's senses also occurs a few lines earlier, to characterize the madness of love. And in the *Laws* (790e–791b), Plato refers to this same loss of reason, when instead of poetic, mantic, or erotic *mania*, he speaks of telestic *mania*, or possession trance: the Bacchantes, he says, are *ekphrones* or "out of their senses," and it is the combined action of music and dance that restores them to their senses, so that they are *emphrones*.

Thus the four kinds of *mania*—that is, of trance—all have the effect of throwing the affected person into a state of unreason. This madness, however, manifests itself in very different ways depending on which *mania* is at work. Neither the poet in his state of inspiration nor the lover prey to mad love is ever described as being in the state of frenzy that manifests itself by foaming at the mouth and rolled-back eyes, as is the case with Agave when she is possessed by Dionysus-Bacchus and is about to dismember her son Pentheus (*Bacchae;* 1122). Neither the poet, the lover, nor the Pythoness is ever depicted in the attitude of crisis characterized by a flung-back head and an entirely arched body, so often seen in the possession scenes painted on vases. None is described as undergoing the effects of music, or as having dance as his or her principal activity. All these manifestations are symptomatic of telestic *mania,* which expresses itself through a set of particular behavior patterns totally different from those produced by the other kinds of *mania.*

The amnesia suffered by a possessee upon emerging from his trance is also one of the characteristic features of telestic *mania.* Witness the dramatic account of Agave's horrified surprise when she learns, from the lips of her father Cadmus, that in her murderous frenzy, having taken her son Pentheus for a wild animal, she had dismembered him and wrenched off his head. But what distinguishes telestic *mania* most radically from the other three is that it is the outcome of an offense, of misconduct toward the god, who then manifests his anger by striking the guilty person with madness. The same could never be said of the other three *mania.* That it is characteristic of telestic madness is formally confirmed by Euripide's text cited above: "Would it be some offense committed against the ardent huntress Dictynna for not having sacrificed a victim for her," the Chorus asks the "engodded" (*entheos*) Phaedra. This is also attested by Plato's well-known text, which we will now examine at length.

Telestic Mania (*Phaedrus* 244d–e)

In the *Phaedrus,* as we saw earlier, Plato distinguishes between four kinds of *mania.* Before proposing a classification (265a–b), he starts by explaining what each kind consists of (244–49). Following a brief exordium celebrating divine *mania* in general, he treats a first type of trance (*mania*), the one that seizes the "prophetesses" and that he will later call mantic—let us say divinatory trance. He then comes to the one that he will term "telestic" trance in his classification. It is this passage that interests us. This text, composed of a few lines (*Phaedrus* 244d–e), difficult to understand, and well-known for its very obscurity, has been the object of a ten-page study by Linforth (1946b), who before providing his own interpretation, summarizes that of his predecessors, all of whom, he says, find it "baffling." Wilamowitz-Moellendorf (1920, 1:411) himself admitted that "he never found any explanation" for this passage, which left him "perplexed"

("Eine Erklarung habe ich nirgend gefunden und bin selbst ratlos"). To my knowledge, no translation or interpretation[9] of it, including that of Linforth, is satisfactory. The most recent translation (1983), proposed not by a Hellenist but by a well-known ethnopsychiatrist, G. Devereux, in his article "La crise initiatique du chaman chez Platon (*Phèdre* 244d–e)" is scarcely more convincing. But it seems that in light of what was said about possession in the first part of this book, a new reading of this text is possible. As presumptuous as it might seem, I will therefore chance a new translation of it here.[10] The reader will forgive me for providing one so close to the Greek that it hardly resembles English, but I deemed it important to follow Plato's train of thought as closely as possible.

The following is what Socrates says:[11]

> Besides [1], indeed from these very diseases [*noson*] and great woes [*ponon*] that certainly originate [*ek*] in ancient offenses [*menimaton*] committed by someone in some lineages [*genon*], [2] trance [*mania*], [the very one] that comes upon those who [usually] indulge in it by giving them prophetic power [*propheteusasa*], secures [*eureto*] deliverance [*apallagen*] through the use of prayers to gods and of cults [celebrated in their honor]; [3] thus [*othen*], resulting indeed in purifications [*katharmon*] and rites [*teleton*], it [trance] brings recovery [*exante epoiese*] to the one who welcomes it [*echonta*] for the present as well as for time to come, [4] securing [*euromene*] for him who was correctly entranced and possessed [*orthos manenti te kai kataschomeno*] release [*lysin*] from [his] troubles.

What does the substance of this text signify? Let us break it down ito its four parts in order and briefly analyze their contents:

[1]: People suffer from diseases and woes that are the consequences of certain offenses.

[2]: Divinatory trance delivers them through recourse to the gods.

[3]: Thus, purifications and rites bring them recovery.

[4]: He who is correctly entranced is released from his troubles.

As we can see, Plato's exposé consists of a series of facts that are in direct relation to trance and that succeed one another in a certain order. This order is exactly the one followed in the first part of this book in order to speak of the dynamics of possession. Broadly speaking, we are therefore dealing in both cases with the same facts. Seen in this way, things become clear. Socrates' discourse, nevertheless, is not. We must therefore now enter into detail and justify our analysis.

[1] What are those "diseases," "woes," and "offenses"? Plato does not say, but the general context and situation to which he implicitly refers do not leave any room for doubt. The "telestic" trance (*mania*) with which he is dealing here is the one he will later say is "inspired" by Dionysus. On the other hand, as we saw (above, 269), for Plato *mania,* which is a disease, is

of two kinds, one due to "human diseases," the other to a "divine state." This being said, how can we concretely conceive the relations that Greeks of his day discerned between Dionysus, the divine state of *mania,* and disease? One of the best-known tragedies by Euripides, *Bacchae,* whose topic, as we know, is Dionysiac trance, provides the answer to our question. Dionysus is depicted as taking terrible vengeance against those in his own lineage who insult his mother's memory, refuse to celebrate his cult, and chase out his followers. Finally, Agave (one of his mother's sisters), struck by *mania,* dismembers alive her own son Pentheus, also made mad by Dionysus. Offense, madness (here, madness crisis, in other words, disease), woe (what more horrible woe for a mother?)—this perfectly illustrates Plato's text, with the exception that in the *Bacchae* Agave's murderous frenzy is provoked not by "ancient" faults, that is to say, those committed by others long before her, but by her very own.

It is this reference to the ancient aspect of the fault that has frustrated the majority of commentators.[12] The difficulty is easily solved if we recall that Plato considered *mania* crisis as resulting from fright, and fright as the sign of a "defective disposition," or to put it more simply a certain "weakness of the soul." He expressly states this in the *Laws* (790–91); we will return to the subject later. The present text of the *Phaedrus* tells us that Plato saw in this weakness of the soul, which predisposed one or another individual to trance, the consequence of an ancient fault committed in the lineage; in other words, he considered it to be hereditary, at least in part. The difference between the concrete example of trance described by Euripides in the *Bacchae* (fault attributable to the person himself) and the abstract tableau drawn by Plato in the *Phaedrus* (fault attributable to the lineage) is due to the fact that Euripides refers to legendary time, when the cult of Dionysus was in the making,[13] whereas Plato refers to historical time, when this cult had already long been instituted. Let us say metaphorically that in this passage of the *Phaedrus,* it is not Agave that Plato has in mind, but her descendants.

In sum, the first part of the present text describes a situation corresponding to the one seen so often in the first half of this book as being at the origin of possession, that is to say, "histories of illness" that result in "crises." As for the *Bacchae,* the crisis that affects Agave is particularly tragic, to be sure, but Greek antiquity offers numerous comparable examples.

[2] The second part of the text poses the problem of knowing just exactly who the people are whom Plato designates—rather enigmatically, we should say—as "usually indulging in trance," which gives them "prophetic power." Without exception—at least to my knowledge—translators and commentators alike have understood that the people concerned were the same as those mentioned in the previous phrase; in other words, those suf-

fering from the woes of *mania*. Therein lies the error, for this is not the case, for two reasons.

First, in his general discussion of *mania,* which almost immediately precedes our passage, Plato begins precisely by speaking of prophetic trance, and he most clearly indicates those whom it affects, giving as examples the Delphic oracle and that of Dodona. Consequently, the people he has in mind are the diviners. But here he refers to the diviners in general and not necessarily to the two just mentioned, for as Dodds, who is evoking Plato, tells us: "Nor was prophetic possession confined to official oracles. Not only were legendary figures like Cassandra, Bakis, and the Sibyl believed to have prophesied in a state of possession, but Plato refers frequently to inspired prophets as a familiar contemporary type" (1951, 71).

The second reason for considering that *mania* having "prophetic power" concerns diviners and not the diseased springs from the very logic of the system, which would have it that everywhere, and not only in Greece, the diseased come to consult diviners and ask them what to do. In this respect, Boyancé (1936, 66) cites a case that perfectly illustrates the rule and concerns Athens itself:

> The legend that concerns the introduction of a cult originating in Eleutheria conforms to the habitual scheme: A fault; the Athenians refuse to welcome with honor the statue of the God brought to them by a certain Pegasus; the result is a disease that in this case affects not the spirit but the body. . . ; recourse to a prophetic and inspired authority, this time as so often before, the Delphic Oracle. The consequence in the institution of the cult and the healing of the disease.[14]

Exactly what role did these diviners have? Among the Greeks as elsewhere, it is clear that they were first asked to identify the deity responsible for the woes afflicting the diseased person in order to know to whom prayers should be addressed, a preliminary requisite to any hope for healing.[15]

[3] After the sick persons have sought consultation, the diviners, having expressed their opinion, prescribe purifications (*katharmoi*) and rites (*teletai*). What exactly were these *teletai* so characteristic of this *mania* that Plato would call it *"telestikē"*? Or, if one prefers, what were these rites so characteristic of this trance that Plato would call it "ritual?" In the *Bacchae,* rites are frequently mentioned. In the beginning verses of the tragedy, Dionysus presents himself and says: "To this of Hellene cities first I come, having established in far lands my dances and rites, to be God manifest to men" (*Bacchae* 20–23).

The word *teletē* is frequently translated as "initiation," but Boyancé (1932, 42) and Dodds (1960, 75–76), who both take a great interest in *telestike,* agree that the word generally designates the ritual of mystery cults. Prayers, sacrifices, purifications, dances, and songs are thus part of the *teletē*. But Boyancé, who examines these rites in the Orphic context, in which they play an important role, emphasizes that they are expected to be effective. The word *teletai*, he writes (1932, 48), seems to designate "rites whose thrust is to more or less force the deity, rites whose most important part is recourse to effective formulas." He tells us elsewhere (ibid., 47, 161) that they are chanted formulas. But force the deities to do what? To manifest their presence. And Boyancé asks: "What exactly was this presence which, to our way of thinking, is the main goal of these rites that are mainly vocal and baptized by the name of *teletai*?" (ibid., 54). He answers: "We can only think about what the science of *teletai*, which became *telestikē*, is for the Neoplatonists. It essentially consists in provoking the arrival of the deity, but this operation is a very material one: the god animates the statue representing him and *telestikē* is the art of consecrating statues." It is not unreasonable to think that in Dionysiac cults the word *teletai* also served to designate rites aiming at "provoking the arrival of the deity," but this time in a different way: by arousing possession trance. For Dionysianism, *teletai* could thus signify, in part at least, the art of consecrating not statues but initiates. We cannot state it definitely, but we can at least hypothesize it.

Whatever the case may be, rites necessarily imply accomplishing a series of actions in a certain order, respecting the prescribed order, *correctly* following a certain traditional behavior. This aspect of things must above all be retained here; we shall soon see why.

Let us now turn to the second part of [3]. The problem is to know exactly who is the one "welcoming" this trance and what aspect of trance, prophetic or telestic, is involved.

Evidently, this trance that "brings recovery" is the one to which Plato actually refers, in other words, "telestic" trance. As for the one to whom this trance "brings recovery," he can only be the one who needed it, that is to say, one of the people referred to in [1]. This sick person only recovers, the text says, if he "welcomes this trance for the present as well as for time to come." What does this mean? Obviously, that the person concerned will have to, from then on, regularly comply with the rituals of telestic trance. In other words, he will recover only if he has been initiated and integrated into the cult of the god responsible for his woes; in brief, only after he has become member of what the Greeks called a *thiasos*, let us say a "college of the possessed."

[4] We have just seen that the one who "welcomes" telestic trance "recovers." But how is he "released from his troubles?" The last part of the text states this clearly: by being "correctly entranced and possessed," in other words, by correctly (*orthos*) observing the rites of the trance; in short, by practicing ritual trance. This is undeniably how this phrase, which has frequently been badly translated, must be understood. Let us

emphasize here that if, in his last sentence, Plato speaks of a correct way of being entranced, he also implies there is an incorrect one. Otherwise his text would be meaningless. For Plato, there thus existed two opposed aspects of trance, one ritualized and the other not. Among the Greeks, we once again find the opposition of ritualized versus nonritualized trance, which, as we saw in the first part of this book, is one of the universals of possession.

Now that we have completed our analysis, the scheme underlying Plato's text can be rewritten in a different way, one that will more clearly identify the nature of telestic trance. The episodes in the text succeed one another in the following manner: [1] diseases and woes (i.e., nonritualized trance crises) due to the offended god's anger; [2] consultation of the diviners, who through prophetic trance identify the god in question and prescribe the adequate prayers and cults needed to "secure deliverance" of the sick person; [3] purification and rites, which imply initiation and integration of the sick person into a "college of the possessed"; [4] practice of ritualized possession trance, healing.

Before going further and leaving this highly instructive text, let us observe that the obscurity of this passage of the *Phaedrus* (244d–e) which has caused so much ink to flow is due ultimately to the fact that Plato, who will define four types of *mania* much later, here describes only its different aspects. And at this stage, which is that of divine *mania* in general, he does not distinguish between them. From one end of the text to the other, *mania* is the grammatical subject, but Plato does not specify the form of *mania* involved. It is up to the reader to know that in [1] he speaks of telestic trance in its nonritualized aspect, in [2] of trance in its divinatory aspect, in [3] of both aspects one after the other, first of divinatory trance which prescribes the rites, second of telestic trance which brings recovery, and lastly in [4] of ritualized telestic trance.

For Plato, telestic trance thus appears to be profoundly ambivalent. It is at one and the same time sickness and healing of sickness, which should not surprise us. Let us say, using Zempléni's term, that its main dimension is therapeutic. But among the Greeks this "therapeutic dimension" could very well be a later aspect of possession trance since the latter did not always have the ambivalent character, both divine and shameful, that it had in the days of Plato. He himself tells us so, still in the *Phaedrus* (244b), where we can read: "madness was accounted no shame or disgrace by the men of old who gave things their names."

It is clear that if Plato feels obliged to write that in olden times *mania* was "accounted no shame nor disgrace," this is because in his time it was, if not by everyone at least by some, and not without conflict as the very subject of the *Bacchae* tragedy demonstrates. Indeed, Plato himself seems to have had ambivalent feelings, if not toward *mania*—"madness" in general—at last toward its telestic form; in other words, toward possession trance. These feelings explain, at least in part, the conception he had of the relations existing between this form of trance and music and dance. It is therefore important to know them.

In the *Phaedrus,* which, as we know, is the dialogue in which he sets forth his conception of love, Plato precedes Socrates' discourse on the four forms of divine madness (*mania*) with a shattering preliminary statement. Having said that, contrary to what certain people think, the beloved would be wrong to prefer the lover "in a calm state of mind" (*sōphronei*) to the one "made mad" (*mainetai*) by love under the pretext that madness is an evil, Socrates declares: "In reality, our greatest blessings come to us by way of madness [*manias*] which indeed is a divine gift" (*Phaedrus* 244a). Here we are back to the conception of madness as a "divine lot" (*theai mora*) resulting from a "divine force" (*theia dynamis*), an idea we already encountered in the *Ion* (5534c). A fine "praise of folly," as Erasmus would have put it!

But is it sincere? Dodds (1951, 64) sees it as a "conscious paradox," a deliberate provocation that "startled the fourth-century Athenian reader hardly less than it startles us." But matters may not be as simple as that. If we look more closely, we quickly see that everything depends upon the kind of madness we are talking about. Socrates, as we saw, distinguished between four different kinds. Everything indicates that his eulogy of "erotic madness" is perfectly and unreservedly sincere. "Of all forms of *enthusiasm,*" he tells us, it is "the best." Through it, when one "sees beauty on earth, remembering true beauty, one feels one's wings growing" (*Phaedrus* 249d–e). For Plato, indeed, the madness of love is the direct result of contemplating beauty, and beauty—that of the young beloved—is the best access to the good and the true, which is to say that which is most important in the world, the essential, in the strict sense of the word. It is thus easy to understand why Plato considers mad love—or erotic madness as he calls it—as a gift from the gods, as an inspiration, as an *enthusiasm,* and why he should present it as such. I personally do not see any paradox in this at all.

Things are less clearcut, however, as soon as we move from erotic madness to poetic madness. Here, the least one can say is that Socrates is laughing up his sleeve as he pokes fun at the unfortunate Ion. When he tells him, with utmost seriousness, that it is Homer who possesses him, he asks him: "When you recite epic verses correctly and thrill the spectators most deeply . . . are you not beside yourself, is your soul not transported by enthusiasm?" (*Ion* 535b–c). And Ion acknowledges that something of the sort does happen within him: "Whenever I recite a tale of pity, my eyes are filled with tears, and when it is one of horror or dismay, my hair stands up on end with fear,[16] and my heart goes leaping" (ibid., 535c). This is like the shiver running up the spine of the officer-cadet hearing his national anthem, or of the veteran hearing the Last Post. So Socrates is in fact describing something real, something that exists, and is therefore only half-joking. Indeed, elsewhere (*Phaedrus* 245a), again with reference to possession and the madness of the Muses (*Mousōn katōkochē te kai mania*), he says: "But if any man comes to the gates of poetry without the madness of the Muses [*manias Mousōn*], persuaded that skill alone will make him a good poet, then shall he and his works of sanity with him be brought to nought by the poetry of madness, and behold their place is nowhere to be found." Here again, I see nothing paradoxical. Music—or rather "music technique" (*mousikē technē*) for "music," meaning "of the muses," was originally an adjective—being another aspect of poetry, is also "a science of love matters" (*erōtikōn epistēmē*), with respect to "harmony and rhythm" (*Symposium* 187c). Both music and poetry therefore proceed in part from love, and it is thus logical that both erotic and poetic madness should be almost equally dear to Plato's heart. It is still true, however, that he never jokes about the first whereas he does on occasion about the second. Ah, one may say, but Ion isn't really a poet, "a creator," he is just a rhapsodist and this is why he can be ridiculed. The fact remains, however, that both possession and enthusiasm are being mocked through him, and whether one likes it or not, Socrates is no longer completely serious here.

As for mantic *mania,* that is to say, divinatory frenzy, Plato seems to hold rather the same opinion of it as of poetic frenzy. It is hardly necessary to say much more than that. Let us simply say that on the whole he believes in it. Not that he holds the prophetesses of Delphi or Dodona in any particular esteem. Indeed, he claims that while "they were mad they conferred great benefits on Hellas," but immediately thereafter he adds that while they were "in their senses" they conferred "few or none" (*Phaedrus* 244b).

Things are quite different, on the other hand, when Plato deals with telestic *mania,* in other words, with possession trance. Once and only once is it qualified as "inspiration," and this is because it is part of divine *mania* in general. It is not even once called "enthusiasm." It is "possession." This is the word Plato constantly uses to speak of it, and that's all. This is already significant in and of itself, but there is more. To what exactly is this *mania,* which like all divine *mania* is a gift of God, tied? To fright, Plato says in *Laws* (790e), a fright resulting from a certain "weakness of the soul" and that is the "practice of cowardice" (ibid. 791b). Plato puts those who suffer from this fright in the same group as crying children rocked to sleep by their nanny—a comparison hardly flattering for the Bacchantes. How then shall we classify those Bacchic dances which "mime drunken people" and whose rhythms (*rythmoi*) are equally "appropriate to illiberality, and insolence or madness or other evils" (*Republic*

400b)? Well, it would be best to "separate it off both from pacific and from warlike dancing, and to pronounce that this kind of dancing is unfit for our citizens" (*Laws* 875c–d). Plato thus did not hold these bacchic dances in great esteem.[17]

Thus, when Plato says that *mania* is for us "the greatest blessing and a gift from God," there is indeed "a conscious paradox." In making this statement, he sincerely has in mind the three *mania,* erotic, poetic, and mantic; as for telestic *mania,* his feelings are certainly mixed.[18]

Plato uses two words to designate the possessed, or, more generally, adepts of possession cults: "Bacchantes" (*bacchoi*), which of course is derived from Bacchus, and "Corybanters" (*korybantiōntes*), or those who act as Corybantes, the two words being more or less synonymous as he uses them. Oddly, however, he never uses the word maenads (*mainades,* from *mania*)—that is to say, the mad, frenzied, or crazed female companions of Dionysus so often depicted in paintings and symbolizing the trance state in Greek religion—even though they occupied the place they did in ancient Greek literature. Why?

Perhaps because the word *mainades* designates very particularly, it would seem, Dionysus' permanent companions who had come with him from Lydia (*Bacchae* 55), whereas *bacchae,* which also designates them, could be indiscriminately applied to all female adepts of his cult—or at least this is what emerges from a reading of Euripides. The words "Bacchant" and *baccheuein* ("to behave like a Bacchant") were not only reserved for Dionysus-Bacchus; they were of general use and could as well apply to the worship of another *daimōn,* in particular to the Corybantes[19] and to adepts of Cybele worship. If Plato abstains from any reference to the maenads, it is perhaps because they have no connection—or in any case have much less connection than Bacchants or Bacchantes—with the therapeutic dimension of trance. To speak of "Bacchantes" or of "those who behave like Corybantes" (*korybantiōntes*), and thus implicitly to refer to the cult of Cybele, "Mother of the Gods," is, on the contrary, to refer to a form of possession whose therapeutic dimension is primordial.

Dodds points out that the worship of Cybele should, in fact, be viewed from this angle. Having observed (1951, 77) that other deities besides Dionysus could "cause mental trouble" and that "presumably all could cure what they had caused if their anger were suitably appeased," he tells us that "by the fifth century the Corybantes at any rate had developed a special ritual for the treatment of madness. The Mother, it would appear, had done likewise (if indeed her cult was at that time distinct from that of the Corybantes)." In *The Wasps* (119–20), what is Aristophanes' point of reference when he wants a typical situation to express a son's efforts to cure his father, Bdelycleon, of his *mania* for judging? Quite naturally, the Corybantes. The son makes his father "corybantize," but the latter resists and "runs off with the drum." What does Plato do, also with an intent to mock, when he wants to characterize Phaedrus' *mania* for speechifying? He depicts him as delightedly "syncorybantizing" with another person "whose sickness [*nosounti*] is wanting to listen to speeches" (*Phaedrus* 228b–c). All this sufficiently demonstrates, I trust, how far "corybantizing" and being afflicted by *mania*—as well as being cured of it—were, in Plato's time, synonymous.

Now that we have dealt with the words, we can come to what Plato thought about the relation of dance and music to trance.

Music and Trance: Plato's Theory

Plato never gathered together his ideas about the relation of trance to music and dance into an organized and, as it were, autonomous whole. The fact remains, however, that these ideas do form a coherent whole that is nothing less than a theory. This becomes quite apparent if one takes the trouble to collate and logically articulate a number of passages dealing with telestic madness that occur in the *Phaedrus* (something we have already seen at length), in the *Laws,* and in the *Ion.*[20] This is what I now propose to do, and the best starting point is a passage from the *Laws* (790d–791b), consisting of about twenty lines, which should be quoted in full.[21]

Dealing with the exercizes that should be used to form the souls of very young boys, Plato examines the methods of raising infants, and, in this context, advocates the virtues of continuous movement, which is "in all cases salutary" but especially in the case of the newborn "because it is as if they were always navigating." Experience, he says, has brought home the advantages of this method to "those who nurse small children" as well as—and here we come to the passage that interests us—

> to the women who ritualize [*telousai*] in the healing [*iamata*] of the Corybantes. For when mothers have children who suffer from insomnia and want to go to sleep, lull them to rest, they bring them not stillness, but this very movement [*kinēsin*], for they rock [*seiousai*] them ceaselessly in their arms [they bring them] not silence, but melody [*melōdian*], [so that they] "en-aulize" [*kataulousi*] the children just as [is done to] Bacchantes out of their senses [*ekphronōn*], by using this cure [*iaseis*] [constituted by such forms] of movement [*kinēseōs*] as singing-and-dancing [*choreia*][22] and "musia" [*mousē*]."

The reason behind all this, Plato goes on, is that:

> the sufferings [*pathē*] of both are, in brief, frights; frights [*deimata*] that come from a defective disposition [*hexin phaulēn*] of the soul [*psychē*]. So whenever one applies an external shaking [*seismos*] to sufferings of this kind, the external movement [*kinēsis*] overpowers the internal

movement [*kinēsin*] of fear [*phoberan*] and madness [*manikēn*] and by
thus overpowering it, it brings about a manifest calm in the soul and
a cessation of the grievous palpitations of the heart, which had existed in
each case. Thus, it produces very satisfactory results. It [the
movement][23] brings sleep to the ones [the newborns] while to the others
[the Bacchantes], set to dancing [*orchoumenous*] and listening to the
aulos [*auloumenous*], it brings wakefulness [and], with the help of the
gods, made favorable by happy auspices, and to whom each one
offers sacrifices, it completes [for them] the enjoyment [*ekein*] of a sound
state of mind [*hexeis emphronas*] instead of a state [*diatheseōn*] [that
is] in our eyes madness [*manikōn*].

Just a word first to justify two oddities in this translation: the terms "en-
aulize" and "musia." The Greek *kataulousi* is always translated, whether
in English or in French, by words referring to song or speech (such as "to
cast a spell"), whereas in fact it refers to a musical instrument, the *aulos*.[24]
It is all the more important to respect the Greek text because the *aulos,* as
we shall see later on, is the instrument par excellence of trance among the
Greeks, hence the word "en-aulize." As for the word *mousa,* the reason it
has been rendered here by "musia"—meaning here "thing of the Muse"—
and not, contrary to customary usage, by "music" is simply because it does
not actually mean "music" (cf. Bailly's dictionary), but rather "muse" first
and foremost, and hence "science," "art," or "song," or else "persuasive
words." There is every reason to think that the tunes played on the *aulos*
during possession ceremonies were, as everywhere else, "mottoes," or
more precisely "persuasive words." And what could there be in common
between the melody made by nurses to the babies they are rocking—in
other words lullabies—and the *aulos* themes played to the Bacchantes,
other than the fact that both are "persuasive words"? If *mousa* had to be
translated, in the present context, by an already existing term, then "persuasive words" is the one we ought to choose. Nevertheless, I prefer—still
in this particular context of course—to use "musia," which still stays very
close to the word's origin and does not prejudge what exactly Plato had intended to say. But in any case, there is no reason to translate it by "music."
Furthermore, to do so would be to misrepresent Plato, since whereas he
constantly uses the word *mousikē,* as we know, he abstains from doing so
here. To conclude, we need to remember that in this passage there is no
mention, strictly speaking, of music. It will be readily agreed that this is
important.

Movement, on the other hand, is repeatedly mentioned. Indeed, it is almost the main subject matter of the passage since it is to movement that
song, dance, and "musia" ultimately lead, as Plato expressly indicates
when he writes: "this cure [constituted by such forms] of movement as
choreia and *mousē.*" But movement also has a central place in his general

theory of health. It is thus very significant to note that movement should also be at the very center of his theory of the relation between music and trance.

In the *Timaeus,* which as we know contains an account of his general theory of the world system, humans included, Plato, after having dealt with human psychology, anatomy, and physiology then goes on to describe the diseases to which man is prone, those of the body first, then those of the soul (*Timaeus* 86g), and it is here that we find the definition of madness and its two aspects mentioned earlier. Immediately after that, he tackles the problem of health (87c). In order to maintain it, he observes, nothing is more important than to preserve a correct relationship between soul and body, and the means to this end is "never to move [*kinesin*] the soul without the body or the body without the soul, so that, each defending itself against the other, the two sides will retain their balance and their health" (88b). He then gives two concrete examples: "It is therefore necessary that the mathematician, and anyone who strenuously performs any intellectual activity, should also give movement [*kinesin*] to his body by practicing gymnastics. While the man who is diligent in molding his body must in turn provide his soul with movement by cultivating music [*mousikē*] and philosophy in general, if either is to deserve to be called both fair and good" (88c).

Moving on then from the particular to the general, he sets out his principle of the complementarity—or the antagonism—of internal movement and external movement (*Timaeus* 88c–e):

> The various parts, likewise, must be treated in the same manner, in imitation of the form of the Universe. For as the body is inflamed or chilled within by the particles that enter it, and again is dried or moistened by those without, and suffers the affections consequent on both these movements, whenever a man delivers his body, in a state of rest, to these movements, it is overpowered and utterly perishes; whereas if a man imitates that which we have called the nurturer and nurse of the Universe, and never, if possible, allows the body to be at rest but keeps it moving, and by continually producing internal vibrations, [he] defends it in nature's way against the inward and outward movements. . . . [88d–e]

And he concludes: "Wherefore the movement that is best for purgings and renovations of the body consists in gymnastic exercises; and second-best is the movement provided by swaying vehicles such as boats or any conveyances that produce no fatigue" (89a).

All that, however, only concerns the "composite living creature and the bodily part of it" (89d). But now we find that the same treatment should be followed for our "three kinds of soul" (*psychē*) that "are housed within

us in three regions" and each of which "has its own movements" (89e).
"We must therefore see to it that they all have their movements relatively
to one another in due proportion." As for the "most lordly kind" of our
souls, which "raises us up from earth," it too must retain "its own congen-
ial. . .movement." These movements (*kinēseis*) which have an affinity
with the "divine part within us. . .are the intellection and revolutions of
the Universe. These each one of us must follow," and when they are dis-
torted they must be rectified "by learning the harmonies and revolutions
of the Universe" (90a–d).

This summary of the Platonic theory of movement as the basis of health
in man's body and soul makes it fairly clear that his other theory, that of
movement as the basis of Corybantic healing, is nothing other than a particular case, a particular application, of the first. For the second does in
fact contain the two broad principles of the first: on the one hand that of
rhythmic rocking, on the other that of the antagonism between the two
sets of movements, external and internal, that counterbalance one another and thus reestablish equilibrium when it has been lost. The disturbances affecting those afflicted by telesic *mania* spring from the effect of a
fright on a weak soul. This fright is an internal movement (*kinēsis*). Dance
and "musia" then intervene as an "external shaking" (*seismos*), and by virtue of their specific movement, which overcomes the earlier one and "over-
powers" it, restore calm and tranquillity. But how exactly does this external movement achieve such effects? Plato does not explain this here. But
there is justification for thinking that, in accordance with terms of his general theory set forth in the *Timaeus,* they derive not only from the virtue
sui generis of the rocking movement, but also from the fact that this movement is inseparable from the "harmonies and revolutions of the Universe."
By virtue of their movement, dance and "musia" are thus able, in short, to
reintegrate into the ordering of the Universe the individual who had become separated from it by the disordered movement of fright. To be sure,
Plato feels bound to add (but giving the impression that for him it is just a
matter of form) that the desired result does not occur without the benevolence of the gods. In any case, however, the *teletai* (rites) are aimed precisely toward this end. Such is the theory of Corybantic cure put forward by
Plato in the *Laws.* "This is," he concludes, "to put it shortly—quite a plau-
sible account of the matter" (781b).

Following this text bearing upon the curative function of trance, and
upon the central role played by movement and, therefore, above all, by
dance (since music plays a secondary role and moreover is not even mentioned by that name, we should stress), let us turn to another text, this
time one that relates dance to what we shall call, for the sake of convenience, music, even though, here again, it is also not given that name. We
read in the *Ion* (536c): Those who are corybantizing (*korybantiōntes*)

"have a sharp ear for one tune [*melous*] only, the one which belongs to the god by whom they are possessed [*katechontai*] and to that tune they respond freely with gesture [*schēmatōn*] and speech, while they ignore all others." What does this passage tell us? In the first place that the possessed person reacts to one tune and one alone. Why? Without doubt because it is *his*. Taking advantage of what we have found to be the case everywhere else in these matters, I shall call this tune his motto. When he hears this musical motto, this tune, how does the "corybantizer" react? The text, and even more so the context—which I hope I may be forgiven for not quoting—indicate the answer to this quite clearly: he goes into trance.[25] And how does he manifest this trance? By finding "gestures and speech" enabling him "to respond freely" to this tune,[26] and, consequently, by dancing. We are therefore well aware of the role played by music in triggering that trance. It does not operate by means of some *sui generis* virtue or other that produces emotional effects of a specific kind capable of putting people beside themselves. It is not as *music*—the word is mine and does not figure in Plato's text—that it acts, it is as a *melody* that has a meaning to which it is necessary to respond; in short, it acts as a coded signal.

On the basis of the data given by the three above-mentioned dialogues (*Phaedrus, Laws,* and *Ion*), Plato's theory of the relations between trance and music can now be formulated as follows: "People who are psychologically somewhat fragile, and who as the result of god's anger suffer from divine madness, cure themselves by practicing ritual trance, which is triggered by a musical motto and takes the form of a dance; music and dance, by the effect of their movement, reintegrate the sick person into the general movement of the cosmos, and this healing is brought about thanks to the benevolence of gods who have been rendered propitious by sacrifices."[27]

Formulated in this way, Plato's theory on the relation of trance to dance and music appears at first to be very different from the one usually set forth; I shall later explain how. In the second place, it seems to coincide broadly with the theory proposed in the first part of this book, except on one essential point, which is that of the role assigned to possession itself in the healing process.

Let us begin with what the two theories have in common. On the whole they coincide with respect to the role allotted to music. Music does play a part, granted, but it is no more than one element among others, which include rituals, dance, movement, and, of course, the benevolence of the gods. Music's role is so far from being predominant that the word music appears only once in Plato's texts. (I shall later return to Plato's way of referring to it in the context of possession, since it is significant.) It is the support of dance. Music also triggers trance; but never once is it presented as doing so by means of an emotional charge of any kind. It triggers trance because it is a motto, in other words a signal.

Let us now come to the divergences. The central point of my theory is that music, by acting as both the signal for trance and the support for dance, essentially allows the possessed person to publicly identify himself to the god possessing him or her. It is this process of public identification with the god that is for me the mainspring of possession trance, and when this possession has a "therapeutic dimension" of any importance, it is this public identification that is the principal agent of the cure. In Plato the gods play a part, it is true, but only—and this barely indicated—in order to strike people with madness. At the healing stage their role is limited to viewing things with benevolence. At the outset, when defining the four *mania*, Plato does mention "enthusiasm" and "inspiration," and *mania* is presented as caused by the gods. Here, however, in the texts concerned solely with telestic *mania*—possession trance—nothing of the sort is evoked. Telestic *mania* appears to be emptied of its religious content. Seen in terms of its therapeutic dimension, it appears as an almost purely profane and mechanical affair. If I had to draw a parallel between Plato's theory and my own, I would say that, for him, the healing process is achieved by reinsertion of the individual in the cosmos as a result of the movement of dance and music, which reestablishes harmony with the universe, whereas for me healing is achieved by the reinsertion of the individual in society as a result of the movement of music and dance, which provokes identification with the god. The difference can be expressed as in figure 5.1.

To sum up, Plato's theory is both physical and metaphysical, whereas mine is both psychological and sociological; both are equally physiological.

The question that confronts us now is whether possession among the Greeks displayed certain characteristics that would explain why Plato ignored what I see as one of its universal characteristics: identification with the god. If this were the case, then the Greek system would be an exception that would certainly have to be taken into account. If this were not the case, then we would first have to prove it. This is what I will try to do now.

Dancing and Identifying Oneself with the Gods

Both the vocabulary and the facts demonstrate that telestic *mania* as described by Plato is indeed possession trance in which the subject identifies himself with the god possessing him.

The verb *korybantiaō*,[28] translated by Bailly as, "to be agitated by a Corybantic transport," according to Jeanmaire properly means "to Cory-

Plato's theory   Theory in present work

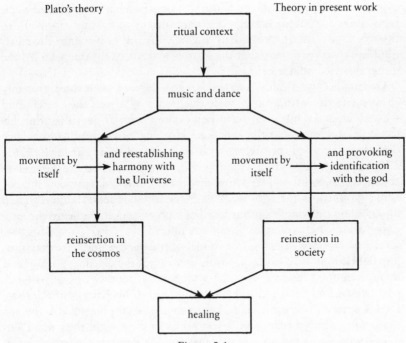

Figure 5.1

bantize" or "to act like a Corybant," since *korybantiōntes* should be trans-lated, he says, as "Corybantizers" or "those who act like Corybantes." And what does "acting like Corybantes" mean if not behaving like them, in other words apparently identifying with them internally?

Similarly, the word *baccheiōn*, "Bacchant," and the verb *baccheuein*,[29] which Jeanmaire translates sometimes by "acting like a Bacchant" (1951, 58), sometimes, more logically it seems, by "acting like Bacchus" (1949, 466), express the idea that by "acting like Bacchus," in other words by "being a Bacchant," one identifies oneself with Bacchus. The process and the state of identification with the god possessing the entranced person, which are at the very center of any possession cult, are clearly expressed by the Greek vocabulary. But there is more.

Among the numerous epithets of Dionysus, we find *Bromius*, the "Roarer," for he was the "bull-god, lion-god, earthquake-god" (Dodds 1960, 74). In the *Bacchae*, describing the mad running and dancing of the maenads in the mountains (the *oreibasia*), led by Dionysus Bromius, Euripides has the chorus say: "Whosoever leads the worshiping companies [*thiasos*] is Bromius."[30] According to Dodds (ibid., 82), this means that the one who leads the *oreibasia* "is identified with the god." And Dodds adds: "Some degree of identification with the god seems to be implied in calling human participants in Dionysiac rites *Bacchae* and *Bacchoi* . . .it is possible . . .that the supreme degree of such identification, open only to the *exarchos,* was expressed by giving him the holy name Bromius" (ibid.). Let us recall here that the *exarchos* was also the one who led the dithyramb (Jeanmaire 1951, 235).[31]

Originally, says Dodds (1961, 83), the *oreibasia*[32] was most probably "a women's rite with a single male celebrant," who was the exarch, and who as we have just seen identified himself with Dionysus during his trance. But what about the maenads? Nothing would lead us to believe that they identified themselves with Dionysus. But, as Gregoire (1961, 225) observes: "Just as the God is a bull, his she-sectarists see themselves changed into cows, and we know that the *Proitides*[33] let out cow moos." Why? Nonnos, in the *Dionysiacs* (8)[34] reports that Semele, impregnated by Zeus and carrying Dionysus, used to moo whenever she heard the lowing of a bull. Now then, as Jeanmaire notes (1951, 347), Semele is presented by Nonnos as being "the model of the Bacchantes." We may thus justifiably think that when they were entranced, the maenads, or some of them, identified themselves either with Semele, mother of Dionysus, or with a cow. For his part, in his introduction to his edition of *Bacchae,* Dodds writes: "There must have been a time when the maenads or thyiads or *Bacchae* really became for a few hours or days what their name implies—wild women whose human personality has been temporarily replaced by another" (1960, xiv). We could say the same of possessions in Greece, which, at least originally, had no direct relation with Dionysus, and stemmed from pre-Dionysiac cults, that of the nymphs in particular. All of this (together with the facts that will be cited subsequently) readily demonstrates, I trust, that telestic *mania,* "inspired by Dionysus" and about which Plato speaks, is indeed a possession trance corresponding to the definition given at the beginning of this book; in other words, it is "identificatory."

Before ending on this point, we must add that although telestic trance—whether it is Dionysiac in the general sense of the term or pre-Dionysiac is of little matter—is indeed "identificatory," the originality, the newness, and at the same time the scandalous aspect of trance tied to the cult of Dionysus stems from its close association with wine and drunkenness. Pentheus himself, the tragic hero of the *Bacchae,* exclaims with virtuous indignation: "When in festivities wine is served to women, I say that then there is nothing wholesome in their mysteries" (1. 261–62). Symbols of telestic trance in Plato's days, the Bacchantes must also be seen as the promoters of what we should call alcoholic trance, which in our days certainly is one of the most widespread forms of mania.[35]

Let us now turn to dance. Be it in writings or paintings, the Bacchantes and the maenads are usually represented as dancing.[36] Evidence from vase paintings[37] show that among the Greeks and elsewhere (and we have already spoken of this "elsewhere" in a previous chapter), possession dance had two main aspects, which I shall here again call, abstract and figurative. The abstract aspect is constituted by a repertoire of movements devoid of any figurative function, in other words representing nothing other than themselves: wild spinning, wide swinging of the arms, abrupt flinging back of the head—the movement "that dislocates the neck"[38] described by Pindar in a dithyramb—violent arching of the body, absent and convulsive attitudes: these are the principal—and well-known—features of the abstract part of possession dancing among the Greeks. As we can see (and this is an often-repeated point, by Jeanmaire in particular), there is great similarity here with the behavior still observed in so many possession dances, from Bali to Brazil, passing through the Middle and Near East, the Mediterranean basin, and both black and white Africa. In this way, savagery and aggression are externalized by means of scant gesticulation that makes use above all of movements expressing agitation and frenzy. Presumably among the Greeks as elsewhere this was the way of expressing the "fury" of the god, and hence his terrible and redoubtable nature—ultimately, his power. Athenaeus, the Egyptian-born Greek who lived in Rome during the later years of the second century A.D., whose *Banquet of the Deipnosophists* is an invaluable repository of information on dance in antiquity, classified possession dances under the generic heading *maniodeis orcheseis,* which we might translate by "frenzied dances." L. Sechan, the great specialist of Greek dance, translates it as *"danses furieuses"* (1930, 83), making it quite plain that he considered violence as its most important feature.

However, possession dance also had another equally important aspect, which consisted in executing figures that were either symbolic or imitations of the behavior of certain divinities or *daimones,* and also of certain animals. For Plato, to imitate "Nymphs, Pans, Sileni and Satyrs" by means of mime is the very definition of "Bacchic dance" (*Laws* 815c). We have the evidence of a famous cup, made at the time of the Median wars, that depicts a figure with the dress, hair, and accoutrements of Dionysus-Bacchus, playing the lyre, dancing with his head flung back in the characteristic trance attitude, and flanked by two naked and staggering Bacchantes. Is it the god himself who is thus represented? Is it a Bacchant, and thus an *exarchōn?*[39] In this last case, it would mean that Dionysus also could be imitated while dancing. But Dionysus was not always represented in his human form. There is evidence that in Thrace, if not in Athens, during certain ceremonies people wore ox horns in order to imitate the Bull-Dionysus (Pearson 1918, 127). The panther, another wild animal, was likewise imitated by means of dance. There is a red-figure vase that depicts a maenad dancing with a pair of clappers in each hand and wearing a panther skin.

"Is it not clear," Sechan observes of this figure, "that she resembles this great wild animal less as a result of this external attribute than on account of the lithe and feline movement of her dance, which must have been punctuated, imagination tells us, with sudden catlike bounds" (1930, 74 and fig. 11). One cannot help but think that some maenads were possessed by a panther at one moment or another of the ceremony.

It might seem surprising that a maenad—a companion of Dionysus, one of those he addresses in the *Bacchae* (55–56) with the words "O my sisterhood of worshipers, whom I lead with me from barbaric countries, . . . who live and travel at my side"—can be possessed by a panther, or rather, for this seems to express better the spirit of the system, by the soul of a panther. Without making any diffusionistic connection between the two facts, I would like to cite an exactly parallel case observed in Dahomey, when, during a ceremony for Sakpata the divinity of earth and smallpox, a woman embodying one of the "kings of the waters" (*tǫxǫsu*) before my very eyes publicly performed a panther dance, thus demonstrating that at that moment she was possessed by this wild animal, and consequently identified herself with it. The fact that in Greece a woman embodying a companion of Dionysus is depicted as possessed by a panther, or that in Dahomey a water divinity fleetingly embodies the spirit of a wild animal, shows, once again, that the themes of possession are universal and that the fury of wild beasts is one of its favorites. It further demonstrates that possession is accompanied everywhere by a broad movement of exchange, by a coming and going of souls,[40] a process that is certainly within the logic of a system whose mainspring is a change of personality.

The dance repertoire of the maenads has another aspect as well. The latter are depicted performing what Maurice Emmanuel has called the "joined hands dance" because of this characteristic gesture that still remains enigmatic (unless I am mistaken) but that undoubtedly had a precise symbolic meaning. As for the dances performed by those who imitated satyrs and sileni, they were made up of a variety of steps. These dancers, according to Sechan, "also on occasion practiced the dance with a forward bending and back arching of the body. But in general they favored abrupt crouching on one leg, followed by leaps that straightened the bent leg and bent the previously straight one, wild caperings in which they often had maenads as partners, together with various contorsions and swaying movement of the hips accentuated by angular movements of the arms" (ibid., 173).

Here, however, a cautionary remark is in order. Jeanmaire, whose authority on the subject of Dionysianism is well known, asks (1951, 292) if in their analyses of these orgiastic dances, the authors I have been quoting (and others too) have not perhaps committed the error of "sometimes reasoning as if the choreography of the Bacchants and Bacchantes was a learned choreography, or at least one that was regularly taught and whose elements could be broken down into a set series of steps and attitudes." In other words, for Jeanmaire the Bacchic dance could only be disorder. In fact, besides the evidence already cited, other arguments also run counter to his thesis. The reader will pardon me, I hope, for taking him once again to Benin, but as an eyewitness I can confidently say that in this country the possession dance performed during public ceremonies—which often constitute what amounts to theatrical performances: opera-ballets whose sumptuousness is displayed in a large square specially set up for the event, and before an audience of several hundred people—makes use of an extremely complex choreography whose steps and figures, diligently learned, are all charged with symbolic meanings. This applies, moreover, not only to the *orisha* cult (Yoruba) but equally to the *vodun* cults (Fon and Gun), and also, in fact, to many other African cults, such as that of the *holey* among the Songhay of Niger, for example, as Jean Rouch will attest, or that of the *zār* as described by Riya Salima in *Harems et Musulmanes d'Egypte.*[41] We have no reason to believe that among the Greeks, where possession also displayed many institutionalized aspects, the Dionysiac dance was any less "learned" than other dances, whether religious or profane, or that it consisted of no more than a few elementary movements conveying agitation and frenzy. The indications I have listed so far tend to prove just the contrary, and comparison with what we know happens elsewhere demonstrates that this was simply not the case. On this point, Jeanmaire seems to have been less perspicacious than he usually was. Now that I have concluded this digression—and it was not without importance—I shall return to my argument.

In the art of dance, "orchestics," the Greeks made a distinction between two fundamental elements (Sechan 1930, 64): the "movements" on the one hand (*phorai*), the "gestures, figures, attitudes" (*schemata*) on the other. We may reasonably presume that within the context of possession, *phorai* served to denote the nonfigurative movements (the abstract aspect of dance) since it is clear that *schemata* or "figures" denoted its figurative aspect; Plato uses the latter word in the *Ion* (536b) when describing the dance of the "corybantizers" who, in order to conform to the tune of the god possessing them, "have no difficulty finding the right gestures [*schematon*] and speech." We have already seen how varied these *schemata* were. Contrary to what Plato would have us believe with his usual ill will toward telestic *mania,* they did not consist only in "miming the actions of drunk people." Of course, one would expect that in Dionysiac rituals drunkenness would indeed be a habitual theme of imitation, the *mimesis,* which was an essential feature of dance among the Greeks. Plato tells us so himself (*Laws* 816a).[42] But Bacchic orchestics was by no means confined to drunkenness and frenzy. If it had been, why would Plato have stressed, as he does in the *Ion* (536b) that "corybantizers" (read: the possessed in general) "have a sharp ear for one tune only," the one which belongs to the god by whom they are possessed. And what merit would there be in their "responding freely" to that tune with gesture and speech, unless those figures were both varied and characteristic? Here Plato is flagrantly contradicting himself.

Indeed, it seems that Plato's ambivalent feelings concerning telestic *mania*—or if one prefers, possession trance—lead him to contradict himself. On the one hand he celebrates *mania* in general as being a "gift of the gods"; on the other, he takes every opportunity to cast a negative light on the behavior of telestic *mania*. To be sure, he considers the latter as being both sickness and the way to cure sickness, but he does not attribute the curing process to the intervention of the gods, who are only asked to be "benevolent." Rather, he attributes it only to the dialectics of movement, which is a purely profane explanation. Ultimately, the real paradox in Plato is that he withdraws the gods from possession, or more precisely, from its therapeutic dimension, whose importance he himself fully recognizes. The reason is that, as Dodds has shown (1951, 217–18), he is divided between his search for rationality and his desire to find a slot for the irrational in his system. His moral fiber disapproves of the excesses, frenzies, and unbridled behavior of telestic trance. Everything happens as if within himself, Plato does not really believe in possession; as if he cannot really admit that these "mad" behaviors are due to the presence of a god—or rather a *daimōn,* since for him the only real gods are the Demiurge and the planets.

Despite its contradictions, Plato's theory does have the immense merit of showing that possession essentially is a process through which the individual is reinserted into the whole that surrounds him, and, as a corollary, that the role of music and dance is to reconcile the torn person with himself. Whether the "whole" referred to in this reinsertion process is the cosmos, as Plato thinks, or the society, as I do, is of secondary importance. Whether in the first case reinsertion is due to harmony with the universe, resulting from movement, or whether, in the second case, it is due to identification with a god, the primary function of dance, is also of little importance. In both cases, the "symbolic efficacy," as Lévi-Strauss would say, is of the same order and direction.

To end, let us note here, since this involves another aspect of the *mimēsis* of which Plato spoke, that imitation of the gods occupies an essential place in Strabo's "theological excursus" (book 10 of his *Geography*), which according to Jeanmaire (1939, 596) constitutes a veritable "theory of orgiastic cults." A product of "enthusiasm," "the state of happiness indicated by the word *eudaimonia,* is, above all, imitation of the divine state,"

Jeanmaire writes in the summary he gives of this text. Defined as "the art of the Muses in the broadest sense," in other words including "dance, music, and song," music is regarded by Strabo as a way of establishing "contact with the divine by means of the pleasure it procures and because it is art at its most perfect."

Plato and Possession Music; the *Aulos*

Curious though it may seem, the word music (*mousikē*) does not occur once in Plato's writings in the context of possession. The only word approaching music—and approaching it very closely, but differing nevertheless—is *mousa,* which occurs once, and only once, in the *Laws* (790e), and which I translated earlier as "musia," for reasons I gave at that time. Plato speaks too willingly of music and uses the word itself too frequently elsewhere for this fact not to be significant.

When referring to what I am calling music in this book—and how, among the Greeks or anywhere else, is one to talk about possession without mentioning music?—what terms does Plato use? As we saw, he uses "musia," "aulos" (in its various forms), "melody," and "rhythm." Of these, however, *aulos* is by far the most frequently used. In direct or indirect[43] association with trance, it occurs eleven times in his works, whereas *melos,* in this or a derived form, appears only four times[44] and the word *rythmos* once.[45]

It is important to stress that whereas Plato links trance closely with melody or a melodic instrument, he rarely associates it with rhythm. In connection with trance, not once does he make any reference to such percussion instrument as drums, cymbals, or clappers, all of which are frequently mentioned or depicted in this context elsewhere. Again, this fact is significant.

For Plato, it is the tune, the melody played by the *aulos* that counts. It is when he hears it that the "corybantizer" begins to dance. Plato makes no mention either of the sound intensity of the drums or clappers (instruments the Greeks must surely have played just as loudly as other peoples) or of the frenzied aspect of the rhythm (which also must have gone through the same paroxysmic phases as elsewhere in the world) as the dancing figures painted on Greek vases eloquently attest. Indeed, Plato accords such slight importance to rhythm in possession rituals that when it comes to identifying rhythms, or more precisely, to saying which of them "is appropriate to illiberality and insolence or madness or other evils" (*Republic* 400b)—since that is how these things appear to him, we must remember—he simply refers the reader to Damon and passes on. In fact generally speaking, the ethos, as it was to be called later, of rhythms is of scant interest to him altogether: "But which [rhythms] are imitations of which sort of life, I am unable to say" (*Rep.* 400a–b). When Plato writes about possession, it is to the *aulos* first and foremost that he makes reference. Rhythm leaves him indifferent, and he says nothing about percussion instruments. Aristotle was to take much the same course in the *Politics* (8), in which he deals with rhythm merely in passing, and as a wholly secondary aspect of music seen in the context of its relation to enthusiasm.

But it is not only in the work of these two great theoreticians of the relations between music and trance that the *aulos* is presented as the instrument par excellence of *mania*. The same is true for the works of the tragic poets. Aeschylus, in the only surviving fragment of his tragedy *The Edonians*,[46] mentions the *bombyx* and of its melody (*melos*) whose call "leads to madness [*mania*]." (The *bombyx* was a type of *aulos,* a single clarinet with a long body and removable reed; it had movable metal rings—*bombykoi*—that acted on the side holes rather like modern keys.[47] Sophocles, for his part, says of Ajax, when he was seized by a murderous frenzy, that he was literally "synaulized" by "divine madness" (*Ajax,* 610). Euripides, in the *Bacchae,* specifically names the *aulos* several times, and also the *lotos* (160), which was probably a particular variety of the *aulos*. But to be honest, although in this tragedy wholly centered on possession he talks of the *aulos* as an instrument typical of Dionysus worship, he also says the same of the drum, "that hide-stretched orb" (ibid., 123), and nothing is ever explicitly said about the exact relation that either instrument had with trance. In *Heracles,* on the other hand, the murderous frenzy of the hero is directly related, three times in succession,[48] to the *aulos*. Moreover, it is explicitly stated that no drums will take part in the sinister dance that Lyssa promises (*Heracles,* 891). Thus the bloodthirsty *mania* that grips both Ajax and Heracles, when the latter are in the power of Lyssa, the "rage,"[49] is presented as linked with melody and not, in any way, with percussion.

All this, once again, contradicts the myth that trance is triggered by drumming and its supposed effects on the brain's alpha rhythm. The trances with which we are dealing here have a quite different explanation, despite Neher's and his disciples' opinions.[50] The unanimity shown by Plato and Aristotle on the one hand, and by Aeschylus, Sophocles, and Euripides on the other, in presenting the *aulos* as the instrument of trance is certainly significant, and it must reflect what was commonly believed at the time and ultimately, the actual musical practices current in Greek possession cults. Whether an *aulos, bombyx,* or *lotos,* it was a melodic instrument that the Greeks credited with triggering trance. Neither rhythm, nor sheer volume, nor the frenzy of the percussion instruments—all of which were frequently used in possession ritual as we know from so many paintings—were seen as having this effect.

What exactly was the place of the *aulos* among the ancient Greeks? Both textual and pictorial evidence clearly show that it was closely associated with trance, but that it was not linked to it exclusively, and that it was not reserved solely for possession rituals; far from it. In fact the *aulos* was a very popular instrument in Greece, at least in its simple forms; we may well suppose that the instruments of more complicated construction, such as the *bombyx* Aeschylus mentions, were played only by top-flight professionals. And although after the fluctuations in popularity it underwent in Greece at the time of the Persian wars—Aristotle (*Politics* 8. 6) explains this very clearly—it did become the object of a kind of craze among the upper classes,[51] it was a generally despised instrument. Whether they were men or women—for it is often depicted as being played by women—those who played it during banquets were either slaves or people of very low estate. What Eriximachus, in the *Symposium* (176e) says when he proposes "that we should send away the flute girl [*aulos* girl] who has just come in— let her play to herself or, if she likes, to the women of the household," clearly demonstrates the small regard accorded to *aulos* players. This same *aulos* player was to return later (*Symposium* 212), accompanying a band of revelers creating a great din and supporting a very drunk Alcibiades. The role assigned to her is significant. In about 500 B.C., in other words more than a century before the *Symposium* was written, Pratinas of Phlius, the master of the Athenian satyric chorus, had already written: "Song, the Muse had decreed it king, let the *aulos* keep its second rank for it is its servant. Let it only take command in unruly processions, and the fistfights in which drunken young men indulge on the doorsteps of whorehouses." The *aulos* was thus, broadly speaking, linked with debauchery.[52]

It was also associated, nonetheless, with military exercises, with war, and consequently with courage. It accompanied the pyrrhic dance, which had spread from Crete, said to be its country of origin, to all of Greece, and in particular to Sparta, where it was considered "as a propaedeutics of war" (Moutsopoulos 1959, 146), and to Athens, where "it enjoyed great success in the Panathenian festivals." Plato was particularly appreciative of this dance which was responsible for "physical beauty and nobility of character in the young, because it imitated the gestures of valiant warriors" (ibid.). When accompanying the pyrrhic dance, the *aulos,* it is true, combined its sound with that of the lyre, but it was nevertheless so closely identified with this dance that "it was referred to indifferently by the two terms *aulos* and *pyrrhikine*" (ibid.). Moreover, a vase depicts an *aulos* player in the midst of armed, charging warriors, playing his pipes toward the sky (Séchan 1930, 107). Lastly, the *aulos* was also sometimes associated with a sowing dance (ibid., 100).

The *aulos* appears, then, to have been a popular instrument associated not only with trance but also with the theater, debauchery, war, and agrarian rites. The least we can say, therefore, is that its use was not a specialized one. As to its timbre and the manner in which it was played, we can say, without fear of error, that they were as piercing and as shrill as they

still are throughout the Mediterranean basin in our own day. Paintings de-
pict *aulos* players blowing their instruments with puffed-out cheeks which
indicates that, as is almost universal with this instrument, they practiced
circular breathing, which enables one to play without taking breaths, and
thus without stopping. As played in the Mediterranean manner, let us say,
the double clarinet and the oboe have very vehement intonations, a force-
ful and rasping tone, and an emotional intensity enhanced still further by
the fact that the instrument can be played for hours on end without interruption. In Turkey, a bagpipe—another form of the clarinet or oboe—is
used to incite camels to battle. It is tempting to think, in view of its shrill
volubility, its eloquence, its intensity, which makes the air positively vibrate and can be deafening, and its insistence, which can become almost
obsessive, that this instrument is particularly suited to the task of making
people's heads spin and to triggering trance. This would explain the close
association of the *aulos* with possession. In fact, such an interpretation
might as well be the pure product of our imagination. Nothing proves that
the sound of the *aulos* is experienced in this way by people actually hearing
it, and nothing in the texts demonstrates that this was the case in ancient
Greece. To be sure, Aeschylus, as we just saw, says that its calls "lead to
madness," but Euripides in the *Bacchae* (127–28) speaks, on the contrary,
of "the sweet calling breath of Phrygian flutes [read *aulos*]."[53] If the role of
the *aulos* in triggering trance had been due to its musical characteristics,
and in particular to its timbre, then its relation to trance would have been
doubly exclusive. Its use would have been reserved solely for possession
and, reciprocally, possession would have been induced by no other means.
But this was not the case. We have seen that the *aulos* was used in a great
many other contexts. Trance likewise was occasionally accompanied by a
quite different instrument. We know that in Greece the opposition between *aulos* and zither, between *aulos* music and zither music, between
Dionysus and Apollo was strongly emphasized. And yet, as surprising as it
may be, we find that the lyre could occasionally be associated with Bacchic
trance. This is shown by a painting I mentioned earlier, the one on the red-
figure cup in the style of Brygos and dating from the time of the Persian
wars,[54] representing Dionysus in a state of trance and playing a seven-
stringed lyre. Once again we see that in ancient Greece as elsewhere, the
relations between music—here the instrument of music—and trance were
not ruled by natural constraints but by cultural arbitrariness. It is nonetheless true that this representation of Dionysus holding a lyre is surprising.
Why is the god playing this instrument? To what mythological context
does this refer? For all I know, the question awaits an answer.

Let us now pass on to Plato's thoughts on the *aulos*. Taking as his starting point the passage in the *Symposium* (215c) in which we are told that
the melodies[55] of Marsyas played on the *aulos* are the only ones capable of

inducing possession by reason of their divine origin, Moutsopoulos (1959, 10) concludes that "thanks to this religious aspect of their art, aulos players, having been banished from *The Republic,* reappeared in the *Laws*"—a conclusion somewhat swiftly drawn. It would be very surprising if Plato, whose feelings concerning trance were so mixed, had seen in its association with the *aulos* a good reason for rehabilitating the instrument. The matter should be viewed somewhat differently. The *aulos* is indeed condemned in *The Republic* (399c–d), but this judgment is only made as part of a general condemnation of all "polyharmonic instruments,"[56] a condemnation that applies just as much to "instruments of many strings" as to the *aulos*—the most 'polychord' of all." And Plato asks: "Do not panharmonic instruments imitate the *aulos?*" We know that Plato accused *aulos* players of having introduced all sorts of innovations into music, notably new "harmonies" requiring more notes than the only two modes that "should be kept," that is to say, the Dorian and the Phrygian. In this passage, then, Plato has in mind instruments of recent and complicated workmanship, furnished with a great many side holes (possibly the *bombyx* with its long tube and mobile rings mentioned earlier). But he is not attacking the simple *aulos,* with its small number of holes, any more than he is the lyre or the zither when they have a small number of strings. He is attacking the virtuosos and their sophisticated instruments that upset tradition. He is not attacking traditional instruments in any way. And this explains why, when he is dealing with the organization of competitions "for both men and horses" (*Laws,* 764d–e), he groups "rhapsodists, zither and *aulos* players" together and thinks there should be "a separate umpire" for this group. It is therefore not quite correct to say that the *aulos* is banished from *The Republic* and reappears in the *Laws.* If we look more closely, we see that a different instrument is involved in each of the two cases: in one it is indisputably the instrument played by virtuosos; in the other it is the traditional folk instrument. The two were very different.

Nonetheless, the musical instrument dear to Plato was the lyre or zither, in short a stringed instrument (as long as there were not too many strings!). By their very nature as stringed instruments they were associated with ideas concerning the simple relations of lengths measured on a vibrating string, and hence to mathematical speculation about numbers; thereby they were connected with the highest aspect of music, the one concerning the relations of man with the cosmos and the great laws of the universe.

The *aulos,* on the other hand, is a musically approximate instrument, and the relation between its sounds—sounds that are easily altered by blowing differently or by differently covering the side holes—are more difficult to express in numbers. In the *Philebus* (56a) we read that the art of the *aulos* is one of adjusting its harmonies not by measurement but by "empirical conjecture." Added to its association with trance and debauchery, this aspect of the *aulos* would certainly not have led Plato to rank it high among musical instruments. However, in his respect for tradition and traditional music, he accepts the *aulos* willy-nilly, and carefully marks its place in the *Laws,* as we just saw. Meanwhile, his real feelings burst forth in *The Republic* (398–99) when he proscribes it, without stipulating that he is in fact referring to the modern, virtuoso instrument. Forgetting what he has just said about "instruments of many strings or whose compass includes all harmonies," and which "we shall not need in our songs and airs" because they are responsible for "dirgelike modes of music that are useless even to women," he asserts that "in preferring Apollo and the instruments of Apollo to Marsyas and his instruments"—meaning the lyre and zither to the various forms of *aulos*—he is simply "purging" the city of the "luxury" infecting it.

One could not judge the *aulos* more severely. Plato, nevertheless, nurtured a tender feeling for this instrument. Witness in the *Crito* (54b) the last words he has Socrates utter before his death. Resisting the appeals of Crito, who urges him to flee, Socrates decides to submit to the sentence of his judges, however unjust it might be; he tells Crito what the voice of his conscience is dictating to him and concludes: "That, my dear Crito, is what I seem to hear, just as it is said that those who corybantize seem to hear the *aulos*." As we see, Plato's feelings about the *aulos* were as mixed and as contradictory as those he had for possession.

As for Aristotle, he was not very fond of the *aulos* either, though for different reasons. Recalling the story (*Politics* 1341) of Athena who threw away the *aulos* after she invented it because, as she played it, she saw the reflection of her disfigured face in a spring (which showed that she was blowing it with puffed-out cheeks, the usual technique of *aulos* playing), Aristotle notes that although the goddess certainly did this out of annoyance because of the ugly distortion of her face, the real reason was that "education in flute playing has no effect on intelligence," something that would indeed disgust Athena, the inventor of the sciences and arts! (According to another version of the legend,[57] Athena flung the pipes away from her with these words: "Far from me, shame and taint of my body, I do not indulge in such indecency!" which again is hardly complimentary to the *aulos*.)

Elsewhere, again in the *Politics* (1341a), other reasons lead Aristotle to depreciate the *aulos*. This time, the instrument—which should be used only when "cathartic rather than educational effects" are required—should be excluded from the educational training of young men because one cannot speak while one is playing it; this obviously implies that such a defect does not apply to the lyre or the zither, since both are the instruments par excellence for accompanying singing. The *aulos* is thus condemned to be an instrument played only by professionals, slave musicians, or people of low estate. In fact, Aristotle's entire chapter on the education of young men, and particularly education through music (in the *Politics*), is impregnated through and through with a very marked class prejudice. Nobles and common people, slaves and free men are constantly being contrasted: "But professional musicians we speak of as vulgar people, and indeed we think it not manly to perform music except when drunk or for fun" (1339b), and further on he writes: "we do not consider performing to be proper for free men" (1341b). Still further on (1342a), dealing with theatrical music, he concedes the necessity of providing "cathartic" harmonies and melodies (meaning Phyrgian, and thus suited to the *aulos*) in order to satisfy the tastes of "the vulgar class composed of artisans and laborers and other such persons."

Plato, as we have seen, had little esteem for Bacchic dances—accompanied by the *aulos*—which are unsuitable for citizens." We also saw the lack of respect he had for the *aulos* player in the *Symposium*. In the *Theaetetus* (173d) he associates the instrument with the hetaera. For Plato as well as for Aristotle, both of high social status, the *aulos* was contemptible because it was the instrument of the lower classes and of slaves. In a sense, the *aulos* had in ancient Greece the same position the accordion now has in France. As for Dionysiac songs, they were essentially popular, as Nietzsche saw quite well in *The Birth of Tragedy*. Here once again we find what was said earlier about the highly popular character of possession music.

Let us return to the relation of the *aulos* to *mania*. Apollo was seen among the Greeks as the inventor of the lyre and Marsyas the Silenus as the inventor of the *aulos*. And about the melodies[58] of Marsyas, Plato categorically says: "whether played by a fine *aulos* player or a paltry *aulos* girl, they are the only ones capable of inducing possession, because of their divine origin, and to indicate those who are recipients of the deities and their [proper] rites" (*Symposium* 215c). Why is this? Because they "are themselves divine." An explanation as unexpected as it is peremptory! But who provides it? Alcibiades, who is drunk and delivering his celebrated and highly ironic speech in praise of Socrates. In other words, it should not be taken seriously. In short, Plato tells us that tunes on the *aulos* entrance people, and this is corroborated by too many other sources for us to doubt it; but he abstains from explaining this particular effect of *aulos* music. This fact is important and deserves to be stressed. Although Plato has a theory of the effects of music and dance on the curing of madness, as we have seen, he lacks one to explain the effects of music on the triggering of trance (though as we shall see, others would later formulate one in his place). Aristotle, on the other hand, had very precise ideas on the subject, so we will now turn to him.

Aristotle, the Ethos of Modes, and the Phrygian Mode

Plato tells us that if the "productions" of Marsyas have the strange power of causing trance, this is "because they are themselves divine." His explanation is a bit brief. Aristotle proposes a different view of the matter. In the *Politics* (1340a), having talked about the tunes composed by Olympus,[59] "which make our souls enthusiastic," and having given a long account of the imitative virtues of music and the nature of "harmonies"—or musical modes—he makes the general statement that "the Phrygian mode makes men enthusiastic [*enthusiastikous*]" (1340b). Marsyas the Silenus and his pupil, Olympus, are both, as we know, Phrygians. The *aulos* is Phrygian in origin. If the tunes of Marsyas and Olympus induce trance, they must do so because they are in the Phrygian mode—a more interesting explanation, it will be conceded, than Plato's. And all the more so because it is part of a general theory of music's effects based on the idea that music is able to "represent" and "imitate" states of the soul. Melodies (*Melē*) "do actually contain in themselves imitations of character" (*mimēmata tōn ēthōn*), Aristotle tells us, and in "melodies there are differences, so that people when hearing them are affected differently and do not have the same feelings with respect to each of them" (1340ab). The same is also true of rhythms, he adds. Returning a little later on to the Phrygian mode, he writes (1342b): "the Phrygian mode has the same effect [*dynamin*] among harmonies [*harmoniōn*] as the *aulos* among instruments, both are orgiastic and passional [*orgiastika kai pathētica*]. . .all Bacchic transport [*baccheia*] and all movement of this sort belongs to the *aulos* more than any other instrument, and find their suitable accompaniment in tunes in the Phrygian mode among the harmonies."

Being "passional" or "pathetic," the Phrygian mode is thus opposed to the Dorian mode, which is "ethical." Properly speaking, then, the Phrygian mode is not endowed with *ēthos* or moral character, but with *pathos* or passion. For this reason, unlike melodies in the Dorian mode, which the man or youth of high birth may learn because they are "ethical" (*ēthikōtatai*) and therefore suitable for educational purposes, those in the Phrygian mode must only be listened to, and their performance must be left to musicians of servile or low condition. It is worth noting, in passing, that here we return, though by an unexpected path, to a fact we established in an earlier chapter, namely that possession music is music one listens to and that is played by others.

Aulos music is Phrygian, then, and it excites "enthusiasm" among those persons in whom the effect of the "sacred melodies" (*hierōn melōn*) incite that kind of emotion. Those persons are then thrown into a state comparable to that produced by administering a remedy or purge (*katharsos*), and the result of these "purgative" or "cathartic" melodies is to produce a feeling of liberation in those to whom they are administered. Briefly summarized, this is the well-known theory of the relations between music and trance that Aristotle advances in book 8. 7 of the *Politics*.[60] Clearly it is very different from Plato's. Not a word here of either dance or movement: everything centers upon a theory of the effect (*dynamis*) of music, which is ethical when the mode is Dorian, orgiastic when the mode is Phrygian. In Plato, this aspect of the matter is not even mentioned, the reason being that he does not hold the same views as Aristotle on the ethos of modes.[61] Aristotle is at the same time clearer and more liberal. For him, the Dorian alone is "ethical," which is to say moral and worthy of figuring in the educational program of well-born youths. The Phrygian, being "orgiastic" and "passionate," must be excluded from such a program, and should only be listened to when played by employees of low estate or slaves. This said, however, all modes are good provided they are used in the correct way at the right time.

In Plato, things are rather different: he too places the Dorian above all the other modes, but his opinion of the Phrygian, which is much less clearcut, fluctuates over the years. In the *Laches* (188d–e), the Dorian is presented as the only mode that "is truly Greek," while the Phrygian is presented as being as little worthy of respect as the Lydian and certainly rated lower than the Ionian. In *The Republic* (399), which is to say much later in his life, Plato rejects both the Ionian and Lydian as being "soft" and fit only for drinking to, so that the only two with which he is left are the Dorian and Phrygian, of which he says: "Leave us these two modes—the enforced and the voluntary—that will best imitate the utterance of men failing or succeeding, the temperate, the brave—leave us these." Here, then, Plato is putting the Dorian and the Phrygian on the same footing. It is also worth noting that whereas, as we have seen, Aristotle identifies the *aulos* with the Phrygian mode, Plato, on the contrary never once associates the words "Phrygian" and "*aulos*." Similarly, Aristotle's repeated emphasis on the Phrygian's connection with enthusiasm is matched by Plato's total silence on this subject: the latter never once associates Phrygian music and trance. And just as the explanation of trance onset through the effect of the ethos of modes is central in Aristotle, so again it is entirely absent in Plato.

Plato's and Aristotle's interpretations of the relations between music and trance are thus quite different. Plato's theory of movement in harmony with the cosmos carries on the Pythagorean tradition. By systematizing the ideas inherited from the past concerning the ethos of modes, and at the same time relativizing them, which is to say giving them a much more psychological than moral content, Aristotle branches off in a quite different direction. We are not concerned here with deciding which theory is the better. What is interesting is to observe the extent to which the views of the two philosophers differ on the subject of music's relation to trance, even though they are separated by only about fifty years, and they both interpret what must have been currently observable facts presenting much the same aspect to each of them.

For Aristotle, then, it is the Phrygian mode that triggers trance, by its *sui generis* virtue. This being so, a question naturally poses itself: What were the specific musical characteristics of this mode that enabled it to produce such effects? That is the question I shall now try to answer.

First, it should be noted that the term Phrygian undoubtedly changed its meaning over the centuries in ancient Greece, and that if it designated a certain mode in the time of Plato and Aristotle, it certainly designated another one in the time of Aristoxenes. Needless to say, our question applies only to the, let us say, primitive Phrygian mode, the one to which our two philosophers referred. Let us thus turn to two sources dealing with data considerably earlier than Aristoxenes: first, the comparative table proposed by F. Lasserre (1954, 40) of the six Greek modes as they would have been at the time of Lasos of Hermione, which is to say at the end of the sixth century; second, that presented by J. Chailley (1960, 42) of Plato's six harmonies as transcribed by Aristides Quintilian in the second century A.D.[62]

If we restricted ourselves to these data, which represent the traditional views on the Greek modes, the question we raised would remain an enigma. Aristotle makes the most clear-cut distinction between the Dorian and the Phrygian with respect to their psychological effects. One would therefore expect the two modes to be equally distinct with respect to their musical structures. But this is not the case. If we are to believe these two tables, the Dorian and the Phrygian would then both have the same sequence of intervals (tones, quarter-tones, thirds), with the single difference that the final interval (going up the scale) would be a major third in the Dorian and a full tone in the Phrygian. Thus as Chailley observes (1956, 158), the Phrygian would have differed from the Dorian "solely by its final upper note, a *re* instead of a *mi*." Lasserre's table, on the other hand, establishes a difference of relative pitch between the two modes, with the Dorian being a fourth lower than the Phrygian. Quintilian's table shows no difference of this kind. In any case, this difference is not significant with respect to musical expression, since it does not affect the relations between the notes that constitute the mode. Clearly, then, the Dorian and the Phrygian, according to our two tables, were almost identical in structure. Their expressive possibilities would thus also have been much the same. Only a very experienced ear could have made a distinction between them. Under these conditions, it is difficult to see why the Phrygian should have been the mode of madness, let us say, and the Dorian that of serenity. That two modes so indistinguishable from each other musically could have been endowed with two ethos as different, and indeed as opposed to one another as Aristotle described them, remains incomprehensible.

For Aristotle (*Politics* 4. 3), since it is to him that we must turn once again, the difference between Dorian and Phrygian is comparable to that between a north and a south wind. We are not, therefore, dealing with mere nuances. In his eyes (or ears), the difference between what was called the Dorian and Phrygian in his time must have been musically ear-shattering. As we have seen, the traditional interpretations of what the Greek modes were offer no explanation at all of this difference, but another solution exists. Indeed, the very data underlying the problem have been recently renewed by Samuel Baud-Bovy's research based on a first-hand study of Greek peasant music as it can still be heard today, which in itself is an extremely interesting and innovative procedure. Commenting on the coexistence in Greece of two different musical systems, one pentatonic and without semitones (anhemitonic), the other diatonic with semitones, Baud-Bovy (1978, 189) advances this hypothesis: "that such an opposition already existed in the music of ancient Greece, illustrated by the rivalry of Apollo and Marsyas, with the *aulos* of Marsyas the Microasian, a diatonic instrument by nature, opposing itself to Apollo's lyre, whose strings, however many in number, certainly did not produce anything other than sounds belonging to the anhemitonic systems." According to Baud-Bovy,[63] the primitive Dorian must have been "a pentatonic anhemitonic mode, whereas the Phrygian was a diatonic mode. Apollo and his lyre triumphing over Marsyas and his *aulos* would then symbolize a victory of the Ancients over the Moderns." There is every reason to believe that this Phrygian mode with semitones was a heptatonic. The Dorian versus Phrygian opposition would thus be the same as that distinguishing between a pentatonic mode without semitones and a heptatonic mode with semitones. Musically, the difference is considerable. It it comparable to the one made today in Java between the *slendro* and *pelog* modes. And it is much more marked, for instance, than the already very perceptible opposition between major and minor mode in Western music. Under these conditions, one can readily understand why the Greeks so clearly, and in so many respects, distinguished between the Dorian and Phrygian. The difference was quite perceptible.

We now need to know why this Phrygian "harmony," having the clear-cut musical characteristics just described, was in Aristotle's terms "pathetic," "orgiastic," and "enthusiastic"; in other words, since this is our concern here, suitable for inducing trance. Musically, it is clear that a mode able to make tone/semitone contrasts must offer much greater expressive possibilities than one that lacks this possibility. The *aulos,* a Phrygian instrument, is obviously more expressive than the lyre, a Dorian instrument. The Phrygian *aulos* players, as Louis Laloy[64] observes, must have been the "true gipsy [fiddlers] of antiquity." The instrument's technical possibilities, the quality of its timbre, and the wealth of its inflections, in conjunction with the expressive possibilities of the mode, certainly allowed players to produce melodies of great emotional impact. The Phrygian undoubtedly was—and here we concur with Jacques Chailley—as much a style as a mode. To use Isobel Henderson's terms (1957, 382), the word *harmonia* did not only designate a certain scale but also an "idiom." Should we conclude from this that Phrygian melodies were so charged with expressivity and emotional content that they were capable of inducing trance by virtue of this quality alone? This would mean accepting the idea that music has a power *sui generis,* an idea refuted at length in earlier chapters. But this, one may say, is nevertheless Aristotle's theory! Not quite, I would reply. True, he writes (*Politics* 1340a) that the tunes of Olympus make men's souls "enthusiastic" and enthusiasm is an affliction (*pathos*) of the soul. True, he repeats elsewhere (1342a) that under the influence of these "sacred melodies" certain persons are "possessed" by a form of agitation known as enthusiasm. But he presents this effect of the Phrygian only as a particular—and, without doubt, extreme—case of a more general action tending to produce emotion in those inclined to "pity or terror."

The well-known passage in the *Politics* (1342a) in which Aristotle's views on the relation of music to trance are expressed, is quite significant. The *katharsis* that occurs in possession rituals, as a result of "enthusiastic" harmonies and "sacred melodies," is presented as being of the same order as that which is at work in the theater. (In passing, let me point out that this is probably the earliest text associating possession and theater in this way.) More generally still, these "purgative melodies," which arouse "a pleasurable feeling of relief" in emotional people, provide men with "harmless delight." The Phrygian mode thus covers a very broad musical field, one that includes trance music, theater music, the equivalent of variety show music (I mean those songs that move souls subject to "pity and terror," just cited), and last, dance music, when the latter is agitated or unbridled in character. Moreover, as it emerges from book 8 of the *Politics,* this Dorian/Phrygian opposition subsumes a whole series of other oppositions: calm vs. agitated, virile vs. effeminate, worthy vs. unworthy, aristocratic vs. plebeian, beauty vs. banality, educational vs. entertaining. The Phrygian side of this opposition could be summed up in one word: release. For Aristotle, then, Phrygian does not mean only "enthusiastic" in the religious sense of the term, but rather "orgiastic" in its general and rather late sense. When Aristotle writes (1341a) that the *aulos*—and therefore the Phrygian mode— is not "a moralizing but rather an orgiastic influence," so that it should only be used for purposes of "purification rather than instruction," he is certainly not thinking only of Dionysiac ceremonies. He is also thinking of theatrical performances or banquets; in short, all situations in which people seek release. On the contrary, when he specifically targets possession (*Politics* 1339b) and the music that induces it, he does not merely talk about the Phrygian, but is much more specific: the tunes of Olympus are the ones that make our souls "enthusiastic." Naturally, this must be set alongside the passage I have often quoted from the *Symposium* (215c) in which we are told that only the tunes of Marsyas are capable of "inducing possession." Why this insistence on the two names? Obviously because, by using them, Aristotle and Plato are indicating *ipso facto* that it is not just any Phrygian melody or just any *aulos* tune that triggers trance.

By thus specifying that only the tunes of Olympus and Marsyas are capable of inducing trance, both writers obviously have a particular repertoire in mind. What might its characteristics have been? The texts tell us nothing. But the reference to two legendary[65] if not mythical characters implies that the repertoire in question was ancient and traditional. This is not all, however. Marsyas and Olympus, and particularly the first, are strongly branded, if one may say so, as Phrygians. To mention Marsyas is almost to name Phrygia. And what was Phrygia if not precisely the homeland of Dionysus?[66] "From the fields of Lydia and Phrygia, fertile in gold, I traveled first to the sun-smitten Persian plains," he tells us himself in the *Bacchae* (14–15). And a little later: "O my sisterhood of worshipers, whom I lead with me from barbaric countries, from Tmolus, bastion of Lydia, who live and travel at my side. Raise the music of your own country, the Phrygian drums invented by Rhea the Great Mother, and by me." And lastly, in a later passage the chorus describes the Corybantes as "wedding their frenzies to the gentle breath of the Phrygian pipes." In the time of Plato and Aristotle, "Phrygian melody" clearly meant "melodies in the Phrygian mode," but not necessarily "melodies originating in Phrygia." Evidently this is what was meant by "melodies of Marsyas" or "of Olympus." As we have seen, the Phrygian mode was probably very recognizable as music, but it was less by virtue of being in the Phrygian mode than by virtue of originating in Phrygia that these melodies were endowed with the power of "inducing possession." In other words, their effect was due less to their musical characteristics than to the fact that they were signs: signs of Phrygia, the land from which Dionysus himself had come; in short, from the cradle of Dionysus worship. This process conforms with the general logic of possession which frequently makes a point of revealing the foreign origin of the god responsible for trance through all sorts of external signs. Possession is essentially identification with another. To assign that other a precise homeland is to assert his identity and thus his reality. As we saw in an earlier chapter, in Benin, when peopole belonging to Gun tribes are possessed by Yoruba divinities, they speak Yoruba and sing Yoruba songs. In South Africa, when the Thonga are possessed by spirits of Zulu or Ndau origin, then they sing Zulu or Ndau tunes. In Greece, in order to become possessed by Dionysus, one needed tunes originating in Phrygia.

Let me sum up. Dionysiac possession and the Phrygian mode are so closely associated in the literature of ancient Greece that this relation between music and trance would seem particularly interesting to us, since it springs from indigenous thought and attributes the onset of trance to a specific characteristic of music. In this case we would then have found—at last—an example in which the power *sui generis* of music is explicitly held responsible for trance. Things would seem all the more explainable because (1) this specific musical characteristic—the Phrygian mode—is easily recognizable and constitutes one term of a very clear opposition; and (2) this Phrygian mode seems to have, unlike the Dorian—the other term of the opposition—much greater expressive resources, thus making it more capable of producing an emotional arousal that can easily be imagined as leading to trance. A careful examination of the texts, however, demonstrates that none of this is actually the case. Whereas the texts confirm that all the melodies inducing trance were in the Phrygian mode, they by no means say that all melodies in the Phrygian mode induced trance. The writings of Plato and Aristotle effectively establish the first relation, or imply it; they do not establish the second. Indeed, had they done so, they would have run counter to the most elementary good sense, as a *reductio ad absurdum* will easily demonstrate. To assert that the Phrygian mode triggered trance by the operation of some mysterious musical power would have been also to assert that half of Greece was permanently thrown into this state. For, as all the facts show, *aulos* players of both sexes—and consequently Phrygian music—did not limit their activities just to Corybantic rituals. Their services were constantly sought particularly for banquets (or *symposia*) at which there is no record whatsoever of possession ever taking place. Both Aristotle and Plato, then, wisely refrained from asserting any such absurdity. Others, however, have not hesitated to do so for them, and in their name. By recognizing, not without good cause, that music possesses great imitative powers, and by attributing ethos endowed with powerful effects to the modes, Aristotle opened the path to all sorts of exaggerated theories. During the Renaissance, in their wild admiration for antiquity, people hurled themselves down this path in an aberrant way. And it is to these aberrations, survivals of which are still discernible today, that I shall now turn.

6 The Renaissance and Opera

From Marsyas to Claude Le Jeune; or, The Effects of Music

Let us now leave Plato and Aristotle in order to move on two thousand years, or almost, to the Renaissance, when in Italy, as in France, Greece and the Greeks were being rediscovered. It is a Greece that had been strangely transformed, no doubt, over the centuries, in Alexandria first, then Rome, then by the early Church Fathers and their successors, but one in which we still find our principal themes: first "enthusiasm" or trance and possession, and second the ethos of modes and the Dorian/Phrygian opposition; in other words, the effects of music.

The Renaissance occupies an important place in the history of the relations between music and possession for two reasons. First, it is the wellspring, unless I am much mistaken, of the ideas some people still hold nowadays about these relations; this is what we shall first try to demonstrate. Second, it was during the Renaissance that opera had its birth, as we all know; and in my opinion opera is nothing other, in many respects, than one of the avatars of possession. For in opera possession realizes one of its essential aspects, namely the identification of the subject with the hero by the combined means of music and drama. As Michel Leiris has so clearly shown, possession is fundamentally theatrical. Reciprocally, opera, as theater, is a form of possession. But this is a vast subject, and one that would lead us too far astray. I shall therefore limit myself to a brief sketch of the manner in which the problem can be raised in a short section at the end of this chapter.

Before coming to the Renaissance, however, let us briefly consider some of the Latin and Greek writings that form milestones, as it were, along the path taking us from Marsyas to Claude Le Jeune, from Pythagoras to Mersenne, and from Plato to Pontus de Tyard. Our Ariadne's clew will be the Phrygian mode we examined at such length in the last chapter, on the one hand, and, on the other, a certain story about music and trance that will illustrate its effect in a very significant way.

Although he lends the greatest importance to what Aristotle later termed the ethos of modes, Plato, as we have just seen, never posited the slightest relation between the Phrygian mode and trance. Aristotle, on the contrary, did so, but in a rather nuanced manner. Let us say that, for him, the relation between the Phrygian mode and "enthusiasm" clearly exists, but that it nevertheless admits of a fairly large margin of indetermination. With Plutarch, four hundred years later, the final step has been taken: this relation is raised to the status of a rule. In his *Erōtikos* (758–59), Plutarch cites the theory of the four aspects of *mania*, as it is set forth in Plato's *Phaedrus*. He then adds an observation that is of particular interest to us on "the furor termed martial or bellicose," about which he says: "everyone knows which god sent it and provoked its Bacchic transports."[1] Then, having pointed out that "the soldier, once he has laid down his arms, sheds his warlike madness" (*polemike mania*), he adds: "In the same way, for Bacchic and Corybantic leaping dances, it suffices to change the rhythm by abandoning the trochee, and the air by abandoning the Phrygian mode, for them to lose their violence and draw to an end."[2] If in order for trance to cease all that is necessary is to abandon the trochee and the Phrygian mode, then no doubt intoning them is all that is required for inducing it. We see that the relation between *mania* on the one hand and the Phrygian mode and trochaic rhythm on the other, is seen as resulting from a quasi-mechanical effect of music.

Fifty years earlier—since it was written down by Dion Chrysostom[3]—there was an anecdote in circulation that one could see as a custom-built illustration of Plutarch's rule. I shall not give it in this version, to which I did not have access, but in another one, written down three centuries later, in the fourth century, by a Church Father, Saint Basil, archbishop of Cappadocia. In recounting this anecdote, he wished to demonstrate the necessity for study and exercise in order to develop the body and mind. Having first compared athletic training to the study of music, and having poked fun (I'm not quite sure why) at Marsyas and Olympus, he praises Timothy,[4] "a master in the art of manipulating sounds. So much so that he was able at will, simply by the power of his music, either to arouse or to suppress men's ardor." He adds: "it is said that one day when he was playing his *au-los* in the Phrygian mode before Alexander, during a banquet, he caused him to rise and rush to his weapons; then caused him to return to his guests again, thanks to a relaxed harmony."

The fact that Alexander was well known for his irascible temperament does not alter the facts: this anecdote quite plainly describes a trance, a martial "furor" such as Plutarch describes with reference to "enthusiasm." It is as if one were reading Michel Leiris's *L'Afrique fantôme*, and seeing Malkam Ayyahu being suddenly possessed by a warlike *zār* upon hearing a gunshot. Indeed, Alexander's behavior has all the abruptness and all the conventional aspects of possession. The sudden alienation that invades him is devoid of all logical reason. It is not caused by anger. It has no motivating cause other than the music. Such behavior is evidently similar to that described by Plato in the *Ion* (536c), when he observes that those who are corybantizing "have a sharp ear for one tune only, the one which belongs to the god by whom they are possessed, and to that tune they respond freely with gesture and speech, while they ignore all others." The Corybantes behave like automatons, and it is indeed like an automaton that Alexander behaves. The only difference is that in the case of the Corybantes there is overt possession, whereas such is not the case with Alexander. The music acts by means of *its own power alone*, without the aid of any ritual, simply by the effect of the Phrygian mode in the first place, then by a change of mode.

We shall find that this anecdote resurfaces in the Renaissance, in almost identical form, but in a modern context. Before coming to this, however, let us turn to another story, different, but derived from the same model, and significant in another way. It is even more interesting since it appears in writings even earlier than those cited for the previous example, notably in Cicero. There are a number of variants;[5] I shall use the one by Boethius, which is the most complete. It appears in the introduction to book 5 of the *De institutione musica* (1867, 184–85), which deals with the moral effects of music. Boethius asks, "Is there anyone who does not know the story about the young man from Taormina who, drunk and excited by the sound of the hypophrygian mode, was calmed by Pythagoras who brought him back to his senses by changing the music to a spondee?" And he explains: "Whereas a prostitute had been locked up in the house of a rival and whereas he [the young Taorminian], in a frenzy, wanted to burn the place down, Pythagoras, who was watching the night sky as usual and observing the course of the stars, having realized that excited as he was by the Phrygian mode,[6] he [the young man] would refuse, despite the many warnings of his friends, to change his mind, advised that the mode be changed, thus tempering the frenzy in the young man's soul and [restoring him] to a peaceful state of mind." Less gloriously but just as naïvely stated, this is really the story of Timothy and Alexander all over again. Cicero's version tells us that this Phrygian music was played on the *tibia*, in other words on the *aulos*,[7] which could not be more in keeping with a context of drunkenness and orgy. Alexander was seated at a banquet. The young Taorminian was drunk. Although there is no question of possession, both contexts are nevertheless Bacchic, in the vulgar sense of the term, if not actually Dionysiac. But this time, and this is just as important, we are also in the context of Pythagoreanism, or, more probably, that of Neopythagoreanism (since nothing proves that Pythagoras was ever really the leading figure in so ludicrous an adventure), and this merits a closer look.

Pythagoras thus advises that the music's mode be changed, and that the Phrygian be replaced by a spondee; in other words, he orders the *aulos* player to switch to the Dorian mode.[8] We thus are dealing with a classic example of the ethos of modes. But the presence of Pythagoras lends it a quite different dimension.[9] In the domain of music, Pythagoras represents, as we know, both the theory of consonance and that of the "harmony of the heavenly bodies,"[10] the two being closely allied. And the Boethius version tells us that at the time of the incident Pythagoras was observing the stars; so it really is the Pythagoras-of-the-harmony-of-the-heavenly-bodies who is involved. This version of the anecdote therefore bears upon Pythagorean theory as well as that of the ethos of modes.

The harmony of the heavenly bodies (though we really ought to say the "scale" of the heavenly bodies, since this is what the words really meant)[11] is originally, let us recall, the idea that the law of numbers, which governs the consonance of the principal intervals (octave, fifth, fourth) of the scale, also governs the relations between the distances of the planets. It is the mystery of the *tetraktys*, that is to say of the four first numbers which, through the series of ratios[12] 1/2, 2/3, and 3/4, engenders both the consonances of octave, fifth, and fourth, and the harmony of the universe. It is also the idea that the seven strings of the lyre correspond to the seven planets; a number obtained by adding to the five planets proper the two luminous bodies, moon and sun. This theory, however, was merely germinating in Pythagoras' discovery of the relations of consonance, he himself never formulated it. It was Plato who did so, without referring to Pythagoras moreover, and who in the *Timaeus* gave it its final, grandiose, and esoteric expression (the relation to music is not at all obvious), and thus ensured its fame. The theory was then taken over and modified by many writers, Cicero and Boethius[13] among others. So behind the naïve and ludicrous story of the young Taorminian, drunk, excited, and then calmed down by the *aulos*—a degraded image of the relations between music and trance—we find not only Pythagoras but also Plato, and with them what was later to be called "the music of the spheres." Of all the Neopythagoreans who wrote on music, Boethius is certainly one of those who most influenced the ideas held during the Renaissance about its effects. It is now time to turn to them.

There has never been a period when musicians, poets, and "humanists"—all united at this time by one and the same desire, that of reviving Greek art—have been so deeply concerned about the power of music as the Renaissance. In Italy, as in France, the main concern was to rediscover the secret power that music was believed to have had in antiquity. People referred, with utmost seriousness, to the story of Orpheus taming the wild beasts with the spell of his songs and to that of Amphion displacing stones with the sound of his lyre to build the walls of Thebes. Even the kings put their word in. Like the emperors of ancient China, they held music responsible for public morality. In his *Lettres patentes*,[14] which created the Academie de Poesie et de Musique in 1570 in Paris, Charles IX declared: "It is of great importance for the morals of the citizens of a town that the music current in the country should be kept under certain laws, all the more so because men conform themselves to music and regulate their behavior accordingly; so that whenever music is disordered, morals are also depraved, and whenever it is well ordered, men are well tutored." Created to "restore the usage of music in its perfection," that is to say, in the style of antiquity, this Académie was intended to make its "Listeners . . . capable of higher knowledge, after they had been purged of whatever may remain in them of barbarity." One might think one is reading the *Li Ki* (Memorial of the Rites) of the ancient Chinese. In fact, via Florence and the work of Ficino, adapted to French taste by Pontus de Tyard, what is being revived here is Plato's *Laws* and *The Republic*. And in the "purged" we just read, we may also recognize Aristotle's catharsis from the *Politics*. With these *Lettres patentes*, which merely repeat the terms of the letter in which Baïf requested the creation of the Académie by the king, the whole program of the Pléiade poets was given official recognition. Through them, Ronsard's very theory of the union of poetry and music was made state policy; hence their importance.

Intimately associated with poetry, music was seen in the Renaissance as a decisive factor of civilization. It raises the soul and refines manners. By what means? Essentially by its capacity to arouse emotions. Among the ancients, Pontus de Tyard writes in his *Solitaire second ou discours de la musique*, "music served as an exercise to temper the soul into a perfect condition of goodness and virtue, arousing and calming, by its native power and its secret energy, the passions and affections, while its sounds were borne from the ears to the spiritual parts." Such is the model to be followed. Thanks to the intimate union of words and melody, of "measured verses" and music, also "measured," it is possible to obtain the three desired "effects," which are, Baïf writes in his letter to Charles IX, to "tighten, untighten, and calm men's minds." The supreme aim of music is thus clearly defined: it should move us. And the result of these "effects" is described for us by Ronsard[15] in his hymn to the cardinal of Lorraine, a poem in which, in praising the cardinal's musician, called Ferabosco, the poet also praises what he sees as the ideal in the field of music:

> Oh heavens, what sweetness, what ease and what pleasure
> The soul receives when it feels itself seized
> By the movement, the sound, and the voice combined
> That your Ferabosco on three lyres conjoins
> When the three Apollos, singing divinely
> And gently wedding the lyre to the voice
> Suddenly, with agile throat and hand
> Make Dido die again through Virgil's verse
> Almost dying themselves; or with louder trill
> Rethunder the sieges of Calais or Guienne

> Your brother's victories. Thus there is no soul
> That does not leave its body and swoon away
> At their sweet song, just as, up there in the skies
> At the god Apollo's song, the gods all swoon
> As he plays his lyre. . . .

The ideal, as we see, is that music should make one swoon. And what is swooning if not falling into ecstasy or trance, in short to be beside oneself? "There is no soul that does not leave its body." Again we are reminded of that great coming and going of souls we encountered earlier[16] in Haiti and Africa.

Exaggeration, one may say. A mere figure of speech that should not be taken seriously. Not at all! The literature of the time is replete with references to *fureur* and *furore*, words that translate the Greek *mania*, and that alternate with "enthusiasm." In his *Histoire et chronique de Provence* (1614, 583E), Nostradamus (not the astrologer but his son) writes that the troubadours derived their poetic invention from "a certain inspiration and divine frenzy called enthusiasm by the Greeks." A century later, in his *Le Parnasse ou l'Apothéose de Corelli*, François Couperin was to express in music "the enthusiasm of Corelli caused by the waters of Hippocrene." How are we to explain this rather unexpected resurgence of "enthusiasm?" Largely by the influence of two "humanists" somewhat forgotten today, but who in their time played a decisive role in this return to antiquity that so profoundly marked artistic life in the Renaissance: Ficino, the great translator of Plato, and then Pontus de Tyard,[17] the masterthinker, so to speak, of the Pléiade. Tyard's book *Solitaire premier, ou Discours de Muses et de la fureur poétique* was published in 1552 and reprinted in 1575, and its title evidently echoes that of Ficino's commentaries on the *Ion*[18] published earlier under the subtitle "vel furore poetico."

This "poetic furor" is nothing other than Plato's poetic *mania*, which was attributable, as we saw, to the Muses. Both Ficino and Tyard resuscitated the Platonic theory of the four aspects of *mania*, which, via Latin, became *furore* or *fureur*. In resuscitating it, however, they also transformed it somewhat.[19] Times had changed since Plato. Of the four aspects of *mania*, three had become rather difficult to celebrate: First, erotic *mania*, totally identified with pederasty by Socrates; second, prophetic *mania*, which had acquired a whiff of fire and brimstone; last, telestic *mania*, that of possession, which of course was no longer overtly practiced, under the penalty of being brought before the Inquisition. Of these three, however, the last was to survive the best, owing to a certain amount of clever juggling that enabled Bacchus, with the help of communion wine, to become identified with Jesus, and Dionysianism with religious fervor.[20] But the only one that had remained at all easily defensible was poetic *mania*, with the result that it eclipsed the other three, and "poetic furor" came to be the only state representative of "enthusiasm." Let there be no mistake, however: this poetic "furor" was still very close to religious frenzy, and was regarded as an inspiration, in the religious sense of the term, as a visit from the spirit; in other words, as a trance state, if not as possession.

Let us now return to the "effects" of music. If in the Dorian mode, music will incite men to moderation and virtue, thus exerting the moral influence referred to in the *Lettres patentes*. If Phrygian, it will unleash the passions, enthusiasm, and ultimately violence. Here, in a much simplified form, we recognize the theory of the ethos of modes as set forth by Aristotle. The poets and musicians of the Pléiade took it very seriously indeed. "If it please God to be able by the Dorian mode to extinguish the furor that the Phrygian may have aroused," Claude Le Jeune writes in the dedication of his *Dodécacorde* to Turenne.[21] Forty years later, Marin Mersenne himself, having first expressed the opinion, in his *Harmonie universelle*,[22] that "bad music [meaning Phrygian] should be banned from society," wishes that "magistrates would institute prizes and rewards for those who practice none but Dorian music." In that time of religious wars it was apparently the secret hope of Baïf that the psalms in "measured verses" would disarm the rebellious Huguenots and that the pacifying effect of the Dorian mode would restore harmony between Catholics and Protestants.[23] The least we can say is that Renaissance man took music seriously!

Nothing better illustrates how these "effects" of music were regarded in their relation to the ethos of modes, on the one hand, and to "furor" on the other, than two anecdotes that relate events of the time but are based on the model that had previously inspired the stories about Timothy and Alexander and about Pythagoras and the young Taorminian. Both these Renaissance anecdotes follow the same basic scenario: first, music that renders you beside yourself; second, music that restores you to yourself. It is quite evident that they are both, in fact, simply new avatars of the stories related by Saint Basil and by Boethius some thousand years earlier. They do differ in one respect, nevertheless, in that the first falls into the ecstatic tradition, the second into that of trance.

The first we owe to Pontus de Tyard (1555, 113–15), who after quoting the very two anecdotes already mentioned, that of Pythagoras and the young Taorminian, then that of Timothy and Alexander, passes on to a story told to him at first hand by a contemporary, the count of Vintimiglia. The count tells how, in Milan, where he had been invited to "a sumptuous and magnificent feast, held in honor of that city's most illustrious company," he heard a lute player who had "so divine a fashion of touching" and making "the strings die beneath his fingers," that all those who heard him "remained deprived of all feeling, apart from that of hearing, as if the soul, having deserted all the seats of sensibility, had withdrawn to the edge of the ears, so as to take its pleasure more easily in so ravishing a symphony."

And the count of Vintimiglia adds: "still had we been there, if this same man [the musician], changing his mind I know not how, had not revived his strings, and little by little invigorating his play with gentle force, sent back our soul and feelings to the place whence he had drawn them: not without leaving great astonishment in us all, that we had recovered from an ecstatic transport of some divine furor."

Doubtless one must allow for a certain amount of literary license in this story; but it would be an error to see it as no more than hyperbole and misuse of language. The emotion experienced was so great, we are told, that it was of the order of an "ecstatic transport." "Such power is very certain," Pontus de Tyard adds with respect to this music, "and I can myself bear witness to such things." If he insists so much, it must be because the facts are seen as hardly believable. So extraordinary, in fact, that Mersenne[24] in turn was to use them as proof of the power that "measured music" in the antique style could exert. Tyard also refers to "divine furor," or in other words enthusiasm. Here, certainly, we are in the realm of trance.

The second story is more significant still. We owe it to Artus Thomas,[25] Sieur d'Embry, author of a volume of *Commentaires* on the life of Apollonius of Tyanus, the famous first-century Neopythagorean. It takes place in 1581. Sumptuous festivities had been organized for the marriage of the duc de Joyeuse, favorite of Henri III. The *Ballet comique de la Reine* by Beaujoyeulx—a prefiguration of opera—was presented at the royal court for the first time. There was also music contributed by Claude Le Jeune, the musician most closely associated with the Pléiade, along with Jacques Mauduit. As though to authenticate the story he is about to relate, Thomas, like Tyard, begins by referring to that of Timothy and Alexander, taking care to mention that it was through the Phrygian mode, then through the "sub-Phrygian," that Alexander was first aroused to furor and then restored to himself. He then continues:

> I have several times heard the Sieur Claudin Le Jeune tell . . . that there was once sung an air (that he had composed along with the parts) at the magnificences provided for the wedding feast of the late duc de Joyeuse . . . which air, being tried in a concert played for that purpose, caused a gentleman present to grab his weapons and swear aloud that it would be impossible to prevent him from going out to do battle against someone; and that then they began to sing another air[26] in the sub-Phrygian mode that made him as tranquil as before: an event that has been further confirmed to me since by several who were present, so much do the modulation, the movement, and the conduct of the voice, conjoined together, have force and power over mens' minds. [Thomas 1611, 281]

This same story was repeated a few years later by Titelouze, who wrote an account of it to Mersenne (who was very interested in the "effects" of music) in these terms: "I remember having heard the late Claudin le Jeune, an excellent musician, when talking of the effects of ancient music, say that he believed it was with measured verses, and that he himself, with measured French verses such as Baïf and others composed, once sent a captain into a furor by musical movements that he had joined to appropriately fashioned words."[27]

With this anecdote we are once again, as we can see, in the direct line of Plutarch's rule: changing the musical mode is enough to trigger trance or cause it to cease. This is how a continually strengthening tradition arose; according to it music could induce trance as it does in possession rituals, but outside the framework of any ritual and without reference to possession—in other words, without context and by its own power alone; or again, as Pontus de Tyard himself wrote, by the simple play of its "native power" and "secret energy."

Moreover, based as it is on the Timothy and Alexander scenario, which derives from the same model as that of Pythagoras and the Taorminian, the story of the duc de Joyeuse's gentleman should also be placed in the same Neopythagorean perspective as the latter. Ficino (who naturally also cites the Alexander story), Pontus de Tyard, and Mersenne had all read Boethius,[28] and they were all deeply impregnated with Pythagoreanism and Neoplatonism (a Neoplatonism that sought, moreover, to reconcile Plato and Aristotle). It is this context that explains the success of our story, and it is in such a context that it should be read: the ethos of modes, of course, but also "furor," or in other words trance, and "music of the spheres," which is to say the mystique of numerology and astrology— these are the messages concealed within it, with that taste for secrecy so typical of the Renaissance, a time when knowledge and esoterism naturally went hand in hand. Ronsard's *Préface sur la musique*,[29] which he dedicated to Charles IX, provides a very significant example of this. Writing about the Phrygian and Dorian modes, the poet naturally cites, among other stories, the one about Timothy and Alexander. In the space of four pages there are four mentions of "the harmony of the universe" or of the heavens, and two of "furor"; he who is not "stolen out of himself" by "a sweet-sounding instrument or the sweetness of the natural voice, . . . has a twisted, vicious, and depraved soul," and he who "does not honor Music as a small part of that which so harmoniously (as Plato says) moves all this great universe" is not "worthy of seeing the light of the sun." Ronsard's importance for the French Renaissance lends great interest to this musical declaration of faith. As we see, it closely associates trance or ecstasy with the harmony of spheres.

This said, the principal role in producing the "effects" of music, as they were conceived in the Renaissance, was nevertheless assigned to the ethos of the modes. Whether in the case of Alexander or that of the duc de

Joyeuse's gentleman, furor and the return to normalcy are attributed to the successive effects of the Phrygian, then the Hypophrygian modes. In the story of Pythagoras and the Taorminian it is the Dorian, a more classical view of things, that ensures the "furious" young man's return to his senses. All our stories are thus centered around an antithesis between two modes that have opposite effects; the first, in all cases, is the Phrygian, which remains, whatever century we are in, the mode of "enthusiasm." I shall now examine the problem of the opposite effects produced by these two modes.

To begin with, the problem was by no means the same in the Renaissance as in the time of Aristotle and Plato. No fifth-century Greek could ever confuse the Dorian and Phrygian. The two terms designated two quite distinct modes[30] and whatever each one may actually have been (a matter to which we shall not return), there was no ambiguity at the word level. By the time of the Renaissance, however, this was no longer true. The general opinion of the age was, it is true, that the ecclesiastical modes in use were nothing other than the ancient Greek modes, but unanimity ended there. The greatest confusion reigned as to which was which. According to Glarean, the Dorian was the mode of *re*, and the Phrygian that of *mi*; according to Galileo and Doni it was the reverse, and according to Zarlino something different again: the first was the mode of *do* and the second that of *re*.[31] All were agreed, however, in making the Phrygian the mode of unreason and the Dorian that of moderation and wisdom. Pontus de Tyard supported Glarean's system, Mersenne that of Zarlino. As a result, Pontus de Tyard was convinced that enthusiasm was triggered by the *mi* mode and Mersenne, sixty years later, that it was triggered by the *re* mode, the very mode which for Tyard precisely had the power of calming it. In other words, each man attributed diametrically opposite effects to the same mode! The absurdity of this situation seems to have escaped Mersenne, and his faith in the ethos of modes does not seem to have been affected in the least.

Paradoxically, Claude Le Jeune, to whose music his contemporaries attributed such powerful effects, was much more cautious in this respect. His sweeping statements, quoted earlier, about the power of the Dorian mode to "extinguish the furors that the Phrygian may have aroused," were much more an expression of contemporary opinion in general than of his own. In the rest of his *Dédicace*, he remains very prudent indeed, and even writes that the "diversity of opinion" concerning the names of the modes had prevented him from using them in the nomenclature of his *Dodécacorde*. This alone implies that he was skeptical about the Dorian versus Phrygian opposition. And indeed, he believed much more in the ethos of rhythm than in that of mode. In his *Préface sur la musique mesurée*, which introduces *Le Printemps* (1603) we read the following:

> Rhythmics, on the contrary, was brought to such perfection by them [the ancients] that they drew miraculous effects from it: moving by this means the souls of men to such passions as they wished; which effects they wished to represent to us in the fables of Orpheus, and of Amphion, who softened the cruel hearts of the most savage beasts, and gave life to the woods and stones, so as to make them move and place them where they chose. Since then, this Rhythmics has been so neglected that it has been completely lost . . . until Claudin Le Jeune, who was the first to embolden himself to draw this poor Rhythmics back out of the grave within which it has so long lain, in order to make it equal to Harmonics.[32]

But by "Rhythmics" we must understand the rhythm of words as much as that of music, or, in other words, the "union of music and poetry." As we saw, this is also what Titelouze expresses when he reports the story about the duc de Joyeuse's gentleman to Mersenne: ". . . and that he himself [Claude Le Jeune] with measured French verses . . . once sent a captain into a furor by musical movements that he had joined to appropriately fashioned words."

We are once again back to our story. But this one (that of the gentleman suddenly seized by furor upon hearing a tune by Claude Le Jeune) differs in one respect from that of Alexander, who also becomes "furious" upon hearing Timothy play: the music played by Timothy was instrumental (he played the *aulos*) whereas that of Claude Le Jeune was vocal. As we discovered in the previous chapter, among the Greeks the music of *mania* was primarily instrumental and the musical instrument was almost always the *aulos*. In this respect the Timothy/Alexander story fits perfectly into the tradition. The story of Claude Le Jeune and the gentleman, on the contrary, does not. This is a significant fact, and we will examine it now.

The great idea of the poets and musicians of the Pléiade was that in antiquity music derived its expressive power from its intimate union with poetry. In other words, for them the only true music was sung music, music in which words played a principal role. It is therefore only natural that they should have shown such interest in Orpheus. Ficino, Pontus de Tyard, Dorat, Ronsard, Claude Le Jeune all refer to him as the very symbol of the power of sung poetry.[33] Mersenne also gives him the place of honor in his *Harmonie universelle* by making him the subject of its frontispiece, on which he is depicted surrounded by savage beasts held by the spell of his song.

From Orpheus—going back for a moment to ancient Greece—sprang what was later called Orphism. Without going into the very controversial question of what exactly it was,[34] I shall simply record what Boyancé (1936, 39) has said on the subject, namely that all "the activities of the Orphics may be subsumed under the idea of incantation." Elsewhere (ibid., 33), he also writes that "the idea of incantation is that which establishes the deepest bond between the legend of Orpheus and the religious practices of the Orphics." For them, Orpheus represented above all else the power of incantation, which is to say the magical efficacy of the chanted word. We learn from Plato (*Republic* 2. 364b–c) that the various charlatans and soothsayers who claimed Orpheus as the source of their powers were nothing other than magicians, and that it was in their incantations, their "epodes," that their principal power resided. These epodes, which they sang while performing the appropriate sacrifices at the request of a client, were what we now call Orphic hymns. These hymns in verse form were, to a large extent at least, what the Renaissance humanists were thinking about when, within the framework of a general return to Greek music, they advocated, in the name of musical efficacy, a return to the union of poetry and music. A poem published in 1609 by an Italian friend of Ronsard, Bartolommeo Delbene, who helped organize Henri III's Académie du Palais (an extension of the Académie de Poésie et de Musique),[35] is very revealing in this respect. In it he describes the "City of Truth," an allegory placed under the sign of Aristotle, the ideal model of the Académie. The fourth and last temple of this city is that of intelligence. Upon entering it, one penetrates into the realm of "enthusiasm" and of "poetic furor," symbolized by the "Union of Poetry and Music." Standing in this temple is a statue of Orpheus casting a spell over savage beasts with the charm of his music, and there is a space on the pedestal for the inscription of an Orphic hymn.

For the poets and musicians of the Pléiade, then, the effects of music were governed by three factors: the ethos of modes, the harmony of the spheres, and the power of incantation. The power of music is thus seen as being at once moral, religious, and magic. It is within this general conception, therefore, that we must situate the effect that Claude Le Jeune's music had upon the "furor" of our gentleman. Those who use this anecdote as the perfect illustration of the power of "measured" music in the ancient style are consequently making simultaneous reference to Plato (the theory of enthusiasm), Aristotle (the theory of the ethos of modes), Pythagoras (the theory of the harmony of the spheres), and to Orpheus (the practice of incantation). Whether explicit or not, these references explain why they took this anecdote so seriously. For them, it illustrates their general representation of the relations between music and human behavior.

For us, the story of our gentleman has a quite different meaning. We have said that among the Greeks possession music was principally played on the *aulos*, wordless most of the time, and intended to make people dance. Plato, when referring to such music, uses the words *melody* or *rhythm*, never the word *epode*, which he reserves for completely different contexts. For him, incantation and possession are two totally distinct domains. Incantation is used in the service of magic—or shamanism, if, like Boyancé (1936, 59) and Dodds (1951, 147), one wishes to see the Orphic priests, and even Orpheus himself, as shamans—but never in that of possession. In this respect, the situation in ancient Greece perfectly illustrates the rule formulated in an earlier chapter.[36] So by attributing our gentleman's trance to a kind of music that is not only vocal but reputedly Orphic, and therefore in the incantatory tradition, our story flatly contradicts precisely what it claims to prove, namely its conformity with trance music as it existed in antiquity. It runs contrary to the manner in which the relations between music and possession are practiced, whether among the Greeks or elsewhere. In this respect, then, it could be said to be a "bad story." But this is not important. What is important is that, by claiming to be in conformity with the Greek model, and at the same time by attributing the trance to the incantatory nature of the music, it leads one to believe that trance music among the Greeks was incantation. This is where the confusion lies, a confusion entirely symptomatic of the general confusion that the furious ferment of ideas in the Renaissance created in so many areas.

A music capable of triggering trance by the power of its "secret energy," as Pontus de Tyard would have it, or by the effect of the "hidden relations" of the modes with the soul's "affections," as Saint Augustine wrote,[37] or by the play of the law of numbers, or by its invisible links with the harmony of the universe, or by its incantatory powers; in short, a music that acts mysteriously—such, ultimately, is the theory that underlies our anecdote. It is for this reason that it is so significant, and that I have spent so much time examining it. The ideas it reflects are far from having lost all credit in our own day, and this is the point to which I will now turn.

"Incantatory airs whose effect was irresistible on certain subjects, whatever the skill or the mediocrity of the musician . . .";[38] "possessed thrown into trance by the demoniacal call of the incantatory melody"; a possessed person who "obeys the incantation of this music"—all these phrases demonstrate that for Jeanmaire it is the theory of the incantatory power of music that explains the fundamental role it plays in the possession process. Elsewhere, speaking of the musical theme specific to the possessing spirit, Jeanmaire (1949, 470–71) tells us that "this theme particular to each of the various demons by which each dancer believes himself haunted thus automatically triggers the onset of trance in the hitherto apathetic possessed person." Automatic behavioral response, haunting, incantation—all this adds up to a whole that constitutes, for Jeanmaire, the climate, so to say, of possession among the Greeks. Yet, as we have seen, there is no mention whatsoever of incantation in either Plato or Aristotle! To attribute the effect of music on trance to its incantatory power is to interpret the evidence in a totally arbitrary way. It means introducing magic where it does not belong. Above all, it means being quite mistaken about the formal characteristics of the music concerned. The music that triggered "the bounding dances of the Bacchantes and Corybantes," as Plutarch wrote,[39] was evidently stimulating, extrovert, dynamogenic. Incantatory music is by definition introverted, slowly turning around upon itself, proceeding by fascination, and developing itself in immobility. To see the music that induces trance as incantatory music is therefore a major musical misconception. It is amazing that Jeanmaire, despite his perspicacity and his admirable scholarship in the field, should have made this error. The reasons for it are clearly the power of the Orpheus myth on the one hand, but also, and above all, that of the ready-made ideas generally held about music, and to which even the best minds are not always immune. Many others have made and are still making the same error of interpretation. Their excuse is that they are following a tradition dating as far back as the Renaissance, and that has been maintained by writers as eminent even as Combarieu, who in his great work *La musique et la magie* devotes several pages to incantation in his chapter on the ethos of modes (1909, 228, 233) and concludes that among the Greeks the latter was simply "a legacy from ritual magic."

Linforth, to cite only one more example, makes an error of the same order. In his very important article on Corybantic rites in Plato, he refers several times to the "intoxicating" nature of trance music,[40] and to its "intoxicating spell." Spells, incantations—we are still faced with the same general conception of things, that which consists in attributing trance to a more or less inexplicable power *sui generis* in music, which acts in some way physiologically, like a drug, like an intoxication, like a magic potion. Not once does Plato mention incantation (*epōdai*) or intoxication in his texts on Corybantism. Linforth is yielding here to the same temptation as Jeanmaire, which attributes to music the magic power of triggering possession, something which neither the writings the Greeks nor ethnographic data justify.

It is this same Renaissance Neoplatonic tradition that has influenced— or perhaps given direct rise to—another interpretation of how music is related to trance. But here it is the mystique of numbers that is involved.

The theory of the harmony of heavenly bodies rests, as we saw, upon the belief, a purely intuitive one, that the movement of the planets and the relations of consonance are governed by the same law of numbers and by the same mystery of the *tetraktys* (which one might translate as "fourthness") that designate the ordering of the first four numbers in accordance with the ratios $1/2$, $2/3$, and $3/4$ (which would now be called superpartials), which are those of consonance. In a word, it is mystical numerology. When Alain Daniélou (1975, 14) writes that all music used to induce trance, always and everywhere, utilizes rhythms based on the numbers 5, 7, or 11, he is making use, whether he says so or not, of a theory of numbers that is admittedly different from that of Pythagorism, but that is essentially the same in spirit. In discovering the laws of consonance, Pythagoras gave proof of a great scientific mind. In developing the theory of the "harmony of the spheres," which is pure bunkum, the Pythagoreans and Neopythagoreans were merely dabbling in bogus science. They, nonetheless, were taken seriously for a long time. It seems that even Kepler believed in the music of the spheres.[41] But then, was he not as much an astrologer as an astronomer?[42]

In appealing to Plato, and in invoking *mania* under the name of *fureur poétique*, the poets and musicians of the Pléiade renewed the ties with the Greek trance tradition, but their version of it—need I say?—was literary and watered-down. Parallel to this aristocratic current at the level of the court and the salon, however, was another one, popular this time, that continued to keep the practice of trance alive in Western Europe in much less civilized forms. Tarantism in Italy and Spain, epidemics of Saint Vitus's dance elsewhere, demoniac possessions occurring sporadically in many places, and culminating later in those at Loudun—all these were very virulent manifestations of trance that have a greater connection with telestic traditions—those of Corybantes and Bacchantes—than with the poetic tradition of *mania*.

After a long eclipse, the latter made a new appearance, not so many years ago, again accompanied by music—of course—but this time by an international publicity campaign as well: Beatlemania. The recipe is apparently a good one, since it has been revived even more recently by yet another rock group that labels its show "Starmania." Of course, the word in this context means nothing more than "madness." Yet its use is nevertheless significant, and revealing of a certain desire—or a certain nostalgia—for trance. Learned tradition? Popular tradition? Juncture of the two? That is what remains to be seen.

LETTER ON A OPERA

Opera, as we saw earlier, can be regarded in certain respects as the last avatar of possession ceremonies; or the opera singer (and this comes to the same thing) can be regarded as the most recent of the roles so far played by the possessee. This would mean, all things being equal, that opera is for the German, the Frenchman, or the Italian what the *bori* is for a Hausa and *hau bong* is for a Vietnamese. If the reader doubts that this is so, nothing could be more likely to convince him, I feel, than the letter about to be put before him. It was written[43] by a young ethnomusicologist from Benin, at present living in Paris, to a friend and colleague back in Africa. It fell providentially into my hands at the very moment when I was preparing to deal with this very aspect of the matter. I am reproducing it here just as it was written, with no additions other than a few notes to clear up certain allusions in the text that would otherwise remain obscure.

My dear Asogba,

What an adventure! I went to the Opéra yesterday. I thought I'd gone raving mad! No one had warned me, so I had no idea what I was in for: imagine my surprise when I found myself bang in the middle of a possession ceremony! You would have thought you were in Porto-Novo, in the Place Dèguè, attending the annual feast for Sakpata, or at Alada attending the ceremonies of Ajahuto, or at Abomey for "The Grand Customs." Of course it's not the same thing at all, that's obvious. Of course the differences are immense. Never mind! I still think that a performance at the Opéra and a *vodun* ceremony in Benin are in many respects *fundamentally* quite comparable. That's what I want to explain to you now, since no one here seems even to suspect it, and everything else can wait.

Let's take psychology first. You will agree that the essential aspect of this, in possession, is identification with another, the invasion of the field of consciousness by a person other than the one one is normally, so that one is no longer oneself but this other, and so one behaves in every way like him. This is precisely what happens on the stage during an opera. Last night, in *Elektra*, which was the opera I attended, Birgit Nilsson was no longer Birgit Nilsson but Electra. You will say, yes, but that doesn't happen only at the opera, it's just the same in the theater, or also in movies. That's true to some extent. But what makes the opera a particular case, and links it so closely with a *vodun* ceremony—I almost wrote performance—is its relation to music. In both cases it is in fact the music that organizes the performance, gives it the structure that governs its development, dictates the movements, regulates the alternation between tension and relaxation. Just as a man or woman embodying a *vodun* takes his or her cue from the music to dance out his or her identification with the possessing divinity, so the opera singer takes his or her cue from the orchestra in order to express in song the character he or she is enacting. It is music that gives life to both of them. Neither one nor the other could incarnate his character without being constantly supported or even carried along by the orchestra. Their experience of their role is essentially a musical one, which is not the case in either the theater or the movies. You know how crucial the function of the musicians is at home, in all possession ceremonies. One has the feeling that they are the ones who lead the play, that under their power the possessed are but puppets receiving their orders. All things being equal, I get the feeling that the conductor and orchestra have an exactly comparable function in opera.

The big difference, from the point of view of its relation to music, evidently, is that in a *vodun* ceremony the possessed dance and don't sing, whereas in the opera the performers—I nearly wrote possessed again—sing and don't dance. We could say that in *vodun* [or *bori*, or *hàù bóng*] possession is expressed through dancing and that in opera it is expressed through singing. Or again, that the actor playing the *vodun* embodies his character by dancing it and that the opera performer embodies his by singing it. For he does embody it. Open the article on opera in Fasquelle's *Encyclopédie de la musique* and you will read: "It is not the reality of the characters on stage that is important in an opera, but the degree to which a singer-interpreter succeeds in evoking, *by embodying* [and those are the writer's italics, not mine] the inner character in the drama." I am tempted to think that singing a part implies a greater investment of the self in the dramatic action than when one merely acts it. It is not for nothing that the French call opera "lyric theater." To use Jakobson's terms, I would say that lyricism means that the emphasis is placed on the "addresser" of the musical message, on the "I." The opera house, the lyric theater, is thus the place where the first person expresses itself. It is the triumph of the profound expression of the self, at its most affective, most irreducibly personal level. To express that *self* it is therefore important to be totally invaded by it, and this invasion of the self probably never occurs more fully than in this lyric-dramatic situation, in which it is permissible to live it out totally in public, precisely because one embodies a character that is not oneself. It is obviously the presence of the spectators that gives full meaning to this extraordinary adventure that the opera singer lives out when singing on stage.

Does this intensity constitute trance? To answer this question one would need to ask the singers themselves. Would they or could they, answer? Once themselves again, once the curtain is down and the performance over, do they remember what they have experienced, or are they subject to the same amnesia that our *vodun* adepts experience regarding everything that happened while they were possessed? Ultimately, the point is to know whether the opera performer lives his role and sings it in a state of dual personality, so that he is simultaneously himself and the person embodied, one governing and controlling the other, or whether, on the contrary, he is solely the other and no longer himself at all, in which case we are dealing not with dual personality properly speaking—or, as Freud puts it, "double consciousness"—but with a personality change due to substitution. It is a question that has been hotly debated ever since Diderot, I believe. However, we mustn't lose sight of the fact that opera performers are professionals, that changing personalities is part of their trade, and that this is not the case with the *vodun* adept, even though he too has sometimes undergone a very long training period.

Let us assume then—first hypothesis—that while on stage embodying the hero he represents, the opera singer is in a trance, and let us call it, in this context, a lyric possession trance. This trance is quite clearly extremely controlled. It is not preceded by any crisis. Could this be the only type of trance displaying this particularity? And if so, would it be less of a trance for that reason? As you know, the trance in *vodun* cults is not necessarily preceded by a crisis. Indeed, this is one of the factors that helps in distinguishing between possession by a lineage *vodun* and possession by an "exogenic" *vodun*, to use Luc de Heusch's term. In Senegal, in the *ndöp*, only neophytes have crises; theoretically the women who officiate never do. So the fact that it is devoid of crisis would not be enough of a reason for seeing lyric possession trance as an isolated case within the general framework of possession. (Parenthetically, crises do in fact occur quite frequently in the opera house, or so I'm told. However, they take place in the wings; in short they are not part of the performance. In other words they are nonritualized crises, or just "tantrums," but that's another problem.)

Now let us change our hypothesis and say that the opera singer is not in a trance. Lyric possession would then be a form of possession without trance and we would have a type of possession that is completely different, psychologically speaking, from that at work in possession by a *vodun*. In this case, should we say that we can no longer speak of possession at all? I don't think so. The crucial thing, ultimately, is that, from the spectator's viewpoint, the entire event happens in such a way that the opera singer is seen to be truly embodying his character, or is, in other words, totally possessed by that character. Indeed, if the spectators believe in this incarnation, the singer is a great actor. We are therefore at the frontier of possession, but still within it. Or to put it more accurately (since we must not argue as though possession constitutes a fact in and of itself), let us say that lyric possession has enough points in common with religious possession for both to be considered as belonging to one and the same very general state of consciousness.

So, if seen in relation to possession as a state of consciousness, an opera performance and a *vodun* ceremony are appreciably equivalent, how is it then that they are so different? Is it, ultimately, because one is aimed at the realization of an aesthetic need and the other at that of a religious one? But is this difference a real or an illusory one? What if the aesthetic function in one type of society were the same as the religious function in another? Has art not been, for a very long time, the main technique of religion? It is no wonder that, as the religious function atrophies, art becomes an end in itself. We have heard often enough that Greek drama originated in the cult of Dionysus, that modern Western theater had its origins, in part at least, in the Christian Mysteries, and that Japanese Nô is but a theatrilization of possession. I know nothing about the history of opera, but I will once again quote from Fasquelle's *Encyclopédie de la musique* (my great source of information, as you can see!), in which the article on Comic Opera states that its origins lie in the medieval *Fête des fous*, or Feast of the Madmen. Weren't these "madmen" purely and simply possessed persons? Unless I'm much mistaken, there are a great many reasons to think so. . . . But let us leave aside these historical problems about which I know nothing, and get back to the question at hand. I tend to think that the difference between a performance at the Opéra and a *vodun* ceremony is largely circumstantial and dependent on the context.

I have already told you the ways in which the opera seems to be closely akin to a possession ceremony. I would also like to explain the ways in which the possession ceremonies that you and I know now seem to be akin to opera. A moment ago I mentioned Alada[44] and the annual ceremonies for Ajahuto.[45] Now think back to the feast for Ajagbe that we attended together a few years ago and let me tell you how I remember it. In the late afternoon, Akplogan,[46] sumptuously clothed in a blue and gold brocade robe, left his house in grand procession, preceded by spear carriers. Seats had been prepared for him and his entourage on one side of the public square where the dances were to take place, and in the center there stood an enormous kapok tree. As they arrived, the various families of Alada and the surrounding district, who had also come in procession, went to greet Akplogan before taking their places nearby. The various merchants set up their stalls slightly behind the audience. Little by little the square—I almost wrote the auditorium—filled up. Drums, rattles, and iron bells were gathered at their appointed place, but no one seemed to pay any attention to them. When the time came, however, musicians appeared and began trying them out: hammer-blows on the drums to stretch their skins, test-drumming to judge the effects, bell-calls sketching out a rhythmic phrase. A certain vibration in the air that we both love so much had taken over. As I sat in the Opéra, I experienced this same impression of music awakening when the musicians took their places in the pit and began to prelude, as it were, each performing in his own corner, one playing a few notes of a scale, the other a brief arpeggio. The music slowly took possession of the place, just the way it does back home. Unfortunately, I have no idea what exactly was going on backstage, since the audience isn't allowed there, as you can imagine. But I was suddenly reminded of that wonderful evening in Alada, to which I shall now return. You had gone to say hello to your kinfolk, who had just arrived and settled themselves in a spot—I almost wrote a box—near Akplogan. You were making your social rounds, in short, just as I saw it done last night at the Opéra. Since I know very few people in Alada, I went for a stroll. I was intrigued by a half-open wattle door behind which there seemed to be a great deal of coming and going. I slipped through it. And I was backstage! There's no other way to put it. You know that the Sakpatasi[47] have skirts worn tightly at the waist? Two of them were adjusting their skirts, busily knotting the little fastening strings, then swaying their hips to see whether they hung right. Further on, a woman who was also, visibly, a *vodun* devotee was making herself up, helped by a companion holding a mirror. Elsewhere, a Legba[48] was arranging his necklaces, checking the fastenings of the vast panoply of objects they always wear, and adjusting the tilt of his straw hat. Elsewhere again, a group of women was swarming around a figure whose back was turned to me and whose loincloth was being arranged. All these people were gaily chattering, some standing, moving from one group to another, others seated on small stools. Suddenly my presence was noticed, and with cries and exclamations from all present I was gently but firmly shown the door. I'd had a terrific time. I had really seen what it was like backstage and all that went on there in preparation for a performance. I had discovered that our great ceremonies in honor of the *vodun* are just like theatrical performances in that they require a quite a bit of preparation and involve a great hustle and bustle behind the scenes, during which the adepts, who prepare to go into trance and to be possessed by their gods, behave just like actors backstage in other countries.

The drums began to beat. The feast began. The ritual actions had taken place that morning: invocation of the ancestors, divination, offerings, libations, sacrifices, prayers. The evening would be devoted exclusively to dance. It became dusk. First came a very calm parade, accompanied by drumming that rose and fell. It was as though the entire troupe had to be presented to the audience. If I remember correctly, Khèvioso,[49] recognizable by his *récade*[50] in the form of a stylized brass ax, led the way, unless it was Lègba with his enormous phallus of polished wood around his neck. There were about ten of them in all, all richly costumed, the men wearing short variegated skirts, rather like tutus, the women in long crossover skirts made of multicolored cloth, arms weighed down with silver bracelets, neck and ears bedecked with necklaces and pendants. As they moved past, the audience acclaimed them, shouting out mottoes at the top of their lungs, their voices mingling with those of the singers standing near the drums. After circling the dancing area two or three times, half walking, half dancing, the procession disappeared backstage again. There followed a fairly long pause, filled only by drumming and rather loose singing. Night had fallen. In the dark, one could scarcely make out people's faces, since the only source of light in the square was the gas lamp placed besides Akplogan. Further back, the tiny lamps of the stall keepers pierced the darkness here and there with their small yellow flickers.

Suddenly, Khèvioso burst into the square, eyes rolling, a white kerchief knotted around his head, brandishing his brass ax in threatening gestures, running and leaping in all directions, driving back any children who happened to cross his path. Sacred furor of the god of lightning! His brass ax, taut curve and tongue of fire, flashes in the night. Khèvioso spins around on himself, hurtles first this way, then that. His eyes roll frenziedly in his head, white flashes shining through the darkness with a moist gleam. His

feet make the dust fly. Drums, rattles, and iron bells had joined in frenetically, encouraging, with the greatest agitation, the dancer's wild dashes
and turns.

Meanwhile, without anyone noticing, another dancer—excuse me, a
female divinity, but which?—had also taken possession of the stage, moving forward with tiny steps, scarcely dancing at all, and very reticently,
with little sways of the hips, arms curved out in front of her to part the
panels of her pagne. Apparition full of charm and gentleness, making the
most touching contrast with Khèvioso and his violent demonstrations of
virile energy. Then it was time for Lègba's entrance, as fantastical as ever,
so that one never knows whether he's serious or joking. Straw hat and tutu
both dyed purple and both of a somewhat unlikely shape. Lègba pirouettes, stops suddenly, legs apart, holds his bizarre pose; then shoots off unexpectedly in a new direction. Everything about him is disconcerting. His
expressions force you to laugh, but you're not quite sure why. Other dancers—I mean other gods—come on stage one after the other. Now there is a
pantheon of five or six divinities dancing together, each in the style befitting his or her character. Lègba, who had vanished, makes a showy
reentry, holding his huge wooden phallus in front of him with both hands,
and taking over the center of the square, he performs an obscene dance
with utmost vigor. General but not excessive hilarity ensues. And so the
performance continues, with entrances, exits, crowd scenes alternating
with solo exhibitions. All executed with a very great freedom of movement and, certainly, with a great deal of improvization. Since I was enjoy-
ing the show as a dilettante, never having been initiated into any cult myself, the esoteric aspect of these dances naturally escaped me. And yet,
with all those gods parading about, we certainly were being treated to a
tremendous lesson in mythology. Yet one still had to know how to read it.

I recently described that evening to some friends—white people, of
course—here in Paris. "But what about trance in all that?" they asked.
Well, you know, I told them, come to think of it, there was no more—but
no less—of it than at the Opéra. I doubt whether someone who was really
a stranger to the country, and hadn't been told beforehand, would have
even suspected that the people he saw dancing were in a state of possession. And yet, as you and I both know, they were. The dancers always are
in such ceremonies. But entry into trance takes place backstage—whether
it is with or without crisis is secondary—and from then on it is scarcely apparent most of the time, except by certain small signs recognizable only to
those experienced in such matters. Perhaps there is a slight fixity to the
gaze, perhaps it is bizzarely elsewhere. That's all, apparently at least. I
couldn't say what goes on in their heads.

As I told you, so far I've seen only one opera. That's not much of a basis
on which to make valid comparisons with our *vodun* feasts. The differences from opera to opera are very great, it seems, because the repertoire

is vast. But that's true of our ceremonies too! Very often, I'm told, operas
involve a certain magical element. The action can move outside everyday
reality. Things happen that are scarcely believable. To limit myself to
Mozart, I'm told this is true of two of his operas: *The Magic Flute*, which
as its title indicates has a fairytale atmosphere, and *Don Giovanni* which,
toward the end, also brings into play a fabulous character, the Commen-
datore. And this supernatural, fabulous element is also at work in our
ceremonies. I would even think that it is essential. Remember that ceremony for the resurrection of a Sakpatasi, at Porto-Novo? What could be
more fabulous, more unbelievable than a resurrection? But what theater!
What staging! The open space at the center of the square black with people, the mats so carefully arranged on the ground, the high priest, all in
white, sitting at one end with two pots full of magic water at his feet, the
corpse swathed in its shroud, making its entry on the square borne rigid
on outstretched arms, set down on the mats before the high priest, then
the priest's seven calls, summoning, in dramatic tones, the body to waken,
the truly "deathly" silence of that great crowd awaiting the miracle, the explosion of joy, the delirium that sweeps through it at the first sign of returning life, the frenzy of the drums, suddenly liberated again, the whole
thing preceded by a slow setting of the scene, by choruses, dances, processions, and ending in a general dance accompanying the resuscitated Sakpatasi's first steps, the songs, the joyous sound of all the instruments. And
even though the ceremony was very much part of a possession cult, since
the corpse was that of a girl killed by the *vodun* who wanted her for his
wife, there was in fact no question of trance. Yet possession certainly lay
at the very heart of this drama. Dead to her former life, the girl was being
reborn to another existence, that of the wife of a god, a wife whom this
god would henceforth ritually possess at each of his feasts. A change of
personality, through possession, was the very substance of the ceremony,
and the whole thing was presented, I now realize impregnated as I am
since yesterday with opera, as a musical drama. It is impossible to conceive of it without song, without dance, and without musical instruments.

   Of all the *vodun* ceremonies I have seen back home, this is the one that
provides the best example of dramatization and theatrilization. It is significant, it seems to me, that it had as its theme this resurrection, taking
place within the framework of a possession cult and consisting, ultimately, in the birth of an actress.

   There is another good example of theatrilization among our ceremonies: the "Grand Customs" of Abomey, which also involve a very elaborate theatrical production.[51] Imposing processions, tremendous choruses
as they move from the square to the temple, and all very similar, if I can
believe what I'm told, to what one sees in *Boris Godunov*. Long, unbroken
succession of dances consisting of quite varied allegorical and symbolic fig-

ures whose deepest meaning is not really understood except by initiates. There are dramatic episodes recalling the great feats of the princes of the blood and warriors of former kings, redoubtable fighters who decapitated their enemies without pity, and who are still embodied today by entraced women in the course of these festivities. At a specified moment in the ceremony—which lasts almost an entire day and is repeated on several successive days for weeks on end—each dancer (although she is not the woman one sees; but the character by whom she is possessed and who "dances on her head") in turn breaks away from her group and simulates such a combat in the center of the square. This takes the form of a saber dance in which the movements are precise, lightning swift, but very stylized, preceded by a dance circling the square and followed by a return of the dancer to her group supported on the shoulders of two of her companions, who move forward to help out the exhausted warrior. All action is accompanied, of course, by choruses and drums. Here, however, contrary to what we saw in Alada, there is no improvisation. The entire performance is as strictly regulated as an opera-ballet would have been, I am told, in the days of Louis XIV.

I expect you're wondering by now what I'm hoping to prove with all these comparisons, which you may think very superficial. Don't worry, I'm not going to start arguing that performances at the Paris Opéra have their origins in ceremonies for the *vodun* in Alada, or anywhere else. What strikes me is that possession ultimately seems to occupy fairly comparable positions in two states of civilization as far removed from one another as the one in Paris, on the one hand, and Porto-Novo on the other. But despite appearances, or rather ready-made ideas, this is in fact the case. Everyone willingly agrees that possession occupies a very important position in the traditional religion of our country; but you will find precious few people ready to accept the idea that possession also occupies an important position in the social life of contemporary France. The Opéra stands in the very heart of Paris; its budget is more than a hundred million new francs a year (a tenth of our entire national budget!) and this is where foreign heads of state are taken when they come on official visits. If my analysis is correct, therefore, this Théâtre National de l'Opéra of theirs is nothing other than the French temple of lyric possession. Nonreligious, wholly profane possession, but possession all the same, and comparable to that observed among us, since once again opera consists in people embodying, or behaving so that others believe they are embodying, imaginary characters with whom they identify in public by means of behavior closely associated with music. You may tell me that none of this is really important at the Opéra, that what matters is to show off one's dress or one's wife, to see if the performers sing well and if the sets are beautiful. But all things being equal, the same is true at home! At home, possession takes place in the course of a performance very comparable to an opera. An opera performed here involves behavior very comparable to possession. The fact that possession among us is totally sincere (in theory at least), and that it may be totally insincere here (but can it ever be?), does not change anything at all.

The fascination that possession exerts on the minds of men is what intrigues me. I had naïvely thought it was hardly ever found outside of, let us say, "archaic" societies, such as our own. My visit to the opera has shown me I was quite wrong. How is it that this cultural trait is apparently a universal in human societies, whatever the stage of their development? To what deep need does it correspond? What fundamental function does it perform? Could it be the *katharsis* Aristotle wrote about? This, I must say, is what I was tempted to think when I heard (to my great surprise!) the prodigious outpouring of enthusiasm that exploded in the auditorium as soon as the last note had been sung. One would never find anything like that at home, I thought to myself. That unending applause, those yells of approval intrigued me a great deal. Were they a manifestation of collective frenzy?

As you may have gathered, I still must clear up a lot of points. Ethnologists here in Europe are beginning to ask themselves (it is high time!) what the "indigènes" think of their interpretations. So I hope to find a few native Parisians who will tell me what they think of the ideas I've had and the questions that came into my head as I observed them at the opera. I'll write again and tell you what I find out; it should be interesting. But I shan't necessarily take what they say at face value, you can count on that. Why should the mere fact that they are natives place them *ipso facto* in a better position than us to understand what is going on among them?

"First came a very calm parade, accompanied by drumming that rose and fell" (p. 246).

". . . the women in long crossover skirts made of multicolored cloth, arms weighed down with silver bracelets, neck and ears bedecked with necklaces and pendants" (p. 246).

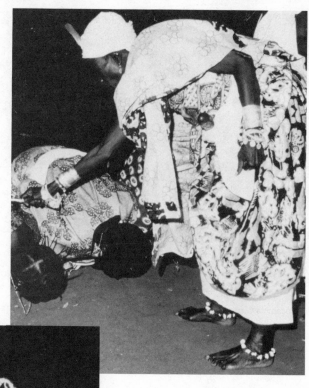

"I doubt whether someone who was really a stranger to the country, and hadn't been told beforehand, would have even suspected that the people he saw dancing were in a state of possession" (p. 247).

"Lègba pirouettes. . . . Everything about him is disconcerting" (p. 247).

"Suddenly, Khèvioso burst into the square . . . , a white kerchief knotted around his head, brandishing his brass ax in threatening gestures, running and leaping in all directions. . . . Sacred furor of the god of lightning! . . . His eyes roll frenziedly in his head, white flashes through the darkness with a moist gleam. His feet make the dust fly. Drums, rattles, and iron bells had joined in frenetically, encouraging, with the greatest agitation, the dancer's wild dashes and turns" (pp. 246–47).

7 Music and Trance among the Arabs

Of all the peoples in the world, the Arabs[1] are undoubtedly those who have associated music and trance the most closely: first, in their religious life, with Sufism,[2] in which trance (*wajd*), which for many adepts occupies a very large place in the search for God, is achieved very often through music; and second, in profane life, in which musical emotion (*tarab*) traditionally leads, very frequently, to trance behavior.[3] These two aspects of the relations between music and trance among the Arabs are what we must now examine.

RELIGIOUS TRANCE

Kitb ādab al-samāᶜy wa al-wajd, "Book of the Right Usages of Audition and Trance,"[4]—such is the title given by Ghazzali (al-Ghazzali, known as Algazel during the Middle Ages) to the eighth section of his renowned *Ihyāᶜ ulūm al-din,* "Book of the Revivifying of the Sciences of the Faith," which dates from the early years of our twelfth century and constitutes one of the most important writings on Sufism. "Audition," let it be clear from the start, means audition of what we have here decided to call "music." To be sure, one could not have found a book more closely connected with the problem of the relations between music and trance.[5] But before coming to it, let us first examine the words *samāᶜ* and *wadj,* which I have translated as "audition" and "trance," whereas Duncan B. MacDonald, to whom we owe the English translation of this work, most often renders them by the terms "listening" and "ecstasy."

The Word *Samāᶜ*

Given the context in which Ghazzali uses it, the word *samāᶜ* is in fact untranslatable,[6] for two reasons. The first is that it denotes a very particular thing, peculiar to Sufism, which is the ceremony made up of prayer, music, and dance that brings dervishes together for the purpose of adoring God and practicing trance. This ceremony is called the *samāᶜ* and, taken in this sense, it is similar to the word *islām* in that it has no equivalent in French or English. The second reason is that Ghazzali's book is above all an attempt to justify *samāᶜ* and his justification rests upon the ambiguity of the word, or rather upon the fact that the word has two meanings, a very particular one, which I have just given, and a general one, which is "listening" or "audition." If "audition" (*samāᶜ*)—"of poetry and music" is understood—is lawful in the eyes of the faith because it can cite illustrious precedents in its support, then the *samāᶜ* (ceremony) is also lawful.[7] This, in extremely simplified forms, is his argument. Now we must look at the meaning, or rather the meanings, of *samāᶜ* even more closely.[8]

The relation between *samāᶜ* as ceremony and trance (*wajd*) is so close that the word *samāᶜ*, in this sense, also signifies the trance state. One can in fact say "to go into *samāᶜ*" or "to be seized by *samāᶜ*," or again, "to be in that state."[9] Molé writes (1963; 148) that the term is practically equivalent to "ecstatic dance," At the beginning of the first chapter of his book (Mac-Donald 1901; 200), Ghazzali says, "know that the *samāᶜ* . . . bears as fruit a state in the heart that is called trance [*wajd*]." Taken to its limits, *samāᶜ* can also mean "music," or something very like it, since one can say[10] "hear *samāᶜ*"—which is surprising since it runs counter to the very logic of the word, for such a usage amounts to the same thing as saying "hearing the audition." But, once again, *samāᶜ*, which derives from the root *s.m.ᶜ*. (hear, listen) denotes, in its first and general sense, the act of hearing or listening, without reference to any particular acoustic phenomenon, or, let us say, "audition." Granting this, in the Sufi texts that interest us here, the verb "hear" (*s.m.ᶜ*) in its various forms always includes an implicit object, which is either poetry, the Koran, or music, though a particular kind of music only. But which one? In order to answer this, I must first digress on the word "music."

The Arabic word *mūsīqī*—which comes directly from the Greek, need I say?—does not appear even once in Ghazzali's book.[11] This is clearly not because he does not know the word; at the time he was writing his book, the translation of Greek authors into Arabic had already been going on for a hundred and fifty years. It is because he is avoiding it. For several reasons. First, because in his time the word *mūsīqī* denoted the rules or the art of music but not music itself as a product of that art, or, if one may say so, as a concrete thing. In order to refer to what we would call music in the concrete sense, Ghazzali talks either of song (*ghinā*) or of instruments used for entertainment (*malāhī*), depending on whether he has vocal music or instrumental music in mind. And so of course, he had many other words at his disposal, such as "entertainment" (*lahw*), in the sense of "entertainment music,"[12] "melody" (*lahn*), or "sound" (*sawt*), for example, without mentioning the names of the various musical instruments. But he does not have a word that covers a very general concept comparable to that we convey by the use of our word "music." (Although, as we all know, this word can have different, and even opposing meanings on occasions, according to who is using it.)

If Ghazzali does not use the word *mūsīqī* it is also because this word, referring as it does to the rules for composing music, relates much more to the music maker than to the listener. And it is precisely the listener he is interested in, not the musician—for a very good reason, indeed, since in the eyes of the faith the musician is always a suspect, if not blameworthy person. His third and last reason for not using *mūsīqī* is that it does not connote any moral value. The rules of music apply to all kinds of music; not only to that played for spiritual purposes but also to that played at "gatherings where wine is drunk" (Mole 1963; 174) in which the songs are mere "amusement and futility." From Ghazzali's point of view, which is essentially that of finding a moral justification for *samāᶜ*, it is indispensible to make a distinction between what we might term "light" music and "serious" music. Only the latter is lawful. To confuse the two by using the same term to cover both would thus be aberrant. That which is lawful consisted of; first, the cantilation (*taghbīr*)[13] of the Koran, of course; second, sung poetry, on the condition that its sentiments and thoughts were sufficiently elevated; and third, accompanied song, provided that the musical instruments utilized were permitted, which is to say instruments that were never associated with blameworthy musical practices. But this is not all. Another restriction must be added to these. It is permissible to hear only that which one hears when one is oneself in a certain state of inner purity. It is not only what is sung or played that counts; it is also the disposition of the listener. Heard with a pure heart, music can be lawful even though it would not be if one listened to it in a lascivious state of mind. This delimitation of the repertoire (Koran, poetry, accompanied song), made all the stricter by a proviso applying to the listener's own intention, is precisely what is conveyed by the word *samāᶜ*. This conceptual patterning of reality to which it corresponds is comparable to no other, and certainly not to that of the word "music."

Thus, in a Sufi text, the range of things possible for "audition" (*samāᶜ*) is restricted to poetry, the Koran, and, let us say, serious music, and these three things combine, for this very reason, to constitute a particular category of sound. This category, which is covered by no particular Arabic word (unless it is *samāᶜ*), may thus be defined, in the context of Sufism, as the category of the objects of audition (*samāᶜ*). This category of sounds, as we have seen, is not only constituted by the different intrinsic qualities of its three components; the fact that it is heard also plays a role. It exists only insofar as it is perceived by the ear and insofar as it affects the hearing. Twice, on the first page of his book, Ghazzali stresses the importance of the ear: "There is no way of extracting their hidden things save by the flint and steel of listening to music and singing, and there is no entry into the heart save by the antechamber of the ears" (MacDonald 1901). The category is, therefore, not constituted at the level of the message itself, nor at that of its sender, but at the level of its receiver, or, if one prefers, at the level of perception.

Why is this? Apparently because the three components of this category of sound are all capable, from the listener's standpoint, of the same effects. This is what emerges from a reading of the "Book of the Right Usages of Music and Trance," which clearly shows that the Koran, poetry, and serious music are all three equally capable of inducing *wajd,* which is to say trance, and of doing so in any context, not only during *samāᶜ* (the ceremony) but also outside it. However, let us observe that the manifestations of this trance will be very different depending on whether the "audition" takes place during *samāᶜ* or outside it. This is a point of great importance for our purposes, and we shall return to it.

The Word *Wajd*

This word, which is more often translated as *extase* or ecstasy, but which I shall render as "trance" for reasons I shall explain later, is only used in the Sufi vocabulary and is derived from the root *w.j.d.,* "to find, to meet with."[14] Speaking about the "reality of trance" (*wajd*) for Sufis and the relation of "audition" to the soul, Ghazzali writes: "*Wajd* is an expression of what is found [*yūjadu*] through audition [*samāᶜ*]" (ibid., 719). This discovery, this encounter, involves something that is in close connection with the deepest part of one's being, or that is in intimate harmony with the situation being experienced. It manifests itself suddenly, like an illumination (I imagine that Saint Paul on his way to Damascus was experiencing *wajd*). It is revelation or inspiration. Its relation to "audition," Ghazzali says, derives from the fact that it "produces purity of heart and the purity is a cause of revealing" (ibid., 723). Trance (*wajd*) consists of "Revelation proceeding from the Truth," he says elsewhere (ibid., 720),[15] and the man who experiences trance achieves it "because he has found [*wajada*] what was lacking with him."

How does this trance manifest itself? Let us begin with the case in which it is induced by audition of the Koran. "The stories indicating that trance [*wajd*] has shown itself in the possessors of heart at hearing the Koran are many," Ghazzali tells us (ibid., 733), and then cites several of them, beginning with three anecdotes concerning the Prophet himself. The latter is depicted as follows: "his eyes were flowing with tears . . . ; then he fell, fainting," and weeping, while listening to three different passages from the Koran. "And much is transmitted from the Companions and the Follower concerning ecstasy through the Qurᵓān. Of them were some who fell swooning, and some who wept, and some who fainted, and some who died in their fainting." He then recounts: "And 'Umar heard a man reciting, *Verily the punishment of thy Lord surely descends; there is none to keep it back!* [Qur., 52: 8]. Then he cried with a great cry and fell fainting, and was carried into his house and ceased not to be sick in his house for a month. And Ṣāliḥ al-Marrī recited to Abū Jarīr, and he sobbed and died. And ash-Shāfiʿī heard one reciting, *This shall be a day when they shall not speak and shall not be permitted to excuse themselves* [Qur., 77: 35]; then he fainted. And ʿAli b. al-Fuḍayl heard one reciting, *A day when mankind shall rise up for the Lord of the worlds!* [Qur., 83:6] and he fell fainting . . . ." "And similar stories are transmitted from a number of them," Ghazzali adds (ibid., 735).

"So, too, is the case with the Ṣūfis," Ghazzali tells us: "One night of Ramaḍān ash-Shiblī was in his mosque, and he was praying behind an Imām of his, and the Imām ricited, *And, verily, if We willed We would bring to thee him whom We inspired* [Qur., 17:88], and ash-Shiblī shrieked a great shriek, the people thought that his soul had fled; his face grew red, and his shoulder muscles quivered, and kept saying, 'With such words He addresses the beloved,' repeating that over and over" (ibid., 735).

"Audition" of the Koran does not have the power of inducing trance solely among devotees. The following story concerns a slave girl, a *tar*[16] player, who were numerous among the Arabs of that time. This story does not come from Ghazzali, of course, but from a quite different source.[17] As she passed close to a Koran reader who was chanting the verse, "Truly hell surrounds the impious," the girl threw away her *tar,* uttered a cry, and fainted. When she came to, she broke her instrument into pieces and embraced religious life.

Trance induced by the "audition" of poetry manifests itself in the same way: by cries and fainting; occasionally, too, by madness and self-destruction. For instance, Ghazzali recounts a story of how the famous Abū-l-Husayn an-Nūrī, hearing at a gathering a certain line from a poem on the subject of religious love, "arose and constrained himself to an ecstasy, and ran wildly on, and happened upon a cane-brake which had been cut, but the stems in which remained like swords. Then he kept running in it and repeating the verse until the morning, and the blood flowed from his legs so that his feet and shanks swelled. And he lived after that a few days and died" (ibid., 716–17).

Now we come to an example of trance brought on by singing (ibid., 708). The scene is set in the vicinity of Baghdad, beside the Tigris. On the verandah of a fine residence there is a man; before him a slave girl is singing. Beneath the verandah a very handsome young man is listening. He asks the slave girl to repeat the line she has just sung: " 'Every day thou changest!' Then she repeated it, and the youth kept saying 'This, by Allah, is my changing in my state with Truth!' and he sobbed a sob and died."

One last example is also very representative of the situation in which trance results from the shock of hearing sung words that unexpectedly correspond precisely to the dramatic situation in which the hearer finds himself. The coincidence triggers an inner upheaval so intense it can be fatal. This story, taken from Isfahāni's *Book of Songs*[18] and wholly profane in character, is that of a woman whose husband is taking her away against her wishes, to the country where he lives. The wife, "having heard a singer reciting some lines by Abu-Katifah, sighs convulsively and drops dead." The lines of poetry were: "I spend the night in grief and moan . . . thinking of my fellow countrymen, who live so far away from me."

All our examples thus far are of unexpected trances linked with situations in which the Koran, poetry, or a song was heard accidentally, as it were. The audition (*samāᶜ*) was fortuitous. It did not occur during a *samāᶜ* in the sense of a "ceremony." When, on the contrary, trance does occur during such a ceremony, it may still manifest itself by cries, tears, and fainting (and eventually even by death), but Ghazzali tells us that according to the "right usages" (*ādāb*) one should not abandon oneself to trance unless it is really too strong; one should always try to dominate it. "Then think not that he who throws himself upon the ground in agitation is more perfect as to trance than he who is still and does not agitate himself; yet, often he who is still is more perfect as to trance than he who is in agitation," he writes (ibid., 1902; 6).

The second part of his book is devoted, first, to the "effects" (*āthār*) of *samāᶜ*, then to the "right usages" that should govern it. The latter are five in number (ibid., 159) and relate to (1) the time, place, and participants in the *samāᶜ*; (2) the precautions to be taken regarding the presence of neophytes (*murid*) to whom the *samāᶜ* could be injurious; (3) attention and inner concentration; self-control, consisting in not yielding to the trance unless it is impossible not to (absence of external manifestations may be a sign of the trance's weakness, but it may also be a sign of the subject's strength of will); (4) control of tears and dancing, neither of which should be indulged in unless it is impossible to restrain them; similarly with the tearing of garments, which should not be practiced except within certain limits; (5) courtesy toward other participants and the behavior one should observe while dancing.

Let us look for a moment at that curious manifestation of trance called *tamzīq,* which consists in tearing one's clothes. The same behavior, which the evidence suggests is a stereotype, can also be observed outside the *samāᶜ* ceremony. One famous example is that of a certain Umayyad caliph (living in our eighth century) who, so the story goes, was so affected by the music of a great singer of the day that he tore his clothing. The singer was given a thousand pieces of gold as a reward, Farmer tells us (1929; 85),[19] but at the same time the caliph warned him: "When you return to Al-Medīna you may be inclined to say, 'I have sung before the Commander of the Faithful and so entranced him that he tore his garments,' but, by Allāh, if a word escapes your lips of what you have seen, you will lose your head for it." We see how much this form of trance behavior, however conventional and stereotyped it may be, is regarded as irresistible. It is also interesting to note that it is both and at the same time highly valued—even a caliph may be subject to it—and somehow shameful—it must not be disclosed. During a *samāᶜ*, one can tear one's garments only if the need is irrepressible, and only on the condition that the remaining pieces of clothing are still usable afterwards (MacDonald 1902; 10).

We have seen that outside the *samāᶜ*, trance manifests itself quite often not only by fainting but also by sudden death. Ghazzali (ibid., 4) also reports on a case of death during a *samāᶜ* caused by struggling too hard to overcome trance. "It is related," he tells us, "that a youth used to accompany al-Junayd,[20] and whenever he heard aught of the mention (*dhikr*)[21] of God he would cry out. Then al-Junayd said to him, 'If you do that another time, you shall not accompany me.' And thereafter he kept putting pressure upon himself until from every hair of him there would drip a drop of water, and he did not cry out. And it is related that he choked one day through the force of the pressure upon him and sobbed a single sob, and his heart broke and he died."

Whether trance takes place during or outside of the *samāᶜ*, we see it can produce the same manifestations: sudden death, fainting, cries, tears, tearing of garments. The only difference is that "right usages" of the *samāᶜ* consist in not succumbing to trance but precisely in controlling these agitations and manifestations: "Think not that he who throws himself upon the ground in agitation is more perfect as to trance than he who is still and does not agitate himself; yet, often he who is still is more perfect as to trance than he who is in agitation." But after having stated in the first lines of his first chapter (ibid., 1901; 200) that the fruit of the *samāᶜ* is trance, Ghazzali adds: "and trance bears as fruit a moving of the extremities of the body, either with a motion that is not measured and is called agitation or with a measured motion which is called clapping of the hands and swaying of the members." In other words, he establishes an opposition between "agitation" (*idtirāb*)—or "nonmeasured" motion—and "measured" motions—or dance—to which trance leads when it is controlled. "Agitation," with its ensuing cries, tears, fainting, and madness, is observed above all, as we have seen, when trance occurs outside the *samāᶜ* or, in other words, when there is no ritual. Let us say that, from our perspective, this is a nonritualized crisis or trance. Dancing, on the contrary, is observed only during the *samāᶜ*, which is to say during a ritual. Let us say that this is a ritual trance. So once again we find the opposition between ritual and nonritual trance, which is familiar by now and which we have encountered so often in matters of possession. Nonritualized trance is frequently lethal (as Zempléni tells us), even within the *samāᶜ* ritual, when it is so violent that it cannot conform to the ritual (as with the young follower of Al-Junayd). Ritual trance, on the contrary, consists in a state of plenitude and exaltation.

The kind of trance, Ghazzali tells us, that is "found with Hearing (*samāᶜ*)" (ibid., 719), and which is a "Revelation proceeding from the truth" (ibid., 720), is at the same time "Witnessing of the Watcher" (i.e., knowledge of God), presence of understanding, beholding of the unseen (ibid., 723), communion with the secret, and relation to what is lacking. It is pleasure (ibid., 230; the word appears thirteen times on this very page) and purity of heart—love, or rather passion, for God. It is not, of course, a possession trance, and Ghazzali (ibid., 178) who clearly has Hallādj in mind,[22] denounces the heresy of the man who claims to be "inhabited" *(hulūl)* by God and to become "one" with him. It is a trance, however, in the sense in which we defined our terms at the beginning of this book, and not an ecstasy, since it manifests itself by movement ("it bears an excitation of the bodily extremities like a fruit"), is produced by sensorial stimuli (sounds), and is achieved not in solitude but in the company of other participants (the *samāᶜ* has three essential ingredients according to Al-Junayd [ibid., 1902; 1]: time, place, and company).

Perhaps, in order to distinguish it from possession trance, we may call it a trance of communion or a "communial" trance. It is not conceived as the effect of God occupying a person—which would be totally impious—but as the result of a more or less immediate relation to God, one that can have the shattering nature of a revelation, the calm nature of contemplation, or even, at the very limit, the nature of a union. The word "communial" seems to me capable of covering all three.

Although it is a trance, then, and not an ecstasy, one might say that when *wajd* is completely controlled, mastered, sublimated, it is nevertheless at the very frontier of ecstasy. This frontier is crossed when *wajd* becomes *fanāᶜ,* which lies somewhere beyond and is a state of annihilation (Molé 1963; 269), or "disappearance" of human qualities in God. This state of ecstasy is frequently the result of another practice known as *dhikr,* which is often closely associated with *samāᶜ.*

The Word *Dhikr*

In a very general way *dhikr*—a word often translated as "recollection"— may be defined as an exercise of piety consisting in repeating the divine name in order to recollect God and at the same time to make him recollect one's existence, in the hopes of attracting his blessing. The word *dhikr* in fact derives from *dhakara,* "to recollect, remember." The practice of *dhikr,* like that of *samāᶜ,* has been the subject of many works by Arab authors, particularly by the Sufis.[23] To be sure, our interest in this practic is limited to its use as a means of attaining the trance state.

If we broadly schematize[24] this very complex question, we can say that *dhikr* has two principal aspects: solitary *dhikr* and collective *dhikr* (Gardet 1952; 649). The first is also called the *dhikr* of the privileged and the second the *dhikr* of the commoners. The first, the solitary, that of the privileged, displays three different degrees of ascetic discipline and ultimately leads to what we have agreed to call ecstasy. The second, the collective, that of the commoners, is on the contrary an attempt to reach the trance state and contains only one degree of ascetic discipline. Solitary *dhikr,* which uses a very elaborate technique of breath control[25] and which involves the silent and inner repetition of the divine name, leads to a state of annihilation, *fanāᶜ,* which consists in a total absorption of the self into God (ibid., 1953; 205ff.). Attained in solitude, silence, and immobility, this ecstasy—or as some say, following Mircea Eliade (1948; 93), this "enstasy"—is accompanied by hallucinations that are mainly auditory when the *dhikr* is of the second degree, and visual when it reaches the third, the one called "inner" or "secret" *dhikr.* Clearly this form of *dhikr* is of no interest to us here, since it is practiced in silence.

The "collective" *dhikr* or *dhikr* "of the commoners" (*dhikr al-ᶜawāmm*) (Gardet 1952; 650), on the contrary, is of utmost interest to us since it is closely associated with music and dance. This is the *dhikr* (or *zikr*)[26] often also called "public" (in opposition to the other, which is "secret"), since it is practiced by a number of dervish brotherhoods from India to Morocco. Its very spectacular aspects, with its violent trances during which the dervishes pierce their flesh, walk on burning coals, grasp red-hot pieces of iron without burning themselves, swallow broken glass—in short give visible proof of their invulnerability—have been described innumerable times. These practices were introduced into *dhikr* at a relatively late date, sometime around our twelfth century, it seems. The style and repertoire of the singing, the use of musical instruments, the dance techniques, the demonstrations of, let us say, fakirism,[27] vary from brotherhood to brotherhood, each having developed its own particular form of *dhikr* over time. But among those that practice collective *dhikr* aloud, the manner of intoning the divine name by shouting, if not howling, it out remains more or less the same everywhere. Hence the name of "howling dervishes" that has sometimes been applied (very improperly, I might add) to the members of these brotherhoods.

Nothing could be more different from the *samāᶜ* described by Ghazzali very early in the twelfth century, or from the *samāᶜ* of the Mawlawiyya[28] (the "whirling dervishes") as it was instituted some hundred and fifty years later by Jalāl al-Dīn Rūmi, then the *zikr* of the Rifāᶜiyya or the *ḥaḍra*[29] of the ᶜIsāwiyya, as they can be observed in our day. We will now turn to the relations between music and the diverse manifestations of trance that characterize these two broad types of ritual, *samāᶜ* and *dhikr*. But before we do so, we must first explain in greater depth the opposition we posit between *samāᶜ* and *dhikr*.

According to Massignon, in the course of time the practice of *dhikr* gradually replaced the *samāᶜ* among the Sufis. "The masters of mysticism," he writes (1934; Tarika), "gradually abandoned free musical séances [*samāᶜ*] . . . for fixed recitations of litanies based on the Koran [*dhikr*]." We shall return to this point before long, but let us specify first of all that *samāᶜ* and *dhikr* are as different from one another as the words used to designate them, and second, that they have coexisted in the past and still coexist today. As Molé states (1963; 150), *dhikr* and *samāᶜ* "must be carefully distinguished, even though a certain correlation does exist between them, and despite the fact that anti-Sufi polemicists frequently confound *samāᶜ* and public *dhikr*." Ghazzali, in his treatise on *samāᶜ*, refers on several occasions to *dhikr*. His brother Ahmad also mentions *dhikr* in his short description of a *samāᶜ* séance (Robson 1938; 105). In both of these cases *dhikr* seems to be an episode within the general framework of the *samāᶜ*. This was some nine centuries ago. More recently, Brunel (1926; 116) found that in Morocco the *dhikr*, accompanied by very violent trances, was practiced by the ᶜIsāwiyya, whereas the *samāᶜ*, with very calm trances, was practiced by the Tijāniyya. In our day, in Iraq, the word *dhikr* is the one used to denote the trance rituals practiced by the Qādiriyya and the Rifāᶜiyya, while *samāᶜ* is used for those of the Yezidi[30] (Hassan 1975; 221ff. and 250–51), about which we admittedly have little information, but enough to presume that they are very different from the first.

It is clearly by the extension of its original meaning that the word *dhikr* has come to denote not merely the "mention of the divine name," as Gardet puts it, but also the entire ritual during which this recitation occurs, when it is collective and performed aloud. In the West, and also in some Muslim regions of the East and of Africa, *dhikr* has become known as a ritual that is more or less open to the public and that gives rise to spectacular manifestations, and it is in this sense, consequently, that the word is most often understood outside the narrow circle of Sufism.

This being so, there nevertheless has been, and still is, a great deal of uncertainty in the use of the two words. For example, *dhikr* is often used nowadays when referring to the *samāᶜ* of the Mevlevi. Judging from the extracts quoted by Molé (1963; 232ff.), the ancient writers spoke only of *samāᶜ*, so that the house where the dervishes met was called *samāᶜkhāna* and the principal dancer *samāᶜzan* (he who makes the *samāᶜ*). Inversely, in the fourteenth century, Ibn Batutah, in the story of his encounter with the Rifāᶜiyya in India, gives the name *samāᶜ* to the displays of fakirism customary among this sect, whereas today we would speak of *dhikr,* or, better yet, *ḥaḍra.* This last word, which means "presence" (not that of God, as one might think, but that of the Prophet), and which in many brotherhoods designates the weekly *dhikr* séance, has, according to Trimingham, "taken the place of the term *samāᶜ* of older usage" (1971; 204).

It is not only with respect to terminology, however, that things have changed over the centuries. As Massignon says, there have been even greater changes in the ritual practices themselves. The practice of *samāᶜ,* as described by Ahmad (brother of the great Ghazzali), which took the form of a "spiritual concert" that gave rise to highly controlled mystical emotions closer to ecstasy than to trance,[31] progressively lost ground to collective *dhikr,* which became an extremely violent affair that generated rather frenzied trances. This change, which began in the twelfth century, consisted, Trimingham says, in "the mechanization (if one can put it that way) of mystical experience" (1971; 199), which from then on became accessible to "the ordinary man in a relatively short space of time, by rhythmical exercises involving postures, control of breath, coordinated movements, and oral repetitions." It is worth observing, in passing, that this evolution paralleled a similar trend in the domain of possession, in which, it has often been said, violent trances are signs of a relatively late stage in the cult's development.

Samāᶜ Music according to Ghazzali

In writing his "Book of the Right Usages of Audition [*samāᶜ*] and Trance [*wajd*]," Ghazzali had in mind readers who already knew perfectly well in what a *samāᶜ* consisted, so that he did not bother to provide a full description of such a ceremony. However, the allusions he makes to the way in which it was conducted are numerous enough to give us some idea of it. His younger brother, Ahmad, on the other hand, who also wrote an apology for the *samāᶜ,* has provided us with a very succinct scheme (Robson 1938; 105–13). Information can also be gleaned from other texts[32] that deal with the *samāᶜ,* either to defend it or, on the contrary, to condemn it. We thus have enough data to be able to say that at the end of the eleventh century a *samāᶜ* was a kind of "spiritual concert," as Mokri (1961; 1014) terms it, in which the music was mainly sung, sometimes by a soloist, sometimes by a chorus, but which also included an instrumental element of varying importance. The concert took place under the direction of a master (*shaikh*) who led the ceremony and was at the same time the spiritual director of the faithful who attended. The solo singing was provided by a cantor, the *qawwāl,* chosen for his musical talent and beautiful voice. The concert consisted of several successive phases, some vocal, some instrumental, some a combination of the two. The faithful listened to the music seated, in a state of great inner contemplation, and allowed themselves to be gradually overcome by trance (*wajd*), which they did their best to control. When the trance became too intense, they rose (MacDonald 1902; 9) and began to dance. Return to calm and normality was brought about by the sound of music suitable for that purpose (Robson 1938, 112), after which everyone went home filled with a memory of "the revelation of what appeared to them in the state of their absorption in trance" (ibid., 113).

Besides the singing, what musical instruments were used? Ghazzali and his brother Ahmad are more or less in agreement on this point. Ahmad (Majd al-Dīn) says that all instruments (*malāhī*) are "forbidden by common consent" with the exception of the tambourine (*duff*), whose "permissibility" is based upon two solid references to tradition (*hadīth*) (ibid., 111, 175), and the transverse flute (*gaṣab*), which he calls the "Persian flute" (ibid., 96). "As for the reed-pipe (*mizmār*), it is forbidden to listen to it on account of what has come down in the tradition, that He (Allāh bless him, etc.) heard the sound of mizmar and stopped his ears" (ibid.). Ghazzali also proscribes wind and stringed instruments (MacDonald 1902, 237) as attributes of "people who drink and of *Mukhannaths* [professional musicians]." He also forbids the hourglass drum (*kūba*) on the same grounds, but confirms the lawfulness of the tambourine, either with jingles or without. He also lists as permitted the small flute (*shāhīn*) accompanied by the kettledrum (*tabl*), instruments that were used, in conjunction, to accompany pilgrim chants (ibid., 220–21) and consequently licit because of their connection with religious practices.

This exclusion of all musical instruments apart from the drum and the flute was what Ghazzali and his brother (and others too) advocated in their concern to protect the *samāᶜ* from the accusations leveled against it by certain very hardline Muslims. Despite what they say, however, the *samāᶜ* as spiritual concert was not always restricted solely to the drum and flute. We know that other instruments were used from the work of one of the great historians of Arab music, al-Masᶜudi,[33] who wrote about fifty years before Ghazzali. He tells us that when asked what he considered to be the best form of *samāᶜ* from a musical point of view, a governor of the ᶜAbbāsid caliph of the time replied: "The best music is that of the four-stringed [lute] when it accompanies a good song rendered by a perfect voice" (quoted in Farmer 1929; 140). We are thus informed on the canons of beauty with respect to *samāᶜ* during the "Golden Age" of the ᶜAbbāsids.

Three hundred years later, Jalāl al-Dīn Rūmī, the famous Persian poet and founder of the brotherhood of whirling dervishes, would celebrate in his poems on the *samāᶜ* the *rebab*—a stringed instrument—the flute, and other instruments as well;[34] we shall return to this point later. Thus, with regard to the musical instruments used in the *samāᶜ*, practice varied a great deal over the years. Doubtlessly it also varied a great deal with respect to place and circumstance.

Let us return to Ghazzali, however, and stick to his views for the moment: for him, the music for a *samāᶜ* is essentially vocal, and can be accompanied only by a drum, and eventually a flute. This being so, how did Ghazzali conceive the relation of this music to *wajd* in the framework of the *samāᶜ*? What role did music play for him in the arousal of trance? To answer these questions, we need to consider his ideas on the effects of music as a whole, as they are expressed in various passages of the "Book of Right Usages."

Although of little importance at first glance, since it occurs only incidentally in his discourse, there is one observation by Ghazzali that provides the key to his entire theory. He makes it in the course of his long account on why song, or rather sung poetry, is more suited than the Koran for inducing *wajd*. There are seven reasons for this, he says (MacDonald 1902, 738), and the "fifth is that the measured melodies are helped and strengthened by the rhythms" of the drum (ibid., 742), something that can never happen with the recitation of the Koran since it can never, as we know, be accompanied by an instrument of any kind. He then adds—and this is the important point for us—that "even a weak trance is not aroused except by a powerful cause, and it only becomes strong by a combination of these causes [which he has enumerated], and each one has a share in the arousing" (ibid., 743). For Ghazzali, then, music does not exert its power, one might say, at any one point; its action is not single but multiple; it creates not one effect but a cluster of effects. It acts at several levels and by virtue of several qualities. How? First, at the physiological level, through the pleasure caused by its sound as an acoustic phenomenon, when it is beautiful. This effect is a "secret that belongs to God, Most High," Ghazzali tells us (ibid., 218). "Some sounds [*aswāt*] make to rejoice and some to grieve, some to put to sleep and some to make laugh, some excite [*itarāb*][35] and some bring from the members movements according to the measure, with the hand and the foot and the head" (ibid.). This effect, he goes on to say, is independent of the meaning of the words, since, for one thing, purely instrumental music (he specifies the lute or *'ud*) is capable of creating the same effects, and, for another, the child in its cradle, who has no understanding, is calmed by pleasant sounds, and even camels, in spite of their "stupidity of nature," are so affected by the singing of their cameleer that they forget the weight of their burden and the length of the journey; indeed, excited in this way, stretching out their necks and with ears only for the singer, they can "kill themselves from the force of the pace."[36] Yet these songs sung to camels, Ghazzali tells us (ibid., 217), are nothing other than poems provided with pleasing sounds (*aswāt tayyiba*) and rhythmic melodies (*alhān mauzūna*). Therefore music, by the action of its sound alone, without reference to its meaning, is capable of wonderful effects. But it is the understanding (*fahm*) of what one hears that opens the path to ecstasy. This understanding is capable of attaining different degrees, which vary with the state (*hal*) of the listener (ibid., 705). There is understanding, we might say, with regard to the words themselves, the meaning relating to oneself, and the meaning relating to God. Only the very highest degree of intelligence, which is reached only after passing through all the other stages, enables one to attain total trance or annihilation (*fanāᶜ*). In addition to the physical pleasure of the music's sound and to the profound understanding of the words being sung, there is one further element that must be added if the music is to arouse trance. The listener, as he hears it, must be penetrated with love (*mahabba*) of God: "It is in him who loves God and has a passion for Him and longs to meet Him . . . and no sound strikes upon his ear but he hears it from Him and in Him," that music gives rise to *wajd* (ibid., 229).

Pleasure (*ladhdha*), divine love, and beauty are the three words that recur constantly in Ghazzali's account (ibid., 230–33) of how "audition" produces trance, after he has first described how, in other contexts, it can arouse profound love, joy, grief, courage, warlike feelings, and how, in other circumstances, it can also be a summons to pilgrimage. The cause of these states (*ahwāl*) that invade the heart when one is hearing music is the secret of God Most High, Ghazzali tells us (ibid., 230) and "consists in a relationship of measured tones to souls" (*al naghamāt al mauzūna*). And "knowledge of the cause why souls receive impressions through sounds," he adds, "belongs to the most subtle of the sciences of the Revelations which Sufis are granted" (ibid.). The pleasure (*ladhdha*) given by music is something that only madmen, the insensitive, and the hard of heart do not experience. Such people are amazed that it is possible to feel pleasure and go into trance as a result of listening to music, and their amazement is like that of the impotent man who marvels at "the pleasure of sexual intercourse, and the youth [who] marvels at the pleasure of governing." Because "in the case of him whose power of perception is imperfect, that he should have pleasure through it cannot be imagined" (ibid.). We clearly see just how sensual Ghazzali's theory on the relations between music and trance is. Elsewhere, when he explains what the onset of trance owes to understanding of the words as opposed to the pure sound of the melody, Ghazzali still talks about pleasure (ibid., 707): one faints "from the force of joy, pleasure, and gladness," he says. But this joy, this pleasure, this gladness, are associated with love of, or rather passion for, God. Pleasure, understanding, love of God—these, then, are the three components of trance (*wajd*), which is a revelation of God when it is the result of the "audition" of music, poetry, or the Koran.

If singing (ghinā͎ᶜ), writes Ghazzali, has greater power than the Koran to cause trance, this is due to seven reasons (ibid., 738–48): (1) because the verses of the Koran do not always match the state of the person hearing them, so that he may not understand them; (2) because the Koran is so well known that there is no surprise effect when one hears it; (3) because the sound (*sawt;* i.e., of the voice) is more pleasurable when it is measured (has a regular meter) than when it is not measured, and such "measure" is what distinguishes poetry from the Koran; (4) because the variety of "measured poetry" has great expressive power, even if the melody is purely instrumental and consequently has no meaning; (5) because "measured melodies are helped and strengthened by the rhythms" of the drum, whereas the Koran never is; (6) because song can be used more freely than the Koran; (7) because "the Koran is the word of God" and because "it is uncreated"; because its composition does not lie in the realm of language since it is a miracle, whereas poetry, which is composed by men, is in harmony with their natural qualities.

If both the Koran and sung poetry can induce trance (*wajd*), this is because both are capable, through the medium of a pleasant voice (ibid., 742), of making us meet (*w.j.d.*), of revealing to us, that which is in profound harmony with ourselves; but if sung poetry is more capable of doing this than the Koran, this is especially because poetry is measured and has rhythm. With respect to the arousal of trance, rhythm and measure are thus regarded as an important dimension of music. But it is not more important than the quality of the sound, the beauty of the voice, and the meaning of the words. It is the combination (ibid., 743) of several causes that gives birth to trance, as we have just seen. The drum, whose rhythm helps the melody and strengthens the measure, is merely one among many others, an interesting point we need to remember. Although for Ghazzali the drum is the only instrument, except for the small flute, that could be played in the *samāᶜ*, it nevertheless only occupies a somewhat secondary place in his list of the effects of music and, ultimately, in his theory of the relations between music and trance. This is a further example of the inanity of the theory, already mentioned several times in this book, that the drum is always and everywhere the principal, if not the only, cause of the arousal of trance.

Whereas in the *samāᶜ*, as it is conceived by Ghazzali, music is principally vocal, in the *samāᶜ* as it was conceived by Jalāl al-Din Rūmi one hundred and fifty years later, the music is at least as much instrumental as it is vocal, if not more so. In the *samāᶜ* of the Mevlevi, the famous whirling dervishes of Konya in Turkey, the music is in fact provided by an instrumental ensemble generally comprising at least two transverse flutes (*ney*), a bowed string instrument (*rabāb*), a plucked string instrument (*tanbūr*), two pairs of small kettledrums (*kudum*), and cymbals (*zim*).[37] It is the flute, however, that plays the principal role and that characterizes the music of this brotherhood to the highest degree. "Listen to the flute. . . . It complains of the separation," says Rūmi in the first line of his great mystic poem, the *Mathnawi*. And elsewhere, speaking of the *rabāb* he says: "It is only dry string, dry wood, and dry skin, but from it speaks the voice of the Beloved."[38] All of the second part of the Mevlevi's *samāᶜ*, that which gives rise to the whirling dance, is accompanied by instrumental music combined with a chorus of singers. The drums of course play an important rhythmic role, but they are played *moderato,* and their presence is always fairly discreet, which conforms to the general esthetics of the ceremony. Unlike the séances of so many other Sufi brotherhoods, the *samāᶜ* of the Mevlevi is in fact remarkable for its extremely restrained character, and although the spinning of the dancers is sometimes rather spellbinding in its visual effect, the spectacle provided by the dance as a whole is always impregnated with great calm. Everything about it is extremely controlled, restrained, ordered, in the image of that great celestial mechanism which, as we know, it symbolizes by imitating the spinning motion of the planets. In this cosmic serenity, although the dancers may be in a trance, there are almost no outward signs of it. The trance is so interiorized that one is more inclined to speak of ecstasy than trance; and this indeed is the word most used in this instance, whether in French or English, to translate the word *wajd.*

The word *samāᶜ*, as I have said, signifies in its general sense the act of hearing or listening—"audition." The *samāᶜ* as ritual consists essentially in hearing or in listening to music, with the aim of attaining that kind of illumination, of divine contact, that is termed *wajd*, or trance. To be sure, this "audition" is not totally passive, since it requires attention, inner contemplation, and concentration (ibid., 3–4). Moreover, once the trance state has been attained it is exteriorized by means of dance, which is nothing other than a way of translating music into action. However, the fact still remains that the person participating in a *samāᶜ* listens to music but does not take part in making it either as musician or as musicant, except perhaps when he claps his hands. Reciprocally, the musicians—singers or instrumentalists—are there solely to provide the music and do not really participate in the *samāᶜ* in that they are not seeking to attain *wajd*. The roles are thus strictly divided: on the one hand there are dervishes, who listen to the music and expect to enter into trance because of it; on the other, the musicians, who make the music and expect nothing from it. In this respect, the situation in the *samāᶜ* ceremony is identical to the one that can be observed in possession ceremonies, and like the latter it is diametrically opposed to the situation that characterizes shamanism.

The Practice of Dhikr

Although the practice of collective *dhikr* undoubtedly varies a good deal from one brotherhood to another, it nevertheless retains certain constant features, not only in its general organization but also in the manner of reciting the *dhikr* proper.[39] According to Trimingham, "the *ḥaḍra* [the *dhikr* ceremony as a whole] at its simplest consists of two parts: a) the reading of the office (*ḥizb*,[40] *wazīfa*, etc.) of the order and other prayers, perhaps interspersed with music and songs (*amāshīd*);[41] and b) the *dhikr* proper, accompanied throughout by music and songs and generally introduced with a special prayer[42] called 'The Opener' " (1971, 204–5). Like the *samāᶜ*, the *dhikr* takes place under the direction of the brotherhood's spiritual leader, the *shaikh*, assisted by one or several singers[43] (*munshid*) who take over in the sung parts of the ritual.

The first part (*ḥizb* or *wird*) of the ceremony constitutes a sort of preparation for the second. A state of contemplation and musical fervor is created by means of prayers (which are, in fact, chanted) and of chants which are taken up in chorus by the participants seated in a circle on the floor around the *shaikh*. A certain tension arises from time to time, fugitively, at moments when Allah's name is chanted, while torsos sway back and forth, prefiguring the essential feature of the second part. This introduction can vary in length according to circumstances, but it seems that, except for the moments of tension just mentioned, it remains musically slack, if one can put it that way, from beginning to end.

The second part, on the contrary, involves an almost uninterrupted crescendo marked out by moments of paroxysm of ever-increasing intensity. Everything is now organized around the rhythmic recitation of the *dhikr*, which from then on will alternate with sung sections, sometimes solo, sometimes choral. At a sign from the *shaikh*, the men—for it seems that the *dhikr* is exclusively a male affair[44]—rise. Still keeping their circular formation, which may be tight or lax, depending upon whether the men are holding each other's hands or shoulders, the participants all join in unison in a rhythmic intonation either of the first part of the profession of faith (*shahāda*); *Lā ilāha illā Allāh* ("There is no god but God"), or of the name of Allah, or of such other words as *huwa* (Him) or *hayy* (Living). The words are half-chanted, half-shouted to a very pronounced rhythm, which the men obtain by strongly exaggerating their respiratory movements as they breathe in and then out. Produced far back in the throat, the voice used is very raucous. The sound that escapes from their chests as they rise and fall to the rhythm has been described by Ferchiou as "a collective rasp" (1972; 55). In certain cases, this general and raucous panting is—as the Arabs express it themselves—very similar to the sound of a saw moving back and forth.[45] This effect is produced by means of a specific practice said to date back to the twelfth century and to have been promoted by Ahmad al-Yasavi, the founder of the Yasaviyya order and who came from Turkestan. In order to produce this "rasping saw dhikr" (al-dhikr al-minshāri), we are told in a nineteenth-century treatise by the founder of the Sanûsiyya (Trimingham 1971; 197), "the hā is expired very deeply, then hī aspired as low as possible." But there are many different ways of vocalizing the syllables that serve as the basis for the recitation, and they vary during the course of the "spiritual concert."[46] Trimingham (ibid., 210) describes the rasp during the final phase of the dhikr as being like the noise of a "rasping saw" or "pectoral barking." But perhaps it would be more correct to speak of "roaring." Whatever the case may be, the essential fact is that this great hubbub has an air of savagery and animality about it. As they roar, the participants sway back and forth or from left to right, with their necks disarticulated and their heads violently hurled about by the movement. It is the shaikh who controls the alternation of song and rhythmic recitation, which follow one another without break and are accompanied by various dance figures (spinning, facing one another, splitting up into small tight groups, or forming a circle, sometimes stamping on the spot, sometimes not), and it is he who also regulates the rhythm and general acceleration of the movements. "Under his drive," Ferchiou (1972; 55) writes in her description of a Sāduliyya ceremony in Tunisia, "the exercise of the dhikr reaches its paroxysm: faces streaming with sweat, eyes almost closed, the faithful are drawn into a rhythmic frenzy, and then comes the silence of their ecstasy."

In other sects, on the contrary, this is the moment when the fakir begin to display the most frenzied manifestations of trance. These manifestations do not, in fact, have very much in common with the communion trance that is, as we have seen, the aim of the dhikr, and these practices are the ones we must now examine. As we shall see, these fakirist practices, already alluded to earlier, constitute a very particular aspect of Sufism. Although they have nothing in common with the dhikr in the strict sense of the term (repetition of the divine name), they do nevertheless form an integral part of the ritual commonly designated by this term, or by the term ḥaḍra, which in this case is practically synonymous with dhikr. As we have seen, in the dhikr in the strict sense it is characteristic for the adepts to be the musicants of their own trance. As we shall see, this ceases to be true, however, of the fakirist section, if I may so put it, of the ritual. Our problem, therefore, is to find out why this should be so. And the answer is that in the case of the fakir we are no longer dealing with communion trance but with possession trance, which means that, logically, the relation of the trance subject to music should no longer be the same. In order to prove this, however, we need to examine the evidence in greater detail.

Fakirist Practices and Possession

All brotherhoods do not indulge in fakirist practices to the same extent. In Tunisia, for example, as we know, the Saduliyya brotherhood abstains from them totally. Among those who do go in for such practices, the Rifāʿiyya, founded in the twelfth century in Iraq, and the ʿIsāwiyya, founded two centuries later in Morocco,[47] are both famous for the spectacular and amazing nature of their exercises. It is with the first of these that we will begin our examination of the relation of music to this particular form of trance that one might term fakirist.

The account given by Christian Poche (1974; discography) of a *zikr* ceremony recorded among the Rifāʿiyya in Aleppo is very significant in this respect. The ceremony (*ḥaḍra*) in question included the skewer ordeal,[48] which is a rite of transition, or initiation, that novices (*mūrid*) are obliged to undergo. It is this trial that interests us here. The trial consists in the *shaikh* piercing the neophyte's flank with a skewer, so that the point goes right through the flesh and out the other side, without, however, leaving a wound or drawing a drop of blood. The deed takes place in an ambiance of noisy effervescence, and the exaltation of the participants is maintained by continual singing, cries, invocations, and a ceaseless beating of drums. The novice is put into a trance, Poche writes, so that he can "identify himself with Ahmad Rifāʿi," the founder of the brotherhood. If, as we stated in the first part of this book, possession essentially involves identification through trance with a god, an ancestor, a hero—whomever—then this identification with the founder of the brotherhood conforms perfectly with the definition of possession. We must therefore view the Sufi adept in this case, however unexpected or misplaced this may seem within the Muslim context, as truly possessed, and as being not in a communion trance—the supposed aim of the *dhikr*—but in a possession trance. The fact that Sufi religious discourse, unless I am much mistaken, remains silent on this aspect of things does certainly present a problem, but it does not change anything. The facts, if Poche's account is accurate, are there and speak for themselves. We shall return to this point later.

What is interesting from our point of view is that, corresponding to this episode of possession, there is a particular kind of music that is very different from that used in the rest of the *ḥaḍra*. As Poche's record notes clearly indicate, drums play the principal role during this ordeal episode. A significant fact is that these drums (actually frame drums) are called *mizhar*, a word meaning (Poche, ibid.) "he who makes appear." "The entry of the rhythm in double time drives the novice irresistibly toward the center of the circle," where he is to undergo the skewer ordeal, Poche tells us. No mention, as one can see, of *dhikr* or recitation. In this summons by the drums, using a rhythm dictated by convention, we see the usual musical mechanism of possession at work. I shall return later to the role of the drums in order to summarize Poche's interpretation and to advance a slightly different one of my own—which of the two is correct is relatively unimportant for the moment. The important point is that first we are dealing with possession, and second, with a relation to music quite different from the one that characterizes the *dhikr,* as described in previous pages.

This skewer ordeal was observed in Iraq, in the fourteenth century, among the Rifāᶜiyya, by the well-known Arab traveler and geographer Ibn Batutah.[49] But his record of the ceremony is not limited to this trial. The author adds that, among the dervishes in trance; "some took a great serpent and bit at its head with their teeth until they had severed it." For his part, P. de Felice (1947; 163–64) writes the following while describing a ceremony he witnessed among the ᶜIsāwiyya of Algeria,[50] in about 1910: "These madmen are first presented with knives and daggers, with which they pierce their arms and cheeks, without a single drop of blood flowing from their wounds. Then they are offered great scorpions and grey vipers on dishes covered with sieves. They throw themselves upon those creatures and devour them. One of them, before consuming his share, ran to and fro with a snake hanging on to his tongue; a second did the same with a scorpion." Brunel (1926; 21) writes that Ben ᶜAisā (or Ibn ᶜIsā), founder of the brotherhood of the ᶜAissāoūa (or ᶜIsāwiyya), "had the gift of captivating ferocious beasts and rendering venomous snakes harmless." We are thus faced once again with a case of "fakirism" that relates to identificatory possession: it is by identifying himself with the founder of his sect that the ᶜAissāoūa dervish acquires the power of facing the trial and of enduring the snake bites. There is every reason to believe that this also holds true for the Rifāᶜiyya.

But the Rifāᶜiyya have not only the peculiar ability—I was going to say the specialty—of undergoing sword and snake bites unharmed: they can undergo fire in the same manner. In Trimingham's words (1971; 86), their ecstatic practices render them "immune to sword and fire." In his description of the above-mentioned seance he witnessed among the Rifāᶜiyya, Ibn Batutah writes: "Loads of wood had been set ready and were lit; they [the dervishes] danced into the fire. Some of them rolled in it; others placed it in their mouth until the fire was extinguished." And he adds: "Such is their rule, and this is how the congregation of the ᶜAḥmadiyya[51] is distinguished." But this is all he says on the subject. So how is this "immunity" conceived?

This time we have no information that would provide an answer to the question. By analogy with the two preceding ordeals—that of the skewer and that of the serpent—which both have their origin in a particular power of the patron saint of the dervishes, one could presume the same holds true for the fire ordeal. The saint may have shown, in one or another circumstance, his resistance to fire. Following the same logic as in the two previous cases, his entranced devotees, by identifying themselves with him, would give proof of the same power. This, however, is pure hypothesis and must still be verified.

I had to linger somewhat on this last case because among all the deeds of "fakirism," the fire ordeal is probably the most frequent and most spectacular. It would indeed be particularly interesting to know how this resistance to fire is conceived, on what sort of "collective representation" it is based. The question can also be raised for the Anastenarides,[52] adepts of a Christian sect well known for its practice of the glowing embers[53] ordeal. During the course of their great annual spring feast, the Anastenarides customarily practice a ritual that consists in walking barefooted over a bed of burning coals without burning themselves. The adepts prepare for this ordeal by entering into trance, aided by musical accompaniment in which drumming plays an essential role. Apparently, at least, this trance is a possession trance, since the adept is "seized by the saint" (Kakouri 1965; 22), whose icon he carries at arm's length above his head, as though better to identify himself with him. Would the imaginary representations that inspire the Anastenarides who walk on the coals without being burnt be those of their identification, conscious or not, with the saint possessing them? (Their insensibility to fire, as a physiological fact, is another matter, and one that does not concern us here.) The hypothesis is once more tempting. Would the biography of the saint—Constantin, most often, but not always—include an episode relating to immunity from fire? This here again is pure hypothesis, but it might well deserve an inquiry. According to a study of the Anastenarides recently carried out by a team from the University of Salonica, the people concerned say that they are moved by a "divine power" (S. Baud-Bovy 1981, personal communication). In this case, the Anastenarides should be seen not as possessed but as inspired. With respect to the dervishes involved in the practice of dhikr, we have seen there was room for hesitation between possession and inspiration trance. Let it be repeated once more, concerning the subjects treated here, that the distinctions, however necessary and useful they may be, are always somewhat blurred. The Anastenarides are but one more example of it.

Let us now return to the Rifāᶜiyya and move on to the music of the ḥaḍra. Ibn Batutah does not say anything about the music that accompanied the séance he describes. He only notes that at the beginning the dervishes "recited the *dhikr.*" After that, they "started the *samā*ᶜ⁵⁴ (I said earlier what we should think of the use, somewhat unexpected here, of the word *samāᶜ*) during which, as we saw, they rolled about in glowing embers. We are thus dealing here with a *ḥaḍra* divided into two parts, the first one devoted to the recitation of the *dhikr* proper, the second to fakirist music and practices. Dermenghem and Barbes, in turn, make the same distinction when they describe the *ḥaḍra* of the ᶜAissāouā in Algeria, a *ḥaḍra* whose second part is devoted, precisely, to the "games" of fire and timber.⁵⁵ As regards the music (which is treated at length in their description), it is the chorus that plays the principal role during the first part (1951; 291–92), and "it is mainly in the second part of the ceremony that the instruments (drums and flutes) will play a part." We have just seen that drums play the principal role among the Aleppo Rifāᶜiyya during the skewer ordeal. This predominance of the instruments during the part of the *ḥaḍra* devoted to fakirist practices is something we shall also find among the ᶜIsāiyya of Morocco, to whom we shall now turn.

Before we do move on to Morocco, however, where the evidence of possession is even greater than in the cases we have considered so far, let me make it quite clear that I have no intention of reducing all manifestations of Sufi fakirist practices to possession. Nothing is ever as simple as that. I simply wish to show that in certain cases at least these manifestations can be interpreted in such a way, and that, at the same time, the relations of the adept to the music follow the logic of possession trance (as outlined in the first part of this book), and not that of communion trance. It is this correlation that it is important for us to isolate.

Among the ᶜIsāwiyya, the public *dhikr* is practiced⁵⁶ either in the course of the weekly Friday meetings (*ḥaḍra*) or during feasts (*lemmāt:* "gathering") "offered by private persons very often on the occasion of family ceremonies," or, lastly, during the great feast (*mūsem*) held every year to commemorate the brotherhood's founder. In all these cases, the *dhikr,* which in its broad lines conforms to the description already given and is therefore completely Muslim, merely precedes other ritual actions that, on the contrary, have nothing to do with Islam. Brunel's work, in fact, shows that a large part of the ᶜIsāwiyyas' religious practice is based upon belief in possession by various spirits, usually those of such animals as the lion, lioness, jackal, boar, camel, and so on. As a neophyte, each adept is given the name of one of these, and from then on he must "imitate the behavior and manners of that animal exactly" during the brotherhood's weekly ceremonies (Brunel 1926; 170). The origin of these beliefs should probably be sought in black Africa.⁵⁷

"The *ḥaḍra* [the weekly ceremony just mentioned] is divided into two essentially distinct parts," Brunel tells us, "the *dhikr* proper and an ecstatic dance" (ibid., 94). It is the *dhikr* that enables the adepts to go into trance. The transition from this communion trance to the one that succeeds it, which is manifestly a possession trance, takes place fairly abruptly, but without causing any real break in continuity. It is characterized above all, it seems, by the more or less progressive ("surreptitious" Brunel calls it; ibid., 95) intervention of musical instruments: drums (*thbol* and *bendaïr*) and oboe (*ghaïta*). These give the signal for another dance, the *rbbāni*, which is relatively slow and is somewhat akin to that of the *dhikr,* since it essentially involves "a sort of rhythmic pounding, now on one foot, now on another," then "in a downward bending movement," while "a raucous and troubling cry of Allah breaks away from their chest." And "there are no variations on this dance," Brunel observes. Thus we are in the presence here of what I proposed, in an earlier chapter, we should call an abstract dance.[58] This serves as a kind of "preparatory exercise" for the next dance, which is figurative this time, and directly related to possession. The figures of this new dance change with the Tā'ifāt, or "groups," to which the dancers are attached. Sometimes the dance involves two performers who face one another; in this case, they execute spinning leaps, then pretend to "repel one another reciprocally like two opposed forces," a choreographic figure alluding to the son of Ben ʿAisa, a "famed sailor" who "when the sea broke upon the shore, hurled himself daringly toward it," so that "the mass of powerful water crashed against his breast." Sometimes the dance involves "extraordinary leaps" accompanying the gesture "of disembowelling and tearing out," which are executed by the *frrāssa:* "those who devour,"[59] who are lions (*sbuā*), panthers (*nmoūra*), or jackals (*dhïab*). Other dance figures corresponding to the behavior of various animals capable of possessing the adepts—boars, jackals, and so on—also occur, of course.[60] Those who embody the camel, the *jmāl,* reproduce "the movements of the animal they are representing in the most detailed manner" (ibid., 204). Their specialty is to chew cactus leaves bristling with spines, or barley, or wild artichokes. They also sometimes quarrel among themselves—"They butt one another with their shoulders and roar, bite one another savagely, and exchange violent kicks"—and sometimes "hurl themselves, head down, at the gates and batter at them with great violence" (ibid., 205).

There is no point to going any further: clearly this second part of the *ḥaḍra,* which Brunel describes as devoted to "ecstatic dancing," has no connection with the first, which was devoted to the *"dhikr* proper." What we need to remember, once again, is that the relations between trance and music totally change from one part to the other. In the *dhikr,* the musicants are the adepts themselves: they are the ones who make the music that governs the exercise that causes them to enter into a trance. In the "ecstatic dancing"—which, all things considered, we might as well call the "possession dance"—it is no longer the adepts who provide the music, by singing, but the musicians, who do so by playing drums and oboes.

Before leaving religious trance among the Arabs, and passing on to profane trance, perhaps it would be useful to review the relations between possession and Islam as they emerge from the examples we have examined thus far. In the case of the ʿIsāwiyya, we are clearly dealing with a phenomenon of religious syncretism. Let me simply say that such things are by no means unique, that no one is surprised when they occur within a Christian framework, and there is thus no reason to be any more surprised simply because they occur within an Islamic context. In Bahia, those who take part in the *candomblé* have no difficulty in practicing possession and at the same time declaring themselves Roman Catholics. True, numerous Christians wax indignant over this fact, but then a number of Muslims are equally ready to express stern disapproval of the Sufi practices I have termed "fakirist." The two cases are thus symmetrical in this respect. However, although both ʿIsāwiyya and adepts of the *candomblé*, each in their own way, provide us with absolutely clearcut examples of syncretism, both openly combining possession and adoration of God, the situation is not always as clear in other cases.

When, in the course of a *ḥaḍra,* one section is devoted to the practice of *dhikr,* which is a recitation of the divine name and communion with God, and another is devoted to the ordeal of being pierced with a skewer, which is an initiation rite and identification with the founder of the brotherhood, in the first case we are indisputably dealing with a Muslim act of faith whereas in the second something else is involved. But what exactly? That is the question, and it has several possible solutions.

I have suggested we view the trance during the ordeal episode as a case of possession. Those involved would undoubtedly be both surprised and indignant at this suggestion. To be sure, they experience this privileged relation with the brotherhood's founder—with the saint—merely as a particular aspect of an overall situation, which is adoration of Allah. The saint is no more than a mediator in this adoration, and this is why there is nothing shocking about identifying oneself with him. It is nonetheless true that this identification, which involves going into trance and temporarily taking on the personality of someone who is the object of the group's devotion for the purpose of obtaining his blessing, conforms exactly to the definition of possession proposed at the beginning of this book. I shall go no further than this, acknowledging all the while that the ambiguity of this case somewhat shades the presence of possession, but the latter nonetheless exists. So that a *ḥaḍra* in which *dhikr* proper and fakirist practices succeed one another, in whatever order,[61] should be seen as in some way juxtaposing communion and possession trance. This is what causes the singularity of these ceremonies. Such a juxtaposition is likely to be a source of ambiguity, so that it is not always clear whether it is the first or the second type of trance that is at work. But the existence of transitional or ambiguous stages does not alter the fact that two types of trance are clearly involved, or, if one prefers, two types of religious bonds with the deity. The interesting point for us, let me repeat, is that the relations between the trance subject and the music vary according to whether the first or the second type is involved. During the *dhikr* proper, which is to say during communion trance, the adepts are the ones who are the artisans of their own entry into trance, which they induce by their own singing and dancing; during the fakirist practices, they no longer do so themselves but others have the task of providing the music, and of inducing their trance. In short, in the first case the adept is a musicant and in the second he is musicated.

The Jinn and "Poetic Furor"

Alongside the possession trance associated with Islam through the popular forms of Sufism we have just examined, there is another kind, parallel with Islam, but also sometimes associated with it. This is the possession trance brought about by those ill-defined beings—let us say those "genii"—known in Arabic as *jinn*. [62] A pre-Islamic survival, belief in the *jinn* has become confused, or combined, with a number of other more or less similar beliefs that are, or have been, current in the various countries in which Islam prevails. The *jinn* are held responsible for certain illnesses, which they cause by taking possession of people, and the individuals possessed in this way tend to organize themselves into schools or colleges. This is true, among other examples, of the female college of the Tidjān-iyya[63] in Tunisia, described by Sophie Ferchiou (1972; 57 ff.): the "spirits" responsible for the possession and called *ʿennēs el ohra* ("the other people") answer for the most part to the definition of *jinn*. [64]

Seen in this way (for there are other aspects, some associated with magic), the *jinn,* or rather the cults of which they are the object, scarcely constitute anything more than variations on the general theme of possession. And these variations would probably tell us no more about the relation between music and possession than what we have already learned in the first part of this book. I shall therefore not linger over them. Moreover, Farmer (1929; 7) tells us that "the *jinn* were evidently conjured by means of music," which takes us back once more to the exorcism problem, which we also discussed in part one—the more reason for moving on. Let it simply be understood at this point that in the subsequent general table of trance (cf p. 290), trance relating to *jinn* cults should of course be placed in the category of possession.[65]

Belief in the *jinn,* however, presents two other aspects that are completely different and particularly interesting from our point of view: first, that of the *shaāᶜir majnūn,* or "poet-soothsayer possessed of the *jinn*" (ibid., 21) who performs the function of prophet or augur[66] (in his early days Muhammad had the reputation of being one); and second, that of the musician, or more correctly of the composer or poet, who receives his inspirations from a *jinn.* Like his master, the celebrated Ishāq al-Mawsilī, the most famous of the Andalusian ninth-century musicians, Ziryāb, "believed that the *jinn* taught him his songs in the middle of the night. When thus inspired he would call his two favorite singing-girls, Ghazzālan and Hīnda, and bid them commit to memory music which had come to him by these means" (ibid., 130). A good example of what the Renaissance was later to call, following the Greeks and Romans, *furor poeticus.*

Possession by the *jinn* as expressed in popular religious practices, the clairvoyance of the augur, and the inspiration of the poet, can be seen as equivalent to three of the four kinds of *mania* described by Plato: the telestic, mantic, and poetic. But what has happened to the fourth, the one Plato himself placed above all the others, the erotic,[67] which, to be sure, is associated with love, but with love as a contemplation of beauty and through this of goodness and truth? This obviously parallels communion trance, the *wajd*—the paroxysmic expression of the love of God. The four types of trances thus far observed among the Arabs thus correspond to the four sorts of *mania* practiced among the Greeks. A great deal could be said about this correspondence, which is certainly not totally fortuitous, and about this quadripartite division of trance. I will simply observe that although the first three categories of trance, those due to the *jinn,* certainly owe nothing to the Greeks, the fourth, that which is due to God, paradoxically does owe them something, in part at least. It is generally accepted that the birth of Sufism is somewhat related to Neoplatonism. Contemplation of a beautiful youth as a means of attaining trance, a practice especially advocated by Ghazzali's brother Ahmad,[68] might well be a more or less direct heritage from Plato.

This is the end of this digression, the purpose of which was to show that as far as trance is concerned, the situation among Arabs of the eleventh century and that among the ancient Greeks, had certain similarities, despite their enormous differences. After this brief mention of the "poetic furor" of musicians, which, though it is occasioned by genii, has no close association with religion, let us now move on to an examination of completely profane trance.

PROFANE TRANCE

Up to this point, the trances we have examined in the *samāᶜ*, the *dhikr*, or the *ḥaḍra* have all been religious. They are designated either by the word *wajd*, a term that comes from the scholarly Sufi tradition and is not in very wide usage, or by the word *ḥāl*. Among the Arabs, however, trance can be produced by music outside of any religious context. It is then referred to as *ṭarab*.

The Word *Ṭarab*

Nothing can better explain what *ṭarab* is, in the sense just indicated, than the following anecdote taken from the *Kitāb al-aghānī* ("The Book of Songs"), a famous collection composed by Isfahānī in our tenth century. The scene is set in Medina, two centuries earlier, under the Umayyad. The famous singer, Jamīla,[69] was in the habit of entertaining the best poets and musicians of her time in her home, among them the great erotic poet ᶜU-mar ibn-Abī Rabī'a. One day, during a concert at her house, she began singing some erotic verses he had written:

> "As Jamīla sang, all those gathered there were seized by *ṭarab* [ecstasy]: they began to clap their hands, beat time on the floor with their feet, and sway their heads, shouting: "We offer ourselves in sacrifice for thee, oh Jamīla, to protect you from all evil. . . . How sublime your song and your words!" As for the poet 'Umar, he began to shout out: "Woe is me. Woe is me. . . ." He tore his robe from top to bottom, in a state of total unconsciousness. When he came to, he felt ashamed and began to apologize, saying: "By Allah, I could not restrain myself, for that beautiful voice made me lose my mind." The other guest answered him: "Console yourself, the same happened to us all, and we fainted. But we did not tear our clothing." [Jargy 1971, 25–26]

Clearly the external manifestations of *ṭarab*, the profane trance, are in all points similar to those of *wajd*, the mystic trance, when the latter is expressed by fainting, loss of consciousness, cries, and tearing one's garments *(tamziq)*. Beside themselves with emotion, people start to clap their hands and dance. Indeed, *wajd* and *ṭarab* sometimes resemble one another so closely that that *ṭarab* may also used to signify mystic trance. This is the case in certain areas of Iraq. A distinction is then made between *tarab kaïf* and *tarab rūhī*, "entertainment trance" and "spiritual trance" (Hassan 1975; 305).

Just as *wajd*, as we have seen, may display different degrees of intensity, so that its manifestations vary from the most abandoned and spectacular form of frenzy, including even sudden death, to the most controlled and interiorized expression, so *ṭarab* can likewise lead to the worst extremes of madness, even death, or, on the contrary, be reduced to a pure and simple musical emotion of which no sign, or almost none, is externally visible.[70] Nowadays, however, especially in urban settings, trance as an expression of musical emotion, of *ṭarab,* is less customary than it was in the past. It still occurs, nevertheless, mainly in country districts. In certain areas around the Euphrates, for example, we are told by Schéhérazade Q. Hassan (1975; 125), people gather every evening in the villages to sing, and it is usual for the men to go so far as to "weep with ecstasy." In Iraq, too (ibid., 32), in the small folk orchestras, the professional drummers often break their drums[71] on their own heads "at the moment of ecstasy"; a form of destructive behavior that naturally makes one think of *tamziq,* the rending of one's clothing, which we have encountered before, and which in Sufi territory we found as a manifestation of mystic trance (*wajd*), during the spiritual concert (*samāᶜ*).

Ṭarab and music are so closely associated that the word *ṭarab* has in fact come to signify music. Thus in our day, in Iraq (ibid., 123), musical instruments are as often referred to as *ālāt il-ṭarab,* "instruments of trance," as they are *ālāt il-mūsīqa.* This usage is by no means recent, as is attested, among other examples, by the treatise of Ibn Abī l-Dunya, the great ninth-century music censor, who already called musical instruments *ālāt al ṭarab* (Robson 1938; 12). And even as early as the time of the first caliphs, in the seventh century, Farmer tells us (1929; 51), music was also called *ṭarab.* The great historian Masᶜudi, in the tenth century, wrote, when wishing to express a certain caliph's passion for music, that he was deeply in love with *ṭarab* (ibid., 60). And there is another more recent example: a book about music published in Baghdad in 1963 and entitled *Al-ṭarab ᶜind il-ᶜArab* ("*Ṭarab* among the Arabs"), is not at all about trance, contrary to what one might expect, but about singing.

It is high time I pointed out that the word *ṭarab* derives from the verb *ṭariba,* which means "to be moved, agitated" (Kazimirski's dictionary). Of someone "moved by the memory of his homeland and longing to return there" (ibid.), one would say he is *ṭarib,* and of "camels hurrying to reach camp again"—excited no doubt by the riders' songs mentioned by Ghazzali[72]—one would say they are *ṭarib. Ṭariba* also signifies "to excite, to want to move," and hence (Kazimirski) "to sing, to make music." *Muṭrib* and *muṭriba,* literally "he" and "she who moves people," are the words for musicians, male and female. The famous Egyptian singer Omm Kalsūm, whose records sold by the millions, was a *muṭriba,* and it was quite usual for those listening to her to be seized by *ṭarab.* For *muṭrib* and *muṭriba,* are, in fact, applied to makers of popular music only, not to makers of learned music,[73] and of course more to singers than to instrumentalists.[74]

On the other hand, *muṭrib* can also sometimes mean "music." There is a tenth-century Arab treatise[75] in which we read that the Greek word *mūsīqī* denotes what in Arabic is called *muṭrib*. In Iran, the word *moṭrebi* is applied to light or popular music (During 1975; 141–42).

The fact that it is possible, when speaking about music, to use the word *ṭarab* (which in fact denotes the emotion or trance to which it gives rise), and when referring to musicians to use *muṭrib* (which means literally "he who arouses *ṭarab*"), demonstrates clearly enough the close ties that unite music and trance among the Arabs. For them, both words can be synonymous. We saw earlier, in the case of the *samāᶜ*, that music was the great mover of mystic trance; and now we find that it fulfills the same function for profane trance. In both cases, we should note, it is the expressivity of the singing that is the operative factor, working through the combined action of the beauty of the voice and the emotional power of the words. The instruments have little, or even nothing, to do with it. Indeed, contrary to what one might expect from the expression *ālāt al-ṭarab*, "the instruments of trance," which in fact means musical instruments, as we have just seen, trance, as a manifestation of musical emotion, is so closely associated with singing that the musical instrument is sometimes regarded as unfavorable to the inducement of *ṭarab*. In classical singing, that of the *maqāmāt*, "only the great singers can attain joy and ecstasy [*ṭarab*] in the presence of instruments," Schéhérazade Q. Hassan tells us (1975; 125). She also tells us that in the villages near the Euphrates mentioned just now, "where love of singing constitutes a genuine mystique," the musical instrument is "a thing of shame": in their singing sessions, rhythmic accompaniment is provided "solely by a string of beads." In other words, *ṭarab*, profane trance, is no more linked with frenzied drumming than is *wajd*, mystic trance. Just as Ghazzali says that the triggering of *wajd* during the course of the *samāᶜ* is linked with the spell of the voice and the power of the words, so is the triggering of *ṭarab* in the course of a concert of popular music. This is so true that the Iraqi proverb *bait il ṭarab mā kharab*, "the house of the *ṭarab* does not know misfortune," means in plain language, "the house where one sings does not know misfortune" (ibid., 124).

THE ENGENDERING OF TRANCE

The relation of trance to music and dance among the Arabs, as it has emerged in this chapter, would seem to be somewhat complicated. This complication is more apparent than real, however, and the data as a whole can be seen to fit into a fairly simple pattern if we simply rearrange them in accordance with, on the one hand, the different conditions under which trance occurs, and, on the other, certain modalities of music and dance. From our viewpoint here, it is possible to reduce both of these sets of data to a small number of oppositions. This is what I now intend to do.

The conditions under which trance occurs may be either profane or religious, and when they are religious they can be either "communial" (meaning that they consist in a relation of communion with Allah) or fakirist (meaning that they relate to the fakirist practices I have described and which fall into the category of possession). If they are communial, they can be either ritualized or nonritualized. If they are ritualized, they can occur within one of three frameworks: "classical" *samāᶜ*, the *samāᶜ* of the Mevlevi, or the *dhikr* in the strict sense of the term.

As for the music that accompanies the trance, it can be made either by the person who is in trance or preparing to enter it, or, on the contrary, by other persons specifically charged with this task. Placing ourselves in the position of the trance subject, who is thus either the "addresser" or the "addressee" of the music, we shall say that in the first case he is a "musicant" and in the second he is "musicated."

Lastly, dance—and it is that of the entranced person that interests us here, needless to say—may either precede entry into trance and prepare it, or, on the contrary, follow it and thus serve to manifest it. We shall say that it can be either the cause of the trance or its effect. It can eventually be both, one after the other, but in this case it changes in character, so that it is no longer the same dance that is involved.

This being granted, what kind of correlations can we find between the first set of data (conditions of trance occurrence) and the second (modalities of music and dance)?

Profane trance, that which is found outside any religious context, is triggered by hearing music (nonreligious music, of course), or, more precisely, singing. The circumstances are of little importance, and the trance occurs sometimes completely unexpectedly, sometimes, on the contrary, in answer to a high degree of expectation. Its most characteristic manifestations are weeping, fainting, and the rending of garments. It can also happen that the trance subject, who is beside himself, will begin to clap his hands and strike the ground rhythmically with his feet in a dance. What is involved, then, is a stereotyped (but not ritual) pattern of behavior that expresses in a particular way the emotion experienced when listening to music. We shall call this trance "emotional trance."

As just described, emotional trance is passive, both from the standpoint of music and that of dance, since it is only while listening to music, not while making it oneself, that one enters the trance state, since most of the time this state solely involves fainting, weeping, or rending one's garments, and also since although there may be movement—hand-clapping and dancing—this movement is only a manifestation, which is to say a sign or consequence, and not a cause of the trance. The person in trance is to be regarded, then, as essentially "musicated" and only very accessorily as a "musicant." This rule is not absolute, however. Emotional trance is sometimes observed in musicians while they are playing. Scheherazade Q. Hassan describes Iraqi drummers breaking their earthenware drums on their heads "at the moment of ecstasy (*ṭarab*)." This would seem to be a case of emotional trance in a musicant rather than in a musicated person. Is it an aberrant case? To answer this we would first have to know whether these particular musicians are entranced by their own drumming or whether, on the contrary, the trance is due to the words of the singers they are accompanying. Both are equally possible. In the second case, despite appearances, we would be dealing with emotional trance induced in a musicated person, which falls perfectly well within the category just described. The musician would, in this instance, experience the odd situation of being what one might call—no pun intended—a musicated musicant.

Now let us move on to religious trance, beginning with communion trance. As we have seen, it can occur outside any ritual context, and I cited a number of examples of people being unexpectedly seized by *wajd* simply upon hearing someone singing a verse from the Koran or some verse of religious poetry. The manifestations of this trance are much more violent than those of the ritualized *wajd,* since they can include sudden death, fainting, and fits of madness. The difference between the two is the same as that which distinguishes nonritualized trance from ritualized trance in the possession cults we examined in the first part of this book. The nonritualized/ritualized opposition can therefore be used once again, within the framework of Sufism this time, in order to distinguish the kind of trance that occurs outside the *samāᶜ*, and which can be lethal, from that which occurs within the framework of the *samāᶜ* and which, apart from very rare exceptions, is not fatal. In fact, this nonritualized communial trance displays much more the characteristics of a crisis (and I am thinking here of what we called the "prepossession crisis" in the first part of this book) than of a trance. It never leads to dancing. The relation of the subject in a trance—or in a crisis—to the music is a passive one. The subject is a musicated person, not a musicant.

Ritualized communion trance occurs inside the framework of three distinct rituals: what I have called the "classical" *samāᶜ,* which conforms with descriptions dating from the time of the two Ghazzali brothers; the *samāᶜ* of the Mevlevi, which is a later form; and the *dhikr.* In the classical *samāᶜ,* the adept is entranced (*wajd*) by the "audition" (*samāᶜ*) of music. His relation to the music is thus once again passive. But here, unlike the nonritualized communion trance, the trance is necessarily, or almost, transformed into dance, so that ultimately dance can be seen as the outstanding sign of its ritualization. Let us once again recall what Ghazzali writes at the very beginning of his "Book of the Right Usages of Audition and Trance": The trance [*wajd*] "bears as fruit a moving of the extremities of the body, either with a motion that is not measured and is called agitation, or with a measured motion which is called clapping of the hands and swaying of the members." The opposition he establishes here between disordered movement, which is mere agitation, and the ordered ("measured") movement that constitutes dance could not be more clear. One might almost think that in this passage Ghazzali had the nonritualized and ritualized distinction in mind. In the last part of his book, in which the "right usages" are actually prescribed, he deals exclusively with dance. He does not say a word about agitation. Thus dance ultimately constitutes, for Ghazzali himself, the very blossoming of trance. Seen in its relation to music and dance, the trance that occurs during the *samāᶜ* thus appears as both the effect of music and the cause of dance. I shall come back to this later, but let me say here and now that this is usually the case in possession as well.

The situation is not the same for the *samāᶜ* of the Mevlevi, however, and we shall not turn to it. Contrary to the "classical" *samāᶜ* as it is possible to reconstruct it from the writings of Ghazzali and his brother Ahmad, the *samāᶜ* of the Mevlevi (the "whirling dervishes") is characterized by the fact that dance is not the result of trance but in fact its cause. In the classical *samāᶜ* it is trance that incites the participants to dance, in the *samāᶜ* of the Mevlevi the opposite is true. Just like the classical *samāᶜ*, the *samāᶜ* of the Mevlevi begins with a section devoted to prayers and invocations, then to music, which the dervishes listen to seated and motionless. At a given moment, they rise and walk once around the room, still to the sound of music, after which, having removed their robes, they begin to spin. The important thing to stress is that they do not wait until they are entranced before they begin to spin, in other words, to dance. Quite the contrary, it is the whirling motion of the dance itself that leads them to ecstasy, or, as I would prefer to say, to trance. This trance is therefore the result of the adept's own action. In relation to his entry into trance the adept is thus active. He is the actor, through his dance, of his own entry into trance. The subject's will is involved in a way that is not found in the classical *samāᶜ*, in which the adept simply undergoes the effects of the music by going into trance in the first place, then by translating it through the movements of his dance. Seen from the perspective of the onset of trance, the difference is considerable.

Induced Trance vs. Conducted Trance

In order to express this important difference, I propose we use the two opposed terms "induced trance" and "conducted trance." Induced trance will signify a trance into which the subject is led through an action external to himself; conducted trance will be that into which the subject leads himself through his own action; in other words, the trance is self-induced.

Clearly the trances we have listed up to now—(1) profane (or emotional) trance; and (2) communial trance, both (a) nonritualized and (b) ritualized in the classical *samāᶜ*—were all induced trances. The communial ritualized trance in the Mevlevi *samāᶜ*, on the contrary, is a conducted trance. But, one may say, in the Mevlevi *samāᶜ* there is also audition (*samāᶜ*, in fact), not just dancing. The Mevlevi are "dancers," it is true, but they are "musicated" and not "musicants." My reply would be that the important aspect to remember is the factor that engenders trance, which in this case is dance and not music, which is not the case, I repeat, in classical *samāᶜ*. This being so, I acknowledge that this case is not totally devoid of ambiguity.

This ambiguity becomes even more evident when we move on to another case that is completely unambiguous and that constitutes, one might say, an example of purely conducted trance. This is the *dhikr* of the Sāduliyya of Tunisia, as described by Sophie Ferchiou. In this case there are no musicants other than the adepts themselves. They are the ones who sing the prayers, the incantations, and the songs that form the first part of the ritual that serves as a preparatory stage for the *dhikr* proper. As for the exercise of the *dhikr* itself, which, as we have seen, is an indissociable mixture of dance, rhythmic recitation, and song, again the adepts are the only ones who take part in it, without the support of a single musician, either with his voice or an instrument. Unlike the practitioners of the Mevlevi *samāᶜ*, who go into trance as a result of their own dancing but who need musicians to provide the music for the dance, the practitioners of the Sāduliyya *dhikr* are the musicants of their dance, and thereby are the sole artisans of their entry into trance.

The Sāduliyya *dhikr,* then, is a perfect example of conducted trance. There certainly are others, and it would seem that the Algerian Rahmāniyya is one of them.[76] But in certain brotherhoods it is usual to engage other musicians. This is true of the Halveti,[77] who secure a flutist and a drummer for the introductory section of *dhikr* in particular. It is also true of the Rifāᶜiyya—those of Aleppo at least[78]—among whom the hymn singer *(munshid)* is a lay person, not a member of the brotherhood.[79] Drums— this time played by members of the brotherhood—may also be beaten to strengthen the rhythm of recitations or songs. The drummers then station themselves a little outside the circle of those who are taking part in the exercise of the *dhikr,* and they do not generally go into trance. In this case, should we say that since the practitioners of the *dhikr* are not the only musicants of their dance (since they are partially "musicated"), they can no longer be seen as the sole artisans of their entry into trance? And would it then follow that we cannot consider the *dhikr* as belonging to the category of conducted trance? Would the rule cease to be general? I think not. In all these cases, the essentials remain: in order to enter into trance the subject must recite the *dhikr,* sing, and dance in the manner described. This is what remains invariable, whatever the brotherhood concerned. It is this that defines the *dhikr.* The rest—singers engaged from outside, the use of the drum—should be seen as accessory and consequently as not invalidating the rule.

Last, there is the case of trance linked with the manifestations of fakirism practiced by certain brotherhoods after the exercise of the *dhikr* and which, through a misuse of language, is sometimes included under the same term. I have already stated how we should view this trance: it is distinct from communion trance, even though it may follow it closely, sometimes without a break, and in practice mingling with it to some extent. We have seen that in every case this trance is associated with music that is not provided by the subject himself (the subject is not the musicant of his own trance) and that the dance is the expression of trance but not its cause. Unlike the communion trance produced by the *dhikr,* which is a conducted trance, the "fakirist" trance is an induced trance, as, by the same token, are communion trance (produced by the classical *samāᶜ*) and profane trance.

This being so, the system of the relation of trance to music and dance among the Arabs may be expressed schematically by figure 7.1: "induced trance" signifies that the subject is "musicated," in other words entranced by the music provided by those other than himself, and that his dance is moreover the effect, not the cause of his trance; "conducted trance" means that the subject engenders his own trance, either through dance or through the effect of both his dance and his own action as a musicant.

Communion Trance: Between Possession and Shamanism

The induced trance/conducted trance opposition, as it has just been isolated, takes us back to a similar distinction made in the first part of this book[80] with respect to possession and shamanism. Viewed in their respective relations to music, it will be remembered that the possessed person was defined as "musicated" and the shaman as a "musicant." Communion trance, shamanic trance, and possession trance can thus all three be characterized by reference to this one opposition, "induced/conducted," but with one proviso: whereas this opposition allows us to distinguish between shamanism and possession, in the case of communion trance, this opposition operates from within, since it distinguishes between the two aspects that this category of trance may have, depending on whether it occurs within the context of the *dhikr* or, on the contrary, within that of the classical *samāᶜ.* Communion trance thus seems to lie between possession

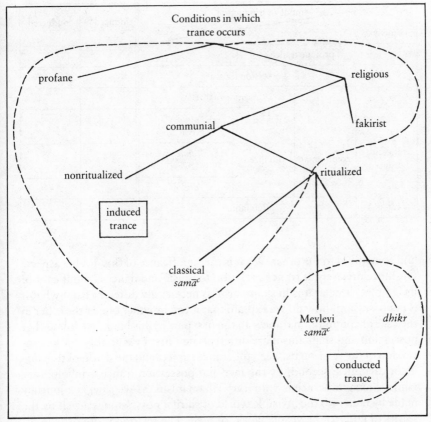

Figure 7.1

(to which it is akin in both the classical *samāᶜ* and in its nonritualized form) and shamanism (to which it is akin both in the *dhikr* and in the Mevlevi *samāᶜ* form).

As for profane or emotional trance—*ṭarab*—which is always induced, it must clearly be placed on the side of possession. Mediumship, for its part, must be set as I have said, outside of this broad opposition altogether.

A general diagram of the relation of trance to dance and music may now therefore be constructed (fig. 7.2) by correlating the contents of the various trances examined up to now with their mode of engendering, i.e., either induced or conducted (these two words being taken in the senses assigned to them earlier with reference to fig. 7.1).

Viewed from the perspective of its relation to dance and music, communial trance thus seems to oscillate between two poles, that of possession and that of shamanism, or, rather, it is sometimes similar to the one

mode of production content				induced	conducted
profane trance				+	
religious trance	communial	possession trance		+	
		nonritualized		+	
		ritualized	*samā^c* (classical)	+	
			samā^c (Mevlevi)		+
			dhikr		+
	shamanic				+

Figure 7.2

and sometimes to the other. What is the significance of this double aspect? Or, more precisely, if trance's relation to music and dance is significant of its content, if what it is in shamanism is necessarily different from what it is in possession, how do we explain that it can be either one or the other in the case of communion trance? In the first part of this book, we found that possession and shamanism are differentiated first by a doubly marked inversion of the relation between the trance subject and the world of the spirits or divinities; second, by the fact that possession trance is involuntary while shamanic trance is voluntary. Shamanism, as we saw, is a journey made by man into the invisible world of spirits; possession is a visit by the spirits or gods to the visible world of men. The relation is opposite in direction, but it operates on a footing of equality, since in both cases a religion of immanence is concerned. Men, spirits, and gods are all of the same essence, of which they represent different avatars, some visible and some invisible. This is why the relation of man to the spirits can be either one of submission or of domination.

In a religion of transcendence, like Islam, which excludes the possibility of identifying with God, and even more so that of dominating him, it cannot be the direction of the relationship that leads, by reversing itself, to two ways of engendering trance, one induced, the other conducted. How, then, are we to explain that, even here, two processes are at work in opposite directions? It appears that it is of no great importance whether the relation between the two worlds, the visible and the invisible, is one of immanence or one of transcendence. Both cases lead to one and the same alternative: either the relation is experienced as something undergone, or it is experienced as something willed. In the first case the trance technique is passive, in the second it is active. Let us say, for brevity's sake, that among the Arabs the *dhikr* represents the shamanic path to communion trance, and that the classical *samā͑* represents the possessional path to it.

An Aside on Christianism

To complement the outline just given on the relation of trance to music and dance in Islam, we should now examine, in a similarly systematic manner, what happens in those other two religions of transcendence, Judaism and Christianism.[81] The subject is a vast one, much of it lies outside our present purpose, and it does not present the clear advantage, as was the case with Sufism, of having a preexisting written theory of these relations. Let me simply say, limiting myself to Christianism[82] and staying close to the categories we have just examined, that the trance of the Shakers in the United States, and of the Shlustes in Russia, as it was practiced in the nineteenth century, would clearly have to be placed alongside the *dhikr,* on the shamanic side, in the category of conducted trances. Like the Sāduliyya, indeed, both Shakers and Shlustes[83] were at once the musicants and dancers of their own entry into trance. On the other hand, the trances observed among black (and sometimes white) Americans[84]—Baptists, Pentecostalists, and others—would be placed more on the side of induced trance, and therefore of possession, as a result of the important role played by musicians (singers, organists, etc.), and the preacher in the ceremonies. But in this area things appear to be extremely fluid. This is because the profoundly syncretic nature of these cults, in which European and African contributions are inextricably mingled, complicates even further an already complex situation since the ideas of Incarnation and the Holy Ghost not only weaken the notion of transcendence in Christianism, they also open up a great many different possibilities in the area of mystical relations with God.

At the beginning of the twentieth century, there was the Welsh Revivalist movement, a Christian movement in which mystic trance played a considerable role.[85] Trance was triggered both by the singing of the participants themselves and by the action—often described as decisive—of the preacher. We are dealing with a kind of trance that was both conducted—since the participants were musicants of their own entry into trance—and induced, but this time by means of words, not song. Unlike the ceremonies of the Shakers or the Shlustes, those of the Welsh Revivalists did not, apparently, include dance. On the contrary, in the famous epidemic of Saint Vitus' Dance[86] (or Saint John's Dance or Saint Guy's Dance) that swept Europe and Germany especially during the Middle Ages, dance was of course the primary sign of trance. But was it the cause of this trance or, on the contrary, its effect? The second hypothesis would appear to be the right one. These dances did not, in fact, occur without music, and since the music was provided by musicians, the dancers were consequently musicated, meaning that their trance was induced. This is clearly evident in a drawing by Bruegel the Elder,[87] the *Epidemic Dance in Moelenbeek,* which depicts a woman falling into a trance as a result of the music being played for her by a bagpiper. I know of nothing in Europe that is as close to a black African possession scene. Except for the costumes and the particular instruments being used, one would think it depicted a *ndöp* ceremony in Senegal. There, we need not hesitate, the subject is a musicated person, and we are indisputably on the side of possession. But a question does arise. Whereas in Bruegel's drawing we are undoubtedly in Christendom, we are not necessarily within Christianity and transcendence.

I shall go no further. These few examples should have sufficiently shown that the diagram used to situate the relation of trance to music and dance in Islam can also be applied effectively to Christianity.

Music as Emotion or as Excitation

Let us return to the Arabs. As we have seen, trance practices among them are exceptionally numerous. From this great diversity, however, two broad patterns emerge: that of the *samāᶜ* and of the *dhikr.* The *samāᶜ* consists in listening to music—which is essentially singing—for purposes of triggering trance and then expressing this state in dance. Also in view of attaining the state of communion trance, the *dhikr* consists in reciting the name of Allah while singing and dancing. These two operations are quite different. Nevertheless, they achieve the same result. There is a paradox here, and it is this paradox that we must now examine.

How, in these two cases, are we to explain the action of the music, or, more correctly, of the singing since the music is often reduced to singing and since in any case, singing always plays the essential role? The problem does not pose itself in the same way with respect to dance: in the *samāᶜ* it is the result of trance; in the *dhikr* it is its cause. We shall return to this point later.

Before anything else, however, we ought to ask what the Arabs themselves thought on this subject; and not just the Sufis, moreover, since profane and religious trance, from the viewpoint of their relation to music, ultimately have a certain number of points in common. The problem therefore does not only interest philosophers of religion like Ghazzali; it also concerns music theorists in general. And as we know, the Arabs have had some very illustrious ones. What were their ideas on the relation between music and trance?

Arab Musicologists and the Effects of Music

The first of the Arab philosophers[88] to have dealt with music, al-Kindī[89] (who died in A.D. 873), thought its effects were of three sorts: those that "dilated" the movements of the soul, those that "contracted" them, and those that "calmed" them. It was in exactly these terms, borrowed from the Neoplatonists, that seven centuries later, Baïf, as we saw, presented the program of his Académie de Poésie et de Musique to Charles IX. In addition to theories on the ethos[90] of modes, the harmony of the spheres, and the efficacity of numbers, al-Kindī also proposed a theory on the relation between sounds and the four elements, the four seasons, and the four humors. The power of music could thus be explained, according to him, through a vast set of psychological, physiological, and cosmological causes.[91]

Al-Fārābī (born in A.D. 872), certainly the greatest of the Arab musicologists, also thought that music was capable of arousing every passion, but for very different reasons. Deeply influenced by Aristotle, he refuted "the Pythagoreans' opinion that the revolutions of the planets and stars give rise to sounds that combine harmoniously" (Erlanger 1930; 28) and in his huge book on music he did not make the slightest mention of the correspondences between sounds and the elements or humors. His theory of the effects of music is purely psychological and rationalist: "Man and animal, guided by their instinct, emit sounds that vary with their emotions, as when they are joyful or fearful. Man's voice is guided by other moods. It can express sadness, tenderness, anger. Inversely, these sounds, these notes, will give rise to the same passions, the same moods in the auditor, and will have the power to exalt, erase, or calm them" (ibid., 14). Significantly, his chapter on the "effects of melody" and "their relation to passions" forms part of the discourse he devotes to "vocal melodies." This amazingly modern discourse intended "to show how to adapt the phonemes of a logos to a given melody and, inversely, how to adapt the notes of a melody to the phonemes of a given logos" (Erlanger 1935; 55). Nothing is more important to Al-Fārābī than a perfect relationship between melody and words. "One seeks the musical effect," he writes, "in order to better reach the goal of poetry" (ibid., 65). We find here, though via a different path from that of Neoplatonism, a fundamental aspect of what seven centuries later would be the musical theory of the Pléiade: the union of music and poetry.

The anecdotes about the effects of music that we found circulating in Paris or Milan in the sixteenth century were already circulating six centuries earlier in Baghdad. In one variant al-Fārābī himself is the hero of the story.[92] It so closely resembles the story of the Milanese lute player recounted by the count of Vintimiglia (was it perhaps the model?) that it is worth quoting here: One day the famous philosopher, who was not only a musicologist but also an excellent musician, presented himself in disguise at the home of the famous vizier Ibn ᶜAbbād. There he sat himself upon the ground

> amidst the shoes of the people present. It was a gathering of friends, and they took him for a jester. He grabbed the instrument away from one of the singers, and, having tuned it while he was being mocked, began to play tunes that made those listening laugh so heartily that their souls almost flew away with joy. He then played melodies so melancholic that they shed tears and their hearts were about to break with sadness; then he finished with a tune that put them all to sleep on the spot, and left them as though dead. On the neck of the instrument he wrote these words: "Abū-n-Nasr of Fārāb visited your house and then left." When they awoke, worried and stupefied by the amazing things they had witnessed, they read what he had written; then they sent people to seek him out everywhere, but in vain, which only furthered their stupefaction.

A literary stereotype, of course, that should only be taken for what it is, but which is nonetheless significant: in the Baghdad of that time, as in Milan later, what mattered was that music should be expressive, that it should move the soul.

But what connection does all this have with trance, one may ask? Very little, even nothing at all up to now. We might perhaps say that in the story of the musician plunging his listeners into the deepest of sleeps, we brush up against trance, in its hypnotic form, just as we brushed up against it, we will recall, under the form of "divine furor" in the story of the Milanese lutenist. Even so, we have to admit that in both cases we do so from afar. We are even farther away from it in the writings of al-Kindī or al-Fārābī. True, both speak of the effects of music on the "passions" of the soul, but this certainly does not mean they are referring to trance, by which I mean that total upheaval of one's inner equilibrium that occurs in *wajd* or *ṭarab*. We know that al-Fārābī, who was very favorably disposed toward Sufism, wrote a book on the *samāᶜ*, but it has unfortunately been lost.[93] This means that we shall never know what he thought about the relations between music and trance, which is a great pity.

As for Avicenna, to move on to the last of this great trinity of Arab musicologists working in the ninth and tenth centuries, he breaks with his predecessors by not making the slightest mention in his work of any theory of the effects of music in relation to the cosmos or to numbers.[94] Other authors after him, as we know, returned to these ideas, notably Safi al-Dīn (thirteenth century), to name only the most famous. But with the exception of the Brothers of Purity, to whom we shall return in a moment, none of them was to deal with trance.

Yet one might have expected that at least one of them, al-Hasan al-Kā-tib (a writer of second rank, to be honest, who wrote in the early eleventh century), would have treated the subject, since his work[95] begins with a chapter on *ṭarab*. But he does nothing of the kind. The *ṭarab* with which he is concerned is only "musical emotion" in its most intellectualized and anodyne form, and has very little to do with the dramatic and sometimes lethal crisis with which we are concerned. He also touches on trance, however, like the writers mentioned earlier, with two stories[96] that we also encounter several centuries later in the writings of Pontus de Tyard or of Ronsard. One of them closely resembles the Timothy and Alexander anecdote we examined in the chapter on Renaissance theories; the other is a verbatim version of the story of Pythagoras and the young Taorminian, quoted in the same chapter. Both were borrowed from Nicomachus. The striking thing about al-Kātib's use of these two stories to illustrate the omnipotence of music, however, is that their original purpose, as we saw, was to demonstrate the opposed effects of the Phrygian and Dorian modes. And these two modes are quite foreign to Arab music. Neither Pontus de Tyard nor Ronsard was very convincing with his rehashed version of these old Neopythagorean tales. We have already explained why. We see that for similar reasons al-Kātib is no more convincing than they.

To my knowledge, the only piece of Arab writing dealing not with Sufism but with general musical theory that takes into account the relations between music and trance is the famous letter of the Brothers of Purity *(Ikhwān al-safā)*, "a group of philosophers, scientists, mathematicians, and littérateurs who flourished at Al-Basra during the second half of the tenth century" (Farmer 1929; 214). This *Epistle on Music*[97] (one of a long series of other epistles) revives, developing and amplifying them in the process, all the ideas then current on the influence of music, its effects on illnesses, on the harmony of the spheres, and on the relation of the four strings of the lute *(ᶜud)* to the seasons, elements, and humors. It is a veritable treatise on musical astrology. The writers of this epistle[98] defined their own work as follows: "In this epistle we discuss music; we show also how notes and melodies, by means of harmonious and rhythmic association, influence the listener's soul in the same way as medicines, potions, and theriacs act upon the bodies of animals. We also explain how the rotational movement of the celestial spheres and their friction against one another engenders melodies as pleasing as those of lute strings and flutes. The purpose of these melodies is to arouse in the pure and rational, human and royal souls an ardent desire to rise up to these sites where they will be separated from their bodies, through that separation known as death." Clearly, then, trance is not the principal preoccupation of this epistle. It does nonetheless have a place in it, and a significant one at that. The last part of the epistle is an isolated chapter that has no connection with anything preceding it and that is entitled "The Diverse Effects of Music."[99] It deals exclusively with the Sufis and *wajd*. Several anecdotes are quoted, all very similar to those told by Ghazzali, in which Sufis are seized by trance and commit their souls, or faint upon hearing one or another passage of the Koran or of sung poetry. Although the title of the chapter attributes these effects to melodic modes, these modes are never specified. The sung or recited words, on the other hand, are quoted meticulously. The soul rejoices and is exalted, we read, "when it listens to descriptions that correspond with the object of its desires and to melodies that are in harmony with the object of its delectation." Given the necessary union of melody and words, it is the meaning of the words, above all else, that is really important. This being so, no explanation is provided for trance as a particular effect of music. It is presented as a fact, and that is all. "May God aid you, oh brother, to understand . . . his hidden secrets." This is how the letter ends.

Our excursion among the Arab theoreticians, however interesting it may have been, has not really solved our problem. We will thus return to it.

Samāʿ and Emotional Trance

As we have seen, two broad models emerge from the diversity of trance forms among the Arabs, the *samāʿ* and the *dhikr:* two practices that could not be more different from one another (what could there be in common between listening to singing, seated and impassive, and singing oneself, even howling, while flinging oneself about like a madman?) but that both paradoxically result in the same thing, namely "communial" trance. Let us examine them again more closely, one after the other.

We shall begin with *samāʿ*. "Audition" (*samāʿ*) of a song or of a chanted recitation with religious content triggers trance (*wajd*), which can be either expected—in which case it is *samāʿ* ritual, which results in dance— or, on the contrary, unexpected—in which case it is crisis or fit, which leads to death or madness. By means of what power does this singing trigger trance or crisis? Ghazzali tells us clearly, and all the anecdotes we have read confirm his statements: it is through its beauty—the quality of the voice in particular—on the one hand, and on the other through its meaning, which has no moving qualities in and of itself but owes them to the subjectivity of the auditor. It moves him because it is in perfect accord with his inner state at that moment, which is that of desiring and seeking God. He experiences the situation as an abrupt meeting—the very meaning of the word *wajd*—a revelation, an illumination. Hence the emotional aspect of the process, an aspect all the more marked because this meeting takes place in a context itself imbued with passion, since love of God, which inspires this desire and this search, is always more or less impregnated with eroticism—whether it is sublimated or not changes nothing.

In profane life *ṭarab* corresponds to *wajd*—religious trance associated with the "spiritual concert" that *samāᶜ* represents. The story quoted earlier about the poet seized by *ṭarab* while listening to the singing of the celebrated Jamīla shows that in this case it was also the beauty of the voice and the erotic context—profane this time—that were at work. Whether *ṭarab* or *wajd*, the trance manifests itself in the same ways: by dancing; by that odd form of behavior *(tamzīq)* that consists in tearing one's garments; by a dead faint, or possibly by all three in succession. Like *wajd*, *ṭarab* can be fatal if it is triggered by an unexpected encounter with a sung text: witness the story of the wife taken away from her homeland by her husband and who, upon hearing some lines relating to her situation, was seized by *ṭarab* and died. Here again it is the meaning of the words and their dramatic content, related to the listener's subjectivity, that are responsible for the trance.

Let me sum up. Both the spiritual and profane concert can give rise to a trance that will in both cases manifest itself in the same way. Unexpected audition of a religious song or unexpected audition of a profane song—both can trigger a fatal trance. *Wajd* and *ṭarab*, religious trance and profane trance, thus seem to be totally homologous, except for their content. We can thus say, that from our perspective, we are dealing with nothing more than two forms, one religious, one not, of one and the same trance. We can say that *ṭarab* is *wajd* minus references to God; or, reciprocally, that *wajd* is *ṭarab* plus references to God. Seen now with respect to their relation to music and dance, *wajd* and *ṭarab* are also homologous. Both are "induced" trances in which the subject is "musicated," song is the operative factor, and dance is the expression (not the cause) of trance. In both cases it is esthetic and passionate emotion that triggers trance. In short, in both cases we are dealing with "emotional trance," and it is this emotional trance that we will examine in the remainder of this chapter.

One observation may perhaps be useful here. Believers will doubtlessly consider that to merge *wajd* and *ṭarab* under one heading in this way is equivalent to removing God from religious trance, and that to do so is aberrant, since it is precisely an encounter with God that produces it. This is not the case. Whether one is a believer or not, the fact is that *wajd* and *ṭarab* are triggered and manifest themselves in the same way, and their relation to music and dance is the same. The revelation can thus be that of God, of beauty, or of truth; what counts, ultimately, is the emotion it arouses and the trance that ensues. This being said, believers are free to think that when it is religious, emotional trance is radically different from when it is profane, and others may think the contrary. The two positions are equally compatible with my interpretation of the facts.

This practice of emotional trance among Arabs brings us to a situation we have not yet encountered in this book. We must now therefore talk about musical emotion and examine its particular faculty of causing the Arabs to become entranced.

In his preface to Erlanger's great work (1930; ix), Carra de Vaux, after first having stressed the essentially melodic nature of traditional Arab music, observes: "With such restricted means, music produced an enormous impression upon Middle-Easterners. A simple distich accompanied by the lute, a few introductory notes sung by a beautiful voice, possibly a voice with the slightly raucous and guttural timbre as they love it in the Middle East, was enough to throw the listener into a state similar to that of ecstasy; he quivered, wept, fainted, he thought he was going to die. Arab literature is full of anecdotes bearing witness to this hyperesthesia of the musical sense." It is indeed hyperesthesia that is involved, it seems, at least relative to what we late-twentieth-century Europeans see as the norm. But to what should we attribute it? I trust everyone will agree we cannot see it as some natural and innate quality of the Arab temperament. We are clearly dealing with a sociocultural phenomenon (even though one could just as easily interpret our relative indifference to music as resulting from a veritable form of anesthesia of our musical sensibility; in which case this would then be *our* culturally specific characteristic). This hyperesthesia, we have said ever since the beginning of this chapter, is largely regressing in our day in the cities. This is proof, if proof were needed, that it does in fact stem from a certain kind of upbringing, tied to a certain type of society.

Moreover, although this musical hyperesthesia is certainly much more widespread among the Arabs than elsewhere, there are other examples of it in the world. In our day, in the realm of Western pop music, the behavior of fans electrified by their idols (such as Janis Joplin or Elvis Presley), beside themselves, yelling, and even smashing up the auditorium, may be seen as a cultural (or countercultural) equivalent of the tears, fainting, and garment rending of the Arabs.

An even better comparison is to be found in what Rousseau[100] had to say about the effect of the "Ranz des vaches" upon Swiss soldiers. When he talks of this "air so dear to the hearts of the Swiss that playing it in their Troops was forbidden on pain of death, because it made those who heard it weep, desert, or die, so ardent a desire did it arouse in them to see their country again," is he not in fact describing a completely typical case of ṭarab? For, one will recall, the word ṭarib, meaning subject to ṭarab, is applied to the person "moved by the memory of his homeland" and "longing" to see it again. I have just referred a second time to the story of the woman who is taken far away from her kin by her husband, and who dies suddenly upon hearing someone sing verses about homesickness. We may be sure that Isfahānī, who recounts this story, would have found nothing at all astonishing in a Swiss soldier who passes from life to death simply upon hearing the "Ranz des vaches." He would have perceived no "hyperesthesia of the musical sense" in the event. For him, the fact that an emotion of a certain type could be so strong as to bring about instant death was part of the natural order of things, just as much, for instance, as seeing a caliph having his best friend's head cut off in a moment of violent anger. It is characteristic of all cultures that they should repress or, on the contrary, encourage, the expression of emotions, and that they should decide which among them should or should not be valued. The person who could explain why Arabs have so strongly developed their musical emotivity would cast light on what is certainly a fundamental aspect of their civilization. The fact that for them song (*ghinā͑*) and trance (*ṭarab*) are so closely associated that the two words can be used synonymously is certainly indicative of a very deeply embedded feature of this civilization. In the absence of further information, let us simply recall that Arab singing is aimed particularly, and above all, at moving, or rather at overwhelming the listener, and that the latter is in turn encouraged by his upbringing to cultivate this emotion, sharpen it, exacerbate it as it were, and not only give it free expression but make it explode, and express this explosion in the most spectacular way. Such conditioning evidently predisposes someone to trance. It does not, however, explain it. In order to do this, I will venture a hypothesis.

It is clear that for Arabs music possesses the emotional power with which we are concerned here only insofar as it is associated with words, which is to say with meaning. At the same time, however, it is because they are cast into a musical form that the words have this impact, which they would lack on their own. Two complementary factors are therefore at work: on the one hand meaning, on the other the sensitive form of the meaning. One is nothing without the other. Only melodies that have a meaning, melodies to which "something exterior to them corresponds," al-Fārābī says, are perfect (Erlanger 1935; 95). This was also Plato's opinion, for whom purely instrumental music was merely an aberration, as we know. But although the meaning can sometimes be culturally specific (when it relates to the inaccessibility of God, for example), sometimes universal and thus natural (when it expresses homesickness), its sensitive form (in other words the musical form it is given) is always cultural. It is therefore only insofar as it refers to culture that the musical form affects, and even overwhelms, the listener. Such a cultural reference thus suddenly confronts the individual with what formed him, what fashioned his sensibility, with everything that is consequently anterior to him, all he has always known, and all that transcends him. This experience confronts his fleeting, imperfect, unfinished individuality with permanence, with completeness and with ontological plenitude. It makes him aware in the most sensitive way—because it is done through his senses—of the existence of two opposing realities, his own and another, one that is both and at the same time close yet in opposition to his. The dichotomy between what he is and what he is not—to which he obscurely aspires—is then felt with heart-rending acuteness. Trance, or rather crisis, is undoubtedly due to this acute and intense impression of being inwardly torn apart; it constitutes a response to an inner state that has become untenable, and for which it is an outlet. Two paths are thus possible. Either this contradiction between the two present realities cannot be resolved and the crisis, which cannot blossom into trance, leads to madness and death, or the other reality does not merely erupt into the realm of consciousness but totally invades or occupies it. In this case it is illumination, which can be so brief as to merge with the crisis—collapse, swoon—or, on the contrary, can be of a certain duration and manifest itself either by the rending of garments[101]—a highly stereotyped behavior pattern—or by dance.

Possession trance, for its part, is associated with a division of consciousness in relation to a general conception of the structuring of the person in which the latter is thought to possess several "souls." Emotional trance is not linked with this ideology, but in its religious form it is clearly related to the idea of God, which is also that of transcendence. This transcendence could well be but one specific aspect of a more general representation of the world, which conceives the latter as irreducibly dualistic. Plurality of soul or duality of the world, the trance that results from them is in both cases the sign of a certain experience of being torn, and this possibly constitutes the common denominator of these two forms of trance that in other respects are so very different.

This being so, and regardless of whether my hypothesis is acceptable or not, one thing must nonetheless be remembered: for an Arab music has the power of inducing trance only because it is a vehicle for words, and because these words are charged with meaning. As Rousseau would say,[102] "he must understand the language spoken to him before what he is being told sets him in motion," which proves that it is not "the physical power of sounds" that is at work here. Thus we find that in this respect what we said about the relations between music and possession in the first part of this book also applies to emotional trance.

Dhikr and Excitational Trance

Whereas the ritual of samāᶜ can be said to pave the way for trance through purely psychological means, the ritual of *dhikr* appears to do so mainly through physiological means. True, the repetition of the name of Allah, or substitutes for it (*dhikr*), is an exercise that occupies the mind, but in the collective *dhikr* intoned aloud, which is the one that interests us, it is the involvement of the entire body in very violent practices that manifestly constitutes the most important part of the exercise. These practices essentially have two aspects: half-spoken, half-sung recitation, and dance, the two being coordinated by rhythm, which is very heavily stressed. All this has already been described, so we need not go over it again. Let me just recall the central characteristics.

Contrary to what usually happens in both speech and song, in which vocal emission occurs only while breathing out, here the vocal cords vibrate as much during exhalation, with only the briefest interruption at the moment when the movement is reversed. The voice is guttural. The raucous and racking panting resulting from it recalls the sound of the back-and-forth movement of a saw. In fact, this chanting appears to be some sort of vocal exercise in which the constantly forced modulation of the breath plays a very important role. It seems likely that breathing in such a way—sometimes for as much as several hours on end—is likely to produce certain physiological effects. To my knowledge, they have not been studied scientifically. It seems justified, however, to assume that the ensuing pulmonary hyperventilation is likely to produce disturbances that might be of the order of a "dizzy spell," let us say. The hyperactivity of the vocal cords, moreover, in conjunction with overstimulation of the hearing system, which necessarily results from vibrations in the throat that are internally transmitted, also undoubtedly contribute to modifying the vascular and neurological balance of the encephalon. As for the dancing, which consists of a sequence of fairly elementary figures, it too is characterized by an alternating movement consisting of swaying the entire body from right to left and left to right while the head oscillates from one side to the other. Here again, it seems likely that such movements can in the long run cause disturbances of equilibrium and result in the "spatial disorientation" to which Zempléni refers with respect to the *ndöp*.

The *dhikr* ceremony can thus be seen as a corporeal technique aimed at bringing about changes in the individual's physiological equilibrium that will lead to certain perturbations. The convulsive aspect, so often described as being typical of this kind of trance, naturally makes one think of something like orgasm.[103] Experienced in a state of consciousness entirely occupied with the idea of God, whose name is repeated throughout, any resulting dizziness, any convulsion, naturally could be interpreted, given the mystic exaltation involved, as an abrupt encounter with God. This being so, and whether the psychophysiological process that occurs is evident or not, this trance is nonetheless attained largely by means of the hyperexcitation of a set of neurovegetative functions. I therefore propose that we call it "excitational" trance, to distinguish it clearly from the one attained through the classical *samāᶜ*, which I have called "emotional" trance.

The collective *dhikr* thus appears to be a very specific singing and dancing technique—in other words a musical technique in the global sense of
the term "music"—practiced with the aim of achieving a certain effect
upon oneself, namely that of triggering one's own trance. To call this
trance attained by the practice of *dhikr* "excitational," as I have just done,
amounts to advancing a theory, however elementary it may be, on the "effects" of the music concerned. Before going any further it would be worth
asking at this point if the Arabs themselves have ever advanced any theory
on this subject.

The musicologists of the golden years—al-Kindī, al-Fārābī, and Avicenna—who as we have seen, are all silent on the effects of music in the *samāᶜ*, are all equally mute on the subject of such effects in the *dhikr*, for the
excellent reason that the collective *dhikr*, which does not date back beyond the twelfth century, was unknown to them. The same applies to
Ghazzali and all those who wrote on the *samāᶜ* before him.

There could, however, be a number of Sufi texts, which, when set
alongside the oral evidence given by *dhikr* practitioners, may enable us to
formulate a theory of the *dhikr*. This theory, according to B. Mauguin,[104]
could be formulated as follows: "In a *zikr*, the function of the music, both
vocal and instrumental, is to activate the various centers in the human
body. It is not perfection of form that is being sought; the only thing that
matters is the circulation of acoustic energy, the perception of a basic
rhythm, and awareness of vibratory phenomena which, when intensified,
are alone able to eliminate the superficial level of the self. It is as though
the ancient masters would have known—a knowledge whose origin is difficult to explain—that certain nerve endings important to the psyche are
located in the throat. In this way, breathing, accelerated and subjected to a
musical rhythm, becomes a powerful factor in mind control." The importance given to the "nerve endings in the throat" tends to indicate that
chanting—with its rather particular technique—would tend to be the
prime factor in the process. But whatever the case may be (for one would
like to know more on these ideas and their origins), we are presented with
a neurophysiological theory on the effects of music in the *dhikr*.

Depont and Coppolani, in their by no means recent description of this
ritual (1897; 156–57), associate rotation of the head (which is swung
from side to side then lowered onto the chest) with the "raucous sounds"
of the voice, compressed by "cerebro-spinal congestion"; "the blood beats
harder and harder in their temples, the participants collapse heavily, roll
on the ground," they write, and this is "ecstasy."

Gardet (1955; 203), to whom we owe the most thorough published
study on the *dhikr* to date, thinks that it should be regarded (I am summa-
rizing a great deal) as "a set of verbo-motor and respiratory means" acting
"on the cerebro-spinal nervous system" in order to in some way bring the

"conscious . . . into harmony . . . with the subconscious," thus imposing the "desired monoideism" on the one as on the other. In a note referring to certain psychiatric research, he emphasizes, as support for his theory, the interdependence of the vegetative and the cerebrospinal nervous
systems. So although Gardet's personal position is far from being that of
an unbeliever, his theory of the *dhikr* as trance technique, as we can see,
clearly allots the largest place to physiology.[105]

What are we to make of these various theories? First, there is no avoiding the fact that none of them—and my own is no exception—is scientifically well founded, and that they all presume, with an admixture of intuition and common sense, that if the *dhikr*—a practice expressly intended
to induce trance and in most cases succeeding in doing so—brings into action such a specific corporeal technique, this is because the physiological
upheavals it produces have the power to provoke that trance. How so?
That is what we need to know, for this is precisely the point on which we
are ignorant. This does not, however, invalidate the hypothesis. Let us
therefore accept it and move on to investigate its implications.

In the *dhikr* we may have, at last, acquired proof that a certain musical
and dance practice—a very ritualized one to be sure, but this does not
matter—has the power of producing trance unaided. If music is indeed capable of such effects in this context, the first thing we must then ask ourselves is if it might not be capable of doing so in other circumstances, and
if we ought to consequently revise all we have said thus far in this book
about its relation to possession. Let me answer right away that this is not
the case. According to my hypothesis, the condition *sine qua non* for music to act as it does in the *dhikr* is that it be a *practice* on the part of the
trance candidate, something it never is (with one exception that does not
invalidate the rule, as we saw[106]) in the case of possession. Music in the
dhikr operates as a corporeal technique, not as an organization of sounds,
hence its characteristic of being strictly indissociable from dance. The
dhikr cannot, then, in any case, be seen as an example that would demonstrate that sounds in and of themselves have the power of producing
trance.

Taking account, then, of the fact that it is the practice of music and not
the music itself—not the message but the act of emitting the message—
that is responsible for trance, we must now go on to investigate whether
this practice, which certainly is a necessary condition for the ritual to induce trance, is also a sufficient condition; in other words, if, in order to go
into trance, it is enough to practice *dhikr* in the correct manner. Or again,
to pose the problem in another way, whether the practice of *dhikr* induces
trance automatically, as has been claimed. For this is how it is generally
conceived, and it is precisely this mechanization (if one may so put it) of
trance for which the *dhikr* is criticized.[107] In this case we are once again

faced with a situation entirely comparable to the one we encountered earlier in the case of possession,[108] where the "right tune" (the musical motto) is often thought to have the power of automatically triggering trance. In fact, as we saw, this is not at all the case. And the same is true, as we shall see, of the *dhikr*.

Let us begin with the most astonishing case, which is mentioned by Trimingham (1971; 211) at the end of his description of the dhikr among the Mirghaniyya in the Sudan. This brotherhood practices a collective *dhikr* that conforms in all points to the general picture given in this book, including the vocal emission, since in the final stages, Trimingham tells us, the words are reduced to a barking noise from the chest, or to the rasping sound of a saw. And then he very unexpectedly adds that this brotherhood is in no way seeking to produce "ecstatic phenomena."[109] Up to now, all aspects of the execution of *dhikr* were seen as answering to a very precise objective, that of inducing trance. Suddenly we are faced with an example of *dhikr* that does not have this aim at all. This is in itself surprising, but it provides the answer to our question: if *dhikr,* practiced here and there in the same manner, sometimes leads to trance and sometimes does not, this means that it does not induce trance automatically; in other words, something else has to be added to it. But what? Before we tackle this question, let us take another look at the evidence.

That *dhikr* should be routinely practiced without any intention of triggering trance certainly is a paradox—and one that raises an interesting problem. At the same time, the facts show that the sheer practice of *dhikr* is not enough to induce trance automatically, or at any rate that it does so only given certain conditions. This is corroborated by another piece of evidence that is probably an everyday occurrence but that I myself witnessed only once,[110] namely that those taking part in "classical" *dhikr*—that is, one intended to induce trance—do not all necessarily become entranced. Some do, others may not. Yet all, apparently, are performing the same exercises in the same way. Moreover, it is well known that the effects of *dhikr* do not manifest themselves in the same way in every brotherhood. Among some, the trance to which it normally leads is unbridled, convulsive, and paroxysmic; among others, it is relatively calm and consists in little more than a gentle and ephemeral daze. This is the case, notably, among the Derqawa d'al-Jadida in Morocco,[111] whose exercises—swaying of the body, roaring, etc.—are just as violent as those of the ʿIsāwiyya, for example, yet never lead to comparable violence in the trance state. Finally, one other aspect of the matter: we saw that in possession the neophyte is the one who responds almost without fail to the summons of the "right tune," whereas the officiant remains impervious to it, or only submits to it with difficulty; the same is true in *dhikr*, in which the ordinary adepts go into trance whereas the *shaikh* does so only rarely.[112]

These few observations should have sufficiently demonstrated that the *dhikr,* which usually leads to trance, can also not lead to it, and that, moreover, the manifestations of the trance are variable. As a hypothesis, I suggested earlier that the musical practice of *dhikr* is responsible for the triggering of trance; now I find myself forced to say that the same practice is not always followed by the same effect, which means either that my hypothesis is false or that it is inadequate. If the same cause does not always produce the same effects, it necessarily follows that either the relation is illusory or that it has been disturbed by some other element, or again that the cause in question is not the only one at work. It is difficult to accept that the hypothesis is illusory, because this would mean the general hyperstimulation provoked by this "excitational" practice is unrelated to the triggering of trance. Why then is it systematically sought after? Let us consequently remain faithful to our hypothesis but try to improve on it.

To begin, however, I would like to reject one possible objection that might be raised, namely that in the field of human behavior no law can be verified other than with a fairly wide margin of uncertainty, and that in this case, it would be futile to continue our quest: since the context inevitably varies from one brotherhood, session, or man to another, it follows that the effects of this practice would also vary. My answer is that we are not dealing with such a case. If the practice of *dhikr* among the Rifāʿiyya is expressly intended to produce trance, and they consider that the cause-and-effect relation between the two is self-evident, and if among the Mirghaniyya, on the contrary, the same *dhikr* is practiced without any attempt to induce (and, to be sure, attain) the trance state, we are faced with a problem, whether we like it or not. This practice, as I said, is above all a corporeal technique. As such, in and of itself it should have the same physiological impact, broadly speaking, on everyone. The problem, therefore, is the following: either it produces trance, as in the first example, in which case why does it not have the same effect in the second? Or else it does not produce trance, as in the second example, in which case why do the participants in the first practice it, since trance is their sole aim?

This contradiction is resolved if we accept that this excitational practice is—in the context of the *dhikr,* naturally—a necessary condition for triggering trance but is not sufficient in and of itself. In other words, there is another cause involved, not physiological this time—since the physical practices of *dhikr* remain the same in all cases—but psychological.

Let us accept, then—and this is my first hypothesis, which of course demands verification—that the practice of *dhikr* gives rise to physiological disturbances, but let us add that the latter constitute no more than preparations for trance. Our second hypothesis will be that these preparations only bear fruit if they are conceived as a prelude to trance or, and this amounts to the same thing, only if trance is seen as the normal end result of these disturbances. Trance would then only occur when two conditions are met: first, that one practices (to be sure) *dhikr;* second that one perceives *dhikr* as something that results in trance. In other words, if the model demands that the *dhikr* engender trance, then it does (Rifāʿiyya); if the model does not require trance in its program, then trance is not engendered (Mirghaniyya).

What a useless truism, one might say. By no means. This interpretation of *dhikr* as functioning to generate trance in fact proposes that the practitioner attains the trance state only because he conforms to a model suggested to him, in other words, because he identifies his behavior with the model. In order for the disturbances brought on by the physical practice of *dhikr* to lead to trance, it is necessary that the intention to transform them to trance should exist somewhere in the practitioner's conscious or unconscious mind. Transition into the trance state would thus be a deliberate act on his part—which does not necessarily mean that it is a conscious act. The overall process could thus be described as taking place in two stages, even though they may not be distinct from one another in reality. The effervescence caused by the practice of the *dhikr* would lead the individual to such a state of instability or inner confusion that it would take very little to topple him into that particular state called trance. It would lead him to the threshold of this state, but, without any intention on his part, it would be insufficient in and of itself to effectuate the passage. An intention to enter into trance is indispensable to this conversion of the quantitative into the qualitative, this phenomenon of crystallization that characterizes *dhikr.* The musical practice of *dhikr*—song and dance—could thus be seen as comparable to the operation required for bringing a liquid to its saturation point in order to cause a change in its state; in both cases a further and quite distinct operation is necessary for the change to take place. In the case of trance it is the will—be it conscious or unconscious—to take the step.

Thus entry into trance, in *dhikr,* would be a deliberate act, but one necessitating long preparation. The hypothesis enables us to solve economically the problem raised by the existence of *dhikr* practiced without a quest for trance. The reasoning behind this is as follows: when practiced without any intention of going into trance (Mirghaniyya), *dhikr* does not in fact induce it; when it does trigger trance (Rifāʿiyya), it is because an intention to go into trance was already present. This hypothesis also resolves the problem raised by the fact that the practice of *dhikr* does not have the same effect—among the same people and during the same ceremony this time—on the *shaikh* as on the adepts. As a general rule, as I said, the latter (or the majority of them) go into trance; the *shaikh* does not. This is because the adepts had an intention to do so whereas the *shaikh* did not. (This does not, of course, preclude the possibility that the adepts may have the intention of going into trance and yet fail to do so, or that the *shaikh* may go into trance without having intended to do so at the outset. We cannot always do as we wish.) Logic, clearly, is on our side. But the explanation may very well seem somewhat simplistic to the unconditional supporters of the spontaneous trance theory. And it does undoubtedly pose the problem—hackneyed but inevitable—of the sincerity of trance. I have mentioned this aspect before. We must return to it now.

Willed Trance, True Trance?

Ghazzali, in the second part of chapter 2 of his "Book of the Right Usages of Audition and Trance," poses this problem in very clear terms. For him, not only can trance be sought deliberately—indeed, this is the very definition of *samāᶜ*—but the actual entry into trance may be feigned. This does not mean that the trance is insincere; everything depends on the purpose for which it is feigned. Since trance, for Ghazzali, is a form of behavior that is learned—and practiced in accordance with "right usages"—it is only natural that in order to learn it, one begins by simulating it. There are two sorts of *wajd,* he tells us (McDonald 1901, 730), one that is spontaneous and one that is forced, the latter being in turn divided into two categories: one that is blameworthy (because it is hypocritical) and one that is praiseworthy. "And this is why, the Apostle of God commanded him who did not weep at the reading of the Koran that he should force weeping and mourning; for the beginning of these States is sometimes forced while their ends thereafter are true." Nothing is earned "except by effort and practice," he adds, "thereafter it becomes nature through custom" (ibid., 731). At the end of his book, in the part that expressly sets out the "right usages," he returns to this point and states, first, that one "should not rise [in order to dance], or raise his voice in weeping while he is able to restrain himself" (McD 1902:8) and second, that "if he dance and force weeping, that is allowable whenever he does not intend hypocrisy by it; for forcing weeping induces grief and dancing is a cause of joy and liveliness."

Ghazzali is not speaking of *dhikr*—or at least not collective *dhikr*—but of *samāᶜ*. Let us say that, in our terminology, he is talking about emotional and not excitational trance. In emotional trance, the relation between trance and that which triggers it—the emotion—is evidently less close than in excitational trance, in which the excitation that triggers the trance appears to be at one and the same time its cause and its symptom. For Ghazzali, emotional trance was a learned form of behavior, which one acquired by first beginning to simulate it. He could have had even greater reason to think the same in the case of excitational trance, in which not only does one mime the excitation of trance before it happens, but one also chants the name of God in such a way that it is difficult to know whether he is being invoked to manifest himself or whether he is being addressed because he is already there. In both cases, however, one must still understand how, by what process, the transition from simulated to real trance takes place.

Life provides many examples of emotions that begin as feigned or imaginary but then become real, often against one's will. One can frighten oneself in play, then end up being genuinely terrified. The same is true of anger, grief, and even joy, although this is rarer and more difficult. At a certain point, one no longer knows quite what the truth is, but by the end one's consciousness is undoubtedly totally overwhelmed by the emotion. On the basis of what? Of nothing! It is more difficult, however, to understand how the same mechanism could work for trance. Perhaps because one is in the habit of thinking of it in all-or-nothing terms, unlike emotions, which we customarily conceive as having varying degrees of intensity; perhaps also because we have had no personal experience of trance. I, anyhow, have not. But if trance is a state of great emotion, accompanied by certain mental representations and certain physiological disturbances, then it is conceivable that disturbances of the same order, artificially provoked by exercising *dhikr*, and accompanied by the same representations, would greatly aid the transition into the trance state.

In trance, be it communion or possession trance, the individual's behavior is so radically different from his normal behavior it seems as though some other person were involved: he was standing—he falls; he felt pain—he is impervious to it; he was clothed—he tears off his garments. It is fairly easy to accept this substitution if one thinks of it as involuntary: if the individual who is its theater undergoes it, if it takes place against his will, because it is stronger than he, because he is borne along by an emotional torment that has deprived him of all control over himself. It is rather difficult to accept that he may be an accomplice in this change or, even more than he is actually the instigator. One thus tends to read into his behavior an insincerity, a duplicity that is incompatible with the reality of the substitution. In short, one thinks that the person is an imposter. This is apparently an error. Trance can be willed. Everyone will agree that *dhikr* involves a deliberate attempt to attain the trance state. By the same token, we should not be astonished to learn that it is also, partially and for good reasons, a simulation of trance. This is an apparent contradiction that we have to take into account: trance can be voluntary, but this does not mean it is necessarily insincere.

Let me add that if collective *dhikr* is a deliberate attempt to provoke trance, "solitary" *dhikr* appears to be a no less deliberate attempt to achieve ecstasy. On this point, however, the Sufis themselves, already divided as to the relative value of the two forms of *dhikr*—collective or solitary—are even more divided on the question of whether *dhikr* involves a deliberate quest for or a spontaneous realization of trance. Al-Hallāj, as we know, insisted that trance must never be actively sought, but that it should always be a gift from God—a conviction shared, later on, by Saint Teresa of Avila (though without the same results, fortunately for her).

Let us return to music. The keystone of collective *dhikr,* if one may so express it, is a particular musical practice. If the Sufis see this form of *dhikr* as inferior, this is because it is, we might say, easier than solitary *dhikr,* which is not only practiced alone but also in silence and immobility. The fact that music—or more precisely the practice of music—occupies a central position in the first and is totally absent from the second, is not fortuitous. If collective *dhikr* is easier than the solitary, this is because the practitioner of collective *dhikr* is supported—literally at times—by his companions, whom he supports in turn. This great enterprise of autosuggestion, namely *dhikr,* is based on the synergic effect of music. It is within music and through it; it is by means of the coordinating power that music alone possesses that the fusion of all these wills and all these desires is realized, a fusion that prefigures for each one the communion with God. I have made it plain enough by now: the singing and dancing practices in *dhikr* should be seen as acting in a very real way on the physiology of trance. Their efficacy in the field of its socialization, in other words of its normal and regular realization, is certainly no less decisive. There is absolutely no need, in order to explain their role, to lend them some undefined, mysterious power.

Fakirism and Identificatory Music

In the last few pages we have concentrated on the orthodox form of *dhikr,* if that is the correct way of putting it. But, as we have seen, there are others, and it can happen that *dhikr* will include episodes much more akin to possession than to Islam. This is true, as we saw, of the skewer ordeal described by Poche[113] among the Aleppo Rifāʿiyya, during which the neophytes, whose flanks are pierced, identify themselves with Ahmad Rifāʿi, the order's founder. During this episode it is not the chanted recitation of the *dhikr* that is heard, but a mixture of songs and drumming,[114] in which the principal drum instrument is the *mizhar,* whose name means "he who makes appear." According to Poche, this drum plays an essential role in the neophytes' entry into trance. "The vigorous beating of the *mizhar,*" he writes, "gradually overcomes all physical resistance and . . . produces a sort of anesthesia that facilitates submission of the body to the discipline of the ceremony, particularly during the sword ordeal. The loudness of sound produced by the instrument, which can be heard from quite far away, causes the accompanying song to be more deeply impressed upon the mind and body of the faithful identifying themselves with him."

Through his songs, the *shaikh* urges the candidate to prepare himself for the ordeal. Invocations to the "saint" mingle with the tireless beating of the *mizhar*. Finally, "the entry of a rhythm in double time irresistibly urges the *murīd* to move to the centre of the *halga* [circle]" where the ordeal itself is to take place. With respect to the relation between the music and the entranced person, the situation is thus quite different here from that which characterizes the *dhikr* proper: it is not the musical practice of the *dhikr* by the adept himself that leads him into trance, it is music that is played for him. The practitioner is completely musicated; he is absolutely not a musicant. Moreover, the situation is also different from that of *samā*ᶜ (where again the adept is a musicated person, not a musicant), since it is not the emotion—both aesthetic and mystic—experienced while hearing a religious song that triggers trance. This is done by songs urging him to be courageous, or exalting the saint, or else by codified drum calls, in short, music that has the same characteristics as that found in the possession rituals described in the first part of this book.

The fact that the ordeal in question takes place during a ritual identified by the word *dhikr* does not alter the situation: we are not dealing at all with a communion rite, but with a possession rite, and within the logic of the system, it is possession music that must be at work.

Now let us move on to the ᶜIsāwiyya, whose *dhikr*, or rather *hadra* (ceremony) includes aspects that are even less orthodox than those of the Rifā-ᶜyya. The second part of this *hadra* consists of figurative dances and demonstrations of fakirism (ordeals of hot coals, daggers, and so on) that must all be viewed, as I have said, as manifestations of possession. The music is no longer provided (even in part) by the adepts but only by musicians especially appointed to the task. One does not hear recitation of the *dhikr*, contrary to what happened during the first part of the *hadra*, but instrumental music performed by drums and wind instruments—the oboe (*ghaita*) among the ᶜIsāiyya of Morocco,[115] the transverse flute (*guecba*)[116] among those of Algeria. There is every reason to believe that the figurative dances and the demonstrations of fakirism (which are their equivalent) are performed to specific musical themes. Brunel (1926; 98) makes a very significant observation on this point. Talking of a particular region where the *hadra* of the Gnawiyya[117] is practiced, he notes that "upon hearing the tune appropriate to this *hadra*, the adepts are seized by *hāl*.[118] They are then offered daggers, which they seize . . . [in order to perform] their favorite exercise, which consists of striking their calves with the points of these weapons until the blood flows." Nothing is said about the musical characteristics of this tune, undoubtedly because none is especially remarkable and because it does not significantly differ from other tunes in the repertoire, except for the fact that it is "appropriate." We are justified in thinking, then, that this "appropriate tune" is nothing other than the "right tune" to which we have referred on several occasions in other chapters, in other words, it is the "agreed-upon" air, which has the value of a signal and is recognized as such, but which is not endowed with any particular expressive property peculiar to it. If the adepts go into trance when they hear it, it is not because the tune has emotive powers specific to it, but because it is the tune of the Gnawa, and because at its cue one adopts the conventional form of behavior—that is, one grabs the daggers. This "appropriate tune" should therefore be placed in the category of musical mottoes, and we have already examined the mechanism by which they act to trigger possession trance.[119] This mechanism is namely that of a code, in which the signal triggers a response as a result of the meaning that has been arbitrarily assigned to it, and not by some intrinsic power acting upon the auditor's emotivity.

Let us now specify this interpretation of the role that music plays in the part of the ᶜIsāwiyya ḥaḍra in which possession is at work; it is one that I deduce from Brunel's description and is by no means his interpretation of the facts. Quite the contrary. A "furious tempest of drums and oboes" that puts the dancers in such a state that "they can scarcely retain their balance";[120] "din";[121] "dizzying music" that, together with the "demoniacal dance" of the tahhayor (generic term for trance dances among the ᶜIsāwiyya), plunges everyone "into an acute neuropathic state";[122] spectators who dance "in the grip of the terrifying staccato music of the ghaïta and the thobol (oboe and kettledrum) and are seized by "this contagious madness" and "this ecstatic frenzy" which "none can resist";[123] "hysterical crisis" that abates "suddenly with the ghaïtas' last notes"[124]—such are the terms that Brunel uses to describe how the music functions in this ritual. Moreover, on several occasions he also mentioned the acceleration of tempo, so that the dances always begin fairly slowly and then gradually speed up. Clearly he provides us with a general picture of the relations between music and trance that is extremely similar to the one that emerged from so many other ethnographical descriptions cited in the first part of this book. And in this picture, as in all the others, it is imperative to distinguish between facts and interpretations of facts. The facts are not to be doubted: the music is extremely violent, it is markedly rhythmic in character, accelerates, accompanies dances that have the same formal characteristics, and the dancers are finally entranced. Thus far one can argue with nothing: these are the facts and they have been recorded. On the other hand, as soon as one makes this music and dance responsible—and entirely responsible—for trance, one is interpreting the facts, and it is this interpretation I in fact dispute.

Music and dance on the one hand, trance on the other, go together. There is a relation of contemporaneity that is undeniable. But by making this relation into one of causality, Brunel commits an error, since in the same culture area, namely Morocco, music and dances that are just as violent and make just as much use of *accelerando* are performed every day without necessarily leading to trance, possession, or demonstrations of fakirism. As for the manner in which he arrived at this error, it involves a process that has two phases. First, he attributes certain characteristics to the music that it does not have, but that it seems to have because they are characteristics of the accompanying trance. Second, having made this confusion, he then considers trance to be an effect of the music precisely because it has these similarities. In short, the procedure is as follows: this man is mad; he dances and listens to music; therefore there is something mad about this music; this being so, it is this music that makes the man mad. Needless to say, this very system of interpretation that is projected onto the facts remains implicit. It is because one is watching trances that can indeed be terrifying that one labels the music as "terrifying" too. It is because entranced people stagger about that one refers to trance as "dizzying" and that one speaks of the "furious tempest unleashed by the drums." It is because the spirits possessing the adepts are regarded as demons that the dance is labeled "demoniacal." In other contexts, the same music and the same dance would be described as "violent" certainly, but they would not be considered as either "terrifying" or "demoniacal."

As we know, the *ahwach* is the customary dance of a large number of the Berber "tribes" in the Moroccan High Atlas mountains.[125] It is danced on the spot. Standing closely packed one against the other, the dancers bend their knees in time with one another, accompanying each beat with a sort of pounding of the ground and a back-and-forth swaying of the body very similar to the one Brunel describes in the *rbbāni* trance dance. It makes use of music that has an extremely marked *accelerando*, also comparable to that used in the "ecstatic" dances of the ʿIsāwiyya described by Brunel. Beaten for all they are worth, the drums *(bendir)* also make a "din" one could well term deafening, if not actually dizzying. From the formal point of view, then, the *ahwach* displays all the features to which Brunel attributes the triggering of trance. Moreover, he also describes the trance dance of the ʿIsāwiyya as a "dance of jubilation" (1926; 122, 225).[126] And an intense impression of jubilation is also what emerges from a successful *ahwach*. Yet the fact remains that the *ahwach* is not a trance dance at all.[127]

Another argument, this time concerning the musical instruments, further strengthens my skepticism with regard to Brunel's theory about the effects of the music. He attributes these effects largely to the oboe *(ghaïta);* yet it so happens that the flute is sometimes used in its place. In his description of the ʿIsāwiyya's annual feast in Morocco, Brunel (1926; 122) closely associates the "hysterical crisis" with the *ghaïta*. The crisis, he writes, abates "suddenly with the final notes." He also emphasizes the *ghaïta's* "nasal sound" (ibid., 98) and denounces its "hatched and frightening" music, which, accompanied by the drums, leads to "frenzied tempests." As we know, the *ghaïta,* the oboe of the Maghreb, is an instrument with a piercing, very intense sound. Clearly, it is its piercing quality and its timbre *sui generis* that Brunel interprets as being responsible for triggering trance.[128] Yet among the Algerian ꜤIsāwiyya it is not the *ghaïta* that is used for the *ḥaḍra* and trance dances but the transverse flute, an instrument whose sound is always rather weak.

In their description of trance dances among the Algerian ꜤIsāwiyya, Dermenghem and Barbès (1951; 309) talk about the "irresistible beating" of the *bendaïr,* and thus attribute the same effects to the drums as Brunel does. As for the flute (*gueçba*), it accompanies the drums "discreetly," they tell us, and its song is "so gentle that it can pass unperceived." They also add, however, that this song is "so pure that the nostalgic appeal of its melody colors the imperious rhythm of the percussion instruments with great efficacity." What sort of efficacity would this be? In Morocco, it was the violence of the oboe that combined with the drums to trigger trance; in Algeria it is the gentleness of the flute. Some explanation seems to be called for. The truth is that both these interpretations are equally subjective.

We are once again confronted with the findings in the first part of the book on the nonspecificity of the musical instruments associated with possession.[129] In practice, as we saw, they all can serve this purpose. This example further confirms this.

I should add that in Morocco, among the Gnawa, another brotherhood that has numerous "points of resemblance" (Brunel 1926; 234) with that of the ꜤIsāwiyya, it is not even a wind instrument, but a stringed one, the *gembri,* a small lute, that is used as the melodic instrument in the band accompanying trance dancers. Here again, however, the *gembri,* which is "the fundamental instrument" (Lapassade 1975; 30 n. 3) of the orchestra, and which produces only rather weak sounds, is "generally" covered (ibid., n. 5) by the "deafening" music of metal castanets and drums. How do we explain the fact that an instrument can play a "fundamental" role in a possession[130] ritual and yet be scarcely heard? Clearly because the function of the *gembri* (like that of the oboe and flute earlier) is to announce the musical mottoes of the genii responsible for the possessions, and because all that is needed in order to produce the desired effect is for the adept consecrated to a particular genius to recognize that spirit's tune (which is easily conceivable, however great the surrounding din). This is the only hypothesis through which this paradox can be solved.

Even though the musical motto, or in other words the melodic aspect of Gnawa music, plays the essential role in triggering trance, it is nevertheless only its rhythmic aspect—which is much more spectacular—that

caught the attention of the Living Theatre[130] some years ago. It seems that
it was also this aspect that attracted a young Moroccan, Pacca Abderha-
man, founder of a pop group whose aim is also to induce trance through
music, but in a profane context.[131] And this is further proof that such erroneous ideas concerning the preeminence of rhythm in the relation between
music and trance reign everywhere. To repeat once again: these ideas are
the reflection of a much too simplistic view of things.

8 Conclusion

If it has taken so many pages to make this inventory of the relations between music and trance, it is because they are so extremely varied, because they often contradict one another from one case to another, and because it is extremely difficult to formulate any rule about them without a counterexample immediately contradicting it. At the same time, things had to be shown in all their complexity so as not to fall prey to interpretations of the most reductive and erroneous sort. At least one fact has been established: that these relations are not simple. Although they are complex, this does not mean that they defy all logic. And elucidating this logic is the task that now remains. The only way to do this is to seriate the questions, which we shall do by successively examining all the principal types of trance as they have been defined in the previous pages, starting with their ideology, and by relating these trances to the manner in which they are engendered (induced/conducted trance), the dynamics of their manifestations, the kind of music associated with them, and the role played by dance. Among all these types of trance, possession trance is the one that seems to have the most paradoxical relations to music. I shall therefore examine it last, and at greater length.

Music in Its Relations to Emotional, Communial, and Shamanic Trances

Among all the types of trance we have discussed, emotional trance—profane or religious—as we observed it among the Arabs is undoubtedly the one that has the most direct and evident relation to music. Upon hearing music that has a strong emotional power over him, the subject, overwhelmed by emotion, goes into trance. From what source does the music draw this power? From the meaning of the words and from the perfection of their relation to the music. The emotion is not only affective; it is to an equal extent aesthetic, and calls upon either the subject's sense of the beautiful, or his sense of the divine, or upon both simultaneously. In this case music is pure message, and it in fact produces trance by virtue of a *sui generis* power. It must nevertheless be emphasized that this power is indissociable from that of the words—it is the "union of poetry and music," as they said in the Renaissance, that is at work. The relations between music and trance are thus, in this instance, as simple as they can be. The only problem they present is that of knowing why musical emotion so commonly leads to such conduct among the Arabs and does so less frequently elsewhere. The answer is clearly that this behavior among the Arabs is a cultural phenomenon, an expression of emotions that have been learned, stereotyped, and assigned a certain value. And although the phenomenon is less usual elsewhere, we do have some examples of it. In Europe, I cited the "Ranz des vaches" and its effect on the Swiss. We have also recently learned that in Melanesia, among certain New Guinea Papuans and also among the 'Are'are of the Solomon Islands,[1] musical emotion frequently gives rise to certain forms of trance. In the West, the emotional impact of military bugle calls, which can reduce the bravest men to tears, is another example. There is also justification for thinking that the more or less hysterical behavior of pop music fans can be categorized as musical emotion that has become an accepted and valued stereotyped form of behavior.

† Of all the arts, music is undoubtedly the one that has the greatest capacity to move us, and the emotion it arouses can reach overwhelming proportions. Since trance is clearly an emotional form of behavior, it is not surprising that musical emotions should prove to be destined to some extent, under the pressure of cultural factors, to become institutionalized in this form. This would mean that we are dealing here with a relation between music and trance that, although strongly influenced by culture, is nevertheless based on a natural—and thus universal—property of music, or at least of a certain kind of music. Moreover, in emotional trance it is music alone that produces the trance. This trance, which frequently is nearer to nervous crisis than to true trance, is of short duration, since it does not result, or only to a very small extent, in dance. Contrary to what happens in the case of other sorts of trance, music does not function to maintain it.

Communial trance, as I have said, occurs in two forms, induced and conducted. When induced—meaning that the subject is a musicated person and not a musicant—it is always emotional, but can be either ritualized or not. When it is ritualized and blossoms into dance, it is the classical Arab *samā^c*. Music brings about the trance as a result of the emotional power—entirely steeped in religious feeling in this case, to be sure—of the sung poetry; it then prolongs it—maintains it, we could say—during the dancing by means of its rhythm. It therefore has two effects: first, triggering the trance; second, maintaining it—the two resulting from two very distinct actions, first that of the words, then that of the rhythm.

When communial trance is conducted, in other words when the subject is a musicant, we have the Muslim *dhikr* or, among Christians, the trance practices of the Shlustes, the Shakers, and various other sects. Here, the

role of the music in producing trance is of a quite different kind. Being indissociable from dance—for it can only be made while dancing—it is
above all a corporeal technique. The dancer and the musician, or more
precisely the dancer and singer, are merged in one and the same person. It
is both the subject's own singing and dancing that lead him to trance. The
dhikr is a certain way of singing. But this singing, which calls for a particular technique of breath control, is at the same time a recitation of the
name of God (among Christians it refers to the Holy Ghost or Christ). The
words also play a role (and many would say that it is the essential one) and
are, here again, bearers of emotion—religious emotion, naturally, but at
the service of a religion of love and fervor conducive to many ambiguities.
In content and in form this music is above all invocatory. If one dissociates
it from the meaning of the words, this music—singing and dancing combined—seems to have the function of creating excitation. What we are
dealing with then is a very particular form of autoexcitation, since it
makes use of breathing, a certain overstimulation of the vocal cords, a
very accentuated rotary movement of the neck and head, and a whole variety of physical movements that must certainly consume (or liberate?) a
great deal of energy. There are two musical characteristics specific to
dhikr: a particular sort of vocal delivery (the "saw" *dhikr*)—which raises
the question of whether or not it has neurophysiological repercussions—
and a systematic use of *accelerando* and *crescendo*, the object of which is
to increase the emotional tension. Although it is not as monotonous as
people tend to claim—even if only because the increasing agitation just
mentioned contributes to a renewal of the musical interest—repetition
(and above all the repetition of words) also plays a role. Let us say, to sum
up, that music, words, and dance create at the same time a great physical
effervescence and a state of "monoideism" that, in combination, create
psychophysiological conditions apparently very favorable to the occurrence of trance. In this case trance is quite deliberately sought for, and if it
occurs—which is not always the case, for the "mechanism" is not automatic, even though it is certainly very efficacious—it is only very rarely
that it does so in an unexpected manner, unlike emotional trance, which
very often does occur unexpectedly.

In the case of both induced communial trance (*samāᶜ*) and conducted
communial trance (*dhikr* and other comparable rituals) the onset of trance
requires a certain amount of theatricality. But the theater involved is as it
were an intimate—or innermost—one. For although there may be an audience (varying in size depending on the case, and sometimes completely
absent), the presence of spectators is not indispensable. Here the theater is
constituted by the small group of adepts taking part together in the practice of either "audition" or sung recitation and dancing. The kind of *dhikr*
practiced aloud—in other words the one that interests us here, since it is

the one that leads to trance, whereas the other leads to ecstasy—is termed "collective." *Samāᶜ* is likewise a group practice, not only because there are always several people taking part in it together (I know of no account of *samāᶜ* organized around a single individual), but also because the gathering is necessarily divided into at least two sections, "auditioners" on the one hand, musicians on the other.

The Mevlevi *samāᶜ*, as I have said, is a particular case in that it is akin both to classical *samāᶜ* and at the same time to *dhikr*, since the dancers are not the musicians (or the musicants) of their own entry into trance, whereas their dancing is the principal means of triggering it. Contrary to what happens in classical *samāᶜ*, dance is not the result and expression of trance; rather, trance is the result of dance. The music here certainly is emotional since both words and instruments are impregnated with love of God. But it is the dance, ultimately, that is the triggering factor. The role of the music thus is twofold. First, it creates a general state of mystic emotion—the emotion at once religious and carnal that is so characteristic of Sufism—and second, it provides the dance with the acoustic stimulus without which it could not even take place. Let us say, to sum up, that here the role of music in the triggering and maintenance of trance is indirect rather than direct, contrary to what happens in both classical *samāᶜ* and *dhikr*.

Now let us move on to shamanism, in which the trance, as in *dhikr*, is conducted, since the shaman is the musicant of his own entry into trance (the fact that he is aided in his role by an assistant who takes over when the moment arises, notably when he loses consciousness, does not invalidate this rule). The relations between music and trance are organized, here again, in accordance with a particular system, but matters are more complicated than they have been up to now. The shaman's musical instrument is endowed with symbolic meanings related to his journey, or, more precisely, to the world or worlds he visits during his trance. If the drum—supposing the instrument is a drum, for even in central Asia, remember, it can be some other instrument—plays a role in triggering trance, this is not, despite what may have been said to the contrary, the result of some mysterious neurophysiological action specific to that instrument, as I have shown only too often, nor of some kind of "obsessive" monotony that also exists only in the imagination of certain authors. Musically, the shamanic drum—or any other instrument used in its place—essentially functions to support his singing, to provide the rhythm that is the primary support of his dancing, and to dramatize or punctuate the action. In short, its role is precisely the same as the one it plays in theater music of any kind, with the single exception that here it is charged with symbolic meaning, and that this symbolic meaning is in turn charged with a certain emotional power. But even in this case we are still in the realm of psychology and cultural conditioning.

As for the shaman's singing, it has several different aspects; sometimes it is invocatory, when he has to summon his auxiliary spirits, sometimes descriptive or narrative, when he is relating his journey, but its specific characteristic is that it is incantatory. The shaman is a magician, and his singing brings to life the imaginary world of the invisible. Without song, the shamanic imaginary system would be inconceivable. (The imaginary system of possession, on the contrary, can dispense with it and make do with purely instrumental music, which operates by means of coded signals whose verbal equivalence is secondary.) Moreover, for the shaman, singing is his principal means of communion with his audience, that audience without which he could not perform and which supports him with its choral responses, for it is the alternation of his calls and their replies that creates the reciprocal warm-up, the climate of emotional excitation, that is indispensable to the onset of the trance. Lastly, for the shaman, to sing and play the drum (or rattle) is to stimulate himself to dance. Beneath the often considerable weight of his costume, this dance takes on the proportions of an exhausting exercise, responsible, beyond doubt, for certain losses of consciousness. To shamanize, in other words to sing and dance, is as much a corporeal technique as a spiritual exercise. Insofar as he is at the same time singer, instrumentalist, and dancer, the shaman, among all practitioners of trance, should be seen as the one who by far makes the most complete use of music.

But the power of music alone cannot be held responsible for the shaman's entry into trance, anymore than in the case of the Sufi. This trance must still be willed. Let us remember what Shirokogoroff observed on this point: the *accelerando* and *crescendo* of the music, intended to intensify the general emotion, do not lead to trance unless the shaman has decided that they will at the outset. Neither the music nor the dance produces trance mechanically or automatically, and this explains why the shaman—just like the Sufi—so often resorts to the use of a drug in order to obtain "lift-off," as it were, at the start of his journey. With a drug, the mechanism is different and more reliable. Music and dance on their own are certainly the instruments of a more authentic, and more meritorious, trance; but they also are much more chancy.

With the shaman we are dealing with someone whose trance—or, more precisely, nervous crisis or fit—is not necessarily linked to music. Every shaman, before becoming a shaman, has undergone sudden and unforeseen crises that occurred outside of any ritual context, and that were in fact the very sign of his vocation. The crises, or trances, that he will regularly experience after having been officially established as a shaman, will be no more, in part at least, than reenactments of previous crises. And it must be emphasized that the crisis—that particularly dramatic aspect of trance—does not require music to trigger it. The psychic upheaval that it manifests thus obeys a purely internal logic of the state of consciousness.

This means that the role of the music is much less to produce the trance than to create conditions favorable to its onset, to regularize its form, and to ensure that instead of being a merely individual, unpredictable, and uncontrollable behavioral phenomenon, it becomes, on the contrary, predictable, controlled, and at the service of the group.

As observed among the Bushmen, trance has yet another set of relations to music. As in shamanism, to which it is kindred in at least one aspect of its ideology (journey of the soul and ascent into the upper world), we are dealing with a conducted trance in which the subject is the musicant of both his own dance and his own trance. As in communial trance (as manifested in *dhikr*, for example), it is a collective practice; but the singing, which is the main support for the dance and has no instrumental accompaniment other than the dancers' own leg-rattles, is divided between the men who dance and will go into trance and the women who do not dance, are seated, provide the greater part of the choral singing, and do not go into trance. The singing, which is symbolically associated with one or another healing ritual, is wordless. It is vocalized on syllables devoid of meaning and does not constitute a particular musical category. The same type of singing that is usually intoned in everyday life is used for the healing dance, which gives rise to trance. This singing is neither invocatory nor incantatory, and it is not its emotional power that is at work, but the ardor of its collective execution, because of which the curative power of the singing "boils" and thus attains its full efficacy. The psychological effervescence, the emotion necessary for the onset of trance, is thus derived from the collective fervor of the singing. As for the dancing, which like that of the shaman or that of the *dhikr*, though for different reasons, is an exhausting exercise, it also contributes to the physiological preparation of trance. Here again, music and dance, taken together, constitute a corporeal technique aimed at attaining trance.

"Underlying all our mystic states," Mauss writes (1936),[2] there are "corporeal techniques," "biological methods of entering into communication with God." If we substitute the words "religious trance" for "mystic states" and "communication with God" to make our generalization clearer, it is evident that for the Bushmen of southern Africa, as for the shamans of central Asia, the Russian Shlustes, the Sufis of the Near East, or the Shakers in the United States, trance is very largely a matter of corporeal technique, in which singing and dancing, in combination, are the two principal elements. But it would be a fundamental error to reduce these various forms of trance to no more than various forms of corporeal technique using various combinations of song and dance. The technique operates only because it is at the service of a belief, and because trance constitutes a cultural model integrated into a certain general representation of the world. Here we have an essential intellectual datum, which underlies both the psychology and physiology of trance. This is why entry into trance always seems to depend upon a kind of restrictive clause: however well prepared one may be, physically and psychologically, one must still be prepared intellectually, and have made the decision (more or less unconsciously) to succumb to the trance state.

The great difference between emotional trance on the one hand and communial (conducted) and shamanic trance on the other, is that in the former the sole responsibility for the onset of trance rests upon listening to music—or, more precisely, to sung poetry—while in the case of the other two it is not listening to music but its practice that is involved; furthermore, it is not the practice of music alone that is the operative factor, but this practice in combination with dance. In the first case the music is in no way a corporeal technique; in the other two it is fundamentally and precisely that. Moreover, in the first case the music is essentially emotional; in the other two, whether invocatory (communial trance) or incantatory (shamanic trance), it is much less emotional, or only indirectly so. In the case of the Bushmen it seems it is not emotional at all, which raises a problem I shall leave open.

Things look quite different, however, in the case of possession.

MUSIC IN ITS RELATIONS TO POSSESSION TRANCE

The reader will remember that in the first part of this book, we found that the relations between music and possession can assume an extraordinary number of different forms. At the moment of the actual triggering of trance, which is often but not always marked by a crisis, it took on the most contradictory aspects. The crisis sometimes appears to be the direct result of the music's frenzy, sometimes quite unconnected with it; music sometimes appears to be the means by which the crisis and fall (in the *ndöp*) are provoked, some times, on the contrary, as the means by which the crisis is brought to an end (as in tarantism); sometimes it appears to be an almost mechanical means by which trance is provoked (in public *candomblé* ceremonies), sometimes it seems to play no part in it at all (the morning trance during the *candomblé* reclusion period); the adepts sometimes appear to be incapable of resisting the summons of the music (when they are neophytes), sometimes, on the contrary, it is a point of honor not to succumb to it (when they are officiants); in one ceremony an adept goes into trance at the sound of his motto, while another, apparently subject to the same objective conditions, does not; in one cult (*candomblé*) each god responds only to the musical theme (motto) specific to him, yet there also is a theme that can mobilize all the gods indiscriminately: one dance (in the *zār* cult) is reputedly a classic means of inducing trance, yet is also performed to provoke the coming out of trance; in the *rab* cult, the drummers appear to be playing a determining role in the onset of possession when great public ceremonies are involved (*tuuru* and *ndöp*), yet play none whatsoever when the ritual is on a smaller scale (*samp*) since they are strictly excluded; sometimes the instruments are held responsible for the onset of trance, sometimes the singing; here it is one type of instrument that is characteristic of possession music, there it is another. In other words, although music indisputably plays a role—more or less decisive depending on the case—in the onset of trance, it seems impossible to establish any constant relation of cause and effect between the two. The only rule that appears to be truly general is that the music must be made for the possessed and not by them, or, in other words, that trance is induced and not conducted.

If we now go on to examine trance, not at its moment of onset, but when it is at its height, things become clearer. We could sum them up by saying that no matter which cult is concerned—if we set aside the initiation period which has its own particular logic—possession music is dance music whose melody is associated with the divinity held responsible for the trance. The relations between music and trance constitute themselves in two different ways depending on whether trance is at its moment of onset or, on the contrary, when it is in full bloom. They are also of two different kinds depending on whether the possessed person is at the initiation stage or not. In order to understand the reason for this state of things we must now look at the relations between music and possession with respect to the logic that governs the system since, indeed, a system seems to be at work. In order to do this, however, it is indispensable to be able to refer to a general theory of possession trance. To my knowledge, no such theory exists.[3] However presumptuous it may seem, I will therefore run the risk of offering one here, less for its own sake (even though I believe it does account fairly well for a number of facts) than because one is needed anyhow. Good or bad, it will have the merit of occupying, until something better comes along, a position that another theory of this kind is bound to hold in this system.

Provisorily, then, let us view trance, as it is observed in possession cults, as a socialized form of behavior resulting from the conjunction of several constituents: (1) at the level of the individual: a given innate to the structure of consciousness making it susceptible of being invaded by an emotional event that submerges its normal state and leads to hysteriform behavior; (2) at the level of collective representations: (a) interpretation of this event as a sign of the will or presence of a spirit or divinity; (b) exploitation or, to use Roger Bastide's term (1972, 94), domestication of the event, with the intention of establishing it as a mode of communication with the divine; (c) identification of the entranced subject with the divinity held responsible for the trance; and (d) theatrilization of this identificatory behavior.

The way in which these constituents are brought in to play varies a great deal from cult to cult, depending on the cult's history, the circumstances in which it was gradually constituted, the context in which it developed, the individuals who affected its evolution, its possible contacts with neighboring or foreign cults, and still a great many other things. For many adepts the original emotion that gave rise to the mental upheaval around which the cult structured itself may well not or no longer be a spontaneous form of behavior but, on the contrary, a form of learned behavior, a stereotype. This does not alter the fact that in the genesis of all possession cults, and therefore all possessional trance, there must, in the beginning, have been an emotional state experienced by an individual and capable of being experienced in turn by others, whether spontaneously or as the result of a learning process. The relation of music to this emotional state is extremely variable since it is integrated into the cult in varying ways. Initiation, according to whether it is very important (in the *vodun* cult, for example) or, on the contrary, nonexistent (as in tarantism) governs the emotional behavior and its relation to music sometimes in one way, sometimes in another. Although emotion is something experienced by individuals, in this instance it manifests itself only within the logic of the cult into which it has been integrated. This is what explains the disconcerting variability of the relation between music and the onset of trance.

The trance itself, in other words the period during which the subject settles himself, so to say, into his other persona and totally coincides with it, has, on the contrary, a quite stable relation to music. In its fullest form, by which I mean the form it displays during public possession ceremonies, trance most often consists in dancing to the sound of music that belongs to the possessing divinity or, if there are several persons, to the sound of music that corresponds collectively to all the divinities present. Here the function of the music is obvious. It is due to the music, and because he is supported by the music, that the possessed person publicly lives out, by means of dance, his identification with the divinity he embodies. The music at this point is thus neither emotional, nor invocatory, nor incantatory: it is essentially identificatory. By playing his "motto," the musicians notify this identity to the entranced dancer, those around him, the priests, and the spectators. The language the music speaks is understood by all, and each person decodes it at his or her own level. It is through this music, and through the dance to which it gives rise, that recognition of the divinity's presence is conveyed to the entire group, a recognition that is indispensible because it authenticates the trance and confers upon it a character of normality. Music thus appears as the principal means of socializing trance.

The onset of trance very frequently obeys this logic as well, of course. It is upon hearing *his* tune, *his* motto (or rather that of *his* god) that the possessed person most often enters into trance. But the exceptions to the rule are so numerous that it is impossible to ignore them. Except in the case of "old hands," going into trance constitutes, for the individual concerned, such an event—I would even say such a psychophysiological adventure—that in order to make the transition successfully, a large number of favorable conditions must be present. The individual equation—to be or not to be disposed to enter into trance—then plays a decisive role in the process, and this is what explains why music, which also has a part in it, indisputably, but which is no more than one element among others, should ultimately play so very variable a role. Sometimes it is its identificatory character that is at work, and then we are in the realm of cultural convention. Sometimes it is its power to create, through its ability to excite and agitate (hence the frequent use of *accelerando* and *crescendo*) a certain state of effervescence that seems to be particularly propitious, very understandably, to the onset of trance. And in this case we are in the realm of the natural. Sometimes it is its association with a particular circumstance, or idea, or character, charged, for the adept, with emotional power. And then we are in the realm of the individual.

In the triggering of trance, music contributes sometimes through one of its aspects—most often, again, its identificatory aspect—sometimes through another, sometimes decisively, sometimes accessorily. In extreme cases it may not contribute to it at all. This is true of tarantism, where, it will be remembered, the trance—or, more correctly, the crisis (and fall)—usually occurs outside any relation with music. This is an extremely significant fact. On the other hand, the tarantulee, when no longer in crisis but in trance, dances to the sound of the tarantella, and it is in fact this tarantella (as long as it is the "right tune") that ends the crisis and causes it to develop into trance. Although it is conceivable that a subject can enter into trance without music, it is inconceivable that a subject could experience the trance itself without music. Let us say that, in possession, music is the condition *sine qua non* of the trance experience. This is so for two reasons. First, because possession trance is a change of identity, because that change of identity has no meaning for the subject unless his new identity is recognized by everyone, and because it is the music that signals it. Second, because this new identity must be manifested and because dance is (usually with costume, but not always) its principal and frequently sole expression. Provided, then, that it is not absolutely fleeting (I am thinking of Malkām Ayyahu's trances, described by Leiris, which often lasted no more than an instant, just long enough to express it with a gesture, word, pose), provided that it has *duration*, this trance, which is the experience of another identity, has an absolute need for music in order to continue to exist, since it is music that, through its identificatory character, maintains the illusion and that, through its function as support of the dance, enables it to be manifested.

The major function of music thus seems to be maintaining the trance, rather in the way an electric current will maintain the vibration of a tuning fork if tuned to the same pitch frequency. Here, however, music is not just physically (on a purely motor level) "in tune" with trance. It is even more "in tune" on the psychological level, since its action consists in putting the individual experiencing his transitory identity "in phase" with the group that is recognizing this identity or imposing it upon him.

Whereas in conducted trance—shamanism and even more so communial trance of the *dhikr* type—music appears as a corporeal technique, here it is above all a technique of communication. Since shamanic trance involves changing worlds, the shaman's adventure is first and foremost an individual affair. It could even be practiced in solitude. And this is why the shaman is of necessity the musicant of his own trance.

Possession trance, on the contrary, consists in a change of identity, and this change would of course be meaningless if it were not recognized by the group. Moreover it is, or is supposed to be, undergone, not willed. This is why the music is provided by the group, since the possessed person only exists as such for the group and because of it. In this relation, then, the music is the instrument of communication between subject and group; but the communication that takes place is particularly characteristic in that the two interlocutors speak simultaneously—one through music, the other through dance—and that the dialogue is addressed to a third party, the spectators. This third party is just as indispensable to the blossoming of trance as the two others, since possession cannot function without being theater.

Music has often been thought of as endowed with the mysterious power of triggering possession, and the musicians of possession as the withholders of some mysterious knowledge that enables them to manipulate this power. There is no truth whatsoever in this assumption. It is nonetheless true that possession cults, as institutions, are mechanisms that make use of great musical skill that has developed over a long period of time. The role of this music is multiple. At the level of the ceremony—or, if one prefers, of the theater—it creates a certain emotional climate for the adepts. Second, it leads the adepts toward that great mutation, occuring at the level of imagination, that consists in becoming identified with the spirit possessing him. In this operation, which is so aleatory and which is subject to so many variables, the relation between music and trance often appears quite strained. Third and last, it provides the adept with the means of manifesting this identification and thus of exteriorizing his trance. It is at this stage that music is indispensable. Why? Because it is the only language that speaks simultaneously, if I may so put it, to the head and the legs; because it is through music that the group provides the entranced person with a mirror in which he can read the image of his borrowed identity; and because it is the music that enables him to reflect this identity back again to the group in the form of dance. There is no mystery to it at all. Or, if there is, then it lies in the trance state itself, as a special state of consciousness; and if we must seek for an explanation of this, it may be found in the overriding power of a certain conjunction of emotion and imagination. This is the source from which trance springs. Music does nothing more than socialize it, and enable it to attain its full development.

Notes

CHAPTER ONE

1. On the universality of trance, see Erika Bourguignon 1973, 9–11.
2. Taber's *Cyclopedic Medical Dictionary,* 9th ed, 1963.
3. *Dictionnaire des termes techniques de médecine,* 16th ed., Maloine, 1955.
4. Cf., for example, the captions to photographs 13a and 13b.
5. *The Book of the Right Usages of Audition and Trance.* We will deal with this work at length in chapter 7, "Music and Trance among the Arabs" in part two.
6. Speaking of states of hyperexcitation of the central nervous system, Bourguignon notes (1973, 5) that trance attains "an extreme in the ecstatic state of mystical rapture." She is here following her own definition of ecstasy in a previous work (1965, 41). Borrowed from the dictionary of psychological and psychoanalytic terms by English and English (1958), this definition is: "Religious and emotionally marked trances are called ecstasy."
7. See pp. 182–83, among others.
8. In the *Dictionnaire des religions* (Larousse 1966), only the term "extase" figures, presented as (mainly for oracles) the result of trance. In the *Dictionnaire de spiritualité,* which is in the process of being published and has not yet gone beyond the letter L, a great deal of space is alloted to the word "extase"; various articles, totaling 140 columns in all, appear under this entry. The word "transe" occurs several times under the entry on shamanism (1961, cols. 2049–50)—and this is significant.
9. In his article on the definition of shamanism, Johan Reinhard (1976, 16) tackles the problem of how to distinguish between trance and ecstasy, but without attaching quite the importance to it that I have here.
10. Cf. "Vie écrite par elle-même," chap. 20 in *Oeuvres complètes* 1949, 193; *Obras complètas* 1948, 138.
11. Ibid. 1949, 308.
12. My italics.
13. Theresa of Avila 1949, 413.
14. *Dictionnaire Bailly* (1894). Cf. the index to Plato, *Oeuvres completes,* "Les Belles Lettres," vol. 13.
15. On the meaning of *ekstasis* in Greek antiquity, see Dodds 1951, 94–95.
16. See the word "transe" in *Le Petit Robert* dictionary.
17. On the ecstasies of the early Church Fathers, see J. Kirchmayer (1961).
18. Mireille Helffer (personal communication).
19. Andras Zémpleni is the one who told me of the existence of these practices among the Wolof. They are totally distinct from the much better-known practices of the *ndöp,* which of course involve trance. Evidently the *khalwa* is a borrowing from Sufism, and the word, meaning "reclusion, retreat," was used to form the name of the Khalwatiyya (cf. Trimingham 1971).
20. This is Gardet's suggested translation for *sirr* (1952, 673). The public *dhikr,* which leads not to ecstasy but to trance, will be discussed at length in part two.

21. On *nembutsu* compared to other forms of mystic prayer, see Gardet (1952 and 1953).

22. In his study on the nature of yoga, printed as an introduction to Thérèse Brosse's work (1963, i–xviii).

23. "Enstasis" is a word invented by Mircea Eliade (1948, 93) to translate the Sanskrit *samādhi*, whose meanings he defines as "union, totality; absorption into, total concentration of the spirit, conjunction." In *Le chamanisme* (1968, 326) he makes a clear distinction between "enstasis" and "ecstasy": for the shaman, "the final aim always is ecstasy and the ecstatic journey of the soul into the various cosmic regions, whereas the yoga seeks enstasis, the ultimate concentration of the spirit, and 'escape' from the Cosmos."

24. The quote is translated from the French since I did not have access either to the German edition (1921) or the English translation, which is said to be quite good.

25. The accounts they both left of their experiences of possession have been published. Oesterreich quotes large extracts from them, taken either from the *Histoire des diables de Loudun* (1716) or from the *Bibliothèque diabolique*, published late in the last century by the pupils of Charcot.

26. In a later chapter dealing with exorcism, I shall return to this reprobate form of trance.

27. I say "in principle." On this subject see the reservations expressed by M. Leiris (1958) in his chapter, "Consciousness or Lack of It in Protagonists of Possession Seances." However, I should point out that these reservations apply solely to the *zār* cult as observed by Leiris in Ethiopia.

28. In this case, we return—albeit by another path—to the concepts of Fischer (1969) and Ludwig (1968) to which Erika Bourguignon (1973, 5–8) refers her readers in her presentation of "altered states of consciousness." The first is based on a continuous scale of neurophysiological factors determining a greater or lesser degree of awakening of the central nervous system. The second is based on a similar continuum, but one that is expressed in terms of the inducement of these "altered states."

29. In her description of these Shakers, Jeannette J. Henney, from whom I have taken the data, makes no distinction between the two states and calls them both "trance." Yet there are, as she herself clearly indicates, two very different states involved. This is a case—among many others—in which the distinction I suggest making between trance and ecstasy could have been usefully employed.

30. In India (C. Malamoud, personal communication), the person seized by the inspiration of the Veda is called, in Vedic Sanskrit, the "trembling one." Oddly, in his well-known book, *The Drums of Affliction* (1968), in which trembling plays a central role and manifestly constitutes a form of trance behavior, V. W. Turner never once uses the word trance.

31. Signified/signifier: I am using here, of course, the well-known distinction made by Saussure between the two aspects of the sign.

32. cf. *A Patristic Greek Lexicon* (1961, s.v. *"energeia"*).

33. Michel de Certeau (1970, 33, 158, 205).

34. Or, sometimes, fallaciously. For it can happen not only that the trance is feigned (a subject to which we shall come later), but also that the extraordinary powers attributed to it are merely illusionist's tricks. This explains why the famous "magician" Robert Houdin was sent to Algeria, in 1856, to beat the "marabouts" at their own game. (cf. Sergent 1952, 125–44 and 185–86). There are indisputably cases of fraud. However, this is merely a marginal and insignificant aspect of trance.

35. More precisely, of "conversion" hysteria as it has been known since Freud. The mechanism of the conversion, it will be remembered, "consists in a transposition of a psychic conflict and an attempt to resolve that conflict into somatic symptoms, either motor (e.g. paralysis) or sensorial (local anesthesia or pain, for instance. . . .) Symptoms of conversion are

characterized by their *symbolic* meaning: they express repressed representations in physical form" (Laplanche and Pontalis 1967, s.v. "conversion").

36. Cut out of the *Mental Disorders Diagnostic Manual* of the APA in 1952, it was replaced by "conversion symptom," notes Ilza Veith (1973, 6), who makes several interesting references to possession.

37. *D.S.M.* III, *Diagnostic Criteria Draft* . . . , American Psychiatric Association. Prepublication 1.5.78.

38. See the issue of *Confrontations psychiatriques* entitled *Hystérie* (1968).

39. In his essay entitled "Normal et anormal" (1956), reprinted in 1970, p. 15.

40. In this passage, Bastide is concerned with possession rather than shamanism. It is still true, however, that he is talking about trance in general.

41. In his study on symbolic efficacy—which, as we know, is an interpretation of a shamanic text—Lévi-Strauss (1958, 222) recalls that Freud himself had already considered that "description of psychoses and neuroses in terms of their psychological structure would one day give way to a physiological or even biochemical conception of them."

42. On the concept of "altered states of consciousness," its origin, and its applications, see Bourguignon's introduction (1973).

43. The same word is used in Bengal to denote the famous sect of inspired musicians who call themselves *baul* ("madmen"). On the music of the *baul*, see the record made by Georges Luneau (discography).

44. The word "representation" is of course taken here, and in the general course of this book, with the meaning attributed to it in sociology ever since Durkheim.

45. Éveline Lot-Falck 1963 (1977, 7).

46. All references are to the second edition (1968) of his book on shamanism, not to the first edition (1951).

47. For a very broad critical view of Eliade's positions on shamanism, see Éveline Lot-Falck 1973, 1–2.

48. Used as though they were synonymous, as we have seen.

49. L. Delaby (1976, 130), according to Shirokogoroff. On the shamanic journey as related to that of the spirits and to the life of the hunter, see Delaby 1977.

50. See C. MacDonald, "De quelques manifestations chamaniques à Palawan" (1973, 11–20) and various contributions to the issues where this study has appeared.

51. To my knowledge, Dodds was the first to formulate clearly the distinction that ought to be made between shamanism and possession: "some writers . . . use the terms 'shamanism' and 'possession' as if they were synonymous. But the characteristic feature of shamanism is not the entry of an alien spirit into the shaman; it is the liberation of the shaman's spirit, which leaves his body and sets off a mantic journey or 'psychic excursion.' Supernatural beings may assist him, but his own personality is the decisive element" (1951, 88 n. 43).

52. On the general relation of the shaman to his "guardian spirit" and "auxiliary spirits," see Eliade's chapter (1968), "Acquiring Shamanic Powers." For the Tungus in particular, see L. Delaby 1976, 83ff.

53. The place of "possession" in shamanism and its specific characteristics in that context are set forth in various passages of Eliade's book, notably pp. 23, 89, 388, and 399 of the 1968 edition.

54. Presented in "Possession et chamanisme" and developed in parts 3 and 4 of "La folie des dieux et la raison des hommes," studies that follow one another in *Pourquoi l'épouser?* (1971).

55. For Eliade (1968, 388), the importance that the incorporation of spirits has acquired in Tungus shamanism is a relatively recent thing, attributable to foreign influence. Tungus melodies are said to betray a "Chinese origin," he notes (ibid, 200) citing J. Yasser (1926), which "confirms Shirokogoroff's thesis concerning the strong Sino-Lamaist influences on

Tungus shamanism." Shirokogoroff's work, we must remember, concerns the Tungus of eastern Siberia and Manchuria.

56. "Shamanizing to the lower world is practised among all Tungus groups," Shirokogoroff (1935, 306) observes at the end of his long description of a shamanic journey to the lower world.

57. On the problem of the definition of shamanism and the relative importance that should be accorded in that definition to the journey of the soul as opposed to possession, see Johan Reinhard's article (1976, 12–18) which includes a critical examination of Eliade's ideas on this point. Without going into detail, let me say that the views expounded in this article are somewhat at variance with my own, and that the reason lies partly in what I shall have to say later about possession.

58. The Gold are a subgroup of the Tunguso-Manchu family, whose territory lies in eastern Siberia. Cf. Delaby 1976, 7 and 12.

59. Cf. Delaby 1976, 67.

60. Italicized in the original.

61. Described in this way, the situation is not specific to the Tungus alone. It has broad analogies with that among the Yakut. Cf. E. Lot-Falck (1970) and the distinction made between "incorporation and possession," and between the *mänärik* "plaything of the spirits" and the "tamer" shaman.

62. Johan Reinhard 1976, 16.

63. For Laurence Delaby (personal communication) the difference lies above all in this last distinction.

64. In "Formes et transformations de la possession" and "Vers le chamanisme" (1971, 255–76).

65. *Ecstatic Religion* (1971), photo 11b.

66. See P. Verger (1957, 150–58 and photos 83–86).

67. On the word *wajd*, see p. 258ff.

68. Segurola (1963) s.v. *vodun.*

69. Cf. P. de Félice 1947, 160).

70. On the importance of identificatory behavior in Haitian voodoo, see Louis Mars (1953, 218) and his inventory of the "types of identification in some cases of possession."

71. On these two words see the second part of this book.

72. On these flagellants, see the summary of P. de Félice (1947, 204–7) and the long reviews by Robert Hertz (1928, 229–49) of K. K. Grass's book on Russian sects.

73. Cf. M. de Certeau (1970), the chapter "Le théâtre des possédées" and p. 289.

74. Although -*si* certainly stems from -*asi* meaning "female," "wife," in *vodunsi*, as in various other words formed in the same way, the suffix -*si* actually indicates a state of dependence rather than the state of being a wife. *Vodunsi*, in fact, designates boys as much as girls. However, this is not the place to discuss this point in detail.

75. "Individual" in the sense A. Zempléni uses the word (1966, 316), meaning "one whose starting point, original cause, lies in an individual problem," but nevertheless affects the "familial unit."

76. Herskovits (1938, 2:146–47) gives an example observed among the Fon. In this instance the child-to-be was consecrated to Sakpata.

77. Nago: a subgroup of the Yoruba.

78. For many reasons I think that among the Gun (as among the Fon) this recruitment as a consequence of a "history of illness," as Jane Belo would say in the case of Bali, or, by personal vocation, one might say, in opposition to "impersonal vocation," is to be found alongside the other. But it seems certain that it by far the less frequent. Akindélé and Aguessy do not even mention it in the passage they devote to this aspect of *vodun* worship (1953, 113–14).

79. In Africa at least, though not in Brazil. Cf. G. Cossard (1970).

80. Michel Leiris (personal communication).

81. On this point, see G. Rouget 1961, 5 n. 9. According to Abbé G. Kiti (1968, 28), three dialects "very different from one another" are learned, each being used exclusively during various periods of the initiation. "Speaking in tongues" in Christian trances obviously is a practice to be linked with the use of secret languages. On glossolalia, see the article on the "don des langues" in the *Dictionnaire de spiritualité* (1976, vol. 9, cols. 223–27).

82. Concerning the use of the word "crisis" (for *crise*) in the present context, the situation is slightly different in French from what it is in English, in which the existence of the word "fit" sometimes makes things a little clearer. A few examples chosen at random will suffice to show that, as a whole, however, the problem remains quite comparable in both languages. In the introduction to her book, Jane Belo, who often uses the word "fit" (1960, notably pp. 223–24), writes (ibid, 4) about Balinese "occasional trancers" that "it was sometimes possible to observe in these *crises* [italics are mine] of involvement an analogy to sexual excitement," while Robin Horton, speaking of the Kalabari in Africa, refers (1969, 24) to "times of communal crisis" when the priest was "apt to become spontaneously possessed," a quite different use of the term, as we can see. On the other hand, "crisis," which is an important entry in the index—from which "fit" is absent—of *Religious Movements in Contemporary America* (Zarzetsky and Leone, eds., 1974), refers to trance in general but also to "crisis cults," which perfectly illustrates our point.

83. *Loa bossal,* by analogy with *bossal,* "slave," a term that during the days of the slave trade in Haiti designated a slave recently imported and not yet baptized (M. Leiris, personal communication). The word itself derives from the Spanish *bosal* meaning "wild, untamed" (Metraux 1958, 326).

84. A. Zempléni (personal communication).

85. Cf. S. Tidjani (1950, 299–305) and P. Verger (1957, 95).

86. In the *zār* cult "the agitation of the *gurri*" is comparable to the movements of a slaughtered chicken or an animal fatally wounded by a hunter as it struggles before its "soul comes out of it" (Leiris 1958, 81, n. 1).

87. Not to be confused with *bori,* the possession of the Hausa.

88. *Sinri:* genii of illness who possess the sick person.

89. In other words, that of the priests themselves.

90. *Bia,* a notion that includes simultaneously "shadow," "reflection," and "soul" (Rouch 1973, 531).

91. Later on, we shall see what, according to the myth, caused the first crisis incurred by the first totemic priest.

92. This will be dealt with later, in the chapter on exorcism.

93. This is curiously similar to the ritual for Sakpata in Dahomey. After the adept has been publicly resurrected, the worms that have fallen from the shroud enveloping the "corpse" are carefully collected (Tidjani 1950, 301).

94. Maximilien Quenum (1938, 93) gives another interpretation of this episode. According to him, the novices "regarded themselves as having been forcibly torn from the delightful company of their gods," and this is why they go into "a furor" and smash everything in their path. According to Ségurola (see under *ahuan-uli*), who is clearly using Quenum's text, this episode forms part of the ceremonies marking "the end of a stay in a fetishist convent." See also Le Hérissé 1911, 135.

95. On this point, see R. Bastide 1972, 94.

96. For the Wolof, cf. the film *Le N'doep;* for the Mundang, cf. an unreleased film by Alfred Adler, Marie-José Pineau, and Andras Zempléni.

97. Cf. M. de Certeau 1970, 61 and 207.

98. Littré, *Dictionnaire de la langue française* (1978), s.v. "obsession."

99. Cf. Seǵurola 1963, under *vodun*. The author adds the following comment to his translation: "Term employed to convey that the person in question believes himself to have received a warning from the fetish that he has been personally selected to enter the fetish's service."

100. Still unpublished, unhappily; let us hope that it will be soon.

101. In Portuguese *chamar o ere* (Cossard 1970, 164).

102. Metal bell, a sacred instrument.

103. On the very disputed origin of the word *ere,* see Bastide 1958, 199 n. 72 and 1972, 62 n. 3.

104. I am quoting on the basis of Bastide (1958, 184).

105. "During initiation the person in the *santo* state is mute and expresses him/herself by signs only"; Gisèle Cossard (personal communication).

106. Reading the text, one gets the impression that the novices returning from their bath are singing in the *santo* state, which would contradict the information given in the previous note, that novices in the *santo* state are mute. Clearly there is a slight error in the wording of the description.

107. Ọmọtun may well mean "child once more," implying that the novice has returned to the child state. Abraham's *Dictionary of Modern Yoruba* (1958) indicates that *tun* expresses the idea of beginning again rather than "newness," but this is a point that needs further checking.

108. Cf. Bastide (1958, 199ff.) and P. Verger (1957, 72–73).

109. The god of lighting, one of the principal *orisha.*

110. In Haitian voodoo, a direct descendant of *vodun* worship, initiation is much briefer (cf. Métraux 1958, 171–88) and does not occur at the same stage of the adept's life. Simplifying a great deal, one might say that it is more a confirmation than an initiation. In Haiti, the adepts are not trained to the practice of possession from early childhood on, contrary to what often happens in Benin. This in part explains why initiation is so different on the two sides of the Atlantic. Even so, Haitian initiation does present a number of features that conform to the African model.

111. On initiation into the *vodun* cult, see Herskovits (1938, 2:111ff.), Akindélé and Aguessy (1953, 113ff.), Verger (1954, 322ff.), and Kiti (1968, 26ff.). Nowadays an agreement with the Marxist-Leninist government of the Popular Republic of Benin has fixed the period of initiation at three months at most.

112. Although this word, now used traditionally in this context in French, can give rise to confusion, I shall continue to use it here to designate what is called in Benin, in Fon- and Gun-speaking territory, *huŋkpáme* (the god's enclosure) or *hunxwé* (the god's house) or *kúxwé* (the house of death), in which *hun* (blood, divinity, secret) is in practice synonymous with *vodún,* and in which *kú* denotes the symbolic death that marks the beginning of initiation.

113. Or, more fully, the "new wives of the divinity," the *hunsi yoyó,* but also "husbands" since in this context *-si* denotes dependence without sexual connotation, and applies to boys as well as girls.

114. I refer to them as being female since girls were in the majority, but there were a few boys as well.

115. I say "presumably" because I can't rule out the possibility that these "new wives" may have gone elsewhere at a later date in order to perform the same ritual. The fact remains that once their initiation is over, the new initiates will never sing this song again.

116. About Siligbo, see Akindélé and Aguessy 1953, 123.

117. With one difference: Le Hérissé is describing three new adepts of whom only one is in the very first stage of initiation, while the other two are at a slightly more advanced stage, whereas Verger's photograph is of four adepts all at the very first stage.

118. Gisèle Cossard 1970, 172–74, 181, etc.

119. The film *Sortie des nouvelles de Sakpata* (Rouget and Rouch 1963) includes in its second part the first of these ceremonies, which consists in going to take a ritual bath in the sacred stream. Jean-Luc Magneron's film *Vaudou* shows several aspects of initiation in Dahomean convents, but in a context so confused and falsified that this piece of evidence, however beautiful to look at on occasion, unfortunately remains of little use.

120. Cf. Rouget 1961, 3–4. The first part of the film *Sortie des nouvelles de Sakpata* shows the novices performing these begging dances, followed by givings of thanks, but before their official graduation and within the convent enclosure.

121. Cf. the description of it by Herskovits (1938 2:165–66). This ritual was filmed for French television in 1971 by J. Lallier and M. Tosello, in collaboration with P. Verger. It is the same rite that is observed, with variations, in the *candomblé* as described by G. Cossard (1970, 189 and 143) and in Haitian voodoo by Métraux (1958, 181–87).

122. Which of course does not form part of the category of "song" in the Fon and the Gun thought system. But I shall leave this aspect of things aside, important though it is.

123. This repertoire is the subject of a study, in preparation, by the present author.

124. More precisely for the *vodun* Sakpata of a particular village.

125. Do^6 (la^4 = 440 Hz).

126. For reasons that would take too long to cover here, it has so far proved impossible to issue a record of these "long thanksgiving songs." However, some examples of the short type have been issued (Rouget 1961); it at least gives some idea of the strangeness described here.

127. I do not wish to conceal the fact that there is an element of interpretation in this way of presenting things. Once again, they are not well known. The interpretation offered here is based on the hypothesis that what happens in *vodun* worship is comparable to what has been observed in *orisha* worship, and particularly in the practice of the *candomblé*. It has the merit of providing an account of a number of facts that would otherwise remain incomprehensible. It nevertheless still requires verification.

CHAPTER TWO

1. This is a point about which a great deal has been written during the last ten years. It seems, however, that the last word is very far from having been said. On this subject, see in particular K. P. Wachsmann (1971) and B. Nettl (1977).

2. Recent research has revealed the scope and complexity that such a taxonomy can attain in a Melanesian society (cf. Zemp 1978 and 1979). At the moment, however, research of this kind is still exceptional.

3. See note below.

4. In line with J. Molino (1975, 47), J.-J. Nattiez, in his work on musical semiology (1975, 50ff.) proposes that musical analysis should be divided into levels—poïetic, neutral, esthesic—likewise inspired by linguistics. For various reasons (the choice of terms in the case of "poïetic" and "esthesic," the validity of the concept in the case of the "neutral" level) this terminology does not seem to me to offer sufficient advantages (although it does have some, incontestably) to be preferred here to that proposed by Jakobson.

5. This is the case with the trance observed by M. Leiris (1934, 114) during a hunter's funeral rite. "The aspirant guardian of the family totem" is described as turning somersaults, rolling in the dust, and standing on his head, after which he is "led away in convulsions."

6. Germaine Dieterlen and Amadigné Dolo (Dogon of Sanga); personal communication. A photograph published by G. Dieterlen (1941, pl. XIV) shows a future *binu* priest hanging by his feet from the roof of a barn, which he has climbed during his trance. Apart from the *binu* priests, both priests and priestesses of Amma (god of creation) on the one hand (cf. Dieterlen 1941, 240–45) and certain "wives of the Sigi" on the other (cf. Griaule 1938, 268ff.; Leiris 1948, 131ff., 353ff.) are also subject to trance. Only the trance of the *binu* pirests (cf. Dieterlen 1941 and de Ganay 1942) is described as regularly associated, after "ordination," with a set musical repertoire. I am tempted to think, for various reasons too complicated to

go into here, that the trance of the *binu* priests alone ought to be seen as falling into the category of possession in the sense it is used in this book.

7. Cf. p. 98.

8. Griot: a West African French word meaning a professional musician belonging to a certain caste.

9. "The greatest of all the *bori* gods" (Monfouga-Nicolas 1972, 105).

10. Andras Zempléni (personal communication).

11. A female *ndöp* initiate.

12. If one had to compare *bori, candomblé,* and *vodun* worship as systems developing in time, then one could say that in the *bori* it is possession that counts primarily, with initiation playing only a limited role, that in *vodun* worship, on the contrary, it is initiation that counts the most, while possession occupies a statistically small amount of time, and that the *candomblé* represents a sort of compromise between the two, since initiation in the *candomble* is more important than in the *bori,* and possession is more frequent than in *vodun* worship.

13. Cf. pp. 43 and 150–51.

14. Cf. p. 47.

15. The woman in charge of the initiation of novices alongside the "father of the saint." The latter is the cult's principal priest and head of the religious community. The adepts are the "saint's daughters." In this syncretism characteristic of the *candomblé,* the word "saint" (Portuguese *santo*) designates the divinity, the *orisha.*

16. A double or triple bell with internal clapper that only "the father of the saint, or persons carrying out particular duties, have the right to shake" (Cossard 1970, 70).

17. With reference to "wild trances," R. Bastide (1958, 252 and 1972, 94) observes that in the *candomblé* there are "leather chants," a term alluding to the leather-thonged whips whose ultimate aim is "to create a violent ecstasy in those guilty of some taboo violation or of some lack of respect." In practice, the "savagery of the crisis" triggered by these chants has no connection with the "wild" possession we are dealing with here. So the example of these "leather chants" does not run counter to the observations I have just made.

18. P. Verger (personal communication).

19. This can be both seen and heard perfectly in the film shot by P. Verger and Y. Bellon for French television in the Sakété region of the Popular Republic of Benin in 1974.

20. Analogous cases of conventions have been reported in Bastide (1972, 93–4) for the *candomblé* in Brazil, and in Blacking (1973, 44) for possession among the South African Venda.

21. Adler and Zempléni (1972, photo facing p. 129 and personal communication).

22. Jane Belo's descriptions are always so painstakingly detailed that one is justified in thinking that if there had been instruments involved she would have said so. The fact that the music is purely vocal is corroborated by recordings of *sanghyand dedari* and *djaran* (nymph spirit and horse spirit) in which one hears only choral singing, mingled with those rhythmic cries made famous by the *ketjak* (cf. G. Fresnais, *Bali,* discography).

23. Cf. p. 108.

24. I shall deal with the *dhikr* at length in part two.

25. In chapter 5, "Music and Trance among the Greeks."

26. *Pizziche terantate,* literally "tarentian stings," is the term that metaphorically designates the tune to which the person bitten by the tarantula must dance, so closely associated are the music for the spider and the one for its bite.

27. Bells: not our church bells, of course. I am thinking here above all of the simple or double iron bell, held in one hand and struck with a wooden stick held in the other, which is so common throughout black Africa.

28. Fiddle: any instrument with bowed string(s) and a neck.

29. I shall return at length to the drum in a later chapter, pp. 169–76.

30. Cf. later, in chapter 5, "Music and Trance among the Greeks."

31. Samuel Baud-Bovy has written to me, for which I am very grateful, "that the instrument Dionysus plays is not the Apollonian lyre but the instrument, of a quite different type, which Wegner calls barbiton. This barbiton occurs only in depictions of banquets, as an accompaniment to drinking songs, and in the hands of Eastern Greek poets, Alcaeus, Sappho, and Anacreon. . . ." The lyre mentioned in the next example, however, is, as I have indicated, the classic five-stringed type.

32. Here I am talking about the "government oracle," which is the principal Tibetan oracle. For oracles of lesser importance it seems that these horns are not blown. In these cases a bell or cymbals are used (Nebesky-Wojkowitz 1965, 435 and 438), sometimes accompanied, as the horns are, by drumming.

33. Cf. p. 155.

34. In the cult observed by P. Simon and I. Simon-Barouch (1975, 40) there was no lute because there was no one there to play it and the drum was not of the required type.

35. Cf. Moutsopoulos (1959, 131 n. 1) and Jeanmaire (1951, 37).

36. As transcribed (p. 181), the *arebate* rhythm includes bursts, if one may so put it, of demisemiquavers at crotchet = MM112. In other words, the smallest beat unit of this rhythmic theme is MM 896, or very close to fifteen strokes a second, which does seem extraordinarily fast, even when there are, as in the case here, intermittent and very brief bursts. It is doubtful that this kind of rapid cadence can be done with bare hands; *arebate* must, therefore, be drummed with sticks.

37. On the *adarum* rhythm, which certainly deserves a study of its own, see P. Verger (1957, 22 and 243). The *adarum* can be heard on the *candomblé* record made by G. Béhague (see discography).

38. My italics.

39. My italics.

40. At least this is what emerges from the recording by L. Berthe, available in the Musée de l'Homme collection. See discography.

41. A double iron bell with external clapper, part of the orchestra and different from the sacred *adza* mentioned earlier.

42. Unpublished films and recordings.

43. One of them published; see record *Ogoun, dieu de fer.*

44. See p. 106.

45. By "rhythmics" I mean the ensemble of the rhythms and the rhythmic traits characteristic of an ethnic group or a region, as well as of a musical style or a composer, the rhythmic system being that which rules the rhythmics.

46. Nago: one of the Yoruba dialects.

47. John Levy, notes for the record *Musique bouddhique de Corée* (see discography). This is the chant called "The Peak of the Vultures," a sort of requiem intended "to prepare the soul of the departed for its entry into paradise."

48. This is also made plain by the music of the film about this cult made by R. Morillère and the two writers (see filmography).

49. On possession among the Zulu, see S. G. Lee (1969).

50. *Ndöpkat;* female initiates to the *ndöp.*

51. Cf. p. 66.

52. *Binu boy* "drum of the *binu,*" not to be confused with *binu boy* (high tone), meaning "name of the *binu.*" See G. Calame-Griaule 1968, 36.

53. Dieterlen 1941, 224 n. 1, and 226 n. 4.

54. Nommo: one of the two primordial twins created by Amma, the god of creation. Nommo is the master of water and words. He is the focal center of the *binu* cult. See G. Calame-Griaule 1968, 203.

55. On the importance of the musical or verbal "motto" and its "power of evocation" in black Africa among the Peul, outside the possession context, see Christiane Seydou (1972, 28).

56. Unless these dance rhythms are functioning as collective mottoes for the gods? This is merely a hypothesis; one cannot tell with so little data.

57. On the Sardinian *argia,* see Clara Gallini's book (1967).

58. Thonga and Tsonga are two different transliterations of the same name. Tonga, however, denotes a quite different ethnic group.

59. The mottoes are frequently played on an instrument by a musician and/or sung by the musicants.

60. Let us leave aside the spectators, whose participation in the music is secondary, at least from the point of view of what concerns us here.

61. This ceremony has been described in detail by P. Verger (1957, 150–58 and photographs 83–86); the music has been published in disc form by G. Rouget (see discography).

62. This ceremony has also been described in detail by P. Verger (1957, 316–21) and, from another angle, by G. Rouget (1965, 70–76); the music has been issued on disc (see discography).

63. Marion Kilson does not specify at what moment in the ceremony these songs are sung, or which of them might be used in this context to summon the gods and trigger possession. The collection of songs she published (a considerable number: 243) is extremely heterogeneous; four-fifths were not collected in their situational context, and only three were in fact sung by adepts in a state of possession. It is therefore difficult to say what relation there may be between these songs and possession as such.

64. *Wadāgā:* possession séance.

65. The *dhikr* will be dealt with at length in part two of this book.

66. Here, the least one can say, however, is that the music triggering the possession trance is not exactly made up of the genius mottoes! Moreover, the behavior of the possessed is very particular: "When, angered by the repetition of God's name," Sophie Ferchiou writes, "the genius responsible for the possession wishes to manifest its anger, one sees the 'patient' beat her thighs or scratch her cheeks like a mourning widow."

67. This air will henceforward be his, H. A. Junod notes (1936, 2:441), and adds that this song will later be the means by which his crises are provoked or cured. He does not make clear, however, whether the song is sung by the possessed person himself in order to induce or heal these crises.

68. A. Zempléni (personal communication).

69. See pp. 248–49 and G. Rouget 1955 (discography).

70. In the context of divination, not possession, Germaine Dieterlen (1951, 221–22) records an identical fact among the Bambara, where it is the diviner's harp that is the communicating instrument.

71. The information was acquired via a Wolof interpreter, and Michel Leiris himself feels it should be treated with caution. With the proviso that it requires verification, however, it certainly merits inclusion here in view of its interest in relation both to the water drum's symbolism and its organology.

72. The iron bar is probably arranged slantwise in the water container; the lip of the upturned gourd, which floats on the water and is struck, rests against the bar, which is reminiscent of the positioning of the gourd and rod in the gourd drum of the Songhay (Rouch 140; Surugue 1972, 52), which is also a possession drum but rests on sand rather than water. As among the Malinké (see below, p. 116), who also use the water drum for possession dances, among the Bambara, the instrument is beaten by women.

Among the Koniyaké, a subgroup of the Malinké, the water drum is beaten by men and used for profane dances performed by girls (Rouget, discography 1972). As we know, in the Popular Republic of Benin, Cuba, and Brazil, it is an instrument used for funerals, and it is played by men. We thus see to what a great extent the symbolism of an instrument as specific as the water drum can vary from one region to another: an example—if one were needed—of the largely arbitrary nature of this kind of representation.

73. I have done no research into what may have been written on the relation between dance and possession. Let me simply observe here that in her "Panorama of Dance Ethnology," which is by no means new since it dates from 1960, Gertrude Kurath gives in all (p. 240, *Psychology*) only two references concerning possession: Sachs and Herskovits.

74. M. Leiris gives a much more precise indication of what the *gurri* is in a later publication (1974, 43): the *gurri* (from the verb *agworra*, "to low, to roar, to weep while howling") is a form of behavior typifying the possessed person and a conventional sign indicating the arrival, then the departure of the spirit. It consists in violent movements—rotation or swinging of the upper torso—accompanied by noisy exhalation and rhythmic gesticulation, which the majority of *zār* are supposed to have those whom they put into trance execute, and which displays different forms depending on the different categories of *zār*.

75. "A man divided, that may well be the origin of the theatrical character" A. Schaeffner writes (1965, 42) in his study of pretheater.

76. A vast subject that could only be adequately treated, of course, in an interdisciplinary manner. From the overall standpoint taken in this book and to speak only of French sources, no satisfactory work has been devoted to it so far. The book by Robert Francès on the perception of music has quite different concerns. The author himself presents it in fact (2nd ed. 1972, 414) as constituting a "prolegomena to a theory of esthetic judgment" and as using the data of experimental and social psychology (ibid, 402), and ignoring, or almost, those of physiology, while making no use of comparison.

77. Here I am following A. Carapetyan 1948, 148.

78. A very ancient form of divination practiced by the Tibetans consists in reading the displacement of seeds placed on a drumskin when the latter is caused to vibrate under the effect of a nearby drum beaten by the soothsayer, who simultaneously invokes the appropriate divinities and requires them to answer his questions (Nebesky-Wojkowitz 1956, 457–60).

79. On this topography of our inner sensitivity, see Husson, *La voix chantée,* p. 60.

80. A particular theory about the neurophysiological effects of drumming will be examined in chapter 4, "The Strange Mechanism."

CHAPTER THREE

1. Although they lie outside the scope of this book since they deal with New Guinea, I would refer the reader here to the six articles dealing with possessed persons, mediums, and shamans edited and introduced by B. Juillerat for the *Journal de la Société des Océanistes,* 1977.

2. See pp. 102–14.

3. Cf. in M. Eliade's work (1968) the principal references to music on pages 111–12, 115–16, 144–53, 161–65, 234, 237, 243–45, 257, 390–91. For the Tungus in particular, see the analytic bibliography in L. Delaby 1976.

4. On the music of the Araucan shamans, see Maria Ester Grebe 1973.

5. Information kindly supplied by Laurence Delaby.

6. On this point, see E. Lot-Falck 1961.

7. Roberte Hamayon, according to Zangalov (personal communication).

8. Notes to the record *Séance de chamanisme.* Recorded by H. Le Besnerais. Text by S. Dreyfus (1954, 2). See discography.

9. L. Delaby and R. Hamayon, to whom we owe the posthumous publication of the work of Lot-Falck, refer to Vasilevič (1968). The origin of the word shaman has, of course, been the subject of a great many different hypotheses.

10. The third means "inhaling the auxiliary spirits, curing the sick, searching for the patient's spirit," and is therefore of less interest for us here than the first two.

11. I am thinking here of the Sanskrit word *saṇgita,* which includes vocal music, instrumental music, and dance (Bake 1957, 196).

12. A detail kindly supplied by Laurence Delaby (personal communication).

13. The bibliography on the shamanic drum is considerable. See M. Eliade (1968, 128, 144–45, and 390 nn.).

14. Italicized in original. Eliade is here contrasting *musical magic* and *noise magic,* with reference to the use sometimes made of the drum to "drive out the evil spirits." We shall return to the subject when dealing with exorcism.

15. "The drum speaks," the Tungus say (Delaby 1976, 109).

16. We will deal at length with this problem, which is very important, at the end of the first part of this book.

17. See note 30 below.

18. See Anne Chapman's notes for the two records of Selk'nam shamanic songs she has published (discography).

19. Shirokogoroff constantly uses the word *ecstasy,* never the word *trance.* What he is describing is nevertheless what I proposed to call "trance" in this book.

20. Cf. in particular ibid., pp. 326 and 309, the first passage concerning a Tungus shaman, the second a Manchu shaman.

21. Ibid., p. 306.

22. I imagine Shirokogoroff means alcohol here. Elsewhere (1935, 306) he describes the shaman as swallowing a large shot of vodka before setting out on his descent to the lower world.

23. In consequence, it is never played outside the context of a shamanic ceremony, since it could provoke the inopportune visit from spirits "who would then seize upon people incapable of mastering them" (ibid., 302).

24. Information provided by Anne Chapman, who acquired it both from her own personal research in Tierra del Fuego and from reading Gusinde.

25. Notes to the recording made by Le Besnerais and based on evidence collected by him. See discography.

26. The song can take on yet other aspects. Among the Buryats, for instance, unlike the shaman's invocation song which "obeys musical rules," the "song for the journey is a formless and continuous sequence of sounds, intersected by moans, sighs and cries (copied from birds, creatures that can pass without hindrance from one world to another)." See R. Hamayon 1978b, 24.

27. See discography. One side of the record is devoted to the "Holy Ascension," in other words the shaman's journey to the upper world. Unfortunately, however, this is not a fieldwork document but a reconstruction made for the purposes of a "folk music concert" in the U.S.S.R. in 1969. The violent and frenzied side of the trance so often described in relation to Siberian shamans is naturally absent. This said, the remainder is certainly very representative of Yakut shamanic music. Being seventy-eight years old, but of incredible youthfulness, the singer, S. Zverev, clearly remembers the time when shamanizing was still common. One presumes he shamanized himself. Even down to the shaman's great yawns as he incorporates the auxiliary spirits, one might think that this side of the record was specially made to illustrate the two shamanic journey narratives reproduced by Eliade (1968, 189ff. and 160ff.), one from the Yakut, one from the Altai Tartars.

28. Side B, band 9 of J. Hurault's record. See discography.

29. It has not been possible to establish the text of most of the other eighteen, which makes the proportions of the first sixteen even more significant.

30. On the style of these songs and its kinship with that of songs among Siberian tribes (Tungus, Chukchi, Yukaghir, Samoyed, Ostiak) mentioned in this chapter, see A. Lomax and his "cantometric" analysis at the end of Anne Chapman's notes, as well as his book *Folk Song Style and Culture.* It is undeniable that the evidence he invokes must be taken into ac-

count. It fits in perfectly with Lévi-Strauss's observations (1966, 326) on "the ancient paleolithic cultural stock" common to Asia and the New World.

31. Cf. p. 17ff.

32. This is the case in particular with the description Avicenna made of a shamanic divinatory seance among the Turkoman. Cf. J.-P. Roux (1963, 290), in which certain quotations from ancient texts, used in his article on shamanic dance, are very instructive.

33. See p. 28.

34. See 1 Samuel 10:5–6. We shall return to this later.

35. See 2 Kings 3:10–15.

36. *Le théâtre sacré des Cévennes* cites innumerable examples (Misson 1707).

37. On divinatory trance in shamanism, see E. Lot-Galck 1968.

38. A medium presented by Nadel, wrongly in my opinion, as a shaman.

39. Cf. p. 000.

40. This subject will be discussed at length in part two of this book.

41. More precisely, among the !Kung Bushmen, a group referred to in the two studies quoted here. Let us recall that the Bushmen are people of small stature who live by hunting and gathering in the Kalahari desert in southern Africa.

42. "Medicine man," "medicine song," and "medicine dance" are the terms used by Lorna Marshall. In reality, according to Marshall's data, it would be more proper to translate the Bushman terms, more literally, as "power man," "power song" and "power dance" in which "power" or "potency" would be a rendering of the word *n/um*.

43. Even when they do have this power, which is extremely rare, the women do not act as "medicine women" (Marshall 1969, 366 n. 1).

44. Although, as we have seen, these dances are not always specifically aimed at healing a sick person—very far from it—they do nevertheless, in all cases, aim at defending and protecting the individuals and the group.

45. Four examples of medicine or healing songs, presenting different aspects of this music, have been issued on disc with transcriptions (cf. discography). See also the work of Nicholas M. England (1967).

46. Cf. *Bushman Music* (see discography).

47. Cf. *Séance de chamanisme* (see discography).

48. Cf. *Musique. . . Wayana de Guyane* (see discography).

49. Recordings archived at the British Institute of Recorded Sound, London, and the Département d'ethnomusicologie du Musée de l'Homme. Audrey Butt herself says of these chants (1962, 41) that the shamans explicitly claim that the chant and its rhythm aid the spirit to take flight.

50. *Bori,* in Hausa, means "boiling." Among the ancient Greeks, the Pythia was "regarded as a living cauldron who boiled under the god's influence" (Jeanmaire 1951, 452).

51. Cult in the sense the term is used in this book, since, as is evident in Michel de Certeau's work, the possession of Sister Jeanne des Anges and her companions was in fact integrated into the mass as part of the performance, and indeed became its "high spot." But it figured rather like an anticult. Moreover, Michelet, in his *La sorcière,* has shown the great importance that must be given to sorcery in these affairs, something that removes them even further from possession as I have defined it.

52. I am speaking here of a traditional Dahomey, one not torn apart by conflicts between the traditional religion, Christianity, and Islam. This Dahomey no longer exists. But its traditional religion is still sufficiently alive for it to be possible to ignore this aspect of things here.

53. One cannot quite rule out, however, the possibility that in *vodun* ceremonies such as those held for the graduation of the new initiates—ceremonies entirely centered around possession—the role of the *nonvito* or "she who calms the mother" is in fact to exorcise malevolent powers. We can ignore this point here, however, first because it is an entirely personal

interpretation that remains to be proved, second because the intervention of the *nonvito,* in these circumstances at least (the only ones I have been able to observe, moreover), is so discreet as to pass almost unperceived.

54. Is he in trance at this moment? What exactly does he drive out of the dead person's house? Does the ritual require music? I am unfortunately unable to answer these questions.

55. The same situation can be observed in southern India. Cf. L. Dumont (1957, 353ff.).

56. Junod's italics.

57. As presented by R. F. Gray (1969, 171), the *shetani* cult among the Segeju of Tanzania would seem to be an exception, since he describes it as aimed at "exorcism" of the spirit responsible for the possession. In fact, everything indicates that here again there is, at least, pact making involved. The use of the word "exorcism" is thus no more justified in the case of the Segeju than in that of the Thonga.

On the other hand, the case cited by John Beattie (1969, 164–65) among the Banyoro is quite clearly a real exception and would thus seem to invalidate what I have said. In fact, however, the process of exorcism, or rather of destruction (Beattie's term) concerns a category of spirits (ghosts) that is very marginal in the overall picture he gives of possession among the Banyoro; and this overall picture—including what he has to say about the use of music (ibid, 166)—is in perfect accord with what I stated here.

58. According to Sachs (1940, 106–8), the instrument David played—the *kinnor*—was neither a harp nor a zither, contrary to what is found in the many translations of the Bible, but in fact a lyre.

59. The word "harp" here translates the Hebrew word *nevel.* Sachs (1940, 115–17) considers that it was probably a vertical angular harp. On the other hand, the instruments here called "flutes" are in fact clarinets.

60. Dhorme observes in a note (1956, 1143) that "the music is at the service of inspiration."

61. A fact pointed out to me by Elena Cassin.

62. Particularly E. De Martino. See his chapter "Ethnological and Folklore Parallels."

63. The *argia,* its Sardinian equivalent, is now also well known, thanks to the work of Clara Gallini (1967). Unhappily, I became aware of it too late to make use of it in this book to any large extent.

64. Our quotes refer to the French translation, *La Terre du remords,* published in 1966. Let us recall that the original Italian edition has an accompanying record made by Diego Carpitella who contributed the chapter "The Choregrapho-Musical Exorcism of Tarantism," and made a film of a tarantism séance which was shown in Paris, in 1960, on the occasion of the Sixth International Congress of Anthropological and Ethnological Sciences.

65. Elena Cassin (see bibliography), in her account of this work, has shown the merits of the book and the inadequacies of the main thesis.

66. These data are taken from "Neuropsychiatric Considerations on Tarantism," written by Dr. Giovanni Jervis and featured in De Martino's book as an appendix.

67. *Muzak,* no. ?:58–59.

68. The Gnawa will be discussed in chapter 7.

CHAPTER FOUR

1. In various passages in the article "Music," particularly that (1768, 314) in which, having cast doubt on the fidelity of transcriptions, he poses with great lucidity the problem, central to ethnomusicology, of the interpretation of musical systems.

2. The passage of the *Dictionnaire* quoted here already appears, under a nearly identical form, in the article "Musique" of the great *Encyclopédie* of Diderot. Of his *Dictionnaire,* completed in 1764 and published in 1768, Rousseau writes, in the first page of his "Preface," that "the bases of this work were quickly set forth fifteen years ago in the *Encyclopédie.*" He further states, on the last page, that its manuscript (which was composed in three months)

"left his hands" in 1750. It is thus in 1750 that the first draft of the above mentioned passage of this *Dictionnaire* was written.

For its part, the *Essai sur l'origine des langues, où il est parlé de la melodié et de l'imitation musicale* appeared in 1781, after the death of Rousseau. The date of its composition has not yet been ascertained and there has been much dispute about it. According to C. Porset (1970, 15), the *Essai* was sketched out "during the writing of the second *Discours* [in 1754, consequently] . . . and resumed in 1756, perhaps as an *Essai sur le principe de la mélodie.*" In the *Confessions*, Rousseau writes that in 1761 he was still working on the *Dictionnaire*, but that he had just finished the *Essai*. So it is between 1750 and 1761, at the latest, that Rousseau changed his mind about the effects of music. We still need to know when exactly Rousseau wrote the text concerning the division of music into two kinds, natural and imitative, a text that conciliates his two theses, that of the physical and that of the moral effect of music, or rather that shows how each completes the other. This text appeared in the 1768 edition of the *Dictionnaire* and then in 1782, in the *Supplement à l'Encyclopédie*.

3. My italics.

4. In the *Dictionnaire*, page 308, at the end of the passage concerning the distinction made by Rousseau between natural and imitative music, one can read: "As long as we search for moral effects in the physics of sounds, we will not find them there and we will discuss without hearing one another," a sentence which, obviously, prefigures the one of the *Essais* cited above.

5. *Essai sur l'origine des langues où il est parlé de la mélodie et de l'imitation musicale* (ed. Porset 1970, 179). Rousseau is clearly replying here to the writings of a certain Burette, who held the opposite view, then very fashionable. Porset reproduces a significant passage from Burette's work in his edition of the *Essai*, p. 164.

6. Porset 1970, 165.

7. See the section "What Music?" in chapter 2.

8. To be sure, Needham's thesis is presented here in a much abbreviated form.

9. Needham refers here to three articles on percussion instruments that appeared in the *Encyclopaedia of Religions and Ethics* (1912), and particularly that by Crawley ("Drums and Cymbals"), of which elsewhere (1967, 609) he praises the psychological and "even neurological" orientation.

10. Printed the following year in *Man*, n.s. 3, no. 2 (1968): 313–14.

11. Needham (1967, 613 n. 1) is here using observations made by Francis Huxley. I shall return later to these perturbations of the inner ear.

12. We shall return to the word "driving" in the next section.

13. Among those who have been convinced by Neher's thesis, I should also cite G. Devereux (1970, 58), who cites it as authoritative in his general interpretation of trance, and, more recently, F. Schott-Billmann (1977, 140).

14. Quotation taken from Neher (1962, 155).

15. It should be noted that a germ of this theory of the conditioned reflex already existed in a remark made by Nina Rodrigues, who, parallel with his interpretation of hypnosis, also wrote: "There are initiates who cannot hear the music or song with which their first *Santo* state coincided . . . without that state manifesting itself" (1935, 111).

16. Taken from P. Verger 1957, 76.

17. Is the music powerless without the reinforcement of a special set of social circumstances? Blacking asks himself (1973, 45). For him, the answer would be, on the contrary, that if music remains without effect in certain cases this is due to certain social inhibitions.

18. My italics.

19. A weight technique also used, in different forms, by Tibetan oracles and Siberian shamans.

20. Misprinted as "psychological" in the published text. The context indicates that it should be "physiological," and the author has confirmed this.

21. G. Cossard (personal communication).

22. *Abo:* a potion made of various plants with "the property of provoking and reinforcing the trance state" (ibid, 181).

23. Zempléni's thesis consists of more than this single consideration of the music's effect, however. He lays stress throughout his work on the importance of the *bak* or sung mottoes.

24. Italicized by Dr. Aubin (1948). Quotation taken from Leiris (1958, 18, n. 2).

25. Cf. his various films on possession.

26. Cf. B. Surugue (1972, 49ff.).

27. See pp. 128ff.

CHAPTER FIVE

1. No reference to a particular edition of Plato's work will be made here since the quotations given in this book come from different sources. Some were borrowed from the Loeb collection or from translations by Jowett, Hamilton and Cairns, or by Dodds. Others were translated directly from the French (Edition des Belles Lettres: Collection Budé) which is often closer to the Greek text. Still others were translated by Eric de Dampierre and myself. The same applies to the other Greek authors cited.

2. Concerning the translation of *psyche* by "soul," see Dodds (1951, 138–39).

3. The most ancient usage of the word *enthousiasmos* is known to us through Democritus, who gave "for the first time a really scientific and rationalist explanatory essay of enthusiasm," writes Delatte (1934, 33 and 28) in his study on the conceptions of enthusiasm among the Presocratic philosophers.

4. That *Entheos* should be translated in this way is stressed by Dodds (1951, 87, n. 41). He points out that the word never means that the soul has left the body and has become resident "in God," as Rohde sometimes seems to suppose. It always means that the body has a god in it, just as *empsychos* means that it has a *psyche* in it. "Deus inclusus corpore humano," Cicero wrote (*De divinatione* 1. 67. See Dodds 1951, 88n. 45.

5. Phaedra, who is secretly dying because of her love for Hippolytus, son of Theseus, her husband.

6. Dictynna was worshiped in Crete, Phaedra's own country. A deity of the heights, she was confused with the Mother (L. Meridier, trans. of *Hippolytus*, "Les Belles Lettres," Paris 1927, 34).

7. Such as *daimon,* from *daimonao* "to be in the power of a god, to be possessed," a word used by Aristophanes and Aeschylus, but one that does not occur, unless I am mistaken, in Plato.

8. From which we have the word *cateuque,* which signifies the possessed person in Montanism. (Cf. Lacarrière 1961, 293).

9. Without pretending to be exhaustive and without including the German authors whom I only know through Linforth, I will cite Robin, Jeanmaire, Croissant, Boyancé, De Martino, Hamilton and Cairn, Jowett, and Fowler. Strangely enough, Dodds, who cites Linforth several times both in *The Greeks and the Irrational* and his commentary on the *Bacchae,* does not mention his study on *Phaedrus* 244d–c.

10. Since I do not know Greek, which I can hardly spell, I owe this translation to Eric de Dampierre, whose long familiarity with Plato's language on the one hand and with ethnology on the other has particularly well prepared him for such enterprise. May he be warmly thanked for his friendly and precious help.

11. The division of this passage in four parts, numbered 1 to 4 is mine, and is only meant to facilitate commentary.

12. Particularly L. Robin in his translation of the *Phaedrus* (1933, 32 n. 2) and Linforth (1946b, 164–65), to quote only these two authors, whose interpretations do not solve the problem.

13. Cf. Boyancé (1932, 65), who, speaking of the establishment of the Dionysus cult, writes: "Everywhere the God is a victim of unfriendly reception, which is viewed as a real crime of impiety. Everywhere, as punishment, a frenzy takes hold of the *thiasos,* feminine ones most of the time. And everywhere, the establishment of the Dionysus cult is the remedy for this punishment and the indirect consequence of this fault."

14. Strangely enough, Boyancé does not draw from this legend (which he reports à propos, precisely, of our *Phaedrus* text) the expected conclusion. Falling in the common error, he writes: "Plato . . . sees at the origin of these purifications a madness which results from 'ancient faults,' but which in a prophetic frenzy, knows how to disclose the liberating Gods" (1932, 63–64).

15. This has been seen very well by Jeanmaire in *Le Satyre et la Ménade* (1949, 467).

16. Let us recall here that in the myth the first trance of Dionysus is attributed to a fright. Let it be noted too that fright is often what causes a horse to run wild, something which might well be viewed as an animal equivalent of human trance (see above, p. 13).

17. In his study entitled *Le Satyre et la Ménade* (a study to which this present chapter owes a great deal), Jeanmaire notes that the "bacchic dances belong to an order of things about which the philosopher [Plato], even if he disapproves of them, within himself did not feel completely free to express himself" (p. 165).

18. Speaking of the evolution of Plato's ideas concerning *mania,* Jeanne Croissant (1932, 20) observes that there existed for him a certain "hierarchy" in the "mystic facts," and that when Corybantism and Bacchism were involved, he was "nearer disdain than respect."

Linforth, ignoring the evident, defends a totally opposite position. He claims that, where trance is concerned, he cannot find a single note of disapprobation in Plato's writings, and is of the opinion that they imply nothing but gratitude for something admirable, so that everything should be put on the side of approbation and nothing on the other. Pushing this aberration to its limit, he also thinks (1946b, 171) that Socrates, wishing to make the reader forget the "degrading" aspects of possession, is led to emphasize "the divinity of Madness herself."

19. On Corybantes and Corybantism, see in particular Jeanmaire 1951, 138ff.

20. The famous passage in the *Symposium* (215c–e) merely corroborates the others. I shall therefore not take it into account in what follows, since it would add nothing relevant to our present purpose.

21. The translation of this text follows the same principles as those previously adopted for *Phaedrus* 244d–e.

22. *Choreia* indeed means, for Plato (*Laws* 654b), both dance and singing.

23. The subject of the long sentence that follows could well be not "movement," but rather "all that," meaning "all that has gone before."

24. Let it be understood once and for all that for the Greeks the word *aulos* designated a clarinet, usually a double clarinet, with divergent pipes mostly; occasionally an oboe, but always a reed instrument. Never a flute, contrary to what one generally read in texts dealing with ancient Greece, including musicological ones, even though this error has been repeatedly pointed out for many years now. Such, at least, is the present state of our knowledge.

25. Cf. Dodds, who writes: "If the rites of a god X stimulated him [the patient] and produced a catharsis, that showed that his trouble was due to X; if he failed to react, the cause must lie elsewhere" (1951, 78–79). "Hence the importance attached to discovering the identity of the possessing Power" (ibid., 98).

26. Linforth translates (1946a) as "words and gestures to suit that tune."

27. On the basis of the same two passages of the *Laws* and *Ion,* Dodds (1951, 98 n. 102) presents the relationship between music and telestic trance in the following manner: "the Corybantic rite included (1) a musical diagnosis; (2) a sacrifice by each patient to the god to whose music he has responded, and observations of omens; (3) a dance of those whose sacrifices were accepted, in which the appeased deities [perhaps impersonated by the priest?] were

believed to take part." He thus fully recognizes the role of music as a "diagnosis," that is to say as a way to identifying the deity, but does not show music and dance as the way, for the corybantizer, to identify himself with the deity. But indeed, Plato does not do it either.

28. Linforth, in his article on Corybantic rites (1946a, 138–140 and 152–54) discusses the meaning of this verb at length. His main purpose in doing so, however, is to refute certain theories interpreting the word as meaning to be afflicted by the sickness of the Corybantes. His viewpoint is thus quite different from ours here. That said, for him the "fundamental" meaning of the word is "possession by the Corybantes." As a consequence, he translates it sometimes as "possessed by the Corybantes" and sometimes by "taking part in the rites of the Corybantes." As for *korybantiõntes,* he translates it as "Corybantic devotee." There is no indication that for him it means "to Corybantize."

29. Regarding the verb *baccheuein,* Dodds writes: "*baccheuein* is not to have a good time, but to share in a particular religious rite and [or] have a particular religious experience—the experience of communion with a god which transforms a human being into a *Bacchos* or a *Bacche*" (1951, 271 n. 1).

30. H. Grégoire in his translation of the *Bacchantes* (Coll. Belles Lettres, Paris 1961) prefers another reading of this line, but considers it as still "acceptable." In his edition of the *Bacchae,* Dodds, on the contrary, does not consider the possibility of two different readings. I defer to his opinion.

31. I am referring here, of course, to the pretheatrical form of the dithyramb, which originally must have been a sung and danced round accompanied by sacrifices.

32. *Oreibasia:* wild running about and dancing up in the mountains, considered by Dodds (1951, 76 and 270ff.) as being "the prototype of the ritual madness."

33. "Proitus' daughters, struck by Dionysiac madness, are Argian Bacchantes, just as Minyas' daughters are Bacchantes from Orchomene and Dadmus's daughters Theban Bacchantes," writes Jeanmaire (1951, 74).

34. Quoted by Jeanmaire (1951, 347).

35. We here again find a topic—trance and drugs—that has already been evoked, very briefly, in the first part of this book. Let us recall that in his book entitled *Poisons sacrés, Ivresses divines* (1936), Philippe de Félice was probably the first to have dealt at some length with this vast problem (about which much has been published since).

36. About the maenad's dancing, see the chapter "Les danses orgiastiques" in Séchan (1930), and also Lawler's study (1927). Since the publication of these two still classic works, other studies have of course been published; I did not have the opportunity to consult them.

37. Cf. Dodds 1960: "Evidence from Vase Paintings," in *Bacchae* xxxv–xxxvi.

38. Cf. Jeanmaire 1951, 239.

39. Cf. Jeanmaire 1951, 235.

40. Coming this time not from the Greeks but from the Romans and concerning not telestic but erotic *mania,* an example of this movement of the coming and going of the souls is provided—in a rather unexpected way—by Cato the Elder who said, Plutarch reports in his *Erõtikos* "the soul of the lover lives in the body of someone else [that of the beloved]." Cf. Flacelière, notes for the translation of the *Erõtikos* 1953, 130 n. 72).

41. Jeanmaire quotes a long passage of it in his *Dionysos,* p. 308.

42. On the Platonic theory of *mimēsis,* see J.-P. Vernant (1975).

43. Directly in the *Symposium* (215–16), *The Laws* (790e), and the *Crito* (54d). Indirectly in *The Republic* (399d–e).

44. Three in the *Ion* (536bc) and one in *The Laws* (790e).

45. In *The Republic* (400b).

46. Cf. Jeanmaire (1939, 579), quoting after Strabo, and D. W. Masaraki 1974.

47. On the *bombyx,* see D. W. Masaraki 1974.

48. Lines 871, 879, and 897.

49. Concerning *Lyssa* "The Rage," which plays such an important role in the triggering of "wild" trance among the Greeks, I cannot help but think of the great expiatory rite practiced by the *vodun* worshipers in Benin (formerly Dahomey) and known under the name of *oma,* a Fon and Gun word signifying "the rage." Cf. Adandé and Verger 1953.

50. On Neher's theory, see above pp. 000ff.

51. For more details on these fluctuations, see Lasserre (1954, 50–52).

52. Pseudo-Plutarch, Lassere's translation (1954, 46).

53. Translated by Dodds 1960.

54. Cf. M. Emmanuel 1914, 397. The figures on this cup are reproduced on the cover of Jeanmaire's *Dionysos.*

55. To be exact, not the "melodies" but the "things" or "productions" of Marsyas.

56. Let us leave aside here the problem of an appropriate translation of the word *harmonia.*

57. Preserved in a fragment of a dithyramb by Melanippides the Younger. Cf. Lassere (1954, 51).

58. Or more exactly, since the word "melody" here again does not appear in the Greek, the "things of Marsyas."

59. Olympus was the favorite pupil of Marsyas. The tunes Aristotle speaks of were thus the same as those mentioned by Plato. This is made clear, moreover, in the *Symposium* (215c).

60. Upon this point, see the chapter "The Physiological Bases of Musical Catharsis," in Jeanne Croissant's book *Aristote et les Mystères,* 1932.

61. The word *ēthos* taken in the context of the music does in fact not form part of Plato's vocabulary; he never speaks of the ethos of a mode. Aristotle, on the other hand, does so constantly. On the notion of *ēthos* seen from a comparative viewpoint, see the short account by Curt Sachs (1943, 248, 252).

62. One may well ask oneself, of course, if what Aristides Quintilianus calls "Plato's harmonies" really does correspond with these harmonies. But this is another problem (Cf. I. Henderson 1957, 349).

63. Personal letter. On this point, see the article since published by S. Baud-Bovy, in 1978.

64. Quoted by S. Baud-Bovy (1967, 20).

65. In Lasserre we read (1954:31): "Until the time of the sculptor Myron, and probably until that of Plato, the Silenus Marsyas was generally regarded as the inventor of the double-piped flute [read: *aulos*] . . . Aristoxenes, however, taking early poetic sources as his basis, without doubt, substitutes for Marsyas his father Hyagnis. But aulody itself, and sometimes auletics, claims as its founder Olympus, the son or pupil of Marsyas, whom chronographers put some 200 years before Homer . . ." (1954, 31).

66. Whether Dionysus really did come from Phrygia or not is of little concern to us here. The important thing is that he was believed to have done so. On the very complex problem of the origin of Dionysus worship, see in particular Jeanmaire (1951).

CHAPTER SIX

1. Quotation from R. Flacelière 1953.

2. Quotation from Jeanmaire's *Dionysos* (1951, 290).

3. Cf. Yates 1947, 38.

4. Reference is clearly being made to Timothaeus of Miletus, a famous Greek musician who lived in the fourth century B.C., known for the boldness of his musical innovations and mocked by Pseudo-Plutarch in his *De Musica* (cf. Lasserre 1954, 145). Perhaps it is worth noting in passing that if, as we are told, Timothaeus died in about 357, then it is somewhat unlikely that he could have caused Alexander to rise from the dinner table, since Alexander

was not born until a year later! But this is of slight importance. Our story is significant for its symbolic content.

5. Lasserre (1955, 76) quotes five variants, but Jamblique gives another, quoted by Boyancé (1936, 125–26).

6. Here it is the Phrygian mode that is held responsible for the young man's frenzy, whereas a moment before it was the Hypophrygian. This fact has been interpreted by M. Dabo-Péranic (*Encyclopédie de la musique*, Fasquelle, s.v. "hypophrygien") in a way that seems to be without foundation. Even less wellfounded, it seems to me, is the theory defended by Lasserre (1955, 62–63), according to which the Phrygian scale is said to have been that of reasonableness and moderation. But this is another problem.

7. The versions of Philodemus, Galien, and Quintilian also specify it. Cf. Lasserre 1954, 76.

8. To tell the truth, of the five versions cited by Lasserre (1954, 76) only Galien's specifically says that the second tune, the one that calms the young Taorminian, is Dorian. The others, including Jamblique's, all speak of spondee. This spondee, Lasserre and Boyancé (who refers on this point to T. Reinach) both say is the same thing as the "Song of Libation" (since spondee meant libation, hence the name of the rhythm that usually accompanied it). Both also refer to Olympos who, according to Pseudo-Plutarch (*De Musica*, 11) invented the enharmonic scale when playing this song. This would mean that spondee refers here not to a rhythm but to a melodic genre. But Pseudo-Plutarch indicates that in performing this "spondiasm" Olympos was in the "Dorian tonality" (*De Musica*, ibid.; Lasserre 1954, 137). We are thus brought back once more to the Dorian that Galien openly specifies, and this is what we need to remember.

9. Two of the six variants, that of Galien and that of Mart. Capella, attribute the affair to Damon, not Pythagoras.

10. And not the "music of the spheres," contrary to what is too often incorrectly stated.

11. Cf. the article by T. Reinach (1900) on the music of the spheres.

12. Length ratios of vibrating strings.

13. Boethius, through whom the harmony of the heavenly bodies became known as *musica mundana*. The latter, the music of the universe, formed, according to his theory, along with *musica humana* and instrumental music *(constituta instrumentis)*, one of the three parts of music seen as a whole.

14. I quote from the text reproduced by Frances A. Yates (1947, 319) in her book on the French academies of the sixteenth century, a work from which a great deal of the information used in this chapter is taken.

15. Pierre Ronsard, *Oeuvres complètes*, ed. Blanchemain (1966, 5:96).

16. See p. 42.

17. Let me observe in passing, since it is worth stressing, that Pontus de Tyard was not only the author of obscure allegories collected and published under the rather misleading title *Discours philosophiques*. His reputation as an enlightened man, and his prestige among political leaders of the time was such that Henri IV, at the time when he was preparing to convert to Roman Catholicism, wrote to him to confide in him and to ask his advice. Cf. Yates (1947, 222).

18. The dialogue by Plato in which poetic *mania* is treated, as we saw in the previous chapter.

19. On the reinterpretation of Plato's four *mania* by Ficino, see Yates (1947, 81) and the long extract she adds in a note from his commentary on the *Symposium*.

20. On this point, see Yates (1947, 92).

21. *Dodecacorde:* collection of psalms composed in the twelve ecclesiastical modes, published at La Rochelle in 1598. Cf. H. Expert (1900).

22. *Harmonie universelle* 1636, sig. A vi recto.

23. On this point, see Yates's (1947) chapter, "The Religious Policy."

24. In *Questiones celeberrimae in Genesim,* Paris 1633, col. 1532.

25. Probably also the author of an ode on the effects of Claude Le Jeune's music.

26. The story does not say so, but these two "airs" almost certainly belong to *La Guerre,* since it was this piece, composed on the theme of love as a symbolic tournament, that Claude Le Jeune wrote for these festivities. Cf. Lesure (1961, 47).

27. Mersenne, *Correspondance,* ed. P. Tannery, 1932 1:45. Rousseau was to recount these stories in his turn, and comment on them with great humor, in his *Dictionnaire de musique* (1768, 12).

28. Cf. Yates (1947, 2 and 39).

29. Preface to *Mélanges de cent quarante-huit chansons* . . . published in Paris in 1572. Cf. *Oeuvres complètes* of Ronsard, ed. P. Blanchemain, Paris, 1866, 7:337–41.

30. Even though things were already beginning to change. But this is secondary. The changes had not yet resulted in any confusion of terminology, and this is what is significant here.

31. On this point, see Yates (1947, 47–48) and Chailley (1956, 138–39).

32. Quoted in H. Expert (1900).

33. It is true that Orpheus is usually depicted with a lyre. However, as Boyancé (1936, 42) observes, it is "primarily by the power of his singing, not by that of his lyre, which accompanies him only after a certain date" that he creates his effects. According to Plato (*Laws* 3. 677d), it was also, of course, to Orpheus that the invention of poetry was revealed. The invention of the lyre was attributed to Amphion.

34. "Few problems remain as obscure as those regarding the relations between Orphism and Pythagoreanism," Boyancé observes (1936, 93). Dodds, for his part (1951, 147ff.) tends toward the view that the two things are, broadly speaking, so interconnected as to form a single entity, and that what is generally termed Orphism could ultimately be reduced to Pythagoreanism. Here, needless to say, it is not the mathematical aspect of Pythagoreanism that is involved, but rather its moral and religious aspect—insofar as it is possible to separate the one from the other. My comments on Orphic incantations apply equally to Pythagorean incantations.

35. Cf. Yates (1947, 111).

36. Cf. pp. 129–33.

37. *Confessions* (book 10, chap. 33).

38. Jeanmaire is here thinking of the passage (*Symposium* 215) in which Plato, with reference to the tunes of Marsyas, says that they are the only ones that put men in a state of possession and that it does not matter if the *aulos* player is a good or a bad one.

39. Cf. R. Flacelière's French translation (1953, 76).

40. Linforth 1946a, 140, 156, and 158.

41. Cf. T. Reinach 1900, 433, n. 1, referring to the *Harmonia mundi* (1619).

42. On this aspect of Kepler, see Gérard Simon (1979).

43. Or, more precisely, might have been written . . .

44. Alada: city in southern Benin, capital of an ancient kingdom from which the kingdoms of Abomey and Porto-Novo later emerged. Alada is in many respects a veritable conservatory of ancient customs.

45. Ajahuṭo: "Killer of Aja," founder of the dynasty.

46. Akplogan: "Chief of the lance," the principal religious figure of the kingdom, and for this reason often called "Chief of the fetishers."

47. Sakpatasi: "wife of Sakpata," who is the god of earth and smallpox. The Sakpatasi perform particularly elaborate dances. The men execute spectacular, perilous leaps. On the suffix -*si,* see above, chap. 1, n. 74.

48. Lègba: messenger of the gods; trickster and phallic divinity.

49. Khèvioso: god of lightning.

50. Rècade: ornamented scepter, a veritable work of art that is sometimes carried by the kings of Dahomey and sometimes entrusted to messengers to signify the monarch's presence.

51. For one episode from these ceremonies, cf. the recording by G. Rouget and P. Verger, *Dahomey, Musique des Princes.*

CHAPTER SEVEN

1. Since our examination of Sufism will take us as far as Morocco on the one hand and Yugoslavia on the other, in the following pages we will not deal with only the Arabs. Should I have used, in this case, the term Islam to cover this vast field? The manifestations with which we will be concerned are occasionally so far from Islamic orthodoxy that using the word Islam would still not have solved the problem. In any case, the Arabs form such a significant part of the chapter that it is only logical they should figure in its title.

2. Sufism: the word has been defined (Trimingham 1971, 1) as denoting that mystic tendency in Islam that aims "at direct communion between God and man." The definition is schematic but convenient. Among the various etymologies of the word advanced by the Arabs, we should recall the one that identifies the term Sufism as deriving from the word *sūf*, a woollen garment habitually worn by Moslem ascetics. The Sufis are organized into a large number of brotherhoods *(ᶜṭā'ifa),* each of which as its own "way" *(tarīqa).* For a general overview of Sufism, cf. Corbin (1964, 262ff.).

3. Modern life has without doubt made such behavior much rarer, but it still occurs quite commonly in various regions, as, to cite only one example, in the south and central region of Iraq (S. Q. Hassan, personal communication).

4. An English translation of the *Kitāb ādāb al-samāᶜ wa al-wajd* was published in 1901–2 by Duncan B. MacDonald in an article entitled "Emotional Religion is Islam as Affected by Music and Singing." This is the version which I have consulted and to which I refer in the text under MacDonald's name. The last pages of the *Kitāb* also appear in French translation in M. Molé's long article (1963, 193–201) entitled "La danse extatique en Islam."

5. Although Ghazzali is highlighted in this chapter, this does not mean that his work is the only one of its kind, or even the most important. Many other Sufis had dealt with the problem before him, among them, to cite only one, al-Hudjwiri, whose *Kachf al-mahdjūb* ("Unveiling of Sacred Things") has been translated into English by Nicholson (1911). And others were to deal with it after Ghazzali. But for our purpose, which was not to enter into the details of the arguments aroused by the great question of music's "lawfulness," it seemed better to focus attention on a single author, who is in any case quite representative of the Sufi pro-music tendency.

6. In his translation of the *Kitāb,* MacDonald translates *samāᶜ* sometimes by "Listening to Music and Singing," sometimes by "Hearing Music and Singing," sometimes by "Listening," sometimes by "Hearing," sometimes by "Music and Singing"; a rather unsatisfying diversity. His footnote (1901, 236) on translating the term makes his uneasiness quite clear.

Robson (1938) in his English translation of the treatise by Ghazzali's brother Ahmad on *samāᶜ,* translates the words as "audition." Farmer generally translates it as "Listening to Music," but he (1929, 140) also sometimes translates it simply as "music."

In French, L. Massignon (1922, 85) translates *samāᶜ* as *concert spirituel* or "oratorio," terms later taken up by M. Mokri (1961) and E. de Vitray–Meyerovitch (1972). Trimingham (1971) also translates it as "spiritual concert." H. Corbin (1964, 260) translates it as "audition musicale." Molé, in his long article on ecstatic dance in Islam, uses the word *samāᶜ* throughout without attempting to translate it. As we can see, this is not an easy word to translate.

7. The question of whether music in general is or is not lawful in the eyes of the faith, and whether it should be permitted or forbidden, has preoccupied Muslims from the very start, as is well known. And this applies even more to the Sufi *samāᶜ,* since its music is in direct rela-

tion to religious practice. On this extremely muddled issue, see what I feel to be a very good summary made by Farmer (1929, 20–38) in his *A History of Arabian Music,* in the chapter "Islam and Music."

8. The Arabs have written a great deal about *samāʿ,* either to praise or condemn it. A cursory inventory, based on MacDonald (1908), Farmer (1929), Robson (1938), Mokri (1961), and Molé (1963) of the works entirely or partly devoted to *samāʿ,* provides us with a list of twenty-six works, seventeen of which have the word *samāʿ* in their title. One of the oldest is that by al-Hujwiri (d. A.D. 1072), from which Ghazzali makes numerous borrowings. The *Kitāb sharh al-samāʿ* "Commentary on the *Samāʿ*") by al-Fàràbî (no. 165 in Farmer's bibliography, 1940), which is much earlier, since the author died in A.D. 950, has unfortunately been lost.

9. Molé (1963, 148, 227, 235, 237), quoting various Arab authors.

10. Molé (1963, 204) quoting two different Arab authors.

11. In his treatise on *samāʿ,* Ahmad, Ghazzali's brother, uses the word *mūsīqī* once (Robson 1938, 71–122), in a very general sense.

12. *Malāhī,* meaning "instruments of entertainment," in other words "musical instruments" but with a moral nuance in the meaning, derives from *lahw.*

13. For the term *taghbīr,* see Farmer 1929, 33 n. 2.

14. On the meaning of *wajd,* see Gardet (1976, 175–83) and his remarks on Massignon's interpretation of the word.

15. MacDonald translates it both times as "revelation." I am told by R. P. Nwyia that the word "inspiration" is nearer to the Arabic.

16. A lute with a long neck.

17. From a sixteenth-century text quoted by Rouanet (1922, 698).

18. *Kitāb al-aghānī.* Translation by Quatremère, *Journal asiatique* 16 (1935):515 and 517.

19. Farmer is here quoting from Isfahānī's *Book of Songs.*

20. Al-Junaïd: master of Baghdad Sufism, acclaimed as spiritual ancestor by the majority of Sufi congregations (Molé 1963, 169, n.).

21. We will deal with *dhikr* a little further on.

22. A famous Sufi mystic who lived in Baghdad in our tenth century and claimed unity with God, was declared a heretic and crucified.

23. By Ghazzali notably, in another book of his great work on the revivification of faith. For a bibliography on *dhikr,* see Gardet (1952–53 or 1976) and Trimingham (1971).

24. To do so, I shall mainly use the two studies by L. Gardet (1952 and 1953), "La mention du nom divin dans la mystique musulmane." These studies have been edited and published in book form in 1976 in collaboration with G. C. Anawati.

25. On *dhikr* technique, both in itself and compared with other types of mystic orison ("Jesus prayer" of the hesychasts and the *nembutsu* of Japanese Buddhists in particular), as well as its relations with yoga, See Gardet 1952–53.

26. *Dhikr* or *zikr:* orthographical variants that indicate variations in pronunciation.

27. We know that the Arabic *faqir* (Persian *darwish*), which means "poor," designates an adept among the Sufi. It is therefore logical to speak here of fakirism. However, in both French and English the word usually has a pejorative connotation and denotes activities usually regarded as more or less contemptible and fraudulent. Need I say that my use of it here does not include any such nuance. The fact that this particular aspect of fakirs' activities, which consists in public performance of exercises aimed at amazing onlookers because they challenge (or seem to challenge) certain laws of nature—Massignon (1934, 701) refers to them as jugglery—has been severely criticized by canonical Muslims, by most Christians, and by a good number of nonbelievers, has of course not been taken into consideration here. In Morocco, where the word dervish is not used, they say *fagīr* (pl. *fuggarā*).

28. The Turkish form is Mevlevi.

29. We shall return to this word in a moment.

30. The Yezidi form a "heterodox Islamic sect" (Hassan 1975, 234) and are not Sufis. See also Hassan 1976.

31. Ibn Jubair, a twelfth-century traveler, writing in the time of Saladin, describes with wonder the "impassive *samāᶜ*" during which the participants become so "enraptured" in ecstasy "that they can hardly be regarded as belonging to this world at all" (from Trimingham 1971, 10).

32. Cf. Molé 1963.

33. Quoted by Farmer 1929, 140.

34. Cf. Molé 1963, 238ff.

35. Here we once again encounter the word *ṭarab,* albeit in another form; we shall return to it later.

36. Is the camel particularly sensitive to music? One would be tempted to think so upon reading this text, particularly when it is compared to another, by Jalāl al-Dīn Rūmī this time, who in his *Mathnawī* mentions a shepherd who played the flute so well that "the camels themselves made a circle around him" (quoted in E. de Vitray-Meyerovitch 1972, 88). Moreover, in Turkey, we know that they hold (or still held recently) camel fights in which the two animals are incited to combat by two bagpipes played by the respective camelherds, each of whom is pressed against the animal's flanks with the intention of driving him into a frenzy. (I learned this information from someone who observed such fights himself, and who allowed me to listen to his recordings.)

37. Cf. Mauguin (discography).

38. From Eva de Vitray-Meyerovitch (1972, 83).

39. A fact that emerges, at any rate, from descriptions of the Qādiriyya and the Rifāᶜiyya by Depont and Coppolani (1887); the ᶜIsāwiyya in Morocco and Algeria by Brunel (1928) and by Dermenghem and Barbes (1951); the Rahmāniyya of Algeria by Haas (1943), quoted by Gardet (1952); the Shādhilīyya of northern Africa and the Mirghabiyya of the Sudan by Trimingham (1971); the Sāduliyya of Tunisia by Ferchiou (1972); the Rifāᶜiyya in Syria and Yugoslavia by (respectively) Poche (1973, discography) and Mauguin (1974, discography). The performance given in Paris in 1978 by the Khalwatiyya (or Halveti) from Turkey followed the same scenario and enabled me to grasp certain aspects firsthand, thus providing a very useful supplement to my reading.

40. *Ḥizb* means "part, section" (of the Koran). The word *wird* is also often used to denote all that is recited or sung during this first part.

41. It is worth noting that these "songs" (Trimingham's term) are not designated by the word *ghināᶜ,* which is the term usually employed in Arabic for "song" and has almost the same meaning as our word "music."

42. R. P. Nwyia writes me, in a letter, that this is probably the first *sura(h)* of the Koran, the title of which means "that which opens."

43. These singers are not necessarily members of the brotherhood. At least this is not the case among the Rifāᶜiyya of Aleppo (cf. Poch, discography). Moreover the presence of such singers does not always seem to be required. Ferchiou (1972) makes no mention of them in her description of the *dhikr* of the Tunisian Sādulīyya.

44. Female Sufi colleges do exist (Trimingham 1971, 18). Do they practice the *dhikr*? One is tempted to assume so. But perhaps it is not practiced in public, which would explain why there is no description of them, to my knowledge at least.

45. Cf. Trimingham (1971, 197 and 210).

46. On this point, see Gardet (1952, 659).

47. Both of which have spread out a great deal. Cf. Trimingham (1971, 37–40 and 86). On the expansion of the ᶜIsāwiyya, see Brunel (1926, 46ff.).

48. Called *darb shish,* " 'piercing' with the sword" (Poche, 1976, discography). The skewer made of metal with an ornamented chain, is about fifty centimeters long (Poche, personal communication).

49. *Voyages d'Ibn Batoutah,* quotation in Molé (1963, 223).

50. The author refers only to north Africa, but it seems likely that the ceremony took place in Algeria since the Aïssāouā of Morocco do not practice this kind of ordeal, according to Brunel.

51. Al-Rifāʿi's first name was Ahmad, hence this other name for the Rifāʿiyya.

52. Putting the Rifāʿiyya and Anastenarides together is quite legitimate: Sufism and Eastern Christianity are not at all foreign to one another.

53. On the Anastenarides and their ordeal by hot coals, see Kakouri (1965, 7–32).

54. Quotation in Molé (1963, 223).

55. Trimingham writes (1971, 86) that the ʿIsāwiyya borrowed these "ecstatic practices, whereby the dervishes became immune to sword and fire", from the Rifāʿiyya.

56. Or at any rate were practiced in this way in Morocco in 1926. All the information used here is taken from Brunel (1926, 92–122). The ʿIsāwiyya are also called ʿAïssāouā.

57. On this point see Brunel (1926, 233ff.).

58. See p. 000.

59. The ʿIsāwiyya practice a rite involving the eating of raw flesh, the *frīssa* (Brunel 1926, 175ff.) that has often been compared with the omophagy of the Bacchantes.

60. Brunel makes brief allusions to them on various occasions.

61. The one whose music was recorded and published by Poche, mentioned several times in this chapter, provides a very abridged but very significant example, with the one exception that the *wird*—the introductory part—is omitted. The particular feature of the *ḥaḍra* recorded by Poche is that the skewer ordeal precedes the *dhikr* proper, whereas the reverse order is usually the rule: the fakirist practices normally follow the *dhikr.* This is the order followed, among other examples, in the séance described by Ibn Batutah.

62. According to MadDonald and Massé (*Encyclopédie de l'Islam* 1965, s.v. "Jinn") the possibility that this word was borrowed from the Latin *genius* cannot absolutely be ruled out.

63. The Tidjāniyya congregation displays very different features in Morocco and Senegal. On possession among these Tidjāniyya women from Tunisia and its relation to music as they emerge from Ferchiou's description, see p. 000.

64. For a definition of *jinn,* see the article by MacDonald and Massé cited in note 62 above.

65. On possession by *jinn* cf. *Encyclopeadia of Religions and Ethics,* 1918, vol. 10, s.v. "possession," pp. 135–36.

66. Taken from Farmer 1929, who himself refers to Hirschfeld (1902).

67. Cf. p. 000.

68. "In order to go into ecstasy, he liked to set a rose, as a sign of separation, between himself and the face of a young novice" (Massignon 1922, 88). On eroticism in *samāʿ* and its profound ambiguity, see Molé (1963, 155–56).

69. On Jamīla, see Farmer 1929, 85.

70. On the word *ṭarab,* in the context of music, see Shiloah (1972, appendix 2) who writes in particular: "*Ṭarab* comprises quite a scale of affective categories: pleasure, delight, mental pastime, emotional shock, ravishment, exaltation, and ecstasy, which sometimes brings about the death of the listener." The features shared by *wajd* and *ṭarab* are indicated in another work by Shiloah (1967, 192 n. 6). On *ṭarab,* see also Habib Hassan Touma (1976, 52).

71. These pottery drums, are quite inexpensive, and the musicians are careful to buy "several at a time"!

72. Cf. pp. 267–68.

73. *Maqām* singers and instrumentalists are not called *muṭrib* (S. Q. Hassan, personal communication).

74. Contra: Farmer (1959, 2) writes that in the tenth century *al-muṭrib* was the usual word for "musician," particularly if he was an instrumentalist. In Turkey (Mauguin, discog-

raphy) the group of instrumentalists and singers that accompanies the Mevlevi dervishes in their spinning dance is called *mitrib*.

75. Translated by Farmer (1959, 2). The word *mutrib* can thus denote sometimes music and sometimes the musician.

76. At least this is what emerges from the description given by Gardet (1952, 559–60) and derived from Haas (1943). To be sure, however, one would have to read Haas himself, which I have unfortunately been unable to do.

77. To judge from their performance in Paris in 1978.

78. Mauguin (discography) tells us nothing on this point about those in Kosovo, Yugoslavia.

79. Cf. the commentary to Poche's record.

80. Cf. pp. 132–33.

81. Certain very limited aspects of the problem were treated in the first part of this book: the case of David and Saul, that of the possessed nuns of Loudun, and that of tarantism.

82. On "enthusiasm" in Christianity, see Knox (1950).

83. For the first see the nineteenth-century engraving depicting a Shaker dance held in their parish house in New Lebanon (*Les Shakers* 1976); for the second, see the descriptions of P. de Félice (1947) and Hertz (1928).

84. I am speaking from very brief personal experience in Harlem and, above all, from what I have been told by friends with more experience of these things. Ignorance or real absence of evidence? I have not been able to consult descriptions of Baptist or Pentecostal worship that would elucidate the points of interest to us here.

85. For a summary of the "Welsh Revival," see P. de Félice (1947, 273ff.).

86. Cf. also P. de Felice (ibid., 193ff.).

87. In the Albertina Museum in Vienna. Reproduced by F. Lesure (1966) in his illustrated work on music and society.

88. To speak of "Arab" philosophers or musicologists, to be sure, means I am reverting to an obsolete and justly criticized usage (cf. Corbin 1964, 5ff.), but from our present standpoint it has no important drawbacks and has the virtue of simplicity.

89. Cf. Cowl (1966, 137 and 148).

90. Since I have not checked the Arabic text I cannot assert this with certainty, but it seems likely that the word used by al-Kindī is *tāʿthir* or "influence," a term that should be regarded, in this context, as equivalent to the Greek *ēthos* (Farmer 1929, 76). It is the word that, according to Farmer (1940, nos. 25 and 192), figures in the *Book of Musical Cycles* in which it is translated as *ēthos* by Erlanger (1938:43), and also in the *Epistle* of the Brothers of Purity.

On the ideas relating to the "influence" *(tāʿthir)* of music among the Arabs and what they owe to ancient Greece and Mesopotamia, see Farmer (1926 and 1957).

91. On this aspect of al-Kindī's work, see Farmer (1926, 14ff.) and Chottin (1939, 83 and 121).

92. It figures in the *Commentaires* on Safī al-Dīn (Erlanger 1938, 47).

93. Cf. above, note 8.

94. Denouncing the "vague and outdated philosophy" of "those who were unable to recognize the true nature of each science," Avicenna wrote, clearly with the Pythagoreans in mind: "I shall not waste time explaining the principles of the science of numbers. . . . Nor shall I seek to establish a relationship between the states of the heavens, the character of the soul, and musical intervals" (Erlanger 1935, 106). On Avicenna's ideas about the relations between modes and the various periods of the day, see Farmer (1926, 24), who refers to a text that does not appear in Erlanger.

95. Translated and edited by Shiloah (1972).

96. Shiloah (1972, 45 and 46).

97. Translated and annotated by A. Shiloah (1965 and 1967).

98. In the summary they give of their letters at the end of the collection. The text is taken from Erlanger (1930, xxvii).

99. Shiloah 1967, 192–93. The word translated here as "music" is neither *mūsīqī* nor *ghinā* but *anghām*, which means "melodic modes" (Shiloah 1967, 192 n. 1).

100. *Dictionnaire de la musique*, s.v. "Musique."

101. The rending of garments *(tamzīq)*, the curious practice that among the Arabs can be a sign either of profane or religious trance, should undoubtedly be compared with that other form of trance behavior manifested by the Old Testament Hebrew prophets (such as Saul, to take only one example) and also by certain possessed persons among the Niger Songhay (Rouch: personal communication) which consists not in tearing one's clothing but simply in removing it. In other words in stripping oneself naked, which is a radical and expeditious way of changing personality. Since both practices consist in a negation of clothing, perhaps they are both part of one and the same type of behavior as far as personality structure is concerned. If so, then *tamzīq* may well have some link to possession, but this still needs to be proven.

102. Cf. pp. 167–68.

103. This idea is not a new one. Some two thousand years ago, Democritus already observed that "the act of procreation is similar to a small fit of epilepsy." Apparently, at least a fit of epilepsy and a fit of trance may sometimes be likened. Delatte (1934, 66–67), to whom I owe this reference to Democritus, considers that for the latter, epilepsy, "enthusiasm," and orgasm fall under the same order of physiological phenomena.

104. Cf. the notes for the recording he made of the Rifāʿiyya of Yugoslavia already mentioned. The texts in question (Mauguin, personal communication) are being translated.

105. In fact, Gardet, in his study, is mainly concerned with the solitary *dhikr,* which is practiced in immobility, or almost, but is nevertheless an exercise centered on a certain breath-control technique. If what he says is valid for this almost incorporeal form of *dhikr,* then his physiological interpretation is even more applicable to the collective *dhikr,* in which the entire body is involved, and very violently at that.

106. Cf. pp. 109–111.

107. Borrowing the opinion of the famous Sufi martyr Hallāj, and repeating it as if it were his own, Massignon (1922, 86) expresses the most severe disapproval of the *dhikr* that is practiced with the aim of triggering ecstasy "by force and through a mechanical process as it were." Gardet also writes, "any attempt to produce trance automatically, is scorned by true Sufis" (1952, 662).

108. Cf. pp. 71–72.

109. This observation does not appear in the first version of the description, published in Trimingham's *Islam in the Sudan* (1949). When he repeated it in his *The Sufi Orders in Islam* (1971), he did so verbatim with the exception of one short passage. The words: "The recitation and movements naturally control the breathing—an important thing if emotional effects are to be produced," are now replaced by the observation I provided in my text. In other words, it was not till later on that the author became aware of the paradox of this *dhikr* practiced without any thought of producing trance.

110. During a performance given in Paris (1978) by a Halveti group, one of a number they gave during a theatrical tour of France. Dubious evidence, one may say. Not necessarily, since *dhikr* séances are by no means incompatible—very far from it—with the presence of an audience.

111. Formerly Mazagran. I owe this information on the Derqawa to B. Halff.

112. This information, which I owe to Schéhérazade Q. Hassan, applies to the *dhikr* in Baghdad, but it certainly is generalizable.

113. Cf. pp. 273.

114. Bands 1, 2, and 3 on side one of the record (Poche 1976, discography).

115. Brunel (1926, 103).

116. Dermenghem and Barbès (1951, 309). *Guegba* or *qasaba,* Arabic word denoting the transverse flute called *nay* in Persian.

117. The Gnawiyya, or Gnawa, form another brotherhood, very widespread in Morocco, in which blacks predominate.

118. *Ḥāl:* trance state. Cf. p. 268.

119. Cf. pp. 96–102.

120. Brunel (1926, 98).

121. Ibid., 103.

122. Ibid., 225.

123. Ibid., 119.

124. Ibid., 122.

125. On the *ahwach,* see Chottin (1939, 23ff.) and B. Lortat-Jacob (discography).

126. Term also used by Massignon, (1922, 87), who translates *raqs* by ecstatic "dance" of jubilation.

127. In his description of the *ahwach,* Chottin (1939, 25) calls attention to the fact that its "movements are very supple and discreet, and do not in any way resemble the brutal dislocation observed . . . in the course of the ecstatic dances of the Aïsawa. . . ." If brutal, the dance is ecstatic, if supple, it is not? There seems to be reasonable ground for doubt here, since the distinction appears to be quite subjective. Besides, from one dance to the other things change quite significantly depending on circumstances. This being so, Chottin's remarks certainly confirm that the comparison made here between ecstatic dance and *ahwach* is justified.

128. About the ritual music of the ʿIssāwiyya of Morocco, see André Boncourt's work (1980) which appeared as this book was already in press and could not be cited here as it should.

129. Cf. pp. 77–78.

130. Lapassade interprets the Gnawa's possession rituals as falling into the realm of exorcism. His interpretation is thus subject to the reservations made earlier in the section "Exorcism?" in chapter 3.

131. Cf. Castaldi (1976, 58).

132. Ibid.

CHAPTER EIGHT

1. I owe this information to Steve Feld and Hugo Zemp, respectively.

2. Cf. 1960 edition, p. 336.

3. Contrary to what one might expect from its title, Erika Bourguignon's article (1965), "The Self, the Behavioral Environment, and the Theory of Spirit Possession" does not in fact constitute a "theory of possession."

Bibliography

The bibliography, discography, and filmography include only those works mentioned in the course of this book.

Adandé, Alexandre, and Pierre Verger. 1953. Un rite expiatoire: Oma. *Notes africaines* 58: 41–46. Dakar: Institut Français d'Afrique Noire.

Adler, Alfred, and Andras Zempléni. 1972. *Le bâton de l'aveugle*. Paris: Hermann.

Akindélé, A., and C. Aguessy. 1953. *Contribution à l'étude de l'histoire de l'ancien royaume de Porto-Novo* (Mémoire de l'Institut Français d'Afrique Noire, no. 25). Dakar: IFAN.

Anawati, G. C., and Louis Gardet. 1976. *Mystique musulmane. Aspects et tendances—expériences et techniques* (Études musulmanes 8). Paris: J. Vrin.

Anonymous. 1976. *Les Shakers* (Catalogue de l'exposition, "Les Shakers"). Paris: CCI Édition.

Arbman, Ernst, 1963–70. *Ecstasy or religious trance*. Edited by Åke Hultkrantz. 3 volumes. Uppsala: Svenska Bokförlaget.

Aristotle. *The Politics*.

Arom, Simkha, and Geneviève Taurelle. 1968. Culte des jumeaux chez les Ali. Rituel de guérison chez les Ngbaka-Mandjia en République Centrafricaine. *Encyclopédie des musiques sacrées* 1:92–104. Paris: Labergerie.

Aubin, Dr. H. 1948. Danse mystique, possession, psychopathologie. *L'Évolution psychiatrique* 4:191–215.

Augustine, Saint. 1926. *Confessions*. Text established and translated by Pierre de Labriolle. Paris: Société d'édition Les Belles Lettres.

Avicenna. *See* Erlanger 1955.

Bake, Arnold. 1957. The music of India. In *The new Oxford history of music* 1:195–227. London: Oxford University Press.

Barton, George A. 1918. Semitic and Christian possession. In *Encyclopaedia of Religions and Ethics,* 10:133–39.

Basile de Césarée, Saint. 1857. *Opera omnia* . . . Edited by par J. P. Migne. Paris.

Bastide, Roger. 1955. Le principe de coupure et le comportement afro-brésilien. *Anais do XXXI congr. internacional de americanistas,* pp. 493–503. São Paulo.

_____. 1958. *Le candomblé de Bahia* (Rite nagô). Paris: Mouton.

_____. 1972. *Le rêve, la transe et la folie*. Paris: Flammarion.

Baud-Bovy, Samuel. 1967. L'accord de la lyre antique et la musique populaire de la Grèce moderne. *Revue de Musicologie* 53:3–20.

_____. 1978. Échelles anhémitoniques et échelles diatoniques dans la chanson grecque. *Schweizer Beiträge zur Musikwissenschaft,* 3d ser. 3:183–201.

_____. 1978. Le dorien etait-il un mode pentatonique? *Revue de Musicologie* 64:153–80.

Beattie, John. 1969. Spirit mediumship in Bunyoro. In John Beattie and John Middleton, editors, *Spirit mediumship and society in Africa,* pp. 159–70. London: Routledge and Kegan Paul.

Beattie, John, and John Middleton, editors. 1969. *Spirit mediumship and society in Africa.* London: Routledge and Kegan Paul.

Belo, Jane. 1960. *Trance in Bali.* New York: Columbia University Press.

Berliner, Paul. 1975–76. Music and spirit possession at a Shona bira. *African Music* 5:130–39.

Bible. 1935. *The complete Bible: An American translation.* Translated by J. M. Powis Smith. Chicago: The University of Chicago Press. 19??.

Binon, Gisèle. *See* Cossard.

Blacking, John. 1973. *How musical is man?* Seattle and London: University of Washington Press.

Boethius. 1867. *De institutione musica.* Edited by Godofredus Friedlein. Leipzig.

Boncourt, André. 1980. *Rituel et musique chez les Aissaoua citadins du Maroc,* Université de Strasbourg. 2 vols. ronéotypés.

Bourguignon, Erika. 1965. The self, the behavioral environment, and the theory of spirit possession. In Melford E. Spiro, editor, *Context and meaning in cultural anthropology,* pp. 39–60. New York: The Free Press.

_____. 1968. World distribution and patterns of possession states. In Raymond Prince, editor, *Trance and possession states,* pp. 3–34. Montreal.

_____. 1973. Introduction: A framework for the comparative study of altered states of consciousness. In E. Bourguignon, editor, *Religion, altered states of consciousness and social change,* pp. 3–38. Columbus: Ohio State University Press.

_____. 1974. Cross-cultural perspectives of the religious uses of altered states of consciousness. In Irving I. Zaretsky and Mark P. Leone, editors *Religious movements in contemporary America,* pp. 228–43. Princeton: Princeton University Press.

_____. 1976. *Possession.* San Francisco: Chandler and Sharp.

Boyancé, Pierre. 1936. *Le culte des muses chez les philosophes grecs* (Bibliothèque des Écoles françaises d'Athènes et de Rome). Paris: Editions E. de Boccard.

_____. 1946. Les muses et l'harmonie des sphères. In *Mélanges dédiés à la mémoire de Félix Grat,* pp. 2–16. Paris.

Brandily, Monique. 1967. Un exorcisme musical chez les Kotoko. In T. Nikiprowetsky, editor, *La musique dans la vie,* pp. 31–75. Paris: O.C.O.R.A.

Brosse, Thérèse. 1963. *Études instrumentales des techniques du yoga.* Publications de l'École française d'Extrême-Orient, vol. 62.

Brunel, René. 1926. *Essai sur la confrérie religieuse des ᶜAîssàoua au Maroc.* Paris: Paul Geuthner.

Bruno, Jean. 1973. Extase, transe, expérimentation. *Critique* 312:418–46.

Butt, Audrey. 1962. Réalité et idéal dans la pratique chamanique. *L'Homme: Revue française d'anthropologie* 2:5–52.

Calame-Griaule, Gènevieve. 1965. *Ethnologie et langage. La parole chez les Dogon.* Paris: Gallimard.

———. 1968. *Dictionnaire Dogon. Dialecte toro. Langue et civilisation.* Paris: C. Klincksick.

Carapetyan, Armen. 1948. Music and medicine in the Renaissance and in the 17th and 18th Centuries. In D. M. Schullian and M. Schoen, editors, *Music and medicine,* pp. 117–57. New York: Henry Schuman.

Carpitella, Diego. 1966. *L'exorcisme chorégrapho-musical du Tarentisme.* In E. De Martino, *La terre du remords,* pp. 355–65. Paris: Gallimard.

———. 1967. *La musica nei rituali dell'argia.* In C. Gallini, *I rituali dell'argia.*

Cassin, Elena. 1962. Review of E. De Martino, *La terra del rimorso* . . . . *L'Homme: Revue française d'anthropologie* 2:131–33.

Castaldi, Paolo, A. Pesceiti, and A. D'Angelo. 1976. La religione è il pop dei popoli, *Muzak* (?):58–59. Rome (?).

Certeau, Michel de. 1970. *La possession de Loudun.* Paris: Julliard.

Chailley, Jacques. 1956. Le mythe des modes grecs, *Acta Musicologica* 28, fasc. 4:137–63.

———. 1960. *L'imbroglio des modes.* Paris: A. Leduc.

Chapman, Anne. 1972. *Selk'nam (Ona) chants of Tierra del Fuego, Argentina: 47 Shaman Chants and Laments.* Descriptive notes. New York: Folkways Records (cf. discography).

Chéron, Georges. 1931. Le dyidé. *Journal de la Société des Africanistes* 1, fasc. 2:285–89.

Chottin, Alexis. 1939. *Tableau de la musique marocaine.* Paris: Paul Geuthner.

Colson, Elisabeth. 1969. Spirit possession among the Tonga of Zambia. In John Beattie and John Middleton, editors, *Spirit mediumship and society in Africa,* pp. 69–103. London: Routledge and Kegan Paul.

Combarieu, Jules. 1909. *La musique et la magie.* Paris: Picard.

Condominas, Georges. 1973. Postface pour "Chamanisme et possession." *Asie du Sud-Est et Monde Insulindien,* Bulletin du CeDRASEMI, 4, no. 3. Paris: C.N.R.S. et E.P.H.E. (6e section).

———. 1976. Quelques aspects du chamanisme et des cultes de possession en Asie du Sud-Est et dans le monde insulindien. In *L'autre et l'ailleurs. Hommage à Roger Bastide. Présenté par J. Poirier et F. Raveau,* pp. 215–32. Paris: Berger-Levrault.

Corbin, Henry. 1964. *Histoire de la philosophie islamique,* vol. 1. Paris: Gallimard.

Cossard, Gisèle (Gisèle Binon-Cossard). 1967. Musique dans le Candomblé. In T. Nikiprowetsky, editor, *La musique dans la vie,* pp. 159–207. Paris: O.C.O.R.A.

———. 1970. *Contribution à l'étude des candomblés au Brésil. Le candomblé angola.* Paris: Faculté des Lettres et Sciences humaines de Paris, 2 vols. ronéotypés.

Courlander, Harold. 1944. Dance and dance-drama in Haiti. In Franziska Boas, editor, *The Function of Dance in Human Society,* pp. 35–45. New York: The Boas School.

Cowl, Carl. 1966. The Risāla fī khubr tāᶜlif al-ᶜalḥan of Jaᶜqūb ibn Isḥāq al-Kindi (790–874). *The consort journal of the Dolmetsch Foundation* 23:130–66.

Croissant, Jeanne. 1932. *Aristote et les mystères* (Bib. Fac. Philosophie et Lettres de Liège). Liège and Paris: Droz.

Daniélou, Alain. 1967. *Sémantique musicale. Essai de psychophysiologie auditive.* Paris: Hermann.

――――. 1975. Musiques et danses d'extase. *Le Courrier,* October 1975. Paris: Unesco.

Defradas, Jean. 1968. La divination en Grèce. In A. Caquot and M. Leibovici, editors, *La divination,* vol. 1, pp. 157–195. Paris: P.U.F.

Delaby, Laurence. 1976. *Chamanes toungouses* (Études mongoles . . . et sibériennes, cahier 7). Nanterre: Université de Paris X.

――――. 1977. Routes et chemins d'esprit chez les Toungouses. *L'Ethnographie* n.s. 74–75:189–195.

Delatte, A. 1934. *Les conceptions de l'enthousiasme chez les philosophes présocratiques* (Extract from *L'Antiquité classique,* vol. 3) "Collection d'études anciennes." Société d'édition "Les Belles Lettres." Paris: Droz.

De Martino, Ernesto. 1966. *La terre du remords.* Translated by C. Poncet. Paris: Gallimard.

Densmore, Frances. 1948. The use of music in the treatment of the sick by American Indians. In D. M. Schullian and M. Schoen, editors, *Music and medicine,* pp. 25–46. New York: Henry Schuman.

Depont, Octave, and Zavier Coppolani. 1887. *Les confréries religieuses musulmanes.* Algier: Adolphe Jourdan.

Dermenghem, Émile, and Léo-Louis Barbès. 1951. Essai sur la hadhra des Aïssaoua d'Algérie, *Revue africaine* 95:289–314.

Devereux, Georges. 1970. *Essai d'ethnopsychiatrie générale.* Translated by Tina Jolas and Henri Gobard. Paris: Gallimard.

――――. 1983. La crise initiatique du chaman chez Platon (Phèdre 244 d–e). *Psychiatrie française,* n.s. 6:33–35.

Dhorme, Édouard. 1956. *Introduction à La Bible.* Bibliothèque de la Pléiade. Paris: N.R.F., Gallimard.

Dieterlen, Germaine. 1941. *Les âmes des Dogons.* Paris: Institut d'Ethnologie.

――――. 1951. *Essai sur la religion bambara.* Paris: P.U.F.

Dodds, E. R. 1951. *The Greeks and the irrational.* Berkeley: University of California Press.

――――. 1960. *Euripides, Bacchae.* Edited with introduction and commentary by E. R. Dodds. Second edition. Oxford: The Clarendon Press.

Dreyfus-Roche, Simone. 1954. *Chants indiens du Venezuela. Séance de chamanisme.* Cf. discography.

Dumont, Louis. 1957. *Une sous-caste de l'Inde du Sud.* Paris-La Haye: Mouton.

During, Jean. 1975. Éléments spirituels dans la musique traditionnelle contemporaine. *Sophia Perennis* 1, no. 2:129–54. Teheran: Imperial Iranian Academy of Philosophy.

Eliade, Mircea. 1948. *Techniques du Yoga.* Paris: Gallimard.

――――. 1951. *Le chamanisme et les techniques archaïques de l'extase,* 2nd ed. 1969. Paris: Payot.

Emmanuel, Maurice. 1914. Grèce (art gréco-romain). In *Encyclopédie de la musique et Dictionnaire du Conservatoire* 1:377–537. Paris: Delagrave.

England, Nicholas M. 1967. Bushman counterpoint. *Journal of the International Folk Music Council* 19:58–66.

Erlanger, Rodolphe d'. 1930. *La musique arabe*, vol. 1. Al-Fārābi, *Kitāb al-mūsīqī al-kabīr* (Grand traité de la musique), books 1 and 2. Paris: Paul Geuthner.

_____. 1935. *La musique arabe*, vol. 2. Al-Fārābi, book 3 and Avicenna, *Kitāb al-shifāᶜ* (Livre de la guérison) (mathématiques, chap. 12). Paris: Paul Geuthner.

_____. 1938. *La musique arabe*, vol. 3. Ṣafī al-Din, 1: *Al-sharafiyya* (Epître à Sharaf al-Dīn); 2 *Kitāb al-adwār* (Livre des cycles musicaux) (Commentaires). Paris: Paul Geuthner.

Euripides. *Bacchae; Heracles; Hippolytus.*

Evans-Pritchard, E. E. 1937. *Witchcraft, oracles and magic among the Azande.* Oxford: Clarendon Press.

Fārābi, Al-. *See* Erlanger 1930 and 1935.

Farmer, Henry George. 1908. Art. *(Mūsīkī).* In *Encyclopédie de l'Islam.*

_____. 1926. *The influence of music: From Arabic sources: A lecture delivered before the Musical Association.* London: Harold Reeves.

_____. 1929. *A history of Arabian music to the XIIIth century.* London: Luzac and Co.

_____. 1940. *The sources of Arabian music: An annotated bibliography . . . ,* Glasgow.

_____. 1957. The music of ancient Mesopotamia. In *The new Oxford history of music* 1:228–54. London: Oxford University Press.

_____. 1959. The science of music in the Mafātīh al-ᶜUlūm. *Transactions of the Glasgow University Oriental Society* 17, years 1957–58.

Félice, Philippe de. 1936. *Poisons sacrés. Ivresses divines. Essai sur quelques formes inférieures de la mystique.* Paris: Albin Michel.

_____. 1947. *Foules en délire, extases collectives. Essai sur quelques formes inférieures de la mystique.* Paris: Albin Michel.

Ferchiou, Sophie. 1972. Survivances mystiques et culte de possession dans le maraboutisme tunisien. *L'Homme: Revue française d'anthropologie* 12:47–69.

Field, Margaret J. 1969. Spirit possession in Ghana. In John Beattie and John Middleton, editors, *Spirit mediumship and society in Africa,* pp. 3–13. London: Routledge and Kegan Paul.

Filiozat, Jean. 1963. La nature du yoga dans sa tradition. In Thérèse Brosse, *Études instrumentales des techniques du yoga,* pp. i–xxviii.

Firth, Raymond. 1969. Foreword to John Beattie and John Middleton, eds., *Spirit mediumship and society in Africa.* London: Routledge and Kegan Paul.

Foucault, Michel. 1961. *Folie et déraison. Histoire de la folie a l'âge classique.* Paris: Plon.

Francès, Robert. 1958. *La perception de la musique.* 2nd ed. 1972. Paris: Librairie philosophique Vrin.

Frisbie, Charlotte J. 1971. Anthropological and ethnomusicological implications of a comparative analysis of Bushman and African Pygmy music. *Ethnology* 10:265–90.

Gaborieau, Marc. 1975. La transe rituelle dans l'Himalaya central: folie, avatar, méditation. *Purasartha. Recherches de sciences sociales sur l'Asie du Sud* (part 2), pp. 147–72. Paris: Centre d'Études de l'Inde et de l'Asie du Sud.

Gallini, Clara. 1967. *I rituali dell'argia.* Padua: C.E.D.A.M. (with an appendix, "La musica nei rituali dell'argia" by Diego Carpitella and a recording 17/33).

Ganay, Solange de. 1942. *Le Binou yébéné* (Miscellanea Africana Lebaudy, cahier no. 2). Paris: Libr. orient. Paul Geuthner.

Gardet, Louis. 1952 and 1953. Un problème de mystique comparée: la mention du nom divin *(dhikr)* dans la mystique musulmane. *Revue thomiste* 52, no. 1:642–79 and 53, no. 1:197–216.

_____. 1976. *See* Anawati.

Gessain, Robert, and P. É. Victor. 1973. Le tambour chez les Ammassalimiut (côte est du Groenland). *Objets et Mondes* 13:129–60.

Ghazzālī, Abū Ḥamid Al-. *See* MacDonald.

Ghazzālī, Aḥmad al- (Majd al-Dīn). *See* Robson.

Gray, Robert F. 1969. The Shetani cult among the Segeju of Tanzania. In John Beattie and John Middleton, editors, *Spirit mediumship and society in Africa,* pp. 171–187. London: Routledge and Kegan Paul.

Grebé, Maria Ester. 1973. El Kultrún mapuche: un microcosmo simbólico. *Revista Musical Chilena* 27, nos. 123–24:3–42.

Hamayon, Roberte. 1978a. Soigner le mort pour guérir le vif. *Nouvelle revue de psychanalyse* 17:55–72.

_____. 1978b. Les héros de service. *L'Homme: Revue française d'anthropologie* 18:17–45.

Hassan, Schéhérazade Qassim. 1975. *Les instruments de musique en Irak et leur rôle dans la société traditionnelle* (ronéotypé). Paris: E.H.E.S.S. Now published under the same title by Mouton Editeur, Paris 1980.

_____. 1977. Les instruments de musique chez les Yézidi de l'Irak. *1976 Yearbook of the International Folk Music Council,* pp. 53–72.

Henderson, Isobel. 1957. Ancient Greek music. In *New Oxford history of music* 1:336–403.

Henney, Jeannette H. 1973. The Shakers of St. Vincent: A stable religion. In E. Bourguignon, editor, *Religion, altered states of consciousness and social change,* pp. 219–69.

Herodotus. 1945. *Histoires.* Text established and translated by P. E. Legrand. Paris: Société d'édition "Les Belles Lettres."

Herskovits, Melville J. 1938. *Dahomey, an ancient West African kingdom.* 2 vols. Evanston, Northwestern University Press.

_____. 1943a. *Pesquisas etnologicas na Bahia.* Bahia: Museu d'Estado.

_____. 1943b. The southernmost outpost of New World africanism. *American Anthropologist* 45:495–510.

Hertz, Robert. 1928. Sectes russes (C. R. de K. K. Grass, *Die russischen Sekten*). *Mélanges de sociologie religieuse et folklore.* Paris: Felix Alcan.

Heusch, Luc de. 1971. Possession et chamanisme (1964) and La folie des dieux et la raison des hommes. In *Pourquoi l'épouser? et autres essais.* Paris: Gallimard.

Hitchcock, John T., and Rex L. Jones. 1976. *Spirit possession in the Nepal Himalayas.* Warminster (England): Aris and Phillips.

Holtved, Erik. 1967. Eskimo shamanism. In C. M. Edsman, editor, *Studies in shamanism*. Stockholm.

Horton, Robin. 1969. Types of spirit possession in Kalabari religion. In John Beattie and John Middleton, editors, *Spirit mediumship and society in Africa*, pp. 14–49. London: Routledge and Kegan Paul.

Husson, Raoul. 1960. *La voix chantée*. Paris: Gauthier-Villars.

Jackson, Anthony. 1968. Sound and ritual. *Man*, n.s., 3:293–99.

Jacob, François. 1970. *La logique du vivant. Une histoire de l'hérédité*. Paris: Gallimard.

Jakobson, Roman. 1960. Linguistics and poetics. In T. A. Sebeok, editor, *Style in language*. Cambridge, Mass.: M.I.T. Press.

Jargy, Simon. 1971. *La musique arabe* (coll. "Que sais-je?"). Paris: P.U.F.

Jeanmaire, H. 1939. *Couroi et Courètes. Essai sur l'éducation spartiate et sur les rites d'adolescence dans l'antiquité héllenique*. Avesnes-sur-Helpe: G. Deloffre.

_____. 1949a. Le traitement de la mania dans les "Mystères" de Dionysos et des Corybantes. *Journal de Psychologie* 64–82.

_____. 1949b. Le satyre et la ménade. Remarques sur quelques textes relatifs aux danses "orgiaques." In *Mélanges d'archéologie et d'histoire offerts à Charles Picard* . . . 1:463–73. Paris: P.U.F.

_____. 1951. *Dionysos. Histoire du culte de Bacchus*. Paris: Payot.

Jervis, Giovanni. 1966. Considérations neuro-psychiatriques sur le tarentulisme. In E. De Martino, *La terre du remords*, pp. 329–54. Paris: Gallimard.

Jetté, Fernand. 1961. L'extase dans la tradition spirituelle du xiiie au xviie siècle. *Dictionnaire de spiritualité*, pp. 2131–47. Paris: Beauchesne.

Johnston, Thomas F. 1972. Possession music of the Shangana-Tsonga. *African Music*, 5:10–22.

Jordania, Redjeb. 1978. Boris Vian et la chanson. *Musique en jeu* 30:91–110.

Juillerat, Bernard. 1977. Introduction au numéro: "Folie," possession et chamanisme en Nouvelle Guinée. *Journal de la Société des Océanistes* 33:117–21.

Junod, Henri A. 1913. *The life of a South African tribe*. 2 vols. Neufchatel: Imprimerie Attinger Frères.

Junod, Henry P. 1934. Les cas de possession et l'exorcisme chez les VaNdau. *Africa* 7:270–99.

Kakouri, Katerina J. 1965. *Dionysiaka. Aspects of the Thracian religion of today*. Athens: G. C. Eleftheroudakis.

Kartomi, Margaret. 1973. Music and trance in central Java. *Ethnomusicology* 17:163–208.

Kātib, al-Hasan Al-. *See* Shiloah.

Kilson, Marion. 1971. *Kpele Lala. Ga religions, songs and symbols*. Cambridge, Mass.: Harvard University Press.

Kindī, Al-. *See* Cowl.

Kirchmayer, Jean. 1961. Extase chez les Pères de l'Église. *Dictionnaire de spiritualité*, s.v. "Extase." Paris: Beauchesne.

Kiti, R. P. Gabriel. 1968. Consécration à un fétiche au Dahomey. *Études Dahoméennes*, 11:26–32.

Knox, R. A. 1950. *Enthusiasm, a chapter in the history of religion*. Oxford.

Kurath, Gertrude. 1960. Panorama of dance ethnology. *Current Anthropology* 1:233–54.

Lacarrière, Jacques. 1955. L'épouvante: Théâtre et possession au temps d'Eschyle. In *Eschyle et l'Orestie* (Cahiers de la Compagnie Madeleine Renaud-Jean-Louis Barrault), 3ᵉ année, 11ᵉ cahier, 58–65. Paris: Julliard.

————. 1961. *Les hommes ivres de Dieu*. Paris: Arthaud.

Laloum, Claude, and Gilbert Rouget. 1965. Deux chants liturgiques yoruba. *Journal de la Société des Africanistes* 35:108–38.

Lapassade, Georges. 1975. Transe et possession au Maroc. *Quel corps?* 2:27–30.

————. 1976. *Essai sur la transe*. Paris: Jean-Pierre Delarge.

Laplanche, J., and J. B. Pontalis. 1968. *Vocabulaire de la psychanalyse*. Paris: P.U.F.

Lasserre, François. 1954. Plutarch, *De la musique*. Texte, traduction, commentaire précédé d'une étude sur l'éducation musicale dans la Grèce antique (Bibliotheca Helvetica Romana). Olten and Lausanne: Urs Graf-Verlag.

Lawler, Lilian B. 1927. The maenads: A contribution to the study of dance in ancient Greece. *Memoirs of the American Academy in Rome,* 6:69–112.

Lee, Richard B. 1968. The sociology of !Kung Bushman trance performances. In R. Prince, editor, *Trance and possession states,* pp. 35–54. Montreal: R. M. Bucke Memorial Society.

Lee, S. G. 1969. Spirit possession among the Zulu. In John Beattie and John Middleton, editors. *Spirit mediumship and society in Africa,* pp. 128–56. London: Routledge and Kegan Paul.

Le Hérissé, A. 1911. *L'ancien royaume du Dahomey.* Paris: Émile Larose.

Leiris, Michel. 1934. *L'Afrique fantôme*. Paris: Gallimard.

————. 1955. *Fourbis*. Paris: Gallimard.

————. 1958. *La possession et ses aspects théâtraux chez les Éthiopiens de Gondar*. Paris: Plon.

————. 1974. Mazmur le clerc. *L'Ethnographie*, n.s., 68:39–58.

Le Jeune, Claude. 1598. *Dodécacorde contenant douze psaumes de David.* . . . Reproduced in Henry Expert, *Les maitres musiciens de la Renaissance française*. Paris: Leduc, 1900.

Lesure, François. 1961. Claude Le Jeune. In *Encyclopédie de la musique III*. Paris: Fasquelle.

————. 1966. *Musica e società*. Milan: Istituto editoriale italiano.

Lévi-Strauss, Claude. 1949. L'efficacité symbolique. *Anthropologie structurale*. Plon: Paris, 1958.

————. 1960. Introduction à l'oeuvre de Marcel Mauss. In Marcel Mauss, *Sociologie et Anthropologie*. Paris: P.U.F.

————. 1962. *La pensée sauvage*. Paris: Plon.

————. 1966. *Du miel aux cendres* (*Mythologiques* II). Paris: Plon.

Lewis, I. M. 1971. *Ecstatic religion: An anthropological study of spirit possession and shamanism*. Harmondsworth: Penguin Books.

Linforth, Ivan M. 1946a. The corybantic rites in Plato. *University of California Publications in Classical Philology.* 13, no. 5, 121–62. Berkeley and Los Angeles: University of California Press.

————. 1946b. Telestic madness in Plato, Phaedrus 244 DE. *University of California Publications in Classical Philology,* 13, no. 6, 163–72.

Lomax, Alan. 1968. *Folk song style and culture*. Washington: American Association for the Advancement of Sciences.

Lot-Falck, Éveline. 1961. L'animation du tambour. *Journal asiatique* year 1961:213–39.

_____. 1968. La divination dans l'Arctique et l'Asie septentrionale. In Caquot and Leibovici, editors, *La divination* 2:247–77. Paris: P.U.F.

_____. 1970. Psychopathes et chamans yakoutes. In *Échanges et communications. Mélanges offerts à Claude Lèvi-Strauss à l'occasion de son 60ᵉ anniversaire,* réunis par J. Pouillon et P. Maranda. 1:115–29. The Hague-Paris: Mouton.

_____. 1977. À propos du terme chamane. *Études mongoles . . . et sibériennes,* cahier 8, 7–18. Nanterre, Labethno: Université de Paris X.

MacDonald, Charles. 1973. De quelques manifestations chamanistiques à Palawan. In *Asie du Sud-Est et monde insulindien, Bulletin du Centre de documentation et de recherche (CeDRASEMI)* "Chamanisme et possession" (fascicule 2), vol. 4, no. 3:11–18. Paris: Mouton.

MacDonald, Duncan B. 1901 and 1902. Emotional religion in Islam as affected by music and singing. Being a translation of a book of the *Iḥyā 'Ulūm ad-Dīn* of al-al-Ghazzālī with analysis, annotation, and appendices. *Journal of the Royal Asiatic Society* 1901, 195–252 and 705–48; 1902, 1–28.

_____. 1908. Samā. In *Encyclopédie de l'Islam*.

_____. 1908. Dhikr. In *Encyclopédie de l'Islam*.

Majd al-Dīn, Aḥmad al-Tūsī Al-Ghazzālī. *See* Robson.

Mars. Louis. 1953. Nouvelle contribution à l'étude de la crise de possession. In *Les Afro-américains* (Mémoires de l'Institut Francais d'Afrique Noire, no. 27), pp. 213–33. Dakar: I.F.A.N.

Marshall, Lorna. 1969. The medicine dance of the !Kung Bushmen. *Africa* 39:347–81.

Masaraki, Despina W. 1974. Ein Aulos der Sammlung Karapanos. *Mitteilungen des Deutschen Archäologischen Institut Athenische Abteilung* 89:105–21.

Massignon, Louis. 1922. *Essai sur les origines du lexique technique de la mystique musulmane*. Paris: Paul Geuthner.

_____. 1934. Tarīka. In *Encyclopédie de l'Islam*.

Mauss, Marcel. 1936. Les techniques du corps. Reprinted in *Sociologie et anthropologie,* 1960. Paris: P.U.F.

Meinecke, Bruno. 1948. Music and medicine in classical antiquity. In D. M. Schullian and M. Schoen, editors, *Music and medicine,* pp. 47–97. New York: Henry Schuman.

Merriam, Alan P. 1964. *The anthropology of music*. Evanston: Northwestern University Press.

Mérsenne, Marin. 1636. *Harmonie Universelle*. Edited by François Lesure, 3 vols. Paris: C.N.R.S.

_____. 1932. *Correspondance*. Edited by P. Tannery.

Metraux, Alfred. 1942. Le chamanisme araucan. In *Religions et magies indiennes d'Amérique du Sud,* ed. Simone Dreyfus, Paris: Gallimard, 1967.

_____. 1958. *Le vaudou haïtien*. Paris: Gallimard.

Michelet, Jules. 1862. *La sorcière*.

Misson, Maximilien. 1707. *Le théatre sacré des Cévennes.* London: Robert Roger. Reissued by Les Presses du Languedoc. Brignon: 1978.

Mokri, Mohammad. 1961. Soufisme (Le S. et la musique). In *Encyclopédie de la musique* 3:1014–15. Paris, Fasquelle.

Molé, Marijan. 1963. La danse extatique en Islam. In *Les danses sacrées* (coll. "Sources orientales" 6), pp. 145–280. Paris: Éditions du Seuil.

Molino, Jean. 1975. Fait musical et sémiologie de la musique. *Musique en Jeu* 17:37–61.

Monfouga-Nicolas, Jacqueline. 1972. *Ambivalence et culte de possession.* Paris: Éditions Anthropos.

Moréchand, Guy. 1968. Le chamanisme des Hmong. *Bulletin de l'École Française d'Extrême-Orient* 54:53–294.

Moutsopoulos, Evanghélos. 1959. *La Musique dans l'oeuvre de Platon.* Paris: P.U.F.

Nadel, S. F. 1946. A study of shamanism in the Nuba Mountains. *Journal of the Royal Anthropological Institute of Great Britain and Ireland* 76, 1, 25–37.

Nattiez, Jean-Jacques. 1975. *Fondements d'une sémiologie de la musique* (coll. "10/18"). Paris: Union générale d'édition.

Nebesky-Wojkowitz, René de. 1956. *Oracles and demons of Tibet.* The Hague: Mouton.

Needham, Rodney. 1967. Percussion and transition. *Man,* n.s., 2:606–14.

Neher, Andrew. 1961. Auditory driving observed with scalp electrodes in normal subject. *Electroencephalography and Clinical Neurophysiology* 13:449–51.

———. 1962. A physiological explanation of unusual behavior in ceremonies involving drums. *Human biology* 4:151–60.

Nettl, Bruno. 1977. À propos des universaux. *Le Monde de la Musique/The World of Music* 19:8–12.

Nketia, J. H. 1957. Possession dances in African societies. *Journal of the International Folk Music Council* 9:4–9.

Nostradamus, César. 1614. *Histoire et chronique de Provence.* . . . Lyon: Rigaud.

Oesterreich, T. K. 1930. *Possession, demoniacal and other, among primitive races, in antiquity, the middle-age and modern times* (authorized translation of the 1921 original in German).

Oppitz, Michael. 1981. *Shamanen in Blinden Land.* Frankfurt-am-Main: Syndikat.

Pagès, Max. 1973. La libération du corps. *L'homme et la société. Revue internationale de recherches et de synthèses sociologiques* 29–30:153–75.

Pairault, Claude. 1966. *Boum-le-Grand, village d'Iro.* Paris: Institut d'Ethnologie.

Pearson, A. C. 1918. Possession (Greek and Roman). In *Encyclopaedia of Religions and Ethics* 10:127–30. Edinburgh: James Hastings.

Pidoux, Dr. Charles. 1955. Les états de possession rituelle chez les Mélano-Africains. *L'évolution psychiatrique* 11:271–83.

Plato. *Crito; Ion; Laches; Laws; Phaedrus; Philebus; Republic; Symposium; Theaetetus; Timaeus.*

Plutarch. 1953. *Dialogue sur l'amour (Eroticos).* Text and translation by Robert Flacelière. Paris: Société d'édition "Les Belles Lettres."

Porset, Charles. 1970. *See* Rousseau 1781.

Pottier, Richard. 1973. Notes sur les chamanes et médiums de quelques groupes Thai. *Asie du Sud-Est et Monde Insulindien.* Bulletin du CeDRASEMI 4, no. 1. Paris: C.N.R.S. et E.P.H.E.

Pouillon, Jean. 1972. Malade et médecin: le même et/ou l'autre? (remarques ethnologiques). *Nouvelle Revue de Psychanalyse* 1:77–98.

Prince, Raymond, editor. 1968. *Trance and possession states* (Proceedings of the Second Annual Conference, R. M. Bucke Memorial Society 1966). Montreal.

Prince, Raymond. 1968. Can the EGG be used in the study of possession states? In R. Prince, editor, *Trance and possession states,* pp. 121–37.

Pseudo-Plutarch. *See* Lasserre.

Quenum, Maximilien. 1938. *Au pays des Fons, us et coutumes du Dahomey.* Paris: Émile Larose.

Rausky, Franklin. 1977. *Mesmer ou La révolution thérapeutique.* Paris: Payot.

Reinach, Théodore. 1900. La musique des sphères. *Revue des études grecques* 13:432–49.

Reinhard, Johan. 1976. Shamanism and spirit possession: The definition problem. In John T. Hitchcock and Rex L. Jones, editors, *Spirit possession in the Nepal Himalayas,* pp. 12–20. Warminster: Aris and Phillips.

Robson, James. 1938. *Tracts on listening to music.* Being *Dhamm al-malāhī* by Ibn abī ᶜl-Dunyā and *Bawāriq al-ilmāᶜ* by Majd al-Dīn al-Ṭūsī al-Ghazzālī (coll. "Oriental Translation Fund," n.s., vol. 34). London: The Royal Asiatic Society.

Rodrigues, Nina. 1935. *O animismo fetichista dos negros bahianos* (Prefacio e notas de Arthur Ramos). Civilisação Brasileira, Rio de Janeiro. (First published, in installments, in *Revista Brasileira,* in 1896–97. Translated and published in French in 1900).

Roger, Joseph Louis. 1803. *Traité des effets de la musique sur le corps humain.* . . . Translated from the Latin edition (1748) by Étienne Sainte-Marie.

Ronsard, P. de. 1866. Oeuvres complètes. Published by M. Prosper Blanchemain. Paris: Librairie A. Franck, 1866.

Rouanet, Jules. 1922. La musique arabe. In *Encyclopédie de la musique et dictionnaire du Conservatoire* 5:2676–2939. Paris: Delagrave.

Rouch, Jean. 1960. *La religion et la magie Songhay.* Paris: P.U.F.

———. 1973. Essai sur les avatars de la personne du possédé, du magicien, du sorcier, du cinéaste et de l'ethnographe. In *La notion de personne en Afrique noire.* Colloques Internationaux du C.N.R.S., no. 544:529–44. Paris: Éditions du C.N.R.S.

Rouget, Gilbert. 1957. Introduction to *Notes sur la musique des Bochiman comparée à celle des Pygmées Babinga,* établies par Yvette Grimaud avec la collaboration de G. Rouget. Paris: Musée de l'Homme, Département d'ethno-musicologie and Cambridge: Harvard University, Peabody Museum. Notes to the record; cf. discography.

———. 1961. Un chromatisme africain. *L'Homme, Revue française d'anthropologie* 1:30–46.

———. 1962. Musique "vodun" (Dahomey). *Actes du VI ᵉ Congrès International des Sciences Anthropologiques et Ethnologiques* (Paris 1960) 2, 2:121–22. Paris.

———. 1965. Notes et documents pour servir à l'étude de la musique yoruba. *Journal de la Société des Africanistes* 35:67–107.

———. 1971. Court songs and traditional history in the ancient kingdoms of Porto-Novo and Abomey. In K. P. Wachsmann, editor, *Essays on Music and History in Africa*, pp. 27–64, Evanston: Northwestern University Press.

Rousseau, Jean-Jacques. 1765. Musique. In Diderot, editor, *Encyclopédie ou Dictionnaire raisonné des sciences, des arts et des métiers*, vol. 10.

———. 1768. *Dictionnaire de la musique*. Paris.

———. 1781. *Essai sur l'origine des langues, où il est parlé de la mélodie et de l'imitation musicale*. Edited by C. Porset. Bordeaux: Ducros, 1970.

———. 1782. *Supplément à l'Encyclopédie*, vol. 3. Neufchatel and Amsterdam.

Roux, Alain. 1973. La musique pop. In Paul Beaud and Alfred Willener, *Musique et vie quotidienne. Essai de sociologie d'une nouvelle culture*. Paris: Mame.

Roux, Jean-Paul. 1963. La danse chamanique de l'Asie centrale. In *Les danses sacrées*, pp. 281–314. Paris: Éditions du Seuil.

Sachs, Curt. 1940. *The history of musical instruments*. New York: W. W. Norton.

Ṣafī al-Dīn. *See* Erlanger 1938.

Schaeffner, André. 1951. *Les Kissi. Une société noire et ses instruments de musique*. Paris: Hermann.

———. 1965. Rituel et pré-théâtre. *Histoire des Spectacles* (Encyclopédie de la Pléiade), pp. 21–54. Paris: Gallimard.

Schneider, Marius. 1948. *La danza de espadas y la tarentela. Ensayo musicológico, etnográfico y arqueologico sobre los ritos medicinales*. Barcelona: Instituto Español de Musicologia.

Schott-Billmann, France. 1977. *Corps et possession. Le vécu corporel des possédés face à la rationalité occidentale*. Paris: Gauthier-Villars.

Schullian, D. M. and M. Schoen, editors. 1948. *Music and medicine*. New York: Henry Schuman.

Séchan, Louis. 1930. *La danse grecque antique*. Paris: E. de Boccard.

Ségurola, R. P. B. 1963. Dictionnaire fon-français (2 vols., ronéotypé). Cotonou: Procure de l'Archidiocèse.

Sergent, Alain. 1952. *Le roi des prestidigitateurs, Robert-Houdin*. Paris: Éditions du Seuil.

Seydou, Christiane. 1972. *Silâmaka et Poullôri. Recit épique peul raconté par Tinguidji* (Classiques africains). Paris: A. Colin.

Shiloah, Amnon. 1965 and 1967. L'Épître sur la musique des Ikhwān-al-Safā. *Revue des Études Islamiques* 32:125–62; 34:159–93.

———. 1972. Al-Ḥasan ibn Aḥmad ibn 'Alī al-Kātib. *La perfection des connaissances musicales (Kitāb Kamāl adab al-ghinā)*. Traduction et commentaire d'un traite de musique arabe du xie siecle. Paris: Paul Geuthner.

Shirokogoroff, S. M. 1935. *Psychomental complex of the Tungus*. London: Kegan Paul.

Sigerist, Henry E. 1948. The story of tarentism. In D. M. Schullian and M. Schoen, editors, *Music and medicine*, pp. 96–116. New York: Henry Schuman.

Simon, Gérard. 1979. *Kepler astonome astrologue*. Paris: Gallimard.

Simon, Pierre, and Ida Simon-Barouh. 1973. *Hâù Bóng. Un culte vietnamien de possession transplanté en France.* Paris: Mouton.

Stein, R. A. 1962. *La civilisation tibétaine.* Paris: Dunod.

Sturtevant, W. C. 1968. Categories, percussion and physiology. Man, n.s., 3:133–34.

Surugue, Bernard. 1972. *Contribution à l'étude de la musique sacrée Zarma Songhay (République du Niger).* Études Nigériennes 30, Niamey.

Tanner, R. E. S. 1955. Hysteria in Sukuma medical practice. *Africa* 25:274–79.

Tardits, Claude. 1958. *Porto-Novo. Les nouvelles générations africaines entre leurs traditions et l'occident.* Paris, La Haye: Mouton.

Theresa of Avila (Sainte Thérèse de Jesus). 1949. *Oeuvres complètes.* Translated by R. P. Grégoire de Saint Joseph. Paris: Editions du Seuil. *Obras completas.* 1948. Madrid: Editorial Plenitud.

Thomas, Artus, Seig. d'Ambry. 1603. Ode sur la musique du défunct sieur Claudin Le Jeune. Reproduced in Henry Expert, *Les maîtres musiciens de la Renaissance française* (Claude Le Jeune, Le Printemps, Ier fascicule). Paris: Leduc, 1900.

———. 1611. "Commentaires" figurant dans la traduction, par B. de Vigenère, de: Philostrate, *De la vie d'Apollonius de Thyaneen.* Paris: chez la veuve Matthieu Guillemot . . . .

Tidjani, Serpos. 1950. Rituels. In *Le monde noir, Presence africaine,* numéro spéspécial 8–9:297–305. Paris.

Torgue, Henry Skoff. 1975. *La pop-music* (Collection "Que sais-je?"). Paris: P.U.F.

Touma, Habib Hassan. 1976. Quelques notes sur les rapports entre esthétique et improvisation dans la musique arabe. *The World of Music.* 18:51–52.

Tracey, Andrew. 1970. The Matepe Mbira music of Rhodesia. *African Music* 4:37–61.

Trimingham, J. Spencer. 1949. *Islam in the Sudan.* London: Oxford University Press.

———. 1971. *The Sufi orders in Islam.* London: Oxford University Press.

Turnbull, Colin M. 1961. *Forest people.* New York: Simon and Schuster.

Turner, Victor W. 1968. *The drums of affliction. A study of religious process among the Ndembu of Zambia.* Oxford: Clarendon Press.

Tyard, Pontus de. 1555. *Solitaire second, ou Prose de la Musique.* Lyons: Jean de Tournes.

Vasilevič, G. M. 1969. *Evenki. Istoriko-etnografičeskie očerki.* (XVIII-*nacalo* XX v.). (Les Evenki. Aperçus historico-ethnographiques du xviiie au début du xxe s.). Leningrad: Izd. Nauka.

Veith, Ilza. 1973. *Histoire de l'hystérie.* Translated by Sylvie Dreyfus. Paris: Seghers.

Verger, Pierre. 1954. Rôle joué par l'état d'hébétude au cours de l'initiation des novices aux Cultes des *Orisha* et des *Vodun. Bulletin de l'Institut Français d'Afrique Noire* 16:322–40.

———. 1957. *Notes sur le culte des oriṣa et vodun* (Mémoires de l'Institut Français d'Afrique Noire, no. 51). Dakar: I.F.A.N.

————. 1969. Trance and convention in Nago-Yoruba spirit mediumship. In John Beattie and John Middleton, editors, *Spirit mediumship and society in Africa*, pp. 50–66. London: Routledge and Kegan Paul.

Vernant, J. P. 1974. Paroles et signes muets. In J. P. Vernant, editor, *Divination et rationalité*. Paris: Éditions du Seuil.

————. 1975. Image et apparence dans la théorie platonicienne de la *mimésis*. *Journal de psychologie* 2:133–60.

Vian, Boris. 1958. *En avant la zizique . . . et par ici les gros sous*. Paris: Le Livre contemporain.

Vincent, Jeanne-Françoise. 1971. Divination et possession chez les Mofu, montagnards du Nord-Cameroun. *Journal de la Société des Africanistes* 41:71–132.

Vitray-Méyerovitch, Eva de. 1972. *Mystique et poésie en Islam. Djalal-ud-Dīn Rūmī et l'Ordre des Derviches tourneurs*. Desclée de Brouwer.

Wachsmann, Klaus P. 1957. *See* Nketia, J. H.

————. 1971. Universal perspectives in music. *Ethnomusicology* 15:381–84.

Walker, Sheila S. 1972. *Ceremonial spirit possession in Africa and Afro-America*. Leiden: E. J. Brill.

Wilamowitz, U. von. 1920. *Plato*. 2d. ed. Berlin.

Yasser, J. 1926. Musical moments in the shamanistic rites of the Siberian pagan tribes. *Pro-Musica Quarterly* 4:4–15.

Yates, Frances A. 1947. *The French academies of the sixteenth century* (Studies of the Warburg Institute, vol. 15). London.

Zemp, Hugo. 1978. 'Are'are classification of musical types and instruments. *Ethnomusicology* 22:37–67.

Zempléni, Andras. 1966. La dimension thérapeutique du culte des rab, ndöp, tuuru et samp; rites de possession chez les Lébou et les Wolof. *Psychopathologie africaine* 2:295–439.

————. 1972. *See* Adler.

Discography

Unless otherwise indicated, the author cited is responsible for both the recording and commentary.

Anonymous. 1969 (?). *Iz jakutskogo muskal'nogo fol'klora* (Samples of Yakut musical folklore). 30/33. Melodia D 030639-40 (U.S.S.R.).

Béhague, Gérard. 1977 (?). *Afro-Brazilian Religious Songs. Candomblé Songs from Salvador, Bahia, Brazil*. 30/33. Lyrichord Stereo 7315, New York.

Berthe, Louis. 1970. *Barong, drame musical balinais*. Commentary by B. Lortat-Jacob. 30/33. (Coll. Musée de l'Homme.) Vogue LD 763, Paris.

Brunet, Jacques. 1974 (?). *Traditional Music of Southern Laos*. 30/33. (Unesco Collection, Musical Sources.) Philips 6586 012.

Chapman, Anne. 1972. *Indian Chants of Tierra del Fuego*. 2 records, 30/33; produced in cooperation with the Musée de l'Homme. Folkways Records, FE 4176, New York.

Fresnais, Gilles. 1973. *Bali, divertissements musicaux et danses de transe*. 30/33. O.C.O.R.A. OCR 73, Paris.

Hurault, Jean. 1968. *Musique Boni et Wayana de Guyane*. 30/33. (Coll. Musée de l'Homme.) Vogue LVLX–290, Paris.

Koechlin, Bernard. 1975. *Possession et poésie à Madagascar*. 30/33. (Coll. Musée de l'Homme.) O.C.O.R.A. OCR 83, Paris.

Le Besnerais, Henri. 1954. *Séance de chamanisme. Chants indiens Yaruro du Venezuela*. Commentary by Simone Dreyfus-Roche. 30/33. Musée de l'Homme, Paris.

Levy, John. 1968. *Musique bouddhique de Corée*. 30/33. (Coll. Musée de l'Homme.) Vogue LVLX–253, Paris.

Lortat-Jacob, Bernard. 1979. *Berbères du Maroc. Ahwach*. 30/33. (Collection C.N.R.S.—Musée de l'Homme.) Le Chant du Monde LDX 74705, Paris.

Luneau, Georges. 1979. *Bengale, Musique des "fous."* 30/33. (Collection C.N.R.S.—Musée de l'Homme.) Le Chant du Monde LDX 74715, Paris.

Marshall Expedition and Mission Ogooué-Congo. 1957. *Bushman Music and Pygmy Music*. 30/33. Musée de l'Homme LD 9, Paris and Peabody Museum, Cambridge (U.S.A.).

Mauguin, Bernard. 1969 (?). Turkey I. *Musique mevlevi*. 30/33. (A Musical Anthrology of the Orient. Unesco Collection.) Barenreiter Musicaphon BM 30 L 2019.

———. 1974 *Islamic Ritual from Yougoslavia. Zikr of the Rufa'i Brotherhood*. 30/33. (Unesco Collection, Musical Sources.) Philips 6589 015.

Poche, Christian. 1976 (?). *Zikr: Islamic Ritual Rifa'iyya Brotherhood of Aleppo.* Recorded by J. Wenzel. 30/33. (Unesco Collection, Musical Sources.) Philips 6586 030.

Rouget, Gilbert. 1955. *Fête pour l'offrande des premières ignames à Shango au Dahomey.* 30/33. Musee de l'Homme LD 2, Paris.

_____. 1955. *Dahomey, Musique des princes, Fête des Tohossou.* Photographs by P. Verger. 30/33. (Coll. Musée de l'Homme.) Vogue Contrepoint MC 200.093, Paris.

_____. 1958. *Ogoun, Dieu du Fer.* 30/33. (Coll. Musée de l'Homme.) Vogue Contrepoint, MC 20.159, Paris.

_____. 1961 *Dahomey, chants rituels.* 17/33. (*L'Homme* I-3.) Musée de l'Homme LD 17.3, Paris.

Tardits, Claude. 1959. *Invocation à Sakpata.* 17/33. Musée de l'Homme. Paris.

Filmography

See also the short list of film references given by E. Bourguinon (1976, p. 73). An asterisk indicates Paris, C.N.R.S. and Comité du film ethnographique, Musée de l'Homme. These films are also available from the S.E.R.D.D.A.V. (C.N.R.S.).

Collomb, Henri, and Zempléni, Andras. 1967. *Le N'doep.* Directed by Michel Meignant. 16mm, 40 min. Paris: Laboratoires Sandoz.

Garine, Igor de. 1966. *Foulina, les possédés du pays Moussey.* 16mm, 34 min. Paris: C.N.R.S., Office du Film de Recherche Scientifique.

McEwen, Frank. 1970 (?). *Dombatsoko—Le sacrifice des taureaux.* 16 mm. Salisbury: Salisbury Art Gallery.

Morillère, Roger, Pierre Simon, and Ida Simon- Barouh. 1970. *Les génies des quatre palais (Thánh Tú Phu').* 16 mm, 70 min. Paris: C.N.R.S., Comité du Film Ethnographique et Laboratoire Audiovisuel de l'E.P.H.E. V^e section.

Olivier de Sardan, Jean-Pierre. 1973. *La vieille et la pluie.* 16mm, 55 min.*

Rouch, Jean. 1951. *Yénendi. Les hommes qui font la pluie.* 16mm, 30 min.*

———. 1954. *Les maîtres fous.* 16 and 35 mm, 35 min.*

———. 1968. *Le Yénendi de Gangel.* 16 mm, 45 min.*

———. 1972. *Les tambours d'avant: tourou et biti.* 16 mm, 10 min.*

———. 1973. *Horendi: initiation à la danse de possession.* 16 mm, 65 min.*

Rouget, Gilbert, and Jean Rouch. 1963. *Sortie de novices de Sakpata.* 16 mm, 18 min.*

1. Subject Index

2. Index of Religions, Sects, Divinities, and Religious Figures

3. Index of Ethnic Groups and Places

4. Index of Authors, Individuals, and Characters

333112647

Corrigendum Concerning the *Ere* State

This book was already in print when, in April 1985, Gisèle Cossard and Pierre Verger, who both happened to be in Paris, kindly urged me to clear up the confusion between the states of hebetude and of *ere*.

Without entering into detail, it will be recalled that both are altered states of consciousness characteristic of the initiation stage of the *orisha* cult in Brazil and in Africa. In the present book one can read (p. 50) that the "state of hebetude . . . is clearly nothing other than the *ere* state." Such is not the case. Although both are closely linked with initiation, they must be distinguished from one another. To put it briefly, the *ere* state is attributed to an infantine spirit and manifests itself, in a more or less provocative way, by decidedly childish behavior having nothing to do with hebetude.

It is not necessary to go any further here. Suffice it to say that this distinction implies a certain rereading of pages 47–50, 56–57, 66, 70, and 71, but that it does not change anything in the section entitled "The Musical Repertoire of Initiation" (pages 58–62), except that on page 59, line 4, the words "in *ere* state" should be deleted.

333112647

From Siberia to Africa, from antiquity to modern times, music has been associated with ritual trance and altered states of consciousness. What is the nature of this association? Is it universal or culturally specific, neurophysiologically or symbolically based? In *Music and Trance,* a distinguished ethnomusicologist attempts the first extended answer to these questions, which have long puzzled anthropologists, psychologists, and musicologists. He concludes that no simple universal law can explain the relations between music and trance; their interaction depends on the systems of meaning in their home cultures.

Rouget reviews all known ethnographic descriptions of states of possession to test a range of hypotheses about their causes. In his meticulous analysis, he concentrates on West and Central Africa, but also sifts information from Latin America, Russia, the Middle East, and Europe. To organize this immense store of information, he develops a typology of trance. He describes the key characteristics of shamanism, spirit possession, and emotional and communal trances, and he outlines the differences among them. Music is analyzed in terms of performers, practice, instruments, and its ties to dance. Each kind of trance draws strength from music in different ways at different points in a ritual, Rouget concludes. The only universal characteristic is the profound identification an adept feels with the melody that induces and maintains the trance.

Forcefully rejecting pseudo-science and reductionism, Rouget demonstrates that neither the neurological effects of rhythm nor drug use nor mental illness can account for the power of music in trance states. His conclusion is that music's physiological and emotional effects are inseparable from patterns of collective symbols and behavior, and that music and trance are linked in as many ways as there are cultural structures.

GILBERT ROUGET is director of research at the Centre Nationale de la Recherche Scientifique, chairman of the Department of Ethnomusicology at the Musée de l'Homme in Paris, and lecturer at the University of Paris X—Nanterre.

A Chicago Original Paperback

Chicago
Original
Paperbacks

THE UNIVERSITY OF CHICAGO PRESS

ISBN 0-226-73006